THE FALL
AND RISE OF
JIMMY HOFFA

THE FALL
AND RISE OF
JIMMY HOFFA

Walter Sheridan

Saturday Review Press

NEW YORK

To my wife and children

Acknowledgments

I owe a special debt of gratitude to Jack Miller, John Cassidy, Bill Greenhalgh, Adrienne Cowles and Joe Higdon for their friendship and support; to Margo Higdon, Ruth Brazer, Helen Marsili and Rosemary Kennedy for their long and patient hours of typing; to Peter Maas, Margaret Carroll and Stephanie Erickson for their invaluable editing assistance.

Contents

■□■□■□■□■□■□■□■□■

Introduction by Budd Schulberg

━━━━━━━━━━━━━━━━

A SPECTER IS HAUNTING America. No, it is not communism. Despite Wallace, Goldwater and the right-wing doomsday criers, it is not even creeping socialism. It is, as readers of this book will find alarmingly documented, an altogether different sort of creeping disease. Creeping, hell, it's now boldly up on two feet and *running*. Toward what goal? More. More houses? More schools? More day-care centers? Forget it. More money. More power. Power to do what? Enjoy life, liberty and the pursuit of happiness? Not as Jefferson and our eighteenth-century idealists imagined it in those simpler times. Today it is the high life, the deal that brings liberty in the form of "commutation" from the federal pen, and the pursuit of the easy buck—be it at the gangster Xanadus of Las Vegas, or at millionaire retreats built with Teamster money like Moe Dalitz's La Costa Country Club, or at the various White Houses, Dicknixon style. There the Big Money, that unholy alliance of over-and-under-the-table, has enjoyed the friendship of the man who grasped early in his checkered career the sharp-edged triangle of money, power and politics.

Throughout our history Big Money has been decried, by Andrew Jackson, William Jennings Bryan, both the Roosevelts. . . . There are periodic appeals to our idealism, compassion and sense of community. Reform movements rise and fall like the tides. Today our children's crusade turns its back on the sources of wealth and power and wanders into the desert to smoke its pot and live the good life to the music of Led Zeppelin, James Taylor and Joe Cocker. They have chosen to abandon the system rather than reshape it. The old system, their gypsy life-style is telling us, is a rat-race is a money-game is a war-machine conceived in material-

ism and dedicated to the proposition that the race is to the swift
and the poker pot to the swift of hand.

Left behind to fight the network of graft-organized greed that
has infected our profit system are the Walter Sheridans of this
land, unlikely Don Quixotes who tilt not at windmills but at
syndicates and are willing to take on single-handed an army of
hoodlums, fixers, purchasable politicos and business opportunists,
to go it alone if their leaders are shot down and a Mitchellized
Justice Department moves to deliver them and their witnesses to
the enemy.

I first came to know Walter Sheridan in the early sixties when
I went to Washington to discuss with the then Attorney General,
Robert Kennedy, the possibility of adapting his book, *The Enemy
Within*, as a motion picture. Our irrepressible producer, the late
Jerry Wald, had called me in Mexico to say that Kennedy had
chosen me from a list of film writers Wald had submitted.
Kennedy had been impressed with *On the Waterfront* and *The
Harder They Fall* and felt that I would be particularly responsive
to the job of dramatizing corruptive power in America.

It is true that the subject had fascinated me from my high school
days. And *The Enemy Within*, a hard-hitting account of Kennedy's
experiences as chief counsel for the Senate Rackets Committee,
would give me the chance to write not merely a sequel to *Waterfront* but a significant extension of that film on a national scale.
Kennedy's book presented startling evidence of the collusion between Jimmy Hoffa (plus other crooked union leaders), Mafia racketeers and their "respectable" allies in the world of business.

At Kennedy's home in McLean, Virginia, it took time to break
the ice, but gradually we established good rapport. Then, charac-
teristically, young Kennedy asked me when I could begin and how
soon my screenplay would be ready. I told him that I had re-
searched the New York waterfront for more than a year before I
had begun that script; I would not feel ready to plunge into the
writing of *Enemy* until I had fully absorbed this even more complicated material. "But it's all in the book," Kennedy said with an
author's pride. I told him I would like to read the entire hearings
of the Senate Committee. "That's fifty-nine volumes," Kennedy
warned. "Millions of words." When I held out, he passed me on
to his lieutenant in charge of the Hoffa investigation, Walter
Sheridan.

Sheridan turned out to be the most unlikely of G-men. Television and movie fans accustomed to Lee Marvin or Rod Steiger and Efrem Zimbalist as their gangbuster heroes would be badly let down by Mr. Sheridan. So quiet-spoken you literally have to lean forward to hear him, on the surface a diffident, even shy and eminently gentle man.

But Kennedy's book had indicated the tiger that lurked within the deceptively bland exterior, praising Walter as tireless and unbendable, committed to the principle of integrity in government and labor-management. Outraged by the labor racketeering encouraged by political and business connivance, he would work around the clock day after day to stitch together a collar of evidence to fit even the thick, tough necks of the Jimmy Hoffas.

Until the Kennedy investigations, the robber barons of the labor movement had carved up their million dollar pies with impunity. It is one thing merely to dream the impossible dream, quite another to gather together for a convincing indictment all the little jigsaw facts buried by professional deceivers. How Walter Sheridan persevered in this quest, despite bribes, threats and government roadblocks, provides an encouraging lining for an essentially discouraging story.

For months, after Walter sent me the Rackets Committee material, I immersed myself in the testimony of thousands of witnesses who talked (or balked) about pension funds looted of millions of dollars, with a majority of those six- and seven-figure loans going to notorious Mafiosi, of "sweetheart" contracts arranged between greedy company executives and union officials on the take (including, as this book makes clear, President Hoffa himself), of once respectable industries and unions infiltrated by a blatant army of extortionists and enforcers, terrorizing the would-be honest into silence or connivance. It was material, I realized, that made waterfront crime—evil as that was—seem like very small potatoes.

Now I understood more clearly the conclusion Bob Kennedy had reached in his book—that the real enemy within was the increasingly effective alliance of big money, labor racketeers, the mob, and dishonest prosecutors, judges and government officials, without whom billions could not be stolen from our economy—and that this nationwide conspiracy was poisoning the wellspring of the nation. From my talks with Bob Kennedy, Walter Sheridan and their colleagues in the Justice Department, I was convinced of their passionate devotion to this theme—and to the conviction that we could never defeat an external enemy unless we first cut from our body politic the growing cancer of corruption that would finally destroy our society as Rome was eaten away from within two thousand years ago.

When I returned to Washington with all fifty-nine volumes of testimony buzzing in my head, I outlined a possible story line to Bob Kennedy and his staff. But now I felt a further step in research was necessary: to move on from the transcripts to the people behind the transcripts, those who had endured the pressure of belonging to a union whose dictatorship they despised and whose goon-squad violence they feared.

When I discussed this request with Kennedy he again passed me on to Walter, who, in his calm, cautious way, put me in touch with a fascinating union leader, a highly placed officer who had been secretly cooperating with the Kennedy investigation because he had lived his life as an honest trade unionist and had become disgusted with the wholesale looting of union funds, the terrorizing of union members who protested, the Mafia leaders allowed to pass themselves off as union leaders. The roster of Teamster vice presidents read like a Who's Who in American Crime, and "Max," as we shall call our inside contact, had had a bellyfull.

Here, through Walter's sensitive liaison, I was to get a one-on-one insight into the ongoing drama—the tension that runs through so much of Walter's book—a man's conscience struggling to keep afloat in a sea of fear. For the next few months I was to meet Max under conditions that reminded me of my World War II days in the O.S.S. We met in Los Angeles, in a small town in Florida, and in Mexico—using pseudonyms and even taking the precaution of meeting in a third, neutral room in case we were being followed or bugged. His nerves were shot and he was drinking himself through the day, terrified of Hoffa and his henchmen, yet driven by the gut-conviction that mobsters like Johnny Dio and Red Dorfman and Joey Glimco and Tony Provenzano and all the rest of the tribe were poison to the labor movement to which he had dedicated his life. Through Max, I met other Teamster dissidents, all hating Hoffa's guts and all afraid to face his wrath.

Thanks to Max, I was able to personify in my script a reluctant, tormented thorn in the tough hide of the composite labor boss I called Pete Bonner. Alas, the film for reasons that bring me very close to the spirit of this uncompromising book, has never reached the screen. Jerry Wald, who alone had had the courage to produce it, died suddenly, at a time when 20th Century-Fox was fighting for survival after its spendthrift *Cleopatra*. A labor tough walked right into the office of the new head of the studio to warn him that if the picture was ever made drivers would refuse to deliver the prints to the theaters. And, if they got there by any other means, stink bombs would drive out the audiences.

With Bob Kennedy's encouragement, I tried to produce the film myself. One film star phoned to say he loved the script, then came to my house drunk to tell me he was afraid he might be killed if he did it. There have been ever-increasing ties between the mob and some of the film studios and, of course, those studios rejected it out of hand. Finally, I had firm interest from Columbia, the company that had released *On the Waterfront*. On the eve of the meeting with Columbia executives to which I had been invited, every one of the people who was to attend that conference received a letter from William Bufalino, whose activities on behalf of Hoffa are a matter of record (as Sheridan's book confirms). Bufalino is, among other things, a lawyer, but this letter was disturbingly extra-legal. It stated flatly that 20th Century-Fox had wisely abandoned the project as soon as all the possible eventualities had been pointed out to them, and he felt confident that Columbia would be smart enough to do likewise. On the morning of the meeting, a studio secretary called to tell me that it had been canceled, indefinitely. Apparently Hoffa and Bufalino had decided what the American people could and could not see. And the Hollywood "front office"—notorious for its vincibility—had meekly complied.

But that was only a taste of the frustration that Walter Sheridan had suffered over the years as he battled against the invisible empire. The jury tampering in Nashville reads like *Police Gazette* fiction, but it's all too true. The Chicago trial, in which Jimmy Hoffa was finally convicted of stealing more than a million dollars from his Teamsters Pension Fund, is the stuff of high social drama. And the trials and tribulations of Ed Partin, the big and tough Teamster from Baton Rouge who turned on Hoffa, helped to convict him, and then was offered a million dollars if he would perjure himself and retract his testimony—or be destroyed if he refused; all of this must be read, and then reread and digested, to be believed. And remembered. The incredible cast of those working to gain a pardon for Hoffa, and a buy-off or conviction of Partin, include governors, federal judges, Louisiana Mafiosi, Chicago gangsters, Pension Fund lawyer-grafters, senators, congressmen, administration officials, con-men, sleazy go-betweens. Even Audie Murphy and George Murphy get into the act, not to mention gun-totin' William Loeb and his infamous Teamsters-financed *Manchester Union Leader.*

Here is the enemy within, in all its star-spangled unglory.

The enemy walks among us, not as an underworld fugitive but as an adornment of cafe society, enjoying the best tables in New York and Miami, Las Vegas, Hollywood and Acapulco. You'll find him chumming with the celebrities at Le Club or "21" or the Sands, or in the Polo Lounge at the Beverly Hills Hotel. Instead of fearing government pressure, he'll boast of his *in* with the White House. And the "cream" of our society don't shun him, they invite him to their parties. And they hope he will return the favor.

In this painstaking book, Sheridan faces up to the reality that, after all the convictions and sensational disclosures, corruption flows on. George Jackson rotted in jail for nearly a decade for heisting $70. Jimmy Hoffa cops a million, bribes juries, runs with the most dangerous gangsters in America and, thanks to the intervention of his good friend Dick Nixon, does an easy five. This, after the parole board had rejected Hoffa's appeal three times in a row. This, in an election year when Nixon has become anathema to the legitimate labor movement and the Teamsters wind up as his only big-labor support.

The Nixon-Hoffa friendship, beginning when Nixon was Vice President, was emphasized again by his recent attendance at the executive board meeting of the Teamsters. And his Secretary of Labor gave fulsome praise to that gang-ridden union at its most recent convention. "A strange love affair," *The New York Times* has described it. One might call it something even stranger. Sheridan doesn't go in much for adjectives. He's a fact man and his step-by-step account of the Hoffa-Nixon romance will make you want to weep for an America that is now challenged—as Bob Kennedy had begun to challenge her—to reach deep down and rediscover her soul.

Will the dry rot of moral decay leave the field to the Hoffas, the I.T.T. and the Syndicate? The enemy within seems to grow stronger every day. Whether or not a Jack Anderson, a Ralph Nader, a Walter Sheridan can arouse our people from their complacency is the question on which the future course of America may depend.

Brookside
Long Island, New York
July 4, 1972

THE FALL
AND RISE OF
JIMMY HOFFA

Prologue

AT 4 P.M. ON December 23, 1971, James Riddle Hoffa walked out the gates of the federal penitentiary at Lewisburg, Pennsylvania, a free man. Earlier that day President Richard M. Nixon had signed an Executive Grant of Clemency authorizing Hoffa's immediate release from prison. Hoffa turned aside questions by waiting newsmen as to why he thought the President of the United States had intervened on his behalf.

Three times in the preceding two years the United States Parole Board had considered and rejected, by unanimous vote, Hoffa's petitions for freedom. Now, acting on a petition for commutation of sentence, which had been filed only one week earlier, and without the usual consultation with the judges who had sentenced him, the prosecutors who had convicted him, or the Criminal Division of his own Department of Justice, the President had, by the stroke of a pen, sprung Jimmy Hoffa.

It has been fifteen years since I first saw Jimmy Hoffa in the Caucus Room of the old Senate Office Building in Washington, D.C. I was a young, relatively new recruit on the staff of the Senate Select Committee on Improper Activities in the Labor or Management Field, more commonly known as the McClellan Committee. The Committee was set up in early 1957 under the chairmanship of Senator John McClellan of Arkansas to investigate labor racketeering. I was sitting on a folding chair behind Robert F. Kennedy, the chief counsel of the Committee, and his brother, Senator John F. Kennedy, one of the Committee members. Hoffa was seated directly in front of me at the witness table, ready to testify, his patent leather hair combed straight back, glistening in the bright glare of television lamps. He was the ninth vice president of the International Brotherhood of Teamsters, the largest, richest and most powerful labor union in the world. He knew that the following month he would be elected the general president of that union at its convention in Miami. He was cocky and impatient and anxious to be on his way.

I did not know, as I sat there that August day in 1957, that I had already passed the point of no return, that henceforth my life would be inescapably intertwined with those Kennedy brothers and this tough Teamster from Detroit.

For the next seven years I would be intimately involved in what some would call Robert Kennedy's vendetta to get Jimmy Hoffa. It was not a vendetta. It was, rather, a determined and dedicated effort by Bob Kennedy, as chief counsel of the Committee and later as Attorney General of the United States, to cope with a uniquely talented man who used his almost limitless power and resources to perpetuate a racket-infested nationwide empire; to corrupt public officials and private citizens; and to arrogantly violate his own fiduciary trust and the laws of the land for the benefit of himself and his associates and to the detriment of his union members and the public good. For Kennedy to have done less than he did would have been a violation of his own public trust and a dereliction of duty.

The McClellan Committee did not only investigate Jimmy Hoffa and the Teamsters Union, it also conducted an unprecedented inquiry into labor racketeering. In public hearings the Committee exposed cesspools of corruption that had been stagnating unchecked in the netherworld of some segments of labor and management. In all, officials of fifteen unions and over fifty companies were demonstrated to have been involved in illicit practices. The testimony of 1525 witnesses who appeared before the Committee told a fifty-nine-volume story of corruption. Much of that story did have to do with Jimmy Hoffa and his associates in the labor movement, the business world and the underworld.

When Senator John F. Kennedy was elected President, he asked his brother Bob to serve as Attorney General. Bob Kennedy reluctantly acceded to his wishes and agreed to head the Department of Justice. He asked me to go with him as a special assistant.

As Attorney General, Kennedy brought the Justice Department actively into the fight against organized crime, which he had come to recognize as an acutely evil force that thrived on the weaknesses of society, systematically corrupting and eroding its institutions. He saw Jimmy Hoffa's empire as a satellite of this force. He had seen enough first-hand, during the exhaustive probings by the McClellan Committee, to know both the enormity of the problems of syndicated crime and labor racketeering and the difficulty of dealing effectively with them. And having criticized the Department of Justice under the previous Administration for not doing enough about the problems, it was his nature to now assume the responsibility.

He beefed up the Organized Crime Section of the department's Criminal Division, gave it new direction and purpose and designated it as the coordinating nerve center for an all-out drive by all federal investigative agencies against organized crime. He knew from experience that even such an effort would take years to make significant breakthroughs and that a lesser effort would be meaningless. He also began drafting new legislation to bring the interstate activities of organized crime under federal jurisdiction.

He asked me to gather together and head up a small group of bright young attorneys to take a fresh look at labor racketeering, starting with material that had been generated by the McClellan Committee, to evaluate possible violations of federal statutes, with particular emphasis on Hoffa and his empire. This was not the first such group in the Department of Justice. Kennedy's predecessor as Attorney General, William P. Rogers, had set up a similar group to determine which of the many possible violations of federal law uncovered by the McClellan Committee offered the best chance for the successful prosecution of Hoffa. After an extensive grand jury investigation, that group had recommended that Hoffa be indicted and prosecuted for his role in what the evidence indicated was a flagrant misuse of union funds in a Florida land deal called Sun Valley, Inc. The authorization to indict Hoffa was given by the department but was then abruptly withdrawn at the last minute during the campaign in which Hoffa was supporting Vice President Nixon for the Presidency. Shortly after Senator Kennedy was elected President, but before he took office, the attorneys were sent back to Florida by Rogers to bring the indictment. Hoffa felt he had been double-crossed, but Attorney General Rogers obviously did not want to leave behind him what might appear to be a fixed case for Jimmy Hoffa. Thus Richard Nixon's political debt to Jimmy Hoffa was left unpaid.

Shortly after we arrived at the Department of Justice, we

learned that not only was Hoffa misusing the Pension Fund to fraudulently cover up the earlier misuse of union funds in the Sun Valley project, he was also the pivotal force in the dispensing of numerous substantial loans by the fund to persons and under conditions that appeared highly questionable. There was evidence of misrepresentation of facts, diversion of funds and under-the-table payment of substantial cash kickbacks. Based on this evidence, we launched an intensive investigation of the operation of the Pension Fund. It was a major undertaking, requiring grand jury investigations in many of the major cities in the country. At every opportunity Hoffa made public charges that a vendetta was being waged by Robert Kennedy to destroy the Teamsters Union, citing the number of grand juries being utilized by the government.

The Pension Fund at that time had assets of over $200,000,000. It was a trust fund for the payment of pensions to retired Teamsters members. Jimmy Hoffa was a trustee of that fund, with the fiduciary responsibility to Teamsters members to handle their fund judiciously. Most such funds are administered by established investment institutions which, by policy, invest only a small proportion of the funds in real estate, and even then, only in sound ventures. Even within the Teamsters Union, the Western Conference of Teamsters, for instance, delegated the control of its pension fund in this manner, resisting a determined bid by Hoffa to take it over. Control of the huge Central States Fund, however, was retained by Hoffa and his fellow trustees and they invested a majority of the funds in speculative real estate ventures. Millions of dollars were loaned by the fund for the construction or remodeling of hotels, restaurants, shopping centers and other high-risk ventures, many of which culminated in foreclosure. Millions of dollars were poured into hotels and mob-controlled gambling casinos in Las Vegas. Other underworld figures profited from the fund, either by receiving loans themselves or by being cut in on the substantial cash kickbacks that were a condition of many of the loans. It was the biggest slush fund in history, used by Hoffa as a power vehicle for the benefit of himself, his associates and the mob.

In the three and one-half years that followed, investigations of unseemly loans by the Pension Fund and other nefarious activities of Hoffa and his associates went forward. While his battery of attorneys waged a staying action in the courts, and powerful political figures, including United States Senators and Congressmen, sought to intervene on his behalf, Hoffa pushed ahead in his drive for more power.

In the spring of 1962 he was indicted by a federal grand jury in Nashville, Tennessee, for allegedly receiving hundreds of thousands of dollars in payoffs through a trucking company set up in that city in his wife's maiden name. His trial, later that year, ended in a hung jury after one of the most massive efforts to tamper with a jury in history. The trial judge ordered a grand jury investigation, which resulted in the indictment of Hoffa and several others, ultimately including one of his attorneys, for jury tampering. Hoffa was also indicted, along with another group of persons, in Chicago, on a charge of having defrauded the Pension Fund of almost $2,000,000. In 1964 he was convicted of both charges and was sentenced to an aggregate term of thirteen years in prison. By that time over one hundred other Teamsters officials and their associates had also been convicted of various crimes.

When Robert Kennedy resigned as Attorney General in August, 1964, to run for the United States Senate in New York, I also resigned and joined his campaign. After his election I accepted a position as a special correspondent with the National Broadcasting Company. I thought that finally, after seven years, my involvement with Jimmy Hoffa was over. It was not.

For three years Hoffa battled to stay free. Again, the voices of Senators and Congressmen were raised in his defense, demanding an investigation of the Department of Justice. His attorneys filed motion after motion attempting to overturn his convictions. Numerous persons were offered bribes to furnish false affidavits in support of these motions, and some of them did. A $225,000 fund was created and huge sums of money were offered to government witnesses and others, including FBI Director J. Edgar Hoover, to furnish information that might somehow keep Hoffa from going to prison. Some persons who could not be bought were threatened. A threat was even made to the brother of a Supreme Court Justice.

Jimmy Hoffa once said that every man has his price. He was almost right. But because there were some who could not be bought, and because Hoffa was justly convicted in two courts of law, all of these efforts failed. On March 7, 1967, three years after his conviction, Hoffa entered the Lewisburg prison to begin serving his sentence.

Again I thought it was over and again I was wrong. The campaign that had been waged to keep him from going to prison now turned into an even more intensified effort to get him out. The intimidation and attempted bribery of witnesses continued. When the Criminal Division of the Department of Justice began an investigation of these corrupt efforts, a United States Senator threatened to have the head of the division indicted. Another United States Senator, who had received over $100,000 from one of Hoffa's attorneys, used a subcommittee of which he was chairman in an apparent effort to develop evidence to help Hoffa. One of the key witnesses against Hoffa came under continually increasing pressure from investigations by state and, finally, federal agencies. Offers of seemingly unlimited amounts of money to anyone who could help free Hoffa continued, as did the political pressures on every level.

With the election of President Nixon in 1968 things finally started moving in Hoffa's direction. The key witness against Hoffa was indicted twice by the federal government and became the subject of an all-out investigation by several government agencies. As the government kept applying pressure on this witness, Hoffa's agents continued to offer to alleviate his problem if he would agree to help Hoffa. Friends of Hoffa, both within and outside the Teamsters Union, found they now had an access, previously denied them, to both the Department of Justice and the White House. By the following Christmas, after Hoffa's first petition for freedom had been rejected by the Parole Board, active consideration was being given by President Nixon to commuting Hoffa's sentence, but disclosures of this possibility by the press aborted the plan.

After Hoffa's second bid for parole was denied, a series of secret meetings between his representatives and high-ranking officials of the Department of Justice were held. As a result, Hoffa begrudgingly agreed to abandon his intention to seek reelection as president of the Teamsters Union at the 1971 convention and to resign from all of his positions in the union. In return, he was to be paroled at a rehearing by the Parole Board.

Within minutes of the announcement of Hoffa's resignation and the immediate election by the Teamsters Executive Board of his hand-picked successor, Frank Fitzsimmons, President Nixon attended a meeting of the Executive Board in Miami. The new romance between the White House and the Teamsters Union was given further impetus two weeks later when President Nixon sent a delegation headed by the Secretary of Labor, bearing his personal message, to the Teamsters Convention in Miami, which formally elected Frank Fitzsimmons as the new general president.

The Parole Board met the next month to rehear Hoffa's petition. Hoffa and his associates fully expected that the petition would be granted. They thought they had made a deal. But the Parole Board, in a demonstration of its independence, again turned Hoffa down by a unanimous vote, after expressing some concern about the fact that he had received a $1,700,000 lump-sum retirement settlement and that his wife and son were still on the Teamsters payroll for salaries totaling nearly $100,000 a year.

Again, as in 1960, Hoffa thought he had been double-crossed. Emissaries were dispatched to the Department of Justice to register outraged protest. Finally, two days before Christmas, the account was settled, and Hoffa was freed by the President of the United States.

The terms of Hoffa's release forbid him from engaging in "direct or indirect management of any labor organization" until March, 1980, and require him to remain under the supervision of a probation officer until March, 1973. Hoffa will undoubtedly adhere, at least technically, to the latter requirement but he has no intention of conforming to the former. He is determined to find a way to have that restriction lifted so that he can take back what he considers his—the office of general president of the International Brotherhood of Teamsters. The smart money is riding with him.

This is the story of these past fifteen years. It is a chronology of corruption. It is also a sad but realistic testament to the inability or unwillingness of our society and its institutions to persevere over the long haul in contending with the corruptors. In the final analysis, it becomes easier to join them than to fight them.

I decided to write this book when it became apparent that the attempts to corrupt government witnesses and others were going to continue until Hoffa somehow obtained his freedom and that no one was going to really do anything about it. It is now just as clear that even though Hoffa has finally been released through the intervention of President Nixon, these corrupt efforts will continue until he regains the presidency of the Teamsters Union.

PART I

THE RISE

CHAPTER I

The Rise of Jimmy Hoffa

JIMMY HOFFA WAS SEVENTEEN years old when he participated in his first strike. As part of a crew on the loading docks of the Kroger Company in Detroit, Hoffa rebelled against the long hours, low pay and poor working conditions. Though smaller and younger than some of the others, he stepped forward and helped galvanize the individual frustration and discontent of his co-workers into a group protest. They refused to unload a shipment of perishables and forced the company to bargain with them and remedy some of their grievances. Jimmy Hoffa had made his first move as a leader and henceforth would never be anything else.

Hoffa and a group of the men decided to form a local union and obtained a charter from the American Federation of Labor. The following year (1932) they moved into the Teamsters Union and a year later Hoffa was in charge of Local 299 of the International Brotherhood of Teamsters in Detroit. Although it had only a few hundred members, it was the largest Teamsters local in the city.

The International Brotherhood of Teamsters was formed in 1903 and established its headquarters in Indianapolis, Indiana. Its first president, Cornelius P. Shea, served until 1907, when he was succeeded by Daniel J. Tobin, who continued in office until 1952. Under Tobin, the International Union was a decentralized, loose-knit federation of fairly autonomous local unions. As the union grew, local unions in major cities banded together to form joint councils. These were designed as organizational structures and not intended as vehicles to power.

Although Hoffa's newly formed local and many of the others in Detroit were kept in trusteeship by the International during the late thirties and early forties for financial reasons, there was little interference from Indianapolis. Hoffa gained firm control of his own local and gradually extended his influence. He formed a close working relationship and friendship with Owen Bert Brennan, the head of Local 337, the second largest in the city. He then began exerting authority over the other Detroit locals. In the early 1940s he formed and headed the Michigan Conference of Teamsters and pulled all of the locals in the state into his widening power base. In 1945 he was officially elected president of Local 299—merely confirming the leadership role he had acquired during the now rescinded trusteeship. Two years later he became president of Joint Council 43. With his position consolidated as the undisputed boss of the Michigan Teamsters, Hoffa was ready to extend his domain.

The Central States Drivers Council had been formed by Minneapolis Teamster Farrell Dobbs in the late 1930s. Dobbs had the vision to realize that with interstate commerce rapidly expanding, Teamsters organization and negotiation, to be effective, would have to reach across state lines. He saw the driver of the truck that moved interstate (the over-the-road driver, as he was called), rather than the local cartage driver, as the key to the future of the Teamsters Union. When Dobbs left the union to devote himself full time to the Socialist Workers Party, Hoffa took over as negotiating chairman of the Council. He now had the perfect vehicle to expand his power throughout the Midwest.

But Hoffa did not achieve his dominant position without a struggle. From the beginning there were bitter battles with foes both within and outside the union. Dissidents in his own local and local leaders throughout the state who were protective of their own autonomy resisted submission to Hoffa's domination. Externally, depression-wracked companies fought off the organizing efforts of the Teamsters and other unions with strikebreaker goon squads, often led by racketeers. The Teamsters also battled other labor organizations, particularly the United Auto Workers, over the right to organize and represent particular groups of workers. It was a struggle that demanded stout hearts, thick skulls and a lot of muscle. Hoffa decided early in the game that he would always have more muscle than the other guy. He obtained his own racketeers. Some of his business agents, like Herman Kierdorf and his nephew Frank Kierdorf, were recruited right out of prison. Many of the others had criminal records. But the real muscle that everyone understood and feared was the mob—the Detroit Purple Gang and the Mafia. Hoffa formed working relationships with both. He also cultivated friendly relationships with certain members of the trucking industry who sat on the other side of the bargaining table.

In the late forties and early fifties Hoffa extended his control over Teamsters organizations throughout the Midwest and into the Plains States. He shrewdly utilized the Central States Drivers Council to impose his contracts and his will on employers and local unions through areawide negotiations and agreements. At the same time, his skillful and aggressive organizing efforts swelled the ranks of his membership. He leapfrogged the areas of most resistance and then squeezed them into submission by isolated strikes and embargoes. In both organization and negotiation he played one company off against another and used key friendly companies to break the solidarity of the opposition. In return, these companies received preferential treatment in their own dealings with him. Hoffa set up a system whereby he was the ultimate judge of grievances brought by union members against a company. Therefore the company knew that the decision whether to strike over grievances was in Hoffa's hands, and the member knew that control of his welfare rested with Hoffa.

In the late forties a new concept was added to collective bargaining agreements—the health and welfare fund. The Michigan Conference of Teamsters Health and Welfare Fund was established in January, 1949. In November of the same year the Central States Health and Welfare Fund was created. Both funds were administered by trustees representing labor and management. It became a provision of all contracts that, as a fringe benefit, the employer would pay so much per month into the fund which would be used to cover hospitalization and death benefits for union members. To Jimmy Hoffa these potentially enormous sums of money represented additional tools of power. They would also require an insurance company to underwrite them and an agent to manage them.

In 1949 Paul "Red" Dorfman was the head of the Waste Handlers local union in Chicago. He had taken over the local in 1939 when its founder and president, Leon Cook, was shot and killed. The other official of the union at the time was a man named Jack Ruby, who achieved notoriety many years later by shooting Lee

Harvey Oswald. Paul Dorfman represented the Chicago mob and was well connected throughout the underworld. He and Hoffa found it mutually advantageous to form an alliance. Dorfman had a stepson, Allen, who coincidentally decided to go into the insurance business. Prior to 1949 Allen Dorfman had no experience in insurance, no office and no license. His stepfather arranged through Dr. Leo Pearlman, the executive vice president of the Union Casualty Company of Mount Vernon, New York, for Allen to set up the Union Casualty Agency in Chicago in January, 1949. Three weeks later, the day after the Michigan Conference Health and Welfare Fund was established, Hoffa wrote a letter to Dr. Pearlman asking what benefits his company could offer. The real bonanza for the Union Casualty Agency, however, was to be the Central States Health and Welfare Fund, which was created later that year.

In January, 1950, insurance companies were invited to submit bids for underwriting the lucrative new Central States Fund. The Union Casualty Company was not on the list of companies solicited. Thirteen companies responded but the bids were thrown out. During this period Dr. Pearlman was in Chicago wining and dining Paul and Allen Dorfman and Hoffa. On February 2 Allen Dorfman wrote to Pearlman saying, "From all indications, it appears that our efforts to land the Central States business will be successful." Two days later a second invitation for bids went out; this time the Union Casualty Company was included.

On February 13 Allen Dorfman again wrote to Dr. Pearlman and said, "The big thing for us to consider here, Doctor, is to get the contract first. Once we are established with the Central States, the rest will be worked out." Then Dorfman quoted Hoffa as saying, "Tell Doc to get us the Central States drivers' contract, and once we are in, the rest will be good going."

The Pacific Mutual Insurance Company had submitted the lowest bid, but again the bids were thrown out. On March 7 eight of the companies, including the Union Casualty Company, were asked to submit new bids. Pacific Mutual was again the low bidder, so it was eliminated from consideration by Hoffa, who claimed that the company had experienced some financial difficulties in 1936. On March 14, 1950, the insurance for the Central States Fund was finally awarded to the Union Casualty Company.

To give some appearance of legitimacy, the insurance for the Michigan Conference of Teamsters was placed temporarily with the Continental Casualty Company. Allen Dorfman explained the decision in a letter to Dr. Pearlman dated March 17, 1950:

> They are giving the insurance of the above captioned group to the Continental Casualty Company who had submitted bid $3.75. The reason for this—they want to show whomever might have questioned the Central States Conference deal that it was to be given to the lowest bidding company.
> Now, Jimmie [*sic*] has made the following statement to me, which he had brought before his board and has been agreed upon by both them as well as the employers; that if their experience this coming year with the Continental Casualty Company does not prove to meet with their satisfaction, that Union Casualty will then assume the risk.

Dorfman's reassurance to Dr. Pearlman was well founded. On March 8, 1951, the contract for the Michigan Conference Fund was awarded to the Union Casualty Company, even though it did not submit a bid until the following day and despite the fact that Continental Casualty offered to increase benefits without increasing premiums.

Allen Dorfman and his mother Rose formed the Union Insurance Agency of Illinois and became the sole agents for both the Central States and Michigan Conference funds. Almost overnight Allen Dorfman became a wealthy man because of his stepfather's friend Jimmy Hoffa. Millions of dollars flowed into Dorfman's Union Insurance Agency, much of it in excessive commissions and fees. The only victims were the rank and file Teamsters members whose benefits were decreased by the plundering of funds set up for their welfare. The Dorfmans and their underworld friends had become permanent and pivotal members of Hoffa's empire.

Paul Dorfman's underworld influence was not confined to Chicago. He next reached out to the East Coast in a move that would offer possible increased revenues for his family's insurance agency, while at the same time paving the way for a power grab in New York by Jimmy Hoffa.

The UAW-AFL was a splinter union chartered by the AFL and made up of a dissident segment that had broken away from the UAW-CIO in 1939. Anthony Doria, the secretary-treasurer of the UAW-AFL, was invited to attend a dinner by the key officials of the Central States Drivers Council. The purpose of the invitation was to attempt to interest Doria in placing his union insurance business with the Union Casualty Company. At the same time, Paul Dorfman used his influence to persuade Doria to issue a charter for a new local union in New York City. The charter was issued to a former Communist Party member named Sam Zachman, who had previously met with Dorfman at the Hampshire House Hotel in New York. The person who would actually control the local, however, was John Dioguardi, better known as Johnny Dio, a notorious racketeer.

Dio had served three years in Sing Sing during the thirties for his involvement in a series of extortions that included terrorism and strong-arming of trucking companies going back to 1932. After his release from prison Dio worked in and then operated a series of women's dress manufacturing companies in New York, New Jersey and Pennsylvania. At the time the charter for Local 102 was issued on September 18, 1950, Dio owned a nonunion dress company in Pennsylvania. When he sold it, he was paid an additional $11,000 by the new owner to ensure that the company would remain nonunion. It was obviously not his concern for the welfare of the working man that attracted Dio to the labor movement.

Dio then linked up with another notorious racketeer, Tony "Ducks" Corallo, and began to build his own labor empire. More charters were issued for more local unions and Dio staffed them with ex-convicts. Dio was now designated regional director by the UAW-AFL International Union. Dio and his henchmen, operating under the guise of labor officials, proceeded to "negotiate" sweetheart contracts with small business operators in New York City. Most of the employees of these businesses who were forced to become members of Dio's locals were blacks and Puerto Ricans. The paid a $25 initiation fee and $3.50 a month dues and got nothing in return. The "contracts" provided for the bare minimum wage and there were no benefits of any kind. It was pure shakedown and exploitation.

A convention of the International Brotherhood of Teamsters was scheduled to be held in Los Angeles in 1952. There was general agreement among the Teamsters hierarchy that the time had come for aging Dan Tobin to step aside. His logical replacement was Dave Beck, the head of the Western Conference of Teamsters. A possible dark horse candidate was James R. Hoffa. Dave Beck had started out as a truck driver in Seattle, Washington, and, like

Hoffa, had gradually built an organization. He had succeeded in incorporating all the locals and joint councils on the West Coast under a single Western Conference, which he headed. He had held office longer than any of the other eight International vice presidents. Vice president was a title Hoffa did not yet have, but coveted. Beck sought Hoffa's support in his bid for the presidency of the union. Hoffa decided to back Beck and bide his time. With Hoffa's support, Beck became the third president of the Teamsters Union. Beck reciprocated by naming Hoffa the ninth vice president.

In late 1952 Teamsters Local 807 in New York, headed by Tom Hickey, an honest, dedicated labor leader, was attempting to organize cabdrivers in that city. Suddenly Hickey found himself competing with Local 102 of the UAW-AFL under Johnny Dio. Hickey was dismayed to learn that the racketeer-staffed local with which he was contending had the staunch backing of the new International vice president of his own union, James R. Hoffa. While covertly tutoring Dio in tactical ways to outflank Hickey, Hoffa suggested to Dave Beck that Dio and his local be brought into the Teamsters Union to continue organizational efforts with the cabdrivers and that Hickey be directed to desist. Dave Beck, however, with some prodding from AFL-CIO President George Meany, refused to give a Teamsters charter to Johnny Dio's local and supported Hickey in the jurisdictional dispute. Thus Hoffa and Dio were temporarily stymied.

In Chicago, in addition to his connection with the Dorfmans, there was further evidence of the increasing ties between Hoffa's growing empire and the mob, in the person of Joey Glimco. The cabdrivers in Chicago had been organized since the 1930s by Teamsters Local 777. Since 1937 Glimco, though only a trustee of the local, had controlled it with an iron hand and extracted kickbacks from the local union officials' paychecks. The local officials were even required to pay the income tax on the money paid to Glimco in tribute. At the same time, Glimco was extorting similar payments from Teamsters officials and businessmen in Chicago's Fulton Street Market. Glimco, who had been arrested over thirty times for charges including murder, assault with a deadly weapon and extortion, but jailed only once, was a close associate of the leading mobsters in Chicago. In 1952 he ousted the president of Local 777 and took it over himself. Thereafter he used the union treasury as his own. In an incredible under-the-table arrangement with the cab companies, Glimco kicked back a percentage of members' dues to the companies.

Other Hoffa allies in Chicago included Dorfman associate Don Peters, the president since 1941 of Teamsters Local 743, and John T. "Sandy" O'Brien, the president of both Joint Council 25 and Local 710 and a vice president of the International Union. O'Brien instituted a unique way of stealing money from his members. Starting in 1952, he and other officers of Local 710 received a percentage of the dues paid by the membership in addition to their salaries, vacation pay and Christmas bonuses. In 1952 O'Brien's combined income from the local was $43,614.86. By 1955 it had reached $70,376.62.

In St. Louis Harold J. Gibbons headed the Teamsters organization. He had become involved in the labor movement in the early 1930s and had thereafter served as an official in several unions in the Midwest. In 1941 he became the St. Louis director of the Retail, Wholesale and Department Store Employees Union of the CIO. In 1947, as a result of friction within the union, Gibbons took his organization out of the parent body and formed an independent union called the United Distribution Workers Union. A year later the new union merged with Teamsters Local 688 and Gibbons became president of the combined organization. He then went on to gain control of Joint Council 13 and the entire St. Louis Teamsters organization.

In the early 1950s the St. Louis mob decided to move in on Gibbons' operation. In desperation, Gibbons turned for help to Jimmy Hoffa. The two men had never met but Gibbons was aware of Hoffa's reputation for having the right connections in the underworld. Hoffa was able to negotiate a truce and thereby enlisted Gibbons as a key figure and supporter in his expanding empire. It was a strange alliance between the suave, intellectual Gibbons and the brash hustler Hoffa. When Hoffa took over the Central States Conference of Teamsters, Gibbons became his number two man.

To reinforce his own muscle, Gibbons in 1952 recruited Robert "Barney" Baker, a three-hundred-pound former prizefighter. Baker had come up through the tough New York waterfront jungle where he had been a strong-arm man for a group of racketeers who had attempted to take over the piers and truck terminals in the late thirties and early forties. From there he went to the mob-controlled Colonial Inn in Hollywood, Florida, where he served as a doorman and bouncer. There followed a short stint with ill-fated "Bugsy" Seigel who was building the Flamingo Hotel, the mob's first Las Vegas casino.

When Barney Baker joined the Gibbons organization in St. Louis he went on the payroll as an organizer for the Central States Conference of Teamsters. His paychecks were signed by both Gibbons and Hoffa, as the ranking officers of that organization. Baker came to his new task with impressive underworld credentials and was soon in contact with the leading St. Louis Mafia figures. In April, 1953, he was arrested by the St. Louis police and charged with possession of a concealed weapon. The charge was dismissed.

In June, 1953, Jimmy Hoffa was suddenly confronted with the first serious threat to his free-wheeling power quest. A subcommittee of the House of Representatives Government Operations Committee, chaired by Congressman Clare E. Hoffman of Michigan, which had been looking into misuse of union welfare funds and labor racketeering, held hearings in Detroit. Hoffa and Dorfman were subpoenaed and questioned about their relationship and activities in connection with the Central States Health and Welfare Fund. They both declined to answer questions and the subcommittee recommended that they be cited for contempt. Back in Washington, however, political pressures were being brought to bear to restrain the irascible Michigan Congressman from broadening his inquiry. It was decided that the Government Operations Committee did not have proper jurisdiction to pursue the investigation.

Hoffman then persuaded the chairman of the House Labor Committee, Sam McConnell of Pennsylvania, to establish another subcommittee to continue the investigation. Congressman Wint Smith, a conservative Republican from Kansas, was appointed chairman with Hoffman serving as a committee member. Hearings were scheduled for November, 1953, in Detroit. In addition to the activities of Hoffa and the Dorfmans in connection with the Health and Welfare funds, the subcommittee was interested in other phases of Hoffa's operations, such as certain political contributions and the formation of the Test Fleet Corporation, a trucking company that had been set up in his wife's maiden name.

Hoffa was now faced with the revival of a congressional inquiry that he thought had been quietly buried. Since the chairman of the new subcommittee, Wint Smith, was from Kansas, it was not surprising that two Hoffa emissaries, Barney Baker and Gibbons' lieutenant, Dick Kavner, turned up in Wichita, Kansas, at the law firm of former Governor Payne Ratner. Ratner was retained to assist Hoffa in the upcoming Detroit hearings and was assured of future Teamsters business.

The subcommittee held hearings in Detroit in late November. On November 25, the day before Thanksgiving, Chairman Wint Smith was called from the hearing to take a long-distance telephone call. The day after Thanksgiving Jimmy Hoffa appeared as a witness and this time answered the questions asked. But Congressman Smith had already told Detroit newsmen that he was under pressure to conclude the hearings and was quoted as saying, "The pressure comes from way up there, and I just can't talk about it any more specifically than that." Nothing further came of the investigation and Hoffa was once again home free.

In Ohio Hoffa's key lieutenant was William Presser. In the early forties Presser had organized a local jukebox union in Cleveland called the Musical Maintenance Workers Union, which later became Local 442 of the International Brotherhood of Electrical Workers. Presser perfected a system for "stabilizing" the jukebox industry. It involved a collusive arrangement between an "association" set up by jukebox operators for this purpose and the local union to control competition and ensure that the preferred operators acquired and maintained the preferred location. It was mutually advantageous and profitable for the association and the union. The arrangement was enforced by the threat or use of a picket line.

In 1945 a man named Eugene C. "Jimmy" James set up a jukebox local in Detroit with Presser's help. Two years later the Teamsters Union issued a charter to Local 985 in Detroit and Jimmy James took it over as a jukebox local. Shortly thereafter, the wives of Jimmy Hoffa and Bert Brennan went on the payroll of Local 985 in their maiden names at $100 a week each. In attempting to "stabilize" the industry in Detroit James ran headlong into the Mafia, which controlled one of the record distributing companies there. The tensions were eased considerably when James agreed to bring William E. Bufalino into the local. Bufalino was married to the niece of Angelo Meli, one of the Detroit Mafia chieftains. In 1949 Jimmy James left Local 985 and took over mob-controlled Local 46 of the Laundry Workers Union in Chicago.

In 1951 Presser obtained another charter from the Teamsters Union and moved his jukebox operation into the newly formed Local 410 in Cleveland. He opened up a branch of the local in Youngstown, Ohio, and installed as business agent Joseph Blumetti, a former bartender who had been released from the penitentiary in 1946 after serving half of a six-year sentence for white slavery.

Presser found that with a Teamsters local he was able to enforce the arrangement between the jukebox operator association and the union even more effectively. It was only necessary to suggest to a tavern owner that he might not receive his beer deliveries if he did not have the right jukebox in his establishment. With the jukebox industry thus stabilized, Presser went on to become the number one Teamster in the state of Ohio. He became president of the Cleveland cabdrivers' Local 555, Joint Council 41 and the Ohio Conference of Teamsters. He placed three of his brothers-in-law and his son in union positions.

Presser also established his liaison with the mob. Louis "Babe" Triscaro, a former prizefighter, became the president of Local 436 of the Excavation and Race Track Workers in Cleveland. Triscaro, who was associated with leading Mafia figures in Ohio, California and New York, became Presser's right-hand man and served as vice chairman of Joint Council 41.

In Toledo Larry Steinberg, who, like Harold Gibbons, had left the Wholesale, Retail and Department Store Workers Union of the CIO and moved into the Teamsters Union, acquired control of Joint Council 25 there. Steinberg, an honest, dedicated man, adopted a policy of live and let live with Hoffa and Presser and they reciprocated. In Cincinnati Jim Luken, the president of the Milk Drivers Local 98, actively opposed both Presser and Hoffa. In 1954 Presser sent one of his brothers-in-law, Harvey Friedman, to Cincinnati to set up a jukebox local. Luken, who was aware of Friedman's criminal record and objected to his activities and his appointment as a Teamsters official, went to Hoffa, whom he had never met, to complain. Hoffa told Luken that Bill Presser was his man and that if he wanted to get along in the Teamsters Union in Ohio, he would have to take orders from Presser. Luken courageously defied Hoffa and Presser and girded himself for what he knew would be a long and lonely fight for survival.

In late 1954 another congressional subcommittee under Congressman George Bender came to Cleveland to investigate alleged corruption in the Teamsters Union. Again, the investigation died quietly after a very short life. It was not merely coincidental that the Teamsters switched their support to Bender in his race for a seat in the United States Senate.

Hoffa was afforded another opportunity to extend his influence to the East Coast in 1954. The contracts between the New York City and New Jersey Teamsters locals and the trucking companies were due to expire on August 31, 1954. A negotiating committee for the Teamsters headed by Tom Hickey, the general organizer for the New York metropolitan area, was attempting to reach an areawide agreement with the trucking companies that would provide a sizable wage increase for both local cartage and over-the-road drivers. An impasse was reached in the negotiations and Dave Beck sent a group of International vice presidents in to assist. The group was headed by Hoffa, who immediately installed John O'Rourke, his ally in the New York Teamsters organization, to replace Hickey on the negotiating committee. Hickey and his local walked out of the negotiations, which were being held at the Henry Hudson Hotel in New York City. After Hickey left, Johnny Dio, now a familiar figure, appeared at the hotel and told his friend Jimmy Hoffa that he was looking for a job. Hoffa was quoted as responding, "Well, you always know where to get one." Also present with Hoffa was a man from Cleveland named Phil Weiss who used his influence with labor leaders such as Hoffa to make deals with employers. During the negotiations Weiss approached the chairman of the committee representing the trucking companies and told him he could assure they would get a break if they placed their insurance with an agency from Chicago which he would recommend.

Hoffa's interest in the New York negotiations was twofold. He wanted to gain control of the huge Joint Council 16 in order to take over the eastern seaboard. To do this he had to discredit and undercut Tom Hickey and his friend Martin Lacey, the president of the Joint Council, and replace them with his man, John O'Rourke. In addition, he did not want the New York Teamsters to negotiate a wage higher than he had negotiated with some of the same companies in the Central States contract. The bargaining had broken down with Tom Hickey demanding a wage increase of twenty-five cents an hour. The truckers would not agree to more than fifteen cents an hour. Dave Beck had backed Hickey and his committee on the twenty-five-cent figure and had authorized a strike on that basis. When Hoffa took over the negotiations he offered to settle for eighteen cents the first year and seven cents the second year, even though he had no authority from Beck to do so. The Central States trucking companies obviously preferred Hoffa's lower settlement offer and one of their representatives was on hand at the negotiations.

When Hickey and his local broke away from the negotiating committee after Hoffa's takeover, Hickey immediately went out and started signing up individual companies on the basis of a twenty-five-cent increase. The negotiating committee for the New York truck owners, even though they realized they might get a better deal from Hoffa, were fearful of his incursion into their territory and the possible accompanying underworld influence. Therefore they decided they would be better off in the long run dealing with honest Teamsters like Hickey and Lacey—even at a higher price—and they all fell into line and accepted Hickey's twenty-five-cent increase. Hoffa's bid to discredit Hickey and Lacey and take over New York was again temporarily stalled. But he would be back.

Hoffa negotiated his first pension plan as part of his Central States contract in January, 1955. The Central States Health and Welfare Fund, the Michigan Conference Health and Welfare Fund and the growing funds of Local 299 had all served their purposes and would continue to do so. But they were insignificant compared to the new vehicle he was about to acquire. At the time, Hoffa himself did not comprehend the enormity of the economic monster he was creating.

Under the terms of the original contract each employer paid $2.00 per worker each week into the fund. The fund was given the name of The Central States Southeast, Southwest Areas Pension Fund but was commonly referred to as the Teamsters Pension Fund. At the outset no procedure was established in the contract for the administration of the fund nor was any set amount stipulated for retirement benefits. It was subsequently agreed that the fund would be managed by a Board of Trustees composed of six union representatives and six employer representatives. It was obvious from the beginning, however, that through threat of strikes and control of "friendly" employer trustees, Hoffa would exert almost absolute control over the fund.

With his new-found reservoir of funds firmly in control, Hoffa again looked to the East and embarked on a bold scheme to capture control of the stubborn New York Teamsters organization and its 140,000 members.

The election of officers of Joint Council 16 was coming up in February, 1956. Hoffa knew that if he could bring about the election of his man, John O'Rourke, to head the Council, he would finally have won the battle. In November, 1955, Hoffa approached Einar Mohn, the executive vice president of the International Teamsters Union and Dave Beck's right-hand man. Mohn, whose home base was Los Angeles, was an honest man, but one who did not ask too many questions and minded his own business. Hoffa asked Mohn for charters for seven new Teamsters locals in New York. He told Mohn that most of the locals to be chartered were at that time affiliated with the UAW-AFL. Without investigating the matter further, Mohn issued the charters. He did not, as was customary, notify either Martin Lacey or Tom Hickey that new locals were being chartered in their jurisdiction. The charters were given to John McNamara, an official of Local 808 in New York who was a friend of Hoffa and Johnny Dio. McNamara turned them over to Dio and Tony "Ducks" Corallo. The ploy that had failed in 1953 now succeeded. Dio and Corallo "staffed" the new locals with their gangster friends who then were in a position to vote in the Joint Council election for John O'Rourke. Five of these locals did not have a single member. They were "paper locals" controlled by the mob to help their friend Jimmy Hoffa muscle his way into New York.

When Lacey and Hickey got wind of what was going on they called a meeting of the Joint Council. At the Council's direction they sent a letter to Dave Beck demanding an explanation. They pointed out that they had been specifically promised, in a letter from Einar Mohn in June, 1954, that they would be consulted prior to the issuance of any new charters in New York. Beck never responded but four weeks later Mohn sent a telegram in which he said that these and other charters had been issued quickly to accommodate different groups around the country seeking affiliation with the Teamsters as a result of the recent merger of the AFL-CIO. It was an obvious subterfuge, and Lacey, on behalf of the Joint Council, responded with a telegram again demanding a reply to their letter to Beck and more details about the new charters. The telegram stated that in the meantime the Joint Council would continue to refuse to accept the new locals in the Council.

In a countermove a letter was sent to Beck by Dio's cronies on behalf of five of the locals, urging that the locals be recognized as members of the Joint Council with the right to participate in the upcoming election. One of the signers of the letter was Harry Davidoff who had been convicted of extortion and had an arrest record going back to 1933.

Dave Beck finally ruled that the paper locals should be allowed to vote in the election but that the votes would not be counted unless they would affect the outcome. The election was held on February 14, 1956, and Lacey received eleven more votes than O'Rourke. The forty-two votes cast by the paper locals would give the election to O'Rourke. Lacey went into federal court and obtained a ruling that the votes were invalid and that the paper locals should not be seated on the Joint Council.

Hoffa had been stopped again, but only temporarily. His opposition had finally been intimidated and was exhausted by the battle. One year later Martin Lacey, disillusioned and in ill health, declined to run and John O'Rourke was elected without opposition. Tom Hickey would be opposed by O'Rourke for his office as vice president of the International Union at the next Teamsters Convention in September, 1957, and faced almost certain defeat with Hoffa now in control of New York.

Tony "Ducks" Corallo was a member of the hierarchy of the New York underworld. He had acquired his nickname because of his ability to "duck" convictions. He had served only one six-month sentence, for possession of narcotics in 1941. Before Hoffa came on the New York scene, Corallo had already moved into the labor movement and by 1955 controlled five Teamsters locals, although he held office in only one (vice president of Local 239). Sam Goldstein, another labor racketeer, was president of that local but took orders from Corallo. Johnny Dio, although lower in the underworld structure than Corallo, was ambitious and well connected—and he had a friend named Jimmy Hoffa. It was a classic example of Hoffa and the mob using each other for their mutual benefit. During this period Dio and Corallo brought into the labor movement some forty men with an aggregate record of 178 arrests and 77 convictions. By the time Hoffa finally gained control of the New York Teamsters organization, twenty-five of these same men had been convicted on new charges of bribery, extortion, perjury and forgery. These included Sam Goldstein of Local 239, Harry Davidoff, who served as an "official" of one of the paper locals, and Dio himself. There were also other New York Teamsters officials who worked closely with Dio and Hoffa in the Joint Council takeover, such as John McNamara of Local 808, and Abe Gordon and Milton Holt, who were officials of Local 805 which Dio often used as a headquarters. When it was all over Jimmy Hoffa had vastly expanded his empire and was the most powerful vice president in the Teamsters Union and the undisputed heir apparent to Dave Beck. But he was also beholden to another major segment of the Mafia.

Across the Hudson River in Hoboken, New Jersey, a business agent for Teamsters Local 560 named Tony Provenzano, who had close Mafia connections and a bent for shaking down trucking companies, was growing in power and would soon be elected president of the local and subsequently of New Jersey Joint Council 73. He, too, would become a staunch ally and supporter of Hoffa.

At about this same time, in Philadelphia, Hoffa arranged through the International Hotel and Restaurant Workers Union for a charter to be issued for a new local to one Samuel "Shorty" Feldman whose arrest record going back to 1928 included charges of murder, armed robbery, possession of narcotics and burglary. Feldman had been unable to get the charter on his own but quickly obtained it after Hoffa interceded. It demonstrated not only another underworld connection of Hoffa's in yet another city, but also his power to influence the policies of another international union.

Back in Chicago, Paul De Lucia, more commonly known as Paul "The Waiter" Ricca, had been convicted of income tax evasion and was facing deportation by federal authorities. Ricca, a former leader in the Capone mob and an elder statesman of the Chicago underworld, was in desperate need of cash to cope with his legal problems. He had a palatial summer home in Long Beach, Indiana, on the shore of Lake Michigan which he had named Nancette Estate. It included a twenty-room mansion, swimming pool, tennis courts and a twelve-room servants' quarters. In July and August of 1956 the estate was purchased by Hoffa's Local 299 and Bert Brennan's Local 337 for $150,000. The Chicago mob again benefited by this very unusual expenditure of Teamsters members' funds.

The pattern of favors exchanged between Hoffa and members

of the underworld was already well established. The relationship would continue to be a source of power to both sides and the threat it posed to honest trade unionism and to the public welfare would multiply as the ties between Hoffa and organized crime increased.

CHAPTER II

The Corrupters

As THE YEAR 1957 BEGAN, the country was prosperous, hopeful and complacent. President Dwight D. Eisenhower and Vice President Richard M. Nixon had been reelected. The national preoccupation with the threat of Communist infiltration generated by Senator Joseph McCarthy had abated. The threat of organized crime, graphically documented seven years earlier by Senator Estes Kefauver, had been forgotten. It was not a time for boat-rocking.

The International Brotherhood of Teamsters was now the largest, richest and most powerful labor union in the country. Its president, Dave Beck, was well respected and considered a labor statesman. He had moved the Teamsters headquarters from Indianapolis to Washington, D.C., to be close to the center of power and had built a huge new marble building which stood respectfully at the foot of the northwest corner of Capitol Hill within walking distance of the Congress of the United States.

As the new year began, Dave Beck, sitting in his plush new office, should have been as complacent as his fellow citizens. He had come a long way from his local union in Seattle. But Beck was not complacent. He was in a state of panic and was making plans to leave the country. The next convention of the International Brotherhood of Teamsters was scheduled for the coming September in Miami Beach. Beck knew that there was one man who might challenge and beat him for the presidency—the ninth vice president of the union, James R. Hoffa. A bit closer to home, Beck could

look out of his window up the hill to the old Senate Office Building, fully aware that in a basement office on the far side of that
building a young man and his staff had already gathered enough
information and documents to destroy him. The young man was
Robert F. Kennedy.

Outside of the state of Massachusetts and Washington, D.C., few
people had heard of Robert F. Kennedy in January, 1957. He had
been the minority counsel on the Senate Permanent Subcommittee on Investigations but had resigned because of the investigative
tactics of Roy Cohn during Senator Joseph McCarthy's heyday.
When Senator John McClellan became chairman of the subcommittee after the 1954 elections, Kennedy returned as chief counsel.

In 1956, during an investigation into corrupt government pro-
curement practices, Kennedy discovered that racketeer Johnny
Dio and other hoodlums had infiltrated labor unions in the New
York City area. He checked further and received reports from
investigative reporter Clark Mollenhoff and others of corruption
and racketeering in the Teamsters Union and other segments of
the labor movement. Following leads, one of the trails led to the
West Coast and Dave Beck. Accompanied by veteran committee
accountant Carmine Bellino, Kennedy went first to Los Angeles
and then to Seattle. He learned that Beck had used over $150,000
of union funds to improve his huge estate in Seattle, had then sold
the estate to the union, which in turn had awarded it back to him
as a lifetime residence. He also heard that a man named Nathan
W. Shefferman, who operated an organization called Labor Relations Associates in Chicago, had made numerous wholesale purchases for Beck. Kennedy and Bellino moved on to Chicago. Shefferman admitted to Kennedy that he had made many purchases for
Beck but said that he didn't know whether union funds were
involved. His records, which Kennedy subpoenaed, showed that
he had received $85,000 in union funds from Beck to purchase a
variety of items for him wholesale. Other bank and union records
were subpoenaed and analyzed. Bellino was able to establish that
all together Beck had embezzled over $350,000 from the union.

Beck decided to run and hide. He vent first to Europe. While
he was gone, unsuccessful political effcrts were mounted to block
or sidetrack the investigation. Then attorneys for the Teamsters
Union decided to challenge the jurisdiction of the subcommittee.
To obviate this problem, the Senate created a special committee

called the Senate Select Committee on Improper Activities in the Labor or Management Field. It was composed of eight Senators—four from each party. Senator John McClellan was named chairman and Robert Kennedy chief counsel. One of the other Democratic Senators on the committee was John F. Kennedy.

Outside of the state of Michigan and the labor movement few people had heard of James R. Hoffa in January, 1957. It was not generally known that the stocky little former dock worker, working in alliance with the mob, had by 1957 quietly extended his influence across the nation. Having ensured Beck's election in 1952 by his support, he was now ready to take over. He, too, through his intelligence network, had a good idea what Kennedy and the McClellan Committee were up to and he knew that he was very vulnerable. But right now Kennedy was after Beck, so Hoffa decided to try to use Kennedy to eliminate Beck and worry about his own defense later. He went about this by arranging for one of Beck's own attorneys to feed information to Kennedy about Beck. He had the same attorney arrange a meeting between him and Kennedy where he would offer to cooperate with the Committee. But apparently Hoffa did not let it go at that, for in Washington D.C., at 11 P.M. on March 13, 1957, he was arrested by FBI agents and charged with having attempted to plant a spy on the McClellan Committee.

John Cye Cheasty, a New York attorney, had gone to see Kennedy a month earlier and told him that he had just been offered $18,000 by Hoffa to get a job on the Committee staff and feed back information. Cheasty had with him the cash he claimed Hoffa had given him as the first payment and he turned it over to Kennedy. The FBI immediately instituted an investigation with Cheasty serving as a willing double agent. FBI agents monitored conversations between Hoffa and Cheasty and photographed their meetings at which Cheasty handed over documents provided for the purpose by Kennedy and McClellan. When Hoffa was arrested he had Committee documents in his possession. It looked like a perfect case.

In the meantime, Beck had returned from Europe, continued to evade the Committee by claiming illness and then taken off again for the West Indies. Finally in late March he returned to face the music. Both Beck and Nathan Shefferman testified before the Committee on March 26 and March 27. Beck took the Fifth Amendment, claiming that his answers might tend to incriminate him.

Shefferman testified and his answers tended very much to incriminate Beck.

At the conclusion of the second day's testimony, Senator McClellan said:

> ... Mr. Beck has shown flagrant disregard and disrespect for honest and reputable unionism and for the best interests and welfare of the laboring people of his country.
>
> Above all, he has shown arrogant contempt for the million and a half members, the honest laboring people in the teamsters union.

Beck was, to say the least, discredited.

On April 13, 1957, I joined the staff of the McClellan Committee. Three days later I was sent to Chicago to join Pierre Salinger in an investigation of Nathan W. Shefferman. For the next three months Pierre and I probed into the operations of Shefferman and his Labor Relations Associates throughout the Midwest and in New York, New Jersey and Massachusetts. Shefferman posed as a consultant to employers in personnel matters. We discovered that in reality his organization was a creation of the Sears, Roebuck & Company and was engaged in widespread, subtle and sinister union-busting activities on behalf of Sears, its subsidiaries and suppliers and a variety of other clients. Shefferman's services consisted of thwarting organizing efforts of unions or, as an alternative, finding a "friendly" union for his clients. His friendship with Dave Beck and other union officials was very helpful.

Meanwhile, on May 15, Hoffa, Bert Brennan and a New York professional wiretapper named Bernard Spindel were indicted by a federal grand jury in New York City on charges of tapping telephones in Hoffa's Detroit Teamsters headquarters so Hoffa could eavesdrop on his own lieutenants.

Jimmy Hoffa went on trial in Washington, D.C., on the earlier indictment for attempting to bribe Cheasty on June 19, 1957. Something went wrong with the "perfect case." One month later, after only three and a half hours of deliberation, the jury of eight blacks and four whites found Hoffa not guilty. The prosecution had been inept, while Hoffa's attorney, Edward Bennett Williams, had been brilliant. But there were foreshadowings of things to come. Halfway through the trial a Negro newspaper, featuring a front-page pro-Hoffa article and a picture of Hoffa's Negro defense attorney, Martha Jefferson, was delivered to the homes of the black jurors. When the matter was brought to the attention of Judge Burnita Matthews, she was outraged and immediately locked up the jury. Then, near the end of the trial, on the day Hoffa took the witness stand, Joe Louis, the former heavyweight champion, walked into the courtroom and put his arm around Hoffa in the presence of the jurors. His appearance had been arranged by Barney Baker and Paul Dorfman. It undoubtedly had a strong effect on the black members of the jury. In addition, it was later learned that several of the jurors had criminal records. One was arrested during the trial. Amid the tumultuous scene of joy among Hoffa's followers when the verdict was announced, a New York racketeer was heard to say, "Let the lawyers think they won it."

In Chicago Pierre and I learned the news in the two-word headline of the late afternoon paper—"Hoffa Acquitted." When we returned to the office Bob Kennedy had already called and left word for Pierre to call him. He told Pierre to go to Detroit immediately and meet Carmine Bellino. They were to interview Hoffa and subpoena the records of his Teamsters organization. I remained in Chicago to pursue the Shefferman investigation.

Any hope Dave Beck had of hanging on to the presidency of the union vanished when Kennedy discovered that Beck had also profited from a trust fund set up for the widow of a Teamsters official who had been one of Beck's best friends. The revulsion that set in in the ranks of the Teamsters membership over this disclosure sealed Beck's downfall. On May 26, 1957, Beck announced he would not be a candidate for reelection. Now with Beck and the trial out of the way, Hoffa had an almost clear shot at the top in the upcoming convention. Only the McClellan Committee and Robert Kennedy stood in his way.

Several months earlier Kennedy had opened a field office in New York City. He assigned a group of regular staff members under Paul Tierney and Walter May to the office and augmented it by hiring John Constandy from the New York District Attorney's office and several men from the New York City Police Department. He also arranged for several members of the Intelligence Division of the police department to be temporarily assigned to the committee. Kennedy told the group to dig into the infiltration by Johnny Dio and other racketeers of the labor movement in the New York area. By July they had considerable documentation of the Hoffa-instigated Dio-Corallo takeover of the UAW-AFL locals, the setting up of the phony paper locals and the undermining of the local Teamsters leaders in Hoffa's bid to control Joint Council 16. On July 22, three days after Hoffa's acquittal, Senator McClellan announced that the Committee would hold hearings starting July 30 concerning racketeering influence in the New York Teamsters Union.

As the sordid New York story unfolded before the Committee during the first three weeks of August, Pierre and Carmine worked feverishly in Detroit preparing for Hoffa's appearance before the Committee, which was scheduled to follow.

I received a call in Chicago from Pierre.

"Bob wants you to find Joe Louis and interview him," he said. "There is an allegation he was paid several thousand dollars for appearing at the Hoffa trial. Get an affidavit if you can."

I called Larry Fanning, the editor of the Chicago *Sun-Times*, who gave me an address for Louis in South Chicago. I asked Art Kaplan, a staff member who was in Chicago working on the jukebox rackets, and Jack Thiede, a General Accounting Office accountant on loan to the Committee, to go with me.

I was surprised to find that Louis lived in a lower-middle-class black neighborhood in a third-floor walk-up apartment. He was not at home and we waited in the car outside. Two hours later a taxi pulled up and Joe Louis emerged toting a golf bag. He had already gone into his apartment when we entered the first-floor foyer. As we were starting up the stairs a man came in behind us and hollered up toward the third floor, "Hey Joe!"

He was a suavely dressed black man and I recognized him from pictures I had seen.

"Hey, are you going up to see Joe?"

When I replied that we were, he said, "Tell him Julian Black wants to see him." He had been one of Louis' managers and had prospered very well from the relationship.

Louis answered the door himself when we knocked. We identified ourselves and he asked us in. I told him that Julian Black was downstairs and wanted to see him. He went dutifully down the stairs leaving us standing in his living room. The only reminder of the days of his glory was one picture of the Brown Bomber in fighting pose hanging on the otherwise barren walls.

When Louis returned we all sat down and I explained the purpose of our call. I asked him about his visit to the courtroom during the Hoffa trial. He said that he was an old friend of Hoffa's and had stopped in to see how he was doing. He acknowledged knowing Barney Baker but was vague about whether Baker or anyone else had been instrumental in his appearance at the trial. He was emphatic about only one thing—he said he had not been given any money for appearing at the trial. I told him I would like to reduce what he had said to the form of an affidavit and bring it back for him to sign. He said that was agreeable to him.

One of the reasons I had asked Jack Thiede to come along was that he lived nearby, had a typewriter and his father was a notary public. We drove to Thiede's house where I typed up the affidavit and his father then accompanied us back to Louis' apartment. Louis let us in and then resumed a telephone conversation he had been having. He was explaining to someone what we wanted. When he hung up I handed him the affidavit and asked him to read it to see if it was accurate. After he had read it he asked for a pen. He then drew lines through the entire affidavit except for the last paragraph which stated that he had not received any money. I asked him if there was something inaccurate about the rest of it. He did not reply to my question but said that he would only sign the last paragraph and did so.

As we were leaving I told him that Bob Kennedy would like his autograph for his son Joe. Louis said he would give it for his son but not for Kennedy—"He can go jump off the Capitol." Then he took the piece of paper I offered and wrote, "To Joe Kennedy— best wishes—Joe Louis."

I respected his loyalty to Hoffa but there was something sad about the whole thing—the apartment . . . Julian Black's demanding tone. A few months later we would learn that Louis had gone on the payroll of the Mercury Record Company in Chicago as public relations consultant. One of the owners of the company received a sizable loan from the Teamsters Pension Fund.

On Tuesday morning, August 20, 1957, the Caucus Room on the third floor of the old Senate Office Building was filled to a standing-room-only capacity. The glaring television lamps illuminated the front of the red-carpeted, high-ceilinged old room like a stage. At 10:30 A.M. the measured strokes of Senator John McClellan's gavel hushed the buzzing spectators. James R. Hoffa stood at the witness table with white-haired George Fitzgerald, who had been his friend and lawyer for over twenty years. On Hoffa's right, at the overcrowded press table, reporters sat with pencils poised. To the left television cameras prepared to transmit the proceedings live to living rooms, offices and taverns across the country. Senator McClellan sat facing Hoffa, flanked by the full Select Committee. Robert Kennedy, the chief counsel, sat at the chairman's left.

The brief silence was interrupted by Senator McClellan's commanding drawl that was to become so familiar to people across the land:

"The Chair observes that we have quite an audience this morning. You are welcome, but we must maintain order and bear that in mind. . . . Mr. Hoffa, will you be sworn, please?"

Hoffa was sworn in and then read a short statement into the record in which he stated that he had attempted to refresh his memory concerning "many phases of my labor activities" and would answer questions according to his best recollection. He requested the right to refuse to answer questions he considered outside the purview of the Committee. Senator McClellan commented on the latter and then turned to Robert Kennedy.

"All right, Mr. Counsel, you may proceed with the witness."

And so it began. It started out calmly like the first round of a prizefight with each of the determined men feeling the other out. Hoffa had considered taking the Fifth Amendment but had finally decided to testify. His decision was probably influenced by the fact that the AFL-CIO Ethical Practices Committee had recently passed a resolution condemning the use of the Fifth Amendment by a labor official. He was cocky but polite as he answered Kennedy's questions about his arrest record and even called the chief counsel "Bob." Then the questioning moved on to Hoffa's business interests and he tried to avoid the issue by saying that the Hoffman Committee had looked into them. But Kennedy said that the Hoffman Committee had never finished its investigation. As his questions became more persistent, Hoffa's demeanor became more defiant.

In 1947 a trucking company had been formed for Hoffa and Brennan called the J & H Sales Company. Its purpose was to lease equipment to companies hauling new automobiles. The company was set up by Albert Matheson. Matheson and his brother Carney acted as lawyers for the National Automobile Transporters Association, which was composed of these same automobile-hauling companies. The initial capital for J & H Sales was a $1000 "loan" from Albert Matheson. Half of this money was used as the down payment to purchase a new Chevrolet truck. Commerical Carriers, Inc., a Flint, Michigan, car-hauling company, arranged for the truck to be purchased at a fleet rate, endorsed the note and mortage for the balance of the purchase price and then leased back the truck and assigned it to haul Cadillacs, the most lucrative traffic. In addition to representing the parent association, Albert and Carney Matheson were also retained by Commericial Carriers at $1000 a month and negotiated in labor matters for both with Hoffa.

The stock for J & H Sales was originally held in the name of an attorney, James Montante. On May 3, 1947, ten days after the passage of the Taft-Hartley Act, which prohibited payments by employers to representatives of their employees, the stock was transferred to Josephine Poszywak and Alice Johnson, the maiden names of the wives of Hoffa and Brennan. They put up no money and contributed nothing to the company, which was operated for them by Montante and Albert Matheson.

At that time, most of the hauling for Commercial Carriers was done by owner-operators. These men were employees of the company who owned and drove their own equipment, which they leased to the company. In 1948 Commercial Carriers decided to convert to the use of mostly company-owned equipment and informed their employees that they were terminating their lease agreements. The employees, all Teamsters members, went on strike. Bert Beveridge, one of the owners of the company, fired the striking employees and appealed to Hoffa for help. Hoffa sided with the company and forced the men back to work. He then allowed the company to rehire the men as new employees, thus sacrificing their seniority. Seven of the men, whom the company considered the strike leaders, were not rehired.

Shortly thereafter, James Wrape, an attorney for Commerical Carriers, set up the Test Fleet Corporation in Nashville, Tennessee. Wrape became president of the company and E. R. Beidler, the accountant for Commercial Carriers, became vice president and general manager. The only stockholders, however, were Josephine Poszywak and Alice Johnson. The original capital for the company consisted of two dividend checks totaling $3000 issued by the National Equipment Company—the new name for J & H Sales—to the wives of Hoffa and Brennan and a $1000 check issued by Alice Brennan. The $4000 was used as a down payment for the purchase of ten tractors. The balance of the purchase price for the tractors, amounting to $20,000, was financed by a loan from the Mercantile-Commerce Bank and Trust Company of St. Louis, Missouri. Bert Beveridge of Commercial Carriers guaranteed the loan and arranged for the purchase of the trucks at fleet discount prices. The trucks were then leased by Commercial Carriers. They were assigned at first to the Flint terminal to haul Buicks, but a year later were transferred to the Cadillac terminal along with the one National Equipment truck that had been transferred to Test Fleet.

In 1950 National Equipment Company purchased four trucks from Convertible Equipment and Leasing, Inc., a company in which Albert and Carney Matheson were stockholders. These vehicles were leased to Baker Driveaway, a subsidiary of Convertible. This business was not profitable and a year later National Equipment was sold to Convertible by the wives of Hoffa and Brennan for $10,000.

Test Fleet, on the other hand, was extremely profitable and in the nine years of its existence would receive over $1,000,000 from Commercial Carriers. The 1954 investigation by the Hoffman Committee caused no disruption in the Test Fleet operation other than the changing of the name of the company to Hobren.

These were the facts that Robert Kennedy was attempting to elicit from James R. Hoffa on the morning of August 29, 1957. Hoffa acknowledged that these were business ventures of his and Brennan's, that the stock for Test Fleet was held in the maiden names of their wives on the advice of attorneys and that he and his wife did not separate their money—"My wife takes some of my money and I take some of hers." But then he alternated between insisting it was his wife's company and, later, responding to Senator John Kennedy's inquiry about the propriety of the arrangement by saying his "experience of knowing what can be produced out of trucks, by leasing equipment and paying union wages" had made him a better labor official.

He told Senator Kennedy that he was going to dispose of all of his business interests in view of the rules of conduct for labor officials recently promulgated by the AFL-CIO Ethical Practices Committee, even though he didn't agree with them. But the Test Fleet operation was not terminated until the following year and then was done so by Commercial Carriers under a court order.

The simple facts of the matter were that Commercial Carriers, which employed Teamsters members whom Hoffa represented, set up and operated a trucking company for Hoffa and Brennan that yielded great profit at no cost or effort to them. This was done for the purpose of ensuring labor peace and there was an attempt to conceal the arrangement by incorporating the company in Tennessee under their wives' maiden names. On its face it appeared to be a blatant violation of the Taft-Hartley Act.

In the afternoon session of the hearing, Hoffa was asked by Kennedy whether he had any other business interests with Carney Matheson. Hoffa said that in 1952 he had invested $20,000 in cash in a business called P.M.L. with Matheson and another attorney. He said that he had some of the cash on hand and had borrowed the rest but could not recall how much or from whom. Hoffa then recited a list of loans he claimed to have obtained since 1952. They ranged in amounts from $1000 to $25,000, were all in cash, had not been secured by notes, bore no interest and most had not been paid back. The lenders were businessmen, Teamsters business agents, a trucking company owner, Local 299, a stockbroker and a man named Henry Lower.

KENNEDY:	Who is Henry Lower?
HOFFA:	I believe, and don't hold me to it, I won't give the title, but he has a title in Sun Valley, I believe.
KENNEDY:	Sun Valley, Florida?
HOFFA:	Sun Valley, Inc., and I think Mr. Bellino knows.
KENNEDY:	We are counting on you to give us the information.
HOFFA:	I am giving you the best I can give you and if you want it correct, I think that they should assist a little bit, and they have it.
KENNEDY:	That is $25,000 that you borrowed from Henry Lower?
HOFFA:	That's right.
KENNEDY:	Who was Henry Lower? How did you know Henry Lower?
HOFFA:	Henry Lower at one time was a representative of the Teamsters Union.
KENNEDY:	He used to represent the Teamsters Union and what does he do now?
HOFFA:	He now is in real estate.

KENNEDY: Where is he in real estate?

HOFFA: In Detroit, Florida, and I don't know where else.

KENNEDY: When was this loan of $25,000?

HOFFA: I believe it was last year and I haven't got the date and I don't know why it isn't here, but I believe it was last year.

KENNEDY: And he loaned the money to you?

HOFFA: That is right.

KENNEDY: Do the Teamsters have any arrangement or financial arrangement with Mr. Lower or any companies associated with him?

HOFFA: The Teamsters did not owe Mr. Lower or Mr. Lower did not owe the Teamsters, at that time, any money.

KENNEDY: Does Mr. Lower or any of his companies have any relationship, business relationship, with the Teamsters Union?

HOFFA: Only so far as the fact that the Teamsters members can buy lots in Florida, if they care to, from Mr. Lower.

KENNEDY: Anybody can buy lots in Florida.

HOFFA: You asked me a question and I answered it.

KENNEDY: Do you mean that there is no other relationship?

HOFFA: He is not an officer of the Teamsters Union. Let me see. I think without a salary he might be a special agent.

McCLELLAN: Special agent for the Teamsters?

HOFFA: He might be on certain incidents, we may need him to do something and he may have the capacity to advise, but I don't think, Senator, that he is presently an officer, or presently a paid representative.

Hoffa then stated that he had countersigned two notes for Lower, one for $50,000 and another for $25,000, so that he could go into the real estate business. Then:

KENNEDY: He has lots down in Florida that he sells?

HOFFA: That is correct.

KENNEDY: Where did he borrow the money from?
HOFFA: From a bank, I believe, in Florida and he bor-
          rowed the first money from the Commonwealth
          in Detroit, which I co-signed, and I think he now
          has a loan from one of the banks in Florida.

Kennedy then brought out that the records of the Commonwealth Bank in connection with the $50,000 loan to Lower which
Hoffa had co-signed included the following memorandum:

About a year ago we lost a teamster account of $800,000 through
some misunderstanding. We are trying to get this account back and
a welfare account at the National Bank of Detroit that runs over a
million dollars. If we cannot take care of them, they propose to go
to the City Bank and no doubt we will lose more accounts.

The bank records in connection with the second loan to Lower
for $25,000 contained the following notations: "Branch manager,
do you recommend?" Reply: "Only if pressure is applied from
union."

Hoffa said he had no explanation for the notations and could not
make a positive statement as to whether he had pressured the bank
until he talked to the bank officials.

Kennedy then asked, "Mr. Hoffa, on this Lower project of Sun
Valley, did the Teamsters have any connection with that?"

HOFFA: From a sponsoring situation.
KENNEDY: You sponsored that. How did you do that?
HOFFA: We sponsored it on the basis that our members
          could have the first opportunity to buy lots at a
          reduced price, I think, of $250. I am not quite
          positive. Those same lots today are worth $800 to
          $1000.

Then Kennedy asked Hoffa whether he himself had an interest
in Sun Valley.

HOFFA: I have an option to buy an interest in Sun Valley,
          but I have not exercised that option.
KENNEDY: What does that mean?
HOFFA: Exactly what I said.

KENNEDY: You are going to buy the whole of Sun Valley?
HOFFA: What is that?
KENNEDY: It is an option to buy the whole?
HOFFA: No, sir. I have an option to buy a percentage.
         What it is I can't tell you at this moment.

Kennedy then showed Hoffa examples of Sun Valley advertisements which contained such notations as "Every detail of your business transaction can be handled by your local business agent" . . . "Your investment has every safeguard" . . . "Stake your claim in the Teamsters' model city of tomorrow."

KENNEDY: Did you tell them that you had this interest, that
         Henry Lower had loaned you $25,000?
HOFFA: I certainly did not. That was my private and personal business.

Hoffa said that the loan from Lower had been in cash, "because I have always operated my expenditures in cash."

That was the essence of Hoffa's testimony concerning his knowledge of Henry Lower and Sun Valley, Inc. There was a great deal left unsaid.

The original funds for Lower's investment in the venture in August, 1954, came from a $10,000 loan to him by William Bufalino's Detroit Local 985, which had, on the same day, received a loan in the same amount from Jimmy Hoffa's Local 299. From 1954 to 1956, during most of which time Lower was actively engaged in promoting the Sun Valley project, he received a total of $91,000 from Local 299, Local 376 and Joint Council 43. During the period 1955 to 1957, Lower received from the Sun Valley, Inc., a total of $144,000.

To help pave the way for financing his project, Lower had enlisted the support of Robert E. McCarthy, the manager of the Bank of Commonwealth in Detroit. McCarthy wrote a letter of introduction for Lower to the Florida National Bank at Orlando, and then accompanied Lower to Orlando for a Sun Valley promotional barbecue to which the officials of the Florida bank were invited. Lower told the bank officials that the actual owners of Sun Valley were James R. Hoffa and himself. He asked them for substantial loans for the project and assured them that a Teamsters Union account would be opened in their bank that would maintain a balance in excess of or equal to the amount loaned to Sun Valley. Based on these representations, the bank officials agreed to lend the money.

Lower lived up to his side of the deal. On June 20, 1956, Local 299 in Detroit opened an account at the Florida National Bank in Orlando with a deposit of $300,000. On the same day a loan by the bank in the same amount was credited to the Sun Valley account. Subsequently, on November 17, 1956, another $200,000 from Local 299, personally delivered by Lower, was deposited in the Teamsters account at the bank. Four days later a cashier's check in the same amount was issued by the bank to Sun Valley, Inc. The account that Local 299 had opened and in which the $500,000 in union funds had been deposited was a checking account bearing no interest. Throughout all of this, Jimmy Hoffa and Bert Brennan held an option to buy 45 percent of Sun Valley, Inc.

As in the Test Fleet situation, Hoffa's cavalier and sketchy testimony was typical of his attempts to camouflage the facts in what was in this case a gross misuse of union funds. He had financed the original investment with union funds. He had pressured the Commonwealth Bank in Detroit into loaning Lower $75,000 and had in turn received a $25,000 cash loan from Lower. He had allowed Lower to draw huge sums of money from three separate union organizations while he was off promoting Sun Valley. He had deposited a half a million dollars of his members' money in an interest-free account in the Florida bank to induce the bank to make loans in the same amount to Sun Valley. And he had promoted the sale of lots to Teamsters members. He had done all of this with his members' money without ever telling them that he and Bert Brennan had almost a half-interest in the project from which they could conceivably have made a fortune.

As if all that weren't enough, he then allowed Henry Lower to misrepresent to the Teamsters members the true picture of their retirement investment. They were told that roads were paved when they were not. They were told that there would be no assessment for paving when there would be. They were told that all of the lots were high and dry when some of them were under water. Hoffa then allowed Henry Lower to divert $180,000, which should have gone toward the promised land improvements, to his own use. Ironically, one of the purchasers of lots who would suffer from this fraud along with Teamsters members and others was Hoffa's old friend Johnny Dio.

Kennedy moved on to other of Hoffa's business ventures. There was the Columbia Trotting Association, a harness racing track in Columbus, Ohio, in which Hoffa and Brennan had an interest. Hoffa testified that when Brennan bet on horses he would bet a like amount for Hoffa. He said that he had made $5,000 to $10,000 a year this way.

There was also a prizefighter named Embrel Davidson whom Hoffa said he and Brennan owned. Kennedy asked Hoffa whether any union funds had been used in connection with Davidson. "Not with him," was Hoffa's reply, but it was not true.

Kennedy then asked Hoffa about Jimmy James. Hoffa said he and Brennan had loaned James $2000 in cash to start a Teamsters local in Detroit. In turn, James had placed the wives of Hoffa and Brennan on the local's payroll, again under their maiden names, for $100 a week. They had remained on the payroll until they had received $6000. Hoffa was unable to explain why he and Brennan, through their wives, had received a 300 percent profit on their loan to James.

Senator John Kennedy then asked Hoffa about Allen Dorfman, and pointed out that Dorfman's insurance license had been revoked by the state of New York and yet he had collected over $1,000,000 in commissions in connection with the Teamsters Welfare Fund and continued to represent the fund. Although Hoffa, in collusion with Dr. Leo Pearlman of the Union Casualty Company, had been directly responsible for the designation of Dorfman as the agent for the fund, he replied, "We cannot designate to them who is their agent." He stated further, "I understand that sometime early next year he will not be an agent of that company, and the company will probably have a new agent." What actually happened was that insurance companies came and went, but Allen Dorfman remained the sole agent for the Teamsters Fund.

At the end of the first day of the hearings it was apparent that Hoffa and his friend Brennan had been engaged in unethical, if not illegal, business ventures involving conflicts of interest to the detriment of their union members, often using their wives' maiden names as fronts. It also marked the beginning of a litany of some of the names of those who formed the inner circle of Hoffa's empire.

The following day the names of prominent racketeers were

added to the litany. It started out with Hoffa acknowledging that a year earlier his and Brennan's locals had put up $150,000 in union funds to purchase Nancette Estate in Indiana on the southern shore of Lake Michigan. He said that the sole reason for the purchase was to establish a school for Teamsters business agents. He denied knowing that the estate was the home of Paul "The Waiter" Ricca, a notorious Chicago gangster. At the time of the purchase Ricca was in income tax difficulties and in desperate need of legitimate funds. The proposed school for business agents never materialized.

Kennedy then moved on to Hoffa's relationship to Johnny Dio and the efforts by Hoffa to take over Joint Council 16 in New York with the help of Dio and his racketeer friends. This probing wore on for most of the following two and a half days. Hoffa became more and more evasive, claiming over and over again that he could not recall details of his activities with Dio. To refresh his memory, recordings of conversations between him and Dio that had been legally obtained by the District Attorney of New York under court order were played. Hoffa continued not to remember.

Some of the Kennedy-Hoffa exchanges went like this:

KENNEDY: Did you discuss with Mr. Lacey, Mr. Dio getting a charter from the Teamsters?

HOFFA: I cannot recall that, whether or not it was discussed or not, since you don't want my belief, and I can't answer.

. . .

KENNEDY: What hotel was it?

HOFFA: I can't tell you.

KENNEDY: Did he [Johnny Dio] go up in the elevator with you?

HOFFA: I don't know.

KENNEDY: Do you know if he went to your room?

HOFFA: I can't answer that. I don't know.

KENNEDY: You can't remember back—now this is three months ago and you can't remember three months ago whether Johnny Dio was in your room, a man under indictment for throwing acid in Victor Riesel's eyes?

HOFFA: I cannot remember whether he was or not, as I said. It was that period of time and I just don't recall.

. . .

KENNEDY: Mr. Hoffa, can you refresh your recollection at all now in connection with this, or in connection with anything, if Mr. Dio made any arrangements to send people out to your headquarters in Detroit.

HOFFA: To the best of my recollection, I must recall on my memory, I cannot remember.

Finally, in frustration, Senator McClellan decided to read a statement into the record in which he leveled forty-eight specific charges against Hoffa including conflicts of interests, misuses of union funds, association with racketeers, abuse of trusteeships and stifling union democracy.

In the wake of the revelations before the Committee, George Meany, the president of the AFL-CIO, served notice on the Executive Board of the Teamsters Union that if Hoffa were elected as the new president, he would recommend that the union be expelled from the parent body. There were secret conversations among some Executive Board members about dumping Hoffa, and two Chicago Teamsters officials, Tom Haggerty and Bill Lee, announced their intention to run against him. On top of these union problems, as well as certain further confrontation with the McClellan Committee and the wiretap trial slated for late fall in New York, Hoffa was again indicted by the New York federal grand jury for perjury. But he went defiantly forward in his bid for the presidency.

In the week before the Teamsters Convention, which was scheduled to open on September 30, 1957, the McClellan Committee held four more days of hearings on Hoffa and his activities. Hoffa was invited to attend but was not subpoenaed to testify because of the now pending perjury indictment. Hoffa remained in Florida to solidify his support for the election and ignored the hearings.

In the Senate Caucus Room there was more testimony by Detroit Teamsters officials about loans they had supposedly made to Hoffa in support of Hoffa's testimony about his sources of cash. Some of the officials acknowledged that at the time of the alleged loans they themselves were in financial difficulty to the extent that they also had to borrow money. There was also testimony indicating that the delegates to the Teamsters Convention had not been chosen in accordance with the Teamsters constitution. Bert Brennan and Jimmy James pleaded the Fifth Amendment concerning their relationship with Hoffa and other activities. Other witnesses shed further light on the Test Fleet and Sun Valley operations. William Bufalino, the Detroit Teamsters attorney who had taken over Local 985 from Jimmy James, also testified. He was questioned about his first experiences in the jukebox business and it was brought out that he had become president in 1946 of the Bilvin Distributing Company which had been largely financed by his wife's uncle, racketeer Angelo Meli, and other Detroit underworld figures. There was also testimony that Hoffa and Bert Brennan had loaned $40,000 of their locals' funds to John Bitonti, a Dearborn, Michigan, gambler who had been arrested over twenty times.

The most damaging testimony came from Robert Scott, a barber who had formerly served as the secretary-treasurer of the Michigan Federation of Labor and as a Teamsters official in Pontiac. Scott, who said that he had received threatening telephone calls warning him not to appear before the Committee, testified first about activities in Local 614 in Pontiac. He said that Dan Keating, the president of the local, had handled the remodeling of Hoffa's summer home at Lake Orion, Michigan, and had, from all indications, paid for it with Local 614 funds. Scott stated further that business agents of the local also worked on Hoffa's hunting lodge at Iron Mountain, Michigan. And when a grand jury was investigating Hoffa's operations in 1948, Scott said, he had been assigned by Hoffa to determine the nature of the testimony of witnesses. On this assignment he had learned that a man named Turk Prujanski had testified before the grand jury that he had given Hoffa between $5000 and $10,000 to fix the chairman of the Liquor Control Commission. Scott said that when he told Hoffa this, Hoffa said "he would have him taken care of." Then, Scott continued, two of Hoffa's men told Prujanski to leave the state and he went to California. When he was brought back to Michigan on a fugitive warrant, he refused to testify further and was sent to jail for contempt. Scott also testified that Hoffa had asked him to contact the Governor of Michigan to intercede for a pardon for a relative of Detroit mobster Pete Licavoli, and on another occasion Bert Brennan had asked him to put the fix in with Oakland County, Michigan, authorities so that racketeer Sam Finazzo could operate a gambling game. Scott said that when he quit in disgust in 1952 Hoffa told him he would break his arms and legs.

When Turk Prujanski was called before the Committee and asked about his grand jury testimony, his trip to California and his refusal to testify when he returned, he said that he couldn't remember any of the pertinent facts.

On Saturday, September 28, Senator McClellan concluded the hearings by making thirty-four additional charges against Hoffa including misuse of union and welfare funds, obstruction of justice and association with racketeers.

On the same day federal Judge F. Dickinson Letts in the District of Columbia issued a temporary injunction to stop the Teamsters Convention. His action was based on a complaint brought by New York attorney Godfrey Schmidt on behalf of a committee of thirteen rank and file Teamsters from New York and New Jersey charging that the convention was rigged. The Teamsters International enlisted Washington labor attorney Martin F. O'Donoghue to appeal the injunction. The Court of Appeals vacated the injunction and the convention opened, as scheduled, the following Monday at the Eden Roc Hotel in Miami Beach.

A deflated Dave Beck presided over his own demise and backed Hoffa's candidacy. A mood of belligerent defiance pervaded the gathering. Senator McClellan's charges and the threat of expulsion by the AFL-CIO were mocked by the delegates, who overwhelmingly elected Jimmy Hoffa as their new president.

On October 23, acting on a new petition filed by the rank and file committee, with additional documentation, Judge Letts issued a new injunction prohibiting Hoffa and the other officials elected at the convention from taking office. This time the Court of Appeals upheld the injunction and a trial on the merits of the petition was set for late November. Later that week the Executive Council of the AFL-CIO suspended the Teamsters Union until such time as it could "eliminate corrupt influences from positions of leadership."

On October 22 the McClellan Committee commenced hearings on Nathan W. Shefferman and his Labor Relations Associates. The Shefferman hearings lasted for two and a half weeks. When Nathan Shefferman had testified in the Beck hearings earlier in the year, he had stated that his organization had little to do with labor unions or labor disputes. But our investigation had demonstrated rather conclusively that in the vast majority of its activities Labor Relations Associates was involved directly with efforts to keep unions from organizing Shefferman's clients. When Shefferman was asked by Robert Kennedy whether he wanted to correct his earlier testimony, he pleaded the Fifth Amendment, as he did to all further questions. Witness after witness described how Shefferman and his employees, under the guise of personnel consulting, set up company-sponsored committees to screen out union sympathizers, paid strikebreakers and engaged in numerous other illegal activities designed to "bust" legitimate organizing efforts of unions. When there was no way to avoid unionization, they arranged top-down contracts with "friendly" unions at great savings to their clients. The Teamsters Union sometimes played the role of "friendly" union.

Wallace Tudor, vice president in charge of personnel and employee relations for Sears, Roebuck & Company, which had created and subsidized Shefferman's operation, made a candid admission before the Committee:

> I want to state, with the utmost candor and conviction, that many of the activities engaged in by Labor Relations Associates and certain company personnel acting with them were inexcusable, unnecessary, and disgraceful. A repetition of these mistakes will not be tolerated by this company.

This was in sharp contrast to the much less candid statements the top officials of Sears, Roebuck had made to me and Pierre Salinger during our investigation. They had also tried unsuccessfully to persuade Bob Kennedy not to hold hearings. Faced with public disclosure, they had finally severed their connection with Shefferman shortly before the hearing after having paid his organization $239,651.42 during the previous four years.

At the time of the hearings, Shefferman had served some three hundred clients, many of them department stores, but also such prestigious companies as the Morton Frozen Food Company, Englander Mattress Company, the Mennen Company and the Whirlpool Company.

At the conclusion of the hearing Senator McClellan stated:

> The activities disclosed before this committee reflect a great discredit on some business firms in this country. They cannot adopt the posture, as did some of the firms appearing here, that all this was the doing of Mr. Shefferman and his agents. It is a fact that many of these firms did not choose to repudiate or even frown on the

activities of Mr. Shefferman until the public had been made aware of some of his practices.·

. . . It was management who paid the bills for the activities of Nathan Shefferman, and it was management which knowingly utilized the service of Nathan Shefferman with no compunctions or regrets until the revelations in recent months.

Nathan Shefferman, the friend of labor and management, joined his friend Dave Beck in total disrepute.

In late November and early December, 1957, Hoffa was battling for survival on four fronts. On November 25 he went on trial with Bert Brennan and Bernard Spindel on the wiretapping charge in New York City. At the same time, in Washington, the trial on the charges of the thirteen rank and file Teamsters who were seeking to invalidate his election got under way. In Atlantic City, New Jersey, the AFL-CIO Convention opened in early December, with its own trial of Hoffa and the Teamsters high on the agenda.

Their case was not helped by the hearings then in progress before the McClellan Committee where a story of Teamsters violence and corruption in Tennessee was unfolding. The hearings focused primarily on two men named Smith—W. A. "Hard of Hearing" Smith, a business agent with Local 327 in Nashville, and Glen Smith, the president of Local 515 in Chattanooga and president of Joint Council 87. Both men had extensive criminal records and had been involved, according to testimony, in numerous acts of violence including dynamiting, shootings and beatings, in Tennessee and neighboring states.

Frank Allen, the former terminal manager in Nashville for the Terminal Transport Company, testified that he had been viciously beaten up by W. A. Smith two years earlier. He said that at the urging of Joe Katz, the president of the company, he had pressed charges against Smith who was thereupon indicted. Allen said that the case never went to trial because he subsequently withdrew the charges at the request of Katz. Katz then testified that he had asked Allen to withdraw the charges after both Gene San Soucie, the president of Local 135 in Indianapolis, and Jimmy Hoffa suggested that he do so. Katz said that he thought he would have fewer difficulties with the union if he did as they suggested.

The Teamsters career of Glen Smith showed an even more

callous disregard for civility. He became a business agent for
Local 236 in Paducah, Kentucky, in 1946 after having served
two prison terms for robbery and burglary. While an agent, he was
convicted of assault and battery and indicted twice for malicious
destruction of property. He then left Paducah and became secretary-treasurer of Local 515 in Chattanooga. There he was indicted
for conspiracy to commit dynamitings, arson and assault. He then
went back to Paducah and took over Local 236, which had been
placed in trusteeship. He was extradited back to Chattanooga to
stand trial on the conspiracy charges. However, this case never
went to trial because the charges were dismissed by Chattanooga
Judge Raulston Schoolfield after a check for $18,500 drawn on the
funds of the local union was cashed and charged to "attorney fees."
The check was signed by H. L. Boling, the secretary-treasurer of
the local and co-defendant in the conspiracy charge, and countersigned by Glen Smith. According to two witnesses before the
Committee, Boling bragged that the money had been used to fix
the case. Both Smith and Boling pleaded the Fifth Amendment
and Judge Schoolfield declined an invitation to appear before the
Committee.

After the case was dismissed, Smith was sent as an International
organizer to Florida where, according to Committee witnesses, he
was involved in more dynamiting and arson. Then he returned to
Chattanooga and again became president of Local 515 and the
Tennessee Joint Council.

In an interview with Clark Mollenhoff a week later, Hoffa, commenting on W. A. Smith and Glen Smith, said, "Those hillbillies
in Tennessee need somebody tough to keep them in line."

While Hoffa's attorney, Sol Gelb, pleaded his case in the New
York courtroom, John English, the aging, respected secretary-
treasurer of the International Teamsters, pleaded before his labor
colleagues ninety miles to the south for one year's grace for the
Teamsters to clean house. But George Meany, the AFL-CIO
leader, was uncompromising. He rejected a last-minute offer by
Hoffa to step aside in favor of a hand-picked successor or to accept
supervision by an outside committee. He considered Hoffa's underworld connections anathema and would accept nothing short
of the relinquishment of office by Hoffa and other corrupt leaders
with no strings attached. Meany brought the motion to expel the
Teamsters to a vote and the verdict of the convention was five to
one for expulsion. The Bakery Workers and Textile Workers were
also ejected.

Hoffa fared better in the wiretap trial in New York. On December 20 the jury announced that it was hopelessly deadlocked, eleven to one for conviction. Judge Frederick Van Pelt Bryan reluctantly declared a mistrial.

Hoffa had won one and lost one but there remained the serious threat of the rank and file suit, which was going badly. After twenty-two days of testimony, Hoffa's attorney, Edward Bennett Williams, proposed a compromise solution that all parties accepted. Hoffa would continue in office as provisional president under the supervision of a Board of Monitors until a new election could be held. During the interim period certain reforms would be instituted. The Board of Monitors was to consist of one person representing the union, another representing the rank and file committee and a third neutral person, agreeable to both sides, who would serve as chairman. Godfrey Schmidt, the attorney for the rank and file committee, was designated as one monitor by the committee members. L. N. D. "Nat" Wells, an attorney for the Southern Conference of Teamsters, was picked as a monitor by Hoffa and the International. The chairman, appointed by mutual agreement, was retired municipal judge Nathan Cayton of Washington, D.C.

In January, 1958, Hoffa finally assumed office as provisional general president of the International Brotherhood of Teamsters. In the previous year he had survived two trials in federal court, intensive investigation and exposure by the McClellan Committee and an internal revolt. He was confident he could also survive the Board of Monitors. He rationalized the expulsion by the AFL-CIO with the millions of dollars in saved per capita taxes that would build up the Teamsters treasury and he defiantly asserted that the AFL-CIO needed the Teamsters more than the Teamsters needed them.

CHAPTER III

"The Situation Will Clear Itself Up"

▭▭▭▭▭▭▭▭▭▭

In February, 1958, I spent two weeks in Indianapolis, Indiana, and began sifting through the subpoenaed records of the local Teamsters organization headed by Gene San Soucie. While I was looking them over, I noticed a memorandum written by Harold Ranstad of the McClellan Committee staff concerning an Indianapolis attorney named David Probstein who had mysteriously disappeared in 1955. The memo indicated that a check at the local police department had revealed that Probstein had started a business called the State Cab Company in 1954. When he applied for cab licenses, he claimed to have plenty of money behind him but would not divulge its source. On June 6, 1955, he had left by train for St. Louis on what he described to a friend as a "dangerous mission" and had not been heard from since. Ranstad said that there had been some indication that Teamsters Local 135 had some connection with State Cab but that he hadn't pursued it further.

The records showed that Probstein banked at the Fidelity Bank and Trust Company. In reviewing the records of Local 299 in Detroit, Carmine Bellino had found the transmittal of a check for $125,000 in October, 1954, to the Fidelity Bank and Trust Company in Indianapolis. When Bellino called the bank, bank officials at first told him that they could not find any record of such an account. When the bank records were finally located, Frank McKinney, the president of the bank and former National Democratic chairman, told Bellino he didn't know anything about the account. The records showed that on October 27, 1954, a deposit had been made in

the Fidelity Bank and Trust Company in the amount of $125,000
in the name of the International Brotherhood of Teamsters, Local
Union 299. The funds had been placed in a checking account
drawing no interest. The original persons designated as authorized
to draw on the account were Gene San Soucie, president of Local
299, and Norman Murin, secretary of Local 299. San Soucie and
Murin were, of course, officials of Local 135 in Indianapolis, not
Local 299 in Detroit. This authorization had been replaced by
signature cards in the names of James R. Hoffa, president of Local
299, and Frank Collins, secretary-treasurer of Local 299. I decided
to find out a little more about David Probstein before I left Indianapolis. I went to see attorney Joseph G. Wood, Sr., the friend
Probstein had confided in about his "dangerous mission" and the
last person to see him.

Wood described Probstein as a mediocre attorney who had dab-
bled unsuccessfully in politics. He said that Probstein had begun
living beyond his means and had purchased a large house which
was threatened with foreclosure. Probstein had called Wood the
night before his disappearance saying that it was urgent that he see
him. Wood agreed to go to Probstein's house the following morning. There, in his wife's presence, Probstein told Wood that he had
to leave that afternoon for St. Louis and that he then might have
to go East. He said he had been dealing with dangerous people and
felt his life was in danger. He asked Wood to take care of his wife
and family if anything happened to him. He would not tell him
anything further. Wood said that Probstein left that afternoon, a
Sunday, by train for St. Louis. Probstein's wife called Wood the
following Friday and said she had not heard from her husband and
was worried. Wood went to the Probstein home and telephoned
Probstein's brother in St. Louis. The brother said that his son had
seen Probstein in his apartment building's coffee shop the previous
Sunday, the day he went to St. Louis, but that he had neither seen
nor heard from him. Wood said that in going through Probstein's
effects he had found some records of long-distance calls made by
Probstein in April and May of 1955. The calls were made to Detroit
to Harlan Rowe, E. R. Beidler, Herbert Grosberg and James R.
Hoffa.

My interest was increasing rapidly. Harlan Rowe and E. R.
Beidler were, at the time, accountants for the Commercial Carriers
Company and also for the Hobren Corporation, which had been
set up in the maiden names of the wives of Hoffa and Bert Bren-

nan. Herbert Grosberg was the accountant for both Hoffa and Local 299. Wood also had two telephone call slips from the Palmer House Hotel in Chicago indicating that on a previous visit there Probstein had called a Mr. Goodman. The telephone number was that of Philip Goodman, an attorney for Allen Dorfman in Chicago.

Unknown to me, Martin Ulhmann of our staff, who for months had been plodding through the maze of Dorfman's financial operations in Chicago, had one week earlier written a letter and sent it along with a subpoena to the Indiana National Bank in Indianapolis. In the letter he asked for records in connection with loans made by Allen Dorfman to the account there of one David Probstein. The pieces of the puzzle were starting to fit together. Probstein had obviously had dealings with both Hoffa and Dorfman, had left on a mysterious mission in fear of his life and had failed to reappear.

I talked to Probstein's wife, Edith. It had been three years since her husband's disappearance and she was obviously resigned to the fact that she would never see him again. She said that her husband had met and become friendly with Gene San Soucie about 1954. She also recalled meeting Allen and Paul Dorfman at a going-away party for an Indianapolis Teamsters official the same year. The next thing she knew, her husband had started the State Cab Company and told her that the Teamsters Union was backing it. They had then purchased a new home, which she didn't think they could afford although her husband told her they could. Her husband made trips to Chicago and Detroit in connection with his business but never told her much about it. She had the impression that when her husband left for St. Louis, he was going to meet some men from the union and he told her he might have to go to New York with them. He called her the following evening from St. Louis and said that he was driving to New York with two men and would be staying at the Statler Hotel. Since he always called her each evening when he was out of town, she became alarmed when she heard nothing further from him. She finally contacted Joseph Wood and together they went to the police. She had heard nothing since.

Other people who had known Probstein filled in more of the story. Probstein had an unsuccessful law practice and spent considerable time investing his and other people's money in delinquent tax property. He claimed to be friendly with Frank McKinney, the president of the Fidelity Bank and Trust Company. He had run unsuccessfully as a Democratic candidate for minor political offices. In 1954 he started the State Cab Company. All employees had to join Local 135 of the Teamsters Union. There had been unsuccessful attempts by the Teamsters to organize other cab companies in town, and this was going to be the first organized company. It was assumed by persons familiar with the situation that the union was backing the company financially. After the cab company materialized, Probstein also formed the Aldor Insurance Agency with Allen and Rose Dorfman from Chicago. A man named Robert Greenfield, who worked for Allen Dorfman, made frequent trips to Indianapolis to confer with Probstein. Local 135 furnished lists of the names and addresses of union members to the insurance salesman, and their employers had supposedly agreed to deduct the cost of insurance premiums from their pay. There were also plans for a loan company that would make loans to Teamsters members, but it never actually became operational.

Probstein had been extremely worried before his disappearance and told people, "You just don't know what a vicious bunch I'm dealing with. They're vicious and you don't cross them."

A few months before Probstein disappeared Gene San Soucie and Gus Zapas, the president of Local 58 of the Bartenders Union, visited the State Cab offices and had a heated exchange with Probstein. Zapas was heard threatening to kill Probstein. Soon afterward Probstein was removed from the company and Zapas took over as president.

Gus Zapas' real name was Gus Zapantis, alias "Gus the Greek." He had come to Indianapolis from Chicago about 1953 and had been hired by Gene San Soucie to work for the Indiana Conference of Teamsters. In 1955 he took over Local 58 of the Bartenders Union. He had been arrested over forty times in Chicago and was closely associated with leading Chicago and St. Louis Mafia leaders. Since he came to Indianapolis there had been numerous bombings in connection with organizing efforts by the Teamsters and Bartenders unions. Zapas had been arrested most recently in July, 1956, at the Claypool Hotel in Indianapolis in the company of a leading gambling figure for threatening a man with a gun. At the time of my inquiry, the case had been continued and was the oldest criminal case on the court docket.

I subpoenaed the records of the Fidelity Bank and Trust Company that concerned Probstein, Dorfman and the State Cab Company. An account had been opened on January 7, 1954, in the name of David Probstein, trustee, with an initial deposit of $20,000 consisting of two unidentified $10,000 checks. The following day $17,-500 of this money was transferred into a new account opened in the name of the State Cab Company. The authorized signature for the State Cab Company was David Probstein, president. On May 10, 1954, a deposit was made in the State Cab account in the amount of $8000. On July 13, 1954, the bank extended a loan to the State Cab Company in the amount of $27,083.28. On September 16, 1954, an account was opened in the name of the Aldor Insurance Agency with a deposit of $3000. The same day another account was opened in the name of the Union Loan and Finance Company, also in the amount of $3000. The signature cards for both accounts bore the names of David Probstein, president, and Allen Dorfman, treasurer. The deposit of the $125,000 of Local 299 funds in a checking account occurred a month later, on October 27.

In Detroit Carmine Bellino ascertained that the Hobren Corporation, owned by Hoffa's and Brennan's wives, had loaned the State Cab Company $8000 on May 10, 1954. This explained the May 10 deposit and also established Hoffa's interest in the company. The questions remaining were the source of the original $20,000 deposit to Probstein, the reason for the $125,000 deposit of Local 299 funds, and finally, what happened to David Probstein.

I determined from subpoenaed hotel records that the man who had gone to Indianapolis from St. Louis in late 1954 to look over the operation of the State Cab Company after Gus Zapas took it over was Ben Saltzman, who at the time was a business agent for Local 405, the taxicab Teamsters local in St. Louis. Saltzman had been involved in the violence during the 1953 St. Louis taxicab strike and had been indicted for seriously beating up a cabdriver. I talked to Saltzman, who admitted going to Indianapolis in connection with the State Cab Company but would not say anything more about it. Barney Baker had been in Indianapolis at the same time.

During the same period Allen Dorfman, Philip Goodman, Dr. Leo Pearlman and Robert Greenfield went to Indianapolis and met with David Probstein. There was considerable shouting and cursing at Probstein and he was given until the first week in June to come up with some money. The following day Gene San Soucie

ordered all the locks at the Aldor Insurance Company changed to
deny Probstein access to the premises.

On May 16, 1955, Jimmy Hoffa's accountant, Herbert Grosberg,
went to Indianapolis and met with Probstein. He reviewed the
books and records of the State Cab Company and returned to
Detroit the same evening.

I went back to Indianapolis in late May and attempted to find
out more about the Probstein and Teamsters .accounts at the
Fidelity Bank and Trust Company. I talked to Francis J Moore, a
vice president of the bank, whose name had appeared on a notation
on the back of the canceled $125,000 Local 299 check deposited in
the bank. Moore could not recall the opening of the David Probstein, trustee, account or anything about the two $10,000 checks
that had initiated it. When I asked for the loan application in
connection with the $27,000 lent to the State Cab Company, I was
told that there wasn't any. Moore said that it was not unusual to
make such a loan without an application but that he probably
would have discussed it with Frank McKinney, the president of
the bank, and the loan committee. Moore said that the State Cab
loan account became delinquent around November, 1954, and he
had started pressuring Probstein to bring it up to date.

Carl Schultz, another General Accounting Office employee assigned to our Chicago office, had been reviewing records of the
Dorfman enterprises along with Martin Ulhmann. For the past
month Carl had been focusing on the Dorfman end of the Probstein case. He found that on August 12, 1954, Allen Dorfman had
issued his personal check for $11,000 to David Probstein, trustee.
The check was deposited by Probstein in a real estate account he
maintained at the Indiana National Bank. He subsequently withdrew $9000 of this amount and deposited it in his wife's account.
She, in turn, wrote a check for this amount, which was used as a
down payment on their house. Dorfman's records indicated that
the money had been given to Probstein to invest in tax-delinquent
property. Probstein's appropriation of the money for his personal
use was one of the reasons Dorfman became upset with him.

Also of interst was a memorandum written by bank president
Frank McKinney on April 24, 1958, which was furnished by the
bank's attorney to Karl Deible, an accountant from the General
Accounting Office who had been assigned to help me. In the
memorandum McKinney stated that he had been approached by

David Probstein in 1953 with a proposition to invest in Probstein's purchase of tax-delinquent property. McKinney said he had thereafter furnished Probstein $7500 of his personal funds for that purpose. McKinney went on to say that when in October, 1954, he heard rumors that Probstein had mismanaged funds entrusted to him by McKinney and others, he demanded an accounting from Probstein. He said that when Probstein was unable to repay his investment, he obtained a demand note dated October 22, 1954, from Probstein in the amount of $6000. The $125,000 deposit by Local 299 five days later, according to McKinney and the bank officials, had nothing to do with Probstein's precarious financial condition at the time. I did not believe them.

On May 20, 1958, Hoffa, Bert Brennan and Bernard Spindel went on trial again in federal court in New York City on the same wiretap charges that had ended in a mistrial the previous December. On June 23, 1958, they were acquitted. One juror, Miss Catherine Barry, had been excused by Judge Thomas F. Murphy on June 6, after she reported to the FBI that she had been contacted by a writer for a labor paper who wanted to talk to her about the case. There was every indication that the perjury charges still pending against Hoffa would be dismissed because of a recent Supreme Court decision in the Benanti case that held that evidence obtained by wiretap by state authorities, even though legal under state statutes, could not be used in federal courts. For the first time in over a year Hoffa seemed to be out of danger of prosecution. He had survived three trials in federal court, now he had only the Board of Monitors and the McClellan Committee to worry about.

In Washington, D.C., Judge Cayton had resigned as chairman of the Board of Monitors. On May 24 Judge Letts appointed Washington labor attorney Martin F. O'Donoghue to replace him. The appointment caused some eyebrow raising because O'Donoghue had served as an attorney for the Teamsters Union in the early efforts to counter the petitions of the rank and file committee. In a column that started, "Jimmy Hoffa's former lawyer is now Jimmy Hoffa's chief monitor," Washington labor writer John Herling commented, "Union, management and government circles were startled by the O'Donoghue appointment which was described as 'incongruous,' 'inappropriate' and as a 'built-in hole in the head.' " A *New York Times* editorial called the appointment "most surprising indeed."

O'Donoghue's name had been proposed by Teamsters counsel Edward Bennett Williams and, surprisingly, had been accepted by the rank and file committee and Judge Letts. Jimmy Hoffa undoubtedly thought he had scored a coup. The rank and file committee, however, apparently accepted O'Donoghue as a man of integrity, as did Judge Letts who described him as, "not only a good lawyer but an honorable man." The committee and Judge Letts were right.

The monitorship under Judge Cayton had been amiable and uneventful. The monitors had reviewed the Teamsters constitution as amended at the 1957 convention, found it to be improved and were considering recommendations for further amendments. Questionnaires had been answered by all International officers concerning possible conflicts of interest. The firm of Price Waterhouse & Company had been retained to review accounting and financial procedures. Of the 109 locals in trusteeship at the time of the 1957 convention, 41 had been restored to local autonomy. The drafting of model local union by-laws had been initiated.

Martin O'Donoghue assumed the office of chairman on May 27, 1958, and held a meeting of the Board on that day. It was agreed at the meeting that all orders or requests between the Board and the International would henceforth be in writing. It was also decided that when the Board referred a complaint of a union member to the International for investigation, it would also specify a date by which the International would have to submit a report of its investigation to the Board.

In spite of the expulsion of the Teamsters Union by the AFL-CIO, Hoffa had been able in the first six months of 1958 to form or maintain working-agreement pacts with nine AFL-CIO unions including the Machinists Union, whose president, Al J. Hayes, held the post of chairman of the AFL-CIO Ethical Practices Committee—the Committee that had initiated the move against the Teamsters. In addition, Hoffa also entered into pacts with the International Longshoremen's Association and the Bakery Workers, both of which had also been expelled from the AFL-CIO. George Meany went off to Europe to attend international labor meetings pondering what, if anything, should be done about the fraternization of his member unions with the exiled Teamsters.

There was no question that Hoffa's grip on the leadership of the Teamsters was firm and complete. He had managed to increase his membership beyond 1,500,000 and to strengthen his union's bargaining position in a period of recession when other unions were faltering. He called a meeting of the International Executive Board and announced plans to strengthen and centralize operations of the International and to broaden the base of organizational effort. He also announced plans for a Conference of Transportation Unity to form an alliance of all transportation unions. With such ambitious goals and the likelihood of the Teamsters' increasing national impact, the question of whether Hoffa would move to clean house of the racketeering influence that pervaded his organization took on new significance.

While I was in St. Louis the hearings on Local 107 of the Teamsters Union in Philadelphia were in progress in Washington. Testimony before the McClellan Committee showed that Ray Cohen, the secretary-treasurer of Local 107 who had been elected a trustee of the International Union on Hoffa's slate at the 1957 convention, had presided over a four-year reign of terror and corruption since taking over the local. Cohen had been elected in 1954 after a campaign of intimidation. He had fired other elected officials and appointed his lieutenants in their places, had set up a goon squad to beat up and terrorize opposition and conduct violent organizing campaigns in companies such as Horn and Hardart, and had perpetuated a wholesale plunder of the local union treasury. All together, $400,000 in union funds was misused. Some of the financial manipulation was carried out in concert with Ben Lapensohn, a shakedown artist who had been fired by Cohen's predecessors because of his extortion activities.

The Committee also found that the Food Fair Company had made a private deal with Cohen in 1954, in direct violation of the rules of the bargaining association of which it was a member. As a result, Food Fair was given a substantial concession in its contract with the union which none of the other members obtained. Shortly thereafter Ben Lapensohn was able to purchase Food Fair stocks and bonds at substantially less than market value. Food Fair also offered other labor leaders preferred treatment on a new stock issue whereby they were able to purchase $90,000 worth of stock for $42,000.

Martin O'Donoghue began putting Hoffa to the test. In his first clean-up directive, he ordered John O'Rourke in New York to hold regular union meetings during the summer months. The members had voted to do so but O'Rourke had refused. He also ordered the indefinite cancellation of a scheduled election in Local 245 in Springfield, Missouri, until he could resolve by investigation allegations that members desiring to run for office were being denied that right. Then he ordered that Ray Cohen, secretary-treasurer of Local 107 in Philadelphia, and Joseph Grace, the local's president, be bonded in accordance with the International constitution or be ousted from office. Hoffa had already agreed to hold hearings concerning the McClellan Committee findings regarding Local 107 as recommended by O'Donoghue. In his approach to Local 107, O'Donoghue initiated what would become his common practice— using the evidence developed by the McClellan Committee as his ammunition to attempt to force reform action by Hoffa.

Next, O'Donoghue directed that all union officials be bonded, a provision of the union's own constitution which had not been enforced. He also recommended that John McNamara, president of Local 295 and secretary-treasurer of Local 808, who had been convicted of extortion, be suspended from office pending the appeal of his case.

O'Donoghue moved the Board of Monitors headquarters out of the Teamsters International headquarters into the Tower Building next to his office. He felt, among other things, that complaining Teamsters members would feel more free to express their feelings away from the watchful eye of the International officials. He also beefed up the Board's manpower by hiring Professor Florian J. Bartosic of Villanova Law School to serve as executive assistant to the Board and recruiting William C. Humphrey as a field examiner to look into election procedures relative to trustee locals.

In July the McClellan Committee held a series of hearings to determine, as Senator McClellan stated, "the extent of racketeer and gangster infiltration of legitimate union and business enterprises." McClellan noted that there had already been considerable indication of such influence in the testimony before the Committee during the preceding eighteen months. He then went on record with a statement about the nature of organized crime: "There exists in America today what appears to be a close-knit, clandestine, criminal syndicate." Noting the "momentous work" done in this area by the Kefauver Committee in 1950 and 1951, McClellan said further, "This criminal conspiracy has operated for many years in America, on rare occasions subjected to the light of publicity but, more often, operating at a level beneath the mainstream of American life. Because we are dealing with a clandestine group, because they are highly organized and disciplined, they present a formidable problem."

The Committee started with the "Apalachin Convention," the name given to the meeting at the home of Joseph Barbara, Sr., in Apalachin, New York, on November 14, 1957. The Committee spent four days probing the participants at the meeting, their connections with legitimate businesses and unions and their relationships with the whole structure of organized crime throughout the country. According to the Committee's investigation, of the fifty-eight persons known to have been in attendance at the Apalachin conclave, fifty had arrest records, thirty-five had been convicted, twenty-three had been imprisoned and twenty-two had been involved in either labor unions or labor-management activities. James LaDuca, the secretary-treasurer of Local 66 of the Hotel and Restaurant Workers Union in Buffalo, was at the meeting. He had previously worked for a taxicab company owned by John Montana, who was also at the meeting. Then he had worked for the Maggadino Funeral Home, owned by Antonio Maggadino, who was also at the meeting. He had also been a business partner in the Buffalo Beverage Company with Montana and Peter Maggadino. (Incidentally, John Montana had, the previous year, been named man of the year by a committee set up by the Buffalo *Courier*.) In 1950 LaDuca's brother had used Local 66 funds to help put down a move by Teamsters in Local 375 in Buffalo to oust Teamsters official Ernest Belles. When Belles was finally removed, it was found that he had misused $35,000 in union funds.

As in the case of other persons attending the Apalachin meeting, LaDuca had been in telephone contact with other major racketeers. One of the persons who had contacted his office about a week prior to the meeting was Gus Zapas in Indianapolis. LaDuca was also an associate of Barney Baker.

John Scalish of Cleveland, Ohio, a close associate of Teamsters official Louis "Babe" Triscaro, was also at the meeting. So were four persons connected with the Hod Carriers Union and Carlo Gambino, a leading New York City Mafia leader who operated a labor relations firm.

While the Committee was thus occupied, Jimmy Hoffa pushed forward with his plan for an alliance of all transportation unions. Working in concert with Joseph Curran, president of the National Maritime Union, and Thomas "Teddy" Gleason of the International Longshoremen's Union, Hoffa announced that representatives of the three unions would meet in Montreal to explain their plans to the Canadian Congress of Labor, and that the unions would also send representatives to the International Transport Federation meeting in Amsterdam on July 23, 1958. Hoffa also began making overtures to the Airline Pilots Association. On July 21 he announced that he had invited Harry Bridges, president of the West Coast International Longshoremen's and Warehousemen's Union, to a meeting on August 14 with the East Coast International Longshoremen's Association. He said that the purpose of the meeting would be to seek a common contract termination date and to study problems in the shipping industry resulting from new technology. Completely uninhibited by the expulsion from the AFL-CIO, Hoffa, having worked out pacts with a number of AFL-CIO unions, was now moving to forge a common front with all transportation unions both domestic and foreign, including some unions that had also been expelled from the AFL-CIO. However, his concentration on new power plays was interrupted by an announcement by Senator McClellan that he would be called to testify before the Select Committee on August 5.

On July 21 Bob Kennedy sent me to Wichita, Kansas, to look into reports that former Kansas Governor Payne Ratner had been instrumental in influencing the termination of the 1953 congressional investigation in Detroit, the investigation that had ended when the chairman of the investigating subcommittee, Congressman Wint Smith of Kansas, announced that "the pressure comes from away up there."

I went to Mr. Ratner's law firm in Wichita and served him with a subpoena for his records. Ratner was initially very cordial and gave me access to all his records. When two days passed and I was still methodically going through them, Ratner's attitude became strained and progressively more hostile.

But my search of the files was productive. A letter dated October 5, 1953, from Ratner to Teamsters attorney Dave Previant started, "I called Jim Hoffa last Tuesday evening and reported to him about my successful interview with the party with whom they wanted me to confer." Expense accounts covering the period from September to November, 1953, captioned "Re: Wint Smith matter"

itemized expenses of Ratner for a long-distance telephone call to
Wint Smith in Makato, Kansas, a trip to Salina, Kansas, for a
conference with Wint Smith and Ratner's trip to Detroit during
the congressional hearings in late November, 1953.

A letter from Ratner to Hoffa in Detroit dated November 30,
1953, three days after the hearings ended, began, "Dear Jimmy: I
listened carefully to all of the evidence last week. It is my considered opinion that you did nothing illegal or improper. I am proud
to call you my friend. . . . Wint told me today that he certainly got
in bad with Hoffman and the staff by having gone along with me
in his treatment of you Friday. . . ."

Another letter from Ratner to Hoffa dated March 11, 1954, said,
"Dear Jimmy: As soon as I returned from Miami, I talked to Wint
Smith by telephone along the lines you suggested. I seemed to get
a favorable response. I did not report to you at the time because
I knew I would be in Washington shortly. . . . I have just returned
from a week in Washington. . . . He said that Hoffman had prepared a citation charge and sent it over to his office for him to sign
but that he had refused to sign it. He declared that it is his best
judgment that there will be no further effort to cite you and, if
there should be, that it will not be successful."

I also found a very interesting memorandum of a call from
Barney Baker which said:

Baker Opr 8 St Louis Teamsters ofs fone Main 1284 re: arranging for
his friend Gus Zatas [*sic*] of Chicago to visit Jack Apple, Federal
Pen. and not have to talk through wire mesh. Exceedingly difficult
to today but was able to arrange for Zatas to talk to Apple without
having to talk through the wire mesh. However, the Federal rule
that a guard must be present so can listen in on the conversation—
But Gov. has arranged for the guard to wander off and if Zatas and
Apple talk in low voice he will not hear the conversation.
Procedure: Zatas has to write Warden Looney just stating he wants
to visit Apple—don't mention Governor's name but Warden will
know what it is and he will write Zatas and tell him he can visit with
Apple. If Zatas has no criminal record should have no difficulty.
However, if Zatas has criminal record might be a little difficult.
Counting on him having Hoffa get in touch with Gov. when gets
out this way.

I called Bob Kennedy and told him what I had found. He said
that he and Carmine Bellino would come out and we would inter-

view Ratner. I had showed Ratner the documents in which I was interested and told him I would like to take them with me. He asked to make copies of them, to which I agreed. I told Ratner that Kennedy and Bellino would be in later that day and would like to talk to him.

I met Kennedy and Bellino at the airport and took them to Ratner's office. He had the documents I had given him on his desk and was very agitated. He handed the documents to Kennedy and Bellino, and as they went through them, I noticed that the memorandum concerning the visit of Gus Zapas to his friend Jack Apple in prison was not among them. I mentioned it to Kennedy and he asked Ratner where it was. Ratner nervously opened his desk drawer and, in obvious embarrassment, retrieved the missing memorandum and handed it to Kennedy.

The interview that followed was strained. Ratner said that he had been introduced to Barney Baker and Dick Kavner of the Teamsters Union sometime in the late summer or fall of 1953. He did not recall who had introduced them. Shortly thereafter he had been invited to attend a Teamsters' lawyers meeting in St. Louis and had been retained to represent the union. He acknowledged contacting Congressman Wint Smith in connection with the Detroit investigation. He said that his purpose was to get the hearings postponed if possible, in view of a pending grand jury in Detroit, and to obtain a more courteous hearing for Hoffa than he had received in the previous investigation by Congressman Clare Hoffman. He denied any knowledge of the arrangements made for Zapas or the contents of the memorandum.

On July 31 the McClellan Committee next turned its attention to the overall supply industry in Detroit, where it found that the Star Coverall Supply Company, after commencing business in 1952 in an already overcrowded field, had been able to take away considerable business from its competitors. Pierre Salinger had learned, and the testimony confirmed, that the reason for the sudden success of Star Coverall was the collusion between the company, one of the principals of which was the son of Detroit Mafia leader Angelo Meli, and Teamsters Union official Herman Kierdorf. Kierdorf, whom Jimmy Hoffa had helped get a parole from prison and then recruited as a Teamsters business agent, used his influence as a Teamsters official to coerce companies into utilizing the services of the Star Coverall Company.

On the morning of August 5, 1958, Jimmy Hoffa appeared again

before the McClellan Committee. Senator McClellan opened the
hearings by noting that since his last appearance before the committee one year earlier, Hoffa had become the president of the
Teamsters Union and that "the potential for good or evil in the
position he holds is tremendous." McClellan further said that "Mr.
Hoffa has aligned himself with certain underworld characters,
who are a part and parcel of the criminal elements and most
sinister forces in this country. When he testified before the Committee, Mr. Hoffa said he would attempt to divest himself of some
of his associations and give this union the character and quality of
leadership and administration worthy of the importance and high
purposes of this great labor organization. In these hearings the
Committee will be interested in ascertaining whether he has been
successful—or what efforts and progress he has made in that direction." Senator McClellan said that he hoped Hoffa's memory
would be better during these hearings than during the last and said
that the Committee had "a right to expect from him candid and
truthful answers." McClellan said that the Teamsters Union had
the power to shut down the economy and that it was "unthinkable
that the leaders of any such powerful organization should have an
alliance or understanding in any area of its activities with racketeers, gangsters, and hoodlums."

In spite of Senator McClellan's remarks, the questioning did not
start out smoothly.

Kennedy:	Mr. Hoffa, did you know Mr. Joseph Holtzman?
Hoffa:	Yes I did.
Kennedy:	He was a close friend of yours, was he?
Hoffa:	I knew Joe Holtzman.
Kennedy:	He was a close friend of yours?
Hoffa:	I knew Joe Holtzman.
Kennedy:	He was a close friend of yours?
Hoffa:	I knew Joe Holtzman.
Kennedy:	He was a close friend of yours?
Hoffa:	Just a moment. I knew Joe Holtzman, and he wasn't any particular friend of mine.

Senator McClellan admonished Hoffa to characterize his relationship with Holtzman. Hoffa said that the deceased man had
been an acquaintance of his since 1934 and that his partner in a
labor relations consultant business, Joe Bushkin, was a friendly

acquaintance. He also acknowledged that two of the cash loans that he had received and about which he had testified earlier were from these two men. He said he had checked with his accountant and determined that he had obtained $5000 from each man, as loans, in 1951 and had returned the money in 1953.

Kennedy then asked Hoffa about Holtzman's role in a 1949 contract dispute between the Detroit Institute of Laundering, representing the laundry operators, and Local 295 of the Teamsters Union and its president, Isaac Litwak. Hoffa was vague in his answers but did acknowledge that he had at one point met with representatives of the Detroit Institute, that he thought Holtzman represented them, that he had probably talked to Holtzman about the labor dispute and that he didn't think that Holtzman had arranged the meeting. He could not remember whether he attended a specific meeting at the Detroit Leland Hotel between members of the Institute of Laundering and the local union where the contract dispute was settled.

A series of laundry owners and former laundry owners then testified that the contract negotiations in 1949 had reached a point of impasse with Isaac Litwak, the head of Teamsters Local 295. The principal point of contention was Litwak's insistence that the companies change from a six-day week to a five-day week, which the companies felt they could not afford. Litwak was threatening a strike. A suggestion was then made by laundry owner William H. Miller that the president of the institute, Howard Balkwill, and the secretary, John Meissner, approach someone higher in the union. Subsequently, at the direction of Balkwill and Meissner, each company agreed to put up $90 in cash for each truck owned by the company over a three-year period. The cash payments for the first year were turned over to John Meissner. In return, assurances were given that the companies could retain their six-day work week and would not have to make any additional material concessions to the union. Hoffa attended the next negotiating meeting and the contract was signed shortly thereafter. The contract did not contain a provision for a five-day week nor any other material concession. A meeting was subsequently held between representatives of the institute and Hoffa in the latter's office at Teamsters headquarters in Detroit. There was almost unanimous agreement by the witnesses on these facts. But when it came down to who received the cash that was collected, the testimony was vague, or in some instances different, from statements previously

given by the witnesses to Pierre Salinger, Carmine Bellino and
Bob Kennedy. Something had caused all of these witnesses simultaneously to change their testimony.

Former laundry owner William Miller had been interviewed by
Salinger two weeks earlier and had furnished a sworn affidavit in
which he stated that when the negotiations with Litwak broke
down, Balkwill and Meissner had set up a meeting with Hoffa and
reported back to him that the contract with no further concessions
would be signed "with the payment of $90 per truck by all mem-
bers of the association to Hoffa."

When Miller appeared before the Committee, as the first witness
after Hoffa, he said that he wanted to make certain changes in his
affidavit because at the time he gave it he "just read it over casually,
not looking it over real good." Miller now stated that although he
had suggested that Balkwill and Meissner meet with Hoffa, he was
not at the meeting and didn't know with whom they actually met.
He said that they did later tell him that the payment of $90 a truck
would obtain the desired contract, but he did not know to whom
the money was to be paid. Thus the only real change Miller made
in his affidavit was to take Hoffa out of it.

Based on Miller's affidavit, Salinger, Bellino and Kennedy had
interviewed Meissner and Balkwill in Detroit a week before the
hearing. Both had denied knowledge of any payoff in connection
with the 1949 dispute, and had become indignant that it had even
been suggested. But when they appeared to testify they knew that
their records had been subpoenaed and that other laundry owners,
as well as Miller, had confirmed that money had been collected to
pay to someone to settle the strike. They had also flown into
Washington the night before the hearing on the same plane as
Hoffa. They had also talked to William Miller. Now they testified
that indeed they had had a meeting to settle the dispute, but with
the deceased Joe Holtzman, not with Hoffa. They denied telling
William Miller they had met with Hoffa. Holtzman had arranged
to settle the dispute for $17,500, which they agreed to pay over a
three-year period and which they collected by assessing the institute members $90 a truck. Balkwill considered it a "payoff" and
"assumed" that some of it went to Hoffa. Meissner considered it
a "fee" to Bushkin and "conjectured" that some of it may have
gone to Hoffa. They also admitted making payoffs totaling $16,000
to another Teamsters official, but he also was dead.

When Hoffa was then recalled to testify, he said that he had refreshed his memory by a telephone call to Detroit. He now remembered intervening in the 1949 dispute to avoid a needless strike, and admitted attending the meeting at the Detroit Leland Hotel. He denied, however, receiving any of the $17,500 payoff. When he was then asked what the items listed on his income tax returns as "collections" represented, he answered that they were gambling winnings from horse bets placed by Bert Brennan. Hoffa said that he did not have any records concerning this money, which totaled $60,000 over an eight-year period. He said Bert Brennan kept the records. Bert Brennan was then called as a witness and took the Fifth Amendment.

Embrel Davidson, the former professional heavyweight fighter, testified that in 1952, after breaking with his former manager, he was introduced by Sam Finazzo, a Detroit fight promoter, to Bert Brennan and agreed to have Brennen as his new manager. He said that Brennan had in turn introduced him to Hoffa, and that he understood Brennan and Hoffa were business associates. He fought under Brennan's management for two years and during that period went on the payroll of the Michigan Conference of Teamsters Health and Welfare Fund for $75 a week as a claims investigator. Davidson said Hoffa was present in the office when Brennan arranged for him to go on the payroll, and although he never did any work for the fund, he collected his check each week. Brennan dropped him in 1954 when he was advised by his doctor not to take an upcoming fight. Davidson identified a photograph of Raffaele Quasarano, a major narcotics trafficker, as a man he knew as "Jimmy" who frequented the Motor City Arena which was operated by Sam Finazzo. He said that Finazzo also claimed to be a good friend of boxing underworld figure Frankie Carbo. On one occasion, while being managed by Brennan, Davidson had a fight in New York City at Madison Square Garden. The night of the fight Brennan stayed at the Lexington Hotel with Raffaele Quasarano. Sam Finazzo was found to have a criminal record of twenty-nine arrests and four convictions. Finazzo, Quasarano and Brennan all pleaded the Fifth Amendment concerning their relationship with one another and with Davidson.

When Hoffa had testified a year earlier he had stated that he and Brennan had a prizefighter named Embrel Davidson in 1952 and 1953. When he was asked at that time, "Were some of the Teamster funds used in connection with him at all?" Hoffa had replied, "Not with him."

Kennedy now called Hoffa to testify. Hoffa said that he had not known that Embrel Davidson was on the payroll of the Michigan Conference Health and Welfare Fund and would see that the money paid to Davidson was returned to the fund. Although he may have been present in the office when Brennan made the arrangements with Davidson, Hoffa said, he did not hear the conversation. He told the Committee that he did not know who else might have been on the fund payroll but then admitted that two private investigators who had been on the payroll sometimes did investigation work for him rather than the fund. He also acknowledged that he had known Sam Finazzo and Raffaele Quasarano for about ten years.

Referring to Hoffa's pledge to clean up the union in his appearance before the Committee in 1957, Kennedy asked whether he had conducted an investigation of his friend Bert Brennan who had since been elected an International vice president at the Miami convention. Hoffa replied that he knew Brennan so well he didn't have to. Kennedy then elicited the information that Herman Kierdorf, business agent for Joint Council 43, had been hired by Hoffa in the early thirties shortly after being released from Leavenworth Prison, had gone back to prison in 1941 on an armed robbery conviction and had returned as a Teamsters official in 1949 after Hoffa interceded with the parole board to terminate Kierdorf's parole supervision, which was not due to expire until 1952. Kennedy then pointed out that the previous week there had been testimony before the Committee about Kierdorf's collusive efforts on behalf of the Star Coverall Supply Company. Kennedy asked Hoffa whether he had investigated this. Hoffa replied that he had asked Kierdorf about it and Kierdorf had denied it.

Kierdorf's nephew, Frank Kierdorf, had also been hired by Hoffa as a business agent for Local 332 in Flint, Michigan, in 1950, shortly after being released from prison where he had been confined for armed robbery. There had been testimony before the Committee of beatings, shakedowns, arson and bombings attributed to Kierdorf. On August 3, two days before the current hearings began, Frank Kierdorf stumbled into a hospital in Pontiac, Michigan, with 85 percent of his body burned to a crisp. Authorities concluded that he had ignited himself while setting fire to a dry-cleaning establishment in an obvious case of arson. He died four days later on August 7, the day Kennedy was questioning Hoffa about him. Hoffa said that he had hired Frank Kierdorf because he needed an experienced business agent. He then admitted that the only evidence he had that Kierdorf had ever been a business agent was that his uncle, Herman Kierdorf, said so. Hoffa was asked whether he had investigated any of the wrongdoings attributed to Kierdorf by witnesses before the Committee. He replied he had asked Kierdorf about the charges and Kierdorf had denied them.

When asked what he had done about Glen Smith and H. L. Boling of Chattanooga and W. A. "Hard of Hearing" Smith of Nashville, Hoffa answered he had not done anything because their cases were on appeal and that "the situation will clear itself up." As for Tony "Ducks" Corallo, the racketeer friend of Johnny Dio's who controlled several New York locals, Hoffa said that he understood that Corallo "is intending to resign from our union."

Kennedy: Have you taken any steps against Mr. Tony "Ducks" Corallo?
Hoffa: As of now, no.

When Hoffa later stated that he had been too busy with other union problems to take any action against such persons, Senator John Kennedy said:

Mr. Hoffa, I don't think there is anything more important. You are now seeking to arrange an alliance with Mr. Bridges, with the west coast union, to extend your power over the transportation system in the United States. You don't seem to be interested in cleaning up corruption in your own union. It is not very difficult to [do]. You have extensive powers. These people are notorious, some of them who came before us. You don't seem to take any action.

Hoffa replied, "There will be action taken in due time."

Senator Kennedy then asked whether on the airplane flight to Washington with earlier witnesses Balkwill and Meissner, Hoffa had suggested that the money they collected had gone to the deceased Mr. Holtzman and not to him. Hoffa did not answer the question directly. Robert Kennedy pursued it.

Kennedy: Do you deny that you said to them, "Remember that you gave the money to Holtzman"?
Hoffa: I don't remember discussing it with them.

Kennedy: Do you deny it?
Hoffa: I am not going to sit here and tell you from mem-
             ory that I did or did not, but I don't believe I did.

Robert Kennedy asked Hoffa whether at the conclusion of the
testimony by Balkwill, Meissner and William Miller, he had said,
"That s.o.b., I'll break his back." Hoffa said that he didn't know
and that he may have been discussing someone in a figure of
speech. A member of the Capitol police force then testified that he
had heard Hoffa make such a statement. Hoffa then claimed that
if he had made such a statement, it was not directed at any witness
or member of the Committee.

Kennedy returned to the problem of Hoffa's failure to clean
house and questioned him about two of Johnny Dio's other cohorts
in the union, Milton Holt, the secretary-treasurer of Local 805 in
New York, and Abe Gordon, the vice president of the same local,
both of whom had taken the Fifth Amendment before the Committee. Hoffa acknowledged that no action had been taken against
either man although Abe Gordon, a friend of his, had been with
him at the International headquarters for the past several days.

The evidence of racketeer influence in the union continued to
pile up. Philadelphia hoodlum Sam "Shorty" Feldman, a Teamsters business agent, and Detroit mobster Maxie Stern pleaded the
Fifth Amendment when asked how they took over a Philadelphia
local of the Hotel Restaurant Workers Union with Hoffa's help.
Two weeks before the hearing Feldman was arrested for interstate
transportation of stolen bonds. Paul De Lucia, better known as
Paul "The Waiter" Ricca, the notorious Chicago Mafia leader, took
the Fifth Amendment when questioned about the sale of his home,
Nancette Estate, to Hoffa's Local 299 and Bert Brennan's Local 337
for $150,000 in 1956. Jerry Adlerman of the Committee staff then
testified that through an oversight, in the purchase of the property,
part of Ricca's estate, including half of the swimming pool and half
of the tennis court, had not been conveyed. He said that after the
Committee began its investigation of the transaction, the Teamsters apparently realized the oversight and acquired the remainder
of the property without paying any additional funds. There was
no record of any specific mention of the Nancette Estate purchase
by Hoffa and Brennan to their union membership until just prior
to the 1957 hearings. On August 14, 1957, at a special meeting of Joint

Council 43, Hoffa announced that "through an oversight" the minutes of a meeting in October, 1956, failed to mention the purchase. A motion was then made that the property, then owned jointly by Locals 299 and 337, be sold, for the purchase price, to Joint Council 43 as a "training center for health and welfare, pension and contract negotiations, and for the general welfare of the local unions affiliated with the joint council."

Then Arthur L. Morgan, a former Teamsters official from Minneapolis, who had testified one year earlier that because of corruption he had taken part of his local union out of the Teamsters Union and formed an independent local, told the Committee about his experiences since that time:

> Since I returned to Minneapolis, my life has been a living hell. Every night practically the telephone would ring all night long, and my wife would get calls that asked if the children were home from school, and she would say that they are, and they would tell her, "Maybe you are lucky tonight, and maybe you won't be so lucky tomorrow night."

Morgan said that the calls had continued even though he had changed his number several times to unlisted numbers, and that members of his local and their wives had also received threatening calls. Furthermore, Morgan testified, Sidney Brennan, who had replaced Jerry Connelly as head of the Teamsters local, was still in office even though he had been convicted of extortion. He said that the same was true of the president of the Joint Council.

Hoffa was again recalled as a witness. After acknowledging he had not taken any action against Shorty Feldman, he said that a committee had been set up to hear charges of misuse of union funds against Ray Cohen and other officials of Local 107 in Philadelphia but that he had not suspended Cohen or any of the other officials from office. Kennedy pointed out that nineteen of the officials of Local 107 had 104 arrests and 40 convictions among them, and that Hoffa also had not taken any action against Al Reger, the secretary-treasurer of Local 552 in New York, who had been convicted of extortion. Joe Glimco, the head of Local 777 in Chicago, a close associate of top Chicago hoodlums, who had been arrested thirty-eight times, was also still in office. Hoffa retorted that he saw nothing wrong with Glimco. He also acknowledged

he had done nothing about the Minneapolis Teamsters officials
who had been convicted of extortion, nor about Frank Matula of
Los Angeles, who had been convicted of perjury.

On the first day of the second week of the hearings, Senator John
Kennedy made an observation:

> Mr. Hoffa, a number of witnesses have taken the Fifth Amendment
> before this Committee, with whom you are involved in transactions.
> The records are never in existence. Your deals were always in cash.
> You refer us to the other witnesses and they take the Fifth Amend-
> ment. It seems to me that you have surrounded yourself in this
> hearing with these witnesses, all of whom take the Fifth Amend-
> ment and you don't have any records. We only have your word as
> to what happened. You operate in cash. It seems to me, then, in a
> sense that you are taking the Fifth Amendment. That is the effect
> of it.

Hoffa, of course, denied this but Senator Kennedy's views would
have a significant effect on the strategy of the Hoffa camp later in
the week. Some Teamsters officials who had intended to take the
Fifth would be told by Hoffa that they had to testify. It would not
last long but it would offer some relief from the monotonous
pattern and also produce some incredible testimony.

Former Governor Payne Ratner of Kansas testified before the
Committee on August 13. He had flown to Texas and met with the
Teamsters attorneys after our interview. Some of them had criticized him for turning over his records and told him he should have
claimed the attorney-client privilege. He was now subdued as he
tried to explain before the Committee why he had removed the
memorandum about the arrangement for Gus Zapas to visit Jack
Apple in prison. He said he had removed it because he didn't think
it had anything to do with the Teamsters. He again denied knowing anything about the memorandum or of having made any arrangements for Zapas. He acknowledged knowing that Barney
Baker was a Teamsters official and that Baker had been one of the
first to contact him from the Teamsters.

The Committee then turned to the State Cab Company in Indianapolis and the missing David Probstein. The officials of the
Fidelity Bank and Trust Company continued to profess their ignorance of the reason for the deposit of $125,000 in the bank on
October 27, 1954. Hoffa then gave his explanation claiming he put

the money in the bank to influence employers in Indianapolis who, he said, knew that Gene San Soucie's Local 135 was in bad financial condition. Hoffa said that he had met David Probstein and acknowledged that on the recommendation of San Soucie, he and Bert Brennan had advised their wives to lend $8000 from the Hobren Corporation to Probstein for the State Cab Company.

Shortly before the hearing Carmine Bellino had discovered the source of the original $20,000 deposited by Probstein in the Fidelity Bank and Trust Company on January 7, 1954. It was this money that had been used to form the State Cab Company. It had consisted of two $10,000 dividend checks, also from the Hobren Corporation, to the wives of Hoffa and Brennan. They had been endorsed by them and turned over to Probstein, who had, in turn, endorsed the checks and deposited them in the David Probstein, trustee, account at the Fidelity Bank. The loan from the Hobren Corporation for $8000 was not made until May 10, 1954.

Hoffa knew that we knew about the $8000 loan. He did not know that we knew about the other $20,000.

Kennedy: Did you, your wife, Bert Brennan, or his wife or Hobren Corporation or Test Fleet Corporation have any other financial dealings with Mr. Probstein?

Hoffa: This is my extent of the financing of Probstein.

Kennedy: And you or any of these companies that you own or operate never had any other financial operations or dealings with Mr. Probstein, is that correct, other than the $8000?

Hoffa: I did not.

Gene San Soucie, who had intended to take the Fifth Amendment, now testified in accordance with Hoffa's new public relations policy. He said that he had brought Probstein to Detroit to meet with Hoffa and Brennan to see if they would assist in starting a cab company, which San Soucie's local union would then hopefully organize. At his request, he said, Hoffa and Brennan agreed to lend Probstein $8000. Then he stated that he knew of no other money going from Hoffa and Brennan to Probstein.

Continuing his testimony, San Soucie said he had hired Gus
Zapas five years earlier. and that he was a representative of the
Indiana Conference of Teamsters. He described Zapas as a
"good mixer"—"He is the kind of fellow that, you might say, is
a man's man. He gets along good with truck drivers." Contrary
to the testimony of other witnesses, who stated that San Soucie
had kicked out Probstein as president of the cab company in
late 1954 and replaced him with Zapas, San Soucie claimed he
had merely sent Zapas, at Probstein's request, to look things
over. He denied ever arguing with Probstein or threatening
him.

His explanation of the $125,000 deposit of Local 299 funds in
the Fidelity Bank and Trust Company was the same as Hoffa's.
He said that he had asked Hoffa for a loan for local 135 so he
could build up the union and impress employers that it was vi-
able, and that instead of granting the loan, Hoffa had deposited
the check for $125,000. It was carried on the financial report of
his local union as a $100,000 loan from the Michigan Confer-
ence of Teamsters. San Soucie said that this was so that word
would get around that the local was solvent. He acknowledged
that he had no authority to draw on the money and could give
no explanation as to why it had been deposited in a checking
account where it would draw no interest or why it was carried
in a fictitious manner at a different amount in the financial report.

Gus Zapas also testified, much to everyone's surprise. He was
questioned by Kennedy as to how he happened to become an
official of the Teamsters Union.

Kennedy: And how long have you been in the labor union
           movement?
Zapas: From the day I started work for the Conference
           in Indianapolis. About 4 or 5 years. I wouldn't
           know for sure.
Kennedy: You went to work about 1953?
Zapas: Somewhere around there.
Kennedy: For the Teamsters?
Zapas: Indiana Conference of Teamsters.
Kennedy: Who hired you for that job?
Zapas: Mr. Gene San Soucie.
Kennedy: What had you been doing just prior to that?

Zapas:	Nothing.
Kennedy:	You had been doing nothing?
Zapas:	No, sir.
Kennedy:	No work at all?
Zapas:	No, sir.
Kennedy:	What had you been doing for the year prior to that?
Zapas:	Nothing.
Kennedy:	For the 2 years prior to that?
Zapas:	I attempted at times to tend bar at various establishments in Chicago. My father owned a few bars but being harrassed by the Chicago Police Department, coming in and questioning at various hours of the day, the employers would not hold me and I never could hold a job.

Zapas said that he had met San Soucie in a bar in Chicago and had been hired as a Teamsters business agent although he had done "nothing" for a year prior to that meeting. Shortly thereafter, while still holding his position with the Indiana Conference of Teamsters, he had been installed by San Soucie as head of the Bartenders Union in Indianapolis. Zapas also acknowledged receiving $1500 from the Laundry Workers Union in Indianapolis "for organizing purposes."

Zapas said that he had known Barney Baker for about ten years and admitted asking Baker to try to arrange for him to visit his friend Jack Apple in prison. He said he did not know how Baker went about it. Then he declared he had taken over the State Cab Company at Probstein's request when San Soucie sent him to look it over. He denied threatening Probstein but admitted arguing with him.

Allen Dorfman testified that he knew David Probstein but denied having had an argument with him and said he could not recall having met with him in May, 1955, in Indianapolis, although he might have. He identified his registration card at the Marriott Hotel in Indianapolis on May 10, 1955. He took the Fifth Amendment concerning any details of his insurance operations in Indianapolis or any financial dealings he may have had with Probstein. He also took the Fifth Amendment when asked if he had had a dispute with Probstein over money.

Big Barney Baker then came to the witness table accompanied

by Hoffa's attorney, George Fitzgerald. In keeping with the new policy, he, too, would testify. Kennedy asked him first about his days on the New York waterfront. He asked him about Varick Enterprises, which had been a shakedown operation for the mob. Baker said that he did not have any connection with Varick Enterprises but knew the people who did.

Kennedy: Who were the people that did?
Baker: A Mr. Dunn.
Kennedy: Cockeyed Dunn?
Baker: I don't know him as Cockeyed Dunn. I knew him as John Dunn.
Kennedy: Where is he now?
Baker: He has met his Maker.
Kennedy: How did he do that?
Baker: I believe through electrocution in the city of New York or the state of New York.

Kennedy then asked Baker about another racketeer, Danny Gentile.

Kennedy: Where is he now?
Baker: I don't know where he would be now. Excuse me. I believe he was implicated with a certain case in New York. He must be in jail.
Kennedy: That is the Hintz killing? You see, we have had the testimony that you were closely associated with these people, Mr. Baker.
Baker: Yes, I knew them real well.
Kennedy: I am just trying to find out and give you a chance as to whether you did. Mr. Gentile is in prison at the present time for the Hintz murder?
Baker: To the best of my knowledge, I believe so.
Kennedy: What about Squint Sheridan? Did you know him?
Baker: Andrew Sheridan, sir?
Kennedy: Yes.
Baker: He has also met his Maker.
Kennedy: How did he die?
Baker: With Mr. John Dunn.
Kennedy: He was electrocuted?
Baker: Yes, sir.

Kennedy: He was also a friend of yours, was he?
Baker: Yes, he was a friend of mine.

In further testimony Baker admitted knowing Gus Zapas, but denied any involvement in the State Cab Company. He also denied that he had ever received any money from an employer. In the last instance, at least, he lied.

We had recently obtained information that in August, 1957, Baker had been staying at the Rambler Motel in Des Moines, Iowa, with a man named Edward Weinheimer who represented a trucking company in McKees Rock, Pennsylvania, called the Esco Company. One day Weinheimer was anxiously awaiting the delivery of some mail. Finally it arrived—three white envelopes which were given to Weinheimer by the motel manager. Shortly thereafter on the same day Barney Baker paid his motel bill with a hundred-dollar bill which he took from an envelope that appeared to be identical to one of the envelopes received by Weinheimer. Just prior to the hearing, we had sent a General Accounting Office employee from Des Moines to interview the motel managers, Mr. and Mrs. Virgil Smith. They confirmed the sequence of events and were subpoenaed to testify before the Committee on the day of Baker's appearance.

At the lunch break during Baker's testimony when I was going over the testimony for the afternoon with Bob Kennedy I told him about the Weinheimer incident and that the motel managers were here, prepared to testify. I said we had not yet been to the Esco Company to determine whether money had been sent by them to Weinheimer. Kennedy suggested that I just call the president of the company and ask him. It was typical of his direct approach.

I called the Esco Company in McKees Rock and asked for the president, George Callahan. When he came on the line, I identified myself and put some direct questions to him. I asked him if a man named Edward Weinheimer had represented his company in August, 1957. When Callahan said that he had, I asked if he had sent three envelopes containing hundred-dollar bills to Weinheimer at the Rambler Motel in Des Moines in August, 1957. There was a pause and Callahan answered, "Yes, I did." He said that he had sent $1000 in hundred-dollar bills, and that the money was intended to help work out some labor problems he was having with the Teamsters Union. When I asked him whether he knew Barney Baker and whether Baker had helped him with his problems, he replied that he did know Baker and that Baker had been generally helpful. However, he was reluctant to tie the $1000 sent to Weinheimer to the help he received from Baker. I then put Bob Kennedy on the phone and Callahan gave him basically the same information, again not quite admitting that the $1000 was to go to Baker to ease his labor situation. Obviously the phone call had caught him unaware and it was apparent that he thought he had already said too much.

That afternoon Kennedy asked Baker about the Esco Company. Baker said that he had been sent to McKees Rock, Pennsylvania, to help in a strike situation and "to arbitrate and get the contract signed and settled." He stated he had met with both the owner of the company and the union. He had known Mr. Weinheimer, a representative of the company from New York, and admitted meeting with him in Des Moines sometime in 1957. Then he claimed he had gone to the Rambler Motel where Weinheimer was staying merely to use the swimming pool and had rented a room for that purpose. He denied that Weinheimer had given him any money and said he had not paid for his room with a hundred-dollar bill from an envelope.

After the motel managers testified, Baker was recalled. He now admitted that he might have used a hundred-dollar bill and that it might have been in an envelope. Kennedy said that he had talked to George Callahan on the phone and that Callahan's story was that he had sent $1000 in hundred-dollar bills to Weinheimer to work out labor problems with the Teamsters Union. Baker then admitted consulting with Callahan about his labor problems.

Baker:	It is my job to try to end strikes, as well as organize them.
Kennedy:	It is your job when you get paid $1000, evidently, Mr. Baker.
Baker:	I never got paid $1000, sir.
McClellan:	Let us nail it down. Did you get $1000 or any part of $1000 from Weinheimer?
Baker:	No, sir.

On Saturday morning Carmine Bellino and I flew to Pittsburgh and then drove to McKees Rock to talk to Mr. Callahan at the Esco Motor Company and to subpoena his records. The records indicated that in addition to the $1000 check that had been cashed on August 14, 1957, two more checks had been cashed—on September 16, 1957, and October 16, 1957. Callahan said that the proceeds from all three checks had been sent to Weinheimer in hundred-dollar bills. The first one, with which we were familiar, had been sent to Des Moines. He could not recall where the others had been sent. The post office records at McKees Rock indicated that on September 16, 1957, two packages were sent by Esco Company to Weinheimer at the Bellcrest Hotel in Detroit. The post office records also confirmed that three packages had been sent to Weinheimer in Des Moines on August 14. There was no record of anything being sent on October 16. Callahan said that he may have handed the third $1000 to Weinheimer, and that he had subsequently loaned Baker a total of $1125 on different occasions.

We checked at the Bellcrest Hotel in Detroit and found that both Edward Weinheimer and Barney Baker had registered there on September 16, 1957. We also found that the dates the moneys were sent or given to Weinheimer corresponded to significant dates in the labor difficulties the Esco Company was having with the Teamsters Union. The company's problems were primarily with Ted Cozza, the president of Local 211 in Pittsburgh. On Friday, September 13, 1957, Cozza, an ex-convict who had been arrested nine times and convicted on three occasions, set a strike date against the company for Monday, September 16. Weinheimer checked into the Bellcrest Hotel in Detroit on September 13. On September 14 he called Callahan and told him that the strike had been called off. On September 16 the second $1000 was sent to Weinheimer at the Bellcrest.

George Callahan appeared before the Committee the following week and gave a reluctant but candid account of his relationship with Weinheimer and Baker. He acknowledged that he knew the money he sent to Weinheimer was to secure labor peace and that he knew that Weinheimer was in contact with Baker. He said that henceforth he would conduct all his business by check. Edward Weinheimer also appeared and took the Fifth Amendment.

Even as Hoffa chafed under the day-by-day outpouring of evidence of continued corruption in his empire, he received two additional jolts from other quarters. The Board of Monitors issued Orders of Recommendation directing Hoffa to file charges against

Bert Brennan, Sam Feldman, Glen Smith and H. L. Boling and to suspend them from office. At the same time, the AFL-CIO Executive Council directed that "any alliance or agreement, formal or informal, between an affiliate of the AFL-CIO and the International Brotherhood of Teamsters be cancelled." The policy declaration stated further that "this above stated principle applies to any proposals for new alliances or agreements between the corrupt leadership of the International Brotherhood of Teamsters and any AFL-CIO affiliate." The latter statement was aimed at Hoffa's proposed Conference on Transportation Unity.

Hoffa responded to his attackers by a ludicrous attempt to improve his image. On August 23, he announced in Washington that he had appointed a three-man "antiracketeering commission" headed by former United States Senator George Bender of Ohio, the same man who had headed the 1954 abortive congressional investigation of the Teamsters in his home state. The other members of the commission were Washington attorney F. Joseph Donohue and a retired Wayne County, Michigan, judge, Ira W. Jayne. Martin O'Donoghue was outraged and issued a statement saying that the creation of the commission raised serious implications and had not been discussed beforehand with the Board of Monitors or the court. He demanded an explanation from Hoffa. Senator McClellan said the commission's good faith could be tested by whether it moved "against Hoffa himself." Bob Kennedy was also outraged and sent me to Ohio to investigate Bender's connection with the Teamsters.

In September, 1954, George Bender, then a Congressman, had headed a subcommittee investigating alleged corruption in the Teamsters Union in Ohio. The publicity would be helpful for Bender, who was running for the United States Senate seat previously held by the late Senator Robert Taft. William Presser, the head of the Ohio Teamsters, and Louis "Babe" Triscaro, his Mafia-connected number two man, both appeared before the Committee. They answered some questions but took the Fifth Amendment concerning their personal finances. The hearings were adjourned and Bender announced that they would resume in Washington on November 9 and that Presser and Teamsters President Dave Beck would be called. At the hearing in Washington Presser again appeared and took the Fifth Amendment. Beck was not called. The hearings were again adjourned and were never resumed. Bender was elected to the United States Senate.

The investigation of the Ohio Teamsters had been a farce. As had the investigation in Detroit a year earlier, it just suddenly ended. To find out why I went first to Jim Luken, the president of Joint Council 26 and the head of Teamsters Local 98 in Cincinnati. Luken, an honest and fearless labor official, had thus far resisted the attempts by Hoffa and Presser to take over the Cincinnati Teamsters organization. He recalled attending a Joint Council meeting immediately following the election of Bender as United States Senator in 1954. George Starling, Luken's predecessor as president of the Council, read a letter that requested the Council to contribute $40,000 for legal expenses for Presser and Triscaro in connection with their appearances before the Bender Committee. Someone present raised the point that their legal fees had already been paid and wanted to know why they needed additional money. The reply, which Luken wrote down at that time, was, "Other money was spent to pull certain strings to see that these charges were dropped."

I found two other Teamsters officials who recalled attending a meeting of the Ohio Conference of Teamsters shortly before Bender's election. They said that the Teamsters Union in Ohio had, up until that meeting, been supporting Bender's opponent, Thomas Burke, and strongly opposing Bender because of his congressional investigation. At the meeting William Presser announced that the Teamsters were switching their support to Bender.

I talked to Thomas Burke. He was reluctant to discuss it but did say that the support of the Teamsters in his race against Bender did appear to wane just before the election. When he lost by a very narrow margin, he appealed to the Teamsters for financial help for a recount. They turned him down.

In the minutes of a meeting of the Ohio Conference of Teamsters, held a few days after Presser's last appearance before the Bender Committee, I found a speech by Presser in which he said that there would not be any contempt citations or perjury charges arising from the investigation. Presser said, "We found, especially during the latter portion of the hearings, that we had a second friend on the Congressional Committee, a friend that did a fair job for the people concerned and his name is George Bender and it has taught me a lesson."

In 1955 Senator George Bender was the guest speaker at another meeting of the Ohio Conference of Teamsters and was warmly greeted by Presser, who said, "To you George Bender, the Republican whose name has been handled around as an anti-labor Senator, if it weren't for this·one man, and his advice . . . we would have a lot of problems that do not exist . . . and Bill Presser is committed to George Bender anywhere down the line."

I flew to Cleveland to talk to Presser. At that time he was the head of the Ohio Conference of Teamsters, Joint Council 41 in Cleveland and Local 555, the taxicab drivers' local. When I got into a cab at the Cleveland airport, and the driver asked me where I wanted to go, I couldn't resist my impulse and quipped, "Take me to your leader." He laughed and drove me to the Teamsters headquarters.

The records of the Teamsters organizations had already been subpoenaed earlier in the year by Art Kaplan in connection with his jukebox investigation. We had an office in the Federal Building staffed by Helen Thorpe and Tom Eickmeyer, two General Accounting Office accountants on loan to the Committee. Records had been turned over to that office on a piecemeal basis, but it had been a constant struggle to get them and many of them were missing. One of the canceled checks that had been turned over was in the amount of $1000 to G. H. Bender dated August 15, 1958, just one week before Bender was appointed by Hoffa to head his antiracketeering commission. The check was endorsed "Retainer for Public Relations, Ohio Conference of Teamsters. G. H. Bender, George H. Bender."

At the Joint Council 41 headquarters I reviewed the correspondence files that had not been turned over to our accountants. I was looking for further documentation of the relationship between the Teamsters and Bender. In an envelope labeled "Christmas list" I found an invoice from the Rudolph Deutsch Industrial Sales Company in Cleveland dated December 8, 1955, for eight "Champagne Masters" at $100 each. The names of eight persons to whom the champagne masters were to be delivered were written on the invoice: Beck, English, Hoffa, Brennan, Connell, Bender, Bliss and Dorfman. John English was, of course, the secretary-treasurer of the International Union. Judge James C. Connell was a federal judge in Cleveland. Ray Bliss was the chairman of the Republican Party in Ohio. The envelope also contained a yellow sheet of paper on which the same eight names were listed along with a first initial for each. I made detailed notes of the contents of the envelope.

I took the file containing the envelope, along with two other files, to Presser and said I would like to take them with me. He said he would prefer to have them photostated first. I agreed to leave them with him for that purpose and said I would return in a few days to pick them up. I left town and returned four days later, on Saturday morning, September 13. From the airport I called Presser at union headquarters. He answered the phone himself and said, "If I knew it was you, I wouldn't have answered it." I told him I would like to come out and pick up the files. He said that since he had told me I could have them, and he was a man of his word, I could come out and pick them up. When I arrived, the files were on a television set in Presser's office. He claimed he hadn't had a chance to have them photostated, in fact, hadn't touched them, but that I should go ahead and take them anyway. As I flipped through the files I noticed that the envelope and the yellow sheet of paper were missing and that the portion of the invoice listing the names had been torn off. The name "Beck" had been erased and it appeared that an attempt to erase the other names had torn the invoice and that the other names had then been torn off.

"I should have known better than to trust you," I said to Presser.

"You have your job to do and I have mine," was his reply. I took the files and left. I returned to our office, got a subpoena and went to the Rudolph Deutsch Company where I obtained the original of the invoice, which, of course, had the eight names listed on it. Bill Presser had been caught obstructing justice by destroying a document under subpoena.

In Washington the pressures on Hoffa were mounting. The rank and file committee that had originally challenged his election now demanded his ouster from the union. Hoffa responded by calling a meeting of two hundred Teamsters officials from around the country for a vote of confidence. All but one of those assembled gave it to him. He then announced plans to hold a new convention and election of officers in February, 1959. Martin O'Donoghue, impatient with Hoffa's delaying tactics and failure to act on recommendations to suspend corrupt officials, reacted by filing a petition with Judge Letts on September 17. The petition asked that the consent decree that had initiated the Board of Monitors be amended to make it clear that the Board had the power to order reforms rather than just recommend them and to order the union to comply with Orders of Recommendation already made. O'Donoghue also sought to dismantle the Bender antiracketeering commission and to block Hoffa's attempt to call an early convention.

The McClellan Committee hearings continued, with Hoffa making almost daily appearances to attempt to explain the evidence of corruption which flowed in seemingly unending testimony. He saw nothing wrong in the payment of $22,000 in union funds for the production of a thirteen-week television series designed primarily to assist the reelection campaign of Detroit Judge Joseph Gillis. The production company paid $1300 of this money directly to the judge. Judge Gillis subsequently presided over criminal actions against Teamsters officials. Hoffa also admitted contributing $11,000 to the campaign of the District Attorney in Detroit. He couldn't recall a conversation with a former prosecuting attorney during which, according to witnesses, he ridiculed the prosecutor for not accepting gifts and said he could frame him or anyone else in three months' time. Hoffa was then attempting to intercede for Local 299 Vice President Frank Fitzsimmons who had been indicted for taking money from employers. When the case came up before Judge Gillis, the indictment was dismissed.

Bob Kennedy asked Hoffa whether Barney Baker's admitted long assocation with a number of major racketeers didn't disturb him. "It doesn't disturb me one iota," Hoffa snapped.

Kennedy then asked Hoffa about a meeting he had with Sol Lippman, the then general counsel for the Retail Clerks Union, one year earlier. Lippman had gone to Detroit to place Local 876 of the Retail Clerks Union in trusteeship and move it out of the Teamsters headquarters. He took this action after Bob Kennedy told him that Hoffa completely dominated the local, negotiated its contracts, staffed it with Teamsters officials and forced it to pay dues to the Teamsters Joint Council. When Hoffa heard about it, he sent for Lippman, went into a tirade and, according to Lippman, threatened to have him killed. A thoroughly frightened Lippman told Kennedy that Hoffa said, "I've got friends who would shoot you in your tracks someday while you are just walking down the street. If I did it no jury would even convict me. I have a special way with juries." Lippman would not testify before the Committee about the threat, however, because he said his union would have to get along with the Teamsters in the future. Hoffa denied making the threat.

Kennedy asked Hoffa to produce the record of his option to buy half of Sun Valley, Inc. Hoffa said he hadn't been able to find it. Kennedy asked Hoffa why he had deposited the first $300,000 of Local 299 funds in an interest-free checking account in the Florida National Bank and Hoffa replied, "Because I wanted to."

One of the last witnesses to appear during the hearings was Richard Pastor, the editor of a labor newspaper in New York City. According to Catherine Barry, a juror in Hoffa's second wiretap trial in New York, it was he who had contacted her during the trial. Pastor took the Fifth Amendment when asked if he had contacted Miss Barry and who had instructed him to do so. After seven weeks of testimony the hearings came to an end on September 18, 1958.

Throughout the remainder of the autumn there were charges and countercharges filed with Judge Letts and in the press relating to the Board of Monitors. Hoffa was seeking to hold an early convention to rid himself of the Board of Monitors. Martin O'Donoghue and Godfrey Schmidt, as a majority of the Board, sought to block the convention and force reforms on Hoffa. There were reports that O'Donoghue would resign if the court did not put more legal teeth into the Board's supervision of the union. Schmidt then moved to abolish the monitorship and put the union in receivership. The other monitor, L. N. D. Wells, who as the International's representative had consistently dissented from the views of O'Donoghue and Schmidt, and who had favored the early convention to end the monitorship, now came out in favor of the monitorship to avoid a receivership. The dissension then spread to the rank and file committee. John Cunningham, the original leader of the committee, filed for the removal of Schmidt as a monitor, claiming he had a conflict of interest. Cunningham was represented by New York attorney Jacques Schiffer, who would soon become one of Hoffa's lawyers. Cunningham, at a press conference, linked the McClellan Committee and O'Donoghue with Schmidt in his critical remarks about the monitorship. It was apparent that Cunningham had split with the other twelve rank-and-filers in their opposition to Hoffa.

Finally, on December 11, Judge Letts ruled in effect that orders by the Board of Monitors had the same effect as orders by the court and extended the life of the Board indefinitely. He ordered the convention called by Hoffa canceled and denied the motion to oust Monitor Schmidt. It was a major victory for Martin O'Donoghue and a stunning defeat for Hoffa.

Hoffa defiantly closed out the year by announcing his intention to organize police departments beginning with New York's Finest.

CHAPTER IV

"I Get What I Want"

════════════════

ON JANUARY 27, 1959, Allen Dorfman appeared before the McClellan Committee and took the Fifth Amendment. Staff accountant Martin Uhlmann, who had spent eighteen months in Chicago untangling the labyrinth of Dorfman's operations, presented his findings to the Committee. In the ten-year period from 1949 to 1959, Allen Dorfman's agency received a total of $4,000,000 in commissions and fees. (In 1948, the year before the golden egg was laid, Allen Dorfman's taxable income was only $5094.) An examiner for the New York State Insurance Department testified that $1,250,000 of the commissions paid to Dorfman were excessive according to the insurance industry code of ethical practices. He also stated that under the same code no profit is allowed on service fees. Dorfman made up to a 53 percent profit, increasing the excessive payments to $1,650,000. The insurance examiner also noted that Dorfman's license to practice in the state of New York had been revoked because the examiners had been denied access to his records. Finally, on three occasions during the ten-year period, the rates of commissions and fees paid to Dorfman were increased while, at the same time, the benefits due to Teamsters members were decreased.

In 1954 Dorfman had taken $50,000 in premiums due to the insurance company and deposited it in a special account, using the funds for his own purposes. When the Committee investigation began in 1957, Dorfman attempted to cover up by forwarding $50,000 to the insurance company in two separate payments.

Dorfman had also issued life insurance policies for Hoffa, Gene San Soucie, Frank Fitzsimmons, Don Peters (the president of Local 743 in Chicago), Irving Green of the Mercury Record Company (who had hired Joe Louis after the 1957 Hoffa trial) and others. Dorfman had advanced the premiums on some of these policies and had not been reimbursed. At the time of the hearing, the latest available records showed that Hoffa owed $726 to Dorfman for a premium paid by the latter eighteen months earlier. The insurance company rejected an application by Johnny Dio after his premium check bounced three times and his policy was covered by a check from one of Dorfman's companies. Gus Zapas made an application for a policy but it was voided when he failed to make a payment.

By 1959 Dorfman's known business network, including the original Union Insurance Agency of Illinois, encompassed fourteen insurance entities and ten other business organizations. The records of Dorfman's agencies and the insurance company indicated that Dorfman had cashed over $300,000 in checks during the period 1949 to 1957. This meant that Dorfman, Hoffa's frequent travel companion, had available to him about $40,000 a year in cash during that period, the disposition of which was unknown.

Dr. Leo Pearlman's Union Casualty Company, the other party to the conspiracy, had also profited neatly from the arrangement. In 1951 the name of the company was changed to the Union Casualty and Life Insurance Company. In 1956 the name was again changed to the Mount Vernon Life Insurance Company, and again in 1958 to the Northeastern Life Insurance Company of New York. When the New York State Insurance Department revoked Dorfman's license his contract was canceled by the company and Dr. Leo Pearlman was eased out. The cancellation of Dorfman's contract, however, was apparently only a device to satisfy the insurance examiners. The Republic National Life Insurance Company of Dallas, Texas, which handled reinsurance for Northeastern, became the middleman for the continued payment of commissions and fees from the Teamsters to Dorfman. The new president of Northeastern acknowledged to the Committee that his company could not afford to lose the Teamsters business and knew that they could not keep it without Dorfman somehow remaining in the picture. One of the people who had convinced him of this was A. Maxwell Kunis, who was an actuarial consultant to both Northeastern Life and Republican National Life and also served as a consultant for the Central States Pension Fund, Joint Council

43 and several other Teamsters organizations.

The Committee then heard testimony from John Cunningham, the original leader of the rank and file committee that had instituted the suit to prevent Hoffa from taking office after the 1957 convention. In the first indication of dissension in the committee, Cunningham had filed a suit in April, 1958, seeking the removal of Godfrey Schmidt, the rank and file member of the Board of Monitors. Cunningham had been represented in that suit by Jacques Schiffer, a New York attorney who had also represented several of Johnny Dio's paper local associates who had taken the Fifth Amendment before the Committee. Cunningham said he had not paid Schiffer any fee. Subsequently Cunningham had filed another suit against Schmidt in December, 1958, demanding an accounting of funds paid to him by the rank and file committee and again calling for his ouster as a monitor. In this action Cunningham was represented by Joseph Williamson, an attorney from Urbana, Illinois, and Washington counsel Raymond Dickey. They had received $12,000 from three Teamsters locals toward their fee for representing Cunningham. In addition, Cunningham had paid them $2500 in cash, which he said he borrowed from Moss Herman, a former Teamsters member. Herman had, in turn, borrowed the money from Jacques Schiffer.

From August, 1958, through January, 1959, Cunningham had, on several occasions, stayed at the Woodner Hotel, which was the Washington residence of Hoffa and other Teamsters officials. His hotel bills had all been paid either by the Teamsters Union directly or charged to Moss Herman's account and later picked up by the Teamsters. In addition, Moss Herman had been receiving cash payments from Hoffa to "cover expenses" and had then loaned money to Cunningham. Cunningham acknowledged visiting Hoffa in his apartment at the Woodner Hotel, but denied knowing that his bills had been paid by the Teamsters and said he had never asked Moss Herman where he got the money he lent him. The undermining of the rank and file committee had begun.

In the running legal battle with the monitors, the International Union appealed Judge Letts' December ruling giving the Board of Monitors the power to enforce its recommendations for reform, contending that the original consent decree had provided only an advisory function for the Board. Pending a decision by the Court of Appeals, a period of cold war set in between the Board majority and the International.

Martin O'Donoghue, chairman of the Board of Monitors, hired three young attorneys, John Cassidy, Laurence Cohen and Leonard Mendelbaum, as staff members and the Board continued its regular meetings, but little was accomplished because both the Board and the International were aware that further meaningful action would have to await the Court of Appeals decision. On March 13 Nat Wells resigned as a monitor representing the International, pleading that the Board consumed too much of his time. He was replaced on March 18 by Washington attorney Daniel B. Maher, a former Assistant United States Attorney.

From mid-February to mid-April the McClellan Committee held hearings on nationwide racketeering in the coin-operated machine industry. These hearings were interrupted for one week during March for hearings on Joey Glimco, the president of Teamsters Local 777 in Chicago, and John T. "Sandy" O'Brien, the secretary-treasurer of Local 710 in Chicago, who was also the second vice president of the International Union. The Committee found that Glimco had conducted a wide-scale shakedown operation in the Fulton Street Poultry Market in the late 1940s and then taken over Teamsters Local 777, the taxicab local, in 1952. He forced officials of the local to pay him tribute amounting to $3000 a month, used over $100,000 in union funds to pay his own legal fees in connection with federal extortion charges, diverted $40,000 of union money to purchase a house for himself and his girl friend and kicked back over $325,000 in local funds to two Chicago cab companies as their "fee" for collecting union dues from the local's members.

In testimony about John T. O'Brien, Committee staff member Jim Mundie described the unique system employed by the officers of Local 710 to enrich themselves at the expense of their members. Three of the officials received a percentage of the dues and initiation fees of every member of the local. O'Brien, who received the highest percentage, pocketed (in addition to his expenses) $471,286.11 in the previous seven-year period.

Glimco and O'Brien, both staunch supporters of Hoffa, pleaded the Fifth Amendment when questioned about their activities.

In investigating O'Brien's operations, in La Salle, Illinois, I found a tough and courageous man named Barney Matual. His story, which he agreed without hesitation to relate to the Committee, epitomized much of what was wrong with the Teamsters Union under Hoffa and why it was so very difficult for the membership to do anything about it.

Matual, a proud, honest man, had formed Teamsters Gas Station Operators and Attendants Local 981 in La Salle in 1936 and had become its vice president and later its president. He had also helped form three other similar locals in nearby Illinois cities. The four locals prospered and lived at peace, with each other and the International, until they were suddenly confronted with a visiting party on December 4, 1954. The intruding group consisted of James R. Hoffa, Paul Dorfman, Kansas City Teamsters boss Roy Williams, Dick Kavner of the St. Louis Teamsters and the three Floyd brothers from Joliet, Illinois (Virgil Floyd, the head of Local 179 in Joliet, had just been convicted of taking money from an employer).

Hoffa called a meeting of the executive boards of the four locals and announced that he wanted them to merge with Virgil Floyd's local. Matual noticed that Kavner was carrying a gun. Matual and the other officers of the four locals protested, delayed for time and said they would take a vote of their members as to whether they wanted the merger. Hoffa said that if they did not agree to the merger, he would force them into Local 179 anyway. The four locals had a combined membership of 701 members. When the vote was taken, with an unusual 100 percent participation, the members voted 694 to 7 against the merger.

Shortly thereafter Matual attended a regular Teamsters meeting at a Springfield, Illinois, hotel. At the meeting he was tapped on the shoulder and told someone wanted to see him in one of the hotel rooms. When he went into the room he found Virgil Floyd and Barney Baker. Baker told Matual that he "had better" work with Floyd. Matual had never met Baker before but had seen him around and understood that he was a strong-arm man for Hoffa. In fear of physical violence, Matual told Floyd and Baker he would think it over.

On April 1, 1955, the date Hoffa had set for the merger of the locals into Local 179, the four locals voted to merge themselves into one local to form a consolidated front, but refused to merge with Floyd's local. The new combined local was designated Local 46 by drawing the number of one of the locals out of a hat. In December, 1955, Barney Matual was elected its president.

Thereafter, Virgil Floyd and his henchmen came to town and

harassed and intimidated employers under contract with Local 46 and threatened Matual. Matual attempted to obtain a permit to carry a gun but was turned down.

The International then sent in an auditor to go over the books of the local even though they had been audited just a year earlier. The auditor attempted to get Matual to sign a blank sheet of paper, saying that the rest would be filled in later. Matual refused. Shortly thereafter the auditor returned with David Sark, an assistant to John T. O'Brien. They said they had a letter from Dave Beck placing the local in trusteeship under O'Brien. Matual refused to accept it. Then O'Brien himself came in and told Matual the local was being placed in trusteeship. When Matual asked what the charges were, O'Brien said he didn't know. At Matual's request, O'Brien arranged a meeting with Beck at the Statler Hotel in Dallas on July 12, 1956.

When Matual arrived at the hotel he encountered Hoffa in the lobby. Hoffa said, "Barney, I get what I want." Matual said he knew then that it was Hoffa who was pushing Beck for the trusteeship. At the meeting Matual and Hoffa almost came to blows. Beck separated them and told Matual that he was going to be placed in trusteeship if it cost $100,000 to do it, "because my boy Jimmy knows what he's doing."

Matual replied, "You might give Local Union 46 a trusteeship, but you will never give me a trusteeship. My father came here from Lithuania looking for freedom. I have it and I am going to keep it." He then walked out of the meeting.

Matual reported back to his membership, who voted overwhelmingly to refuse to accept trusteeship. The International's auditor returned and, in Matual's absence, took all of the cash in the safe and the keys to the office and told the secretary that he was taking over. When Matual learned of this, he had the locks on the office changed and on advice of counsel withdrew all the local's funds from the bank and put them in a trust account.

O'Brien then set up a rival Local 46 and began raiding Matual's local. He attempted to bribe Matual and offered him a job with another local. Finally, on November 22, 1958, the members of Matual's local voted to withdraw from the Teamsters Union and affiliate with District 50 of the United Mine Workers.

Matual then related what happened after in connection with the contract the local had with the Star Union Brewery in La Salle. He met with the officials of the company and asked them to recog-

nize the local union under its new affiliation. John Clinch, the vice
president and general counsel of the company, refused to do so and
the local went on strike. The new Local 46, which had been set up
by O'Brien as a rival local, proceeded to import strikebreakers and
go through Matual's picket line, even though none of the brewery
employees belonged to the new Teamsters local. The mayor of La
Salle and other city officials, alarmed by the outside strikebreakers
and the threat of violence, petitioned John Clinch on behalf of
Matual. But in February, 1959, without consulting with his employees, Clinch signed a contract with John O'Brien, forcing his
employees back into the Teamsters Union. The employees ignored
the contract and continued their strike.

On March 11, 1959, the mayor of La Salle wrote to Bob Kennedy
saying that he had formed a committee of leading citizens which
had met on several occasions with representatives of the Teamsters, Matual's local and the Star Union Brewery in an attempt to
settle the strike. The committee had recommended that the strike
cease and that the National Labor Relations Board be asked to
conduct an election. Matual's local and Clinch agreed, but the
Teamsters International turned down the proposal. The next day,
according to the mayor, Clinch changed his mind, "proving to the
committee that he was either being high pressured or was taking
sides with Teamsters International."

Some light was shed on the reasons behind Clinch's decision
when our accountant, Carl Schultz, found that the International
Teamsters had paid Clinch $4000 to represent a group of dissidents
in Matual's local. Clinch appeared as a witness and said he saw no
conflict in accepting money from the International in its fight
against Matual and then siding with the International against
Matual in his position as counsel for the brewery. He denied that
he had ever agreed to the proposal of the mayor's committee for
an NLRB election. Although he denied talking to John T. O'Brien
about breaking the strike, he could not recall what he talked about
in long conversations, which telephone records indicated he had
had, with both O'Brien and his assistant David Sark during the
month preceding his signing of the contract with O'Brien.

Thus the workings of union democracy under Hoffa were revealed in Barney Matual's story: the attempt to force the decent
members of four locals, against their will, into a local controlled
by a convicted extortionist; the audit, the threats, the intimidation,
the bribery, the misuse of trusteeship; and finally the collusion

with management against union members. As Hoffa said, "Barney, I get what I want." And yet, when Hoffa had been asked by Senator Karl Mundt about the trusteeship of Local 46 in an earlier appearance before the Committee, he had been very vague.

Mundt: Do you know the circumstance of that trusteeship?
Hoffa: Not enough to talk about; no, sir.

Senator Frank Church summed it up in referring to Barney Matual's testimony:

> . . . this witness's testimony indicates how very difficult it is for the rank and file to deal with those in command of the Teamsters International. So often we hear it said, "Why don't these working people rise up and throw the rascals out?" Well, that is much easier said than done. I think this story exemplifies that fact very well.

During the early months of 1959, while the McClellan Committee hearings continued to grind out evidence of corruption in more niches and corners of Hoffa's empire, and while the Court of Appeals continued to ponder the decisive question of the future role of the Board of Monitors, Hoffa was quietly but dramatically putting together his transportation alliance. He had backed off from holding his announced Conference on Transportation Unity because of the strong vocal reaction it had engendered in Congress and from George Meany. But he had continued to forge links with Harry Bridges' International Longshoremen's and Warehousemen's Union on the West Coast and with the International Longshoremen's Association on the East Coast. The former had been ejected by the AFL-CIO for Communist domination and the latter, like the Teamsters, for domination by racketeers. Hoffa had also continued to nurture his alliance with the AFL-CIO National Maritime Union and was attempting to take advantage of the recently patched up feud between that union and the Seafarers International Union under Paul Hall, by courting the Seafarers. In addition, he had helped arrange a $200,000 loan for the Flight Engineers Union during its recent strike with Eastern Airlines and was attempting, through it, to establish a firm beachhead in the air transportation field. He augmented this action with approaches to the Airline Pilots Association and the Airline Stewards and Stewardesses Association. He had also stepped up

organizing efforts among airport workers. In February, for example, the Teamsters Union won an NLRB election in Florida involving seven hundred Pan American World Airways stock clerks.
Such potential harnessing of the control points of the nation's
transportation system and the resultant power to shut it down
completely was awesome indeed.

Hoffa had often discounted expressed fears of a nationwide
transportation strike, stating that it would create a backlash and
thus be counterproductive. But at the ILA convention in Browns-
ville, Texas, Hoffa himself gave frightening credibility to such
concern when he said, "They can talk about secondary boycotts;
we can call a primary strike all across the nation that will
straighten out the employers for once and for all."

In March I headed for Miami to check into reports of corruption
in Teamsters Local 320 in Miami Beach. The local was headed by
a man named Harold Gross. Who was Harold Gross? I checked
with our New York office and found that Gross had been associated with Teamsters Local 138 in New York in the early 1940s
at a time when that local was completely under the control of
Murder, Incorporated, and was engaged exclusively in shakedown
operations. In 1942 Gross had been convicted of extortion and
served three years in prison. He was paroled in May, 1945.

The contracts Gross and his helpers had managed to "negotiate"
contained no benefits for the members. Local 320 had only thirty-
two members, yet Gross and two other officers received $150 a
week each. The local was also paying $164 a month for the rental
of Gross' red Thunderbird. All of this was being subsidized by the
International Teamsters Union, which sent $3000 each month to
Local 320.

In talking to service station operators who had dealt with Gross,
I came upon one who unknowingly furnished the key to the even
more incredible story of Gross' lucrative activities in his other
world in New York City. The man told me he sometimes cashed
checks for Gross and had noticed that some of them were from a
printing company in New Jersey. He said he happened to have one
in his cash register that he had cashed earlier that day. The check
was from the Neo-Gravure Printing Company in Weehawken,
New Jersey. I left for New York that night.

The following day I took a bus to Weehawken. At the Neo-

Gravure Company I talked to Charles Chenicek, the general manager, Joseph Gervase, the assistant general manager, and William Hillbrant, the company treasurer. They said that their company printed Sunday supplements such as *The American Weekly* for various newspapers. They told me that Harold Gross was employed as a platform foreman in their shipping department and had been so employed since 1945. For this he received $143 a week. When I asked them whether Gross was working that day, they acknowledged that he was not and that they had not seen him in some time. Their payroll records, however, showed that Gross was still receiving his weekly checks. They did not have an explanation and were visibly upset by the inquiry. I learned from a reliable source that not only was Gross carried on the payroll while doing no work for the company, but also that both he and Connie Noonan, the racketeer head of Local 1730 of the International Longshoremen's Association, had received a substantial amount of money from the company to ensure labor peace. I subpoenaed the three company officials and the company records. On the advice of their attorney, they decided to cooperate fully with the Committee. The story they told Bob Kennedy, Kenny O'Donnell and me late the following evening, and to which they testified before the Committee two days later, was astounding.

The company had, as they said, hired Gross in 1945 as a platform foreman. In addition to his weekly paycheck, however, Gross also covertly received a monthly check for $460. During the fourteen years of his "employment" Gross had received approximately $100,000 in paychecks. But this was only one part. His brother, brother-in-law and two sons had also been on the payroll for various periods of time. This increased the family take to $226,000.

In addition, since 1952 Gross had received a $4000-a-year cash payment. Mr. Chenicek explained that this annual bite had been Gross' price for "arranging" for the delivery of *The American Weekly* supplement to the *New York Journal-American* during a jurisdictional dispute in 1952 between two locals of the Teamsters Union and the Newspaper and Mail Deliverers Union. He said that both the original agreement and each annual payment had been authorized and reimbursed by the *Journal-American*. These cash payments totaled $28,000.

Next, Gross had received two cash payments of $2500 each for his role in negotiating labor contracts favorable to the company with Connie Noonan's Local 1730 of the International Longshoremen's Association. The contracts provided for lesser wages for the employees than they would ordinarily have received through honest negotiation. Since 1949 Noonan had received a $200 cash Christmas present.

Finally, for their roles in arranging the surreptitious nightime delivery of Sunday supplements during a Teamsters strike, Gross and Noonan had been paid $45,000 in cash during an eight-day period in September, 1948. These deliveries had been made to *The New York Times* and the *New York Mirror*, both of which authorized the payments and reimbursed Neo-Gravure for them. Mr. Hillbrant, the treasurer of Neo-Gravure, said that he understood that two years earlier, in 1946, in a similar situation, cash payments totaling $10,000 had been made to Gross and Noonan but he did not know the details, since he was not there at that time.

Bob Kennedy sent Jerry Adlerman and me to New York to interview the officials of *The New York Times*, the *New York Mirror* and *The American Weekly* and to subpoena their records. We found *The New York Times* officials to be most cooperative. They acknowledged the role of the *Times* in the payoffs and made their records available. At the two Hearst publications, however, we were much less cordially received. The officials of both the *Mirror* and *The American Weekly* were evasive and less than candid in their recounting of the transactions.

At the subsequent hearing, Amory H. Bradford, vice president and business manager of the *Times*, gave a forthright statement of what had transpired, and accepted, on behalf of the *Times*, full responsibility for its actions. He concluded by stating:

> I can say that in the light of the circumstances that have developed since then, particularly many of the facts brought out by this committee, and in earlier investigations of similar situations in New York, the *Times* would not today under any circumstances agree to reimburse any of its suppliers for payments to union officials. We would put the public interest against corruption in labor-management relations above private interests in having any such sections delivered. I would think, looking back to 1948, all we can say is that we hope we have learned something from our own experiences and that of others.

The officials of the *Mirror* and *The American Weekly* were less contrite in their testimony. Warren Kelly, vice president and advertising director for the *New York Mirror*, said he had not inquired at the time who was to receive the money that Neo-Gravure was authorized to pay for the delivery of the supplements.

Kennedy: You didn't care where the $10,000 went as long as you got your magazine sections?
Kelly: Exactly.
Kennedy: Do you think that is the proper attitude for a business executive?
Kelly: I think it is the proper attitude for an executive that wants to sell two million papers.

A former official of the Hearst organization was more to the point. John J. Padulo, the business manager of the Erie *Times-News*, had been business manager of *The American Weekly* from 1952 to 1955. He testified that he knew at the time the payments were being made for labor peace and that it was improper, but felt compelled to make them to ensure delivery of the supplements.

Connie Noonan had been president of Local 1730 of the ILA since it was formed in 1948 to succeed a prior local. Noonan had shared control of the earlier local with Barney Baker's old friends, Edward McGrath, John "Cockeyed" Dunn, and "Squint" Sheridan, all of whom were involved in waterfront rackets. Noonan had also been an officer of Varick Enterprises, the shakedown outfit. He was closely associated throughout the years with the top New York and New Jersey hoodlums. Both Noonan and Gross appeared before the Committee and took the Fifth Amendment. Just as the story of Barney Matual reflected so well the frustrations of attempts by honest Teamsters to resist corruption, so, too, the story of Harold Gross offered a vivid example of the entrenchment of corruption in the Teamsters Union under Hoffa and his continued arrogant fostering and support of it. Gross was a convicted extortionist who resumed his shakedown trade immediately after being released from prison. Over one year after Hoffa was elected president and had pledged to clean up the union, Gross was given a Teamsters local and subsidized by Hoffa with $3000 a month and a red Thunderbird to consort with racketeers in Miami and sign sweetheart contracts, while continuing to collect tribute from a victimized legitimate business in New Jersey.

The final irony of the story was contained in an exchange of letters between Bernard Derow, the secretary-treasurer of Local

320 under Gross, and George Bender, the head of Hoffa's so-called antiracketeering commission. Bender had written a letter in October, 1958, shortly after Gross took over the local, asking if there was any racketeering in Local 320. On November 11, Derow replied:

> Dear Sir:
> There are no cases of racketeering or gangster alliances in this local union.
> We will give you full cooperation on any investigation of this local union.

On December 5 Bender responded to Derow's assurances:

> Dear Mr. Derow:
> Your letter of recent date in response to mine of October 24 has been received.
> The fine report you give of your organization is most gratifying to the Commission. The officials and members of your local are to be commended upon it.
> Thank you sincerely for your fine spirit of cooperation.

Meanwhile, Bob Kennedy sent me to look into the labor contracts Hoffa had negotiated. Hoffa and his defenders had consistently claimed that no matter what charges were made against him, he had always ground out the best contracts possible for his members. At the same time Pierre Salinger went to Pittsburgh to check into reports of payoffs to Teamsters boss Ted Cozza; Paul Tierney was in New York investigating the status of the Dio-Corallo empire; and Walter May and John Constandy were running between Cleveland and Florida inquiring about a company called Akros Dynamics, which reportedly had some unusual Teamsters connections and peculiar involvement in the Sun Valley project.

On June 10 the Court of Appeals finally ruled on the jurisdiction of the Board of Monitors. The three-judge court unanimously held that Hoffa must comply with the reform orders already issued and could be required by Judge Letts to comply with future recommendations of the Board of Monitors. The court also upheld Judge Letts' ruling that a new convention could not be held until other reforms had been accomplished.

The court's decision was a drastic blow to Hoffa, who had hoped to get rid of the monitors and to call for a new convention. The U.S. Supreme Court refused to review the case and Hoffa girded himself for a long legal battle, fully realizing that not only might some of his associates be forced out of the union, but that he, too, could be ousted from office. Martin O'Donoghue, also anticipating extensive litigation, announced his intention to petition Judge Letts for permission for the Board of Monitors to retain an outside law firm. Bert Brennan shrugged off the court decision and said, "I think I'll die in the Teamsters Union."

On June 24 the 1958 conviction of Johnny Dio and John McNamara for extortion was reversed by the New York State Appelate Court. Dio had been sentenced to fifteen to thirty years and McNamara to five to ten years. Dio was still faced with pending indictments for conspiracy to obstruct justice in connection with the blinding of Victor Riesel and for failure to file income tax returns.

On the afternoon of June 25 Jimmy Hoffa again appeared before the McClellan Committee, accompanied by Edward Bennett Williams. During that morning the business manager of the Pittsburgh *Sun Telegraph* had testified that Teamsters official Ted Cozza had been on the payroll of the newspaper since 1950 and had received payments totaling $75,000 plus $25,000 in rental fees for a truck he owned. The company official acknowledged that the payments to Cozza were for labor peace and that Cozza did not work for the company. When an efficiency expert hired by the newspaper questioned the payments, Cozza threatened to run him out of town and the company hired Pinkerton guards to protect their expert. Cozza and his men took the guns away from the Pinkerton guards, called the police and preferred charges against the guards for carrying guns without a license. Faced with this testimony, Cozza took the Fifth Amendment.

There followed testimony by the business manager of the Detroit *Times* to the effect that Joseph Prebenda, the head of Teamsters Local 372, had been on the payroll of that newspaper since 1921. In the previous five years Prebenda had received a total of $36,000 from the company while collecting a salary from the union amounting to $48,000 during the same period. The newspaper official testified that he had kept making the payments to avoid trouble but said that Prebenda did do some work for the paper.

Bob Kennedy then called a series of witnesses who had previously taken the Fifth Amendment before the Committee and concerning whom additional derogatory information had been developed. His purpose in doing this was to show that in spite of Hoffa's pledge to clean house, these persons were still officials of the Teamsters Union and no action had been taken by Hoffa.

Then Hoffa was called as a witness and asked to account for his lack of action against any of these Teamsters officials. Considerable attention was devoted to the case of Glen Smith of Local 515 in Chattanooga. When Smith had appeared before the Committee in 1957 he had taken the Fifth Amendment concerning the $18,500 in union funds that had been used to fix the case before Judge Ralston Schoolfield in which the indictment against Smith and others was dismissed. Smith was subsequently indicted and convicted of income tax evasion in connection with the $18,500. In his income tax trial he had testified in open court that the $18,500 was used to bribe Judge Schoolfield. Smith's attorneys' fees were paid by the Teamsters Union. Judge Schoolfield was impeached and disbarred.

Under pressure from the Board of Monitors, Hoffa had sent a letter on August 24, 1958, to Smith and H. L. Boling, the secretary-treasurer of Local 515 who had been implicated with Smith in the fixing of the case, and suspended them both from office. A representation was made to Judge Letts in November, 1958, that Smith and Boling had been suspended. Yet La Verne Duffy now testified that when he checked the records of Local 515, he found that both Smith and Boling had remained in office throughout 1958. It was not until January 6, 1959, the evening the jury started its deliberations in the income tax trial of Smith and Boling, that the local executive board voted to grant them both a six-month leave of absence with full pay in advance.

On January 9 Smith was convicted and Boling was acquitted. At a meeting of the executive board of the local on January 20 Smith was continued on leave of absence and Boling was appointed to temporarily replace him as president of the local.

Hoffa maintained that he had not known until Duffy testified that Smith and Boling had not been suspended in accordance with his August 24, 1958, letter. He said that an investigating panel he had appointed in October, 1958, to look into the matter had not yet reported back to him and he had assumed all along that they had been suspended.

The conviction of Glen Smith would be subsequently reversed on a point of law by trial judge William E. Miller in Nashville.

Hoffa admitted, however, under questioning by Senators Kennedy and McClellan, that he did have the power and authority under the Teamsters constitution to suspend local union officials, and that besides the Smith and Boling case, he had used that power in only one instance—against Sam Feldman in Philadelphia. He said he would deal with others in due time as they came to his attention. Senator Kennedy then pointed out that Hoffa had pledged two and a half years before that he would clean up the union, and that so far there was no evidence he had any intention of doing so; in fact, the evidence was quite to the contrary.

Bob Kennedy asked Hoffa whether George Bender, as head of the Teamsters antiracketeering commission, had brought to Hoffa's attention the fact that Sam Goldstein was still serving as a union official while in jail. Hoffa said he had not. From August, 1958, to May, 1959, Bender had received $58,000 from the International Union.

McClellan: Has his committee reported anything to you at all that should come before your executive board for its consideration with respect to disciplinary action?

Hoffa: No. He is in the process of investigation.

The Committee then turned its attention to a shadowy man whose fleeting tracks kept emerging on areas of Hoffa's byways. Ben Dranow had operated several small fur stores in New York City, Philadelphia, Wilmington and Baltimore during the forties and early fifties. One of his customers had been the John W. Thomas Department Store in Minneapolis. In 1952 Dranow moved to Minneapolis and became the manager of the fur department of John W. Thomas. In 1953 the Retail Clerks International Association called a strike on the store which was to last four years. Dranow became friendly with Jerry Connelly, the Minneapolis Teamsters official who had taken over Local 548 in 1951 shortly after leaving Miami with Jimmy James where they both had been involved in an investigation of an attempted murder. After Connelly was indicted twice for extortion, in 1954 and 1955, he was replaced as head of the local by Sidney Brennan. Three months later, however, the local was placed in trusteeship under Kansas City Teamsters boss Roy Williams who, in turn, put Connelly back in charge of Local 548. In the early morning hours of February 11, 1956, the automobile of a rival Teamster was dynamited. A jury later decided that Connelly had planned the bombing, and had then taken off on February 6 for Miami where he checked into the Waves Hotel. Two days later Dranow checked into the adjoining room. The hotel bills of both Connelly and Dranow were charged to the John W. Thomas Company. When Connelly was subsequently indicted for the dynamiting, it was Dranow who brought the first $2500 in cash to Connelly's lawyer, for which he was later reimbursed by the Teamsters Union.

Meanwhile Dranow had gained control of the John W. Thomas Company by putting up a note for $17,000 to purchase the stock and he put Connelly's son on the payroll under an assumed name.

On June 6, 1956, while still being struck by the Retail Clerks International Association, Dranow arranged with Hoffa for the John W. Thomas Company to obtain a $200,000 loan from the Michigan Conference of Teamsters Health and Welfare Fund. In January, 1957, through the intervention of Hoffa's friend Joe Bushkin, the Retail Clerks' strike was finally settled. Two years earlier Bushkin had made good on three bad checks of Dranow's totaling $3000 at Las Vegas casinos. In August, 1966, Dranow purchased two fur jackets for $2000 each, charged them to the John W. Thomas Company and sent one to Joe Bushkin and the other to Bert Brennan's wife. Dranow then obtained another loan for John W. Thomas Company—this time from the Central States Pension Fund in the amount of $1,000,000. At the time of the loan, the company was in desperate financial condition and facing bankruptcy. The store ultimately did go bankrupt but not before Dranow had made off with $113,000 of its assets.

Dranow had originally been subpoenaed to appear before the Committee in September, 1957, but he entered a hospital and claimed he was ill. He then disappeared and efforts to locate and subpoena him were unsuccessful until November, 1958, when he finally did appear to testify. He took the Fifth Amendment on all questions concerning his relationship with the John W. Thomas Company and the Teamsters Union. Then he disappeared again. He was now scheduled to testify again on June 29, 1959. That morning he sent a telegram from Miami to his attorney claiming that he had a heart condition and had again entered the hospital.

Subpoenas seemed to make him suddenly very sick. But for a sick man, Dranow had been very active indeed.

After the John W. Thomas Company fiasco, Dranow's next caper was an attempt to bail out Jimmy Hoffa from his entanglements in Sun Valley. The Committee had been very critical of Hoffa's handling of the Sun Valley situation after the 1958 hearings and had referred the matter to the Department of Justice for possible prosecution. His role in the Sun Valley project was certain to be one of the principal charges against Hoffa in any action by the Board of Monitors to oust him from office. Still sitting in a checking account in the Florida National Bank of Orlando was $500,000 in Local 299 funds, bearing no interest. The money had been deposited to induce the bank to make loans in the same amount to Henry Lower for the Sun Valley project. Lower had diverted much of this money to his own use and had not done anything to improve the property that Hoffa was helping to promote as a retirement site for Teamsters members. Hoffa, of course, had an option to buy 45 percent of the project and had concealed this from his members until it was brought out by the Committee. He knew he had to do something about it.

The attempted rescue operation had begun immediately after the 1958 hearings. On October 8 Dranow called the president of the Barnett National Bank in Cocoa, Florida, and attempted to obtain a loan so that he and his associates could take over the Sun Valley project. Dranow said that if the loan could be obtained, he would arrange for the deposit in the bank of $1,000,000 in Teamsters funds in an interest-free account. He was, in effect, attempting to compound the Hoffa-Lower misdeeds by doing the same thing all over again at double the cost to the union. The bank president turned him down.

Dranow then linked up with a New York City certified public accountant, S. George Burris, in the continuing effort to help Hoffa out of his Sun Valley predicament. Burris approached New York land developer Irving Blum and attempted to interest him in the idea of taking over and developing the Sun Valley project. Burris told Blum that seventeen hundred lots had already been sold but that roads would have to be built and other improvements made. Burris said he could obtain funds from the Teamsters Union to help cover these costs. For his assistance in arranging things, Burris was to receive $50,000 over a period of a few years as ac-

counting fees. Blum was interested and went to Florida to inspect
the property. He was introduced by Burris to Dranow, who also
told him that Teamster Union funds could be made available for
improvement of the project. Blum's interest waned when he found
out that the project had been badly mismanaged by Henry Lower
and that there was no ready way to determine which lots had been
sold, who owned which lots or what roads would be necessary.

Burris offered to obtain a loan from the Teamsters Pension
Fund for Blum to purchase an apartment building in Buffalo, New
York, on which Blum had an option, but again there would be a
fee, this time 5 percent of the loan. Blum backed away from both
proposals.

Dranow then approached another land developer, Stanton D.
Sanson of Bal Harbour, whom he had met earlier in Minneapolis
when Sanson was attempting to obtain a loan from the Pension
Fund. At that time, the fund had turned down Sanson's original
application but Dranow told him that he could arrange for the loan
if Sanson would agree to pay him a 5 percent "finder's fee." Sanson
decided to drop the matter. Now, in late 1958, Dranow attempted
to interest Sanson in the Sun Valley project and told him that he
could arrange for a substantial loan from the Teamsters for a
sewage plant, roads and houses. While Sanson was considering the
proposal, he received a call from Dranow, who put Hoffa on the
line. Hoffa told Sanson that it was a "must" that he straighten out
the Sun Valley project and urged him to do what he could.

Sanson had a study made of the project and concluded that it was
hopeless to attempt to rehabilitate it. His analysis indicated that it
would take a survey team to merely locate each lot before any
streets could be built and that the streets alone would cost a minimum of $300,000. He concluded that "nothing could be salvaged"
and turned the deal down.

Showing great persistence, Dranow formed his own company,
Union Land and Home, and purchased all of Henry Lower's stock
in Sun Valley for $18,000 and wrote off the $134,000 that Lower had
misappropriated and owed to the project. Burris became president
of Union Land and Home as a front for Dranow. When Burris, a
C.P.A., testified before the Committee, he equivocated in almost
every response to questions, claiming that he was not sure, could
not remember or would have to check his records. He did acknowledge that he and others had received two loans from the Pension
Fund—one for $735,000 for the Prudential Building in Buffalo, and

the other for $1,400,000 for the construction of a housing project in Fullerton, California.

While S. George Burris was machinating with Ben Dranow to rescue Hoffa from the Sun Valley debacle and arranging loans from the Pension Fund, his son Herbert, an attorney, was enmeshed in a bizarre caper that undoubtedly would have resulted in a highly questionable loan by the Pension Fund had not the Committee's investigation intruded.

In April, 1957, two men, Earl T. Benjamin of Cleveland and William Steiner of California, decided to buy eleven surplus C-74 Globemaster airplanes from the government with hopes of reselling or leasing them. To handle the enterprise, they formed a corporation called Akros Dynamics, Inc. Upon their first payment of $500,000, four of the planes were made available to them in Tucson, Arizona. The rest were to be released as additional payments were made. The venture became engulfed in financial difficulties when their hoped-for sources of additional financing fell through and attempts to market the planes were unproductive.

Finally, in January, 1959, immediately after Castro's takeover of Cuba, Alvin Naiman, a Cleveland businessman who had acquired an interest in the enterprise, introduced Benjamin to Dominic Bartone and Jack La Rue, two mysterious men from Florida who claimed they could sell two planes to the new Cuban government. They were given an option on two of the planes. Then, on February 11, Bartone suggested that he could operate more effectively if he were dealing exclusively with only one person in Akros Dynamics. Benjamin and Steiner thereupon signed over their stock to Naiman as their designee to deal with Bartone. The agreement provided that if Naiman did not succeed in disposing of the planes through Bartone, the stock would be returned. Benjamin and Steiner were unaware, however, that others were active behind the scenes.

Two days earlier, on February 9, Jimmy Hoffa had made two significant phone calls. One was to Roy Williams, a Kansas City Teamsters official who was also a trustee of the Pension Fund and who had received a $17,000 loan from Dranow's Union Land and Home Company. The other was to Ben Dranow in Beverly Hills, California. On February 10 Louis "Babe" Triscaro, Bill Presser's sidekick and an old friend of Alvin Maiman's, flew to Washington and visited Hoffa's Teamsters headquarters. Dranow was also there and made a call to S. George Burris in New York, using the

assumed name of "Morris." A call was also made from the Teamsters International to the office of Alvin Naiman in Cleveland. On
February 11, the same day that the Akros Dynamics stock was
assigned to Naiman, Herbert R. Burris flew to Cleveland at the
request of Dranow and met with Triscaro and Naiman in Triscaro's office. Triscaro had summoned Naiman to his office and told
him he wanted him to meet someone who might be interested in
helping with the plane transactions. Naiman explained the situation to Herbert Burris, who suggested that they go to New York
and present the matter to his father. Triscaro, Naiman and Burris
flew to New York later the same day and met that evening with
the elder Burris, who expressed an interest in the deal. The following morning the four men flew to Miami where Naiman met Ben
Dranow, who was introduced as a banker. They remained overnight and early the next morning Triscaro called Hoffa at the
International in Washington. The four men then met again with
Dranow and it was suggested to Naiman that he turn the company
over to Dranow. Then, at Dranow's suggestion, Naiman flew to
Cuba and met with Dominic Bartone, who appeared to have good
Cuban contacts. Upon returning to Miami the next day, February
14, Naiman signed an agreement, witnessed by Triscaro, conveying the stock of the company to Herbert Burris as the nominee for
Ben Dranow. Naiman was to receive 15 percent of any profits,
which he would share with the other Cleveland principals. All
subsequent dealings by Naiman with Dranow, however, were to
be made through another Dranow front man, Abe Weinblatt.

Naiman and Triscaro returned to Cleveland on February 15. The
next day Triscaro again flew to Washington and Dranow, once
more using the alias of "Morris," called George Burris from the
Teamsters International. Triscaro returned to Cleveland and was
called there the following day by Hoffa.

During the remainder of February and throughout the month
of March negotiations continued with the Cuban government.
Naiman made three more trips to Cuba, accompanied each time by
Bartone, Dranow or Triscaro. All four were in Cuba on March 21
when one of the C 74s was flown in from Arizona to be inspected
by the Cubans. During this period there were frequent phone calls
between Dranow, Burris, Triscaro and Hoffa. On April 1 the Cuban government announced its intention to purchase from four to
ten of the airplanes. Akros Dynamics was still in dire financial
condition, however, and needed funds to service and transport the
planes.

Triscaro suggested to Naiman that it might be possible to obtain a loan from the Pension Fund and arranged for him to go to Chicago, accompanied by Bartone, to meet with James C. Downs, the head of Real Estate Research Corporation, the company retained by the Pension Fund to evelute prospective loans. They understood that Hoffa was to call Downs to pave the way and they asked if he had. Downs said he had not heard from Hoffa and suggested they return later that day. Downs then called Hoffa, who said that he had meant to call earlier and that the Teamsters were interested in making the loan if Downs approved. When they returned, Naiman and Bartone asked for a $300,000 loan to help finance the sale of the airplanes. Bartone told Downs that Ben Dranow, who "worked with Hoffa," had assured him the loan would be granted. Naiman offered to put up his interest in a Canadian crushed stone company as collateral.

On April 24 Downs wrote to the screening committee of the Pension Fund and advised against granting the loan. He had visited the crushed stone company and found that it was already heavily indebted. On May 1 Triscaro arranged to go with Naiman to Washington to see Hoffa. Gene San Soucie, another trustee of the Pension Fund, was also present. In their presence, Hoffa called Downs and questioned him as to whether there wasn't some way that he might approve the loan. He was unsuccessful.

During the preceding month, while the search for funds was in progress, the C-74 had been flown from Cuba to Miami. In early April the Bureau of Customs had become aware of a plot to smuggle arms and ammunition to the Dominican Republic. Further investigation established that the mastermind of the plot was none other than Dominic Bartone. The surplus contraband had been quietly acquired and stored in a Miami warehouse and arrangements had been made by Bartone with the Dominican Republic embassy to purchase it. Bartone obtained a permit to fly the C-74 to Puerto Rico but instructed the pilot to feign engine trouble over the Dominican Republic and land there. He then hoped to dispose of not only the arms and ammunition but also to sell the airplane to the Dominican Republic for $400,000. On May 22 Customs agents moved in and arrested Bartone and his co-conspirators and seized the plane and its cargo just prior to its scheduled departure.

On May 26, in spite of the failure to obtain the approval of James Downs and four days after the arrest of Bartone, a circulation of the trustees of the Pension Fund was initiated and San Soucie sent a telegram to the fund voting to approve the loan to Bartone and Naiman on behalf of both himself and Hoffa. The circulation was completed on June 9 and the loan was approved. However, on June 15, less than two weeks before Hoffa's scheduled appearance before the Committee, better judgment somehow prevailed and Stanford Clinton, the Chicago attorney for both the fund and the Dorfmans, advised Naiman that the loan had been rejected because of a legal technicality.

Alvin Naiman cooperated with Walter May and John Constandy and his assistance was invaluable in piecing the intricate affair together. When he appeared to testify, however, he was understandably nervous and very reluctant to implicate Triscaro and Hoffa any more than was necessary. For instance, Triscaro had billed the hotel expenses of both of them for one of their trips to Miami to Local 436 in Cleveland. With the hearings approaching, they decided that the local should be reimbursed. At Triscaro's request, Naiman gave him a back-dated check for his share of the expenses. When Bob Kennedy asked about it at the hearing, Naiman denied that he had back-dated the check at Triscaro's request, but Kennedy's persistence prevailed:

Kennedy:	Mr. Naiman, didn't you tell me downstairs just several hours ago that the reason you dated it June 1 was because of the request of Mr. Triscaro?
Naiman:	I wouldn't say that.
Kennedy:	Didn't you state that down in the office?
Naiman:	No. You asked me that.
Kennedy:	And didn't you say "yes"?
Naiman:	No I didn't, sir.
Kennedy:	You didn't say "yes"?
Naiman:	No, sir.
Kennedy:	Mr. Naiman?
Naiman:	No, I didn't.
Kennedy:	What did you say then?
Naiman:	I didn't answer that.
Kennedy:	Mr. Naiman?
Naiman:	I didn't answer.
Kennedy:	What?
Naiman:	I didn't answer that question.
Kennedy:	You didn't answer it?

Naiman:	No, sir.
Kennedy:	And I let it go?
Naiman:	No. You kept insisting that he had asked me [to] date it June 1. But he never did ask me.
Kennedy:	Did you deny it?
Naiman:	I didn't deny it and I didn't affirm it.
Kennedy:	Didn't you say "yes," Mr. Naiman?
Naiman:	(No response)
Kennedy:	Mr. Naiman, didn't you say "yes"?
Naiman:	No, I didn't.
Kennedy:	Mr. Naiman, didn't you say "yes" to me when I asked you that? You are under oath.
Naiman:	I can honestly say—
Kennedy:	You are under oath now, Mr. Naiman. Didn't you say "yes" to that when I asked you that down in the office less than two hours ago?
Naiman:	I did say that.
McClellan:	Now you say you did say "yes" when he asked you?
Naiman:	Yes, sir.
McClellan:	Do you now say that it is the truth, that you did date the check back at his request?
Naiman:	Yes.

Later on in his testimony, Naiman again became recalcitrant. He acknowledged going to see Hoffa with Triscaro in connection with the attempt to obtain a Pension Fund loan but denied repeatedly that there had been any discussion with Hoffa about the planes or what the loan was for. Two weeks earlier Naiman had told May and Constandy that they had discussed the planes with Hoffa who had commented that Naiman had involved himself in a miserable deal. Now under further persistent questioning by Kennedy, Naiman said that he could not remember making such a statement. Finally, after he had been dismissed as a witness, he decided he wanted to tell the truth and asked to be allowed to testify further.

McClellan:	All right, Mr. Naiman, I understood you wanted to make some further statement.
Naiman:	Ask me the question, please, Mr. Kennedy.

Kennedy: This is in connection with your visit here when
             you went to see Mr. Hoffa in connection with
             this loan. Was there a discussion at that time
             about the fact that you needed the money in
             connection with these airplanes?
Naiman: Yes, there was.
Kennedy: I will say something for Mr. Naiman. He has
             grown up with a number of these people that are
             involved, and he explained to us, and it is reason-
             able, he does not want to get anybody in any
             great difficulty. We have had a considerable
             amount of difficulty on occasion to try to get
             some of these facts. I think he would like to help
             us, but I think that that has been a problem.

Babe Triscaro again pleaded the Fifth Amendment concerning
his role in the escapade and Bartone was excused from testifying
at the request of his attorney who pleaded that his client was under
indictment for the attempted gun-running and that any questions
asked concerning the matter would be prejudicial to his case. In
addition to the poignant example of a witness caught between the
desire to tell the truth and the fear of reprisal, the story of the
escapades of Ben Dranow and his friends suggested for the first
time the role that the Pension Fund had come to play in Hoffa's
empire. The Committee had not had the time, thus far, to investigate the fund as such. Now, with Ben Dranow as the common
denominator, the emergence of the Burris father and son team and
the disclosure that "finder's fees" were solicited to obtain loans, the
glimpses afforded at the Pension Fund lending procedures were
disquieting.

The name of Abe Gordon had cropped up often during the
investigations and hearings of the Committee. The vice president
of New York Local 805, he had been closely associated with racketeers and was active with them in the local paper venture. Like
Allen Dorfman, he was often wherever Hoffa was—at the trials,
International headquarters, Executive Board meetings—a constant reminder to those who might wonder of the continuing
alliance with the world of Johnny Dio. His cohort Milton Holt, the
secretary-treasurer of Local 805, also a friend of hoodlums, had
been convicted of perjury and had taken the Fifth Amendment in

a prior appearance before the Committee. Both were still Teamsters officials, and the Committee took another look at them.

Testimony by staff members and a business agent of the International Brotherhood of Electrical Workers established that Gordon, while living rent-free in the Concord Hotel in Monticello, New York, a plush resort in the Catskill Mountains, had purchased a plot of land from his cousin in nearby Wurtsboro, New York, with $85,000 from the Local 805 Welfare Fund. The land was worth less than one-fourth of the purchase price. Gordon then constructed camps on the land, using nonunion labor, in spite of protests of local labor leaders. He also owned a trucking company that operated without a union contract and paid below union wages. Gordon served as administrator for the Welfare Fund and had received $225,000 in commissions and expenses from the fund in the previous nine-year period.

Milton Holt was shown to have been in frequent contact with active narcotics pushers, sometimes meeting them at the Local 805 office, and to have been the recipient of a number of loans from businesses with whom Local 805 had contracts.

In New Jersey Hoffa's friend Tony Provenzano had become president of Local 560 in June, 1958, and, one month before the hearings, had been elected president of Joint Council 73. This was another example of Hoffa's peculiar method of cleaning up the Teamsters Union—instead of racketeers being weeded out, they were being brought in and actively promoted. The presidents of two trucking companies testified that they had made shakedown payments to Provenzano to ensure labor peace. A former trucking company president told of making payments to John Conlin when Conlin was president of Local 650 in New Jersey. Now an International vice president of the Teamsters Union, Conlin was in poor health and would soon be replaced by none other than Tony Provenzano. Because of his health, Conlin was not able to testify. Provenzano took the Fifth Amendment.

The question of Hoffa's contracts was the next to be brought under scrutiny. In Detroit I learned that the Trans-American Freight Lines, headquartered there, had made a separate agreement with Hoffa commencing in 1955. The agreement provided that drivers would be paid one and a half cents a mile in lieu of

certain fringe benefits, and for the adoption of a different grievance procedure than that followed by other companies. The special arrangement that Trans-American enjoyed provided that
grievances not settled at a local level were to be referred directly
to Chicago, bypassing the city and state grievance councils. However, I found that in practice, they did not even abide by this
separate agreement but instead sent grievances directly to Frank
Fitzsimmons, the vice president of Hoffa's own Local 299, and later
to Roland McMaster, a business agent of the same local. This was
true whether the Trans-American terminal where the employee
worked was in Detroit, Indianapolis, Cleveland or elsewhere.

The company officials defended the one-and-a-half-cents-per-
mile provision, claiming that it had been approved by the employees, who actually made more money that way. In checking
further, I found that neither claim was completely true. The agreement went into effect on February 1, 1955, without consultation
with the employees, and most of the local unions objected to it. A
meeting then was called on February 13, 1955, which was addressed
by both Robert Gotfredson, the president of Trans-American, and
Hoffa. Hoffa said that he could not understand why most of the
locals had turned down the one-and-a-half-cent agreement and
both he and Gotfredson urged them to give it a try. It was finally
agreed that the provision would be accepted on a trial basis for
twelve weeks, at which time another meeting would be held to
make an evaluation. The second meeting was never held and the
employees were stuck with the separate agreement.

One of the things that Hoffa had stressed at the February 13
meeting was that under no conditions would the drivers be required to give up their good bid runs, of which they were very
protective. (Bid runs are preferential trips that drivers bid for on
a seniority basis.) Yet I found that Trans-American was now putting on the road a large number of new Mack trucks, and that to
get one of the trucks, a driver not only had to sign the one-and-a-
half-cent agreement, but in many cases was losing his bid runs as
well.

When Gotfredson and R. I. Dennis, vice president of Trans-
American, testified before the Committee, they said that the one-
and-a-half-cent agreement had been kept in effect without holding
the promised second meeting in 1955 because there had been no
objections from their employees. But I had found in Trans-

American's files a bulletin dated July 25, 1955, signed by Dennis and directed to all terminal managers of the company.

> We held a meeting with representatives of the Central States Drivers Council yesterday regarding the cent and a half per mile Trans-American rider on Central States Agreement. At this meeting we were given the privilege of reading several letters written to Mr. James Hoffa, vice president of the Teamsters Union, with copies to the Central States Drivers Council concerning our cent and a half per mile arrangement. One of the big complaints seems to stem from the fact that many of our terminal managers and/or dispatchers, as alleged by the unions, are not considering the welfare of our drivers.
> The letters of criticism on the cent and a half rider have been written to Mr. James Hoffa by the local Teamsters Unions in Dayton, Louisville and Columbus.

When asked about the bulletin and his access to Hoffa's correspondence, Mr. Dennis replied, "I am sorry, I can't remember back four years."

Both Dennis and Gotfredson claimed that when the one-and-a-half-cent rider came up for renegotiation in 1958, it had been approved by the union membership. But I knew from my investigation that, at least in the case of some Ohio locals, this was not true. Bob Kennedy asked me to conduct the questioning of Gotfredson and Dennis. I asked Dennis about the 1958 vote by the employees in Cincinnati, at which I knew he had been present. He said that a meeting was held on March 23, 1958, at which the drivers had voted against a continuation of the one-and-a-half-cent agreement. But, he claimed, since a representative number of employees had not been present at the meeting because of bad weather, it was decided to hold a second meeting on June 1, at which a majority of the drivers voted in favor of the agreement.

Walter Schultz, the president of Teamsters Local 100 in Cincinnati, along with Otto Frobe, secretary-treasurer, and business agents James Young and John Mead, then testified. They said that most Trans-American employees, including those of Hoffa's own Local 299, had been opposed to the one-and-a-half-cent arrangement from the beginning. Both Frobe and Young had attended the February, 1955, meeting. They stated that Hoffa had pushed the one-and-a-half-cent proposal, promised a second meeting to reevaluate it and assured them that drivers would not lose their bid runs. They said that there had been no second meeting, even though opposition by the members to the agreement continued and drivers were losing their bid runs.

When the matter was up for renegotiation in 1958, Young said, he obtained the signatures of over 90 percent of the Trans-American drivers on petitions calling for an end to one-and-a-half-cent arrangement and submitted them to Hoffa. Business agents from all affected local unions were then summoned to a meeting in Detroit where they requested a strike sanction against Trans-American if the company would not drop the separate agreement. Strike sanction was subsequently granted subject to the approval of Frank Fitzsimmons in a letter in which he acknowledged the authorized strike sanction but suggested instead that the strike be held in abeyance pending a tour of the terminals by Mr. Dennis and Roland McMaster, a business agent for Local 299.

When McMaster and Dennis arrived in Cincinnati on March 23, a vote was taken and the membership voted against the one-and-a-half-cent agreement. At the request of the company, however, they agreed to go along for another sixty days and another meeting was to be held on June 1. The meeting was not held, however, until August 24, and only after further prodding by the members. At that meeting the membership voted not to take another vote, maintaining that they had already voted in March to reject the separate agreement. On October 30, 1958, Business Agent John Mead again wrote to Hoffa setting forth the opposition of the members of Local 100 to the one-and-a-half-cent agreement. At the time of the hearing, they were still operating under it, were still opposed to it and had never voted for it.

The separate grievance procedure that Hoffa had granted Trans-American was even more flagrant. There had been no pretense of even putting this to a vote of the membership.

In Indianapolis I found a Teamsters member who had been one of the victims of the special grievance procedure. Scott Pickett had driven for Trans-American from 1953 to 1957 as an owner-operator, leasing his equipment to the company. The separate one-and-a-half-cent agreement had provided that drivers were to keep a record over each twenty-eight-day period, and if they calculated that they would have received more money under the regular Central States contract than they actually got under the separate agrement, they were to submit a grievance for the difference. Such grievances were to be settled within ten days. There had been many reports that it did not work this way in practice. Scott Pickett was a good example.

Pickett told me that the first time he put in for the difference it was paid. The second time he was offered 60 percent and accepted it. In both instances he submitted the grievances to the business agent at Local 135 in Indianapolis, who merely referred them to Frank Fitzsimmons in Detroit for approval. The third time he sent in grievances, all of which were documented, they were returned from Fitzsimmons with an offer of only a 40 percent settlement. When Pickett protested, he was told by the local business agent that there was nothing he could do because Fitzsimmons made the decisions.

Pickett then called Fitzsimmons, and getting no satisfaction, made four trips to Detroit attempting unsuccessfully to see both Fitzsimmons and Mr. Dennis of Trans-American. Dennis refused to talk to Pickett and referred him back to his terminal manager in Indianapolis, who told him he could not help him. By this time Pickett was unable to keep up the payments on his truck and lost it. He then decided to seek legal help and retained an Indianapolis attorney, Kirkwood Yockey, in July, 1957. Pickett's grievances for 1955 and 1956 now totaled $1400. Yockey conducted a correspondence with the Trans-American lawyer, and after receiving no satisfaction, served notice that he was going to institute a lawsuit. The company lawyer then called Yockey and told him that the only way he could get any action was to contact either Mr. Dennis or Mr. Fitzsimmons. When Yockey declined to go any further, the attorney told him he would arrange for Fitzsimmons to call him. Fitzsimmons called Yockey the same day and told him that Pickett should proceed through the regular grievance channels. Yockey told Fitzsimmons that Pickett had long ago done that and now he was going to institute legal action. Fitzsimmons asked him not to and suggested he call either Gene San Soucie or Hoffa at the Shoreland Hotel in Chicago. Yockey placed a call to San Soucie at the Shoreland Hotel but was told that he and Hoffa had left for Detroit. It was suggested that Yockey might reach them there. Yockey declined and said that if they wanted to talk to him they could call him.

Yockey then received a call from a man who said that he was a business agent for Local 135 in Indianapolis. He told Yockey that he could not talk to him from the union hall but gave the number of a pay phone and suggested that Yockey call him there. When Yockey did, the man told him that Hoffa and Trans-American had an agreement whereby they would not pay grievances and were "sitting tight on them for a year or two, until they starved the drivers out" so that they would be willing to settle for 50 percent. The man said that Hoffa then took 10 percent and gave the driver 40 percent. The man urged Yockey to stick to his guns and file the lawsuit.

Then, a man who said he was Hoffa, and whom Yockey believed was Hoffa, called him from Chicago. He told Yockey that if they could meet in Chicago the next morning he would settle the claim in cash for 40 percent. Yockey said, "I don't see how you can represent a man in the union and ask him to take 40 percent. Will you give me one good reason why this man should take 40 percent?" "Because I said so," was the reply.

Yockey went ahead with the lawsuit and collected 90 percent of what Pickett was owed.

I had originally talked to Pickett in Indianapolis on May 29, 1959. At the time he was employed as a mechanic for another trucking company. He had been completely cooperative and told me the whole story. The following day he was laid off. His boss told him that he had been told to lay him off by Robert Martin, a business agent for Local 135. Pickett went to see Martin. He told the Committee about the conversation.

Pickett:	He told me not to have anything to do with Mr. Sheridan, that Mr. Sheridan was a phoney; that if anybody wanted to talk to me relative to this Committee, to refer them to San Soucie.
Kennedy:	What else did he tell you?
Pickett:	Well, he told me he was on the way to the racetrack, which was May 30, and he couldn't talk any longer, and for me to get lost.

Pickett had remained out of work for four weeks and was not called back to work until just prior to his appearance before the Committee.

An almost comical situation was found to exist in reference to two interrelated companies. The Chi-East Trucking Company in Chicago and the Midwest Haulers in Toledo, Ohio, were both operated by the same three men. We found that Midwest Haulers had an over-the-road contract with Local 710 in Chicago but did not have any drivers. Chi-East in Chicago, on the other hand, did not have a labor contract but did have the drivers. A former driver testified before the Committee that he was hired by Midwest Haulers but found he was actually working for Chi-East. He became a member of Local 710 under the contract with Midwest Haulers but soon realized he wasn't receiving any of the benefits he was entitled to under the contract. He complained to the Local 710 business agent but got no satisfaction. He then complained to the Central States Drivers Council and was told to put it in writing because "Jimmy Hoffa wanted to clean up locals like that." He sent a letter to Hoffa, which was returned to John T. O'Brien, the head of Local 710, with the notation, "returning this correspondence to you without having taken any action."

George S. Maxwell, a former Presbyterian minister who had helped form the Steel Truck Employers Association in Ohio and served as a labor relations consultant, gave further corroboration of Hoffa's willingness to make exceptions to the written contract. He said that as a representative of the association he negotiated labor contracts with Hoffa and the Central States Council. On a number of occasions he had been able to obtain oral concessions for the companies which were not always approved by the members. He said that in all cases these side arrangements were either made directly with, or approved by, Hoffa.

Maxwell also testified that on one occasion he received a call from Hoffa in which he was told that Local 299 did not want Negro over-the-road drivers coming into Detroit and that if it happened again, it "might not be healthy for the drivers." Maxwell said that he passed the word on to the company in question, heard no more about it and assumed that no Negro drivers were dispatched to Detroit thereafter.

Ross Hill, the Negro driver who had occasioned the warning, and who had since moved to California, also testified and confirmed Maxwell's story. Hill had gone to work for the Northern Truck Lines of Youngstown, Ohio, working out of Detroit, as an owner-operator and had joined Local 299 as instructed by the owner of the company. When it was discovered that he was making over-the-road runs from Detroit to Youngstown, a business agent of Local 299 told the owner of the company that they didn't want Hill in the local. The owner then arranged for Hill to transfer to Local 337 in Youngstown. He continued to make runs to Detroit for a while but was told not to stay around the terminal. This meant that he had to drop his load at the terminal and return to Youngstown the next day on a "deadhead," i.e., empty run. As a result, he finally lost his truck and moved to California. The owner of the company also gave an affidavit to the Committee confirming what had happened to Ross.

These were some of the side deals, the nonenforcement of contracts, the shortchanging of union members and the arrogant disregard of their wishes and welfare that we found in Hoffa's own Central States backyard. But of even greater significance was our discovery that Hoffa, in his drive to expand his influence and power, was trying to bring about uniformity of contracts, on an ever broadening front, with both negotiations and grievance machinery controlled by him. To do this, contracts in new areas of conquest would have to be brought into conformity with his already established Central States agreements. His ultimate aim would become nationwide uniform contracts with common expiration dates, but that was a long way off. The problem was that some contracts outside the Central States, and the state of Ohio within, were already superior, in many respects, to his. To achieve his goal, then, those superior contracts had to be brought down to the Central States level, or at least the negotiation of benefits in these areas had to be slowed down until the Central States scale could catch up. Witnesses before the Committee told how this worked in practice.

There had already been testimony in prior hearings of Hoffa's takeover of the stalemated 1954 negotiations in New York City. The local unions, bargaining as a unit under the leadership of Tom Hickey and John Strong of Local 807, were demanding a twenty-five-cent-per-hour increase. Hoffa took over the negotiations and offered to settle for eighteen cents the first year and seven cents the following year. He subsequently offered seventeen cents the first year and eight cents the year after. He admitted he had no authority to make the offer but said that he was sure he could get it.

Hickey and Strong outflanked him by pulling Local 807, which had been the traditional Teamsters leader in New York, out of the negotiations and began making individual settlements for the twenty-five-cent increase. Eventually all the companies settled for the higher figure.

In an affidavit submitted to the Committee, John Strong, who would have testified but was having a leg amputated, stated:

> Although I did not get this information directly, it was my information that because of the negotiations coming up in the Central States area, Hoffa and the big midwestern carriers had already agreed to a package of 17 and 8 and that an effort was being made to see that the areawide committee of New York and New Jersey affiliated with the Eastern Conference of Teamsters conformed to this pattern.

Joseph M. Adelizzi, the director of the Empire State Trucking Association, a highly respected man in his field who had headed the negotiating committee for the New York trucking companies during the dispute, also testified.

Kennedy: Are the contracts that exist in the Eastern section of the United States, as far as the Teamsters are concerned, higher than the contracts of the Central Conference of Teamsters?

Adelizzi: I would say generally so, and over a long period of time.

Adelizzi then went on to explain why the employers he represented had finally decided to go along with Hickey's higher demands rather than with Hoffa's more lenient ones.

Kennedy: Did you feel that this coming in from the outside and offering a better contract for the employers, the 18 and 7, was an effort to undermine the activities of Mr. Tom Hickey of Local 807?

Adelizzi: It had all the appearances of doing just that.

Kennedy: Was it also felt by you and by some of your colleagues that if you signed up on this basis, even though it would be more profitable to you, it would be, in fact, turning over the trucking business and the trucking industry in New York to the underworld or the mob?

Adelizzi: There was a strong suspicion of that, a strong fear of that.

Kennedy: Isn't that, in fact, the reason why you wouldn't sign and undermine Hickey, that although you had your difficulties and problems with Mr. Hickey, at least it had always been felt that he was an honest Teamster official, and that although you might make a temporary deal which would be profitable to you momentarily, in the long run this would be, in fact, turning over the control of the whole trucking industry in New York?

Adelizzi: For that reason we came to the support of Hickey and the leadership of 807.

We found that a similar situation existed within Hoffa's Central States area in Ohio. Hoffa's incursions into Ohio had been resisted from the beginning but for the most part his opposition found it a long, losing battle. William Dearwester, a truck driver for the Complete Auto Transit Company of Flint, Michigan, told the story of one of the early struggles. He said that in 1948 Carney Matheson was representing Complete Auto Transit and Anchor Motor Frieght, both car-hauler companies, in negotiations with Hoffa. The Ohio Teamsters members would not accept the terms that Matheson and Hoffa had agreed upon, and Matheson was threatening to sue the Teamsters for $3,000,000. Ed Murphy, who represented the Ohio drivers and was chiefly responsible for the high caliber of their contracts, was summoned to Detroit. He was forced to capitulate and returned to Cincinnati, where Dearwester was then located, to report to his membership. Dearwester quoted what Murphy had said:

I have been a member of this organization for thirty-five years, most of the time as an official. I have seen some pretty rotten things pulled both by management and labor. But, this man Hoffa, and I don't know where he gets his authority, just pulled the rottenest deal on you fellows that I have ever seen an official pull on members of his own union.

If it is the last thing I ever do, I am going to find out—I am leaving here by plane, going to Indianapolis—and I am going to find out where he is getting his authority. If it is the last thing I ever do, I am going to try to take the wind out of that man's sails.

We do not know whether Ed Murphy ever found out but

about one year later he died and ultimately Hoffa's man, Bill Presser, took over the Ohio Teamsters—that is, except for Cincinnati.

I had first met Jim Luken in Cincinnati in 1958 while investigating the odd relationship between George Bender and Bill Presser. He had a reputation as an honest, tough, uncompromising person, so I sought his cooperation. At first he was polite but cautious, and understandably so. He had seen other congressional committees come and go and was naturally skeptical. Having refused to knuckle under to Presser and Hoffa, he was fighting to survive and did not need more trouble. He did not approve of what Hoffa represented and was doing but he was loyal to the Teamsters Union and its membership. He respected Bob Kennedy and what he was trying to do but he did not know me. Gradually a feeling of mutual trust developed.

Now, one year later, Jim Luken agreed to tell his story to the Committee. He was a former milk driver who had been president of Local 98 since 1949. When he had refused to go along with the Hoffa forces in 1954, Presser had sent his brother-in-law, Harry Friedman, an ex-convict, to Cincinnati to head up a racket jukebox local and attempt to undermine Luken. Luken made an appointment to see Hoffa, whom he had never met, and expressed objections to having men like Friedman as Teamsters officials in Cincinnati. Hoffa told Luken that if he wanted to get along in the Teamsters Union in Ohio, he should take orders from Presser: "Mr. Presser was his man and that was the way it was and that was the way it was going to be."

As a follow-up to Hoffa's warning, the next day Luken was contacted by Presser, who told him that if he didn't do what he was told, Presser would come into Cincinnati himself and break up Luken's local. Presser also told Luken that if he cooperated he could become the president of the Joint Council in Cincinnati. When Luken replied that the Joint Council already had a president, Presser said, "Resignations can be arranged."

Luken called a meeting of his membership and informed them what had happened. He asked for and received authorization to take whatever legal and financial actions were necessary to protect the local. This involved, among other things, placing the local's funds in a trust arrangement so that Hoffa and Presser could not get at them.

Harry Friedman was eventually convicted of filing false affidavits and sent back to prison. Shortly thereafter, a man named Ralph Vanni showed up in Cincinnati to carry on the harassment of Luken. Vanni approached employers with offers to arrange lower contract rates and told them that it would be to their advantage to help him get rid of Luken. Presser told Luken that Vanni was there to disorganize rather than organize, and that if Luken would cooperate, Vanni would be taken out. But Vanni was caught taking money from an employer and left town.

The Hoffa forces had managed to gain control of the largest local in Cincinnati, Local 100, but Luken retained control of the Joint Council. Finally, in 1958, the Luken followers succeeded in taking over Local 100 in an election that was supervised by Toledo Teamsters boss Larry Steinberg, as a personal representative of Hoffa. Nevertheless, the election was contested by the Hoffa forces and one of the newly elected anti-Hoffa officials was framed on a rape charge. The woman in question subsequently admitted that she had been paid by one of the Hoffa followers to make the false charge and had been promised more if he were convicted. The same man who paid her also blew up his own car and blamed it on the Luken people. He even called the insurance company just prior to the bombing to make certain that they would pay for damage to a car from explosives. Luken himself received numerous anonymous threats: an undertaker was sent to his home to pick up his body and flowers were sent to his "funeral."

The Ohio over-the-road contracts had always been superior to the Central States contract but the difference was gradually being eradicated:

Kennedy: In order to equalize the situation, in order to bring Ohio into the pattern with the rest of the Central Conference of Teamsters, the other contracts have been increasing more rapidly than the contracts in the Ohio Conference?

Luken: Yes, sir, the differential is being eliminated. In six years some of it has been eliminated. I am told by experts that most of it will be eliminated by 1961.

Another example of holding down rates to conform with the

Central States contract occurred in connection with the 1955 and 1958 negotiations between the Anchor Motor Freight Company, the Cleveland car hauler, and the Eastern Conference of Teamsters. Again Hoffa injected himself and recommended that Anchor Motor Freight utilize the services of his old friend Carney Matheson in negotiations. Both Matheson and Patrick J. O'Neill, assistant to the president at Anchor, denied to the Committee that Hoffa had recommended Matheson, and O'Neill denied he had ever discussed the negotiations with Hoffa. However, a memorandum dated June 7, 1955, taken from the Anchor Motor Freight files, was then introduced, which described a three-hour meeting between Hoffa, Matheson, O'Neill and his uncle F. J. O'Neill. The younger O'Neill then acknowledged that the meeting had taken place and that the memorandum had been prepared by his uncle but maintained that he could not recall the points mentioned in the memorandum having been discussed.

The memorandum stated that:

Mr. Hoffa had received copy of demands of eastern conference. Hoffa's general reactions were—
1) Demands were ridiculously high.
2) Hoffa had a personal interest because he did not want the eastern conference to get out of line with the national conference.
3) Hoffa thinks eastern conference will be merged with central conference at next contract inasmuch as there are so few carriers in the East.
4) Hoffa thinks negotiations are going to be rugged. This is always true when multiple contracts are merged, plus much individualism in the eastern union circles.
5) Hoffa states he is chairman of all automotive transportation conferences and no strikes can be authorized by the international union without his sanction. He would not sanction an eastern conference strike, if the employers were reasonable.
6) Unauthorized strikes could occur, but if this did happen he would be called into the picture.
7) Hoffa gave background on eastern union officials.
8) Suggested procedure was to move slow and by steps. Hoffa thought it would be wise to use Carney in negotiations.

The results of these negotiations were attested to by two eastern Teamsters officials, Richard Grabowski, business agent for Local 557 in Baltimore, and Ted Daley, secretary-treasurer of Local 445 in Yonkers, New York. Grabowski testified that as a result of the 1955 negotiations with Anchor Motor Freight, his local lost benefits it had previously obtained. He said that again in the 1958 negotiations, which were taken over by Hoffa, the resulting contract would cost each of his drivers approximately $2000 per year.

Ted Daley testified that his local was opposed to the contract terms in 1955 but was forced to accept them. He said that during this period he heard Patrick J. O'Neill of Anchor Motor Freight tell two other Teamsters members that his uncle had Jimmy Hoffa in his back pocket. Daley went to Hoffa and told him about the statement and Hoffa said that he would "straighten it out." Daley said he heard nothing further from Hoffa about it.

In the 1958 negotiations with Anchor Motor Freight, Daley's local was again opposed to the settlement offered by the company. Hoffa moved in and took over the negotiations with Carney Matheson. Daley asked for sanction to strike and was told he would get it. When it was not forthcoming, he complained to Tom Flynn, the International vice president and head of the Eastern Conference of Teamsters. He was told that Hoffa didn't want a strike. Daley said the contract was finally signed on the company's terms in spite of their opposition.

On the morning of July 14, 1959, James R. Hoffa stepped up and took his place at the witness table for what was to be his last appearance before the Select Committee. Hoffa was grim but confident. He knew that he had weathered over two years of intensive investigation by the Committee and that this was probably the end of it. Corrective legislation was almost certain to pass in some form before Congress adjourned, and the Committee, its purpose served, would then go out of existence. Although the testimony during the preceding three weeks had been very damaging, Hoffa, who had become an expert witness, was completely up to his last test.

He had developed a series of techniques, all of which were effective, in dealing with this tribunal. One was his convenient "forgettery," as Senator Ives had termed it. Another was using the Fifth Amendment by proxy. He didn't take it, but everyone else who might have the facts or the records did. A third was his knack for sliding off into a philosophical or technical discussion of labor problems when the openings were given by certain Senators—

sometimes obligingly and sometimes naively. The most flagrant example of an obliging Senator was Senator Homer Capehart of Indiana who repeatedly came to Hoffa's rescue and was antagonistic to witnesses against Hoffa. On one occasion it became so obvious that it was comical. While the hearing was in progress, someone from the Hoffa group rose and left the hearing room. A few minutes later the telephone rang in the phone booth in the corner of the room behind the Senators. It was for Senator Capehart. When he returned to his place after taking the call, the Senator asked a question favorable to Hoffa that obviously had just been fed to him. Another of Hoffa's ploys was to say that he had an important meeting to attend far away and had to catch a plane by a certain time. Now, in his finale, he would use them all, plus a new one—repeatedly denying that certain testimony had been given, thus requiring the locating and rereading of the questioned record.

Hoffa acknowledged that the one-and-a-half-cent arrangement with Trans-American was a "radical departure" from the regular contract but said he had accepted it rather than have a strike. In spite of the testimony of the Cincinnati Teamsters officials that the agreement was never ratified, Hoffa claimed it was. In spite of Mr. Gotfredson's testimony that the special grievance procedure had not been ratified, Hoffa claimed it had. He said he had been furnished this information by Roland McMaster, the Local 299 business agent who had taken over the handling of the grievances from Frank Fitzsimmons.

Roland McMaster was then called. Hoffa flashed five fingers at him and he took the Fifth Amendment concerning not only the Trans-American situation but also his ownership of trucking companies.

As the day went on, Hoffa became argumentative and defiant. At one point Senator John Kennedy asked him whether the $20,000 in cash he had invested in a business with Carney Matheson had come from the racetrack winnings that Bert Brennan supposedly shared with him. Hoffa said that it could have.

Kennedy: I have never been completely convinced, Mr. Hoffa, to be frank with you, that Mr. Brennan did win this money at the racetrack.
Hoffa: Why don't you ask him?
Kennedy: I did, and he took the Fifth Amendment.
Hoffa: Maybe he has a reason.

Kennedy:	I think he does have a reason. You suggested that we ask Mr. Brennan. Mr. Brennan took the Fifth Amendment when he answered the question, and I have never considered that that was a satisfactory explanation of the cash you had or that several people, business agents, who themselves had to borrow money to survive, that they loaned you $2000 in cash without any note or without any interest.
Hoffa:	Thank you for reviewing the testimony.
Kennedy:	Does it suggest anything to you, Mr. Hoffa?
Hoffa:	It doesn't suggest anything except this fact, that you are trying again, as you have many times in this hearing, to bring a headline about or to embarrass Hoffa. That is all.
Kennedy:	No. I am attempting to give you my reaction, as these hearings come to a close, as to where this cash might have come from.
Hoffa:	Then you ought to read the record.
Kennedy:	I want to make it clear for the record.
Hoffa:	Disprove what I said.
Kennedy:	I can't accept the explanation that this was won in the casual way at the racetrack by Mr. Brennan in view of the fact that Mr. Brennan takes the Fifth Amendment when he is asked.
Hoffa:	Then you disprove it.
Kennedy:	It is extremely difficult because you deal in cash.
Hoffa:	And I am going to continue.

Time and again Hoffa challenged Bob Kennedy's recitation of previous testimony, claiming that he had read the record and that what Kennedy was saying was not in the record. Each time when the transcript was reread Kennedy was right.

But the delaying tactics had served Hoffa's purpose. The time had been spent and he had a flight to catch for an important meeting in Miami. It was all over and he knew it. Senator McClellan adjourned the hearing and issued a statement:

Notwithstanding Mr. Hoffa's previous promises and assurances to the committee, he has failed and still refuses to remove and get rid of high officials in this international organization and in some of its subordinate units. These known criminals and disreputable characters have beyond any question of doubt in many instances betrayed the trust, and exploited the rank-and-file membership, of the organization whom it was their duty to protect and faithfully represent. They have engaged in racketeering practices, have taken bribes, committed extortion, and otherwise been unfaithful to the trust reposed in them and that is associated with their offices. Mr. Hoffa's position as the fountainhead of this corruption has been repeatedly emphasized.

The testimony is crystal clear that in his unrelenting drive for power, Mr. Hoffa had repeatedly shunted aside the interest and welfare of rank-and-file union members while making deals with major employers in the trucking industry. His deals with these employers refute his claim to steadfastness and unwavering devotion to the best interest and welfare of the membership he serves. He and his racketeer—and in some instances gangster—associates continue to do business at the same old stand, in the same arrogant and defiant way, despite the overwhelming demands of the citizens of this country for a cleanup and the elimination of corruption and disreputable practices in this, the Nation's most powerful union.

There can no longer be in the mind of any unbiased person even a last vestige of doubt that strong, remedial legislation is drastically needed in the field of labor-management relations. Such action on the part of Congress is urgent and imperative.

CHAPTER V

Power Politics

══════════════════════

THE SENATE SELECT COMMITTEE on Improper Activities in the Labor or Management Field might have gone out of business one year earlier if the corrective legislation proposed at that time had passed. Ironically, Hoffa and the Teamsters Union, who might thereby have been spared another year of investigation, were part of the lobby that effectively opposed the enactment of the Labor-Management Reporting and Disclosure Act of 1958, sponsored by Senators Kennedy and Ives.

The bill passed the Senate by a vote of 88-1 in June, 1958, but then languished in the House. The Senate also passed, by 88-0, the Pension, Health and Welfare Fund Disclosure Act sponsored by Senators Kennedy, Ives, and Paul H. Douglas of Illinois, which was also referred to the House. The latter, in somewhat watered-down form, cleared the House Education and Labor Committee. The Labor-Management reform bill, however, was held up by Speaker Sam Rayburn for six weeks and finally referred to the same House committee toward the end of the session, where it appeared it would die. The only hope for its survival seemed to be a legislative procedure known as "suspension of the rules," which would allow a vote in the full House without committee recommendation. George Meany and the AFL-CIO leadership supported the bill but some of the individual unions in the organization rendered only lip service. On the other hand, there was a strong lobbying effort being waged against the bill by such strange bedfellows as the National Association of Manufacturers, the United States Chamber of Commerce, the United Mine Workers and the Teamsters. The big business forces objected to provisions in the bill designed to correct the nefarious middleman-type practices exemplified by Nathan W. Shefferman.

When Senator John Kennedy attacked the N.A.M. and the Chamber of Commerce for their obstructive opposition, James P. Mitchell, the Republican Secretary of Labor, chided the Democratic House leadership for being susceptible to pressure from those quarters and urged the passage of the bill. Senator Kennedy responded by accusing Mitchell of playing politics and said that Mitchell had "not lifted a finger" to help in the passage of the bill.

When a vote was finally scheduled in the House in August, 1958, on "suspension of the rules" to allow for a vote on the bill, Secretary Mitchell indicated that he was in favor of the bill. Mitchell's position was cited in speeches on the House floor by proponents of the bill such as Congressman George McGovern. When the vote to suspend the rules was taken on August 18, however, the word was passed on the House floor that Mitchell was actually opposed to the bill and Republican Congressmen were urged to vote against the suspension. The motion to suspend was defeated by a vote of 198-190. Following the vote, the Executive Council of the AFL-CIO issued a statement that said in part:

> An unholy alliance of the N.A.M., the Chamber of Commerce, and the reactionary Republican leadership of the House, the Teamsters and the United Mine Workers wrecked the bill. We deplore the role of Secretary of Labor Mitchell, whose opposition to constructive reform legislation was obviously politically inspired.

President Eisenhower then made a statement to the effect that there was still time to pass the legislation. The AFL-CIO ridiculed the suggestion, noting that Congress was about to adjourn, and stated that the opportunity for passage "was lost because the administration, in alliance with reactionary businessmen and the corrupt Teamsters, killed the measure."

Unfortunately, the ill-fated bill had become a political pawn in the prelude to the 1958 elections, but Hoffa had participated in prolonging the investigations of his own activities by giving the Select Committee another year's lease on life. A new bill was introduced in the spring of 1959 by Senators Kennedy and Sam Ervin which again passed the Senate in short order by a vote of

90-1 on April 25. It was then referred to the House. The lobbyists again went to work, with Hoffa in the forefront leading the attack. He decided, however, that he needed the help of a professional and turned the task over to attorney Sidney Zagri, a graduate of Harvard Law School, who had been brought into the Teamsters organization in St. Louis by Harold Gibbons and had developed his lobbying talents there.

When Hoffa assumed the presidency of the union, he had surrounded himself in the International headquarters with Gibbons-type "eggheads." First Gibbons himself became Hoffa's executive vice president. Gibbons' secretary, Yuki Kato, became Hoffa's secretary. Gibbons' lieutenant, Dick Kavner, was named a general organizer. Gibbons' friend, Sam Baron, was already field director of the Warehouse Division. Larry Steinberg of Toledo and Joe Konowe of New York, both liberal trade unionists of the Gibbons school, also were enlisted as right-hand men to the general president. They were a different breed and a curious contrast to the Abe Gordons and Bert Brennans, with whom they shared the inner circle. Now Sid Zagri came in to woo the lawmakers.

On August 4 the McClellan Committee issued its second interim report charging Hoffa and his associates with twenty-one specific acts of misconduct. Hoffa's response was, "To hell with them," and he summoned two hundred local Teamsters officials to Washington to contact their Congressmen and express opposition to the labor bill.

Meanwhile, the Board of Monitors was moving forward in its own attempt to force internal reform in the Teamsters Union. Larry Smith, a member of Godfrey Schmidt's law firm in New York, had replaced Schmidt as a monitor on July 13. On July 22 the Board, with the approval of Judge Letts, retained the services of Kirkland, Ellis, Hodson, Chaffetz and Masters, a prestigious Washington law firm, to assist in litigation. Herbert J. "Jack" Miller of the firm was assigned the task of representing the Board, assisted by associates Raymond Larroca and Howard Willens. Florian Bartosic resigned as executive assistant to the Board effective August 1 and was replaced by John Cassidy.

On August 11 the Board met with Hoffa at the International and recommended that he suspend Harold Gross, Tony Provenzano and Joey Glimco and immediately discontinue the subsidy by the International to Gross's Local 320 in Miami. The Board also recommended that Hoffa remove the funds on deposit in noninterest-bearing accounts at the Florida National Bank and the Fidelity Bank and Trust Company of Indianapolis. Hoffa said that Local 299 had already been instructed to withdraw the funds. He did not commit himself on Gross, Provenzano or Glimco.

On August 13 the monitors petitioned Judge Letts for permission to investigate the disappearance of records in Local 245 in Springfield, Missouri. Price Waterhouse had been attempting unsuccessfully to audit the local's records since June, 1958. The International had conducted its own audit in January, 1959, at which time all of the records were there. When Price Waterhouse was finally given access to the records on August 3, 1959, those for the years 1956 and 1957 were missing.

On August 31 Hoffa advised the Board by letter that the funds in the Fidelity Bank and Trust Company in Indianapolis had been returned to Local 299 and that the funds in the Florida National Bank were being returned. But on September 1 O. P. Hewitt, Jr., the president of the Florida National Bank, stated publicly that he would not permit Hoffa to withdraw the funds, because they were collateral for loans made to Sun Valley, Inc., which still owed $350,000 plus interest to the bank. Hewitt said that Hoffa had agreed to leave the funds, now totaling $400,000, in the bank until the loan was paid off. Hoffa then filed suit against the bank.

On September 2 the Board of Monitors issued formal recommendations to Hoffa calling for the suspension from office of Gross, Provenzano and Glimco, the filing of charges against them within ten days, the placing of their locals in trusteeship and the auditing of the locals' records. The Board also made a determination to investigate the Florida National Bank situation.

On September 9, following a joint House-Senate conference chaired by Senator Kennedy, the Labor-Management Reporting and Disclosure Act of 1959, also known as the Landrum-Griffin Act, was passed by Congress. The following day, believing that the Committee had fulfilled its purpose with the passage of legislation that provided for the correction of most of the abuses that had been exposed by it, Robert Kennedy resigned as chief counsel of the Select Committee. He wanted to write a book about his experiences with the Committee and to manage his brother's upcoming bid for the Presidency. Carmine Bellino and I had accompanied him two weeks earlier to a conference with representatives of the Justice Department to discuss cases that had been referred by the Committee for possible prosecution. He felt that the department was not proceeding as vigorously as it might and said so. But he also had private conversations with Martin O'Donoghue and felt certain that the Board of Monitors under O'Donoghue would be successful in ridding the Teamsters Union of corrupt influences, including Hoffa, if necessary.

On September 11 Hoffa advised the Board of Monitors that he had conferred with Harold Gross, Tony Provenzano and Joey Glimco, who had denied the allegations against them, and that he had concluded that there was "no emergency present" requiring their immediate suspension from office. He also refused to discontinue the $3000-a-month subsidy to Local 320 in Miami, as the Board had recommended.

On September 14 the Board of Monitors filed an interim report with Judge Letts in which it requested the ouster of Hoffa from office by the court if the allegations contained in the report were found, upon hearing by the court, to be true. The report recited the history of the deposit of Local 299 funds in interest-free accounts in the Fidelity Bank and Trust Company and the Florida National Bank. Also, the monitors had recently learned of, and included in the report, an additional $50,000 in Local 299 funds that had been deposited by Hoffa in an interest-free account in the Commercial State Bank and Trust Company in New York City in 1956 where it lay dormant until withdrawn on September 22, 1958.

Up until this point Martin O'Donoghue had been only a constant and increasing irritant to Hoffa. Now, he and the Board of Monitors suddenly posed a real and direct threat to his continuance in office.

On September 17 Secretary of Labor Mitchell sent a telegram to Hoffa directing him to advise Mitchell within ten days what steps he had taken to remove Teamsters officials with criminal records who might be holding office in violation of the new law. (The law precluded a person from holding union office for five years after conviction of certain crimes.)

The Department of Justice was heard from next. On September 21 Attorney General William P. Rogers announced the indictment in Pittsburgh of Barney Baker and Ted Cozza. Baker was charged with taking money from George Callahan, the president of Exhibitors Service Company in McKees Rock, Pennsylvania. Cozza was accused of taking money from the Pittsburgh *Sun-Telegraph*. Three days later Connie Noonan and Harold Gross were indicted for conspiring to extort money from the Neo-Gravure Company in New Jersey.

On September 28 Hoffa announced that the results of a survey he had conducted in response to the Secretary of Labor's telegram indicated that there were five union officials subject to removal under the Landrum-Griffin Act; that they had been put on leave of absence but would be eligible to return to their posts in 1960. Hoffa also said that he had no intention of removing Harold Gross, Tony Provenzano or Joey Glimco from office as recommended by the Board of Monitors.

At the quarterly meeting of the Teamsters International Executive Board held in Washington, Hoffa announced his intention to establish a political action group within the International "to enlighten our members and their friends as to what is going on over on the Hill in regard to taking away from them their constitutional rights."

On September 30 Allen Dorfman's insurance license was revoked by the state of Illinois. His license had also recently been revoked by the state of Michigan. On October 15 I received a call from a Teamsters official who said that he had received a letter from John English, the secretary-treasurer of the International, in connection with the new bonding provision of the Landrum-Griffin Act. The new legislation provided that all union officials who handled union funds were required to be bonded. The letter, dated October 5, said that the International had investigated the situation and after careful study was recommending that the bonding requirements of the Teamsters Union could best be handled by the Summit Fidelity and Surety Company of Akron, Ohio. The Teamsters official said that he had also received bond applications from English which were to be forwarded to the Illinois agency of the Summit Fidelity and Surety Company. We agreed that it had all the earmarks of an Allen Dorfman operation.

I called Carl Schultz in Chicago who established that the Illinois agency of Summit Fidelity was incorporated in Illinois on October 6, the day after the letter from English went out. The president of the company was Irwin S. Weiner and the secretary-treasurer was Sol C. Schwartz. Weiner, who operated the American Bail Bond Company in Chicago, was also a business associate in three meat-shortening companies of "Milwaukee Phil" Alderisio and Albert Frabotta, both notorious racketeers. These companies also had other major Chicago hoodlums, such as Sam Battaglia and Marshall Caifano, on their payroll.

People we talked to indicated that Weiner was representing himself as the exclusive agent for the Teamsters Union bonding, and that he hoped to obtain the bonding business from about eight hundred local unions. It was estimated that he already had approximately $2,000,000 worth of premiums in applications submitted. It was now obvious that instead of being impeded by the new legislation, Hoffa was using one of its provisions to provide another windfall for the Dorfmans and the Chicago mob.

During our investigation Allen Dorfman's Illinois insurance license had been saved by a last-minute injunction against the insurance commissioner by a state judge.

On November 17 Senator McClellan wrote a letter to Secretary of Labor Mitchell outlining the plot. McClellan concluded, "I believe that these activities again demonstrate very clearly the attitude of Mr. Hoffa and the necessity for close supervision of his official conduct and the strict enforcement of the new law." A copy of the letter was sent to the Board of Monitors and it was released to the press.

On November 16 the Supreme Court declined to hear the petition of the International seeking to overturn the Court of Appeals June ruling backing the authority of the Board of Monitors. The way was now clear for O'Donoghue and the Board to move forward in their attempt to oust Hoffa and his cohorts from office. O'Donoghue announced his intention to seek authority from Judge Letts to take depositions in Detroit and Florida in connection with the Local 299 funds still on deposit in the Florida National Bank. He also designated Washington attorney Paul McCardle to investigate and draw up charges against Bert Brennan for trial before the International Executive Board.

On November 18 Edward Weinheimer, Barney Baker's partner in crime, was indicted by a federal grand jury in the District of Columbia for perjury in connection with his testimony concerning the money sent to him by Exhibitors Service Company during the company's difficulties with the Teamsters Union in 1957. The indictment stated that Weinheimer admittedly conferred with Hoffa and Baker just prior to the payments for the purpose of seeking their intervention in a jurisdictional dispute involving the Exhibitors Service Company.

On December 2 two telephone operators at the Washington,

D.C., Woodner Hotel, where Hoffa and other top Teamsters lived, were indicted. They were charged with destroying, falsifying and concealing records of telephone calls made by Hoffa while the records were under subpoena by the McClellan Committee and the grand jury. They had been caught in the act of destroying such records by Committee investigators on April 10. The indictment charged that they had also altered records and secured and hidden original telephone company records so that the grand jury could not obtain them.

The grand jury investigations and indictments growing out of the activities of the McClellan Committee had been handled at the Department of Justice by the Organized Crime Section of the Criminal Division under William Hundley. To augment this effort, because of the large volume of material relating to Hoffa generated by the Committee, Malcolm Wilkie, the Assistant Attorney General in charge of the Criminal Division, recruited James Dowd, who had served under Wilkie as an Assistant United States Attorney in Texas. Dowd was appointed a special assistant to the Attorney General and was given a small staff of attorneys to assist him. He was instructed to review all of the Hoffa material emanating from the McClellan Committee to determine what case, if any, offered the best chance for successful prosecution of Hoffa. After reviewing the entire McClellan Committee record, Dowd decided that the Sun Valley situation was a flagrant case of fraud and misuse of funds that could and should be prosecuted in federal court. On December 7 Dowd filed a letter in federal court in Washington, D.C., from the Deputy Attorney General, authorizing him to conduct a grand jury inquiry.

Hoffa once again faced attacks on two fronts. Both the Board of Monitors and the Department of Justice were zeroing in on the same target—Sun Valley. Hoffa decided to seek a political solution to his problems.

With the 1960 Presidential and congressional elections approaching, Hoffa had already begun moving in the political arena. His previously announced intention to create a political action group within the union was followed by a promulgation in the November issue of *International Teamster*, the International's official publication, of a call to Teamsters members to wage war at the polls. Fifty-six Congressmen who had voted for the Landrum-Griffin Act were named as the enemies of the union to be defeated in the upcoming elections. Members were also urged to take active roles in the Presidential primary elections, particularly the Wisconsin race, where it was suggested that Senator John Kennedy would be pitted against Senator Hubert Humphrey. Kennedy was described as the "co-author of the union-busting Kennedy-Landrum-Griffin bill."

Having thus marked the foes to be purged, Hoffa then sought political friends who might assist him in warding off his old tormentor, Martin O'Donoghue, and the new threat from Jim Dowd's grand jury.

On Sunday morning, December 13, Hoffa met with former California Republican Congressman Allan Oakley Hunter at the Americana Hotel in Miami Beach. The meeting had been arranged by I. Irving Davidson, a Washington public relations man and promoter who was a friend of Hoffa's. Hunter reported the results of the meeting to Vice President Richard Nixon in an eight-page "Dear Dick" letter one week later. According to the letter, Hunter had been approached by Davidson to serve as the Republican co-chairman along with an unnamed Democrat of a committee to advise Hoffa on the handling of the Teamsters' new political fund. Davidson had suggested Hunter to Hoffa because of his "association and friendship with Nixon." Hunter had told Davidson that he would have to confer with Nixon before discussing the matter with Hoffa. After meeting with Nixon, Hunter had advised Davidson that "it would be best for all concerned" if he "did not accept any official position with the Teamsters Union" because of his "association and friendship" with Nixon. He told Davidson, however, that he was interested in the Teamsters' "program for political action and would be very happy to discuss the subject with Mr. Hoffa."

Hunter briefed Nixon on Davidson's background, stating that he was a registered agent for Nicaragua; a "representative, or agent of sorts" for the state of Israel; had met Hoffa through mutual friends in Pittsburgh; had negotiated a Pension Fund loan for Clint Murchison, Jr., of Texas for an apartment house project; and had "an affinity for interesting and controversial personalities."

The meeting with Hoffa in Hunter's hotel room in Miami was arranged by Davidson at Hunter's request. Upon entering the room, Hoffa had taken his coat off "to indicate he was not recording our conversation" and Hunter had done the same. Hunter told Hoffa that he was not there at the request of Nixon and was not speaking for Nixon, but that he was interested in Nixon's "political future and the effect the activities of the Teamsters Union might have upon it." Hunter told Hoffa he thought that he and Nixon had certain things in common—"you were hated by experts, you were both self-made men, you were both dedicated to your respective fields of endeavor, and you both had a lot of guts." Hunter also told Hoffa that although Nixon "could naturally not condone many of the things that had gone on in the Teamsters," he "did not have the knife out for him personally, and bore no preconceived prejudices against him." Hunter wrote that he told Hoffa, "In my opinion no person could be elected President of the United States without substantial support from the rank and file of labor."

Hunter then asked Hoffa what he "expected of the government" and "what he might do for political candidates whom he favored." According to Hunter, Hoffa wanted only fair and equal treatment rather than being treated as a scapegoat. Hoffa claimed that he was "cleaning up the union as best and as rapidly as is possible."

Hunter said that Hoffa had one specific request. "He didn't know how it could be done but he felt that Judge Dickenson Letts, the federal judge to whom the monitors answer, should be taken out of the case" because he was "too old, incompetent, and completely prejudiced."

Hoffa told Hunter that "outright endorsement" of Nixon "would most likely do more harm than good" but that "open endorsement of local officials of his union in certain cities would definitely benefit a candidate" and that the work of individual members throughout the country would be an asset. "Hoffa stated that in lieu of a positive endorsement, much good could be done by knocking Kennedy, Humphrey and Symington, to name three."

Hunter's letter to Nixon went on:

Hoffa is definitely of the opinion that the Department of Justice under Attorney General Rogers is harassing him and that the large number of investigators and attorneys who have been assigned for special duty in connection with the Teamsters Union activities are working up nothing more than nuisance suits. This, he charges, is discriminatory and unfair. Again, he said, he expects no privileges or special treatment; he just wants to be treated like anyone else. These nuisance suits, he says, have cost the Teamsters Union a great deal of money. He said that the Florida land case, for example, he would win, but that it would cost money and might involve considerable time in court. He said that it's an easy thing to get a Grand Jury indictment but convictions are a different matter. He says that as far as he is personally concerned he has absolutely no worries because he leads a clean life, pays his taxes, and obeys the law.

According to the letter, Hoffa also told Hunter that he was trying to get the monitors to declare that he was holding office illegally and to order a new election. He said that the monitors knew he would win such an election easily and were therefore stalling until the Department of Justice indicted him. Hoffa said that he planned to "release a blast very soon against Judge Letts accusing him of conspiracy."

Hunter said that the meeting ended "on a very friendly note." He told Hoffa that while he was not representing anyone, he would be glad to help in any way he could if Hoffa should desire to contact Nixon or to convey any information to him. Hoffa told Hunter that if he did not wish to contact him directly, he could do so through Mr. Davidson.

Hunter concluded his letter to Nixon by saying that Hoffa "gave the impression that as between those candidates for President on the horizon at the present time he personally favored you." The letter would prove to be a prophetic blueprint for future action.

On December 11, 1959, Harold Gross was convicted in federal court in New York City on six counts of income tax evasion in connection with the money he had extorted from the Neo-Gravure Company. Five days later Hoffa wrote a letter to Martin O'Donoghue in which he stated that "Harold Gross has resigned from all positions in the International Union and its subordinate bodies. In addition, he is being issued a withdrawal card. The initiation of these actions predated by far his criminal conviction on December 10th in New York." A withdrawal card is given to a Teamsters member who leaves a particular jurisdiction or enters another craft. If the member comes back, he is entitled to readmission. Gross was, in effect, taking a leave of absence from the union.

In the same letter Hoffa advised O'Donoghue that he was not going to suspend either Tony Provenzano or Joey Glimco since both men had denied any wrongdoing. He noted that Provenzano had been indicted by the state of New Jersey and that it would be unfair to conduct an investigation while he was under indictment.

In the case of Glimco, he said that to impose a trusteeship on Local 777 at that time would add further to the local's difficulties. (Dissident groups in both Provenzano's and Glimco's locals were attempting to oust them from office.) Hoffa said he would bring charges against Glimco "in the very near future."

On January 2, 1960, in the same Senate Caucus Room where all of the hearings had been held, Senator John F. Kennedy announced his candidacy for the Presidency of the United States. Jimmy Hoffa responded to Kennedy's candidacy by stating that "Kennedy sacrificed the entire labor movement to pacify the Southern politicians for a few delegate votes at the Democratic convention."

The Teamsters International Executive Board met in Washington on January 12 and 13. Martin O'Donoghue reluctantly agreed to meet with the Executive Board on January 13 after heated exchanges with Hoffa by both telephone and letter. After one such telephone conversation, O'Donoghue wrote to Hoffa, "At the outset, I will state once and for all that I will not again subject myself either over the telephone or personally in conference to your cursing, personal abuse or threats . . . the next time you engage in such personal abuse or cursing, either over the phone or in person, I will terminate the conference."

At the meeting the monitors and the Executive Board covered a wide area of subjects, from proposed by-laws to union cleanup, with Hoffa accusing O'Donoghue of stalling and empire building and O'Donoghue retaliating with charges that the delays and costs of the monitorship were caused by Hoffa's lack of cooperation.

Also in attendance was Frank Matula, the recently appointed International trustee from Los Angeles. The unusual fact about his presence was that he was supposed to be in jail in Los Angeles serving a sentence for perjury. He had been sentenced in October, 1959, to six months in jail, five years' probation and a $2500 fine, but had been given a three-week "furlough" by Los Angeles Judge H. Burton Noble so that he could attend the Executive Board meeting. When Los Angeles newspapers expressed outrage at the action, Judge Noble said he did not want to interfere "with the position Matula had spent twenty years attaining."

There was another new face on the International scene. Florian

Bartosic, who had resigned from the staff of the Board of Monitors the previous July to go on the NLRB, was hired by the International as its new house counsel.

On January 20 Judge Letts ruled that Hoffa must go to trial in federal court on the charges brought by the Board of Monitors in connection with the misuse of union funds in the Sun Valley operation. The Board of Monitors asked Judge Letts to remove Hoffa from office if he were found guilty. Edward Bennett Williams announced that he would not defend Hoffa in the trial, since it might conflict with his position as general counsel for the International Union. Hoffa was to be represented instead by James Haggerty of Detroit. Teamsters officials said that Hoffa would seek to have Martin O'Donoghue disqualified because he at one time had represented the Teamsters Union.

In February attorneys for both Hoffa and the Board of Monitors began taking deposition in preparation for the trial. Jack Miller and John Cassidy went to Florida to question bank officials and others and then on to Detroit. They found on arrival there that Bert Brennan was indisposed with the flu and attorney James Haggerty had suffered an apparent heart attack, thus forcing a postponement of the depositions.

Martin O'Donoghue kept pressing Hoffa for action on the Smith and Boling matter in Local 515, the audit of the Michigan Conference Health and Welfare Fund concerning the payments by Bert Brennan to prizefighter Embrel Davidson, the audits of Locals 808 and 295 in New York and the status of the bonding situation. He received little satisfaction, as Hoffa continued to hedge and delay.

On February 15 the federal grand jury investigation of Sun Valley by Jim Dowd and his associates was shifted from Washington to Orlando, Florida. On the same day the St. Louis law firm of Wiley, Craig, Armbruster and Wilburn filed an intervening petition on behalf of members and representatives of Local 618 in St. Louis and some forty other local unions around the country. Associated with the Wiley firm in filing the petition were seventeen other law firms, including that of Payne Ratner of Wichita, Kansas. The petition, claiming to represent 116,000 Teamsters members, attacked the Board of Monitors for delaying a convention and overreaching its authority, and claimed the rank and file committee, which had initiated the action in 1957, and its attorney did not truly represent the Teamsters membership.

When Senator McClellan's letter of November 17, 1959, to Secretary of Labor Mitchell concerning the funneling of the Teamsters' bonding business to the Dorfmans and the mob had been made public, the Dorfman forces had immediately begun scurrying around to find new fronts for their operation. They contacted Los Angeles attorney Jake Ehrlich, who, in turn, contacted Stewart Hopps of San Francisco. Hopps had a reputation in the insurance field as an international highbinder, with a fast-talking facility for moving in and out of companies through front men, and, with the help of phoney foreign corporations, siphoning off assets into his international labyrinth. For this new venture, Hopps brought in Charles Bray, a thirty-one-year-old insurance man from Evanston, Illinois, who had a few years earlier inherited the Central Casualty Insurance Company from his father. Bray then met with Allen Dorfman, Sol Schwartz and Irwin Weiner. They agreed to turn over all of the bonding applications they had received through the Illinois Agency of Summit Fidelity to Bray, who was to serve as the new front. Stewart Hopps also went to Chicago to participate in the arrangements and to assist in putting together a new package. In mid-December of 1959 Bray, Hopps, Dorfman and Schwartz went to Miami where the International Executive Board was meeting. Bray stayed in his hotel room while Schwartz went before the Executive Board to present the new bonding plan. The United Benefit Fire Insurance Company of Omaha, Nebraska, replaced the Summit Fidelity and Surety Company as the underwriter. Under the original setup, United Benefit was to have been one of the reinsuring companies for Summit. Four other companies, including Bray's Central Casualty, would now handle the reinsurance. The plan was accepted by the Executive Board and Bray returned to Chicago and formed the Oxford Agency, Inc., on December 24 to replace the Illinois Agency of Summit Fidelity. On December 31 the Oxford Agency sent letters to all Teamsters affiliates stating that it was taking over the bonding. So the cards had been reshuffled, but the players who would walk off with the loot were still the Dorfmans and the mob.

Throughout this period Martin O'Donoghue persistently attempted to ascertain from the International the details of the bonding program. Each letter he sent seeking more information received evasive responses from International Secretary-Treasurer John English. Finally, on February 11, 1960, English wrote, "All personnel covered by the Act are presently bonded with faithful performance bonds of individual nature by the United Benefit Fire

Insurance Company of Omaha, Nebraska." There was no mention
of the Oxford Agency, Inc. The new agency had obtained office
space, almost overnight, in the Teamsters-owned building at 29
East Madison Street in Chicago, which also housed the Central
States Drivers Council and the Pension Fund. There was also no
mention of what, if any, investigations had been conducted before
bonding such Teamsters officials as Joey Glimco, Tony Provenzano and Ray Cohen. There seemed little doubt that if Harold
Gross' resignation had not been forced by his tax evasion conviction, he, too, would have been bonded.

On February 26 the McClellan Committee released the first part
of its final report which, in part, covered the Harold Gross–Connie
Noonan shakedown of New York newspapers and Gross' role in
Local 320 in Miami.

At about the same time, Hoffa, in Miami, announced that he was
going to demand a nationwide contract covering 400,000 drivers
in the following year's negotiations. Hoffa noted that all the principal regional contracts would expire in a ninety-day period beginning February 1, 1961, and that the trucking industry did not have
the united front necessary to resist his demands. He ridiculed
expressed fears that such a contract might give him dictatorial
powers over the nation's transportation and the ability to command a nationwide strike.

Hoffa followed this up, two days later, with the announcement
that he was going to meet with officials of the Retail Clerks International Association, the Retail, Wholesale and Department Store
Workers, and the Meatcutters Union to discuss the possibility of
master contracts covering the retail field and food chains on a
nationwide basis. He also announced that he was initiating an
intensive drive to organize industrial workers outside the trucking
industry.

While ignoring the pronouncements of the McClellan Committee, Hoffa continued the offense on all fronts. The Board of Monitors suddenly began to come apart at the seams. Monitor Larry
Smith, who had been voting consistently with Martin O'Donoghue to create a majority against the Teamsters monitor, Daniel
Maher, abruptly switched sides, and refused to sign the charges of
malfeasance and nonfeasance that O'Donoghue and the law firm
had prepared against Hoffa. Five days later Andy Boggia, the new
leader of the rank and file committee since the defection of John
Cunningham, also broke with O'Donoghue. Then Hoffa filed a

motion with Judge Letts seeking an order to forbid O'Donoghue from making press releases and public statements.

On the political front, on March 8, the same day Senator John Kennedy was winning his first victory in the New Hampshire primary, Hoffa made a foray into Wisconsin where Kennedy's next primary test would come in five weeks. Speaking before a University of Wisconsin class, Hoffa accused the Kennedy brothers and Senator McClellan of distortion and prostitution of the Committee. Hoffa also addressed a meeting of two thousand Teamsters members and their wives in the Milwaukee auditorium. There he criticized, of all things, the bonding provisions of the Landrum-Griffin Act, which he continued to label "the Kennedy-Landrum-Griffin Act." He said, "This section of the law seemed to be designed to enrich the bonding companies. If Senator John Kennedy's father does not already own a bonding company, he should buy one." While it was true that the bonding provisions of the act did perhaps impose excessive economic hardships on some unions, particularly the smaller ones, it ill behooved Hoffa, who had just concocted a scheme to use the provision to enrich his friends, to complain about the very profits they were reaping.

Hoffa also accused Martin O'Donoghue of trying to destroy the Teamsters Union; described the Kennedy brothers as millionaires who could not understand the problems of the workingman; and criticized Senator John Kennedy's voting record. When asked whether the monitors would remove him as president, as Bob Kennedy had predicted, Hoffa replied, "Bob Kennedy should live that long."

Hoffa reiterated the need for common expiration dates for Teamsters contracts and for the formation of a transportation council. He concluded with a plea for all members and their families to register and vote. "Your union leadership will do all it can to help you, but in the final analysis, you must provide the manpower and the voting power to keep our union strong."

On February 11 Jack Miller returned to Detroit to take the deposition of Bert Brennan concerning the Sun Valley matter, in preparation for Hoffa's trial, now set for April 23. Brennan had acquired Hoffa's knack of "forgettery" and could not recall anything significant concerning the operation. Henry Lower took the Fifth Amendment. While Miller was in Detroit, petitions were being circulated in Local 299 seeking an exoneration by the members of Hoffa's handling of the Sun Valley project. Frank Fitzsimmons, the vice president of the local, announced that the members were enthusiastic in their response to the petitions.

Hoffa continued his whirlwind offensive. On the evening of March 14 he held a rally at Madison Square Garden in New York City. His followers had hoped that it would be the largest demonstration of its kind in history to prove the rank and file membership supported him. However, in spite of every effort to pack the Garden, including exhorting cab drivers to park their taxis and come, half the seats were empty. Of course, the other half were filled with eight thousand enthusiastic Teamsters and Hoffa spoke for eighty minutes. He again attacked Senator John Kennedy for his role in the drafting of the Landrum-Griffin Act and denounced George Meany, Walter Reuther and the news media. He concluded with a call for political action "to elect workers to office—not bankers, lawyers, and millionaires."

On March 16 the *New York Herald-Tribune* published a confidential memorandum, which it said had gone out over Hoffa's name, listing nine Senators and seventy-three Congressmen to be defeated in their upcoming elections. Spokesmen for the union said, however, that the document in question was only a draft that was never adopted by Hoffa and had been "abandoned."

At the Board of Monitors things were going from bad to worse. Picketing of the Board's office by so-called rank and file members had been under way for a week. Anonymous threatening phone calls to Martin O'Donoghue and his family were taking their toll on the already weary Board chairman. O'Donoghue was further demoralized by the announcement that Danny Maher was resigning as a monitor and was to be replaced by attorney William Bufalino, the head of the Detroit Jukebox and Car Wash local. The disintegration of the original rank and file committee continued with the announcement that seven of them had voted to fire Godfrey Schmidt as their attorney. (Schmidt had continued as the attorney for the rank and file group after resigning as a monitor.)

Senator McClellan issued a statement denouncing the selection of Bufalino and said he doubted that "a properly informed court" would appoint him as a monitor. In April, 1959, McClellan had branded Bufalino's Local 985 in Detroit "a leech preying on working men and women to provide personal aggrandizement to Mr. Bufalino and his friends."

Some insight into the undermining of the rank and file committee was provided by Edward McFarland, a tough Irish Teamster who had been one of the original thirteen members. He furnished me with an affidavit in which he stated that he had been offered a "bundle" of money and any job he wanted in the Teamsters Union if he would help in breaking up the rank and file committee and denounce Godfrey Schmidt. McFarland had turned down the offers. He said that he and the others who opposed the firing of Schmidt were not told about the original meeting, where the vote to do so was taken. He also said that Monitor Larry Smith, who represented the rank and file committee, had become increasingly critical of Martin O'Donoghue and had begun opposing O'Donoghue in the Board actions without consulting with the committee. When McFarland had challenged Smith about this, he said that he had checked with Andy Boggia, the leader of the seven who had now repudiated Schmidt. "Whereas formerly Andy Boggia and the rest of the committee had taken the position, along with Godfrey Schmidt, that the removal of Hoffa was of prime importance, they switched almost overnight to the position that local remedies were more important than the removal of Hoffa and that Godfrey Schmidt should be removed as our attorney."

As the Senate Select Committee was about to expire, Senator McClellan introduced a resolution to transfer the functions of the Committee to McClellan's Permanent Subcommittee on Investigations. This was followed by the publication of another segment of the Select Committee's final report on March 28. All of the Committee members subscribed to the findings concerning Hoffa, which stated:

> Time and time again the Committee has found Hoffa to be faithless to the members of his own union. He has betrayed these members so frequently that it has become abundantly clear that Hoffa's chief interest is his own advancement and that of his friends and cronies —a great number of whom are racketeers.
> In addition, Hoffa has used union funds for his own benefit and that of his friends.
> Hoffa has consistently supported the interests of racketeer friends over those of his own members.
> Hoffa and his chief aides have consistently repressed democratic rights within the union.
> The committee is convinced that if Hoffa remains unchecked he will successfully destroy the decent labor movement in the United States. Further than that, because of the tremendous economic

power of the Teamsters, it will place the underworld in a position
to dominate American economic life in a period when the vitality
of the American economy is necessary to this country's preservation
in an era of world crisis. This Hoffa cannot be allowed to do.

After reciting the point-by-point findings of the 1959 hearings
concerning Hoffa and the Teamsters, the report concluded, "From
this point on, the fate and the future of James R. Hoffa rest with
the executive and judicial branches of the Government, the monitors, and inevitably with his own members."

In a flurry of activity in the last two days of March Andy Boggia,
the leader of the majority faction in the rank and file committee,
blasted Martin O'Donoghue in a *New York Times* interview and his
group announced that they had hired New York attorney Robert
Silagi to replace Schmidt. Judge Letts fired Monitor Larry Smith,
stating, "I have been persuaded that you have not had your heart
in the assignment." The International filed a new suit in federal
court calling for a new convention, claiming that the Landrum-
Griffin Act had preempted the functions of the monitorship,
which had become "a burdensome charge against the funds of the
International" and had abandoned its advisory role and "adopted
an adversary and prosecutional attitude." Judge Letts appointed
Terrence McShane, a young New York FBI agent, to replace
Smith as a monitor. Judge Letts also refused to accept the resignation of Monitor Maher, thus temporarily blocking the appointment of William Bufalino. Maher, nevertheless, again submitted
his resignation, stating that he was "unable and unwilling to serve
further," and that as of April 4, "I shall no longer serve on the
board." Smith announced that he was appealing his firing by Judge
Letts and the International appealed the appointment of McShane
by Judge Letts.

As the infighting went on in the beleaguered Board of Monitors,
the preparations went forward for its trial of Hoffa later in the
month. Jake Kossman, a rumpled street-wise Philadelphia attorney, took over the taking of depositions for Hoffa. Hoffa participated in the questioning, and shouting matches erupted several
times between Jack Miller and the witness on the one hand and
Kossman and Hoffa on the other. In his deposition, Martin
O'Donoghue told how he had been threatened in a phone call by
Hoffa. Hoffa responded by calling O'Donoghue a "cry baby." As
O'Donoghue, whose health was failing and who had been told by

his doctor to quit the monitorship, was leaving the session, Hoffa hollered after him, "Good-by, Marty, go see the doctor."

Meanwhile, Sid Zagri's new political operation had not been idle. On April 13 eleven Congressmen made speeches on the floor of the House of Representatives attacking Judge Letts and the Board of Monitors and calling for an early new convention for the Teamsters Union. Congressman James Roosevelt of California suggested that an investigation by a subcommittee of the House Judiciary Committee might be necessary and that impeachment of Judge Letts could result. Congressmen John Dent and Elmer Holland of Pennsylvania said that the monitors were spending $2000 a day or, as Dent put it, $700,000 a year, of union funds. Congressman Abraham Multer of New York cited the same yearly expenditure and termed it "awfully nice patronage" for the court. It was an impressive display of political clout. Some of these same men and others of their colleagues, in both the House and the Senate, would rise and give their remarkably similar speeches again and again in the future whenever Jimmy Hoffa was in trouble. The $700,000 a year figure used by the Congressmen must have come from the Teamsters, and yet in that month's issue of *International Teamster* magazine the entire cost of the monitorship for two years and three months was given as slightly less than that figure. Hoffa's new political action program, now officially designated DRIVE (Democratic, Republican, Independent Voter Education), with Zagri at the helm, was bearing fruit.

The barrage of letters, telegrams and phone calls to Senators and Congressmen intensified. From the Teamsters hiring hall in Seattle came the report that men attempting to obtain employment there were being asked to sign petitions calling for the dissolution of the Board of Monitors and the holding of a new convention. As one man told a reporter for the Seattle *Times*, "What can you do? The implication is, at least, that you either sign or you don't get shipped out through the hall."

On April 15 Senator John F. Kennedy won over Senator Hubert Humphrey in the Wisconsin primary and headed for West Virginia.

In *The New York Times* of April 20 James Reston, commenting on DRIVE in a column headed "A View of the World From Jimmy Hoffa's Window," said, "Nobody is left in any doubt about Mr. Hoffa's preference in this election. He prefers the defeat of Senator John F. Kennedy of Massachusetts. He is against everybody but he is against Senator Kennedy most of all. . . . He will see to it that the 8,000 members of the Teamsters in West Virginia know his views before they vote in the primary there on May 10. But, as he says, everybody is free to take this advice or leave it alone."

On April 28 hearings commenced before Judge Joseph R. Jackson in federal court in Washington, D.C., preparatory to Hoffa's trial on the charges brought by the Board of Monitors relative to Sun Valley, Inc. Ironically, Hoffa's lawyers now cited the Landrum-Griffin Act, which the Teamsters head had criticized so severely, in support of their arguments that only members of the union could either elect or remove its officers.

On the same day Sally Hucks, the Woodner Hotel telephone operator, Moss Herman and attorney Joe Williamson, who had represented John Cunningham before the McClellan Committee, were indicted by a federal grand jury in Washington for perjury and obstruction of justice in connection with the altered and destroyed Teamsters telephone records.

After another day of hearings before Judge Jackson, the often postponed trial of Hoffa faced another and perhaps indefinite postponement when the Court of Appeals on May 2 in a 2 to 1 emergency ruling held that the trial should be delayed until the court heard other pending appeals.

Ten days later the Court of Appeals issued a stay against the firing of Larry Smith by Judge Letts. On the same day Judge Letts reluctantly appointed William Bufalino to succeed Danny Maher as the monitor representing the International.

From the first day of his appointment on, William Bufalino's sole purpose seemed to be to disrupt the workings of the Board, harass its staff and drive Martin O'Donoghue out of his mind. If that was true, he succeeded very well in the first two objectives and almost brought off the third. On May 12, the day of his appointment, Bufalino went to the monitors' office and told John Cassidy that he wanted to be present every day when the mail was opened. "Do you understand that?" he asked Cassidy. Cassidy replied that he had heard what Bufalino said. Then Bufalino countered, "Now, Cassidy, don't get cute with me. We have to work together and you might as well understand it."

On May 16 Hoffa, in a telephone conversation, and Bufalino, at the monitors' office, had heated discussions with Cassidy and both told him they were going to have him cited for obstruction of justice. Bufalino also canceled an appointment that afternoon with

O'Donoghue at his office, claiming that he understood that the office was bugged. On the following day Hoffa called Cassidy and again accused him of obstruction and said he was going to have him prosecuted. Hoffa told Cassidy he was going to ruin him so that he would "never be able to practice law in this town". On May 20 Hoffa once more called Cassidy and accused him and the monitors' staff of "deliberately distorting the facts." He said that he was going to have them cited for contempt and would cut off the payment of Cassidy's salary. On May 24 Bufalino questioned Cassidy about what he had said in his deposition on the Sun Valley case. When Cassidy declined to tell him, Bufalino said that Jake Kossman was going to file a perjury action against him in a couple of weeks.

The Board of Monitors office had always been considered the office of the chairman, and therefore Mr. O'Donoghue's office. The other monitors had always had their own offices and files. Likewise, John Cassidy and the other members of the staff were considered the chairman's staff and answerable to him. Judge Letts had concurred in this understanding. Bufalino challenged all of this and demanded a desk in the monitors' office, a key to the door, access to the mail and files and authority over the staff. After much bickering, a compromise arrangement was worked out whereby Bufalino maintained his office at the International and took over former Monitor Maher's files. When Maher's files were found to be inadequate, members of the staff helped Bufalino reconstruct them and O'Donoghue offered to have his files duplicated if Bufalino and Hoffa decided the cost of doing so was warranted. Bufalino also hired his own staff assistant. The function of opening the mail was retained by O'Donoghue and the staff, who then routed the mail to the individual monitors. Confidential mail for the chairman went only to him. He agreed, however, to a Bufalino proposal that a daily log be kept of all incoming mail, including a notation of the number of confidential items, if any. There were almost daily arguments about the arrangements but they continued in effect throughout the month of May. Bufalino kept pressing for a key to the monitors' office but at one point told Cassidy that he was only doing it on the instructions of Jake Kossman, so that they could bring suit when it was refused.

On May 31 Bufalino came into the monitors' office while staff member Joseph Lang was opening mail. Bufalino grabbed the correspondence and Lang attempted unsuccessfully to retrieve it.

Bufalino then left the office with the mail. Sometime thereafter newsmen and television crews began arriving at the office and told John Cassidy that Bufalino was going to hold a press conference there. Bufalino finally arrived with his left hand heavily bandaged. He claimed that it had been hurt by Lang when they both reached for a stack of correspondence. He said Lang had refused to let him see the correspondence but he had taken it anyway and had delivered it to Judge Letts. Bufalino said that he had been given a tetanus shot by a doctor, but then admitted that the scratches he received were "trivial" and that Lang probably hadn't meant to hurt him. Then he charged that he was being ignored as a monitor and that the court's orders were not being properly followed.

It was a transparently contrived publicity stunt. Martin O'Donoghue filed complaining affidavits with the court in which Joe Lang stated that Bufalino had "lunged across the table and grasped the correspondence." O'Donoghue said, "These incidents reveal clearly the plan to utilize Monitor Bufalino, not in the proper performance of his duties as an officer of this court, but as a tool for creating dissension and controversy in order to hamstring the board."

On June 1 William Presser went on trial in federal court in Cleveland on the charge of having obstructed justice by mutilating the subpoenaed "champagne master" invoice. Senator McClellan and I were on hand to testify for the government. Presser had been convicted in February in Washington, D.C., of contempt of Congress for refusing when before the McClellan Committee to answer the question whether or not he had destroyed other subpoenaed records. Presser testified at the trial that he was in Washington during the period between the day I had left the documents with him to be photostated and the day I returned to pick them up. Therefore, he said, he did not have time to go through the files and mutilate the invoice and denied doing so. However, long-distance toll records which the government had subpoenaed from the telephone company showed that two person-to-person calls had been completed from Hoffa in Washington to Presser in Cleveland during the period in question. On May 7 Presser was found guilty by the jury.

On June 3 the Court of Appeals formally reinstated Larry Smith as a monitor. It also ruled that the Board of Monitors as a whole and not Chairman O'Donoghue should direct the activities of the law firm. The two rulings left O'Donoghue as a minority on the

Board, with his future effectiveness in grave doubt.

It was all downhill from there. Bufalino's harassing tactics continued. He began calling O'Donoghue at home late in the evening, ostensibly about Board business, refused to sign expense accounts and continued to harangue the staff members. On June 10 Hoffa called O'Donoghue and accused him of lying, cheating and trying to destroy the International. O'Donoghue finally said, "Mr. Hoffa, I am not going to take this abuse from you," and hung up the phone.

Finally, on July 11, Martin O'Donoghue submitted his resignation as chairman of the Board of Monitors to Judge Letts, to become effective upon the swearing in of a successor. In his letter of resignation O'Donoghue outlined the progress that had been made in the areas of auditing and record-keeping, by-laws and trusteeships and election procedures, but noted that the problem about which the Board "has made little or no progress is that of cleaning up corrupt influences with the Teamsters Union." He wrote further, "During the past few weeks the task has become increasingly more difficult. The entire past year has been marked by unwarranted personal attacks on me as Chairman by the defendants in their pleadings in the Courts, by the actions of the Defendant Hoffa in his day-by-day relations with the Board of Monitors, but with the advent of William Bufalino to the Board of Monitors, such personal attacks on the Chairman and the Staff members of the Board have even become a disrupting influence on the deliberations of the Board at formal meetings."

O'Donoghue attached to his letter a draft of a comprehensive report which contained, as the judge had directed, a detailed narrative of the Sun Valley case resulting from the depositions and investigation by the Board and the law firm. However, the likelihood of Hoffa's ever going to trial on these charges was now growing increasingly dim.

As the Democratic delegates gathered in Los Angeles in early July, Senator John F. Kennedy, having swept all of the primaries, was the odds-on favorite for the Presidential nomination. But Senator Lyndon B. Johnson, the majority leader of the Senate, who had stayed aloof from the primary trail, was now a declared candidate and hope to wrest the prize from the front runner. There is no question that Kennedy considered him his most serious competition.

I. Irving Davidson, who had arranged the meeting the previous

December between Hoffa and Nixon's friend, Allan Oakley Hunter, was at the convention. He introduced Hoffa to Lyndon Johnson's friend, John Connally of Texas. Hoffa promised Connally that he would support Johnson for the Presidency if he was nominated. The last-minute boom for Governor Adlai Stevenson, which might have stalled the Kennedy momentum, fizzled, however, and John Kennedy was nominated on the first ballot on July 13.

The Republican Convention met two weeks later in Chicago. I. Irving Davidson was also at that conclave and arranged another meeting between Hoffa and Allan Oakley Hunter. After having covered a losing base in Los Angeles, Hoffa now renewed the pledge of support for Nixon, who was also nominated on the first ballot.

On July 21 the Court of Appeals ruled that the civil trial of Hoffa on the monitors' Sun Valley charges could go forward. The court, however, expressed grave doubts as to whether Hoffa could be removed from office by the court, even if convicted. The trial was set for October but there was little confidence that it would actually be held. The Court of Appeals also refused Hoffa's plea for an immediate election but did state that an election should be held as soon as possible and that the parties involved should "consult in an earnest effort to reach an agreed disposition of pending matters," looking toward that end. Pursuant to the court's ruling, Judge Letts ordered the attorneys for the parties to commence meeting on September 6 to work toward a settlement of all pending matters.

On July 23 in Nashville, Tennessee, Judge William E. Miller reluctantly reversed the conviction of Glenn Smith for income tax evasion as a result of legal issues raised by defense attorneys. But in so doing he made the following statement:

> If this case involved the sufficiency of the evidence to establish a criminal conspiracy on the part of Local Union No. 515 at Chattanooga, its officers and members to attempt the bribery of a Criminal Court Judge and to thwart the administration of justice; or if it involved the moral fitness of certain of its officers to discharge the responsible duties entrusted to them, there would be no doubt that the charges were well founded. For the record in this case is a sordid exposé of the illicit affairs of this Local Union and its officers, aided

and abetted by officers of the International Union of Teamsters reflecting a shocking and callous disregard of duty and responsibility under the law. That the defendant Smith as President of the Local was one of the leading figures in such conspiracy, that he attempted to conceal his illegal activities and schemes by false statements and falsification of records, and that he is morally unfit to hold the important position entrusted to him unmistakably appear from his own testimony.

Addressing a meeting of one thousand Teamsters members in Camden, New Jersey, on August 14, Jimmy Hoffa said that they should vote against Senator John F. Kennedy, whom he described as the son of a millionaire "who never knew what it was to work."

On August 25 I resigned from the McClellan Committee staff and joined Senator Kennedy's campaign staff as the coordinator for the state of Pennsylvania.

In the September issue of *International Teamster* magazine Hoffa blasted Senator Kennedy in an editorial: ". . . this man presents a very real danger to our life as a nation if he is successful in buying our country's highest office." The magazine carried an article on the platforms of both parties which stated that while the Democratic platform promised more, "with Senator John Kennedy as the Presidential candidate, the Democratic platform becomes nothing but a 'pie in the sky' document." A third article quoted Hoffa as saying that "Bobby Kennedy is a young, dimwitted, curly-headed smart aleck" and that Senator John Kennedy "is unworthy of the trust to be President of the United States."

On September 7 the Executive Board of the International Brotherhood of Teamsters voted to oppose Senator Kennedy in the Presidential election but not to endorse anyone. A union source was quoted as saying they would not endorse Nixon outright because "we won't do anything to help Kennedy."

On September 22 an article in *The New York Times* reported that Hoffa would begin a nationwide campaign the following week against the candidacy of Senator John Kennedy. According to the *Times* article, Hoffa and Executive Vice President Harold Gibbons planned to hold political meetings in a dozen cities by October 3, and would urge Teamsters members to split their tickets and vote for Richard Nixon for President and Democratic candidates friendly to labor for lesser offices.

While Jimmy Hoffa was going all out to try to defeat Senator Kennedy and thereby elect Vice President Nixon, strange things were happening in Orlando, Florida. Jim Dowd and his group had been laboring on the Sun Valley case since February and had made excellent progress. By September they had developed the case to the point where they felt they were prepared to recommend to their superiors in the Department of Justice, and to the grand jury in Orlando, that Hoffa, Henry Lower and Detroit banker Robert McCarthy be indicted. A prosecutive memorandum was prepared and submitted to Criminal Division chief Malcolm Wilkie, who concurred with their recommendation. An indictment was drawn up to be presented to the grand jury and copies were mimeographed, as is the custom, for distribution to the press and interested parties after the indictment was brought. Dowd and his assistants were sent to Orlando by Wilkie to meet with the grand jury and bring the indictment.

While Dowd was in the grand jury room summing up the case preparatory to asking for an indictment, he was called out to take an emergency telephone call from Washington. The caller was Malcolm Wilkie, who directed Dowd not to bring the indictment and to return at once, with all of his files, to Washington. Dowd was stunned by the sudden turn of events but did as he was told. When he returned to Washington he was told that Justice Department officials wanted to study the case further. For the time being at least, Hoffa's worries about criminal charges concerning the Sun Valley situation were allayed. Meanwhile, it seemed less and less likely that the civil charges brought by the Board of Monitors about the same matter would ever be tried.

On September 27 a short article appeared in *The New York Times* datelined the previous day from Miami. It said that the Everglades Hotel there had been sold at auction to the Teamsters Pension Fund for $2,500,000. Vaughn B. Connelly, the foreclosed owner of the hotel, had borrowed $4,300,000 from the Pension Fund. The article mentioned that the Pension Fund had several other large investments in property in the Miami area. Walter May and John Constandy of the McClellan Committee staff had talked to Connelly the previous year in connection with their investigation of Ben Dranow's efforts to bail out the Sun Valley project. He had lied to them to protect his relationship with Dranow, the fund and Hoffa. Unbeknownst to anyone, he was now having second thoughts which would soon cause serious problems for Jimmy Hoffa.

In addition to Senator Kennedy, Hoffa had marked fifty-six Congressmen for defeat around the country. It appeared that his campaign was not going well anyplace.

A *Wall Street Journal* article on October 10 indicated that Hoffa's exhortations did not seem to be having any appreciable effect on his members or on the candidates they were supposed to work against and that, in fact, his efforts might be boomeranging to the benefit of those candidates.

An article by A. H. Raskin in *The New York Times* on October 18 said much the same thing about the reaction in Chicago, where Raskin had been conducting his own poll. He found that only 10 Teamsters members out of 150 questioned intended to vote against Kennedy because he was "antilabor."

The November issue of *International Teamster*, which came out just prior to the election, devoted an editorial and three full pages to the threats posed by a Kennedy victory in the election.

A few days after Kennedy's election Jim Dowd, who had been summoned back to Washington two months earlier when he was about to indict Hoffa, was now told to return to Orlando and bring the indictment! Dowd set about gathering his material together, shipping back the file cabinets full of documents, reestablishing contact with witnesses and making arrangements to reconvene the grand jury. The following week he and his associates were back in Orlando. On December 7 Attorney General William Rogers announced the indictment of Hoffa, Henry Lower and Robert McCarthy on twelve counts of mail fraud in connection with the Sun Valley project. Hoffa's apparent immunity from prosecution had ended with the defeat of Nixon.

Hoffa did have the consolation of seeing the Board of Monitors die a slow death, however. Terrence McShane had been appointed to succeed Martin O'Donoghue as chairman of the Board, but his appointment had been stayed by the Court of Appeals after objecting petitions were filed by the International and Hoffa. Then the Court of Appeals ruled that either party to the consent decree could veto a suggested new chairman. This ruled out McShane and made it unlikely that a new chairman would ever be appointed. It was now only a matter of time. Martin O'Donoghue received some consolation when he was named "Lawyer of the Year" by the District of Columbia Bar Association.

On the morning of the day Hoffa was indicted in Orlando,

William Hillbrant, one of the Neo-Gravure Company executives who had testified before the McClellan Committee about the shakedown of New York newspapers by Harold Gross and in Gross' trial for income tax evasion, and who was scheduled to testify again in an upcoming trial of Gross for extortion, was in his home in Elizabeth, New Jersey, ready to leave for work. As he left the house, there was an explosion and the automobile he would have driven to work was demolished.

On December 16, President-elect Kennedy announced the appointment of his brother Robert as Attorney General of the United States. Later that day Jimmy Hoffa walked briskly into federal court in Orlando and pleaded innocent to the Sun Valley charges. Reporters asked him what he thought of the appointment of Robert Kennedy as Attorney General. Hoffa replied, "The Attorney General's job will not be another subcommittee for the Senate."

In his editorial in the December issue of *International Teamster* Hoffa was suddenly conciliatory:

> In the aftermath of last month's national elections, all Americans— those who voted for Kennedy and those who did not—will close ranks and work side by side for the welfare of our country and a better world for all.
> In all democratic institutions, there is room for healthy dissent. Yet, when the vote has been taken and the majority will expressed, all members unite for the welfare of the group. Whether it be club, lodge, local union, state or national government, this is the American way.

It is interesting to note at this point the editorial comments of a particular newspaper concerning Jimmy Hoffa and Bob Kennedy. The *Manchester Union Leader* in Manchester, New Hampshire, owned and published by William Loeb, had supported Richard Nixon in both the primary elections and the campaign. In fact, Loeb had been a long-time ally of Nixon's and had, with his friend Senator Styles Bridges, come to Nixon's defense in 1956 when a strong move was launched to knock the then Vice President off the ticket which culminated in the famous "Checkers" speech. Loeb had likewise been highly critical of John Kennedy during the campaign to the extent that Kennedy singled out the *Manchester Union Leader* for attack on the eve of the election.

But the newspaper's editorial comment was surprisingly benevolent concerning Bob Kennedy's appointment and critical of Jimmy Hoffa. A December 12 editorial had this to say about Hoffa:

> Teamster Union President Jimmy Hoffa may be trying his darndest to smooth over his relations with President-elect Kennedy but it seems to us that his actions speak so loud it is difficult to hear what he says.
> No sooner was the ink dry on a conciliatory Hoffa editorial in the December issue of the union's monthly magazine than Hoffa was indicted in Orlando, Florida, for allegedly pouring $500,000 in union funds into a land development scheme and trying to sell the swampy lots to union members.
> Jimmy Hoffa's editorial would have been amusing were the issues of corruption not so serious. At one point in the editorial, Jimmy blandly stated, "In all democratic institutions there is room for healthy dissent."
> S'funny, but most people have the impression that its not too healthy to "dissent" in the Teamsters Union.

In the December 18 issue of his paper, Loeb wrote the following:

> Having earlier suggested Joseph P. Kennedy—Jack's Old Man—for a high role in federal government, we are happy to applaud the elevation of another member of the clan, Brother Robert, to the Attorney Generalship.
> From what we saw of Robert during the campaign, and earlier in his role of counsel to the Senate labor rackets investigation, he may well be the ablest of all the younger Kennedys. . . .

Loeb's attitude toward Bob Kennedy and, more particularly, toward Jimmy Hoffa would change abruptly two years hence, shortly before he received a loan from the Teamsters Pension Fund.

PART II

THE FALL

CHAPTER VI

The New Frontier and the New General President

============

DREW PEARSON'S COLUMN in the *Washington Post* on the morning of January 4, 1961, was captioned "Nixon Figured in Hoffa Delay." Pearson charged that Vice President Nixon had intervened with Attorney General Rogers not to indict Hoffa in Orlando and that Rogers had "sat on" the indictment throughout the Presidential campaign while Hoffa was giving nationwide political support to Nixon. Pearson said that this support was instrumental in tipping the state of Ohio into the Nixon column. Pearson went on to state that after the election Nixon, feeling indebted to Hoffa, had again attempted to influence Rogers not to bring the indictment but that the Attorney General had decided to go ahead with it. Pearson printed the following excerpts from two letters from Allan Oakley Hunter, whom Pearson described as "the secret intermediary between Nixon and Hoffa." The first letter, dated December 8, was to Hoffa:

Dear Jim:
I was sorry to hear of the indictment against you in the Orlando matter. I know for a fact that your side of the case was put before the Vice President and that he discussed the case with the Attorney General, Bill Rogers.
I do not know what was said by the Vice President to Rogers. I do

know, however, that the Vice President has been sympathetic toward you and has felt that you were being subjected to undue harassment by certain parties.

It would be my surmise that Bill Rogers acted as he did for reasons of his own. Mr. Nixon having lost the election, I doubt that he has since been in a position to exercise any decisive degree of influence. As Vice President he has no authority to order the Attorney General to do anything.

The second letter, dated December 20, to a Hoffa associate, was, according to Pearson, a further attempt to placate Hoffa, who was furious at being double-crossed and wanted Nixon to take a public stand against the indictment:

Regarding the "big doublecross," as you call it, I don't think it would do your friend [Hoffa] any good to make the Vice President a party to the matter. I am satisfied that he, as well as Bob Finch, presented the facts to Bill Rogers and that the latter acted as he did in what he believed to be his own self interest.

For the Vice President to have taken exception to his action publicly would have only caused Rogers to defend his position, also publicly. The Vice President felt that that would only put your friend further on the spot.

A few days after the confirmation of Bob Kennedy's appointment as Attorney General, he asked me to serve as one of his special assistants and to come over to the Justice Department to help get things set up. There had been no discussion of what my duties would be, and the thought that since I was not an attorney I would be rarity in the department had not even occurred to me. For the moment the pure excitement of being a part of the new Administration was all-consuming.

Kennedy told me to find three or four bright young attorneys to take a fresh look at the findings of the McClellan Committee and to probe generally into the field of labor racketeering, particularly into the activities of Hoffa and the Teamsters.

The first recruit was Jim Neal, a native of Nashville, who was with a Washington law firm. At the time Kennedy was trying to decide who should prosecute the pending indictment against Hoffa in Orlando. He was uncertain whether to leave the case with Jim Dowd or to bring someone new in to try it. If he decided the latter, Neal would be an excellent prospect to succeed Dowd. So

Neal agreed to come on as a special assistant to the Attorney General with his ultimate role still somewhat nebulous.

Next Bob called Charlie Smith, a black Assistant District Attorney in Seattle, whom he had met in the early days of the McClellan Committee. Bob had been impressed with Smith and his work as the back-up man in the successful state prosecution of Dave Beck. Smith agreed to come with the department.

Kennedy also sought recruits from within the department. He would say at meetings that if there was anyone present who did not feel he had enough work to do or did not find it challenging, he should come and talk to him after the meeting. One such volunteer was Bill French, who was bored to death with his work in the Lands Division. Bob sent him to me. Next was Charlie Shaffer, a young Assistant United States Attorney in the Southern District of New York who was suggested to me by Brother James Kenny, S.J., a mutual friend at my alma mater, Fordham University. Shaffer had finished at the top of his class in Fordham Law School and he, too, agreed to come with us.

In the midst of this recruiting, Kennedy appointed Jack Miller as Assistant Attorney General in charge of the Criminal Division. John Cassidy left the now all but defunct Board of Monitors and joined our group at the same time.

While Bob Kennedy was staffing the Justice Department, Senator McClellan began new public hearings focusing on Tony "Ducks" Corallo and Sam Goldstein and their continuing control of Local 239. The testimony took up where we had left off in June, 1959. At that time, Corallo had finally resigned as vice president of the local, only to be replaced on the payroll by two other men. Sam Goldstein, though in jail, was still president of the local and still collecting his paycheck. When Hoffa had testified on June 26, 1959, he had stated that he was not aware that Goldstein was still on the payroll but hedged about doing anything about getting him off.

Following his testimony, Hoffa had met in Washington on June 30, 1959, with Bernard Stein, the secretary-treasurer of Local 239, to discuss what to do about Goldstein. Stein had then reported back to Corallo that evening in New York City. The conversation between Stein and Corallo had been recorded by the New York Police Department by means of a court-authorized listening device. Senator McClellan now played the recording at the new hearing.

In the recorded conversation Stein quoted Hoffa as saying that Goldstein had to go off the payroll.

Stein: He says, "I don't give a ____ what you do." He says, "Give him the money." He says, "Anything, this guy, he's got to go. He can't stay. There's no other way about it." He says, "I'm going to make a statement." He says that I instructed the local. I says, "Well, I tell you, Jimmy, don't make the statement until you hear from me Monday. . . ." He says, "Well, he's got to go." He said this a half a dozen times. He's got to get off. . . . "First of all," he says, "he hurt himself a lot. . . ."

Corallo: He can't take the local.

Stein: Tony, the guy told me straight out, and I ain't making like my own words. I'm saying his words: "I don't care if you want to—you want to steal, you want to rob, go ahead," he says, "don't get caught." He says, "Listen, you're worried about money. I don't care how you take the money. I don't care how you take it—get it under the table—get it any way you want." And Tony, he says, "Let time go by a year, he can go back on the payroll. . . ."

Stein (later in conversation):   He says, "What do you think it's going to be like this winter?" He says, "It's all forgotten. It's cold as the ice out in the street." He says, "It's all over. All the wind is gone. And this punk kid here, Kennedy,"—he calls him punk kid —"he's got his nose up in everybody's ____. He'll be gone too. In fact, he'll be gone next month, July."

According to Stein, Hoffa was equally unconcerned about the Board of Monitors:

Stein: Yeah, the monitors. "Lookit," he says, and then finally when I got all through I says, "You got to tell me one more thing—about the monitors—what can they do to the local?" And he says, "Listen, the monitors." He says, "Look, if they come to me and they says Sam Goldstein—we want you to do, you know

> something about him—we bring up Sam Goldstein
> on charges. We bring him before the General Execu-
> tive Board and we acquit him, that's all—he's inno-
> cent. We give him a trial," he says, "that's all."

After further conversation, Corallo finally made the decision:
"We're going to take him off the payroll when this is all over, Hoffa
says he can come right back, not as an officer-business agent, business manager. Six months later he can go on as president."

Martin O'Donoghue and Jimmy Hoffa squared off for the last
time on January 24. The forum was the Senate Caucus Room
where both had been called to testify by the McClellan Committee.
O'Donoghue, testifying first, outlined the history of the monitorship and then unleashed a devastating, point-by-point attack on
Hoffa's obstructive tactics. Citing the "flood of litigation" with
which his clean-up efforts had been met, O'Donoghue said that
"unbelievable as it may seem there have been more than thirty-
eight appeals, nine mandamuses, and three petitions for writs of
certiorari to the United States Supreme Court. Mr. Hoffa objected
to the monitors receiving legal and auditing help on the grounds
of undue expenses, yet he employed a veritable bar association to
render legal attacks against the monitors in order to frustrate the
objectives of the consent order." O'Donoghue charged that "there
was also evidence of subversion," noting that "John Cunningham,
one of the original plaintiffs in the case, was apparently induced
to forsake his role as a plaintiff," and his hotel bill at the Woodneer
Hotel, which had earlier been paid by the Teamsters Union, was
"the last I heard, . . . in excess of $11,000."

O'Donoghue then ticked off the scorecard of Teamsters officials
whom he had unsuccessfully pushed Hoffa to censure and concluded by stating that in spite of three years of repeated promises
by Hoffa to clean up the union, "there has not been one significant
step taken by Mr. Hoffa, and there is no indication that Mr. Hoffa
has either the inclination or the ability to do so."

Hoffa, following O'Donoghue to the witness table, was surly
and arrogant. He accused O'Donoghue of having a "warped mind"
and maintained that the Teamsters Union was "as clean or cleaner
than any other." He challenged McClellan's right to hold the hearing and accused him of seeking headlines. When Jerry Adlerman,
who had replaced Bob Kennedy as chief counsel, asked Hoffa
whether he was afraid to remove corrupt officials, Hoffa shot back,

"Hoffa isn't afraid of anybody, including you." He vehemently denied making the statements attributed to him in the recorded conversation between Bernard Stein and Tony "Ducks" Corallo, shouting, "It's a lie!" Tony "Ducks" himself, who had succeeded in "ducking" a Committee subpoena for months, was finally located in a Long Island hideout and summoned before the Committee. He took the Fifth Amendment.

By 1961 the Teamsters Pension Fund had the awesome assets of $200,000,000. During the McClellan Committee investigations we had recognized it as a growing source of power and possible corruption but we had not looked into it in depth. The loan to Ben Dranow for the almost bankrupt John Thomas Department Store at a time when the store was being picketed by another union had been, at best, callous and imprudent. The contemplated loan, interrupted by the Committee's investigation, to the Akros Dynamics Company to finance the sale of airplanes to Castro had been outrageous. The emergence of C.P.A. S. George Burris as a front for Dranow in the attempted bail-out of Sun Valley by Union Land and Home, the involvement of Burris and his attorney son Herbert in the Akros Dynamics caper, and the fact that the Burrises had themselves received loans from the Pension Fund had also pointed to the probability of much more skulduggery beneath the lightly scratched surface.

Vaughn Connelly, the former owner of the Everglades Hotel and the recipient of $4,000,000 in loans from the Teamsters Pension Fund, now corroborated our suspicion by telling the truth concerning all of his fund transactions. Connelly told us he had paid a 10 percent cash kickback to Ben Dranow to get the loan and that Dranow told him that a portion of the money was going to Hoffa. Connelly also said that his loan application had been false and inflated and that funds from the loans were diverted to help bail out the Sun Valley project. Connelly implicated George and Herbert Burris and Cal Kovens, a Miami contractor, in the scheme. It was his understanding that many loans from the Pension Fund involved similar fraudulent practices. Connelly's statement pointed to a possible wide-scale misuse of funds held in trust for the pensions of retired Teamsters members. The potential magnitude of this callous fraud dwarfed all of the chicanery that had heretofore been uncovered.

Two priorities loomed immediately. Ben Dranow was to go on

trial soon in Minneapolis on charges of bankruptcy fraud in connection with the John W. Thomas Department Store and it was important that someone start looking into Vaughn Connelly's allegations about the Pension Fund.

Jack Miller decided that Jim Neal should try the Dranow case. At the same time, Bob Kennedy decided that he was going to reduce the number of attorneys in the Internal Security Division and transfer them into more meaningful areas of the department. He asked me and Jack to interview some of them and to add two or three to our group. As a result, Tom McTiernan, Bill Kenny and Jim Canavan moved into our group. They, along with Bill French and Charlie Smith, who had arrived from Seattle, headed for Miami to begin a grand jury investigation of the Pension Fund. John Cassidy took over all of the administrative work of the group, and Charlie Shaffer went to New York to look into the allegations of jury tampering in the two Hoffa wiretap trials.

On February 28 Jimmy Hoffa finally won his complete victory over the Board of Monitors when Judge Letts ruled that the Teamsters Union was free to call a convention to hold new elections. Hoffa announced that he would call a convention in Miami in mid-May. He also announced that the Teamsters Union would soon embark on a new organizing drive in all industries and areas regardless of jurisdiction. The Board of Monitors, with no chairman, had actually not been functioning for some time. The three-year struggle by a handful of honest attorneys, acting as agents of the court, to clean up the Teamsters Union or oust Hoffa from its leadership had failed. Their noble efforts had been completely frustrated by Hoffa's skillful tactics of evasion and delay and smothered by the massive counterlitigation by the "Teamster Bar Association" which produced the most voluminous docket in the history of the District Court. It had been an excellent training ground in Hoffa's ways for Jack Miller and John Cassidy, but it had taken its toll on the physical health of Martin O'Donoghue and strained the faith of some in the judicial process.

Hoffa turned his attorneys to the task of dealing with the Sun Valley federal indictment in Orlando. His Florida lawyers, Charles E. Davis and former Governor Fuller Warren, filed twenty-eight pages of motions asking, among other things, that the indictment be dismissed on the grounds that the grand jury that had brought the indictment was improperly empaneled. After three days of hearings beginning on March 13, Judge Joseph P. Leib denied a motion by Jim Dowd for the already delayed trial to commence within sixty days, and gave the attorneys for Hoffa and his co-defendants until May 1 to file additional briefs. On hand to argue on Hoffa's behalf, along with his local attorneys, was Jake Kossman, who now appeared to have taken over the role of chief counsel to the Teamsters head.

In New York Charlie Shaffer was making some headway in his inquiry into the possibility of jury tampering in the Hoffa wiretap trials. In connection with the first trial in late 1957, Shaffer learned that former Senator George Bender, who was subsequently named by Hoffa to head his antiracketeering commission, had contacted a former Republican Congressman from upstate New York to attempt to have him intervene on Hoffa's behalf with the Republican United States Attorney in New York City who was trying the case. The former Congressman declined to do so. Bender's action was taken at the behest of Luther White, a black promoter from Cleveland who was a friend of Hoffa's. White had also contacted a black New York newsman for purposes of seeking sympathetic press treatment for Hoffa and entree to black sports figures and politicians on Hoffa's behalf. White, who was known in Teamsters circles as "the man with the card," subsequently received several payments from Ohio Teamsters organizations under the control of Bill Presser, which were charged to "promotional and educational project," "public relations and consultation" and "organizational service." He also received a $5000 loan from the Michigan Conference of Teamsters and a $185,000 loan from the Teamsters Pension Fund.

Shaffer found in connection with Hoffa's second wiretap trial in 1958 that in addition to the known contact by a labor writer of juror Catherine Barry, who was excused by the judge, there were two attempts to contact the husband of one of the other jurors. In addition, he learned that the man who replaced Catherine Barry as a juror was tailed by private detectives who were hired by Hoffa's wiretapper and co-defendant, Bernard Spindel.

Our group in Miami was involved in tracing a group of Pension Fund Loans in which Ben Dranow and George Burris appeared to be the principal manipulators and which seemed to be intricately interwoven with the efforts to bail Hoffa out of the Sun Valley situation. Starting with the revelations of Vaughn Connelly about the Pension Fund loans to his Everglades Hotel, the trail led to other loans in the Miami area, in New Orleans, Los

Angeles, St. Louis and New Jersey. The common denominators were false and inflated loan applications, collection of large fees and diversion of funds by the same group of people. There was evidence that some of the diverted funds had been channeled into the Sun Valley bail-out operation of Dranow's Union Land and Home Company.

In Minneapolis Jim Neal was continuing his preparations for the trial of Dranow for bankruptcy fraud scheduled for May 23.

In Georgia Frank Grimsley, our newest recruit, began looking into the Pension Fund loans to the General Ogelthorpe Hotel in Savannah and the Atlanta Cabana Motor Inn. Prior to joining us, Frank had been serving as an Assistant Attorney General for the state of Georgia where he had been instrumental in the conviction of a number of corrupt public officials. He and I had served together as FBI agents in the early fifties.

In spite of these activities, Hoffa went about his daily nonstop business with a new feeling of confidence. What was to be his last appearance before the McClellan Committee was behind him. He had treated the Committee with disdain and no longer felt any fear of it. The Board of Monitors had been scuttled and was off his back. The Sun Valley case had been postponed and his attorneys told him there was a good chance the indictment would be thrown out because of an improper empaneling of the grand jury. He was certain to be overwhelmingly reelected at the Teamsters Convention, now set to open July 3 at the Deauville Hotel in Miami Beach. Each victory increased his aura of indestructibility.

On May 23 Ben Dranow's trial in Minneapolis could not begin because Dranow did not appear. Jim Neal had been out there for almost three months preparing for trial and was ready to go. Dranow sent word at the last minute that he was in a Miami hospital with a heart attack. Neal was very dubious and flew to Miami the next day with a doctor. The government doctor could find no evidence of a heart attack and even Dranow's own doctors would not say that he had suffered one. When Neal so advised the court in Minneapolis, Dranow's bail was revoked, his arrest ordered and provisions made for a doctor to accompany him to Minneapolis just in case. Former United States Attorney Coleman Madsen of Miami then went into federal court on Dranow's behalf and demanded a hearing to determine Dranow's physical ability to travel to Minneapolis for trial. In the meantime, Neal had learned that Dranow had attempted to bribe two nurses to falsify his medical records to show that his blood pressure and pulse were higher than they were. The hearing was held before federal Judge Choate in Miami on June 8. Both of the nurses whom Dranow had tried to bribe and the government doctor testified. The judge ordered Dranow to leave at once for Minneapolis in the company of United States deputy marshals to stand trial.

On May 28, while Dranow was feigning illness in Miami to avoid going to trial, Bert Brennan died of cancer in Detroit at the age of fifty-seven. Hoffa named Frank Fitzsimmons, vice president of Joint Council 43 and Local 299, to replace him as an International vice president.

Just prior to his death, Bert Brennan had co-signed a letter with Harold Gibbons that was sent to the officers of all Teamsters locals soliciting voluntary contributions of $25 each to be used for Hoffa's campaign expenses at the upcoming convention. Contributions were to be sent to the National Committee for Reelection of James R. Hoffa and John F. English in Washington, D.C. English was Hoffa's running mate, seeking a new term as secretary-treasurer of the International. The soliciting letter concluded, "Please be certain to forward the list of names of persons making the contributions."

When the letter was written, Hoffa had no opposition, but in early June Milton Liss, president of Local 478 in Newark, announced that he was going to run against Hoffa at the convention.

In early June I received a telephone call from a Hollywood television and movie actress who was referred to me from the Attorney General's office. She said that a banker friend of hers had told her about a Pension Fund loan being negotiated for the purchase and redecorating of the Whitcomb Hotel in San Francisco. According to her friend, there was a substantial cash kickback involved.

Charlie Shaffer and I flew to Los Angeles, talked to the actress and her friend, and went on to San Francisco to talk to the purchaser, a Mr. Carl Long. He acknowledged that he had applied for a loan of $3,600,000 from the Pension Fund and had received a letter of commitment for $2,333,000. He said that the loan had been arranged by a real estate man named Vincent Corsaro from Scottsdale, Arizona. He denied that there had been any kickback. We called Corsaro, who agreed to meet us in Los Angeles the following day.

Corsaro told us that he had met a man named Morton Fromberg

in a Miami bar a year earlier. During their conversation, Fromberg had told him that he had an uncle who could obtain mortgage loans from a union pension fund if the borrower was willing to pay certain fees. Toward the end of 1960 he encountered Long, who was seeking funds to purchase the Whitcomb Hotel. He contacted Fromberg in Miami, who agreed to meet with him in Phoenix in late January, 1961, if Corsaro would send him $1500 for expenses. Long agreed and the meeting took place in Phoenix attended by Long, his associate Lemuel Stroud, Corsaro and Fromberg. Fromberg said that the requested loan for $3,600,000 could be presented to the Teamsters Pension Fund trustees at their meeting in Miami on February 8 and could probably be obtained if they were willing to pay 12 points—i.e., 12 percent of the loan, 8 percent of which would have to be in cash. It was to be a fifteen-year mortgage at 6 1/2 percent interest. The terms were agreed to. Fromberg told Corsaro that most of the cash would go to Ben Cohen, a Miami attorney. After Fromberg returned to Miami, Corsaro recontacted him to see if the terms of the loan could be changed to provide for a twenty-year mortgage at 6 1/2 percent. Fromberg said that it could be arranged but it would cost another $20,000. Corsaro agreed.

Ben Cohen's name was familiar to me. In the 1940s he had been connected with the S & G Syndicate, a widespread gambling empire which flourished unmolested in the Miami area until it was exposed by the Kefauver Committee. Cohen had more recently represented Teamsters interests in Miami and was a politically powerful figure.

Corsaro said that when he went to Miami to present the loan application to the trustees, Fromberg introduced him to Cohen, who told him how to present the application and what to say. Cohen had even rewritten the pro forma that Corsaro had given to Fromberg. Corsaro presented his application to the trustees and returned to Phoenix. He subsequently received another call from Fromberg who said that it would take another $25,000 to get the loan approved. Again the principals agreed.

In April Cohen and Fromberg delivered a letter of commitment from the fund to Corsaro at the Whitcomb Hotel in San Francisco. A man named Howard "Whitey" Morris, whom Corsaro had previously met in Cohen's office in Miami, also was there. Cohen demanded and received a $10,000 cash payment for expenses and returned to Miami that evening. He left Morris and Fromberg behind to collect $100,000 in cash as the agreed upon down payment on the money owed for arranging the letter of commitment. Two days later Long cashed a check for $100,000, which was turned over to Fromberg, who was to keep $25,000 for himself and "his people" and give the remaining $75,000 to Whitey Morris for Cohen.

Corsaro said that Long made several attempts to obtain interim financing from San Francisco banks based on the letter of commitment from the fund but was unsuccessful. Corsaro thereupon returned to Miami in late May to see if Cohen could assist them. Cohen was not very sympathetic. Cohen said, "If your people don't have enough good credit to get interim financing, it's not our liability, it's not our problem."

Corsaro told Cohen if that were the case, "Why don't you give me back the money, taking out the necessary expenses?"

"What money?" Cohen replied without blinking an eye.

Corsaro was furious and stalked out of the office. Cohen sent after him and suggested he go with Fromberg to talk to another man who might be able to help them. Fromberg took him to a hospital to see Ben Dranow, who was there trying to avoid going to trial in Minneapolis. Dranow listened to the problem but did not offer a solution. Fromberg and Corsaro then returned to Cohen's office where Corsaro was introduced to George Burris.

Cohen said to Burris, "Go tell Ben that there's $75,000 in it for him if he gets the interim financing." He then turned to Corsaro and said. "Your group will have to give $60,000 and I will give $15,000 of my own if Dranow will get the interim financing." Corsaro was speechless and returned to Phoenix.

In early June, just a few days prior to our conversation with Corsaro, Cohen and Fromberg met with Corsaro and Long in Los Angeles to collect the remainder of their "fees." Long made out a check for $100,000 payable to Corsaro. Corsaro cashed it and on Fromberg's instructions brought $51,120 in cash to Ben Cohen in the lobby of the Beverly Hilton Hotel. Fromberg took the rest. Corsaro also gave Fromberg and Cohen each checks for $23,000 payable to the II.M.C. Investment Company, a Cohen-Fromberg enterprise, and gave Cohen checks for $23,330 for legal fees and $28,330 payable to the Pension Fund for service charges.

According to the earlier agreements, Cohen and Fromberg were to receive in cash 8 percent of the loan, which amounted to $186,640, plus the $20,000 and $25,000 payments subsequently agreed to, for a total of $231,640. They were now $21,640 short. Corsaro told Fromberg he would be able to get the rest of the money later that day. Fromberg left and returned with another man whom he introduced to Corsaro only as "Joe." He told Corsaro that Joe would wait in the lobby of the Statler-Hilton Hotel and that Corsaro should give him the balance of the money there. Later that day Corsaro obtained an additional $13,000 in cash from Long and turned it over to Joe as instructed. He told Joe he would give him the remaining $8640 the following day in Phoenix. Two days later he met Joe at the Phoenix airport and gave him the money.

It was a graphic account of how a loan was actually obtained from the Pension Fund. It was obvious that Ben Cohen, like Ben Dranow, had access to the fund and his own satellite of people, and yet there was apparent interplay as evidenced by the Burris-Dranow incident.

Teamsters officials began gathering at the Deauville Hotel in Miami Beach in late June for the convention. By July 1 most of the more than two thousand delegates and their alternates, families and friends were already on the scene and the working committees were well into their respective assignments of preparation. Familiar names could be found on these various task forces. Joey Glimco of Chicago was on the Arrangements Committee. On the Officers' Report Committee were such paragons as Frank Matula of Los Angeles and Bill Presser and Babe Triscaro of Cleveland. (Of the three, Triscaro could be singled out as not having been in jail nearly as recently as the other two.) But the most important committee, from the standpoint of the future of the Teamsters Union, was the Constitution Committee, whose chairman was none other than James R. Hoffa. Also serving on this committee was Tony Provenzano, who held the distinction of being the most recently indicted International vice president. It was this committee that would offer amendments to the constitution that would vastly increase the centralized control of the International in Hoffa's hands, delete provisions that were troublesome to him, add provisions to sanction his improprieties and generally increase and perpetuate his power at the expense of union democracy.

The new constitution increased Hoffa's salary from $50,000 per year to $75,000 and added the provision that "all expenses of the General President and General Secretary-Treasurer shall be paid by the International Union." It also provided that the International would pay all legal expenses and related costs for any International officer who was "charged with any violation or violations of any law or is sued in any civil actions" if a majority of the International Executive Board decided that the charges or suits were "unfounded," "politically motivated," "filed in bad faith" or "if a majority of the General Executive Board in its sole discretion determines that the expenditures should be made."

While increasing Hoffa's salary and legalizing the payment of his considerable attorneys' fees, the new constitution increased the dues to be paid by each Teamsters member by a minimum of one dollar per month and increased the per capita tax that each local must pay to the International from forty cents per member to one dollar per member. The result of the last was to increase the assessment by the International on the locals from $7,000,000 per year to $18,000,000, or more than double.

The problem of the election of delegates to the convention, which had led to the 1957 suit by the rank and file committee and the three-year battle with the Board of Monitors, was solved by merely eliminating it. Henceforth, the elected officers and business agents of local unions would be delegates to a convention and there would be no election of delegates unless the number of officers and business agents was less than the number of delegates to which the local was entitled.

The previous constitution had provided, "The General President shall devote his entire time to the service of the International Union." Because of this provision, the Board of Monitors had challenged Hoffa's right to continue to hold office in Local 299 and other affiliates while serving as general president. This was remedied by the substitution of a new provision which stated, "The General President and the other general officers may hold office in subordinate bodies and render services thereto."

To cover situations where union funds had been placed in non-interest-bearing accounts, a new amendment provided, "Subordinate bodies may keep their money deposited in non-interest-bearing commercial accounts, savings accounts and safety deposit boxes in the name of the subordinate bodies. The subordinate bodies may also invest in property, real and personal."

Punishment of dissident subordinate bodies who refused to obey the directives of the general president formerly rested with the General Executive Board, which could suspend the subordinate or revoke its charter. A new alternative was added with the phrase, "or imposition of Trusteeship by the General President."

The section dealing with grounds for charges against members and officials of the union was also altered to fit the realities of recent difficulties. "Misappropriation of funds," of which Hoffa had been accused, was replaced by the more difficult to prove "embezzlement." Eliminated were "violation of the oath of office," "gross disloyalty or conduct unbecoming a member" and "activities which tend to bring the Local Union or the International Union into disrepute."

So as not to leave anything to chance, the time when the newly elected officials would take office was changed from the traditional December 1 date to "all officers shall be installed on the last day of the Convention."

Inside the convention hall, the new amendments to the constitution were passed one by one. There was isolated vocal resistance to the raise in dues and per capita taxes and the elimination of the election of delegates. But the vast majority of delegates were hellbent on giving Hoffa everything he wanted and getting on with the election. To a question by one delegate on the new provision whereby local union officials would automatically be delegates to the convention, thus eliminating delegate election by the rank and file, Hoffa gave this enlightening answer:

> I believe that the resolution brought about the request for the change in the constitution and speaks for itself, namely, the fact that every rank and file member has a right to run for both an officer's position and as a delegate to a convention; but it gives a coordinated effort so that when they elect an officer or delegate to this convention, they keep in mind that the one elected must have the responsibility and respect to attend conventions, and so we will be in a position to know whether or not those officers coming here, who have to carry out the provisions of this constitution and conduct the affairs of the union, will be able to come here and participate and know what is going on and what brought about this constitution. This will not eliminate them.

When Jim Luken attempted to take the floor, Hoffa interrupted him ten times in a period of four minutes and each time turned off the microphone into which Luken was trying to speak. Hoffa controlled the microphones from the podium. His final interjection was, "All right, I think you've made your statement, brother."

Another dissenter was gaveled quiet by Hoffa with the quip, "You're out of order, brother. Shut up." When another complained that Hoffa's machine dominated the convention, Hoffa moved to strike his remarks from the record. "Hoffa don't have no machine. Now, we'll have no more of that." But one defender of Hoffa's conduct of the convention was quoted as saying, "Never have I witnessed a chairman who allowed more democracy to creep in."

There were speeches by Congressmen Joseph Karth of Minnesota and Alfred Santangelo of New York. There were greetings sent by Congressmen James Roosevelt of California and Roman Pucinski of Illinois. There were more speeches by Joe Curran of the National Maritime Union, Harry Bridges of the ILWU, John Roosevelt of Bache and Company (who handled Teamsters investments) and Edward Bennett Williams.

After the speech by Williams, a resolution was introduced which listed all of the charges and indictments that had been brought against Hoffa. The delegates were then asked for a vote of confidence in Hoff's integrity. The resolution passed with a roaring acclamation.

The elections were at hand and the name of Milton Liss was placed in nomination by Jim Luken of Cincinnati. John English nominated Jimmy Hoffa, calling him "the man with the most guts in America." There followed a fifteen-minute demonstration of bands, bells and horns and the roaring chant of "Hoffa, Hoffa, Hoffa."

Then it was all over. Halfway into the roll call, Milton Liss, with only fifteen votes—six from his own local—withdrew his name from nomination and Hoffa was elected by acclamation.

Hoffa was at the peak of his power—the undisputed president of the largest union in the world, the highest paid union official in the country, with unprecedented personal control over the union's machinery and its members. He was on record with pledges to organize the unorganized regardless of jurisdiction, and to greatly increase the union's political activity by forming "a legislative lobby second to none" and exerting a major influence on the 1964 Presidential election. He was quoted, while at the convention, by Bob Greene of *Newsday* as stating, "Soon young aggressive men will take over the labor movement. I will be with them. And we are going to take over the political party, Democrat or Republican, that loses the 1964 election. I will lead one of the greatest labor political organizations ever formed in this country."

Hoffa also had claimed during the convention that the Kennedys were continuing their vendetta against him, that there were 150 FBI agents trying to infiltrate the convention and that the Justice Department had "dozens" of female agents in town trying to trap the delegates. He said, "These women are mingling with delegates in hotel lobbies, dining rooms and bars, trying to pick them up and get them into situations where they can be forced to divulge things that are the union's private business. Don't get hooked by these Justice Department hookers."

Now, with the convention behind him, Hoffa said that his critics should get lost, that the Kennedys and the Secretary of Labor "ought to recognize now that the time and effort they've put in trying to destroy the Teamsters have completely failed. It was a waste of time." Hoffa also said that the Teamsters Union would be back in the AFL-CIO in the next eighteen months, and if it was not, he would start his own federation. One of his parting shots was, "I may have faults, but being wrong ain't one of them."

I was in Miami during the convention, but not to check on Jimmy Hoffa's election, which was a foregone conclusion. John Cassidy and I went down to check on the progress of our group. None of us went near the convention. While we were in Miami we talked to Ben Cohen's friend Morton Fromberg. He did not tell us much but let enough slip so that we knew that Ben Cohen had been involved in another Pension Fund kickback in connection with a loan to two real estate developers, Sam Eig and John McKeever, in Montgomery County, Maryland, a suburb of Washington.

As the convention was breaking up and the delegates were heading back to their local unions, seven employees of the Everglades Hotel, across the causeways in Miami, were complaining to a reporter from the Miami *Herald* that Hoffa "wants $75,000 a year for himself but his outfit pays coolie wages here." Vaughn Connelly's former hotel had been taken over by the Teamsters Pension Fund when he could not make the payments on his loans. The employees complained that the elevator operators were only making $41.50 per week, the telephone operator $51 and the dishwashers $46. They said, "The Teamsters assumed $30,000 in back wages when they took over last year," but "he doesn't even know we exist."

Hoffa's victory was made even more complete one week after the convention when Judge Joseph P. Lieb in Florida dismissed the Sun Valley indictment on the grounds that the grand jury that had indicted Hoffa had not been properly empaneled.

One of the delegates to the convention was Joey Glimco, the head of Local 777 in Chicago. Like most of the other delegates who shouted and cheered their approval of Hoffa's stewardship and acclaimed his new constitution which gave him a stranglehold on the union, he was Hoffa's guy. It was not easy to gain and keep control of a local union if you were not Hoffa's guy. The new pension for local as well as international officers, which the convention had just approved, would help keep it that way. But Joey Glimco had been losing his grip, and while he was in Miami Beach voting himself a new pension, there was a revolt under way in his local.

Jim Luken, the head of Local 98 in Cincinnati, like a few of the other delegates, was not Hoffa's guy and had managed to hang on to control of his local by sheer guts and the backing of enough of his members. He had placed Milton Liss' name in nomination and voted for him and his had been among the sprinkling of nays that were drowned out in vote after vote. Jim Luken had had enough and was about to start his own revolt.

There were other pockets of unrest throughout the country in some local unions in cities like Los Angeles, St. Louis, Youngstown and Baltimore that belied the image of unanimity contrived at the Deauville Hotel. Teamsters members and some officials in these locals, chafing under a system they considered oppressive, had placed their hope in the McClellan Committee, the Board of Monitors and the courts. Now all these government channels seemed unavailing and open revolt the only answer. Few would succeed.

Hoffa moved quickly to put out the brush fires. He figured if he could put out one right away, the others might lose heart. The most imminent and serious uprising also happened to be where he was considerably obligated, so Hoffa decided to put his newly crowned prestige on the line at the side of Joey Glimco in Chicago. There was no longer any need for pretense about bringing charges against Glimco, as Hoffa had told the court he would under the monitorship. There was no longer any need to make believe he was going to clean up the Teamsters Union, as he had promised both the court and the United States Senate. That was all behind him now, and Joey Glimco, the Mafia's friend, was also his friend and part of his power structure that was being threatened.

Two years earlier, after the McClellan Committee revelations about Glimco, a former official of Local 777, Dominic Abata, had formed within the local the Democratic Union Organizing Committee which sought to change the local's leadership. It took a great deal of courage to be a part of that effort. Glimco's thugs played for keeps and rifle shots through kitchen windows, beatings in dark alleys and other forms of stark intimidation became commonplace. But in spite of it, the DUOC grew in strength and determination as more and more of the cabdrivers from the five-thousand-member local joined its ranks. They fought in the courts for two years seeking a secret election supervised by the National Labor Relations Board and finally got it. For the first time since anyone could remember, rank and file Teamsters were threatening to do what Hoffa would not—throw the racketeers out of office.

Two days before the election Hoffa broke away from negotiating sessions in San Francisco, where he was also having trouble with defiant locals resisting his areawide contract, and flew into Chicago to address a Glimco rally. Those sharing the platform with him included International Vice President John T. O'Brien, Glimco and Barney Baker. The DUOC was advocating that the local disaffiliate from the Teamsters Union and go independent. Hoffa told the assembled four hundred cabdrivers that Joey Glimco had brought them a "better way of life" and urged them to vote for Glimco and the Teamsters Union. He tore up a copy of that day's Chicago *Daily News* and threw the pieces out into the audience, calling it a "lousy stinking newspaper." The paper carried an editorial aimed at Glimco entitled "Throw Out the Thugs." Hoffa acknowledged that both Glimco and Oscar Kofkin, the vice president of the local, had at one time been indicted for murder, but said that neither had been convicted. Also at the rally was Gus Zapas, who had left his positions with the Teamsters and Bartenders unions in Indianapolis after the McClellan Committee hearings, and was now conveniently the head of Local 46 of the Laundry Workers in Chicago. This was the same racket local that Jimmy James had once headed after he left his Jukebox local in Detroit. The times and scenes changed but the same cast of characters kept showing up. Zapas was arrested by Chicago police when he left the meeting, and Abata charged that Hoffa was importing ex-convicts to terrorize the members.

On July 19 the members of Local 777 voted overwhelmingly to oust Glimco, leave the Teamsters Union and go independent. In his first test since Miami Beach, Hoffa had put his prestige on the line and he lost. Back in San Francisco the following day he blamed Senator Paul Douglas of Illinois, who had supported the DUOC, for the defeat. Hoffa told reporters, "Senator Douglas must hold himself responsible for destroying a well founded Teamsters Union. He stuck his nose in the election and campaigned for the Independent." Hoff said that he would attempt to reorganize the Teamsters local. In Chicago Dominic Abata, who had been under around-the-clock protection by the Chicago police because of a series of threats, called the election "a crack in the dam."

Abata's observation apppeared accurate in the weeks that followed as the firing of his successful challenge ricocheted off several walls of Hoffa's empire. Members of Local 85 in San Francisco booed down a proposal that Hoffa be invited to speak at their meeting to advocate their acceptance of the latest trucking association offer in the bogged-down negotiations. There was considerable suspicion that Hoffa was covertly guiding the strategy of the trucking association in his desperate bid to put together a western areawide contract. There were growing indications that Local 85 and Local 70, the two largest Bay area locals, might lead the majority of the membership of Joint Council 7 out of the Teamsters Union. In St. Louis members of cabdrivers' Local 405, following Abata's lead, voted to disaffiliate from the Teamsters. A shattering blow to Hoffa was struck in Cincinnati, where four thousand of Jim Luken's followers in four local unions voted in open meetings to break away from the Teamsters Union. Harold Gibbons spoke in vain to a packed meeting of 1791 members of Luken's own Local 98 trying to persuade them not to make the break. When the vote was taken, it was 1789 to 2 for leaving the Teamsters Union.

` Luken then petitioned for an NLRB-supervised election to finalize the defection, while at the same time preserving the contractual rights of the locals. George Meany issued a statement supporting Luken and said, "I am confident that in this election these rank and file workers will vote overwhelming to free themselves from the gangster domination of the Teamsters International Union." Hoffa reacted swiftly and angrily. He ordered the assets of the four locals frozen, only to find that Luken and his attorneys had long since placed the assets in trust accounts out of the reach of the International. "The cupboard is bare as far as Jimmy Hoffa is concerned," Luken said. Gibbons accused Luken of mishandling the union's funds. Luken sent a telegram to Secretary of Labor Arthur Goldberg inviting the Labor Department to audit the funds. Hoffa fired off a three-hundred-word telegram to a hundred AFL-CIO unions urging them to repudiate Meany's statement. He challenged Luken to a debate in Cincinnati. Luken agreed but stated, "What's there to debate? The unions have left the Teamsters. They're gone and talk sure won't bring them back. But if he wants to do it, I'll be glad to please Mr. Hoffa."

While Hoffa was thus occupied on several fronts, fighting to hold his union together, other pressures were building. In Washington Secretary of Labor Goldberg challenged Hoffa's figures of increasing membership and said that reports filed with the Labor Department showed that the membership of the Teamsters Union had actually declined under Hoffa's leadership. In Minneapolis Ben Dranow was convicted on eighteen counts of fraud, sentenced to seven years in prison, fined $12,000 and freed on $50,000 bond pending appeal. In Detroit Henry Lower, Hoffa's co-defendant in the recently dismissed Sun Valley case, was indicted for income tax evasion and died three weeks later of cancer.

In Cincinnati the Fifth Circuit Court of Appeals ruled that the Labor Department had the right under the Landrum-Griffin Act to subpoena the records of Local 299 in Detroit. Detroit federal Judge Fred Kaess had ruled earlier that the Labor Department's subpoena was a "fishing expedition."

The Hoffa-Luken debate got under way in Cincinnati on Sunday afternoon of August 27. By that time, Hoffa had forty-one of his lieutenants in town at the Gibson Hotel. Luken led off the debate, tracing his difficulties with the International back to 1954 and up to the present when "the Teamsters International, in my opinion, has thence gone into the position of being controlled by one man. Frankly I don't agree with that one man or that small group of people's ideas of unionism." With reference to the influx of Hoffa's outsiders, Luken said, "Now, we do not feel that our action should have caused this mass invasion, for this mass invasion we do somewhat reluctantly apologize to this community."

Hoffa responded that the International "is not fighting the question of the membership that previously was represented by Luken.

Rather we are in here in a legal position." He said that under the constitution the assets ánd books of local unions that disaffiliate must be turned over to the general president. Hoffa contended that for a number of years Luken "repeatedly refused to carry out the mandates of the constitution," and that "the organizers who are in here are in here because of the large area necessary to be covered. An all-experienced, well-organized campaign will be placed on the streets, TV, radio, the press, to tell the members of the trick that has been played upon him."

When the debate was opened to questions from the press, Hoffa denied that the Cincinnati disaffiliation represented a national trend. "There are a few self-seeking leaders who are attempting to mislead their members into independent unions."

When asked to explain his ideological differences with Hoffa, Luken said he believed that

> the control of the local unions should be vested within its member-
> ship . . . [from] even a cursory study of the current International
> Constitution as opposed to that of 1952, for example, you will find
> that the powers of the International Union, for example, go to the
> point where it goes to state, "If the General President has informa-
> tion that leads him to believe . . ." he may go ahead and do some
> things. Well, some of the things he may do is impose a trusteeship
> upon a local union . . . all officers are removed, and they have no
> appeal except right back to Mr. Hoffa and right back to a committee
> appointed by him.

Hoffa responded that unless Luken was doing something wrong, he should have no fear of trusteeship. He said that Luken, by his own admission, had defied the International for six years but had not been subjected to trusteeship.

When Hoffa was asked to explain the overwhelming vote for disaffiliation by Luken's local, he compared Luken to Khrushchev and said that Harold Gibbons had been prevented from addressing the local because Luken was "afraid of the truth."

Luken pointed out that this was not true; that Gibbons had spoken to the local meeting for ten minutes without interruption and that another vote was taken thereafter, which was the same as the previous vote. Luken compared this to the Teamsters Convention where he had been interrupted by Hoffa ten times in four minutes when he tried to speak.

Luken then pointed out that there were two margarine companies in Cincinnati, one with a contract negotiated by his local, the other with a contract signed in Detroit. He said the one negotiated by his local had an hourly wage scale that was one dollar higher than the other one. In addition, the bakery drivers covered by the Detroit contract had been promised a five-day week four years earlier but were still working six-day sixty-hour weeks.

After the debate Hoffa spoke to a less than half-capacity crowd at the Cincinnati Music Hall and pleaded against splintering of the union. Luken went on television and said that the decision to revolt had been made only after giving up all hope for reform within the Teamsters Union.

> We love and still do the tradition, the institution of the Teamsters Union. We could not believe that any one man through money, connivery, press agent magic could capture this history, and tradition, and convert them to his own private instrument of personal power or wealth.

Hoffa left Cincinnati that night to return to his negotiations with the balky Teamsters on the West Coast. Before leaving, he said, "We will do everything to bring this story to the membership. We will spend as much time and money as necessary." He left Gibbons and his cadres of outside organizers behind for an all-out effort to woo back Luken's members.

Another large-scale rebellion that posed a serious threat to Hoffa's control in the East was under way in Philadelphia. It had actually been in progress for almost four years but had been, for the most part, ineffective. As in Cincinnati, the members had watched and waited, hoping that the revelations before the McClellan Committee of wholesale looting of the union treasury by Ray Cohen and his associates would be dealt with from within by the Board of Monitors and from without by criminal prosecution. By mid-1961 all corrective efforts seemed to have been frustrated and the uprising erupted and spread dramatically. A history of events leading up to trigger point clearly demonstrates how Hoffa, who had used his office, the Teamsters constitution and chicanery to attempt to crush his enemy Jim Luken, employed the same instruments to protect his friend Ray Cohen, an embezzler of union funds.

Following the disclosures by the McClellan Committee, a group of members of Teamsters Local 107 had formed a Betterment Committee under Jim Laughlin, and filed charges against Ray Cohen. Shortly thereafter, Martin O'Donoghue wrote a letter to Harold Gibbons, as an Order of Recommendation from the Board of Monitors, in which he recommended that charges be preferred against Cohen and his associates; that a panel be set up in accordance with the Teamsters constitution to conduct trusteeship proceedings; and that Price Waterhouse be authorized to review the records of Local 107 and the McClellan Committee and that the results thereof be presented to the hearing panel. Secretary-Treasurer John English agreed with the Board of Monitors that the local should be placed in trusteeship and testified before the McClellan Committee that the International was going to step in.

Two months later Price Waterhouse submitted to the monitors a sixty-nine-page report substantiating most of the McClellan Committee charges and enclosed photostatic copies of forged checks and other evidence of embezzlement. Martin O'Donoghue forwarded the report to Hoffa on September 2, 1958, and recommended that charges be filed by September 15, in accordance with the Teamsters constitution, and a hearing conducted by October 1.

On September 8 Hoffa sent Ray Cohen a copy of the report and O'Donoghue's letter, thus giving Cohen all of the evidence against him, and said that a panel would be in Philadelphia on September 11 to "conduct the preliminary investigation." Hoffa's actions were in direct violation of the Teamsters constitution, which provided that "adequate notice at least ten days prior to the date of the hearing shall be given to the local. . . ." Hoffa's violation enabled Cohen to obtain a temporary restraining order to prevent the panel from proceeding. The petition for the restraining order had actually been signed two months earlier, a further documentation of the apparent conspiracy of inaction. The process was further delayed by related appeals by Hoffa which dragged on for over a year.

On September 19, 1959, Cohen and six others were indicted through the action of the District Attorney of Philadelphia for conspiracy to cheat and defraud.

It was not until May, 1960, that Hoffa sent another panel to Philadelphia to conduct a hearing. This time the hearing was held, but it was not Cohen and his associates who were on trial, it was the rank and file members who had brought the charges against him. The Price Waterhouse report was not introduced, the offer of one of the firm's representatives to assist and testify was ignored and neither Cohen nor any other official of Local 107 was called to testify. The hearing was a complete whitewash.

Shortly thereafter, Martin O'Donoghue and John Cassidy went to the International headquarters. O'Donoghue told Harold Gibbons, who had been on the hearing panel, that he did not approve of the way the hearing had been handled. According to O'Donoghue, Gibbons replied, "We've run too long with the hares to start running with the hounds." O'Donoghue then said that Hoffa, who was also present, had a constitutional duty to have the Price Waterhouse material placed before the panel. Hoffa replied, "I know my constitutional duty and you needn't tell me what it is. I know how the hearing should be conducted and that's final."

By May, 1961, when the election of delegates for the Teamsters Convention was scheduled in Local 107, nothing had changed. The Betterment Committee had petitioned in court for the right to review the records of the local but had thus far been stymied. Another group of members of the local decided to act. They ran a slate of their own against Cohen's nominees for delegates to the convention. They did not win but they came close. Encouraged by the show of strength, they formed an organization called The Voice of Teamsters Local 107. As members of other locals joined their ranks, they changed the name to The Voice of the Teamsters Democratic Organizing Committee, and became more commonly known as The Voice.

The leaders of The Voice were Charlie Meyers and Frank Grimm. There was some mistrust between the Betterment Committee and The Voice, partially because Grimm, who had been one of the original members of the Betterment Committee, had admitted publicly that he had been a spy on the committee for Ray Cohen but now claimed he was completely disillusioned with Cohen. The target of both groups was Cohen and his cohorts rather than Hoffa, but The Voice applied for an AFL-CIO charter and there was no question that their combined efforts were a serious threat to Hoffa's East Coast hegemony.

In mid-July, 1961, the Pennsylvania Supreme Court finally ruled on the suit brought by the Betterment Committee and held that the rank and file members of Local 107 had a right to an accounting by Cohen and other local officials of the expenditure of union funds. In August a group of Local 107 members in nearby Wilmington, Delaware, formed a third organization called Teamsters

Committee for Labor Reform, which was allied with the Betterment Committee. The new group filed suit in federal court in Wilmington challenging the appointment by Cohen of business agents and stewards and calling for an election for these offices.

The Betterment Committee and its Wilmington ally, while not drawing significant popular support from the members, were nevertheless having an effect in the courts. The Voice, on the other hand, was more openly aggressive in soliciting members and in early September drew fifteen hundred to a rally in northeast Philadelphia in an impressive show of strength.

While The Voice was meeting in Philadelphia, Hoffa was in Los Angeles. He had put down the revolt in San Francisco and reached a tentative contract agreement with almost the same terms as were first offered by the trucking association. Now he ran into a hornets' nest of angry resistance from Local 208 in Los Angeles in spite of the fact that the local was under the control of Hoffa's lieutenants Sidney Cohen and Frank Matula. When Hoffa attempted to read the terms of the proposed contract for the Los Angeles area to a meeting of the local, he was interrupted repeatedly by boos and shouts of "sellout." At one point he was unable to bring order to the unruly meeing for over five minutes. Some members climbed up onto the platform where Hoffa was speaking during the melee. Finally about one thousand members walked out. Those remaining voted 800 to 150 against Hoffa's proposed contract. At Hoffa's instructions, newsmen were barred from the meeting but a *Los Angeles Times* reporter had sneaked in. When he was discovered some five hours later, he was threatened with violence and thrown out.

In spite of the opposition by Locals 85 and 70 in San Francisco, and Local 208 in Los Angeles, under the new constitution Hoffa needed only the support of a majority of the 104 locals in the western states to make the areawide contract binding on all locals. This he had. Petitions began circulating in Locals 208 and 357, another hotbed of resistance, for the purpose of withdrawing from the Teamsters Union. Some men circulating the petitions were threatened and beaten up. In a Hoffa countermove spearheaded by International Vice President George Mock and International organizers Jack Goldberger and Jim Harding petitions asking that Local 208 be placed in trusteeship were circulated. Some members signed this petition thinking that it was the one seeking withdrawal from the Teamsters Union. In late September Local 208 was placed in trusteeship by Hoffa with Jim Harding serving as administrator. Hoffa had won the battle of the West.

So on top of the Labor Department charge that Hoffa's membership figures were inflated, thousands of Teamsters members were threatening to disaffiliate. Hoffa stalled the exodus by delaying NLRB elections through litigation and barreled forward with his promised expansionist moves. Organizing drives were under way among professional athletes and racing car drivers. The Teamsters continued to make inroads in the airline industry. On September 14 the Teamsters Union signed a pact with the Mine, Mill and Smelter Workers Union, which had been ousted by the AFL-CIO for being Communist-dominated. Hoffa appeared before the convention of the Transportation Workers Union and pleaded his case for the readmission of the Teamsters into the AFL-CIO. Mike Quill, the union president, promised his support at the AFL-CIO Executive Council meeting scheduled for October 9 in New York City. To hedge his bet, in case the parent body turned him down, Hoffa began moving quietly toward a possible merger of the expelled Laundry Workers and Bakery Workers with the Teamsters.

As the AFL-CIO meeting approached, there was increased speculation that a new charter might be issued for a rival Teamsters Union as had been done in the cases of the Laundry Workers and Bakery Workers. The Communication Workers of America passed a resolution urging such a course of action, and Joe Beirne, the president of the union, announced his intention to introduce it at the Executive Council meeting. It was acknowledged in labor circles that a separate charter would mean open war and invite massive raiding by the Hoffa Teamsters. A public statement critical of Hoffa by Secretary of Labor Arthur Goldberg a week before the AFL-CIO meeting implied to some that there was government approval and support for a separate charter.

When the AFL-CIO Executive Council met at the Commodore Hotel, Joseph Curran, president of the National Maritime Union, submitted a resolution by Mike Quill of the Transportation Workers Union urging the readmission of the Teamsters Union. The vote against the resolution was 24 to 3. Only David McDonald of the Steelworkers and A. Philip Randolph of the Sleeping Car Porters joined with Curran in the vote. After the vote George Meany told reporters that the Teamsters Union appeared to be even more dominated by corrupt and criminal elements than it had been when expelled four years earlier. Meany had no comment on the possibility of issuing a new charter. In Portland, Oregon, when he was advised of the refusal of the AFL-CIO to readmit the Teamsters, Hoffa was reported to have said, "Who asked 'em?"

Jim Dowd and his group went back to Orlando to begin working with a newly empaneled grand jury, looking toward the probable reindictment of Hoffa on the Sun Valley charges, and on October 11 Hoffa and Robert McCarthy, the Detroit banking executive, were reindicted for fraud in connection with the Sun Valley project.

On October 23 the Supreme Court agreed to review Bill Presser's conviction for obstruction of justice in the Cleveland case involving the mutilated "champagne master" invoice. On the same day Hoffa filed a $1,000,000 libel and slander suit against George Meany and twenty-four other top officials of the AFL-CIO, charging them with trying to steal away members of the Teamsters Union. A few days earlier Meany had met with Jim Luken in Washington and announced that a charter would be issued by the AFL-CIO to Luken. Meany described the Hoffa suit as "the funniest thing I have heard of in a long time."

The AFL-CIO charter was issued to Jim Luken by Meany in a ceremony at AFL-CIO headquarters in Washington on November 3. Luken said that he and his members were happy and gratified to be back in the AFL-CIO.

Bob Kennedy asked Jim Neal to begin working with Jim Dowd on the Sun Valley case and also to research the Test Fleet case, which the McClellan Committee had developed, to determine whether prosecution should be brought.

Neal joined Dowd in Orlando on November 14 where government and defense attorneys were assembled for a review of documents. One of the pretrial motions filed by Hoffa called for a suppression of evidence derived from electronic eavesdropping. The government had no such evidence but Hoffa's motion was a preview of the bizarre drama about to unfold. On the morning of November 15 Hoffa attorney James E. Haggerty went to his room in the San Juan Hotel in Orlando accompanied by another Hoffa attorney, William Bufalino. Haggerty, a white-haired, conservative gentleman from Detroit who had formerly headed the Michigan Bar Association, was referred to by some of Hoffa's associates as "the bishop." While he and Bufalino were in the room, Haggerty noticed a small black box attached to the foot of his bedside table. The next thing Jim Dowd knew someone was pounding on the door of his room on the floor above and yelling that everyone should immediately get out of the hotel. Haggerty had called the police and reported that there was a box that looked like a bomb in his room and the police had ordered the hotel evacuated. All the occupants ran out and gathered in the street while police and firemen rushed into the building.

The assistant fire chief, using a mattress as a shield, cautiously approached the little box and cut the wires leading to the bedside table. A police lieutenant then carefully opened the box. What he found inside was not a bomb but a wireless transmitter which was not operative because the power source was not connected.

The charges that followed were predictable. Hoffa and his attorneys claimed that the government had installed the device to listen in, from their rooms right upstairs, on Hoffa's attorneys discussing the defense strategy. The fact that the respectable Haggerty had been its victim added to both credibility and outrage. The government attorneys, of course, vehemently denied having anything to do with the device, as indeed they had not. But I am sure that James Haggerty to his dying day thought we had. He was still making references to the incident in speeches three years later as an example of our outlandish tactics. The fact is that the device was planted there, unbeknownst to Haggerty, by Hoffa's wiretapper, Bernard Spindel.

The following day in New York Hoffa charged that there were twenty-nine special grand juries around the country out to get him, and that half of the attorneys in the Department of Justice and half the agents in the FBI were involved in the effort. There were, in fact, at the time thirteen grand juries which either were or had been receiving testimony in connection with Hoffa or his associates. Seven of these were obtaining information about the far-flung Pension Fund loans. Five of the other six either had returned indictments against Hoffa or his associates or would before the year was out. There were sixteen attorneys, including Dowd's group of four, and perhaps thirty FBI agents around the country involved in these activities.

In late November Teamsters officials met with leaders of the Ku Klux Klan in the South in connection with strategy for the trial of the Sun Valley case in Orlando. The Klan leaders promised to cooperate and asked in turn if Hoffa could help them in bringing dissident Klan elements into line.

On December 1 Barney Baker, having exhausted his appeals, surrendered in Pittsburgh and was sent to the federal penitentiary in Sandstone, Minnesota, to begin serving his two-year sentence.

On December 6 the AFL-CIO Convention opened in Miami Beach at the Americana Hotel. Hoffa and the Teamsters International Executive Board were meeting at the same time at the Eden Rock Hotel fifty blocks away. The Building and Construction Trades Department of the AFL-CIO passed a resolution that consideration be given to any union that applied for readmission if it could show that it was in compliance with the constitution, laws, rules, standards and policies of the AFL-CIO. Hoffa told reporters that he would have to know what some of the standards and policies meant before he would apply for readmission.

While Hoffa was in Miami Beach, his accountant in Detroit, Herbert Grosberg, who also served as the chief accountant for the Detroit Teamsters organizations, quit. Hoffa told reporters that Grosberg had quit "because he couldn't stand the constant harassment by Bobby Kennedy." But Grosberg stated publicly that he quit because Hoffa wanted him to violate the law by turning over all of his accounting papers to him.

CHAPTER VII

The "Improvers"

ON NEW YEAR'S DAY IN 1962 Jim Luken in Cincinnati received a telephone call from a man in Baton Rouge who identified himself as E. G. Partin, the head of Teamsters Union Local 5 in that city. Partin made reference to Luken's successful disaffiliation from the Teamsters and said that he and his local were considering doing the same thing. He told Luken that Hoffa, Harold Gibbons and Dusty Miller, the head of the Southern Conference of Teamsters, were "breathing down my neck." He described a meeting he had with Hoffa three weeks earlier in Miami when he complained that "stooges" of Dusty Miller's had filed charges against him in the Joint Council. According to Partin, Hoffa told him to keep his mouth shut and everything would turn out all right. Partin quoted Hoffa as saying, "I have seven or eight guys around the country who know how to shut people's mouths. Sometimes it looks like an accident but their mouths are shut." Partin told Luken he had taken this as a threat.

Partin also said that the previous year he had paid a solicited bribe of $5000 to a New Orleans NLRB attorney to fix NLRB elections. When he took the matter up with Hoffa, he said, Hoffa had approved the deal and given him the $5000 in cash at the Shoreland Hotel in Chicago to pass on.

Luken had never heard of Partin and did not even know if he was who he said he was. He thought the information was significant, however, so he called John Cassidy that evening and related the conversation. Coincidentally, the FBI in Baton Rouge had already begun an investigation of Edward Grady Partin based on allegations of two dissident members of his local, J. D. Albin and A. G. Klein, Jr. Partin was indeed the head of Local 5, and was considered a close associate of Hoffa's. Frank Grimsley of our group and Peter Duffy, an Assistant United States Attorney in New Orleans, were overseeing the investigation. I furnished the information Luken had provided to Grimsley. FBI agents in Baton Rouge told Grimsley that Partin had been uncooperative in the past, so no attempt was made at that time to contact him directly.

Grimsley was also in touch with Sargent Pitcher, the District Attorney of East Baton Rouge Parish, and his chief investigator, William Hawk Daniels, who had been conducting their own investigation of Partin. Pitcher had defeated Partin's attorney, Osie Brown, in the last election for District Attorney. Daniels was a veteran investigator as well as an attorney, having served behind enemy lines with Military Intelligence during World War II. On January 23, 1962, Partin was indicted by Pitcher's grand jury on the charge of forging the name of a Local 5 member on a union withdrawal card.

By mid-December, 1961, Jim Neal had completed his research of the Test Fleet case and had concluded that it was a clear-cut violation of the Taft-Hartley Act, in that Hoffa and Bert Brennan had apparently received hundreds of thousands of dollars through the Test Fleet Company (later the Hobren Corporation), which had been set up for them in their wives' maiden names by the Commercial Carriers Corporation of Flint, Michigan. Although the original conspiracy was thirteen years old, Neal determined that it had continued until March, 1958, when the arrangement had finally been canceled under pressure from the McClellan Committee and the Board of Monitors. The decision was made to proceed with a combined grand jury and FBI investigation to further determine the advisability of prosecution. Since Test Fleet had originally been incorporated in Nashville and corporate reports had been filed there as late as June, 1957, it was decided to conduct the grand jury inquiry in that city. Jim Neal and Charlie Shaffer would conduct the investigation.

Bob Kennedy also asked Tom Sheridan, who headed the Organized Crime Section in the United States Attorney's office in Los Angeles, to review the State Cab case, which the FBI had been investigating, to determine whether a perjury indictment should be brought against Hoffa for testifying before the McClellan Committee that he had no financial interest in the company other than the $8000 loan from the Hobren Corporation. Tom Sheridan immediately asked the FBI to conduct an all-out investigation to try to locate David Probstein.

In early February Shaffer and Neal went to Nashville to begin the grand jury investigation of Test Fleet. Jim Durkin, a young attorney in the Organized Crime Section, was loaned to us to go with Shaffer and Neal to Nashville to help with research "for a few weeks." Because of unforeseen events, Durkin's "temporary" assignment in Tennessee lasted two years.

Meanwhile, open warfare had broken out between Paul Hall, the president of the Seafarers International Union, and Jimmy Hoffa. Hall, who had called Hoffa a "fink" at the AFL-CIO Convention in December, threw down the gauntlet when he issued an SIU charter to Dominic Abata's forty-five hundred breakaway cabdrivers in Chicago on January 18. That afternoon Hall attended a meeting of Abata and his stewards at the Hamilton Hotel to celebrate the new affiliation. After the meeting the group stopped in at the cocktail lounge in the hotel. Abata was accompanied, as he had been for some time because of threats against his life, by two Chicago police detectives. A group of about twenty Glimco loyalists had gathered outside the hotel to picket the meeting. One of them came into the cocktail lounge and started shouting at Abata and Hall. One of the detectives identified himself and asked the man to leave. He responded by taking a swing at the detective. The detectives arrested the man and proceeded to escort him out of the hotel. When they reached the sidewalk the pickets converged on them and one of them struck one of the detectives. Abata and Hall came out of the hotel to render assistance and a swinging brawl ensued. A squad of uniformed police arrived on the scene, broke up the melee and arrested some of Glimco's men, as well as Abata and Hall.

The feud quickly spread to Philadelphia where, two weeks later, Hoffa issued a Teamsters charter to a group of SIU defectors headed by Stephen "Blackie" Cardullo, a former national director of the Seafarers Union. The mutual raiding struggle promised to continue, with Hoffa stating that the Teamsters were going to attempt to sign up all of the SIU members in the Philadelphia area. Hall shot back by calling Hoffa "the greatest enemy of the American labor movement."

Stepping up his activities in the political arena, Hoffa set up a Ladies Auxiliary to DRIVE "(the political education arm of the

teamsters)" headed by his wife Josephine. Together they made a
sweep through the South for a series of DRIVE rallies and "Jo
Hoffa dinners," issuing new charters for DRIVE and the Ladies
Auxiliary.

Hoffa also announced plans for a new nationwide organizing
drive to recruit new members for the Teamsters Union. He said
he intended to concentrate on the many small nonunion companies outside the trucking industry and would personally lead the
drive. Although he vowed not to raid other AFL-CIO unions unless they raided the Teamsters first, Hoffa said that if workers
organized by other unions were dissatisfied with their representation and approached the Teamsters, they would be welcomed. The
Bakery Workers Union, which had also been expelled from the
AFL-CIO and which Hoffa had been wooing to affiliate with the
Teamsters, voted on January 24 to remain independent and to
neither merge with the Teamsters nor seek reaffiliation with the
AFL-CIO. But Hoffa continued to seek a merger with the expelled
Laundry Workers Union, and on March 5 a special convention of
that union, meeting in Chicago, voted to merge with the Team-
sters Union.

A hearing on pending motions in the Sun Valley case was scheduled for March 12 in Tampa. Prior to the hearing, Hoffa subpoenaed Secretary of Labor Goldberg, Senator McClellan, Bob
Kennedy, Jerry Adlerman, John Seigenthaler and various others,
including postal inspectors, FBI agents, members of the press and
former Department of Justice officials. On March 9 Judge Leib
quashed most of the subpoenas after a four-hour hearing in which
Hoffa's attorneys argued that they hoped to show through these
witnesses that the atmosphere had been poisoned against Hoffa
and that the evidence for his indictment had been obtained by
McClellan Committee wiretaps. One of the subpoenas not quashed
was that of Eddie Jones, a former member of the McClellan Committee staff. When Jones appeared at the March 12 hearing he
declined to answer the questions of Hoffa's attorneys about his
activities while with the Committee since he was precluded from
doing so by a recently passed Senate resolution. Judge Leib upheld
the validity of Jones' position. Hoffa's attorneys argued that they
hoped to show through Jones that wiretap evidence had been used
in the indictment. Jim Dowd assured the court that no evidence
had been obtained through wiretapping, but Jones' refusal to testify, even though in conformity with the Senate resolution, gave
propaganda ammunition to Hoffa's charge that Senator McClellan

and Jones were taking the Fifth Amendment.

On the evening of March 23 I was having dinner with my wife at Goldie Ahearn's Restaurant in Washington when I received a call from Al McGrath of the FBI. He told me that they had found David Probstein in Sacramento, California, where he was living under the name of Donald Weber and working for the California legislature. I called Bob Kennedy, who was in Los Angeles with the President, and he suggested that Carmine Bellino and I fly out to the Coast to confer with Tom Sheridan and the FBI agents handling the case. Carmine and I left for Los Angeles late that night. The following morning we went with Tom Sheridan to meet with Bob Kennedy at his hotel. We discussed the case and then Tom, Carmine and I flew up to Sacramento and talked to the FBI agents who had found Probstein. He had readily acknowledged his identity and agreed to cooperate with them. They had already started talking to him and had established good rapport. I was anxious to talk with the man I had sought for four years but decided it could wait a little longer.

David Probstein subsequently told Tom Sheridan about the formation of the State Cab Company and his abrupt disappearance. He said he had gone to Detroit in early January, 1954, with Gene San Soucie and they had met with Bert Brennan. The three of them discussed the idea of forming a cab company and Brennan was told that it would take $20,000 to get it started. According to Probstein, Brennan agreed to get the money and called his wife and Hoffa's wife and told them he was going to bring checks out for them to sign. There was also a discussion as to how the cab company could be formed without showing Hoffa and Brennan as principals.

Probstein and San Soucie then left Brennan's office and waited in the hallway. About an hour later Brennan gave San Soucie two checks, each in the amount of $10,000, drawn on the account of the Test Fleet Company. One was made out to Hoffa's wife, in her maiden name, and endorsed by her. The other was made out to Brennan's wife, in her maiden name, and also endorsed. San Soucie turned the checks over to Probstein and said, "If anything goes wrong with this money, it's trouble."

Probstein said that he and San Soucie then returned to Indianapolis. He took the two checks, endorsed them, "David Probstein, trustee," and deposited them in an account bearing that name at the Fidelity Bank and Trust Company. He then wrote a check for $17,500 on the account and opened the State Cab account.

Then he wrote a check for $12,000 on the State Cab account, cashed the check and used the money as a bribe to obtain twelve cab licenses.

In late January, 1954, Probstein continued, he went to Miami Beach at San Soucie's direction to meet Hoffa. He said that San Soucie picked him up at the Carousel Hotel where he was staying and took him to another hotel where Hoffa was staying. They had coffee with Hoffa in the dining room of the hotel and San Soucie explained how the cab company was being set up.

In April, 1954, according to Probstein, he needed additional funds to purchase cabs and radio equipment. He contacted San Soucie who told him to get in touch with Brennan. He called Brennan in Detroit and told him he needed $8000 for the equipment. He said that Brennan told him to come to his home the following Saturday. He went to Brennan's home as instructed and explained why he needed the additional money. Brennan told him he would let him know and Probstein returned to Indianapolis.

Shortly thereafter, San Soucie gave Probstein an $8000 check drawn on the account of the Hobren Corporation. Probstein signed a note and considered the money a loan to the company. He had not signed a note for the original $20,000.

Probstein said that in the fall of 1954 Hoffa came to the Aldor Insurance office, which was located in the same building as the cab company, accompanied by San Soucie and Gus Zapas. Hoffa asked Probstein how the cab company was doing and Probstein indicated that it was not doing too well. He went on to explain to Tom Sheridan how in mid-December, 1954, he was locked out of the cab company by San Soucie and had nothing more to do with its operation. Shortly thereafter, San Soucie told him to sell the company. He said that one of the purchaser's conditions was that the contract with Local 135 be canceled. Probstein said the contract had never been enforced and San Soucie agreed to cancel it.

Things went from bad to worse and Probstein's debts became insurmountable. In May, 1955, unable to face the situation any longer, he decided to disappear.

In Washington Hoffa minimized the Sun Valley case and predicted that he would be found innocent. "Nobody got defrauded out of a quarter. So where's the problem?" Hoffa quipped. "Stories about the Orlando case make it look like Hoffa put $500,000 in his kick. Which ain't bad if you can do it, but I didn't," he added in an interview with newsmen. He also accused Bob Kennedy of spending millions of dollars of government money in pursuit of a vendetta against him. The Teamsters Union was in good shape, he claimed, and had $1,000,000,000 in assets.

In Des Moines two weeks later Hoffa said that he still considered President Kennedy too inexperienced for his office and the Attorney General unfit for his job and "acting like a little hoodlum."

Later, in Chicago, Hoffa threatened to send one thousand unemployed Teamsters from forty-three locals to drive taxicabs and break a strike which Dominic Abata had called against the cab companies. The two-day strike ended when the companies signed a contract with Abata's newly affiliated local. But three Teamsters cabdrivers, claiming to be acting on their own, filed suit in federal court to set aside the contract. They were represented by Jacques Schiffer, the New York attorney who had represented John Cunningham and funneled money to him through Moss Herman after Cunningham broke with the rank and file committee in the monitor situation.

Following an appearance in court with his new clients, Schiffer told newsmen that Robert Kennedy was responsible for the defection of the cabdrivers to Abata and the Seafarers Union. "By the time we finish this case, there will be a complete unearthing of the Boston bully boy," Schiffer said. He declared they would subpoena Kennedy to appear at a hearing and show "to whom he gave orders and how they came down the line."

Schiffer's out-of-courtroom diatribe continued during the hearings and finally came to the attention of Judge Julius Miner. The judge castigated Schiffer and threatened him with "severe disciplinary measures" if it happened again: "I am perturbed by the conduct of Attorney Jacques Schiffer outside of my courtroom after every session, resorting to flagrant and vile soapbox oratory before television cameras, radio apparatus, representatives of the press, and groups of his followers. . . . Such loose chatter and irresponsible propaganda is obnoxious to this court and is degrading to the legal profession."

Back in Washington Bob Kennedy called a meeting in his office one evening to determine where things stood in relation to Hoffa and to make some decisions. In the Sun Valley case, Judge Leib had taken the results of the March hearing under advisement. Neal and Shaffer had completed their grand jury investigation and had submitted a prosecutive memorandum which concluded that there was sufficient evidence to indict and prosecute Hoffa in Nashville in the Test Fleet case. Based on the information furnished by David Probstein and the investigation thus far, Tom Sheridan concluded that there was no question that Hoffa had committed perjury in the State Cab case when he denied having any interest in State Cab other than the $8000 loan from the Hobren Corporation. But since at the time of Hoffa's testimony in 1958 Bob Kennedy had the two additional $10,000 checks in his possession and did not show them to Hoffa, there were legal precedents by which a challenge might be made to the materiality of the questions and Hoffa's false answers. Charlie Smith, reporting on the Pension Fund investigations, said that the evidence was continuing to accumulate showing that a series of loans had been made by the fund, through Hoffa's influence, which involved false and inflated applications and diversion of funds, some of which were for the purpose of bailing Hoffa out of the Sun Valley situation. In short, Hoffa had fraudulently used the Pension Fund to undo what he had fraudulently done with union funds in the Sun Valley case.

After much discussion Kennedy decided that Dowd would go forward with preparations for trial in the Sun Valley case; Neal and Shaffer would proceed to recommend indictment to the grand jury in Nashville; and Smith and Tom Sheridan would conduct further investigation.

On April 17 George Roxburgh, the Local 299 business agent, was again indicted for extorting more than $2500 from the Interstate Motor Freight System in Grand Rapids, Michigan, during the period 1959 to 1961. At about the same time, the United States Attorney in San Juan, Puerto Rico, was attempting to obtain the subpoenaed records of Teamsters Local 901 there. Frank Chavez, the head of the local, who had been charged with carrying a concealed weapon and attempted murder, claimed that the records had been shipped to the International in Washington. The International claimed it had not received them. In Minneapolis Ben Dranow was convicted in federal court of income tax evasion.

On May 2 Jimmy Hoffa flew into Los Angeles to address the twenty-third Jo Hoffa dinner attended by a thousand Teamsters members and their wives. Hoffa charged that big business and big government were conspiring to "divide and conquer us." He told his audience not to be fooled by "editorials, news stories and television programs about me. Ignore them." He said that there were twenty-nine grand juries out to get him but they would not succeed. From Los Angeles Hoffa moved on to Denver where he told newsmen that the AFL-CIO would eventually be forced to readmit the Teamsters in the interests of a strong labor movement. "Meany can't be that bullheaded," Hoffa said. He then journeyed to Golden, Colorado, to participate in an organizing campaign at the Coors Porcelain Company. While Hoffa was standing outside the company gates passing out leaflets, students from the Colorado School of Mines picketed with signs reading "Hoffa go home" and "Keep Golden clean."

On May 16 I went to Chicago to confer with department attorneys on the Dorfman investigation. We also met with Carl Schultz and Jack Thiede who had left the General Accounting Office to go with the Chicago office of the Labor Department's Bureau of Labor Management Reports (the bureau that had been set up to enforce the Landrum-Griffin Act). In their new posts they had continued to keep track of the key Chicago figures from the McClellan Committee days, including Joey Glimco, Gus Zapas and the Dorfmans.

The Dorfman enterprises continued to flourish and grow. The revocation of Allen Dorfman's license had been overruled by a state court and he continued, through various agencies, to serve as the sole agent for the Central States and Michigan Health and Welfare funds and had the inside track to a variety of other insurance packages in Teamsters affiliates throughout much of the country. Carl Schultz had identified sixteen agencies controlled by Dorfman, with diverse operations which included bonding, high-risk policies, delinquent tax liens, investments and high-figure life insurance.

I intended to fly to Los Angeles on May 17 to confer further with Tom Sheridan and Charlie Smith. While I was waiting for the flight at O'Hare Airport, I called our office in Washington. John Cassidy had been trying to locate me and told me that Sam Baron, the field director of the Teamsters National Warehouse Division, had just been assaulted by Jimmy Hoffa at the International headquarters. He said that Baron had contacted the United States Attorney's office in Washington and was going to swear out a complaint against Hoffa. I canceled my reservation to Los Angeles and took the next flight to Washington. Cassidy met me at the airport and we drove to the United States Attorney's office. Baron was already there talking to Assistant United States Attorneys Bill Greenhalgh and Ed Daley, who were assigned to the Municipal Court in the District of Columbia.

Baron was part of the egghead brain trust (personified by Gibbons) that Hoffa needed and used, blending them into his prag-

matic mixed bag with the Dios and Dranows. He had been in the
labor movement since his early twenties. When he was twenty-
seven he was on the staff of the International Ladies Garment
Workers Union in New York where he experienced his first taste
of labor racketeers and began his struggle against them. He later
became president of a New York local of the Bookkeepers, Stenog-
raphers and Accountants Union and then served in the Spanish
Civil War on the side of the Loyalists. He subsequently became
affiliated with the Textile Workers Union and became an International vice president and a national director in Canada. In 1953
Harold Gibbons brought Baron into the Teamsters Union as field
director of the Warehouse Division. He had an early run-in with
Hoffa—then an International vice president—and quickly developed a repugnance for Hoffa's racketeer friends. When Hoffa was
first attempting to bring Johnny Dio and his cohorts into the
Teamsters Union, Baron, who knew Dio for what he was from his
earlier days, warned Dave Beck about him and blocked his entry.

I had met Baron by accident two year earlier. At that time he
was very disturbed about the continued relationship between
Hoffa and the racketeers. He felt powerless to do anything about
it, but as a dedicated trade unionist, he believed in the Teamsters
Union and hoped desperately that things would change. I met
with him from time to time to discuss the situation. He had considered quitting a year earlier when the Board of Monitors went
down the drain. At that time he asked Bob Kennedy to put him
in touch with someone trustworthy at *Life* magazine so he could
get his story on the record in case anything happened to him.
Kennedy put him in touch with Hank Suydam of *Life* but nothing
came of it at that time.

Baron had told me that his personal revulsion for Hoffa dated
back to the day in May, 1956, when his friend, labor columnist
Victor Riesel, was blinded when acid was thrown at him on a New
York sidewalk. Baron said he was with Hoffa that day in a suite
at the Hotel Sherman in Chicago. Hoffa went into another room
to take a phone call and then came back into the room where
Baron, Gibbons and others were gathered. According to Baron,
Hoffa walked up to him and poked his finger in his chest, saying,
"Hey, Baron, a friend of yours got it this morning."

"What do you mean?" Baron asked.

"That son of a bitch Victor Riesel. He just had some acid thrown
on him. It's too bad he didn't have it thrown on the goddamn hands
he types with."

Johnny Dio was subsequently indicted for conspiring to blind Riesel, but the man who threw the acid was found murdered and other potential witnesses wouldn't talk. The case never came to trial.

Hoffa knew that he did not have Sam Baron's loyalty. But he tolerated him over the years because of Gibbons and because he was an effective trade unionist. Baron had served as the executive secretary of the Teamsters National Council to organize Sears, Roebuck in 1959 and played a key roll in the organizing drive against Montgomery Ward in 1960. He was highly respected both within the Teamsters organization and throughout the labor movement.

Now he sat in the office in the old Municipal Court building in Washington looking rather forlorn with a bruise on his left cheek and a cut over his right eye as souvenirs of his latest encounter with Hoffa.

He told us he had gone that morning at ten o'clock to a conference room adjacent to Hoffa's office for contract discussions with the Kroehler Furniture Company. He had no sooner entered when he heard Hoffa yelling for him from his office. He walked to Hoffa's office and found him in a complete rage.

"What the hell do you do around here?" Hoffa bellowed. "If you don't know, why the hell don't you admit it?"

Baron, in sheer frustration, did not answer and turned and walked out. But Hoffa pursued him and kept yelling. Baron said that he turned and said, "But, Jimmy, I do know what I'm doing."

With that, Baron said, Hoffa shouted, "Nobody talks back to me," and knocked him down with a roundhouse swing to his left eye. Some people in the office grabbed Hoffa and Baron got up and started to walk away, but then, according to Baron, Hoffa broke away, grabbed him, spun him around and hit him again on his left eye, knocking him down again. Baron said that as he got up again he said to Hoffa, "You bum, you would use your muscle." Baron said that Hoffa then gave him a violent shove and knocked him over a chair. This time Baron got out of the room and went down to the basement garage to his car and drove home.

Baron said there were a number of witnesses to the beating, and although he suspected none of them would stand up for him, he wanted to press charges. Greenhalgh issued a warrant for Hoffa's arrest charging him with simple assault. Hoffa surrendered at the police precinct near the International and posted $500 bond.

As soon as San Baron returned home, the phone calls started.

One of the first was Gibbons, sympathizing with his friend but at the same time trying to reconcile him and Hoffa. There were others from friends and some from the press, but the ones that would continue for some time to come were the ominous calls. Sometimes there was nothing but heavy breathing at the other end of the line. Others were anonymous flat threats like "I advise you to drop the charges" and "Hoffa wants to know what kind of coffin you want." Jim McShane, who had been appointed United States marshall for the District of Columbia, assigned two deputy marshalls to guard Baron.

On the following day Hoffa and the Commercial Carriers Corporation were indicted by the grand jury in Nashville in the Test Fleet matter. The indictment charged that Hoffa and the late Bert Brennan had received over $1,000,000 from Commercial Carriers in violation of the Taft-Hartley Act. The same day, Hoffa pleaded not guilty to the Baron assault charge and asked for a jury trial, which was set for June 19. Hoffa was represented at the arraignment by Washington attorney H. Clifford Allder who told reporters that witnesses to the fracas gave statements clearing Hoffa of any wrongdoing.

It had been a bad week for Jimmy Hoffa. He knew that of the two charges, the one that might do him the most harm was that of assaulting Baron, who had many friends in the union. Although outwardly Hoffa was as brazen and cocky as ever, the incident itself could lead to speculation in the ranks that he was losing his cool. As James Wechsler put it in his *New York Post* column, "The spectacle of a leader who has lost the capacity to lead, and strikes out wildly against a modest dissident, can only encourage the spread of heresy. The act of violence was the measure of his growing vulnerability." Hoffa was also aware that one of the sections in the Teamsters constitution which had not been changed at the last convention provided that striking a fellow union member was a ground for expulsion from office.

When Harold Gibbons called Sam Baron he said that Hoffa was sorry and suggested that Baron and his wife take a couple of weeks off and let things blow over. Others suggested that if Baron withdrew the charges he could "write his own ticket" in the Teamsters organization. Baron would not budge. But the difficulty of successfully prosecuting Hoffa for an alleged assault in his own inner sanctum became increasingly obvious as witness after witness swore that the diminutive, aging Baron had been the aggressor— that he was drunk, called Hoffa a son of a bitch and swung at him

—and that Hoffa had merely pushed Baron in self-defense. The saddest thing to Sam Baron was that his good friend Harold Gibbons was one of those witnesses who went to Hoffa's defense.

Publicly Hoffa took the tack of ignoring the Baron charge and attacking the Test Fleet indictment as a further proof of the Kennedy vendetta and a "smoke screen" to cover up the Billy Sol Estes scandal. Speaking in Newark, Hoffa said:

> With Billy Sol Estes, Laos and widespread unemployment as a consequence of administration policies, you would think they would find something more important to do than to pick on us.

In Philadelphia he held a press conference and charged that the Department of Justice had more than seventy-five investigators out to get him and the Teamsters Union. He repeated the smoke screen charge claiming that the Estes case "leads right into the White House" and again accused the President and the Attorney General of conducting a personal vendetta against him. He then addressed a DRIVE meeting of a thousand Teamsters and exhorted them to organize politically to fight the enemies of labor.

Hoffa then flew into New York for a joint meeting of New York and New Jersey Teamsters officials. He was attempting to obtain the authority from representatives of forty locals comprising more than 200,000 members in the New York–New Jersey area to bargain jointly for a uniform wage pattern with common expiration dates. In so doing he could acquire the latest link in his efforts to achieve a nationwide pattern with common expiration dates of contracts. He again disclaimed any potential threat of a nationwide strike but conceded, as he had in the past, that a nationwide bargaining program would enable the Teamsters to get around the secondary boycott provisions of the Landrum-Griffin Act.

On May 23 Judge Lieb denied Hoffa's motions in the Sun Valley case and set the trial date for September 10. The judge changed the venue from Orlando to Tampa.

In Philadelphia The Voice continued to gain momentum and petitioned the AFL-CIO for a charter. George Meany assigned Bill Kircher of his staff, who had worked with Jim Luken, and Bill Taylor, another veteran staff member, to work with The Voice. Jim Dougherty, a young Philadelphia attorney whose father headed the Postal Workers Union, took on the thankless task of representing The Voice. The NLRB was petitioned to hold an election but the combination of stalling tactics by the Teamsters attorneys and the built-in impediments of the bureaucracy rendered progress slow and painful.

On June 2 John Herling, the highly respected Washington labor columnist, addressed a huge Voice rally. Herling praised the labor movement, which he deeply loved:

> In the history of the United States, the part played by organized labor in the dedicated effort to improve the character of our nation, and to raise the standards of life for those who belong to unions and those who may not be union members exceeds that of any other sector of our nation.

He then went on to say that although the labor movement was necessarily a human organization, its humanity "must never be confused with the skullduggery represented by some manipulators, some cynical lawyers, and arrogant and corrupt and insolent men who describe themselves as leaders of labor." He bemoaned the fact that because of the actions of labor leaders like Hoffa there was a tendency on the part of those who sought to weaken labor, and the public in general, to smear the entire labor movement:

> Hoffa is trying to identify himself with the entire labor movement and identify the labor movement with him. That, ladies and gentlemen, is the worst case of mistaken identity you can imagine. He is trying to say that what is good for Jimmy Hoffa is good for labor, and what is bad for Hoffa is bad for labor. That's what he says. The fact is that through his unprincipled strategy, Jimmy Hoffa has been trying to drag the labor movement down to his level.
> . . . he has prostituted the great values that are an inherent part of the labor movement. He has succeeded in kidding the experts and the inexperts. He has bought allies wherever he could find them.
> . . . He wheels with anybody. He makes deals with anybody. He thinks he knows the price of everybody, but the fact is that he knows the value of nothing. . . .
> Hoffa uses intimidation and fury and threats as well as money. He has sought to scare good men as well as bad into submission. By the time he gets through with them, it is hard to tell the difference. . . .

Referring to the Sam Baron incident, Herling wondered why, if Hoffa were innocent, as he claimed, Harold Gibbons had called Baron to tell him that Hoffa was sorry that he had lost control. Herling praised the courageous efforts of The Voice and concluded, "You are not only fighting for your self-respect and your organization, you have dedicated yourselves to the fight to regain the soul of the labor movement."

On June 5 Floyd Harmon, secretary-treasurer of Teamsters Local 614 in Pontiac, Michigan, was indicted for embezzlement of union funds.

On June 6, seven years to the day from the afternoon that he disappeared in St. Louis, David Probstein walked down a corridor of the federal courthouse in Washington and into a grand jury room. Gus Zapas, Allen Dorfman and Frank McKinney were also there, waiting to testify under subpoena. On the day that Probstein would have been declared legally dead, his appearance came as quite a shock.

On the next day Jimmy Hoffa appeared in Nashville for his arraignment and pleaded not guilty to the Test Fleet charges. Commercial Carriers, Inc., pleaded nolo contendere to the same charges and admitted in open court that the arrangement they had with Hoffa was wrong and should have been terminated much earlier. Hoffa's bond was set at $3000 and his travel was restricted to the United States, Canada and Puerto Rico. At a meeting with defense and government attorneys three days earlier, Judge William E. Miller had directed that a hearing on motions would be held on July 23 and that all pretrial matters should be disposed of by August 1. Hoffa told newsmen that he would beat this case just as he had the others.

On June 13 in federal court in Chicago Jacques Schiffer told Judge Julius Miner that Joey Glimco had nothing to do with the filing of the suit against Dominic Abata by the three cabdrivers he represented. The following day Judge Miner ejected Schiffer and barred him from further practice in his court because he had "abused the privilege and breached the confidence" of the court. The judge said he had learned that Joe Coco, one of Glimco's henchmen, had arranged for Schiffer to represent the three cabdrivers and that the Teamsters Union was paying Schiffer's expenses.

Hoffa, in Chicago for a meeting of the Central States Drivers Council, did not comment on Schiffer's ouster, but did tell newsmen that he had instructed all Teamsters Union officials and employees at the International headquarters to refuse to talk to FBI agents. He also offered to let an FBI agent come and live with him in his plush suite at the Conrad Hilton Hotel. Hoffa was quoted as saying, "Attorney General Kennedy can save the taxpayers hundreds of thousands of dollars by assigning an FBI agent to live with me. Then Bobby can stop tapping Teamster telephones all over the country and using hundreds of agents to spy on the Teamsters."

In Tacoma, Washington, one week later, Dave Beck surrendered to begin serving a five-year sentence for filing false income tax returns. Beck, now sixty-eight, boarded a motor launch which ferried him across the Puget Sound to the McNeil Island Federal Penitentiary. He told newsmen as he departed that he intended to be a model prisoner and hoped to be released before his seventieth birthday. He said that he had left his business interests, consisting of extensive real estate holdings, motels and other buildings, in the hands of friends.

On June 21 Morris J. Emanuel, the assistant regional director of the Bureau of Labor-Management Reports in Chicago, testified before the McClellan Committee. Emanuel was Carl Schultz's and Jack Thiede's boss and had been working with La Verne Duffy of the McClellan Committee on an investigation of possible collusion between officials of the American Guild of Variety Artists and nightclub operators. Emanuel testified that an official of the Guild had a $6000 unpaid bill at the Concord Hotel in the Catskill Mountains in New York. In his position in the Chicago office, Emanuel had access to all investigative reports concerning labor racketeering and other violations of the Landrum-Griffin Act, including, of course, those relating to Hoffa and the Teamsters. It would be another year before we found out that he was on the Teamsters payroll.

In New Orleans, on June 22, a federal grand jury indicted Edward Grady Partin, the head of Teamsters Local 5 in Baton Rouge, charging that he had embezzled $1659 in union funds. On the same day in Miami, Cal Kovens and Leon Cohen were convicted of violation of the banking statutes for making false representations in obtaining loans of nearly $740,000 from the Miami Beach Federal Savings and Loan Association.

In Tampa a pretrial conference in the Sun Valley case was concluded on June 26. Judge Lieb set a new trial date for October 15.

On Sunday, July 2, Jimmy Hoffa flew to Nashville to put down a seething rebellion in Local 327. Ewing King, now president of the local, had defeated Don Vestal, the former head of the local, in an election eighteen months earlier. After the election Vestal supporters had gone to Washington to petition Hoffa for a separate charter for another local. They claimed that Hoffa had encouraged them. They had received no further satisfaction, however, and discontent grew within the local and there were increasing complaints about the lack of enforcement of labor contracts.

When Hoffa, accompanied by Dusty Miller and Weldon Mathis, a representative of the Southern Conference of Teamsters, faced the four hundred Teamsters gathered in the War Memorial Auditorium, there were some hostile members in the audience. Hoffa rammed through a vote of confidence for Ewing King. When Vestal supporter Corky Ellis tried to tell Hoffa he was out of order, he was shouted down. Hoffa made a speech on areawide bargaining and urged the necessity of Teamsters unity. The squabbling continued and Hoffa announced that he had to catch a plane. A Teamster shouted back, "You told us you would stay and hash out our problems if it took a week. Now you say you have to catch a plane. Why don't you make up your mind?" Hoffa and Miller took off, leaving Weldon Mathis behind to contend with the dissenters.

In Washington the investigation by the United States Attorney's office of the Sam Baron assault was bogging down. Six witnesses, all on the Teamsters payroll, either swore they saw Sam Baron attack Jimmy Hoffa or refused to testify. The situation prompted one Teamsters attorney to privately label such Hoffa helpers as "the improvers." "They have a facility for improving misdemeanors into felonies," he said. Assault was merely a misdemeanor but obstruction of justice was a felony. It was a prophetic statement.

Sam Baron volunteered to take a lie detector test. He was asked the following relevant questions:

1. Did Jimmy Hoffa strike you with his fist as you say?
2. Did you at any time curse Jimmy Hoffa?
3. Did you drink any alcoholic beverages on May 17, 1962, the day of the assault?
4. Did you drink any the day before?
5. Did you do anything to Hoffa other than push him to protect yourself?

Baron answered "yes" to the first question and "no" to the other four. The polygraph operator gave the following written conclusion: "It is the opinion of this operator after careful evaluation of the charts that the subject was truthful as to the relevant questions stated."

The six witnesses refused to take a similar test and Baron's test could not be used as evidence. Finally, completely frustrated, David Acheson, the United States Attorney, with Sam Baron's reluctant consent, dropped the charge against Hoffa. Said Acheson,

"We like to have a fighting chance of winning a case before we go to trial. We didn't feel we had that chance here." Hoffa had won another one.

On July 19 the United States Court of Appeals in Washington ruled that union funds could not be used to pay for attorneys' fees for the representation of union officials against criminal or civil charges. It also held that attorneys who represented a union could not represent officials of the union as defendants in criminal or civil cases. The decision was a blow not only to Hoffa but also to some members of the "Teamsters Bar Association" who could no longer obtain from the union their large fees for defending Hoffa. For Hoffa, it meant not only that he would have to find another source for paying his attorneys in the future, but also that he might have to reimburse the union for money already spent in his defense.

By late July the various Pension Fund investigations had reached a point where there was sufficient evidence of common denominators in those involved in the Sun Valley bail-out to bring them all together in one case before a single grand jury. The most logical place to try the case, which would have proper venue, was Chicago, where the Pension Fund headquarters was located. Jack Miller told me to call Jim O'Brien, the United States Attorney in Chicago, to make arrangements. O'Brien said that a grand jury was scheduled to convene on August 1 and we were welcome to use it.

Meanwhile, Hoffa's trial in the Sun Valley case, scheduled for October 15 in Tampa, was thrown into a state of confusion when Congress passed a bill creating a new Middle Judicial District in the state of Florida effective October 29. The area encompassed by the new district would include Tampa. The bill became law on July 30.

In answer to Hoffa's motions in the Test Fleet case in Nashville on August 1 Neal and Shaffer made reference to the new law and the confusion and delay it was likely to cause in relation to the Sun Valley case and asked that the Test Fleet case be set for trial on September 15.

Judge William E. Miller denied Hoffa's motions for a dismissal of the indictment and a change of venue to Detroit, but did not set a trial date.

On August 6 Judge Bryan Simpson, the chief federal judge in Florida, issued an order setting over all pending cases set for trial prior to October 29 until a judicial conference could be held to consider the effects of the new legislation. Consequently, three days later Judge Leib removed the Sun Valley trial from his calender.

On August 8 Ben Dranow was sentenced in Minneapolis to seven years in prison for income tax evasion. The sentence was to run concurrent with the seven-year sentence he had received previously for fraud.

On August 10 Judge Miller in Nashville issued an order setting the Test Fleet trial date for October 22 on the condition that the Sun Valley case was not reset for trial by September 15.

Hoffa and his attorneys reacted swiftly to the sudden turn of events. After almost two years of utilizing every legal means available to avoid going to trial in the Sun Valley case—the latest effort being a plea on August 6 for more time to file motions—they now suddenly moved on August 10 (the day after Judge Leib removed the case from his docket) that the trial date be set for the week of October 1. Since the original indictment in December, 1960, the government had repeatedly moved for an early trial date. Now, for the first time, Hoffa decided he wanted to go to trial at once. Judge Leib set a hearing on the matter for August 20.

On the day of the hearing in Tampa, Hoffa's friend Senator Homer Capehart rose on the floor of the Senate to demand an investigation by the Senate Judiciary Committee of what he implied was collusion between the Department of Justice and the courts to deprive Hoffa of a speedy trial in the Sun Valley case.

At the hearing itself attorneys for Hoffa and O. B. Cline, the attorney for co-defendant Robert McCarthy, argued for an early trial date. Jim Dowd, appearing for the government, pointed out that in addition to the serious legal problems created by the new legislation, the defendant Robert McCarthy was not physically able to go to trial. Dowd then read into the record an affidavit from Dr. Archie Bedell who said that he had been Robert McCarthy's personal physician for twelve years. Dr. Bedell described a series of heart ailments suffered by McCarthy since August 3, and went on to say that exposure to a trial of any length within the next four months might well prove fatal.

Dowd suggested to the judge that Cline had not even communicated with his client before announcing that he was ready to go to trial.

Following the hearing, Judge Leib denied the motion by Hoffa that the trial be reset and Judge Simpson issued an order reaffirming his prior pronouncement of a delay of all trials.

On August 21 the grand jury in Chicago, investigating the combined package of Pension Fund loans relating to the Sun Valley case, got under way. Charlie Smith headed the Justice Department group consisting of Tom McTiernan, Jim Canavan, Bill Ryan and Tom Kennelly.

In late August Hoffa was in New York heading the areawide New York–New Jersey bargaining sessions with the trucking industry. He also loaned $100,000 in Teamsters funds to the Flight Engineers International Association to support its strike against Eastern Airlines. Hoffa said that the association was considering affiliating with the Teamsters Union. On August 31 Hoffa went to Atlantic City to address the convention of Teamsters Joint Council 73. He accused the Administration of establishing a gestapo. He claimed that Teamsters members in Massachusetts who were supporting Edward McCormick in his primary campaign against Edward Kennedy for the United States Senate were being harassed by the government.

Hoffa's trial in Nashville was still six weeks away but the "improvers" were beginning to stir. On September 12 Phil Weiss, awaiting trial in a Newark extortion case, checked into the Hermitage Hotel in Nashville. On the same day Henry "Buster" Bell, a huge, balding man who was an International vice president of the International Longshoremen's Association and the head of its Local 1804 in New York, checked into the Traveler's Rest Motel in the horse country on the southern fringe of Nashville. Weiss, Bell and Hoffa were all close friends. Weiss and Bell were actually in Nashville together but stayed in separate hotels as a security measure. Bell had a known fondness for horses and Weiss was in the oil business. They made contacts in both areas to establish their cover story. Weiss checked out of his hotel on the 14th but Bell stayed on another day.

On Friday, September 15, the list of the panel from which the jurors for the Hoffa trial would be picked was completed and mimeographed. Buster Bell returned to New York that weekend.

On September 19 the congressional onslaught against the Department of Justice on Hoffa's behalf, which had been kicked off by Senator Capchart a month earlier, got under way in earnest. Eleven Congressmen, led by Representative William Bray of Indiana, gave speeches in the House of Representatives attacking the Attorney General and the Department of Justice. Again, Teamsters lobbyist Sid Zagri had done his work well. It was a well-orchestrated performance, but there was some duplication in the scripts. (Representative Bray and Representative Thomas Pelly of

Washington both used an identical quote from Clarence Darrow. Representatives Alvin O'Konski of Wisconsin and Fred Schwengel of Iowa used two identical paragraphs in their statements.) In the next two days Representative Glenn Cunningham of Nebraska and Senator Hiram Fong of Hawaii joined in the attack. The statements charged that the government had attempted to delay the Sun Valley case, thus depriving Hoffa of his right to a speedy trial; that as both Congressmen O'Konski and Schwengel identically stated, "the flamboyant headlines engendered by public statements by the Attorney General concerning James R. Hoffa" had poisoned the climate in Nashville; and that the Justice Department had conspired with the courts in a "forum shopping" plot.

The facts were quite to the contrary. It was Hoffa and not the government who had delayed the Sun Valley case for almost two years. Considering only the time since the second Sun Valley indictment in October, 1961, Hoffa had filed forty motions with Judge Leib, and had appealed seven of these to the Court of Appeals and two to the Supreme Court. (In both the Supreme Court appeals he took the position that it would be futile to attempt to try the case at that time, as neither of the appeals could be acted upon until early October.) It was Hoffa, not Robert Kennedy, who had engendered the "flamboyant headlines," with frequent public attacks on the Attorney General. Bob Kennedy had made no public statements about Hoffa since becoming Attorney General. Finally, it was Congress, not the Attorney General, which had created the new judicial district in Florida and it had been the chief federal judge in Florida who had ordered all cases postponed. On September 24 and 25 Congressman Edwin Willis of Louisiana and Senator McClellan made statements in the House and Senate setting forth the facts in the case and defending the actions and integrity of the Attorney General and the Department of Justice.

On September 25, however, Sid Zagri sent a letter on DRIVE letterhead to "All International Vice Presidents, General Organizers, Teamster Lawyers, Joint Councils, Local Unions and Drive Ladies Auxiliaries," attaching copies of the Congressmen's statements as reflected in the *Congressional Record*. The statements by Senator McClellan and Congressman Willis were not included.

On the day Senator Fong became the twelfth member of the United States Congress to voice concern over the deprivation of Jimmy Hoffa's right to a speedy trial in Tampa, Phil Weiss and Buster Bell returned to Nashville on another reconnaissance mission. This time they both stayed at the Hermitage Hotel but on separate floors. Three days later they returned to New York.

During these last days of September Jimmy Hoffa was in New York City and New Jersey trying to push through his areawide agreement. He had broken the united front of the truckers by playing one company off another—a tactic he had employed so successfully in the Midwest. However, in his determination to forge the areawide pact, Hoffa had alienated his old friend and ally John O'Rourke and other Teamsters officials in New York City who were afraid they might be undercut by Hoffa's negotiations. O'Rourke and his followers broke away and began negotiating on their own.

On September 27 Frank Grimsley called me to report that Edward Grady Partin, the head of the Baton Rouge Teamsters, had been arrested by District Attorney Sargent Pitcher on a charge of kidnapping, and was being held without bail in the parish jail. Grimsley said that it was actually a family squabble involving a Teamsters member's children and not an actual kidnapping.

On Sunday, September 30, while the President and the Attorney General were engrossed in the tense and delicate maneuvers to move James Meredith onto the University of Mississippi campus, I received another call from Grimsley. He said that he had just been called by Peter Duffy, the Assistant United States Attorney in New Orleans. He told me that Partin had told Sargent Pitcher that he had some information affecting the national security and that he wanted to talk to someone from Justice. I told Grimsley to go ahead down and see what it was all about.

Grimsley called me the next day from Baton Rouge. He had been talking to Sargent Pitcher and his assistant Billy Daniels, who had in turn talked to Partin. They told Grimsley that Partin said that on a recent trip to Washington Hoffa had talked to him about killing Bob Kennedy. Grimsley said that he was going to talk to Partin that night.

Early the next morning Grimsley called again. He said they had waited, for security reasons, until the middle of the night to talk to Partin and that they had talked from 3 to 6 A.M. During this three-hour period Partin told Grimsley that shortly after he was indicted in June, he had gone to Washington to see Hoffa at his office in the International headquarters. (This would have been at the time that Hoffa was charged with assault by Sam Baron, indicted in the Test Fleet case and faced with the sudden reappearance of David Probstein, all in rapid succession.) He said that while they were alone in the office, Hoffa, who was highly agitated about something, got up from his desk, walked over to the window and beckoned Partin to join him. Partin said that Hoffa had then asked him if he knew anything about plastic bombs. Partin quoted Hoffa as saying, "I've got to do something about that son of a bitch Bobby Kennedy. He's got to go." According to Partin, Hoffa went on to say that Kennedy had guts, that he drove around by himself in a convertible, that he swam in his pool alone at his house in Virginia and that there were no guards at the house. Hoffa said that he had been checking on him. Partin said that Hoffa mentioned throwing a plastic bomb in the car or in the house. According to Partin, Hoffa also said he knew where he could get a silencer for a gun.

Partin also told Grimsley the details of how he had bribed the NLRB examiner with money furnished by Hoffa, the same story he had earlier told Jim Luken. He also repeated to Frank what he had told Luken about being threatened by Hoffa in Miami the previous year.

It was an incredible story. Grimsley said that Partin was perfectly willing to take a lie detector test.

I went to see Jack Miller and he agreed that under the circumstances, a lie detector test would be a good idea. He called Al McGrath at the FBI and explained the situation and asked him to administer a polygraph test to Partin. Then we went up and told Bob Kennedy.

I encountered Kennedy that evening as he was leaving the building.

"What do we do if that fellow passes the test?" he asked with a wry smile.

"I don't know but I think he might," I replied.

He shrugged and climbed into his car.

The FBI does not often give definitive conclusions in a polygraph test. This time they did—two days later. The memorandum from the bureau concluded that from all indications, Partin was telling the truth.

We were now anxious to know more about Hoffa's intentions. Sargent Pitcher, realizing the seriousness of the situation, was eager to cooperate. Partin agreed to use his influence to get the "kidnapped" children back to their mother, although he insisted he had had nothing to do with their being spirited away. Pitcher, in turn, was able to have a reasonable bond set so that Partin could get out of jail.

On October 4 the congressional attack on Hoffa's behalf

resumed. Senator Wayne Morse of Oregon led off, followed by Representative Arch Moore of West Virginia on the following day and Representative John Dent of Pennsylvania on October 6. The first two insisted on Hoffa's right to a speedy trial in Tampa and Congressman Dent criticized a recent Senate resolution making available to the prosecution records of the McClellan Committee.

Commenting on the earlier round of congressional speeches, John Herling said in his labor column:

> Sidney Zagri, the political director of the Teamsters Union, stands in the wings as the ghostly master of ceremonies in one of the strangest colloquies ever to take place on the floor of Congress.
>
> In checking out this strange story, I asked Rep. Bray to account for this surge of sympathy and concern for Jimmy Hoffa. He attributed it to his "social conscience." When I asked him how come that he had this clutch of other congressmen ready and waiting with scripts in hand, he admitted that he had arranged to have them on the floor. Then he said, "I never talked to Jimmy Hoffa in my life." Whereupon I asked him, "Did you speak to Sid Zagri?" "Yes, I conferred with Mr. Zagri. He did provide me with factual material." Herling then asked Congressman Pelly the same question. "I may have gotten into something over my head," Mr. Pelly said.
>
> Then Mr. Pelly explained he read a magazine article on the subject. What magazine? It turned out to be the Teamster Magazine, edited by James R. Hoffa. What was the article? It was a speech on the Senate floor made by Republican Senator Homer Capehart of Indiana who had several weeks before read off the original script of la Zagri.

The October issue of *International Teamster* magazine carried excerpts from all of the speeches and photographs of the Congressmen and Senators who had made them.

On October 8 Partin called Hoffa in Washington to report that he was out of jail. He recorded the call with equipment furnished to him by Billy Daniels.

On the morning of October 16 President Kennedy called the Attorney General and asked him to come to the White House. It was the beginning of the Cuban missile crisis.

That afternoon, at Idlewild Airport in New York City, Phil Weiss and Buster Bell boarded American Airlines Flight 55 for Nashville.

In Minneapolis, that same day, Ben Dranow did not appear in

court, as directed by the judge, and was given until 10 A.M. the following morning to appear. When he did not show up the next day, the judge issued a fugitive warrant for his arrest.

On October 18 Partin called Hoffa again, at the Essex House in Newark. He again recorded the conversation with the equipment furnished by Daniels. Hoffa told him that he had to be in Nashville the following Monday, October 22, for his trial. He told Partin to meet him there that afternoon at the Andrew Jackson Hotel, where he would be staying.

When Frank Grimsley called to report that Partin was going to Nashville, I told him to tell Partin to be on the lookout for any indication of jury tampering or other illegal activity. I also gave Grimsley our office number in Nashville and told him to give it to Partin. If Partin did call, I instructed, he should use the name "Andy Anderson."

On October 19 Phil Weiss and Buster Bell contacted two men, each of whom was acquainted with two men on the jury panel list. This was the first feeler in what would become one of the most massive efforts to undermine a jury in history.

On Saturday, October 20, Larry Campbell, a handsome black business agent for Hoffa's Local 299 in Detroit, arrived in Louisville, Kentucky, one hundred miles due north of Nashville. He was driving a black Cadillac sedan equipped with a two-way radio. He checked into Brown's Tourist Home. Larry Campbell's uncle, Tom Parks, lived in Nashville. It was reasonable to expect there would be black members of the jury.

On the same day Nicholas J. Tweel left Huntington, West Virginia, aboard an Eastern Airlines plane for Nashville. Tweel and his brothers operated the Mayflower Distributing Company, a cigarette vending business in Huntington. Tweel, dark-complexioned, with wavy salt-and-pepper hair, had several months earlier met James Kalil, a fellow Lebanese-American, while attempting to promote a new brand of cigarettes in Michigan. Kalil, a deputy sheriff in Wayne County, Michigan, was an old friend of Jimmy Hoffa's and Allen Dorfman's and had been moonlighting for several years as an insurance agent for Dorfman. Tweel had expressed an interest in obtaining a loan for his business and Kalil had introduced him to Dorfman. On arriving in Nashville, Tweel checked into the Andrew Jackson Hotel.

The entire seventh floor of the Andrew Jackson Hotel had been leased by the International Brotherhood of Teamsters for the duration of the trial, to serve both as living space and temporary International headquarters for Hoffa, his attorneys, staff and associates.

One of Nick Tweel's acquaintences in Huntington was Herman Frazier, the chief of detectives and former chief of police. Frazier was the vice president of the Fraternal Order of Police, a nationwide organization of police officers. One of his close friends on the Huntington Police Force was Lieutenant Nelson Paden, a graduate of the FBI National Academy who specialized in photography, electronic surveillance techniques and polygraph operation. Unbeknownst to the chief of police and most of the citizens of Huntington, Frazier and Paden had, on the side, pooled their talents and formed Huntington Associates, Inc., a private investigating agency. In this extracurricular activity they sometimes utilized the services of Albert Cole, a young sometime insurance investigator.

On October 19 Frazier and Paden had approached Cole and said they were going to Nashville the following day. They told him they thought he could be of service and he agreed to go with them. Since in addition to his other talents, Lieutenant Paden was a licensed pilot, the trio set out for Nashville the next morning in a private plane but encountered bad weather and returned to Huntington. Later that day they took an Eastern Airlines plane to Nashville. They registered at the Noel Hotel, a few blocks from the Andrew Jackson, and occupied adjoining rooms.

Early Sunday afternoon, October 21, Jimmy Hoffa's plush twin-engine Loadstar plane landed in a drizzling rain at the Nashville airport. Don McClott, Hoffa's private pilot, taxied to the ramp and opened the door. Hoffa, briefcase in hand, stepped jauntily down the steps and was greeted by Ewing King, the president of Local 327, and a gathering of well-wishers.

Hoffa told waiting newsmen that the Attorney General was "usurping the powers of his office, making his own policies and starting out just like Hitler did."

Ewing King, a tall, lanky, chinless man, then took Hoffa's suitcase and placed it in the trunk of his red Thunderbird. Hoffa retained possession of his briefcase, and after shaking hands with a cabdriver, climbed into the car with King. They drove to the Andrew Jackson Hotel and Hoffa went to his suite on the seventh floor.

In Baton Rouge, Ed Partin was preparing to leave for his meeting with Hoffa in Nashville the following day.

CHAPTER VIII

Nashville

▭ ▭ ▭ ▭ ▭ ▭ ▭ ▭

ON SUNDAY EVENING, October 21, the eve of the trial, President Kennedy went on television to tell the country, for the first time, of the presence of Soviet-made missiles in Cuba and his decision to blockade any further access of Soviet ships to Cuban ports.

After the President's message, Bob Kennedy called me at home. All of the tension and weariness of the past five days were in his voice as he asked me when I was going to Nashville. I told him that Neal and Shaffer had suggested I not go down until the selection of the jury had been completed. They were concerned that my presence might precipitate an incident and cause a mistrial. (They were being overly cautious because, as it turned out, Jimmy Hoffa did not even recognize me.) There was a pause, and then Kennedy said, "I think you had better go down there tonight."

I arrived in Nashville shortly after midnight and checked into the Noel Hotel. At about the same time Allen Dorfman was at O'Hare Airport in Chicago preparing to board a 1 A.M. flight which would arrive in Nashville in the middle of the night. I went to sleep in the early morning hours thinking about the very real threat of nuclear war and the possibility that Jimmy Hoffa and I would end up very dead together in Nashville, Tennessee.

The headline and lead story on the front page of the Nashville *Tennessean* the next morning began the day-by-day serial on the missile crisis which would continue for the next eight days. At the bottom of the front page of the *Tennessean* was an article about the trial of James R. Hoffa starting that day in federal court. From this and previous stories, the people of Nashville knew the charges for which Hoffa was being tried. They also knew that he had denied the charges and claimed that the events involved were almost fifteen years old and that Robert Kennedy was waging a personal vendetta against him. They were aware that Hoffa was the president of the International Brotherhood of Teamsters and that he and his empire had been under investigation, first by the McClellan Committee and then the Justice Department, for a number of years. They also had read or heard that Hoffa had been tried three times in federal court in the past five years but had never been convicted. But, by and large, the people of Nashville did not really care. Many, if not most, of the citizens considered the trial an intrusion on their normally peaceful, quiet community. Why, they wondered, should all of these people from Detroit and Washington come down here to try this case? What concern was it of theirs? But others were intrigued. To some of them Hoffa represented what they respected and coveted—money and power.

Z. T. "Tommy" Osborn, Jr., the local lawyer Hoffa had picked to help represent him, was a tall, handsome man in his early forties whose prestige had been rising steadily. He had gained some national prominence as the attorney who successfully argued the reapportionment issue before the Supreme Court of the United States. He was scheduled to become the next president of the Nashville Bar Association. He wanted very badly to win this case. He was also convinced that Hoffa was being persecuted. He understood the stakes, but not well enough. He could not have conceived of the corrupt and intense pressures he would be under to win at any cost. Within a year he would lose everything—and would stand indicted and disbarred. Ultimately it would cost him his life.

Judge William E. Miller, who was to preside over the trial, was aware, as he entered the courthouse from the rear parking lot entrance that morning, that this was not just another trial. He felt keenly the national attention focused on his courtroom. He was highly respected among the members of the bar as a man of unimpeachable integrity. His character was such that a plot already being brewed in the Chicago underworld to attempt to bribe him would abort because no one could be found with enough courage to approach him.

The Federal Building in Nashville, an eight-story smooth stone structure, is situated at the corner of Eighth Avenue and Broadway just a few blocks from the Noel and Andrew Jackson hotels in midtown. There are two courtrooms on the top floor separated by elevator banks. On the east side of the building was Judge Miller's court where the trial was to be held. The courtroom on the west side was presided over by the other federal judge, Frank Gray. Our offices were located off a corridor running along the north side of Judge Miller's courtroom, facing Broadway. The jury room was at the end of the corridor. Adjacent to our offices were those of United States Marshal Elmer Disspayne, a friendly, folksy man, and his five deputies. Further up the hall were the offices of United States Attorney Kenneth Harwell, who would sit at the government counsel table with Neal and Shaffer.

Nat Lewin, a former law clerk with Supreme Court Justice John Harlan, had recently joined our prosecuting team in Nashville. He and Jim Durkin would be in and out of the courtroom. Durkin had assembled and indexed all documents so that they would be available at his fingertips. Lewin would lend his legal expertise with his brilliantly quick research facility.

Because of a heart condition, Judge Miller held court only from 9 A.M. to I P.M. This posed the disadvantage of a necessarily longer trial but offered the advantage to the attorneys on both sides of having more time between court sessions for preparation. The first morning of the trial was taken up with the arguing of a motion by the defense challenging the validity of the system utilized for selecting the jury panel from which the jurors would be chosen.

I sat in the back of the courtroom watching the proceedings. Neal, Shaffer and Harwell sat at the government table facing the judge in the front of the room at the left, next to the empty jury box. At the defense table on the right sat Hoffa and his attorneys, Tommy Osborn, James Haggerty, Daniel Maher and William Bufalino. These were his attorneys of record but there were others back on the seventh floor of the Andrew Jackson Hotel, including Jake Kossman and labor lawyer Dave Previant. During the trial their numbers would increase.

I had expected that there would be a large crowd of spectators but there was only a handful of people in the courtroom. The attendance would pick up as the trial progressed, but even then the courtroom would seldom be full. The people of Nashville just were not that interested. There were a few steadies, but for the most part the spectators consisted of a scattering of the curious—Teamsters members, students and attorneys.

While court was in session Ed Partin arrived in Nashville from

Baton Rouge and went to the Andrew Jackson Hotel to wait for
Hoffa. While he was waiting, he went into the coffee shop where
he spotted Allen Dorfman sitting at a table with another man.
Partin walked over and shook hands with Dorfman, whom he
knew. The other man introduced himself as Anthony Quinn.

When the arguments were finally completed in court, Judge
Miller denied Hoffa's motion and adjourned the court for the day.
He said that the selection of the jury would begin on the following
morning.

Early that evening, while Neal, Shaffer and Jim Durkin were
continuing their preparations for trial, the phone rang and I answered it.

"Is Mr. Sheridan there?" asked a voice with a southern accent.

"This is he," I replied.

"This is Andy Anderson. They're fixing to get at the jury."

"Who are *they?*" I asked.

"Allen Dorfman and a man named Tweel."

I knew, of course, who Dorfman was but I had never heard of
Tweel.

"Who is Tweel?" I asked.

"Well, he was in the coffee shop at the hotel with Dorfman and he
said his name was Anthony Quinn. But later, he invited me up to
his room—Room 912 at the Andrew Jackson—and he told me his
real name is Nick Tweel. He's from Huntington, West Virginia,
and has something to do with the cigarette vending business. He
says there's another guy coming in who's an officer in the Fraternal
Order of Police. He says they're here to help Dorfman with the
jury."7 m

I interrupted. "What does he look like?"

"If you want to see him, he's sitting right here in the lobby of
the hotel. I've been sitting here talking to him. I'm in the pay
phone."

I said, "Okay, I'll be right over. How will I know you?"

"I'm pretty big and I've got a handkerchief in my breast pocket
with a 'P' on it," he said.

I described myself and hung up. I walked to the Andrew Jackson
Hotel and entered the lobby. I was self-consciously aware of being
in the enemy camp and tried to be nonchalant. The hotel, located
on a corner, had entrances on both streets. As I walked casually
through the lobby, I noticed two men sitting together. I had only
a fleeting glance of them as I kept moving and went out the other

entrance to the street. As I started back up the street toward the corner, a big man with brown wavy hair came around the corner walking toward me. I looked at his breast pocket and there was a handkerchief with a "P" on it.

I said, "Hi, I'm Walt Sheridan."

"I'm Ed Partin," he replied.

I said, "I'm at the Noel Hotel in Room 542. Why don't you come over there later."

Partin said, "Okay. I'm going up to see Hoffa now. I'll come over when I can get away."

The meeting and conversation had taken less than a minute and we continued on our ways. I walked on to the Noel Hotel and went to my room to wait for Partin.

I did not know what to think. I had never heard of Nick Tweel and had not been able to get a good look at him back in the hotel lobby. The fact that he had been with Allen Dorfman earlier was significant but it did not seem likely that they would bring in an outsider to work on the jury. I thought by this time I knew who all of the insiders were, and there was no Nick Tweel among them.

When Partin got to my room, he sat down on the bed and I sat at the small desk next to him. He was an even bigger man than he had appeared in our brief meeting earlier. As he started to talk, I reached automatically into the desk drawer and pulled out a sheet of Noel Hotel stationary. I began taking notes.

Partin repeated his story of his meeting with Dorfman and Tweel and the subsequent session with Tweel in his room. He went on to say that he had gone to Hoffa's suite after he left me. He had mentioned Tweel to Hoffa and Hoffa said that he was "all right" and "he's up here to help me." Partin said that Hoffa had asked him to stick around for a day or two to make some calls for him. Hoffa then told him, "We're going to try to get a juror—or a few scattered jurors—and take our chances." Partin mentioned that Sid Zagri had been in Hoffa's suite that evening. He also said that he had talked with Ewing King, the head of the local Teamsters Union, and that King told him there was going to be a meeting on the jury that night.

If Partin was telling the truth, there were already three men, including Hoffa, talking about trying to fix the jury. Partin said that he would have to go back to Baton Rouge the next day but would return the day after that. He promised to call me before he left.

Partin, like Hoffa, had come up the hard way. While Hoffa was building his power base in Detroit during the early forties, Partin was drifting around the country getting in and out of trouble with the law. When he was seventeen he received a bad conduct discharge from the Marine Corps in the state of Washington for stealing a watch. One month later he was charged in Roseburg, Oregon, for car theft. The case was dismissed with the stipulation that Partin return to his home in Natchez, Mississippi. Two years later Partin was back on the West Coast where he pleaded guilty to second degree burglary. He served three years in the Washington State Reformatory and was paroled in February, 1947. One year later, back in Mississippi, Partin was again in trouble and served ninety days on a plea to a charge of petit larceny. Then he decided to settle down. He joined the Teamsters Union, went to work and married a quiet, attractive Baton Rouge girl. In 1952 he was elected to the top post in Local 5 in Baton Rouge. When Hoffa pushed his sphere of influence into Louisiana, Partin joined forces and helped to forcibly install Hoffa's man, Chuck Winters from Chicago, as head of the Teamsters in New Orleans.

When we arrived at the office the following morning, Ken Harwell told us that he had received a call the previous evening from one of the women on the jury panel. She told him that she had received a telephone call over the weekend from a man who identified himself as Mr. Allen, a reporter for the Nashville *Banner*. He said he was writing a story about the trial and asked her a series of questions. One of the questions was about her feelings concerning Hoffa and the Teamsters Union. Harwell had reported the call to Judge Miller. I reported what Partin had told me to Ed Steele, the head of the local FBI, whose office was two floors below us. I had the feeling he was somewhat mistrustful of Partin but I asked him to check out Nicholas Tweel.

When the court was called into session that morning, Judge Miller asked the woman about the call. She repeated what she had told Harwell. The judge excused her as a prospective juror and then asked if any other members of the jury panel had received similar calls. Several persons raised their hands. Each of them told of having received similar calls over the weekend from "Allen from the *Banner*." They, too, were excused. Judge Miller expressed his grave concern over the calls and cautioned the prospective jurors not to look at newspaper or television accounts of the trial and not to discuss the trial with anyone. The selection of the jury then got under way. It was a slow, laborious process. Twelve prospective jurors from the panel took seats in the jury box. Each one was then questioned by both government and defense attorneys concerning his or her background and ability to judge the evidence fairly and without prejudice. Hoffa's attorneys had an endless list of questions for each prospective juror—most of them dealing with whether the juror had been prejudiced by prior publicity.

During the mid-morning recess we heard from one of the reporters covering the trial that the publisher of the Nashville *Banner*, James G. Stahlman, was extremely upset about what he considered an implication that one of his reporters had contacted prospective jurors. There was, of course, no *Banner* reporter named Allen. That afternoon Stahlman printed a front-page editorial stating categorically that no reporter from his paper had made such calls and offered a $5000 reward for information leading to the identity of the caller.

By the time the court adjourned for the day only three jurors had been tentatively accepted by both the government and the defense. One of these was a large gray-haired insurance executive by the name of James C. Tippens.

Partin called me from the airport that afternoon on his way to Baton Rouge. He said that later the previous evening he had seen Nick Tweel meet with three men and accompany them into the Andrew Jackson Hotel cocktail lounge. He did not know who the men were. Partin said that when he had stopped in Hoffa's suite that morning to tell him he was leaving, Hoffa told him that he might want Partin to "pass something" for him when he came back. Partin said that Hoffa hit his hip pocket as he said it. Partin took this to mean that Hoffa might want him to pass some money to someone.

The next morning also began with intrigue. James Tippens, who had been tentatively accepted as a juror, went to the judge's chambers before court started to report that he had been approached the previous afternoon by a neighbor who offered him $10,000 in hundred-dollar bills to vote for Hoffa's acquittal. Tippens reluctantly identified the neighbor as Lawrence "Red" Medlin. Judge Miller was shocked. He excused Tippens from jury duty and told him not to discuss the matter with anyone. He then called Ed Steele and told him he wanted Tippens interviewed by the FBI. Steele came and told us what had happened.

Judge Miller then called a meeting in his chambers of Hoffa and his attorneys and the government attorneys. He related to them what had happened. He made it clear that he was not suggesting that either Hoffa or his attorneys had anything to do with the approach to Tippens. But he also expressed his strong indignation that such a thing had occurred. Jim Neal reluctantly suggested that in view of the telephone calls to prospective jurors over the past weekend, followed now by this blatant approach to Tippens, the jury should be locked up. Tommy Osborn objected and said that the calls were probably made by "do-gooders" who took it upon themselves to try to help Hoffa. Charlie Shaffer pointed out that this was not the first time there had been jury tampering in a Hoffa trial, and made specific reference to the second wiretap trial in New York over Bill Bufalino's strong objections. Judge Miller finally decided that he would not lock the jury up at that time and expressed hope that there would be no further incidents. Significantly, Phil Weiss and Buster Bell left late that morning and returned to New York.

The attempt to select a jury dragged on all that day and well into the next. Tommy Osborn had a list of 155 questions which he asked each prospective juror. They included such questions as "Do you watch *The Untouchables?*" "Do you watch the *Huntley-Brinkley Report?*" and "Have you read *The Enemy Within?*" When Neal complained that the defense attorneys were being repetitious in their questioning, Judge Miller said that he had permitted them great latitude but "it is going to reach a point where I am going to call a halt." Finally on Thursday, October 25, Judge Miller took over the questioning himself and said a jury would be selected that day if they had to stay until midnight. A jury of seven women and five men, along with four alternates, was finally seated in a special afternoon session. Judge Miller remarked that it was "the most searching, most complete, the most exhaustive interrogation of a jury that I have ever seen."

On the following morning the opening statements by the government and the defense were delivered. Charlie Shaffer led off for the government, outlining for the jury the case he and Neal hoped to prove against Hoffa. He got to the point early in his statement:

> The proof in this case will show that beginning in 1947 and up until 1958 Hoffa, his union associate and business partner, Bert Brennan, and several people connected with a company who employed Team-

sters Union members represented by Hoffa all participated in a long-range plan, whereby Hoffa would be continuously paid off by the employer.

During Shaffer's recitation of his twenty-page statement he was repeatedly interrupted by Hoffa lawyer Daniel Maher who made motions for mistrial and frequent objections, claiming that Shaffer was prejudicing the jury and making improper statements.

In his opening statement Tommy Osborn claimed that the government's case was based on suspicion and insinuation. He said that Hoffa's dealings with Commercial Carriers were perfectly legal. He said that the facts concerning the Test Fleet operation had been reported to two congressional committees in 1953 and 1957 and that the only thing that had changed since 1953 was "the appointment of a new Attorney General, Robert F. Kennedy."

When the opening statements were completed, Judge Miller repeated his instructions to the jury about not discussing the case with anyone. He then adjourned court for the weekend. The government was to put on its first witness the following Monday.

Back in the office, I received a call from Partin. He had come back to Nashville late the previous night and had gone to Hoffa's suite that morning before court. He said he asked Hoffa if he wanted him to do anything for him. He said Hoffa replied, "No, that bastard went in and told the judge that a neighbor had offered him $10,000. We are going to have to lay low for a few days." Partin, who was calling from a phone booth, said that he was going over to the Andrew Jackson Hotel and would call back later. (Partin had not been in town when the Tippens incident occurred and so could not have known anything about it except through Hoffa. It was beginning to look like Partin's information might be very accurate.)

I went downstairs to the FBI office to talk to Ed Steele and his fellow agent Bill Sheets. They had received a report from West Virginia on Nick Tweel. He was, as Partin said, in the cigarette vending business, with a company called Mayflower Distributors, Inc. They also had a photograph of him which resembled the description given by Partin.

I told them what Partin had just related about his conversation with Hoffa. It obviously tied in with the Tippens approach. Steele and Sheets had interviewed Tippens and believed what he said about the offer by Red Medlin.

The story Tippens told them was that he had found a note left by his secretary that Medlin had called him. He returned the call and Medlin asked him to come to his place of business. Since Medlin was a friend of his, he had not thought anything of it. When he arrived at Medlin's office, Medlin suggested they talk in Tippens' car. It was then that Medlin offered Tippens the $10,000 in hundred-dollar bills if he would vote to acquit Hoffa. Medlin told Tippens that no one would know where it came from.

Thus Steele and the Nashville FBI office were becoming convinced not only that there was considerable activity stirring in relation to the jury, but also that Partin's information appeared to be accurate, so far. Steele, Sheets and I agreed that I would continue the contacts with Partin and report everything back to them so that they might continue to attempt to corroborate Partin's information.

Shortly after court adjourned, Hoffa took off in his private plane for stops in Cleveland, Chicago and Detroit. He was to address a DRIVE meeting in Cleveland on Saturday night and return to Nashville Sunday evening. After Hoffa left, Partin called me again. I told him I would pick him up in our rented car in front of the Western Union office, down the street from the Noel Hotel. He was waiting when I arrived and climbed into the car. We drove some distance away and parked. He said that he had spoken with Ewing King at the Andrew Jackson Hotel and that King was talking about approaching a female juror whose husband was a highway patrolman. King said they lived outside of town and that he knew someone who lived near them who could approach the patrolman. King said he thought he might drive out in the country that weekend. He told Partin that they were getting copies of the jury list to show to people they could trust.

If what Partin was saying was true, there was little question that the onslaught on the jury was continuing. I dropped Partin off a few blocks from the Andrew Jackson Hotel and drove back to the Federal Building. I asked Neal and Shaffer whether the husband of one of the female jurors was a highway patrolman. We looked down the list of jurors and at what background information we had. Juror number ten was Mrs. James Paschal, thirty-five, of Woodbury. Her husband's occupation was listed as "State Highway Patrolman."

Again, there was no way Partin could have known that on his own. I told them what Partin had related about his conversation with King. I said I thought we should ask the FBI to institute a surveillance of King. They agreed and I went downstairs to see Ed Steele and Bill Sheets. They, too, agreed that it was the only sensible thing to do.

I called Jack Miller in Washington and brought him up to date. I had been giving him daily reports on the continuing out-of-court machinations and Neal and Shaffer had been keeping him advised on the progress of the trial. Jack also concurred on the necessity for a surveillance and said he would call Al McGrath at the bureau and get things moving. Beginning that Friday evening, Ewing King's Thunderbird was discreetly followed wherever it went.

We had been just in time and the surveillance paid off quickly. On Saturday morning King left the house at 11:30 and headed north out of Nashville in his Thunderbird. At 2:15 P.M. he pulled into the driveway of a residence near Woodbury, some eighty miles north of Nashville. He went into the house and remained for one hour. He then drove back to Nashville, arriving home at 5:21 P.M. The FBI agents determined that the residence belonged to Mr. and Mrs. Oscar Pitts. "Mutt" Pitts, as the husband was called, was a truck driver working out of Nashville and was a member of Local 327.

On Monday morning, October 29, the government began presenting its case against James R. Hoffa. Jim Neal had intended to call Detroit attorney Albert Matheson as the first government witness to tell how he had set up and operated the J & H Sales Company, the predecessor of Test Fleet, for Hoffa and Brennan. Neal had talked to Matheson as recently as the preceding Friday about his testimony. Although Neal knew that Matheson, a long-time associate of Hoffa's, was reluctant to testify, he expected that as an attorney he would certainly state the facts as they had happened. About fifteen minutes before court was to be convened, Matheson approached Neal and told him that if called as a witness, he would probably take the Fifth Amendment.

Neal was surprised and upset. He decided to let Matheson sit in the witness room and cool his heels and call instead Bertram B. Beveridge, the former president of Commercial Carriers, Inc., as the government's first witness. Beveridge testified how he had arranged with Bert Brennan to set up the Test Fleet Company and that Brennan had told him he "would have to cut Hoffa in on the deal." Beveridge continued his testimony throughout the day's session under direct examination by Neal.

After court adjourned, Partin called. He had been to Baton Rouge for the weekend and had returned to Nashville that morning. Again, what he had heard in Hoffa's suite tied in with what had happened that morning. He said that Hoffa asked someone to call "Al" and tell him to take the Fifth Amendment. He quoted Hoffa as saying they should keep the pressure on "Al," and if he kept his mouth shut, he would be all right.

Partin said that Hoffa was mad at Ewing King because he had tried to call King over the weekend and had been unable to reach him. In talking about the jury, Partin continued, Hoffa had said that he would pay $15,000 or $20,000 or whatever it cost. Partin mentioned that there was a local business agent in Hoffa's suite who talked with a Slavic accent and was carrying a gun.

Ewing King, whom Partin said he had also talked to, told him that the wife of one of the business agents was a nurse and that the husband of the black female juror was a doctor. According to Partin, King said that the business agent's wife knew the doctor, but did not say anything about any contact being made with the doctor.

Once more, however, Partin's information was accurate. The husband of the black female juror, Mrs. Matthew Walker, was the chief of surgery at the Meharry Medical College. Also there was a business agent named Larry Herd whose wife Mamie, a nurse, had been in the courtroom with Ewing King and others every day.

Partin called again that evening to say that Hoffa had told him he, William Bufalino, Larry Steinberg and Chuck O'Brien were going to drive outside of town five or ten miles to make some phone calls. Hoffa told him he wouldn't use the phone booth across from the Andrew Jackson Hotel because it was probably tapped.

Larry Steinberg, one of Hoffa's special assistants, had been in Nashville since the beginning of the trial. He usually stayed at the hotel during the day keeping a check on the business of the International. Chuck O'Brien, a young business agent for Local 299, was considered to be Hoffa's protégé and lived with his wife and family in Hoffa's old house in Detroit. O'Brien told Partin that he had come in from Detroit that day and was going on to Akron, Ohio, to help the Rubber Workers Union with a picket line there.

As the trail went on from day to day, the contacts with Partin continued. I never tried to contact him because it was too dangerous. He always called me from a pay phone. Sometimes he would talk briefly because he did not want to stay in a phone booth very long for fear of being seen. I would usually pick him up at a designated spot and we would drive out of the downtown area. A couple of times I met him in a theater.

On October 30 Nick Tweel called Partin at the Andrew Jackson Hotel. Partin was not in and Tweel left his number in Huntington. When Partin called back, Tweel wanted to know how things were going and told Partin he would return to Nashville the following Tuesday.

Partin said that there was talk in Hoffa's suite that day of trying to get Bill Wade, the former All-American football player from Vanderbilt, or Pat Boone, the movie actor, also a native of Nashville, to come and sit in the courtroom. Partin said that the business agent with the accent who carried a gun was named George. I checked and determined that there was a local business agent who talked with an accent named George Broda. There was no indication that either Bill Wade or Pat Boone was called or that they would have had any inclination to come if they had been.

Partin had to return to Baton Rouge on union business on Wednesday evening, October 31. When he was leaving, Hoffa told him to call Allen Dorfman in Chicago from the airport and find out whether Dorfman had heard from Tweel. Hoffa gave Partin Dorfman's number. When he got to the airport, Partin tried to call Dorfman, using the number Hoffa had given him. It was a wrong number. Partin then realized that he had Dorfman's number in his address book and looked it up. Hoffa had merely transposed the last two numbers accidentally. Partin called the right number and reached Dorfman's office but he was not in.

As Partin was leaving Nashville for Baton Rouge, Phil Weiss and Buster Bell were returning for their fourth visit. They again checked into the Hermitage Hotel.

On Thursday and Friday James Wrape, the attorney for Commercial Carriers who had incorporated the Test Fleet Company in Nashville, testified as a government witness. He was followed to the witness stand by Bert Beveridge, who was recalled for further cross-examination by the defense. The testimony was interspersed with complaints by Hoffa attorneys Osborn, Bufalino and Maher that they suspected their phones were being tapped. Neal said that he had no knowledge of any such activity on the part of the Justice Department.

On Monday, November 5, Partin returned to Nashville as the second week of the trial got under way. The cross-examination of

Bert Beveridge and the redirect examination by the government consumed the court session. That afternoon Partin told me that Hoffa had been berating Ewing King at the hotel because King hadn't done what he was supposed to do in connection with the jury.

On the following day King told Partin that he was supposed to meet with the highway patrolman, the juror's husband, the next Sunday at a spring near the patrolman's house. King said that he was going to borrow some dogs and pretend he was coon hunting in case the FBI was watching him. He also might switch cars with someone for the same reason.

On Wednesday, November 7, I met with Partin again. He had just left Hoffa's suite at the Andrew Jackson. He said that Hoffa told him not to worry because he had the male Negro juror in his pocket—his Negro business agent named Campbell had come to Nashville early in the trail and contacted the juror. Hoffa told Partin that the juror wouldn't take any money but that he wouldn't vote against his own people. The only male Negro juror was Gratin Fields, a stocky seventy-year-old retired railroad company employee. According to Partin, Hoffa thought it looked like they were going to have to settle for a hung jury unless they could get to the foreman. Hoffa went on to say that a hung jury would be as good as an acquittal because the government would never try the case again.

That night Partin had to leave to go back to Baton Rouge and would be unable to return for about a week because of union problems back home. I hated to see him leave with so much going on but there was no choice.

I got together with Ed Steele and Bill Sheets and told them about my latest conversation with Partin, as I had each time I talked to him. I knew that Hoffa must have been talking about Local 299 Business Agent Larry Campbell and I asked them if they could try to find out where he was. We did not know at that point that he had been in Louisville. There was also the problem of covering any meeting between Ewing King and the patrolman the coming weekend.

I called Jack Miller to report the latest information and he suggested I fly to Washington that night. We had been talking daily, but now that we were faced with what was obviously a broadscale effort to tamper with the jury, it was time to sit down and determine just what to do about it.

We met that night and again the following morning with Bob Kennedy. It was decided that we would continue, with the help of the FBI, to corroborate as much as we could of what Partin was reporting about attempts to tamper with the jury through whatever investigation and surveillances were necessary. There would not, however, be any surveillance of Hoffa himself, his attorneys or any juror. It was further decided to submit the proposed course of action to Judge Miller for his approval. I returned to Nashville that evening.

The following morning, Friday, November 9, Judge Miller authorized whatever investigation and physical surveillance we thought would be necessary to follow up on the jury-tampering allegations, but instructed that there should be no surveillance of Hoffa, his attorneys or the jurors.

By now the FBI had established that Larry Campbell had been staying at Brown's Tourist Home in Louisville. I asked Ed Steele to obtain the records of telephone toll calls made from Brown's Tourist Home and also from Campbell's residence in Detroit, Ewing King's residence and the offices of Local 327 in Nashville.

In court that day Albert Matheson finally decided to testify. Matheson acknowledged setting up and operating the J & H Sales and Equipment Company, the forerunner of the Test Fleet Company, to obtain "the good will" of Hoffa and Bert Brennan. Harlan Rowe, the accountant for Commercial Carriers, had testified the previous day that he had agreed to serve as vice president of the Test Fleet Company after he had been informed by the vice president of Commercial Carriers that Hoffa had cleared him for the position. He also stated that he had been instructed by the official to move the Test Fleet records to his office because it was embarrassing for Commercial Carriers and Test Fleet to have the same address.

On Wednesday, November 14, Partin was back in Nashville and called me. When I met with him he said that Ewing King had told him he had not yet been able to set up the contact with the patrolman but was hoping to arrange it for that evening or the following evening. Partin said that King told him Hoffa had been after him and that he had to make contact in the next day or two. Partin told me he later heard Hoffa ask King if he was making any headway and King answer that the man who was supposed to set it up didn't do it. Partin said Hoffa then turned to him and said, "These goddamn people don't have any guts," and that King kept telling him he could get to the man any time he wanted to, but kept stalling.

On the same day in Washington the Supreme Court upheld the conviction of William Presser for obstruction of justice in the "champagne master" case. In Newark Tony Provenzano was indicted by a federal grand jury for taking illegal payments from the Dorn Transportation Company. Provenzano sent a telegram to the Attorney General which read in part:

> I want to congratulate you, for distorting the facts and the issues in your present timely indictment aimed at me and in making sure— despite the fact that this has been a lengthy dragout investigation, to issue the announcement to the Press, TV and Radio as elections are coming up in this local union. . . .

The next day Partin reported another conversation with Ewing King. He said that King told him Hoffa had again been pressing him, stating that he needed some insurance on the jury and that King should go ahead and do what he was told and not pay attention to anyone else. King told Partin that he was arranging to meet the patrolman at the house of a man "they" would never suspect. King said he thought he would have the patrolman and his wife meet with the contact and his wife and that he himself would also be there. That way, King said, they could always claim they were meeting with the patrolman to help him get a raise. In fact, King said, he could tell the patrolman that he would arrange an appointment with the governor about a raise.

Partin said that when he talked to Hoffa after his conversation with King, Hoffa said he had ordered King to get out to meet those people. According to Partin, Hoffa was annoyed that King was still telling him what he was going to do and hadn't actually done anything.

The Hoffa supporters in court that day were a mixture of old and new faces—Ewing King, Chuck O'Brien and Ed Partin were there, as they had been most days since the trial began. Red Vaughn and James Ivey, Local 327 business agents, had also been frequent attendants. So had Mamie Herd, the wife of Business Agent Larry Herd. Joe Konowe, who had come down to relieve Larry Steinberg as office manager of the displaced International, was a new face. So were I. Irving Davidson, Hoffa's friend from Washington, and swaggering Frank Chavez, the tough head of the Puerto Rican Teamsters in from San Juan. Before the day was over Chavez approached a newly hired black deputy marshal and asked him if he knew how the jury operated.

Another week of trial ended with Judge Miller showing obvious impatience at the slow progress. The judge said, "I want to abbreviate the presentation of evidence to this jury. I am concerned about the way this case is dragging out." Tommy Osborn blamed the government, claiming that it was refusing to give the defense records. Neal countered by accusing the defense of conducting exhaustive examination about details concerning which there was no dispute. Judge Miller told the opposing attorneys to get together outside of court and smooth things out to expedite the trial.

At 6:58 Saturday evening Ed Steele, monitoring the surveillance of King, heard the voice of one of the agents in a two-way radio car report, "Topcat is moving." (Ewing King had been given the code name of "Topcat.") King, in his Thunderbird, headed north out of Nashville and stopped in front of a suburban restaurant. King went into the restaurant and shortly thereafter George Broda drove up and parked his blue Chevrolet. Within minutes, they had switched cars, just as King had predicted to Partin. Broda, in King's Thunderbird, took a circuitous route as a decoy, ending up at his home. King, in Broda's Chevrolet, headed for Woodbury. The switch caught the agents offguard and they temporarily lost both cars. But King's car, with Broda driving, was picked up again shortly thereafter as it was returning to Broda's home. The FBI car remained in the vicinity to observe whether there was any further movement by Broda in King's car.

At 9:35 P.M. Broda's car was observed by agents, parked at the residence of Oscar "Mutt" Pitts near Woodbury. There were now four agents in two cars in the Woodbury area. They had to keep moving unobtrusively in and around the Woodbury area so as not to be detected in the small community. Another FBI car was in the vicinity of the King residence in Nashville and another was on the highway between Nashville and Woodbury.

I had been in the FBI office since receiving Ed Steele's call when King first left home. We sat there listening to the cryptic infrequent radio communications from and between the cars. King's car had not moved from Broda's residence. Broda's car was still at the Pitts residence, and there was no activity at the King residence.

At 1:25 A.M. Broda's Chevrolet was observed by agents in front of the Paschal residence in Woodbury. A uniformed patrolman was standing next to the car talking to the occupant. The agents passed by them and identified Broda's car and license number and

Patrolman James Paschal. Paschal's patrol car was in his driveway.

Ten minutes later both the patrol car and Broda's car were gone. About one hour later, the patrol car was back in Paschal's driveway and Broda's car was missing.

Ed Steele notified the car patrolling the highway between Woodbury and Nashville to be on the alert for Broda's car with King driving returning to Nashville. About one hour later the car was spotted heading for Nashville. The agent was able to identify King as the occupant. The agent watching King's house was advised that King would probably be arriving home shortly. The agent pulled up his car across the road leading to King's house and put up the hood, feigning engine trouble. At 4:12 A.M. Broda's blue Chevrolet pulled up to turn in the road. The agent approached the car and said he would be right out of the way. In doing so he was able to identify King as the driver of the car. The agent put down his hood and drove away as King drove up the road to his house.

What Partin had said would happen had happened. Ewing King, the local Teamsters president, who had met Jimmy Hoffa's plane when he first came to Nashville for the trial and who had been in the courtroom practically every day, had switched cars and driven eighty miles to talk to the husband of a juror at 1:30 in the morning. There was no way this could be construed as anything other than a flagrant attempt to tamper with a juror. And if Edward Grady Partin was to be believed—and why shouldn't he now?—Jimmy Hoffa not only had knowledge of what King was doing but had encouraged, and, in fact, directed that it be done.

On that Sunday afternoon a four-day election was finally completed in Philadelphia to determine whether The Voice would prevail and take huge Local 107 out of the Teamsters Union. When the final tally was taken, The Voice had been defeated by less than 600 votes—3,870 to 3,274. It had been an intense, sometimes violent campaign, during which Ray Cohen had been arrested for assault. On Monday, November 19, Cohen, having barely withstood The Voice rebellion, pleaded not guilty to his three-year-old embezzlement charge.

As the search for the missing Ben Dranow went on, two of our attorneys, Paul Allred and Abe Poretz, were conducting a grand jury investigation in Minneapolis looking into his disappearance.

In Chicago Judge Miner dismissed the suit brought by the three cabdrivers against Dominic Abata. Joey Glimco, who had claimed he had nothing to do with the suit, was quoted by newsmen as saying, "We have only begun to fight."

In Detroit Roland McMaster, the secretary-treasurer of Local 299, and William Wolff, the president of the Youngstown Cartage Company, were both convicted of receiving and making illegal payments in violation of the Taft-Hartley Act—the same crime Hoffa was being charged with in Nashville.

Back in Nashville, Walter Hansz, the former treasurer of Commercial Carriers who had testified the previous week that the company was reluctant to cancel the Test Fleet arrangement even though it would have been more profitable to do so because of the fear of labor repercussions, was under cross-examination by Hoffa's attorneys throughout the Monday session.

That afternoon the FBI agents tailing Ewing King discovered that they, too, were being followed. A check of the license number of the car countersurveilling the agents showed that it was registered to one of the business agents of Local 327.

The following morning Hoffa told Partin that King thought he was being followed by the FBI. According to Partin, Hoffa said that he told King all he had to do to get rid of whoever might be following him was to jump them and claim he didn't know who they were. Partin also quoted Hoffa as saying that he wished the patrolman would take money, otherwise he might go either way.

In the courtroom hallway during the morning recess King told Partin about his extracurricular activities over the weekend. He said that he had received a call from his contact on Saturday who told him that the beagle hound King had sold him had dropped dead at ten o'clock. King confided that this was a code they had worked out which meant that King should go to the contact's house at ten o'clock that night. King said he switched cars with George Broda and drove to Woodbury in Broda's car where he went to his contact's house and waited there with the contact's wife and his father while the contact went and arranged the meeting with the patrolman. Then, he said, he met with the patrolman on a lonely road and talked to him in his police car and that the patrolman didn't want any money but did want to be promoted to sergeant. He said the patrolman told him that he couldn't force his wife to do anything but he would talk to her. King told Partin Hoffa was upset that the patrolman wouldn't take any money because money would pin him down.

When he returned to Nashville, King went on, there was a car parked with the hood up blocking the road into his house. He said the driver told him he would be out of the way in a minute and had put the hood down and driven away. King was sure it was an FBI agent and supposed that they would be interviewing him. Then he said that the following Saturday night they were going to ambush the agents. The plan, he told Partin, was for him to lead the agents up an alley where he would have a group of "business agents" waiting. Then they would beat up the agents and say that they thought they were robbers. King said that he and Broda hadn't reswitched cars yet because they wanted to keep the FBI guessing.

King also told Partin that he thought the male Negro juror might be "all right."

Inasmuch as the purpose of the surveillance of King had been accomplished—corroborating what Partin reported by establishing the fact that King did contact the juror's husband—and to avoid any incidents, it was terminated that afternoon.

In Chicago that day two men with close underworld connections were discussing a proposed attempt to bribe Judge Miller. They had been in contact with a person in Memphis about approaching the judge with the offer of a share in a $5,000,000 office building which was being constructed with funds provided by a loan from the Pension Fund.

Partin left for Baton Rouge that evening and said he would return the following week.

Court adjourned for the Thanksgiving weekend after Wednesday's session during which Ray Van Beckum, who had succeeded Bert Beveridge as president of Commercial Carriers, Inc., testified that he had allowed the Test Fleet lease to remain in effect at the Cadillac terminal to avoid any trouble with the Teamsters Union. When Jim Neal asked him if there were any particular individuals in the union about whom he was concerned, he answered, "Mr. James Hoffa and Mr. Bert Brennan."

We all went home for the holiday weekend and it was a tremendous relief to escape from the tension and intrigue for a few days. Jimmy Hoffa also went home to Detroit, but he could not relax because he was campaigning for reelection as president of Local 299. He was being opposed by a Dearborn, Michigan, truck driver named Ira Cook, Jr., who had no chance of winning. Nevertheless, a campaign rally was held for Hoffa on Saturday evening at Cobo Hall in Detroit, attended by two thousand Teamsters members. Ira Cook, at Hoffa's invitation, was on the platform with him at the rally. Cook was loudly booed by the audience and said he felt like "Daniel did when he was thrown into the lions' den."

Hoffa defended his accomplishments as a Teamsters leader and then launched into an attack on Senator McClellan, the Attorney General, whom he referred to as "Bobby boy," and the press for its "barrage of filth and slime" about him.

On Monday, November 26, Herbert Grosberg, Hoffa's former accountant, and George Fitzgerald, who had been one of Hoffa's attorneys for almost thirty years, testified for the government. Grosberg told the jury about the two $10,000 dividend checks from the Hobren Corporation that were endorsed by the wives of Hoffa and Brennan and turned over to David Probstein to start the State Cab Company. Grosberg said that all of his discussions about the money and the cab company were with Hoffa and that he never talked to either Mrs. Hoffa or Mrs. Brennan about it. He said that it was Hoffa who sent him to Indianapolis in May, 1955, to check on the money that had been invested.

Fitzgerald testified that on one occasion, at Hoffa's request, he had given the Teamsters leader his personal check for $15,000 in exchange for a $15,000 Test Fleet dividend check made out to Hoffa's wife.

The testimony of these long-time associates of Hoffa was very damaging to the defense position that it was the wives of Hoffa and Brennan who were the actual owners and benefactors of Test Fleet and Hobren.

When Fitzgerald finished his testimony, Hoffa followed him out of the courtroom and confronted him.

"You're finished, you're fired!" Hoffa said angrily. "Turn over all your books and records to the union."

Hoffa could not fire Grosberg. He had already quit.

That evening at 7:30 Ben Dranow was arrested by FBI agents in the maid's quarters in a home in Miami where he had been hiding. He had shaved his head to change his appearance and was living under the name "Bud Smith." He had made a deal with the unsuspecting owner to buy the house and asked permission to move in until the deal was consummated. He was taken by deputy U.S. marshals to Minneapolis where the fugitive warrant was outstanding and put in jail.

Partin came back to Nashville the next day and called me that afternoon. I picked him up and drove across the river and parked. He said that Hoffa was in a rage and was complaining that all his

friends were double-crossing him. Partin said that he was holler-
ing at Allen Dorfman for not talking to George Fitzgerald a week
ago as he was supposed to. Partin said that just before I picked him
up, Allen Dorfman told him to go out and call Nick Tweel in
Huntington and see if anything was new. I drove down the road
to a pay phone and waited in the car while Partin called Tweel.

When he came back to the car, Partin said that Tweel told him
he had a man in Nashville named Dallas Hall, a tavern owner, who
could help with the jury. Tweel wanted someone to read him a list
of the jurors over the phone. I drove back into Nashville and
dropped Partin off.

I met with Partin again later that evening after first confirming
through Bill Sheets that there was a man named Dallas Hall who
operated a club in West Nashville. Partin said he had gone back
to the hotel and told Dorfman what Tweel had said. He then
accompanied Dorfman to Hoffa's suite and they related the conversation to him. He said that Hoffa told someone to tell Bufalino
to bring in a jury list. While they were waiting, Partin said, Hoffa
asked Dorfman if he was sure Tweel was all right. Dorfman assured Hoffa that he was. Partin said that when Bufalino came in
with a sheaf of photostated papers—there was a separate sheet for
each juror, listing residence, occupation and other background
data—Hoffa gave the papers to Dorfman.

Partin said that he then accompanied Hoffa, I. Irving Davidson,
Dorfman, Chuck O'Brien and Jake Kossman to dinner, walking to
O'Brien's Beefery, a restaurant several blocks west on West End
Avenue. Broadway, the street on which the Federal Building
faced, became West End Avenue two blocks further west where it
crossed the railroad tracks. The railroad station was on the same
side as the Federal Building and across from the Nashville *Tennessean* and the *Banner*.

Partin said that Dorfman tried to call Tweel from the restaurant
but was not able to reach him. After dinner, they began walking
back to the hotel. When they reached the railroad station, they all
went in while Dorfman again tried to call Tweel from a pay
phone. Partin said that while Dorfman was on the phone, Hoffa
was talking to the stationmaster about the height of the station
ceiling. Hoffa jokingly bet him a Coke on the height and said he
was going to have an engineer come in the next day to measure it.

Dorfman was again unable to reach Tweel and they walked on
to the corner across from the Federal Building. Partin said there

were two phone booths on the corner and Dorfman entered the one on the left and again called Tweel. He heard Dorfman use a credit card for the call. This time the connection with Tweel was made and Partin heard Dorfman read the entire jury list over the phone. Partin said that this was about 8:30 P.M.

In court the next day Charlie Shaffer continued the step-by-step presentation of evidence showing that proceeds from Test Fleet and Hobren went to Hoffa or for his benefit. A Detroit bank official testified about the purchase of a cashier's check in the amount of $20,000 with $10,000 in cash and two $5000 Test Fleet dividend checks payable to the wives of Hoffa and Brennan. The check was made out to Dr. Leo Pearlman. Frank Collins, the former secretary-treasurer of Local 299 who had served a prison term for perjury to protect Hoffa in connection with the New York wiretap cases, testified that he had signed Hoffa's name to the requisition for the cashier's check on Hoffa's authority.

Out in Minneapolis that day Ben Dranow was indicted for jumping bail and remained incarcerated in the Hennepin County jail there. In Detroit George Roxburgh pleaded guilty to five counts of illegally receiving money from an employer and resigned as a business agent and trustee of Local 299.

On Thursday, November 29, Dr. Leo Pearlman testified that he received that $20,000 cashier's check concerning which the Detroit banker and Frank Collins had testified the day before. Pearlman said the money represented Hoffa's and Brennan's share in the Northwestern Oil Company. The government rested its case after introducing a chart showing that the gross Test Fleet–Hobren income was $1,042,072 with a profit of $257,759. The jury was excused until the following Monday when the defense would begin its presentation.

That afternoon, Partin called Tweel in Huntington. Tweel said he had talked to the fellow in Nashville and that he was working on it. He told Partin that that kind of thing took time. Partin related the conversation to Hoffa the following day.

As their first defense witness on Monday morning, Hoffa's attorneys recalled Bert Beveridge. The former president of Commercial Carriers had earlier testified for almost one week as a government witness. During that testimony Beveridge said that after appearing in the grand jury in Nashville in May, he had falsely told Hoffa attorney James Haggerty that the government attorneys had played tape recordings for him. He said that shortly thereafter he had told Carney Matheson, who was at the time his attorney, that he had lied about that and that it was not true.

Hoffa's attorneys now tried to show that Beveridge had actually been telling the truth when he told Matheson about the tape recordings and was now lying. Beveridge stuck to his position and said further that Matheson had tried to persuade him to testify falsely in the trial that he had heard recordings.

Matheson then took the stand to contradict his own client. He said he had merely told Beveridge to tell the truth and not to perjure himself. Matheson said that Beveridge had decided to change his story about hearing the recordings so as not to antagonize the government.

Government attorneys had not played any tape recordings for Beveridge at any time. In commenting on Matheson's testimony about a conversation he had with his client, Judge Miller had said, "I must say in advance I don't have too high a regard for a lawyer that would do that."

Matheson admitted on cross-examination the next day that while representing truckers in labor negotiations with Hoffa, he was in several business deals with him. He also admitted making what he termed "incorrect" statements before the McClellan Committee while under oath. He said that he only learned later he was wrong.

Jacques Schiffer then testified that he had advised Hoffa in 1954 that the arrangement between Commercial Carriers and Test Fleet was legal.

As the defense went forward, Hoffa's troops were now pouring into Nashville. Some were to be witnesses and some were not. "What's so funny about that?" Hoffa asked reporter Tom Joyce of the *Detroit News*. "I am running the Teamsters Union from Nashville. I have no choice."

Louis "Babe" Triscaro had come in with John Felice, another Cleveland Teamsters official. P. D. Maktos, a Cleveland Teamsters attorney, had also been in. Now, on December 4, there arrived Allen Dorfman, back from Chicago, with Teamster Don Peters; attorney Larry Burns from Detroit; attorney Morris Shenker from St. Louis; David Wenger, Pension Fund accountant; Tom Flynn, the head of the Eastern Conference of Teamsters; and Ed Partin, back from Baton Rouge. They all stayed at the Andrew Jackson Hotel.

That evening I talked to Partin. There had been a call waiting for him from Nick Tweel when he arrived at the hotel. Partin said that when he returned Tweel's call, Tweel said that his Nashville contact had told him things were hot, that the jurors, Hoffa and everyone else were being watched and that they knew about the phone calls.

Partin said that when he reported this to Hoffa, Hoffa told him to go out to a phone booth and call Allen Dorfman. Hoffa said he thought Tweel was just trying to duck out. Partin went out and called Dorfman's office and was told he was en route to Nashville. When he returned to the hotel, Dorfman was there in the lobby with Don Peters. Partin said that he and Dorfman went up to see Hoffa. Dorfman mentioned that he had used a credit card when he called Tweel with the jury list. Partin said Hoffa called Dorfman a stupid son of a bitch and told him that he only used credit cards when he wanted "them" to know whom he was calling. Hoffa told Dorfman he should have a pocket full of change when he made calls like that. He told Dorfman that he thought Tweel was chickening out.

With the trial now moving toward conclusion, we had to decide what to do about Mrs. James Paschal and Mr. Gratin Fields, the two jurors who might have been corruptly influenced. In the case of Mrs. Paschal, we had proof that Hoffa's associate Ewing King had talked to her husband in a surreptitious manner. We also had information from Partin that King had asked her husband to attempt to influence her on Hoffa's behalf and that he had agreed. We did not know for certain that this was true, nor, if it was, whether Paschal had, in fact, tried to influence his wife. The mere fact of the contact of the husband by King, however, seemed sufficient to suggest that Mrs. Paschal be removed as a juror.

The situation with reference to Mr. Fields, the male Negro juror, while not so clear-cut, was beginning to shape up as another corruptive effort. We had information from Partin that Hoffa boasted that Fields had been contacted by Larry Campbell, one of his business agents. Ewing King had made a similar reference. We had located Campbell in Louisville at Brown's Tourist Home. The first returns on our request for toll call records indicated several calls from a pay phone at the Tourist Home to a man named Tom Parks at the Nashville residence of a Mrs. Mattie Mix. We had then obtained the records of toll calls from the Mix residence, which showed calls from there to the pay phone at Brown's Tourist Home. Bill Sheets then established that Tom Parks, who frequented the Mix residence, was the uncle of Larry Campbell. We did not know, independently of Partin, whether Campbell or Parks had actually contacted juror Fields but the circumstances were pointing in that direction.

In the midst of our deliberations a bizarre incident in the court-room precipitated our first move. It was Wednesday, December 5. The jury had just retired temporarily from the courtroom at the direction of Judge Miller so that the government and defense attorneys could argue a motion. A young man in a raincoat walked into the courtroom and up the aisle. When he reached the swinging wooden gates that separate the attorneys, defendant, judge and jury from the spectators, he walked right through and approached Hoffa from the rear. As he did, he pulled a gun from his pocket, aimed it at Hoffa and began shooting. Fortunately, it was only an air-pellet gun. It all happened very swiftly. The defense attorneys jumped under their table seeking cover. Hoffa, reacting instinctively, first put his arm up in front of his face and then lunged at the assailant, striking him in the jaw. As he fell to the floor, Chuck O'Brien, sitting in the first row of spectators, jumped on the man's back and a deputy marshal hit him on the head with his gun butt.

It was all over as quickly as it had begun. The assailant, identified as Warren Swanson, an itinerant restaurant worker, most recently from Washington, D.C., was taken into custody and sent to a prison medical center for observation. He claimed to have had a vision directing him to kill Hoffa. If he had used a regular gun, he probably would have. Hoffa had welts on his arm from the pellets but was otherwise calm and collected.

Judge Miller adjourned the court and ordered the jurors locked up for the night to avoid their being exposed to publicity concerning the incident. He also said that as a precautionary measure, everyone entering the courtroom henceforth would be searched.

With the jury now sequestered, it was an opportune time to make a motion that Mrs. Paschal be removed as a juror and that the jury continue to be locked up to avoid any further attempts to corrupt it.

The following morning Hoffa's attorneys moved for a mistrial. Judge Miller told them to put their plea in a written motion and he would consider it. Jim Neal then handed Judge Miller a motion and requested that the courtroom be cleared of all press and spectators. The motion asking for the removal of Mrs. Paschal had attached affidavits by FBI agents which attested to the fact that Ewing King had switched cars, driven to Woodbury and contacted

Patrolman James Paschal. Judge Miller read the material and then ordered the courtroom cleared of everyone except the government and defense attorneys and Hoffa. He then directed Marshal Disspayne to bring Patrolman Paschal, Ewing King, Oscar Pitts and George Broda to the courtroom. The two little windows in the doors leading into the courtroom were covered with newspapers and masking tape and the press and spectators milling around the corridor in puzzlement could neither hear nor see what was transpiring inside. Among the spectators was Ed Partin.

Judge Miller had decided to hold a hearing then and there on the motion by the government. King, who had been in the courtroom, and Broda were brought in and held in the marshal's office. Patrolman Paschal was brought quietly in the back way and through the judge's chambers so he would not be seen by the press and spectators. Finally, Oscar Pitts arrived and was placed in one of our offices. In the meantime, the FBI agents who had been on the surveillance of King and Broda the night he met Paschal testified as to what they had witnessed. Hoffa sat grimly silent. Then Ewing King was ushered through the side witness door and took the stand. Hoffa, with his hand by his face, exhibited a quick five-finger sign to King. King took the Fifth Amendment. So did Broda and Pitts. Then Patrolman James Paschal took the stand.

At first Paschal nervously denied talking to King. As the questioning by Judge Miller went on, however, he admitted that he had talked to King at the suggestion of Oscar Pitts. He said that Pitts told him King was anxious to help him get a promotion. He denied that the Hoffa trial was mentioned or that he had said anything about the contact to his wife. Patrolman Paschal was a very frightened man.

The hearing lasted almost four hours. Judge Miller instructed those present not to discuss what had transpired with anyone. He directed that Mrs. Paschal be removed from the jury and replaced by the first alternate juror. He also ordered that the jury remain sequestered for the remainder of the trial. He then adjourned the court for the remainder of the week.

Following the hearing, Bill Sheets and Ed Steele interviewed Patrolman Paschal. He again acknowledged having talked to King about a promotion but stuck to his story that no mention was made of the trial and that he had not talked to his wife about it. When Mrs. Paschal was quietly removed from the jury, she, too, was interviewed. She seemed genuinely surprised and said that her husband had not discussed a meeting with King or the trial with her. King and Broda refused to talk to the agents and Pitts was evasive in his answers.

Later that day Partin told me that Allen Dorfman had commented that having the jury locked up was going to make it tough. He said that Ewing King had found out where the jury was sequestered and that Chuck O'Brien said he was going to try to sneak newspapers into the jury. Partin said that King told him the patrolman had answered the judge's questions just as he wanted him to. King said that he was sure the FBI had not seen him meet with Paschal and that all they had seen was him returning home. King told Partin that Pitts was okay and had told the FBI to go to hell. Partin said that King, Broda and Pitts were interviewed that evening at the Andrew Jackson Hotel by Tommy Osborn.

Partin also said that he had seen a man come out of Hoffa's suite with Fred Ramsey, a city policeman who had been hired by Tommy Osborn before the trial to do background investigations on the prospective jurors. Partin said he heard the man referred to as an "attorney from Lebanon." He described him and noted that he had a college class ring on his finger. It did not mean anything at the time but would later on.

When Hoffa left town for the weekend, according to Partin, he told Chuck O'Brien to stay behind and hire private detectives to find out who was leaking information.

Hoffa's attorneys filed a motion on Friday asking that a mistrial be declared. Hoffa claimed, in an affidavit accompanying the motion, that he was in fear for his life and that the attack on him by the assailant had caused "such shock, stress and strain" that it would affect his "ability to communicate fairly and fully with his counsel during the balance of the trial."

Back in Detroit over the weekend, Hoffa resumed his campaign for reelection. Appearing calm and relaxed, he shook hands with hundreds of Teamsters lined up to vote outside the Teamsters headquarters. He was reelected by an overwhelming majority.

When the trial resumed on Monday, December 10, Judge Miller denied Hoffa's motion for a mistrial, terming the motion "utterly groundless if not fantastic." Judge Miller said that he had a "ringside seat" to the pellet gun incident, and that contrary to the psychological strain and fear expressed by Hoffa and his attorneys in the motion, they had appeared to him to have acted "with unusual composure considering the circumstances."

Newsmen immediately noticed that morning that Mrs. Paschal was missing and her jury seat was occupied by alternate juror Mr. Walter Harper, a retired rural mail carrier. When contacted by newsmen, Mrs. Paschal was tearful and upset and said she didn't know why she had been removed from the jury.

The defense continued with two truck drivers from Detroit testifying that they attended a meeting in the early 1950s at which Hoffa and his attorneys spoke about the Test Fleet situation. They said the attorneys said at the time that the arrangement was legal. They were followed to the stand by the widow of Bert Brennan, who had remarried and was now Mrs. Peterson. She testified that she and Mrs. Hoffa owned the Test Fleet Company. She said that it had been set up in their maiden names to avoid having their business or bank accounts become involved in possible legal actions against their husbands. Her testimony and cross-examination continued over the next two days.

On Wednesday Partin again returned to Nashville. I met with him that evening. He said that Hoffa was concerned about security and wanted someone to guard the door to his suite. The man he picked was Partin. Partin said that Hoffa and attorney Dave Previant had a violent argument in the suite, but that he didn't know what it was about except for hearing Hoffa finally tell Previant to get the hell out of the room. Partin said he had talked briefly to Ewing King and King said he might be called before a grand jury but that it wouldn't matter because the patrolman was sticking to his story.

The following day Charlie Shaffer concluded the cross-examination of Mrs. Peterson. Although she continued to maintain that she and Mrs. Hoffa had owned the Test Fleet Company and that she had participated in its management, she did acknowledge under Shaffer's probing that she had nothing to do with organizing the company, did not know its original directors and had never attended a stockholders' meeting. She also admitted she did not know where the original trucks had been obtained nor what happened to them when the arrangement was canceled in 1958.

David Previant then testified that he had advised Hoffa in 1952 that the Test Fleet arrangement with Commerical Carriers was perfectly legal. This would have been unusual advice for such a capable attorney as Previant to give, and Neal engaged with him in an extended debate about the Taft-Hartley Act and its application to the Test Fleet situation. But there was no question that the testimony by the man with whom, according to Partin, Hoffa had been violently arguing the previous evening was damaging to the government's case.

Ewing King and George Broda, undaunted, continued to come to the trial and sit in the courtroom. Other spectators that day included Allen Dorfman, Chuck O'Brien and Ed Partin.

Following the court session I met with Partin. He told me that Ewing King said he knew a bellhop in the motel where the jury was sequestered. He told Partin that he had approached the bell-hop about sneaking newspapers in to the jury but the bellhop was afraid to do it.

On Friday, December 14, Jimmy Hoffa took the witness stand in his own defense. For one of the few times during the trial the courtroom was full. Hoffa testified that he had nothing to do with the Test Fleet Company and received no benefits from it. He admitted using some of the proceeds from the company, which he said his wife had lent to him, but insisted that he always paid her back in cash later on. He contradicted the sworn testimony of his former friend and attorney George Fitzgerald by stating that the exchange of his wife's $15,000 dividend check for a personal check of Fitzgerald's was the attorney's idea, not his, and that Fitzgerald, not he, was in need of funds at the time. Following Hoffa's direct testimony, the court adjourned for the weekend, with Hoffa scheduled to face cross-examination by Jim Neal on Monday morning.

The case would undoubtedly go to the jury by the end of the following week and a decision had to be made on what to do about juror Gratin Fields. I conferred on the phone with Jack Miller and we decided to have Tom McKeon and Bill French get together with the FBI in Detroit and explore all logical leads, including interviews and the compilation of an up-to-date chronology of pertinent toll calls to show Larry Campbell's activities during the trial. Paul Allred would go to Louisville and do the same thing. The three men flew to Nashville that day and I explained everything we knew to date. Then French and McKeon took off for Detroit and Allred for Louisville.

Assuming that the circumstantial evidence continued to point toward a probable attempt to contact juror Fields, the problem remained as to how to move in court to remove Fields from the jury. There were no eyewitnesses to give affidavits as there had been in the Paschal situation. We did not want to expose Partin by submitting an affidavit from him on Hoffa's statement about Campbell and Fields. Moreover, this would also, in all likelihood, require him to testify in a proceeding similar to the Paschal hearing—which we wanted to avoid and which he, at that point, probably would not be willing to do.

Bob Kennedy, who was kept fully advised of development by me and Jack Miller, decided to send Burke Marshall, the head of the Civil Rights Division, and Howard Willens, Jack's assistant, down to add their thoughts to our think tank. It was finally decided that I would ask Partin to give an affidavit about Hoffa's statement to him. The affidavit would then be sealed and submitted, along with the chronology of toll calls and whatever additional information we had, to Judge Miller with a request that the judge reseal the affidavit after he had read it and that Fields be removed from the jury.

When the trial resumed on Monday, Jim Neal began the cross-examination of Hoffa. Neal had been preparing for this for a long time and knew where Hoffa was vulnerable, particularly in several inconsistencies between his testimony the previous Friday and earlier statements made to other government agencies and hearings. When confronted with the contradictions in testimony by Neal, Hoffa said that his prior statements had been mistakes. For instance, Hoffa testified on Friday that he had never discussed the Test Fleet arrangement with Bert Beveridge or any other official of Commercial Carriers. Yet, when he testified before a federal grand jury in New York in 1956, he had stated that he had discussed it with Beveridge. Hoffa said that his testimony before the grand jury was in error.

Hoffa was, as usual, an impressive, though testy, witness, and Neal did an effective job of eliciting reluctant admissions from him of prior inconsistent statements, casting some doubt on his credibility. How much doubt, only the jury would decide.

On Tuesday both the government and the defense rested and Wednesday was devoted to final arguments by attorneys for both sides. Wednesday evening, while McKeon, French and Allred were en route to Nashville with their corroborative information, I met with Partin to obtain the affidavit. I told him what we planned to do and that we hoped, but could not guarantee, that Judge Miller would respect our request that it remain sealed. Partin knew that he was taking an irrevocable step but agreed to give the affidavit. Partin's signature was witnessed by a notary public whom neither of us had ever seen but who had been recommended to me as a reliable person.

The next day, while final arguments to the jury were being

concluded, we began assembling the chronology of toll calls between Nashville, Louisville and Detroit. At the same time, Nat
Lewin was preparing the motion that would be filed. There was
a series of calls from Brown's Tourist Home and from pay phones
in the vicinity to the Mattie Mix residence in Nashville. There
were corresponding calls from the Mattie Mix residence to
Brown's Tourist Home. There were also calls from Brown's Tourist Home to Hoffa's unlisted phone at his residence in Detroit,
where Chuck O'Brien was living. Mr. and Mrs. Tilford Brown,
who operated the Tourist Home, told FBI agents that Campbell
had talked about going to Nashville to help someone. Mrs. Brown
recalled receiving a call from a Mr. O'Brien in Nashville asking for
Campbell. When she told him Campbell was not in, he asked her
where a private airplane could land nearby. She said that a couple
of days later Campbell left, saying he was going to fly to Nashville
to meet someone at the airport. The FBI agents also found a girl
whom Campbell had told he was in Louisville to help Hoffa with
his trial in Nashville.

When the arguments to the jury were completed for the day, Jim
Neal again asked that the courtroom be cleared of press and spectators so that he might present a motion. The jury had already been
excused for the day and Judge Miller ordered the courtroom
cleared. Neal then handed the motion and the attached documents
including the sealed affidavit to the judge.

Judge Miller looked at the contents of the sealed envelope and
then ordered it resealed over the vehement objections of Hoffa's
attorneys. There then ensued a one-hour debate between government and defense attorneys over the merits of the government's
motion. At the conclusion, Judge Miller ordered Fields removed
from the jury.

On Friday morning when the jury filed in, the press were waiting to see if one of the jurors would be missing, as had been the
case two weeks earlier. They noticed at once that Gratin Fields had
been replaced by another alternate juror. When Fields was contacted by reporters at his home, he told them he did not know why
he had been removed. He said that no one had attempted to contact
him during the trial.

Following the instructions by Judge Miller, the case was given
to the jury and they began their deliberations at 3:01 P.M. It was the
forty-second day of the trial and less than four days before Christmas. At 6:30 that evening, not having reached a verdict, the jury
was sequestered for the night.

The long vigil continued all day Saturday and the jury again retired for the night without reaching a verdict. The tension was mounting and the possibility of a hung jury was becoming evident. Sunday morning the jury reported to the judge that it was deadlocked. Judge Miller asked the jury to persevere and attempt to reach a verdict.

Finally, late that morning, Judge Miller, having again been advised by the jury that it was hopelessly deadlocked, summoned the jurors into the courtroom. As they took their places in the jury box, we all knew that there would be no verdict in this trial.

Judge Miller asked any jurors who thought that a verdict might be reached by further deliberation to raise their right hands. No hands were raised. He then asked all jurors who thought they were hopelessly deadlocked to raise their right hands. All of the jurors raised their hands.

The judge expressed his disappointment but noted reluctantly that "there comes a time when if the members of the jury cannot agree, they cannot agree, and that is it."

The sense of relief on the part of Hoffa, his attorneys and followers was almost audible as they relaxed from the tension that had gripped us all for so long. But the stirrings ceased and the muscles retightened as Judge Miller turned from the jury and grimly continued:

> I have a statement to make at this time which I will read for the record, and it will be made a part of these proceedings, and while I am reading this statement, I ask that no one leave the courtroom or enter the courtroom and that no one stand up or get out of their seats.
>
> The trial of this case having been concluded, I feel that it is my duty to make a statement as to some of the unfortunate events which have marked the trial from its inception. First, I wish to make it very clear that I have no reason to doubt the honesty and integrity of any persons called for jury service in this case or the honesty or integrity of any person selected as a regular or alternate member of the jury. The fine citizens who rendered this service are entitled to the gratitude of the Court and the public for their tireless efforts and for the sacrifices which they have made in serving as members of the jury in one of the longest trials in the history of this court. It became necessary during the latter part of the trial to have the members of the jury sequestered and this entailed additional sacrifices on their part. The remarks that I am about to make are not intended to

reflect in any way upon these splendid people of our community. From the very outset, while the jury was being selected from a list of those summoned for jury service, there were indications that improper contacts had been made and were being made with prospective members of the jury. In one instance the Court was required to excuse a prospective juror who had been examined on voir dire after he very commendably disclosed to the Court that he had been improperly approached.

After the jury was finally impanelled and while the trial was underway, two sessions of the Court were held when all persons were removed from the courtroom except the defendant, the attorneys for both parties, the official court reporter, the courtroom clerk and any witnesses called to testify. At these sessions evidence was presented to the court indicating that illegal and improper attempts were made by close labor associates of the defendant to contact and influence certain members of the jury. . . .

In the public interest and to protect the court as an institution of Government, I have decided that three affirmative steps must be taken by the court at this time:

First, I have signed orders to convene another grand jury soon after the first of the year to investigate fully and completely all of the incidents connected with this trial indicating illegal attempts to influence jurors and prospective jurors by any person or persons whomsoever and to return indictments where probable cause therefor exists.

Second, I have requested the United States Attorney for this District to assemble and present to the grand jury when it convenes all evidence on this matter presently existing and any further evidence which may be obtained as a result of any further investigations.

Third, I am now directing that the entire record of the two closed sessions of the court be immediately unsealed for filing in the Clerk's office as a public record, except for certain documents read only by the Court at the second session which because of their strictly confidential nature cannot be released at the present time. . . .

The right of a defendant in a criminal case to be tried by a jury of his peers is one of the most sacred of our Constitutional guarantees. The system of trial by jury, however, becomes nothing more than a mockery if unscrupulous persons are allowed to subvert it by improper and unlawful means. I d o not intend that such shameful acts to corrupt our jury system shall go unnoticed by this Court.

Judge Miller then told the jury about the pellet-gun assault on Hoffa which had caused the original sequestering and explained that the evidence produced at the first secret session the following day necessitated that the sequestering continue for the remainder of the trial. He then declared a mistrial, excused the jury and adjourned the court.

Jimmy Hoffa walked away from another trial. But this time the "improvers" lived up to their reputations. The charge on which Hoffa had just been tried was a misdemeanor. Jury tampering is a felony.

Back in Detroit on Christmas Eve Hoffa taped an interview with station WWJ-TV which was shown that evening and again on Christmas night. In the interview he attacked Judge Miller as being prejudiced, and Jim Neal as "one of the most vicious prosecutors who ever handled a criminal case for the Department of Justice." He said that it was "a disgrace," in his opinion, "for anyone to make a statement that this jury was tampered with...."

As the year ended, Hoffa received votes of confidence from two quarters. In St. Louis Senator Edward V. Long praised Hoffa in a speech before a citywide Teamsters conference at which a resolution was passed supporting Hoffa and condemning Robert Kennedy. In Manchester, New Hampshire, cantankerous William Loeb, the publisher of the *Manchester Union Leader*, wrote an editorial in which he likened Robert Kennedy to Caesar and attacked him both for the trial of Hoffa in Nashville and for the indictment of Governor Ross Barnett of Mississippi for his resistance, in violation of court orders, to the admission of James Meredith to the University of Mississippi. Loeb said that Hoffa and Barnett were being persecuted because they dared to oppose the Administration. Both Senator Edward Long and William Loeb would be heard from again.

CHAPTER IX

"Bobby Kennedy Is Just
Another Lawyer Now"

━━━━━━━━━━━━━━

ON JANUARY 6, 1963, we all headed back to Nashville to get ready for the grand jury investigation ordered by Judge Miller. We now had time to take a more leisurely look at the fast-breaking events and incidents that had transpired during the trial. While the trial was in progress, I had told the government attorneys only what I thought they needed to know to protect the case, namely, the apparent attempts to influence jurors Paschal and Fields. For the most part, I had worked outside the courtroom with the FBI, pursuing these matters, while they worked in the courtroom try- ing to convict Jimmy Hoffa. Now we all sat down for several days to try to evaluate exactly what we did know about attempts to tamper with the jury and, equally important, exactly how much we didn't know.

On the surface, we were starting with many missing pieces, but we did have a major key to the puzzle in Edward Grady Partin. I was the only one who had talked to Partin during the trial. On each occasion, either while we were talking or immediately there- after, I had made notes of what he said. They were cryptic and written on hotel stationery, envelopes and other pieces of paper, but each one was dated and legible—at least to me. We now re- viewed everything Partin had told me, in addition to the other information we had pieced together, primarily through FBI investigations and toll call records. Carl Schultz came down from Chicago on loan from the Labor Department to set up and maintain a running chronology beginning with the first visit to Nashville of Phil Weiss and Henry "Buster" Bell in September, 1962.

The principal difficulty in investigating a crime of this nature is that of insulation. People like Hoffa who engage in illegal activities are usually careful to make certain that they are well insulated from the actual crime by as many layers of other people as possible. When Hoffa was arrested in the Cheasty case, he was ridiculed by some of his underworld friends for having dealt directly with Cheasty. He was not likely to make the same mistake again.

It became apparent in retrospect that had it not been for Partin, we would have known nothing of the efforts to corrupt the jury other than Tippens' own report to the judge, which led now only to Medlin, and the reports by prospective jurors of the "Allen from the *Banner*" calls. Through the information furnished by Partin, and the follow-up investigations and corroborations by the FBI, we had, in this instance, not only the identities of some of the insulating persons and their involvement, but also a direct link to Hoffa himself.

The attempt to influence juror Betty Paschal was the only one where we seemed to know all the links in the chain. From all indications, Ewing King, at the direction of Hoffa, had gone to Oscar "Mutt" Pitts, who had contacted Patrolman Paschal and set up the meeting with King. Even here, the insulation would have held up if King had not gone himself, under FBI surveillance, to meet with Paschal. But again, proving what happened would require our obtaining the cooperation of one or more of the persons involved.

After a number of extensive interviews both James Paschal and Mutt Pitts corroborated, almost word for word, what Ewing King had told Partin and what Partin had, in turn, told me at the time the attempts to influence juror Betty Paschal were taking place. The three statements also coincided perfectly with what the FBI agents had observed during the surveillances. We now had impressive proof of one instance of calculated jury tampering.

The other situations were even more difficult to prove and there were many unanswered questions. Had Larry Campbell succeeded in contacting juror Fields? Had Allen Dorfman and Nicholas Tweel actually attempted to tamper with the jury? What had

Phil Weiss and Buster Bell actually been up to in their various trips to Nashville? We knew from an informant that they intended to attempt to tamper with the jury but we did not know whether or not they had succeeded. Partin had described a man fitting Bell's description as having been in Hoffa's suite during the trial but he had not met either Weiss or Bell. Finally, how many others might there be whom we knew nothing about?

During the investigation in the weeks and months ahead, the pattern would develop of other instances of insulated efforts to corrupt the jury. Some we would be able to prove and others we would not. But by the time we finished, we would be confident in our conclusion that it was one of the most massive attempts to corrupt a jury in the history of the federal judiciary.

While we were sitting in Nashville contemplating the task ahead, Hoffa was in Miami, leveling a blast at the Attorney General:

> Bobby Kennedy has spent over $12 million in taxpayers' money going to 32 grand juries to investigate the Teamsters and particularly myself. He has used the government, thousands of F.B.I. agents, Treasury and Labor Department agents and local police and prosecutors. His desire is to see me rot in jail but it will never come about. Bobby has two reasons—a personal vendetta and a desire for the union to be subservient to anything he wants done.

In Minneapolis the judge ordered a psychiatric examination for Ben Dranow, whose trial for jumping bail was scheduled for January 28. In Hoboken, New Jersey, Tony Provenzano, whose salary had recently been raised $25,000 in appreciation for his services to the union, was awaiting trial for extortion. Charlie Smith and our other attorneys in Chicago continued their painstaking effort to pull together the Pension Fund case, and Bill French and Dick Coleman were preparing to go to trial in Toledo in the prosecution of Teamsters official James Jameson.

At about the same time we began to receive reports from the FBI that Morris Emanuel, who was in charge of investigations in the Chicago regional office of the Labor Department's Bureau of Labor-Management Reports, was actively furnishing information to associates of Hoffa for money. Emanuel was Carl Schultz's superior in Chicago and had access to considerable information concerning Teamsters investigations. The FBI said that their source was very reliable but also extremely sensitive and could not be used as a witness at that time. I advised Ted Thoma, the director of investigations at the Washington headquarters of the Bureau of Labor-Management Reports, and also told Carl Schultz, Jack Thiede and their associate Jerry Gotch in Chicago so they could keep an eye on Emanuel and attempt to discreetly limit his access to sensitive information.

One of the persons with whom Buster Bell had been in frequent contact, while in Nashville before and during the Test Fleet trial and also by long-distance phone, was a Nashville horse trainer. While he would be a logical person for horse fancier Bell to know and communicate with, he also happened to be a friend of Red Medlin's. Medlin seemed, in appearance and demeanor, a most unlikely person to be offering a large sum of cash to a prospective juror. We met with his attorney, R. B. Parker, to discuss the matter. We told Parker we did not believe Medlin's version of his conversation with Tippens. Mr. Parker said that he could understand our suspicions but that his client insisted that he had merely overheard two strangers talking in a restaurant booth behind him about how a juror could make a lot of money, and then passed on to Tippens what he had heard. But he said he would have further conversations with his client and would be back in touch with us.

A special grand jury was convened on January 17, 1963. The first witnesses included Ed Steele, James Paschal and Mutt Pitts. They were followed by James Tippens and his secretary, who had taken the call from Medlin in which he left the message for Tippens to call him. We also subpoenaed the registrations and records of local and long-distance telephone calls from the Travelers Rest Motel and the Hermitage Hotel concerning Phil Weiss and Henry Bell, and the telephone records of the Teamsters group and Nick Tweel at the Andrew Jackson Hotel.

Through FBI investigations we were able to trace the history of the "Allen from the *Banner*" calls to prospective jurors. The FBI ascertained that Herman Frazier, the chief of detectives of the Huntington, West Virginia, Police Department, Lieutenant Nelson Paden of the same department and Albert P. Cole, a private investigator, had been in Nashville at the beginning of the Test Fleet trial and had stayed at the Noel Hotel. A review of telephone records turned up not only the known missing calls but also some additional calls to prospective jurors that we had not known of.

We now knew that some of these calls had been made from the hotel rooms of Frazier, Paden and Cole and that the others had been made from pay phones near the hotel where they stayed. We also knew from investigation in Huntington that Herman Frazier and Nick Tweel were acquainted. William B. Morgan, one of the prospective jurors interviewed, told the agents that he had also received another call prior to the trial from a man who offered him $25,000 to vote for an acquittal of Hoffa if he got on the jury. He identified the caller as an acquaintance of his who coincidentally had the same first and last name—William T. Morgan.

The FBI interviewed Dallas Hall, who operated the Sportsman's Lounge, a tavern across from Vanderbilt University. According to Partin, Tweel had told him that Hall could help with the jury and this had prompted Allen Dorfman, at Hoffa's direction, to read the jury list to Tweel that night from the pay phone on the corner across from the Federal Building. Hall told the FBI that Tweel had come into the lounge one night at the beginning of the trial with two men and two women. Hall talked to Tweel, but on that occasion nothing was said about the Hoffa trial, according to Hall.

But about one month later, Hall said, Tweel called him long distance and asked if he could do him a favor. He said that Tweel asked him how much he knew about the Hoffa trial, which was then in progress. He told Tweel he only knew what he read in the papers and what he heard people discussing. He said Tweel then told him it would be worth something to him if he could help with the trial. Hall said he promised Tweel to check around and see what he could find out, but that that was only to put Tweel off, as he did not intend to do anything.

Hall told us that shortly thereafter Tweel again called long distance and asked if he had done anything. Hall said that he hadn't. He said that when Tweel asked him if he had seen the jury list or knew who was on it, he answered no, and Tweel proceeded to read a list of names and addresses to him over the phone. Hall said he let Tweel think that he was copying them down but that actually he hadn't. He again told Tweel he would check into it but again didn't do anything.

A few days later, Hall said, he got a third call from Tweel, who again asked if he had done anything. Hall said that when he told him he had tried but couldn't find out anything, Tweel said to forget it, and he had heard nothing further from him.

The FBI then interviewed Helen Rippey, the hostess at the Surf Rider Room at the Andrew Jackson Hotel. She identified a photograph of Tweel and said that he and three other men had dinner in the Surf Rider Room at the beginning of the Hoffa trial. Then she identified the other men as Frazier, Paden and Cole. She said that she and Carol Pettijohn, who was the piano player in the Surf Rider Room at the time, had accompanied Tweel and two of the others to several night spots late that evening, ending up at the Sportsmen's Lounge, where she introduced them to Dallas Hall. According to Miss Rippey, Tweel spent most of the time they were there at the end of the bar in conversation with Hall. She said she heard them talking about horseracing. The FBI located Carol Pettijohn in Florida and she corroborated the information furnished by Miss Rippey.

Mr. and Mrs. Tilford Brown appeared before the grand jury and produced the registration records covering Larry Campbell's stay there. Campbell had arrived at Brown's two days before the Test Fleet trial started and had been there throughout most of the trial. The Browns had already told the FBI about the call from Chuck O'Brien from Nashville during the trial asking where a private plane could land nearby, and that Campbell had said he might have to go to Nashville.

The FBI also talked to a nurse in Louisville, Mrs. Ernestine Williams, who was a daily social contact of Campbell's while he was there. She said that they frequently went to a bar called Joe's Palm Room and that Campbell often made calls from the pay phone outside. She also pointed out other phone booths in the vicinity where Campbell made calls. She said that on at least one occasion he went to a particular phone booth to wait for a call. Campbell had also made calls from her residence, she told the FBI.

Mrs. Williams further related that on one occasion she had accompanied Campbell to the airport in Louisville to pick up Chuck O'Brien. The three of them then returned to Joe's Palm Room and Campbell went out to the phone booth to make a call. She said that O'Brien told her that he worked with Campbell in the Teamsters Union in Detroit.

The records of the telephone company in Louisville showed numerous calls from the pay phones pointed out by Mrs. Williams to the residence of Mattie Mix in Nashville. The records of the

telephone company in Detroit showed calls from the home of
another female acquaintance of Campbell's to the Mattie Mix residence in Nashville. Mattie Mix had already acknowledged to the
FBI that Larry Campbell's uncle, Tom Parks, had a key to her
house and access to her telephone.

It was a slow, day-by-day, piece-by-piece process. A telephone
record would lead to another person, and one person would lead
to another. Some people told the truth, others lied and some were
evasive or would not say anything. Some were involved, others did
not want to get involved. There were also those who were simply
scared to death. Some of the pieces were still missing but the ones
we had were all fitting together into a fabric of corruption.

Dick Coleman and Bill French called from Toledo on January
24 to say that Teamsters official James Jameson had been convicted
of taking illegal payoffs from an employer. On the same day Hoffa
placed Local 71 in Charlotte, North Carolina, in trusteeship. The
newly elected officers of the local had made the mistake of testifying against the previous officers, who had been convicted and
sentenced to prison. Bob Peloquin called from Louisville to tell me
that Teamsters Business Agent Norman Hug of Local 89 had been
convicted of perjury and Business Agent Leslie Atterbury, of the
same local, had been held in contempt of court by federal Judge
Henry Brooks for refusing to answer questions before the grand
jury. Atterbury was represented by the roving Jacques Schiffer. In
Philadelphia the reelection of Ray Cohen and his slate in the contest with The Voice was set aside because of irregularities and a
new election was ordered.

One of the farthest things from my mind at this point was the
status of the Teamsters' bonding situation. Carl Schultz had kept
track of periodic changes in the setup and had kept me informed
from time to time. In the shuffle in late 1959, engineered by Allen
Dorfman, Irwin Weiner and Stewart Hopps, the United Benefit
Fire Insurance Company of Omaha had replaced the Summit
Fidelity and Surety Company as the underwriter, and Charles
Bray's Oxford Agency replaced the Illinois Agency of the Summit
Fidelity and Surety Company as the agent. In 1961 United Benefit's
license to do business in the District of Columbia had been lifted

and the Resolute Insurance Company of Providence, Rhode Island, had taken over the underwriting. In December, 1962, Resolute withdrew and was replaced by Citizens Casualty Company of New York. In the meantime, Charles Bray's own company, Central Casualty, had been placed in receivership by the Illinois insurance commissioner and Stewart Hopps had been indicted in Baltimore for mail fraud in connection with one of his international operations.

Bob Peloquin, Ted Harrington and Dick Coleman had been overseeing a continuing investigation of the Dorfman empire but there had been no contact with any of the underwriting companies. I myself had not been in contact with any of the companies involved since late 1959, when I was still with the McClellan Committee. It therefore came as somewhat as a shock when Hoffa suddenly charged that the Justice Department was putting on pressure to prevent Teamsters officials from being bonded. He specifically mentioned me.

Hoffa made his charges in identical letters, dated January 28, 1963, to Senator Lister Hill, chairman of the Senate Labor and Public Welfare Committee, and Representative Adam Clayton Powell, chairman of the House Education and Labor Committee. In outlining the history of the Teamsters' bonding experience, Hoffa charged that: (1) the license of United Benefit Fire Insurance Company of Omaha, which was revoked in the District of Columbia in 1961, was reinstated after the company stopped underwriting the Teamsters bonds; (2) the Resolute Insurance Company of Providence, Rhode Island, which replaced United Benefit, had canceled its contract with the Teamsters Union after a government official called on the president of the company and questioned what type of persons were being bonded; (3) the Citizens Casualty Company, which replaced Resolute on January 3, 1963, had suddenly canceled on January 8, 1963, claiming that it had not been able to arrange adequate reinsurance; and (4) since Citizens Casualty canceled out, 260 bonding companies had been contacted and none would take the business. Hoffa then went on to say:

> In some instances, they have candidly stated that they did not wish to get in the cross-fire between the Attorney General and the Teamsters Union. In other instances, there was evidence of direct pressure not to bond Teamster officials. One instance in point—On January 24, 1963, the United Bonding Company of Indianapolis,

Indiana, offered to bond each Teamster officer up to $64,000. According to Frank Wright, President of United Bonding Company, Walter Sheridan, Special Assistant to Attorney General Kennedy, called upon him on that date and questioned him regarding the intention of his company to bond the officers of the Teamsters Union. On January 25th, Frank Wright withdrew his offer and when asked his reason, he stated, "I don't want the pressure."

Hoffa asked for an investigation of his charges and promised his full cooperation.

I first learned of the situation when I received a call in Nashville that day from Jack Rosenthal in the Department of Justice Public Information Office telling me what Hoffa had said and wanting to know if there was any truth to Hoffa's charges. I told him that to my knowledge there had been no pressure exerted by anyone on any of these companies. I said that the last contact that I, personally, had with any such company was three years earlier.

Hoffa repeated his charges in an interview on CBS television that evening with correspondent Roger Mudd. Based on the Roger Mudd interview, William Loeb, the publisher of the *Manchester Union Leader*, without fully checking the facts, again came to Hoffa's aid in a front-page editorial headed "Dictatorship U.S.A." It said in part:

> Mr. Hoffa is 100 percent correct. This newspaper made some inquiries in the Boston insurance market and discovered that Boston branches of three large national insurance companies had all been informed by their home [offices not to bond] Teamster locals. It is, therefore, obvious that Attorney General Kennedy and his office have been doing exactly what Hoffa charges: namely, preventing the Teamsters Union from obtaining the bond required under the Landrum-Griffin Act. Under the bill, unless the officers are so bonded they cannot serve as officers of the union.

The House Education and Labor Committee responded to Hoffa's letter by holding a hearing on February 1 and inviting Hoffa and government representatives to testify in a closed session. Attorney General Kennedy sent a telegram to the committee asking that the hearing be public rather than closed, and sent Deputy Attorney General Nicholas Katzenbach to testify on behalf of the Department of Justice.

Chairman Powell opened the hearing by referring to the telegram from the Attorney General and Representative Edith Green of Oregon moved that the hearing be an open one. The motion was seconded and it was so ordered by the chairman.

Hoffa appeared as the first witness, accompanied by Sidney Zagri. Both were placed under oath. Hoffa's letter to the chairman was made a part of the record along with a prepared statement that Hoffa intended to read.

Representative Frank Thompson of New Jersey said that he would like to introduce into the record three communications he had received, "for the purpose of giving Mr. Hoffa the opportunity to answer these statements and to perhaps make any corrections that he might wish to make to his letter, since he is now under oath." The first was a letter from Albert F. Jordan, superintendant of insurance for the District of Columbia, who stated that the license of the United Benefit Fire Insurance Company of Omaha had been revoked as of August 30, 1961, and the company had *not* been licensed in the District of Columbia since that time. This, of course, was at variance with Hoffa's contention in his letter to the committee that the company's license had been restored after it stopped writing the Teamsters' bonding business.

The next communication was a telegram from Jack Hyman, the chairman of the Executive Committee of the Citizens Casualty Company of New York, stating that the bonding arrangement with the Teamsters Union had been canceled because of an inability to arrange reinsurnace and that thirty-two days' notice had been given rather than the fifteen days required by the contract. The telegram concluded: "We have not had any contact with any Government agency."

Finally there was a wire from Frank Wright of the United Bonding Company of Indianapolis in which he stated, "No one has contacted or pressured the company from the Attorney General's office or any other governmental agency. Particularly, this office has received no calls from Walter Sheridan." The wire stated further that the Teamsters' bonding business had never been formally offered to the company. This telegram also directly contradicted the charge in Hoffa's letter.

Hoffa, beginning to read his statement, commenced a quick retreat. He prefaced the statement by saying, "I have to say in advance that I personally have not handled any of the bonding of this International Union. It has been left to the various agents who handle the bonding. . . . The statement I will make is a statement that has been related to myself, and I have not checked the facts. . . ."

Representative Thompson interrupted, "Mr. Chairman, we can hardly proceed with a witness under oath whose testimony is based entirely or is to be based entirely on hearsay, and for which he has already disclaimed any responsibility for its truthfulness or lack of truthfulness."

Representative John Dent of Pennsylvania came to Hoffa's aid, as he had in the past, and suggested that he be allowed to continue. Representative William Ayers of Ohio joined with him. The chairman ruled that Hoffa could proceed with his prepared statement. At one point Hoffa departed from his prepared text with an interjection.

Hoffa: Now, when I make a statement of the Department of Justice, I am again referring to the statements that have been relayed to me by Allen Dorfman, and unfortunately, Congressman Thompson, he was speaking for a man by the name of Irv Weiner, who as an officer of the Oxford Bonding Company, who reported this to him when the bonds were canceled.

Thompson: Mr. Weiner and Mr. Dorfman have connections with several bonding companies, do they not?

Hoffa: I do not think Mr. Dorfman has any connection with a bonding company. I think Mr. Weiner is an officer of a bonding company.

Thompson: Mr. Dorfman made the arrangements with one of the companies, did he not? In what capacity was he acting for you?

Hoffa: I think Allen Dorfman handles the health and welfare for the Central States Drivers Council Welfare Plan.

Thompson: Do his responsibilities in that capacity authorize him to negotiate for bonds for the Teamsters International, which he had done?

Hoffa: We have requested him to assist us in getting bonds.

Hoffa went on with his prepared statement but was interrupted again shortly thereafter by Representative Edith Green.

Green: Mr. Chairman, may I interrupt for a point of clarification? Are these facts of which he is personally knowledgeable, or is he now reporting what he heard from someone else?

Chairman: Mr. Hoffa?

Hoffa: Congresswoman Green, I am reporting what has been related to me by Allen Dorfman, from Irv Weiner, who handled the actual bonding.

Green: You have no personal knowledge of any of this material to which you have so far testified?

Hoffa: No, ma'am, I do not. This is the record of cancellations and coverages is all it is so far.

Later, Representative Thompson had this to say:

Mr. Hoffa, to me that has been an incredible performance, because the hearing this morning is based on your letter which you signed of January 28, and yet you come here and at every point where you in your letter say that there has been coercion or undue influence, you retreat to statements that you know nothing about this, it comes from one Mr. Weiner or one Mr. Dorfman.

You admitted in the course of your testimony that they both profit from this. Obviously, they have an enormous financial interest as long as they can place your insurance and get the agency's allowable fees, and any agency which places insurance or a bond gets a fee and is entitled to it. Now, in the McClellan Committee, there was evidence that Mr. Dorfman obtained over $1,600,000 in commissions for handling of the health and welfare fund of the Teamsters, and as a result, his license was revoked in several states, including the State of Illinois. . . .

Deputy Attorney General Katzenbach followed Hoffa as a witness. He categorically denied that anyone connected with the Department of Justice had in any way attempted to influence companies against providing bonding coverage for the Teamsters Union. "I don't understand that any allegations of that kind have now been made, since Mr. Hoffa seems to have withdrawn most of the statements that he made, or stated that he had no knowledge at all." Katzenbach then made an observation as to "the possible actual reason the Teamsters Union was encountering difficulty in obtaining bonds":

It may be because, as Mr. Hoffa testified, the principal man involved
in this seems to be Mr. Dorfman, and that seems to be the source
of most of Mr. Hoffa's information, although Dorfman heard it
from Mr. Weiner who heard it from somebody else. And perhaps
there are difficulties in dealing with a man of that reputation.
I think it may also be true that the sort of coverage sought by the
union is difficult to obtain, because of the fact that the bonding
company is taking a blind bond, in the sense that they do not know
the people involved, and it is a matter of public record that a number of people employed in this union in positions of responsibility
have had difficulties with the law.

Hoffa had finally succeeded in obtaining a congressional hearing
and it had been a complete flop. In an article in the Chicago
Sun-Times, reporter Thomas B. Ross suggested, as Katzenbach had,
that Allen Dorfman rather than the government might be Hoffa's
principal problem in obtaining bonds.

Back in Nashville the appearance of witnesses before the grand
jury continued. Some testified and some took the Fifth Amendment. Inasmuch as we had, or soon would, subpoena everyone who
had been closely associated with the Hoffa camp during the trial,
it was also necessary to subpoena Partin. If we did not, the omis-
sion would be obvious and suspect. A subpoena was routinely sent
to Partin ordering him to appear before the grand jury on February 14. When Partin received the subpoena on February 5, he did
what he would normally do—called Hoffa. Hoffa told him he
wanted to see him the next day in Washington. Partin immediately
called me and naturally we were both concerned. There was no
reason to think that Hoffa suspected anything, but at the same time
there was certainly no guarantee that he didn't. If he did, there was
the possibility that Partin would be in physical danger. If Hoffa
didn't suspect Partin, he certainly would if he didn't go to Washington. I told Partin to call me back in a little while. I called Jack
Miller and we finally decided that if Partin agreed, he should go
to Washington to see Hoffa but should wear a recording device on
his person in case he were threatened.
    Partin called back and I told him what we proposed that he do.
He agreed. He said that he would be arriving in Washington at 8
A.M. the following day at National Airport. I told Partin I would

arrange to pick him up at National when he arrived.

Early the next morning John Cassidy met my plane and we drove in his car from Dulles to National Airport, arriving just in time to meet Partin. We then went directly to the Justice Department where Jack Miller had arranged for Al McGrath and FBI agent Bruce Fisher to meet us in my office. Fisher had special training in recording devices and had with him a small recorder, slightly longer and wider but not quite as thick as a pack of king-size cigarettes. It was the smallest workable equipment available and was designed to be either taped on the small of the back or thigh or carried in a coat or trouser pocket. Fisher tried every possible way of secreting it on Partin, but Partin was so big and filled his clothes so snugly that there was always a detectable bulge. We finally reluctantly abandoned the effort. Partin decided he would go ahead anyway to the International headquarters to see Hoffa.

Cassidy and I drove him to Union Station, which was within walking distance of the Teamsters building, and let him out.

"Call me as soon as you get out," I said, as he made his hurried exit.

"You mean, if I get out," he answered with a nervous smile.

It was mid-afternoon before Partin called. Throughout the day we had imagined all of the possible things that could be happening. It turned out that the reason he had been in there so long was that Hoffa and his attorneys were working frantically to put together a solution to their bonding problem with the deadline two days away. Partin said that from what he heard, the problem was nearly settled and that the United Bonding Company in Indianapolis was going to handle it.

Partin said that while he was waiting to see Hoffa, he had talked to William Bufalino about his subpoena. He said Bufalino told him to take the Fifth Amendment and gave him a card that contained the exact wording he should use. Partin said that Bufalino told him to check with Tommy Osborn when he got to Nashville.

When Hoffa finally called him and Chuck O'Brien into his office, Partin said, he told them both that somebody was talking too much and they had to be careful what they said and whom they spoke to. Partin told me that Hoffa then asked him if he had talked to Bufalino about his subpoena and knew what to do. Partin said he had. Hoffa then cut off the conversation to get back to his bonding problem.

It had been close, but apparently, at least for the time being, everything was all right. Hoffa obviously was concerned about the grand jury but did not yet suspect any one person. If he had not been so engrossed in the bonding problem there might have been more questions asked. We were all relieved. That evening Partin returned to Baton Rouge and I went back to Nashville.

On February 14 Jimmy Hoffa celebrated his fiftieth birthday. On the same day, in Baltimore, Stewart Hopps, who had earlier helped Allen Dorfman line up the bonding arrangement for the Teamsters, was convicted of mail fraud. In Newark Tony Provenzano was voted another $50,000 raise at a Local 560 meeting attended by 375 of the 14,000 members of his union. A spokesman for Provenzano said that he had not decided whether to accept the raise, which would make his combined salaries total $95,000—more than Hoffa's and only slightly less than that of the President of the United States. In Nashville Ed Partin went before the grand jury and took the Fifth Amendment after checking with Tommy Osborn.

The grand jury investigation in Nashville moved ahead slowly. We had several interviews with Nick Tweel and with Frazier, Paden and Cole. We suspected that Tweel had, on behalf of Allen Dorfman, recruited the other three to come to Nashville. Tweel acknowledged knowing Frazier and that he had encountered him in Nashville but denied having anything to do with Frazier and the others being in Nashville. Tweel also denied having any interest in the trial or the jury. He said that he had come to Nashville to meet with Dorfman on a business deal. He admitted stopping in at Dallas Hall's bar but denied any discussions with Hall about the jury, either at that time or subsequently.

Herman Frazier said that he had been approached in Huntington just prior to the trial by a man he had never seen before who identified himself as Jack Wrather. He said that the man asked him if he would be interested in going to Nashville to conduct background investigations on prospective jurors in the Hoffa trial. He said that he had formed a private investigating agency with Lieutenant Nelson Paden, and felt there would be nothing wrong with Paden and his going to Nashville on the weekend before the trial, on their own time, to conduct the investigation. He said they had recruited Albert Cole to help them.

Frazier said that Wrather told them to check into the Noel Hotel in Nashville, where they would be contacted by another party. He said that the three of them flew to Nashville and did as directed, taking three rooms at the Noel Hotel. According to Frazier, that afternoon another unknown man called them and came up to the room. Frazier couldn't recall the man's name but said he had come there to show them how to conduct the investigation. He said that the man picked up one of their phones, called a prospective juror and asked some questions, identifying himself as "Allen from the *Banner.*" He then told Frazier that they should contact other prospective jurors in the same manner. Frazier said that after the man left he began wondering about the propriety of contacting prospective jurors directly and decided not to do it. He denied that either he or the other two men had made any of the calls.

We thought it was a preposterous story but Frazier stuck with it. In an earlier interview with the FBI Frazier had said nothing about the contact man in Nashville. We did not believe Tweel's story either, but he also continued to maintain he was telling the truth.

Cole originally stated to FBI agents that he had been told by Frazier and Paden that they were going to Nashville to check on prospective jurors. He now denied he had said that. Both he and Paden denied any knowledge of the calls to the prospective jurors.

On February 18 Ben Dranow went on trial in Minneapolis for jumping bail. Abe Poretz and John Cassidy tried the case. Jacques Schiffer, who had taken over the representation of Dranow on the appeals from the previous convictions, was called by the government as a witness. Schiffer acknowledged that he had received telephone calls from Dranow the day before he was scheduled to appear in court and while he was a fugitive. He said that on the first occasion he advised Dranow to appear in court as ordered and in another conversation urged Dranow to surrender. Dranow was convicted the following day and was sentenced to two and a half additional years in prison.

In Philadelphia Hoffa was trying to force an acceptance by the trucking companies of his areawide contract, while at the same time attempting to put down the continuing Voice rebellion. Philadelphia was one of the last areas holding out against his nationwide pact. Hoffa told the truckers that if they didn't sign with him in Philadelphia, he would fight them at their other terminals throughout the country. "They've either got to live with us here or fight with us everywhere," Hoffa declared. In reference to The Voice, he said, "We have to convert them to our way of thinking."

On February 28 Hoffa flew to Pittsburgh to address eighteen hundred truckers and Teamsters at a Traffic and Transportation Association dinner. He was met at the airport by International Vice President Harry Tevis and Theodore Cozza, the president of Local 211 who had been convicted earlier of receiving illegal payments from the Pittsburgh *Sun-Telegraph.*

Hoffa announced that DRIVE would kick off its campaign against new antilabor legislation in Detroit on March 10. He called for a march on Capitol Hill in May to oppose the new legislation. He declined comment on whether the Teamsters Union would support Governor Rockefeller for President in 1964 and said they would have to wait and see what was in the Republican platform. He said that he had just finished negotiating a master contract, except in Philadelphia, with uniform terms for all sections of the country.

He also attacked the Attorney General, charging, "Something is happening in this country by the name of Bobby Kennedy. One man has assigned an elite squad of 23 deputy attorneys general to work his dictates on me."

In Nashville we had finally begun to make some breakthroughs. William T. Morgan finally admitted that he had called prospective juror William B. Morgan at the direction of Buster Bell, and offered him $25,000 to vote for Hoffa's acquittal. Then Bill Sheets discovered that a local black bartender named Nathan Bellamy had been approached by Buster Bell in connection with the jury. Sheets interviewed Bellamy who told him that during the trial a big white man had come into the bar and engaged him in conversation. He said that the man had offered him $30,000 in cash if he could get to either or both of the black jurors. Bellamy picked out and positively identified the man as Henry "Buster" Bell from a group of photographs. A waitress who had been in the bar at the time also remembered the man and also identified Bell from the photographs. Bellamy said that he would be willing to testify in court when the time came but wanted the matter kept in confidence as long as possible.

Shortly thereafter we found out that Tom Parks, Larry Campbell's uncle, had attempted to get to juror Gratin Fields through his children. Parks had set up a meeting with the juror's son, Carl Fields, through Jack Walker, a patrolman in the Nashville Police Department. He had also attempted to set up a meeting with Mrs. Mattie Leath, a daughter of Gratin Fields. Sheets and I talked to Walker, who admitted he had arranged the meeting between Parks and Fields and that he had taken Parks to see Mattie Leath, but she would not talk to him. When we talked to Carl Fields, he at first denied everything. He then admitted meeting with Parks but denied it had anything to do with his father or the trial. Finally he told the whole story.

The insulation was breaking down, and piece by piece a strong case was being built that should stand up in court as proof there had been flagrant, premeditated attempts to tamper with the Test Fleet jury. The testimony of witnesses now demonstrated unequivocally that agents of Jimmy Hoffa had, in fact, attempted to corrupt the jury in a case in which Hoffa was the only person on trial and the only possible beneficiary of such acts. The testimony, along with the results of FBI surveillance and investigation, also corroborated everything Partin had related about these incidents and reinforced immeasurably Partin's incrimination of Hoffa as the architect of the conspiracy.

Still another breakthrough came in the person of Hazel Fulton, who was Nick Tweel's secretary at the Mayflower Distributing Company in Huntington, West Virginia, during the time the Test Fleet trial was in progress. She had previously told us that the conversation she overheard the night Allen Dorfman called Nick Tweel from the phone booth in Nashville concerned an insurance company. After she testified before the grand jury, she approached the sheriff in Huntington and asked him to put her in touch with the FBI. She then told FBI agents that she had testified falsely before the grand jury because she was afraid of losing her job. She now confirmed that Tweel had received a call from Allen Dorfman one evening during the trial and that at Tweel's direction she had, on an extension telephone, taken down a list of names and addresses dictated by Dorfman. She recalled one of the names as being something like Pashall. She said that Tweel had subsequently called a man named Dallas Hall in Nashville.

Further documentation of the Dorfman-Tweel-Hall calls was provided by telephone toll call records which verified that a call was made from the exact phone booth described by Partin to

Tweel and that a subsequent call was made by Tweel to Dallas Hall. In addition, the employees at the railroad station corroborated Partin's description of what transpired there that night including the conversation between Hoffa and the stationmaster about the height of the ceiling.

Meanwhile, FBI reports indicated that Morris Emanuel of the Chicago Bureau of Labor-Management Reports office was maintaining his contacts with Teamsters representatives and continuing to furnish them information. Because the FBI was not yet willing to expose its source of information, there was little that could be done about moving directly against Emanuel. In an attempt to at least neutralize him, the few officials in the Labor Department who were aware of his covert activities decided to send him to Puerto Rico on a special assignment. Emanuel did not suspect that we knew about his treachery and took the assignment as it was offered—as an important mission, which, of course, it was not.

I told Tom Kennelly, who was in Puerto Rico conducting a grand jury investigation in connection with Frank Chavez and Local 901, that Emanuel was coming and to be discreet in his dealings with him. Relative to the Chavez grand jury, Kennelly reported that they had caught Chavez handing out literature to the grand jurors which was defamatory toward the Attorney General and the Administration. Chavez was indicted on March 19 for obstruction of justice.

On March 25 the embezzlement trial of Ray Cohen finally began in Philadelphia. And The Voice forces continued their campaign to unseat Cohen in the upcoming new election.

On March 31 Hoffa was in Wilmington, Delaware, where he spoke to a meeting of workers whom the Teamsters were attempting to organize. Charging that the government had spent $50,000,000 trying to put him in jail and that he had spent $170,000 defending himself, Hoffa said, "Do you think if Hoffa really did all those things, that he'd be standing here today? Instead Bobby Kennedy is going crazy because he doesn't know how to put Hoffa away."

On the following evening Hoffa appeared on the *David Brinkley Journal*, where he told Brinkley that the Attorney General was "just a spoiled young millionaire that never had to go out and find a way to live by his own efforts and he cannot understand resistance to what he wants." Hoffa did offer a backhanded tribute to Kennedy when he said, "There's only one thing I like about Bobby Kennedy: his willingness to work and to fight to win. Outside of that, I don't have any use for him."

During the first two weeks of April we reviewed the evidence we had and Jim Neal started preparing a prosecutive memorandum. Both Larry Campbell and Tom Parks were subpoenaed before the grand jury. Campbell declined to talk to us at all. I talked to Parks both before and after he appeared but he only listened and did not acknowledge having anything to do with the approach to Gratin Fields. We had attempted to talk to Ewing King earlier but he also declined.

On the evening of April 10 Neal, Shaffer, Nat Lewin and I flew to Washington and met the following day with Jack Miller and Bob Kennedy. Neal, Shaffer and Lewin took the position that there was sufficient evidence to indict Hoffa, Ewing King, Larry Campbell, Allen Dorfman, Nick Tweel and Lawrence Medlin, for conspiring to tamper with the jury in one indictment. They proposed that Henry "Buster" Bell be indicted separately for the $30,000 offer to Nathan Bellamy and the $25,000 offer to William Morgan, and that Frazier, Paden and Cole be charged in a third indictment for making the "Allen from the *Banner*" calls. They acknowledged that the Frazier, Paden and Cole situation was the weakest because it would be difficult to prove criminal intent to corrupt the prospective jurors. They also felt that charges against Tweel and Dorfman in the first proposed indictment would present problems because the alleged plot never went beyond Dallas Hall. They felt strongly, however, that there was still sufficient evidence in both situations to warrant indictment with a probable chance of conviction. We discussed the matter at length but no decision was made.

Bob Kennedy was considering the possibility of asking an attorney from Tennessee to head the prosecution team. There were two eminently qualified veteran trial attorneys, both from Nashville, who stood apart from the field—Jack Norman, Sr., and John Hooker, Sr. They were men of integrity who brought outstanding talents and presence into a courtroom.

Following our discussion of the merits of the proposed indictments, Bob Kennedy decided to call John Hooker, whom he knew personally better than he knew Norman. He told Hooker the status of the case and explained that no final decision had yet been made whether or not to go forward with it. He said that in the event it was decided to proceed, he would like Hooker to consider prosecuting the case and therefore thought it would be helpful to have his evaluation of the evidence. He asked Hooker if he could come to Washington the following day to discuss it. Hooker agreed to come that evening. After Hooker was fully briefed on the facts, he jumped quickly to the next logical step. He wanted to talk to Ed Partin. He said that after he had, he would then like to give the matter further thought.

On the following Monday I flew to Nashville, met Hooker and we flew on to Atlanta where I had arranged with Partin to meet us at the airport. The potential witness and the potential prosecutor sat on a bench in the airport lobby for two hours, talking and sizing each other up. Both were impressed. Then Partin boarded a plane back to Baton Rouge and Hooker and I flew back to Nashville. En route, Hooker said he thought that the evidence was strong and that Partin would make an excellent witness. But he still wanted more time to think.

On April 19, Neal, Shaffer and I flew to Washington for another meeting with Jack Miller and the Attorney General. This time Bob Kennedy called in some of his other top advisors to listen to our presentation of the evidence and to voice their judgment on the merits of the proposed indictments. Those present in addition to Kennedy and Miller were Bill Hundley of the Organized Crime Section, Assistant Attorneys General Lou Oberdorfer of the Tax Division, Ramsey Clark of the Lands Division and John Douglas of the Civil Division, and Burke Marshall of Civil Rights, Deputy Attorney General Nicholas Katzenbach and Solicitor General Archibald Cox. When we had completed our presentation of the facts, Kennedy asked each person present for his views. Everyone agreed that there was sufficient evidence to bring the indictment against Hoffa, King, Campbell et al., and also to indict Henry "Buster" Bell. A minority felt there was insufficient evidence to bring the Frazier, Paden and Cole indictment. Relative to the Hoffa, King, Campbell et al. case, there were questions in addition to sufficiency of evidence. The primary one was whether Partin, by being in the position he was, had violated Hoffa's rights under the Sixth Amendment to the Constitution. This amendment, among other things, guarantees an accused person the right of counsel. Interpretation of the Sixth Amendment by the courts had held that the right to counsel precluded the violation of the lawyer-client relationship by a third party. The question of whether Partin had done so was certain to be raised both in the trial court, to prevent his testimony, and in any appellate proceedings, if the prosecution were successful.

If Partin had passed on to me defense strategy which he overheard being discussed between Hoffa and his attorneys, and I had, in turn, passed that information on to Neal and Shaffer during the Test Fleet case, there would be a serious question whether a guilty verdict, if obtained, would have been sustained. The extent and type of defense strategy information passed on would probably be the controlling factor. There was the additional question, however, of whether, aside from the Test Fleet case, Partin's presence in the defense camp had tainted any evidence thereby derived, thus precluding its introduction in any subsequent prosecution such as we were now contemplating.

Bearing on the entire problem was the question of how Partin happened to be in the position that he was during the Test Fleet trial. Was he planted there by the government or was he there because the defendant wanted him there? It was our position that Partin had been invited to Nashville by Hoffa, had remained there, on and off, throughout the trial with Hoffa's knowledge and approval, and had even been singled out by Hoffa to guard his suite in the final days of the trial. It was also our position that Partin had been instructed only to be alert for, and to report, information concerning attempts to tamper with the jury or other illegal activity.

The Sixth Amendment problem had come up at our earlier meeting with Jack Miller and the Attorney General. I had said at the time that I had reviewed the notes of my conversations with Partin during the trial carefully, and with minor exceptions, they related entirely to either the jury-tampering attempts that were in progress or the coming and going of people. I also said that with the same minor exceptions, the only information I had passed on to government attorneys during the trial was that concerning attempts to tamper with the jury which I felt they had to know.

At Bob Kennedy's direction, I spent a full day with John Douglas of the Civil Division going over my notes word by word. When we were through with the analysis, Douglas concluded that over 85 percent of the information obtained from Partin dealt directly with attempts to tamper with the jury and that almost the entire remaining 15 percent dealt with the coming and going of people.

When the final vote was taken in the Attorney General's office, only two persons were opposed to bringing the indictment—Ramsey Clark and Bill Hundley. Clark still believed the Sixth Amendment guarantee might prove a barrier, and felt that even if the prosecution were successful, it would not stand up on appeal. Hundley's reason was more pragmatic. He did not like the idea of a one-on-one prosecution of Hoffa—it would, in the final analysis, come down to Partin's word against Hoffa's. He had seen Hoffa cases come and go and he did not like the odds on this one.

The question of our image was also discussed. How would it look when it was learned that we were receiving information from a man in the inner circle of the defense, no matter how he happened to be there? Bob Kennedy asked what alternative we had at the time. Should we have told Partin we didn't want to hear about jury tampering? And once we had heard about it, should we have done nothing about it? Solicitor General Archibald Cox spoke up and said that he was firmly convinced of both the propriety and necessity of going forward and that he would have absolutely no compunctions about arguing the case before the Supreme Court if and when the time came.

Bob Kennedy then made the decision to proceed toward recommending indictment to the grand jury. He called John Hooker in Nashville, who was still agonizing over his own decision, and told him what had been decided and asked if he would come to Washington the following Monday.

On Monday afternoon, April 22, John Hooker committed himself to what he knew would be an arduous ordeal—he agreed to participate in the prosecution of Jimmy Hoffa. Bob Kennedy decided that Jim Neal, also originally from Tennessee, would share the responsibility with Hooker, backed up by Shaffer, Durkin and Lewin. We all returned to Nashville the following day and began the final preparations for the indictments.

In Philadelphia Hoffa and Ray Cohen finally won their second battle against The Voice, winning the election this time by a substantial margin. Hoffa had spent a major share of his time for the past fourteen weeks in Philadelphia, taking personal command of the struggle. He had brought his top strategists in with him, as well as a horde of organizers. The AFL-CIO had supported The Voice but their money and manpower proved both too little and too late to turn the tide. It was a major victory for Hoffa, who had put his personal prestige on the line. John Herling sounded the alarm in his labor column:

> This week there lies a pall over Philadelphia. The dismay spreads from one end of the country to the other. To many it seemed unbelievable that the bad guys should have trounced the good guys as they have. Of course, I don't mean that everybody who voted for the Hoffa slate was evil and that the good was on the other side. But what we must deplore is the large-scale deception, the huge public relations drive and the cynical confirmation that money and muscle can bring honest men to their knees.
> Mr. Hoffa is crowing loudly this week. The sound ought to scare the living daylights out of conscientious trade unionists everywhere.

On May 9, 1963, Hoffa and five others were indicted in Nashville for jury tampering. The five-count indictment named Hoffa in the first count and charged him with conspiring to influence the jury. The second count charged Hoffa and Medlin with attempting to influence prospective juror James Tippens and offering him $10,000 to vote for an acquittal of Hoffa. Count three charged that Hoffa, Campbell and Parks attempted to influence juror Gratin Fields and offered his son, Carl Fields, $5000 for himself and $5000 for his father if Carl Fields would influence his father to vote for an acquittal. The fourth count charged that Hoffa, Dorfman and Tweel offered money to Dallas Hall to influence the jury. Count five charged that Hoffa and Ewing King attempted to influence James M. Paschal by offering him a promotion to induce him to influence his wife, Mrs. Betty Paschal, a juror. None of the counts accused Hoffa of actually making contacts himself but each of the last four counts did charge him with "aiding, abetting, counseling, commanding, inducing" the others to act.

On the following Monday Hoffa appeared in federal court in Philadelphia where he pleaded not guilty, waived a hearing and was continued on $10,000 bond. He blamed the indictment on the Attorney General whom, he told newsmen, "has a personal vendetta against me and is trying to convict me with planted stories in the press." On the merits of the case, Hoffa said, "Of course I'm not guilty. This indictment talks about ten people and I know only

three of them. Two of them worked for me as Teamster officials
and the other is an insurance agent who represents our central
Teamster conference. Outside of that I wouldn't know the other
seven persons if they walked down the corridor of the courtroom."

That same day, in what was becoming a pattern, the front-page
editorial by publisher William Loeb in the *Manchester Union Leader*
was captioned "Moving Toward Dictatorship." In it Loeb stated:

> The latest attack by Attorney General Robert Kennedy on James
> Riddle Hoffa, head of the Teamsters Union, makes you think of the
> kid who lost the ball game and then accused the other side of cheat-
> ing. Last December, in Nashville, Tenn., almost on Christmas Eve,
> Bobby Kennedy lost another of his many attempts to "hang" some-
> thing on Hoffa. The jury couldn't agree. Now the government has
> just indicted Hoffa on the grounds that he and some of his associates
> conspired to fix the jury. . . .
> The government has now indicted Hoffa numerous times. Each
> time Hoffa has either been acquitted or, as in the last case, the jury
> was divided and a mistrial declared. Under any just and fair system
> of government it would seem that his persecution of Hoffa should
> cease, since the only "crime" that Hoffa seems to be guilty of is that
> he will not knuckle under to the Kennedys and give them slavish
> obedience, that other labor unions in the United States do. The
> Teamsters and the head of the Teamsters, James Riddle Hoffa, are
> as independent and proud as the Kennedys, but since when has that
> been a crime in this country?
> The fight of James Hoffa against the Kennedys is becoming the fight
> of all Americans who want to stay free men and women.

Five weeks before Loeb wrote this editorial, the *Manchester Union
Leader* received a $500,000 loan from the Teamsters Pension Fund.

On Tuesday, May 19, three more indictments were returned by
the grand jury. The first charged Herman Frazier, Nelson Paden
and Albert Cole with making telephone calls to ten prospective
jurors, while posing as reporters for the Nashville *Banner*, for the
purpose of influencing them. The second charged Cole with perjury in that he falsely testified before the grand jury that he had
not told FBI agents the purpose of the trip to Nashville was to
contact prospective jurors. The third indictment charged Henry
"Buster" Bell with conspiring with William T. Morgan to influence prospective juror William B. Morgan with an offer of $25,000,

and also charged Bell with offering $30,000 to Nathan Bellamy to induce him to attempt to influence jurors Gratin Fields and Mrs. Matthew Walker.

Jacques Schiffer and William Bufalino arrived in Nashville to confer with Tommy Osborn. Schiffer attempted to talk to Carl Fields, the son of the juror, but Fields would not talk to him. Fields called us to report the contact by Schiffer and we told him, as we had before, that he was free to talk to Schiffer if he wanted to but he was also free not to talk to him if he didn't want to.

In Chicago our group working on the Pension Fund had completed the grand jury investigation and was prepared to recommend an indictment of Hoffa and seven others on charges of mail fraud. Jack Miller, who had followed the results of the grand jury inquiry closely, concurred and recommended to the Attorney General that the indictment be brought. Since the proposed indictment embodied much of the original Sun Valley case, it was decided that the government would move to dismiss the Sun Valley indictment as soon as the Pension Fund indictment was handed down.

At 12:30 A.M. on June 4, 1963, Ray Cohen was convicted of embezzlement by the jury in Philadelphia. Shortly before noon on the same day the Chicago indictment was returned. Its twenty-eight counts charged that Hoffa and the other seven men had obtained by fraud fourteen loans from the Pension Fund totaling $20,000,000 and had diverted more than $1,000,000 for their own personal benefit. The grand jury charged Hoffa with violating his duty as a trustee of the fund by making false and misleading statements to the other trustees and by using his influence to obtain approval of the loans.

Indicted along with Hoffa were: Ben Dranow; Abe I. Weinblatt, Dranow's alter ego in Miami Beach; S. George Burris and his son Herbert Burris; Samuel Hyman, a Key West Florida real estate man; Calvin Kovens, the Miami builder; and Zachery A. Strate, Jr., a New Orleans builder.

The defendants were charged with devising and carrying out a scheme, beginning sometime before July, 1958, which involved fraudulent misrepresentation in applications for loans, demanding and receiving fees and stock options, and diversions of funds for their own interests. One such diversion, according to the indictment, was for the purpose of the "bail-out" of Sun Valley by obtaining funds to pay off debts and extricate Hoffa from the situation.

Arraignment was set for June 25. Hoffa, in Philadelphia, had no comment. That afternoon government attorneys in Tampa asked that the Sun Valley indictment be dismissed.

Because of his years of trial experience, Abe Poretz was assigned to take over the actual prosecution of the Pension Fund case, assisted by Charlie Smith, Tom McTiernan, Jim Canavan and Bill Ryan.

On June 10 Hoffa went to Nashville for arraignment on the jury-tampering charges. He pleaded not guilty and told newsmen that he didn't think he could get a fair trial in Nashville: "I think it would be difficult to get a fair trial anywhere because of the constant harassment of the Justice Department. It's just another one of Bobby Kennedy's shenanigans."

Late the following night Tony Provenzano was convicted by the jury in Newark of extorting $17,000 from the Dorn Transportation Company. The evidence upon which he was convicted was basically the same as had been testified to before the McClellan Committee five years earlier. While the trial was in progress, Provenzano was reelected president of Joint Council 73.

On Saturday, June 15, Hoffa was in Dallas for meetings with Southern Conference Teamsters officials and a DRIVE rally. He held a press conference at the Dallas Cabana Motel, which had been constructed with a loan from the Pension Fund. Hoffa struck out in several directions: "Bobby Kennedy, being what he is, has constantly brought about indictments knowing full well there was no basis for them." He blamed the Attorney General for contributing to the racial tensions in the country and claimed there was no discrimination in his union. He ridiculed a speech by Vice President Lyndon Johnson against discrimination and blasted George Meany. He predicted that the Teamsters would eventually be back in the AFL-CIO but insisted, "They need us. We don't need them."

On June 25 Hoffa and his co-defendants were arraigned in Chicago on the charges of having defrauded the Pension Fund. They all pleaded not guilty, waived all motions and asked for an immediate trial. Judge Richard Austin, noting that there was a prior indictment in Nashville, asked the government attorneys which case the government intended to try first. They advised the judge that the government intended to proceed first with the jury-tampering trial in Nashville. Attorney James Haggerty, on behalf of Hoffa, noted that the Nashville trial would probably be delayed for some time by numerous motions. Judge Austin then directed the government attorneys to appear in court again on September 4 and advise him of the status of the Nashville case. Hoffa's attorneys then withdrew their offer to waive motions in the Chicago case. Judge Austin set a tentative trial date for October 7 but made it clear that it was up to the government to advise him on September 4 which case it would try first. Besides Haggerty, Hoffa was represented at the arraignment by Chicago attorneys Daniel Ahern and Maurice Walsh, both reputable veteran defense attorneys. Ben Dranow was represented by Jacques Schiffer in spite of the fact that Schiffer had testified against his own client in the bail-jumping trial.

During the hearing Schiffer accused the government of trying the case in the newspapers. Judge Austin responded, "It seems to me you are the one trying to try the case in the newspapers."

After the hearing, Hoffa told reporters, "This is another propaganda device by the government. I'm sure we will present evidence that will show we are not guilty. I hope this does not arouse fears in anyone concerning the pension fund. They waited three years to bring this case. It's peculiar I was singled out of sixteen trustees of the pension fund to be indicted when it takes sixteen to make a decision."

On July 2 I flew to Atlanta and met with Ed Partin at Frank Grimsley's house. He reaffirmed his willingness to testify in the jury-tampering trial. He was under no illusions about what that would mean and the difficulties he would face. However, neither of us realized at this time what unending agony it would actually cause him. I told him I thought the trial would probably be in October and we discussed the interim problems. I also told him that there was no indication thus far that Hoffa suspected him or anyone else, because Hoffa was convinced that we had been tapping his phones and bugging his offices for years—which we had not—and thus would think that any evidence we had linking him with the jury tampering would be from electronic sources. I said that it was helpful that Hoffa had such a phobia about electronic surveillance because it would, as it obviously had, lessen the chance of his suspecting anyone. Partin said that he thought it would be a good idea, nevertheless, for him to be somewhat unavailable during the period before the trial. The principal problem he thought he would have if he just dropped out of sight for awhile was his $300 monthly payments to his estranged wife. He said that he had not told anyone, including his wife, about his role in Nashville, and did not want to involve anyone else even for the limited purpose of conveying the money to his wife. Inasmuch as Partin was entitled to reimbursement from the government for all the expenses he had borne during the Nashville trial and would continue to bear, I decided that we would offset these expenses by making the monthly payments to his wife when he was unavailable. We agreed that when the time came, I would obtain the money from a confidential fund at the Department of Justice, which had been set up by law for such purposes, and send the money to Grimsley, who would, in turn, obtain a cashier's check and send it to Partin's wife. Partin would tell his wife only that he had to be out of town for a while and that while he was gone she would receive her monthly payments by mail.

I told Partin to keep in touch with either Grimsley or me by phone periodically, as he had been doing, and we would keep him apprised of the status of the trial and any other developments. There were no other commitments or promises of any kind made to Partin, nor did he ask for any. But I knew when I left him that day that when the time came for him to testify, he would be there and that he would testify truthfully.

On July 12 Tony Provenzano was sentenced to seven years in prison and fined $10,000.

On July 22 there was a hearing in Nashville on Hoffa's and the other defendants' pretrial motions. Judge Miller had excused himself from the case after the indictment was brought and the hearing was held before Judge Frank Gray.

In their motions the defendants asked that the indictment be dismissed on several grounds. One was that a fair trial could not be obtained because of prejudicial publicity. Another was that illegal evidence obtained from wiretaps had been utilized in the indictment. A third was that I, who was not an attorney, had been present in the grand jury room during the testimony of witnesses and that I and FBI agents had illegal access to grand jury testimony. A fourth was that we had threatened witnesses. There were also motions by the defendants for severance from each other and for a change of venue in the event that the indictments were not dismissed. Finally, they charged that the grand jury which had indicted them had not been properly empaneled.

Neal, Shaffer, Durkin, the court reporter, the grand jury foreman and I all testified in the hearing that I had not been in the grand jury room except when I testified as a witness on March 5. I also testified that I did have access to grand jury testimony and did afford access to the testimony to FBI agents Sheets and Steele for the purpose of pursuing the investigation to which we had been properly assigned. I and the others denied we had threatened any witnesses.

Defense attorneys demanded access to the sealed envelope that had been given to Judge Miller during the second secret session of the Test Fleet trial. They claimed that its contents would show that the government had derived evidence from wiretapping. Judge Gray opened the envelope, read its contents (the affidavit by Partin) and resealed it.

When the three-day hearing was completed on July 25, Judge Gray severed the conspiracy count against Hoffa from the other counts, which meant that there could be two trials: one of Hoffa alone for conspiring to influence the jury, and another of Hoffa and the other defendants together for the substantive counts of attempting to influence the jury. He denied all other motions except the motion for a bill of particulars, which he took under advisement. Judge Gray set the trial for Hoffa and the other defendants for October 14 in Nashville.

On August 21 Hoffa filed a petition for a writ of mandamus with the Sixth Circuit Court of Appeals in Cincinnati, appealing Judge Gray's rulings in Nashville. The government filed in opposition the following day.

I was in our office in Nashville on August 23 when I received a call from Robert Vick. I knew that he was an officer in the Nashville Police Department who, like Fred Ramsey and a retired Treasury agent named John Polk, had conducted background investigations of prospective jurors for Tommy Osborn in the Test Fleet case. Such a practice is perfectly legitimate so long as the prospective jurors or their families are not contacted and no attempt is made to influence them. I also knew that Vick had approached one of the local FBI agents in the past and had two or three conversations with him. The agent, suspicious, had been noncommittal and merely listened to what Vick had to say, which was all quite nebulous.

Vick had called me during the recent hearing. I was also suspicious and put him off until after the hearing. Now he wanted to come in to see me. It was a cautious meeting on both sides, with Vick implying, but not actually stating, that there may have been even more jury tampering than we were aware of in the Test Fleet trial. I told Vick I was going to Washington the next morning but would return in a couple of weeks. He said that he would be in touch with me again.

In Washington Hoffa gathered four hundred Teamsters officials together to gear up for the final push for his nationwide contract which he hoped to make a reality in 1964. He made plans to form a national policy committee made up of ten representatives each from the Western, Central, Southern and Eastern conferences. Negotiations with the trucking industry were expected to begin toward the end of the year. The proposed pact would cover 450,000 Teamsters employed by 14,000 companies engaged in both over-the-road and local cartage.

In Nashville Don Vestal, the former president of Local 327, announced his candidacy for that office, now held by Ewing King. The election was scheduled for mid-December.

On September 4 in Chicago Judge Austin, upon being informed that the Nashville case had been set for trial for October 14 but that the Sixth Circuit Court of Appeals was still considering Hoffa's petition for a writ of mandamus, directed government attorneys to appear again on October 21 to report on the status of the case. He said that if the Nashville trial was not proceeding by that time, he would go ahead with the Pension Fund trial.

In San Juan, Puerto Rico, attorney Frank Ragano of Tampa, Florida, who had represented Florida Mafia leader Santos Traffi-cante in the past and who had been one of Hoffa's attorneys in the Sun Valley case, appeared in federal court as the attorney for Frank Chavez. Ragano asked that the Chavez trial scheduled for October 14 be delayed because he was also representing Hoffa in the jury-tampering trial in Nashville, set for the same date. The judge denied Ragano's plea on the basis that he was not an attorney of record in Nashville and had not participated in any of the pretrial motions.

On September 20 the Court of Appeals denied Hoffa's petition for a writ of mandamus. Hoffa appealed the decision to the Supreme Court.

On September 24 Jimmy Hoffa addressed a Kiwanis Club audience of two thousand people at Cobo Hall in Detroit. He charged that a hearing on organized crime scheduled by the McClellan Committee the following day in Washington would be a "radio and television circus" designed to serve as a propaganda campaign for new wiretap legislation. He said that his phone had been tapped illegally by the government in the past. He told the businessmen in the audience that they should pay more attention to pending legislation that could affect them personally. He charged that the country was moving toward a police state and said, "You're no longer in a neutral corner. When you walk into a Federal Court building, you realize that building belongs to the United States and that everyone in that building is employed by the United States. . . . You don't appear as an American citizen, innocent until proven guilty, but as an American citizen guilty until proven innocent."

On October 2 Judge Gray in Nashville ordered a jury panel drawn for the Hoffa case and held a hearing on the pretrial motions filed by Frazier, Paden, Cole and Bell. On the same day Hoffa petitioned the Supreme Court to issue a stay in his trial scheduled for October 14. On October 3 Judge Gray, after two days of hearings, denied some of the motions filed by Frazier, Paden, Cole and Bell and took some others under advisement. The Court of Appeals granted Hoffa and his co-defendants a delay in trial until October 20 to allow Hoffa time to seek a review by the Supreme Court. The court said that the delay was granted only for that reason and not because it considered that Hoffa's earlier petition for a writ of mandamus had any merit.

The perjury indictment against Albert Cole of Huntington, West Virginia, was dismissed on October 7 by Judge Gray because of a wrong date in the indictment. The indictment charged that Cole had lied to the grand jury about what he had said to FBI agents in an interview on January 1, 1963. We had found in reviewing records for the hearing that the FBI interview had actually taken place on January 31, 1963. It was a technicality but the judge felt that it was a sufficient discrepancy to invalidate the indictment.

With the Nashville case now stalled in the Supreme Court, Hoffa and his co-defendants moved in Chicago for an immediate trial. Judge Austin denied the motion and set a new trial date in Chicago for November 12, providing that the Nashville case had not gone to trial by that date.

In a speech to a DRIVE rally at the Murat Temple in Indianapolis on October 6, Hoffa urged Teamsters in Indiana to become more involved in politics and to support candidates who supported organized labor. He said that neither President Kennedy nor Senator Barry Goldwater was an acceptable candidate for the 1964 Presidential election. He said the Teamsters Union might support either Governor Nelson Rockefeller or Governor George Romney if they ran. He also mentioned Governor James Rhodes of Ohio and Pennsylvania Governor William Scranton as possible acceptable candidates.

Hoffa launched into his usual diatribe against Attorney General Robert Kennedy, referring to him as a "spoiled brat who never had to work for a living and who never tried a case in court."

The prominent office holders seated at the speaker's table with Hoffa included Senator Vance Hartke, Representatives William G. Bray and Richard L. Roudebush, Lieutenant Governor Richard O. Ristine and Indianapolis Mayor Albert H. Losche.

On October 7 Judge Gray denied the remaining motions of defendants Frazier, Paden, Cole and Bell which he had taken under advisement.

On Sunday, October 14, Hoffa was in Detroit for a special membership meeting of Local 299. He pushed through a new set of by-laws for the local which gave him, as president of the local, almost dictatorial control over its activities. He was empowered to hire and fire administrative help and to carry out the business of the local when the executive board was not in session. He told the two thousand members at the meeting that "the authority given the president of this union is as broad as that given to the president of the International Union." He acknowledged that the action "may seem to lay the power in the hands of one individual," but said that this was how the union members had become "some of the highest priced people."

In Nashville the Building and Construction Trades Council, at the request of Teamsters Local 327 President Ewing King, passed a resolution to petition George Meany to readmit the Teamsters

Union into the AFL-CIO. Similar resolutions had recently been adopted in Detroit and Chicago.

Morris Emanuel, the Labor Department official who had, according to FBI reports, been furnishing information to Teamsters representatives, had completed his assignment in Puerto Rico and returned to his post in the Bureau of Labor-Management Reports office in Chicago. It turned out that he had known Abe Poretz in the past and had called Poretz on one of his recent trips to Chicago, seeking to renew their acquaintance. Inasmuch as the FBI was still reluctant to surface its informant to expose Emanuel, we decided on another ploy. When Poretz returned to Chicago on October 15 to continue trial preparations, he took with him several copies of a list of potential government witnesses. The documents were treated by the FBI with an invisible solution that would leave indelible blue telltale marks on a person's hand if picked up. If Emanuel came to see Poretz as he had expressed his intention of doing, he would be left alone in the room where the documents lay exposed on a desk. There were enough copies of the document so that it would seem that one would not be missed, but Poretz, of course, knew the exact number. If, after Emanuel left, one or more of the documents were missing, he would be arrested by FBI agents as he left the building.

Emanuel did come to see Poretz and was left alone in the room with the documents. Poretz arranged it so that he could view Emanuel's actions from an adjoining office. Emanuel eyed the documents and got up and walked around the desk but he did not touch them. After a reasonable length of time Poretz returned to the room.

We decided to let the matter go at that for the time being and, with the cooperation of select Bureau of Labor-Management Reports officials, to continue to isolate Emanuel as best we could from any vital information

In San Juan, Puerto Rico, a mistrial was declared in the trial of Frank Chavez for obstruction of justice when the jury was unable to reach a verdict.

On October 18 Hoffa filed his petition in the Supreme Court for a review of the decisions made on his pretrial motions in Nashville by Judge Gray and the Court of Appeals.

On October 25 Nicholas Tweel filed a motion in Judge Gray's court in Nashville charging that his indictment was based on information obtained from wiretaps. Tweel attached an affidavit in which he claimed that in his questioning before the grand jury by Jim Neal, "I was questioned about my conversations, both on the telephone and in person with Mr. Dorfman, and in such a fashion as to suggest that Mr. Neal already knew the content of my conversations." Tweel made a similar charge about a subsequent interview with Neal, Shaffer, Durkin and me, stating, "And again their questions indicated that they had exact knowledge of the content of certain conversations. . . ."

The truth, of course, was that we did have reasonably good knowledge of the content of Tweel's conversations with Dorfman and Dallas Hall. Ed Partin, Hazel Fulton and Dallas Hall had told us what the conversations were about.

While we waited for the Supreme Court to act on Hoffa's petition for review, we continued to prepare for trial in both Nashville and Chicago.

On October 29 Hooker, Neal and I met with Ed Partin at a motel in Columbia, Tennessee, fifty miles south of Nashville. Partin drove to the meeting from Baton Rouge as a security precaution, to avoid the necessity of his utilizing the airport at Nashville or any other airport, where there was always the risk of chance observation. Hooker and Neal reviewed with Partin the testimony he would give at the trial. They were impressed both with his memory of the facts and his ability to express them. We returned to Nashville late that afternoon and Partin drove back to Baton Rouge.

During my trips to Nashville I had from time to time had conversations with Bob Vick, the Nashville police officer who had been one of Tommy Osborn's jury panel investigators in the Test Fleet case. He and others had also been hired by Osborn to do a background investigation of members of the grand jury that had indicted Hoffa. In these conversations Vick became more explicit about his suggestion that there may have been additional jury tampering in the Test Fleet case. He finally reached the point of saying that he had engaged in activities in connection with the Test Fleet jury, at the direction of Tommy Osborn, which he considered improper.

Vick said that the procedure followed by him and the others in investigating the backgrounds of the prospective jurors was perfectly proper and involved the common practice of contacting attorneys, sheriffs and others in the area in which the prospective juror resided to attempt to establish what type of person he was. However, he said, it did not end there. After the jury was chosen, he told me, he had, at Osborn's direction, continued to contact acquaintances of some of the jurors. He said specifically that he had contacted an attorney named Harry Beard, Jr., in Lebanon, Tennessee, who was acquainted with the husband of one of the jurors. He had asked the attorney guarded questions about the finances of the juror and her husband and how they intended to pay for their children's education. He had also wondered out loud whether the attorney thought that the juror's husband might be interested in working with them on a land development deal. He said he had made these inquiries at the direction of Osborn. And when Beard expressed an interest in being of assistance, Vick said he had suggested that he go see Tommy Osborn at his office. Vick told me he knew Beard had been to see Osborn but he did not know what transpired thereafter.

From this experience and others not quite so pointed, Vick said he was convinced that Osborn had succeeded in fixing the Test Fleet jury. He said he was sure that what he knew was only a part of what had transpired, and that, in his opinion, Osborn would also attempt to fix the jury in the upcoming jury-tampering trial. I told him if he obtained any evidence of that to let us know.

It was all too much. We didn't know what to think. Ed Steele of the FBI interviewed Beard, who admitted having been contacted to help with the background check on prospective jurors but denied anything further. We also checked, as best we could, on other similar leads provided by Vick but came up with nothing concrete.

The jury panel list from which the jurors for the upcoming trial would be chosen had now been drawn for Judge Gray's court. There was a similar panel for Judge Miller's court. Tommy Osborn had already hired two investigators to begin the background investigation of Judge Gray's panel. On the chance that the panels would be switched at the last minute, he now hired Vick to start doing the background checks on Judge Miller's panel.

On November 5 Nicholas Tweel abruptly withdrew his motion contending that his indictment had been based on wiretap information. In a letter to Judge Gray, his attorney, Dave A. Alexander of Franklin, Tennessee, said that "other matters have occurred and additional information has been secured indicating that the motion should be striken." We worried immediately that they may have discovered some other explanation for our apparent knowledge of Tweel's conversations and may have zeroed in on Partin. However, there were no overt indications of this.

In Washington the following day Hoffa announced that he would seek a $600,000,000 increase in wages and fringe benefits over the three-year period to be covered by the new national agreement. Hoffa made the statement after a meeting with his seventy-five-man bargaining policy committee at the International headquarters. He said that he hoped to begin the negotiations with the trucking industry in Chicago later in the month. A spokesman for the industry was quoted by newsmen as saying that Hoffa's demands were "outrageous."

I was in my office in Washington on the morning of November 7 when Murray W. "Dusty" Miller, the head of the Southern Conference of Teamsters, called me. He said he was in town and would like to drop over. I was surprised but said that I would be glad to talk to him. John Cassidy had maintained a friendly relationship with Nat Wells, who represented the Southern Conference, since their days on the monitorship. John and I had gone to Dallas the previous year, at Wells' invitation, to talk to him and Miller about the grand jury investigation we had in progress there at the time. It had been an amiable meeting but had not been productive of anything on either side.

When Miller came in, I asked Cassidy to join us. The conversation was very general and friendly. Toward the end of it, Miller brought up Partin's name. We didn't bat an eye. He wondered why Partin hadn't been prosecuted yet on the federal indictment. We indicated that we were very concerned about that too and couldn't understand either why it was taking so long. I mentioned to Cassidy that we would have to check on that. The conversation then moved on to something else.

When Miller left we were convinced that he had been trying to feel us out about Partin and that that was the real purpose of his visit. We also felt reasonably sure that we had passed the test. We felt it was likely that they were checking out different people who had been in Nashville to assure themselves that there was no one they had to worry about. We were not sure, however, whether Miller was acting on behalf of Dorfman, with whom he was very friendly, or Hoffa, or both.

Later that day I received a call from Bob Vick in Nashville. He said that Tommy Osborn had just instructed him to offer a prospective juror $10,000—$5000 now and $5000 after the verdict, if he became a member of the jury, to vote for the acquittal of Hoffa. I told Vick I would be in Nashville the following morning and he should meet me at the office.

It was almost too incredible that an attorney like Osborn would offer money to a prospective juror in a jury-tampering trial. Jack Miller was not in so I went to talk to Howard Willens, his assistant. I explained what Vick had said and told him I thought I should go to Nashville that night. He agreed. I called Jim Neal, who was in Nashville, and told him, and also Al McGrath in the FBI. Neal said that he would call John Hooker, Ed Steele and Bill Sheets, and we agreed to meet in the morning. I left for Nashville at 2 A.M.

Vick met us in the office that morning and explained what had happened. He said that he was in Osborn's office going over the jury panel list with him and he mentioned to Osborn that he knew one of the prospective jurors on Judge Gray's panel, a man named Ralph Elliot from Springfield. He said that Osborn told him to go talk to the juror and tell him that he would receive $5000 now, and if he got on the jury and voted for Hoffa's acquittal, he would receive another $5000. We asked Vick whether he would be willing to put what he had said in the form of an affidavit. He said that he would and did. I believed Vick but Hooker and Neal didn't know what to think and didn't really want to believe that Osborn would attempt to bribe a juror. I didn't either but I thought that he probably had. As things now stood, it would be Vick's word against Osborn's and most people would certainly be inclined to believe Osborn. One way to resolve the doubts would be if a subsequent conversation could be recorded.

Ed Steele went to see Judge Miller and showed him the affidavit. He was shocked. He authorized the FBI to place a recording device on Vick and to institute a surveillance while Vick went back to talk to Osborn.

Vick went to Osborn's office after Bill Sheets had taped a recording device on the small of his back. FBI agents observed Vick enter Osborn's office and saw him come out about an hour later. He was kept under observation while he walked several blocks to where two agents were waiting for him in a car. They then brought him back to our office. Vick said that he had talked to Osborn and that he had repeated the instructions about offering the money to the prospective juror. Bill Sheets removed the recorder from Vick and opened it. We all gave exasperated sighs. The tape was all unraveled in the machine and was useless. The recorder had obviously jammed when Vick sat down in Osborn's outer office. The first part of the tape was very clear—Vick entering the office and being greeted by the secretary—then it went dead.

There was no choice but to try it again. Bill Sheets and Ed Steele took a detailed signed statement from Vick about his most recent conversation with Osborn. We called and talked to Bob Kennedy and Jack Miller. They agreed that the matter had to be resolved and that the only practical way to do it was to attempt again to record the conversation.

The following morning Special Agent Bruce Fisher, who had attempted unsuccessfully to place a recorder on Ed Partin when he had been summoned to Washington by Hoffa earlier, arrived from Washington with a new recorder. Fisher taped the device on Vick's lower back, a little higher up than the first one, and Vick again set out for Osborn's office under FBI surveillance. It was a Saturday morning and Osborn was not in nor was he expected. We would have to wait until Monday.

On Monday morning we met again in our office with Vick. The same procedure was followed and Vick left once again, with the recorder in position, for Osborn's office. The agents observed him enter the office at 9:30 A.M. and exit one-half hour later. He was never out of the sight of the agents except for that half-hour. As soon as he reached the car where they were waiting, the agents removed the device and returned it to our office with Vick. This time it had worked.

There was no mistaking that it was Osborn's voice:

Osborn: Did you talk to him?
Vick: Yeah, I went down to Springfield Saturday morning.
Osborn: Elliot?
Vick: Elliot.
Osborn: (inaudible whisper)
Vick: Huh?
Osborn: Is there any chance in the world that he would report you?
Vick: That he will report me to the FBI? Why, of course, there's always a chance, but I wouldn't got into it if I thought it was very, very great.

Osborn: (laughs)

· · ·

Vick: . . . So he got to talking about the last Hoffa case being hung, you know, and some guy refusing ten thousand dollars to hang it, see? And he said the guy was crazy, he should've took it, you know, and so we talked about—and just discreetly, you know, and course I'm really playing this thing slow, that's the reason I asked you if you wanted a lawyer down there to handle it or you wanted me to handle it, 'cause I'm gonna play it easy.

Osborn: The less people the better.

Vick: That's right. Well, I'm gonna play it slow and easy myself, and er, anyway, we talked about—er—something about five thousand now and five thousand later, see, so he did, he brought up five thousand, see, and talking about how they pay it off and things like that. I don't know whether he suspected why I was there or not, 'cause I don't just drop out of the blue to visit him socially, you know. We're friends, close, and kin, cousins, but I don't ordinarily just, we don't fraternize, you know, and er, so he seemed very receptive for, er, to hang the thing for five now and five later. Now, er, I thought I would report back to you and see what you say.

Osborn: That's fine. The thing to do is set it up for a point later so you won't be running back and forth.

Vick: Yeah.

Osborn: Then tell him it's a deal.

Vick: It's what?

Osborn: That it's a deal. What we'll have to do when it gets down to the trial date, when we know the date—tomorrow, for example, if the Supreme Court rules against us, well, within the week we'll know when the trial comes. Then he has to be certain that when he gets on, he's got to know that he'll just be talking to you and nobody else.

· · ·

Osborn: All right—so we'll leave it up to you. The only thing to do would be to tell him, in other words, your next contact with him would be to tell him if he wants the deal, he's got it.

Vick: Okay.

Osborn: The only thing it depends upon is him being accepted on the jury. If the government challenges him, there will be no deal.

Vick: All right. If he is seated.

Osborn: If he is seated.

Vick: He can expect five thousand then.

Osborn: Immediately.

Vick: Immediately. And then five thousand when it's hung. Is that right?

Osborn: All the way, now!

Vick: Oh, he's got to stay all the way?

Osborn: All the way.

Vick: No swing. You don't want him to swing like we discussed once before. You want him.

Osborn: Of course, he could be guided by his own—but that always leaves a question. The thing to do is just stick with the crowd. That way we'll look better and maybe not have to go to another trial if we get a pretty good count.

Vick: Oh. Now, I'm going to play it just like you told me previously, to reassure him and keep him from getting panicky. You know—I have reason to believe that he won't be alone—you know?

Osborn: You assure him that, one hundred percent.

Vick: And to keep any fears down that he might have—see?

Osborn: Tell him there will be at least two others with him.

· · ·

Osborn: We'll keep it secret. The way to keep it safe is that nobody knows about it but you and me—where could they ever go?

Neal, Sheets, Fisher and I flew to Washington that night. Sheets and Fisher took the recorder and tape to FBI headquarters to have it transcribed and to maintain the chain of evidence. The next morning we met with Jack Miller and Bob Kennedy. Neal had called Judge Miller, who was at a judicial conference in New York, to report what had happened. The judge said that he would return to Nashville the following evening. Now that it was apparent Vick was absolutely accurate in this instance, we knew that what he had told us about Osborn's meeting with lawyer Beard during the Test Fleet case should be pursued further. It was decided to conduct additional investigations and to present the entire matter to the grand jury if Judge Miller approved. It was also likely that Judge Miller would take some action on his own when he returned. We knew that whatever action was taken could result in a delay of the Hoffa trial. (That morning the Supreme Court had refused to consider Hoffa's petition for delay.)

We returned to Nashville to see Judge Miller. Bill Sheets and Ed Steele gave him a copy of the transcript and played the recording for him. Judge Miller shook his head sadly while he listened. It was a painful experience for everyone. We had gone to Judge Miller initially because he was the chief judge and also to avoid the possibility of prejudicing Judge Gray in connection with the Hoffa case. After hearing the recording, however, Judge Miller decided to bring Judge Gray into the matter. The recording was then played for Judge Gray, after the background had been explained to him.

The following morning Judge Miller's secretary called Tommy Osborn and asked if he would come to the judge's chambers that afternoon. When Osborn arrived, he found both Judge Miller and Judge Gray awaiting him. They told him that they had received information "of a substantial nature" that efforts were being made to tamper with prospective jurors for the Hoffa trial, and that the information indicated that he himself was implicated. They told Osborn that he did not have to answer any questions and that anything he said could be used against him. They also told him that he had a right to have an attorney present.

Osborn told the judges that he was familiar with his rights and was perfectly willing to answer any questions. They then asked him if he was aware of any efforts to influence potential jurors. Osborn said that he was not. They then asked him if he himself had made any such attempt or had talked to another person about doing so. Osborn replied that he had not. He was then asked specifically if he had discussed with anyone an effort to influence a prospective juror by the name of Elliot. Osborn again stated that he had not.

The judges thereupon served Osborn with a show-cause order

directing him to appear on November 25 for a hearing to show cause why he should not be disbarred. They gave Osborn the choice of an open hearing or one in chambers. He chose the latter.

Osborn returned to his office and tried to call Vick. However, just before Osborn's meeting with the judges, Vick had moved into a room at the Holiday Inn on West End Avenue accompanied by Ed Steele and Bill Sheets. Marshal Elmer Disspayne sent a deputy marshal out to Vick's home to stay with his wife and children. Osborn's desperate calls to Vick's home went on until midnight.

The following morning John Polk went to Vick's residence on Osborn's behalf, looking for him. He was informed by a deputy marshal that Vick was not there and was not available. Later that morning Osborn asked to see Judge Gray and appeared in Judge Gray's chambers accompanied by his law partner, Raymond Denny, and attorney Jack Norman. They asked Judge Gray to furnish them the information upon which the show-cause order had been based. Judge Gray, acting with the concurrence of Judge Miller, who had gone back to the judicial conference in New York, advised Osborn and his attorneys of the sequence of events beginning with Vick's affidavit on November 8, their authorization of investigation and the utilization of an electronic device, and the subsequent affidavits and recording.

Over the weekend John Hooker met with Osborn's attorneys at their request, as they sought desperately to find a way to save Osborn's future as an attorney. It was a sad, grim situation from everyone's standpoint, but realistically there was little that could be done to improve it.

On Monday morning Judge Gray set the trial for Hoffa and his co-defendants for January 6 in Nashville. The following day Osborn advised Judge Gray that he would like to appear again in chambers and make a statement. An appointment was made for late afternoon to allow Judge Miller time to return from New York.

When Osborn appeared before Judges Miller and Gray, he was again advised of his rights. Osborn asked that he be permitted to make a statement and that the show-cause hearing be held then and there. He then admitted having conversations with Vick on November 8 and November 11 concerning attempts to influence prospective juror Elliot. He said, however, that the idea to approach Elliot had been Vick's and not his, and that he had not actually decided, in his own mind, to go through with it. The affidavits and recording were made a part of the record of the hearing and Osborn acknowledged that it was his voice on the recording and that the transcription of the conversation of November 11 was accurate. The affidavits of FBI agents Ed Steele, Bill Sheets and Charles Grigsby concerning the surveillance of Vick were also introduced, and they testified as to their accuracy. Osborn declined to cross-examine the agents. He also declined the offer by the judges to call Vick as a witness.

The next evening, while Osborn was in Washington conferring with Teamsters officials and attorneys, Judge Miller issued a lengthy memorandum disbarring Tommy Osborn from further practice in federal court. Judge Gray issued a shorter memorandum concurring in Judge Miller's action. Judge Miller outlined the chronology of events and concluded that Osborn had talked to Vick about influencing a prospective juror; that he had lied to the court both in his original answers on November 15 and his subsequent statement on November 19; that he had not made a complete disclosure about approaches to other prospective jurors (here the judge cited Osborn's statement to Vick to assure Elliot "there will be at least two others with him"); that he had not been entrapped by Vick, and that it wouldn't make any difference even if he had; and, particularly in view of the recent indictment for jury tampering in the prior case in which he was an attorney, "that the respondent, in the light of this immediate history and in this context and atmosphere did himself engage in a brazen attempt to bribe and improperly influence a prospective juror is an indication of such a callous and shameful disregard of duty, such a lack of moral fitness and sense of professional ethics as to warrant no lesser punishment than the removal of his name from the roll of attorneys permitted to practice law in this court."

A member of the board of directors of the Nashville Bar Association was quoted by reporters as stating that the Nashville legal profession was in "a profound state of shock." He said that Osborn had been the leading candidate to become the next president of the association in December. "Tommy would have been elected," he said.

At about 1:30 P.M. the next day as I was sitting in the jury room behind Judge Miller's court, which we were using temporarily as an office while his court was not in session, Carl Schultz came running into the room. "Walt, there has just been a news flash that the President has been shot in Dallas!"

I called Bob Kennedy's office but he wasn't there and they didn't know any more than we did. I called John Seigenthaler at the *Tennessean*. He said that the President had been shot in a Dallas motorcade and was in the hospital. He didn't know what his condition was. He invited us to come over to his office. By the time we arrived, there was live coverage from Dallas and the reports indicated that the President had been critically if not mortally wounded. We sat down and watched and waited. Then a short while later came the announcement by Malcom Kilduff that the President was dead.

In Washington, at the International Brotherhood of Teamsters headquarters, Harold Gibbons and Larry Steinberg ordered the flag lowered to half-mast and the building closed, and everyone was told to go home. Then they called Jimmy Hoffa in Miami and told him what they had done. He flew into a rage and became very abusive. He told them he was not going to be a hypocrite and that they should not have done what they had. He also yelled at his secretary for crying. When he was finished, they hung up and left the building.

On Sunday the stunned nation continued to watch the uninterrupted live television coverage as the flag-draped coffin was borne on a caisson up Pennsylvania Avenue from the White House to the Capitol Rotunda. Our group stood out in front of the Justice Department with the crowds that lined the street as the somber procession went by.

Jimmy Hoffa was in Nashville that day to speak at a rally for Ewing King, a few blocks from where memorial services were being held at the same time for the late President. Hoffa attacked King's opponent, Don Vestal, and praised King. He said, "Ewing, if I can come back here anytime before the election, or if you need speakers, or if somebody wants to debate, you just blow the whistle and we'll be here. The International Union is behind you."

Later that day, in a television interview, Hoffa charged Judges Miller and Gray with the entrapment of Tommy Osborn. "I feel that it's a travesty on justice that the government, the local officials and the judges should have any part of trying to set up and entrap him and be able to take away from me a competent lawyer to represent me in this case."

When Hoffa was asked about Attorney General Kennedy, he replied, "Bobby Kennedy is just another lawyer now."

On November 30 Hoffa was in my home town of Utica, New York, where he addressed the thirtieth anniversary dinner of Local

182 and paid tribute to the president of the local and joint council, Rocco De Perno. Hoffa told newsmen that "Bobby Kennedy is out. He will no longer have the veto power of the presidency behind him." He said that Kennedy was "just one of nine men now" in President Johnson's Cabinet.

On December 2 we were back in Nashville for a grand jury investigation of Tommy Osborn's activities. We talked to attorney Harry Beard, Jr., of Lebanon, Tennessee, again. This time he admitted that after being contacted by Bob Vick during the Test Fleet case, he had gone to see Tommy Osborn. He said that Osborn told him to offer $10,000 to the husband of a juror in the Test Fleet case if the juror would vote for the acquittal of Hoffa. Beard, a mediocre country lawyer, said that he was astounded by the proposal but was also flattered that Osborn had approached him. He told Osborn that he would see what he could do. Beard said that he did not contact the juror's husband and never really intended to. After thinking the matter over for a few days, he returned to Osborn and told him that he hadn't yet been able to talk to the juror's husband. Beard said that by this time he was afraid either to report the matter to the government or to tell Osborn he wouldn't follow through. Therefore, he said, he decided to tell Osborn that the juror's husband wanted $50,000, figuring that Osborn would reject this as too costly and let him off the hook. He said he went to Osborn a third time with his concocted story, and that on a subsequent and last visit to Osborn, the $50,000 "demand" was rejected.

On December 4, after furnishing an affidavit about his dealings with Osborn, Beard appeared voluntarily before Judges Miller and Gray in chambers and gave them a statement to the same effect. On the following day Judges Miller and Gray denied a petition by Tommy Osborn for a rehearing. Nashville *Tennessean* reporter Nellie Kenyon reached Osborn in Miami Beach where the Teamsters International Executive Board was meeting. Osborn said he would appeal the decision.

While Hoffa was in Miami Beach for the Executive Board meeting, a revolution was quietly brewing in the hierarchy of the International led by Harold Gibbons and Larry Steinberg, both still chafing from Hoffa's abuse on the day President Kennedy was assassinated. In a front-page story in *The New York Times* on

December 6, reporter John Pomfret quoted informed sources as saying that Gibbons, Steinberg, Dick Kavner and an official in the Warehouse Division of the International, Ferguson Keathley, had all quit their jobs with the International. Keathley had married Hoffa's secretary, Yuki Kato, who was formerly Gibbons' secretary, and according to the article, she also had quit. Hoffa immediately denied the story. Gibbons and the others refused to comment.

In Nashville, on December 6, the grand jury indicted Tommy Osborn on three counts of jury tampering. The indictment charged that Osborn had directed Vick to offer $10,000 to prospective juror Ralph A. Elliot; directed Harry Beard, Jr., to offer $10,000 to D. M. Harrison, whose wife served as a juror in the Test Fleet case; and directed investigator John Polk to arrange a meeting between Osborn and Virgil Rye, whose wife also served on the jury, for the purpose of attempting to influence her vote in the trial.

In Miami Beach Hoffa again denied the continued reports of resignations but admitted that Gibbons, Steinberg, and Keathley had "asked to be relieved" of duties with the International in order to return to their local unions.

On December 11 Hoffa filed a motion in Nashville asking that Judge Gray excuse himself, charging that the judge was already convinced that efforts had been made to tamper with jurors in the Test Fleet case. The motion also asked for a delay in the trial on the basis that Hoffa needed time to find an attorney to replace Osborn. Hoffa also asked for a change of venue, claiming that because of the recent publicity he could not receive a fair trial in Nashville.

The next day Judge Gray denied Hoffa's motion charging that he was biased and then voluntarily withdrew from the case. Both Judge Miller and Judge Gray had already recused themselves from the Osborn case. Judge Gray was replaced in the Hoffa case by Judge Frank W. Wilson of Chattanooga, who immediately announced that he would hold a hearing the following Friday in Nashville on Hoffa's remaining motions.

On December 14 the Board of Governors of the Tennessee Bar Association voted unanimously to begin disbarment proceedings against Tommy Osborn. The Nashville Bar Association took the position that disbarment proceedings by it were not necessary at that time since Osborn had agreed not to practice law in the state courts and to surrender his license if the federal disbarment were upheld on appeal.

On December 18 Judges Miller and Gray issued an order disbarring Harry Beard, Jr. In the order they stated:

> We are painfully conscious in this case, as in any case of a similar nature, of the deep tragedy involved to the attorney personally and to the members of his family. Yet, if the courts are to survive as instruments for the administration of justice, the strictest disciplinary action in such cases is imperatively required and demanded.

A hearing on Hoffa's motions for delay and change of venue was held by Judge Frank Wilson in Nashville on December 20. The government opposed both motions. At the conclusion of the hearing, Judge Wilson took the matters under advisement. He said that he would rule on the motions as soon as possible and that in the meantime both sides should be prepared to go to trial as scheduled on January 6.

On Christmas Eve Judge Wilson granted Hoffa and his co-defendants a delay until January 20. Four days later he also granted their motion for a change of venue and transferred the case to Chattanooga.

The rumors and reports of unrest and revolt within the Teamsters International continued. Gibbons, Steinberg and the others were still scheduled to leave their International posts on the first of the year. Hoffa was still denying that they had resigned, stating that they had merely asked to be relieved of their assignments with the International. Gibbons was still saying "no comment" to questions about the change in his status.

There was, indeed, a growing movement within the Executive Board of the International to throw Hoffa out of office. A majority of the board was sick to death of carrying Hoffa's self-created troubles and his racketeer friends on the shoulders of the Teamsters Union. They were fed up with taking the vindictive abuse he heaped on them in increasing measure. They had grown to detest his ever tightening dictatorial control over their lives and their local unions, and they detested themselves for somewhere along the line deciding to take it. Some of them were angry and ashamed, but they were also growing old and tired and were too willing to trade their manhood and self-respect for the pot of gold that the general president had arranged for them in their very generous pensions just a few years down the road.

They were fragmented into groups which did not trust each other or themselves. There were secret meetings among some of the board members and the would-be successors put out feelers testing the extent and strength of their constituency. There was common agreement that in a showdown secret vote the only two Executive Board members that Hoffa could count on with certainty were Frank Fitzsimmons and Tony Provenzano. But there was no showdown because the others could not agree among themselves whether to move or whom to support if they did. They were mature, intelligent men but too many of them were physically afraid of Hoffa and his friends. As one of them put it—he did not want to go out feet first in a box. So the revolt simmered and died and the result was a passive consensus to wait and see how the trial in Chattanooga came out. If he is convicted, they said to one another, then we will throw him out.

On December 30 an article by the late Ed Woods, Washington correspondent for the *St. Louis Post Dispatch,* appeared on the front page of that newspaper. It said that Hoffa had tried but failed to arrange a deal whereby he would have quit his office as general president of the union, and perhaps even the union itself, if the government would drop the charges against him in Chattanooga and Chicago. The article said that the government had flatly rejected the deal.

When Hoffa read the article he was furious. He called Ed Woods at 10 A.M. on New Years Eve from Detroit. He asked Woods what in the hell he was trying to do and told him that he had got himself "a nice lawsuit." He asked Woods why he had made no attempt to check the story with him. When Woods replied that he had tried unsuccessfully to reach him, Hoffa said, "That's a goddamn lie. You are deliberately trying to screw up my trial." The conversation ended with Hoffa shouting at Woods what he could do to himself. The article was completely accurate and true.

CHAPTER X

"The Very Soul of This Nation"

CHATTANOOGA IS LOCATED 137 miles southeast of Nashville on the northeastern border of Georgia. Unlike Nashville, Chattanooga is an industrial city with a diverse manufacturing economy. The workers in the plants are, for the most part, organized by various unions. As in Nashville, there is a strong Teamsters organization represented by Local 515. The president of the local in 1964 was George Hicks, a big, burly Teamster, loyal to Jimmy Hoffa and a close friend of Ewing King.

The United States Attorney's office is directly across the hall from the single Chattanooga courtroom. On January 3, 1964, John Hooker, Jim Neal and I went there to meet with Jack Reddy, the United States Attorney, to begin preparing for trial. That evening we went to Nashville to gather our files together and arrange for the exodus to Chattanooga.

On January 6 Hooker, Neal and I had another rendezvous with Partin at the Holiday Inn in Columbia. Frank Grimsley had met with Partin occasionally in Baton Rouge or New Orleans and I had kept in touch with him by telephone, but it was the first I had seen him since we met at the same location three months earlier. In the meantime, of course, the President had been assassinated and it was no longer a Kennedy Administration. Although Robert Kennedy was still the Attorney General and was being touted in the press as a potential Vice Presidential candidate in the upcoming election, there was no question that the power structure had changed radically from what it was when Partin had agreed to be a witness. I did not know whether Partin had enough faith in the new government to risk what he was being asked to do for it. He knew full well the potential consequences of testifying publicly as a vital witness against Jimmy Hoffa. We had told him we would protect him physically, but how good was that commitment now, and for how long? How much, if any, obligation would President Lyndon Johnson feel toward the public service of Edward Grady Partin? I am sure Partin thought of these things before we met that day.

But he did not raise any of these questions when we met. He had obviously made up his mind to go forward and told us he would be in Chattanooga when we asked him to come. Neal and Hooker went over his testimony with him again. We had not yet decided whether to put him on as our first witness or our last, but were inclining toward the latter. We told him that we would give him sufficient notice and we agreed that he should drive from Baton Rouge to Chattanooga at that time. Ed Partin made his commitment to the government of the United States that day and kept it. He had been promised nothing in return but a fair shake. The government of the United States would not, in the long run, keep its side of the bargain.

On January 9 we moved to Chattanooga. Bill Sheets went with us and Ed Steele was to follow in a few days. The FBI had agreed, at our request, to their being assigned to Chattanooga for the entire time of the trial because of their familiarity with the case. (Steele would have to make occasional trips to Nashville because of his responsibilities there, but would be in Chattanooga much of the time.) That afternoon a jury panel of two hundred names from which the jury would be selected was drawn in Judge Wilson's court. Only the first initial and last name of the prospective jurors were announced by the clerk of the court as the names were drawn. Judge Wilson ruled that the panel list containing the full names and addresses would be kept secret from both the defense and the government. James Haggerty, Hoffa's attorney from Detroit, was in the courtroom that morning along with Harry Berke, who had been retained as local counsel by Hoffa. Berke, a fifty-two year-old Chattanooga trial lawyer, had been the subject of disbarment action by the Tennessee Bar Association in 1961 but his right to practice law had been upheld by the state Supreme Court.

Back in Nashville, George Broda and other former business agents of Local 327 under defeated President Ewing King were circulating petitions calling for the formation of a separate local. Don Vestal, the new president of the local, had announced that he would not rehire the former business agents when he took office on January 20. In another move against Vestal, a group of King's followers had petitioned the International for a new election. Hoffa had taken jurisdiction over the dispute and appointed a three-man panel to investigate the complaints.

In Newark, New Jersey, the members of Local 478 voted in a referendum to turn down Hoffa's proposed national contract. Milton Liss, the president of the local who had been a candidate against Hoffa at the last Teamsters Convention, had persistently opposed the national contract on the basis that his local would lose benefits by accepting it.

In St. Louis, Harold Gibbons, who had resigned his International post as executive assistant to Hoffa on January 1, made a statement in the *Missouri Teamster* denying a rift with Hoffa. Gibbons said, "My personal relationships with President Hoffa have been excellent in the past, are now, and shall continue to be in the future." Gibbons said that he had resigned the $35,000 a year job with the International because he wanted to get back to his own local union.

On January 11 a former law partner of Judge Wilson's was approached by a person prominent in Tennessee state political circles and offered $5000 if he could influence the judge to postpone the Hoffa case for sixty days. The offer was declined. The improvers were back at work.

Two days later Harry Berke filed a motion on behalf of Hoffa asking for a delay in the trial. It cited prejudicial publicity and the fact that his new attorney, Berke, had not had sufficient time to prepare for the trial.

We assumed that there would be efforts to tamper with the jury in Chattanooga even though this was a jury-tampering trial. Based on our past experience, we realistically had no choice but to make that assumption. We were hopeful that the judge would sequester the jury. If he did, we would only have to be concerned with the period prior to the selection of the jury. We decided to do what we could, based on what we had learned from the jury-tampering activities in the Test Fleet case, to minimize the likelihood of a successful repetition of such efforts.

One thing we had learned was that several of the persons who had been involved in the jury-tampering plots in Nashville had been in the courtroom during that trial. For identification purposes, we decided to set up two locations in buildings across from the courthouse. from which FBI agents could photograph persons entering the courthouse. We also decided—again based on the Nashville experience—to institute a surveillance, once the trial began, of George Hicks, the president of Local 515 in Chattanooga, and William Test, the former president of the local. The main purpose of the surveillance was to discourage Hicks and his associates from engaging in any efforts in connection with the jury—if they should have any such intentions—and to detect them if they did.

In the early morning hours of January 16 in Chicago Jimmy Hoffa and the negotiating committee for the trucking companies finally reached an agreement on the terms of the new nationwide pact and averted strikes which Hoffa had threatened to call, on a selective basis, at midnight on the 15th. The agreement on a three-year contract which would expire on March 31, 1967, called for a twenty-eight-cent wage increase over three years. Hoffa said that the increase, including added fringe benefits, amounted to forty-five cents an hour. He had originally sought a sixty-cent-an-hour wage increase and an equivalent increase in fringe benefits.

On the following day Hoffa flew into Chattanooga accompanied by Chuck O'Brien. He was met at the airport by cheering Teamsters members carrying placards and banners with such inscriptions as: "We'll always be for Jo and Jimmy Hoffa," "Welcome to Chattanooga" and "Thank you Jimmy for the contract." After posing for photographers and talking with waiting reporters, Hoffa climbed into a Teamsters Cadillac with George Hicks and led a forty-car caravan into the city behind a police escort.

That evening Hoffa was interviewed on a live television program. The accommodating interviewer led him through thirty minutes of talk about his wife, his family and his innocence. It was a big propaganda plus. After the program Hoffa left and returned to Detroit.

The Court of Appeals denied a petition that had been filed by Jacques Schiffer on behalf of his client Tom Parks, asking for a delay in the trial. Schiffer claimed that he had a conflicting obligation in Chicago in connection with the Glimco-Abata NLRB case. The Court of Appeals did act favorably, however, on a petition by attorney R. B. Parker on behalf of Lawrence Medlin asking that Medlin be severed from the case and that his trial remain in Nashville. There was now one less defendant in the Chattanooga case.

On Saturday, January 18, Judge Wilson held the scheduled pretrial meeting with attorneys for the defense and government in his chambers. After the three-hour conference he issued an order denying a defense motion that the jury panel list with full names and addresses be released. He said it would not be released until the following Monday morning when the trial and selection of the jury began. He also denied a motion by Nicholas Tweel for a sixty-day delay in the trial.

Now, fifteen months after the Test Fleet trial started in Nashville, we were again in Tennessee, ready to begin another trial. Jim Durkin was still there (it was now two years since he had gone to Nashville to help out "for a few weeks"). Nat Lewin was also there. He had been grudgingly dubbed "Instant Law" by Hoffa's attorneys because of the unique speed and accuracy with which he could ferret out pertinent case citations and legal precedents. Bill French, Tom McKeon, Frank Grimsley and John Cassidy also came in to lend assistance. Carl Schultz and Jack Thiede were also there, hard at work compiling and recording toll calls and maintaining the chronologies.

As in Nashville, a temporary headquarters of the International Brotherhood of Teamsters had been set up, in the Patten Hotel, a few blocks from the Federal Building. William Bufalino had advanced the operation a few days earlier and the combined living-working space for Hoffa, his attorneys and associates was now filling up. Hoffa arrived and moved in on Sunday evening, January 19. He was accompanied by his wife, his son James and his daughter, Mrs. Robert Crancer.

At 9 A.M. the following morning the trial began. The defendants and their attorneys crowded around the defense table at the front of the courtroom on the left. Hoffa was flanked by attorneys James Haggerty and Harry Berke; Jacques Schiffer sat next to his client Tom Parks; attorney Cecil Brandstetter from Nashville was with Larry Campbell; Ewing King was represented by Chattanooga attorney Harold Brown; Chicago attorney Harvey Silets was with Allen Dorfman; and Nicholas Tweel was squeezed in between his two attorneys, Dave Alexander of Franklin, Tennessee, and Henry Grady of Chattanooga. Behind the defense table, against the front left wall in the section reserved for visiting attorneys, sat the defense back-up group of Jake Kossman from Philadelphia, Frank Ragano from Tampa and Harry Berke, Jr., from Chattanooga.

At the government table on the right side sat John Hooker, Jim Neal and Jack Reddy. As in Nashville, Jim Durkin and Nat Lewin would be in and out of the courtroom assisting them.

The trial judge, Frank Wilson, was regarded as a fair, scholarly and patient man of gentle manner but of tough fiber and immense integrity. Most of the first morning was taken up with last-ditch arguments by defense attorneys of motions to dismiss the indictment and to dismiss the jury panel. Judge Wilson denied the motions and then announced over strong objections by defense attorneys that the jury would be locked up for the duration of the trial. The list of the names and addresses of all the prospective jurors which had been kept sealed was given to the government and defense attorneys and the press.

The prospective jurors then filed into the courtroom and filled it to capacity. The selection of the jury got under way. The clerk of the court called out the names of twelve prospective jurors and they were questioned one at a time in the jury box by attorneys for the government and the defense and by Judge Wilson. Four of the first twelve were excused by Judge Wilson. One other was tentatively accepted by both defense and government attorneys after two hours of questioning. He and the remaining seven who had not yet been questioned were locked up for the night.

The surveillance by the FBI of George Hicks and William Test had been started that morning. A surveillance was also instituted of John Cleveland, a heavyset black Teamsters official from Washington, D.C., who had arrived in town the previous evening and who did not seem to have any obvious reason for being there. The agents were specifically instructed not to surveil any defendant or attorney.

The second day of the trial began with Judge Wilson announcing that he was going to take over the questioning of the prospective jurors from the defense and government attorneys unless they speeded up their examination. Unlike in Nashville, there was great public interest in the trial and the courtroom was completely filled. An overflow of people, unable to find seats, milled around in the corridor outside the courtroom. Some of the steady Nashville trial watchers from the Test Fleet case were there including former Local 327 Business Agent John Ivey and Mrs. Mamie Herd, the wife of another former business agent. The spectators as a whole seemed to be a cross section of Chattanooga—old and young, black and white, but a majority were female. By the end of the day six jurors had been tentatively seated.

The following morning Judge Wilson announced that he was taking over the questioning of the prospective jurors to expedite matters. He observed that at the rate they had progressed during the first two days, it would take three weeks to select a jury. He overruled strenuous objections by the defense attorneys. Jacques Schiffer, however, refused to accept the judge's ruling and went into a tirade. "There seems to be an undue rush to force these defendants to trial," he said. Then, pointing at the government attorneys and raising his voice, he said, "This is not Russia. These men have a constitutional right to due process of law. There is something going on in this case, your honor . . . the government wants a drumhead court-martial trial."

Later in the day Schiffer was again on his feet, charging that federal agents were tapping his telephone and surveilling the defendants and their attorneys. Jim Neal responded, "The government states categorically, without any reservation, that no phone is being tapped and that no counsel or defendant is being surveilled." "I don't believe it," snapped Schiffer.

In the courtroom a new face appeared in the support group of attorneys behind the defense table. It was Morris Shenker, the veteran defense attorney from St. Louis, who had been a sometime behind-the-scenes advisor in Nashville and was steadily rising in prominence in the hierarchy of the Teamsters Bar Association. The tall, gray-haired, distinguished-appearing attorney had represented some of the leading racketeers in St. Louis and was active in Democratic political circles there. Shortly after Hoffa was indicted for jury tampering, Shenker had approached Paul Allred, who had resigned from our group to return to private practice in St. Louis. He offered Allred a $25,000 retainer fee to become a consultant for the defense in the jury-tampering case. Allred turned him down and immediately called me to report the offer.

Another attorney who was not in the courtroom but who had been in and out of Chattanooga conferring with Hoffa and his attorneys was Tommy Osborn. Hoffa told reporters that Osborn was there to furnish information he had previously obtained and was doing so voluntarily without a fee. William Bufalino spent most of his time at the Patten Hotel supervising the displaced International headquarters.

Chuck O'Brien arrived at the airport the following morning and was followed by FBI agents to the Patten Hotel. The surveillance was terminated at that point and was not reinstituted. Frank Chavez, the Teamsters official from Puerto Rico, and George Broda from Nashville also showed up in the corridor outside the courtroom.

During the noon recess on the fourth day of the trial Hoffa was the principal speaker at a luncheon held at the Patten Hotel by the Sertoma Club, a local civic organization. After an introduction by local Teamsters President George Hicks, Hoffa praised his new nationwide contract and criticized the McClellan Committee, the newspapers and the Attorney General. He said that none of the businessmen at the luncheon could stand up under the type of investigation to which the Teamsters Union had been subjected. His remarks were received warmly. After the luncheon Hoffa told newsmen that Local 299 in Detroit would soon build a $1,000,000 four-story clinic to provide dental and eye care for Teamsters members and their families.

On Friday, January 24, in a court session extended until 7 P.M. by Judge Wilson, a jury of eight men and four women was finally chosen. By the noon recess on Monday the four alternate jurors had been selected and the testimony of witnesses was ready to begin. As soon as the jury had been selected, all surveillance was terminated.

The government called James Tippens as its first witness, but defense attorney Harry Berke argued that testimony by Tippens about Hoffa would be hearsay. Judge Wilson ruled that for the time being he would not allow testimony by Tippens, at least not until a connection had been established between Hoffa and Lawrence Medlin, who had allegedly made the offer of money to Tippens and whose case had been severed from the trial.

The government then called James T. "Jack" Walker to the stand. Walker said that he had been a patrolman on the metropolitan police department in Nashville for four years. He pointed out Parks in the courtroom. He testified that Parks had come to his home driving a two-tone 1956 green Buick shortly after the Test Fleet trial had begun and that he had talked to Parks in the car.

He said that Parks had asked him if he knew Gratin Fields, the juror in the Test Fleet case. When Walker said that he did, Parks then asked him if Fields needed money. Walker said that he told him he didn't know. He said that Parks then told him that the "big boys" wanted to talk to him because they needed one more person to hang the jury.

Walker went on to tell how Parks had come back a few days later and that at Parks' request he had called Carl Fields, the son of the juror, and asked him to come to his house about a job opportunity. He said he had introduced Parks to Fields and had then left the room. Walker said there had been a subsequent meeting between Parks and Fields at his printing shop that evening. This time, Walker said, Parks and Fields went across the street and talked in Parks' car. Later that night, at Parks' request, Walker called Fields to find out if he had done anything. He said that Fields told him he had not talked to his father and was not going to because he was afraid. When Walker called Parks back and reported this, Parks told him that he wanted to know what Gratin Fields was going to wear to court. Parks said that he had given Carl Fields some money and he thought he would come through.

Walker said that when he heard nothing more from Fields, Parks asked him to contact Carl's sister, Mrs. Mattie Leath, a daughter of Gratin Fields. He said he called Mrs. Leath, a social worker, at her office and arranged to meet her there on her lunch hour. He said that Parks drove him to the meeting and remained in the car while he went in to talk to Mrs. Leath. Walker said that he asked her if Carl had talked to her about his meetings with Parks. She said that he had but that she didn't want to have anything to do with it. He said that she told him if there were any further contacts she was going to the police or the FBI. Walker said that he then left and Parks drove him home. Walker testified that when Parks had first approached him, he had said that "they" would be willing to pay $10,000 to contact the juror Gratin Fields.

Walker was followed to the witness stand the next day by Carl Fields. He corroborated Walker's testimony of how he came to meet Parks. He said that Parks had asked him if he would talk to his father and influence him to vote for the acquittal of Hoffa. He said that Parks told him it would be worth $5000 to him and $5000 to his father if he would do it. He said that he told Parks he would not talk to his father. He said that Parks then asked him if he could find out by nine o'clock that night what kind of suit or what color tie his father was going to wear to court the next morning because he had to make a call to Louisville. Fields said that Parks gave him five twenty-dollar bills and told him he would give him another $100 if he could find that out for him. He said that he called Parks later, at the number Parks had given him, and told him he wasn't going to help him. He asked Parks if he wanted the $100 back and Parks told him he could keep it for his troubles.

Fields said that he had given a statement to Tommy Osborn in which he denied that Parks had asked him to talk to his father but that the statement was not true. He said he had also lied to the FBI and government attorneys initially because he didn't want to get involved.

The next witness was Mrs. Mattie Leath. She described the meeting with Jack Walker and said that he wanted to know what kind of clothes her father was going to wear to court. She said that when she asked him why, he replied, "Well, it is a fellow out in the car who wants to know." She saw a two-tone green Buick out in front, she said, but could not identify the occupant. She testified that her brother, Carl Fields, had told her, her mother and her sister that he had been approached by a man named Tom Parks and that "Parks had offered him a sum of money to try to talk to Daddy." She said they discussed it among themselves several times during the trial but did not mention it to Gratin Fields, the juror.

Both Jack Walker and Carl Fields testified that they had been interviewed by Bill Sheets and me. Defense attorneys now demanded that we be called as witnesses to determine what we had done with our original notes. Sheets had taken notes, incorporated them into an official FBI report and then, as was the policy of the bureau, destroyed the notes. I had not taken any notes in these interviews since I knew that Sheets was.

The next morning, January 29, Sheets and I were called, with the jury absent, and questioned by Judge Wilson. Sheets explained what he had done with his original notes and that it was the policy of the FBI to do so since the same information was contained in his report, which had been turned over to the defense attorneys by the government prior to the testimony of the witnesses. I testified that I had not taken notes nor otherwise recorded the interview.

Schiffer then went into another tirade about the government destroying evidence to protect a "frame-up" of his client. Neal objected heatedly to the accusation. Schiffer shot back, "This is the kind of case that cannot be tried with silk gloves. When I find that my client is being framed by the government with the help of Mr. Neal and the Attorney General and all of those assisting them . . . I'm not going to still my tongue." The exchange continued with Neal and Schiffer accusing each other of filibustering.

The tension in the courtroom, already high when the trial began, was continuing to grow. The defense attorneys were on their feet repeatedly, sometimes together, sometimes separately, objecting to testimony or questions by Neal and Hooker. Many of the objections represented the legitimate, tough, inch-by-inch fighting of defense attorneys for their clients. But Schiffer, by far the most active and loudest, was more and more often going beyond the bounds of either validity or decency and appeared to be attempting deliberately to wear down the judge's patience and cause a mistrial.

The next witness, Mrs. Mattie Mix, led to another verbal brawl which consumed much of the day. Mrs. Mix had delivered a letter to Neal, Hooker and Reddy that morning, signed by her, in which she stated she would take the Fifth Amendment if called as a witness. When they talked to her about it, she said that Schiffer had given her the letter to sign and had told her that if she testified, the government attorneys would embarrass her with questions about past associations and things that happened a long time ago. When Neal and the others assured her that this was not the case, she agreed to testify.

When she was called as a witness, Schiffer immediately objected and asked that the jury be excused. He then said that Mrs. Mix had conferred with him about one year earlier and complained of having been harassed and accused of perjury by the FBI. He said that as a result she had written the letter stating that she would take the Fifth Amendment if called as a witness.

Hooker: Did she write it, Mr. Schiffer, or did you write it?
Schiffer: I dictated it and she signed it and I offer it as evidence.
Neal: This is an effort to obstruct justice . . . she testified freely before the grand jury.

The judge ordered Mrs. Mix to take the stand. She said that Schiffer was her attorney. She was vague on how he happened to have become her lawyer but said that it was since she had been subpoenaed to testify. She also admitted that she had agreed to testify in her conversation with government attorneys that morning.

The jury returned to the courtroom and Mrs. Mix testified. She admitted that Parks took his daily meals at her house, had a key to the house and used the telephone. She also stated that there were calls to Louisville on her phone bill and that she did not make them.

Mrs. Tilford Brown, the proprietor of Brown's Tourist Home in Louisville, testified next about Larry Campbell's stays at the Tourist Home, that he made and received calls on the pay phone there and that he told her in November, 1962, that he might go to Nashville over a weekend.

Mrs. Ernestine Williams of Louisville testified that she was with Campbell on a daily basis while he was in Louisville and that he did not appear to be working. She told of their frequenting Joe's Palm Room and that Campbell made phone calls from the pay phone there. She also described in detail other phone booths in the vicinity where Campbell also made calls and identified photographs of the phone booths. She described going to the airport with Campbell to meet Chuck O'Brien. She said that Campbell also made calls from her residence and identified calls on her phone bill to the Mattie Mix residence in Nashville. She said that Campbell told her he would pay for the calls. She told the court that Campbell had confided to her that "his boss was in trouble."

J. J. Isaacs of the Southern Bell Telephone Company then testified concerning subpoenaed records of the company which were placed in evidence, showing a series of twelve calls, from October 22, 1962, to November 13, 1962, made to the Mattie Mix residence from the phone booths identified by Mrs. Williams. There were also three calls to the Mix residence from Mrs. Williams' residence, all on November 14, 1962.

The next witness was Mrs. Mary K. Reeves of Detroit, who, like Mrs. Williams, was a nurse. She said Campbell paid her phone bill, acknowledged that there were calls on the bill in November, 1962, from her residence to the Mix residence in Nashville and said that she did not make the calls. She said she did not know if Campbell made the calls. Neal then elicited the information that she had testified before the grand jury that she assumed he made the calls because he paid the bill.

Arthur H. Schneider of the Michigan Bell Telephone Company then identified records showing a series of calls from Detroit. At

12:49 A.M. on October 22, 1962, the day the Test Fleet case began, there was a call from a phone booth in Detroit to a phone booth in Louisville which Mrs. Ernestine Williams had identified as one of those where Campbell made calls. Immediately thereafter, at 12:51 A.M., there was a call placed from a pay phone in Detroit with the same exchange, to Hoffa at the Andrew Jackson Hotel in Nashville. Hoffa was not in and the person calling talked to the party who answered. Both calls were charged to the same credit card number, that of Local 299 in Detroit. On October 25, 1962, there was a call from a pay phone in Detroit to the same pay phone in Louisville as above, followed four minutes later by a call from a pay phone in Detroit to Hoffa's suite at the Andrew Jackson Hotel. Three minutes after that there was a call from a pay phone in Detroit to the same pay phone in Louisville. Again, all three calls were charged to the same Teamsters credit card. In addition, there were records of fifteen calls from the same pay phones in Louisville to Larry Campbell's residence in Detroit.

On Thursday, January 30, the government moved on to count four of the indictment, which charged Hoffa, Dorfman and Tweel with attempting to corrupt the Test Fleet jury.

Carol Pettijohn testified that she had been a piano player at the Surf Rider Lounge at the Andrew Jackson Hotel during the Test Fleet case. She told about meeting Tweel there and said that she and Helen Rippey, the hostess, had accompanied Tweel and two other men to several night spots, the last of which was the Sportsman's Lounge. She said that Miss Rippey, who knew the proprietor, introduced them all to him. She recalled that his first name was Dallas. She said that Tweel spent most of the time talking to Dallas at the end of the bar.

Helen Rippey, the next witness, corroborated the testimony of Miss Pettijohn and identified the proprietor of the Sportsman's Lounge as Dallas Hall. She said that she heard Hall and Tweel talking about horseracing.

The government then called Hazel Fulton, who had been Nick Tweel's secretary at Mayflower Distributors in Huntington during the Test Fleet case. Her testimony was interrupted, however, when attorney Harvey Silets objected to her testifying about the call from Allen Dorfman, claiming it was hearsay. Judge Wilson took the motion under advisement and ruled that for the time being she could testify only about her conversations with Nick

Tweel. Neal and Hooker decided to withdraw her as a witness until the judge ruled on the Silets motion.

The last witness of the day was Mrs. Mary Meyers, an employee of the Illinois Bell Telephone Company, who identified toll call records that indicated that an emergency call had been made from the residence of Allen Dorfman to Nick Tweel at his unpublished residence number at 10:55 P.M. on October 21, 1962, the night before the start of the Test Fleet trial. The records also indicated that two calls were made to Mayflower Distributors in Huntington from phone booths in Nashville, charged to Allen Dorfman's credit card, on the evening of November 27, 1962. (That was the night when, according to Partin, Dorfman, at Hoffa's direction, called Tweel from the railroad station and then from the phone booth across from the Federal Building, and read him the jury list.) One call, of short duration, was made at 7:57 P.M. and the other, placed thirteen minutes later, lasted for eleven minutes and forty seconds.

Records of two other calls were also introduced. One was from Dorfman at the Andrew Jackson Hotel to Tweel in Huntington on November 29, 1962. The other was from Dorfman's office in Chicago to Tweel in Huntington on December 4, 1962.

On Friday morning, January 31, 1964, Judge Wilson announced that he was overruling the objection by attorney Silets and would allow Hazel Fulton to testify. When she took the witness stand, she said that she had answered two phone calls at Mayflower Distributors one evening in November, 1962, from a man who identified himself as Allen Dorfman. She said that since the first call was a bad connection, he told her he would call back, and a few minutes later he did and talked to Tweel. She said that Tweel then asked her to pick up an extension line, and that when she did, the man, who had identified himself as Dorfman, read a list of names, addresses and occupations to her, which she took down. She said that most of the addresses were in small towns around Nashville. The only name she could remember was something like "Pashall." She recalled that one of the other women on the list was a retired schoolteacher. She said that when the call was completed, she had typed three copies of the list of names and given them to Tweel at his direction. She stated that she then placed a call for Tweel to Dallas Hall in Nashville.

Miss Fulton then testified that sometime thereafter Tweel had dictated a statement to her which she had signed. The statement, a copy of which she had furnished to the government, said that the phone call from Dorfman concerned the organization of an insurance company.

Hooker: Is that true?
Fulton: No, sir.
Hooker: Who told you to put that in your statement?
Fulton: Mr. Tweel dictated the statement.

She said that she had given a similar statement to Tweel's attorney at his request and had testified before the grand jury falsely about the conversation. She said that Tweel had told her that under no circumstances was she to say she had taken down a list of names. Miss Fulton said that after her grand jury testimony she had gone to the sheriff in Huntington and then to the FBI and told them the truth.

Harvey Silets then conducted a slashing cross-examination which went on into the afternoon session. He emphasized the fact that she had admittedly lied under oath, asked her if Robert Kennedy had given her money, and delved into her personal life, bringing out that she had been married three times and attempting to cast her in the role of a poor mother and heavy drinker.

On redirect examination by Hooker, Miss Fulton said that she had not been threatened, promised anything or given anything by the government. She said that Tweel was the one who furnished her the information about the formation of an insurance company concerning which she testified before the grand jury.

Hooker: Why did you testify falsely?
Fulton: Mr. Tweel was my employer and I didn't want to lose my job.

The next witness was Dallas Hall. He related how Tweel and the others had come into the Sportsman's Lounge during the Test Fleet trial. He said that he and Tweel had talked about horses and race tracks. He told the court that Tweel called him several weeks later and told him it would be worth something to him if he could help him with the Hoffa trial, and that although he told Tweel he would try, he never intended to do so. He said that Tweel called back again sometime thereafter and asked him if he had a list of the jury. He replied he did not and Tweel proceeded to read a list of names, addresses and occupations to him over the phone. He said that he pretended to take them down and again told Tweel he would see what he could do to put him off. He said that he received one more call from Tweel wanting to know if he had done anything, and when he said he hadn't, Tweel told him to forget it.

Richard Chichester of the Chesapeake and Potomac Telephone Company of West Virginia then testified concerning records which showed that a person-to-person call had been made from Mayflower Distributors to Dallas Hall in Nashville on November 27, 1962, and that subsequent calls had been made from Tweel's phones or charged to Tweel's credit card on November 29, November 30 and December 6, 1962.

The trial then moved on to the charge concerning the approach to Patrolman James Paschal. A photograph taken by the Nashville *Banner* was introduced showing Ewing King meeting James R. Hoffa at the airport on October 21, 1962, the day prior to the start of the Test Fleet trial.

William M. Hobbs, Jr., a special agent with the FBI, testified that he followed Ewing King when he drove his Thunderbird to the residence of Oscar Pitts near Woodbury, Tennessee, on October 27, 1962.

Neal: Was a juror from Woodbury?
Hobbs: Yes. Mrs. Paschal.

The second week of trial was concluded and the court adjourned for the weekend. Jim Neal told reporters that the government would finish its case the following week. Jimmy Hoffa and William Bufalino flew to Detroit for the weekend.

We had decided that Partin would be our last witness. As things were progressing, it appeared that he would take the stand early the following week. I called him and told him to start driving north and that Frank Grimsley would meet him in Birmingham, Alabama, to accompany him into Chattanooga. We arranged to meet on the outskirts of Chattanooga near Lookout Mountain on Sunday afternoon.

Partin arrived on schedule with Grimsley and Emmett Tucker, a trustee of Local 5. Tucker had agreed to take a trip with Partin but did not know until they arrived in Chattanooga where they were going or for what purpose. We proceeded up the winding road to the top of Lookout Mountain, where I had arranged for a cabin for Partin. Two deputy marshals, who had been assigned to around-the-clock protection of Partin, were waiting at the cabin.

Later that afternoon Hooker and Neal joined us and again reviewed Partin's testimony with him. It was getting down to the wire and Partin was slightly edgy but otherwise alert and confident. We were reasonably certain that the defense had no idea he was near Chattanooga.

On Monday, February 3, William Loeb wrote another front-page editorial captioned "A Threat to Every American." In it he criticized the locking up of the jury in Chattanooga and blamed all of Hoffa's problems on Robert Kennedy. Loeb went on to say:

> It is well known to the general public that this newspaper has a loan from the Central States Southeast Southwest Pension Fund of the Teamsters Union, and nasty minded people might say that this editorial was written because of that, or at Mr. Hoffa's request. However, just as Mr. Hoffa has never once suggested that this newspaper change its stand in favor of Sen. Goldwater to support Gov. Rockefeller, whom Mr. Hoffa prefers, in the same way he has never asked for any support from this newspaper in his personal troubles.

The trial reconvened on Monday, February 3. FBI agent J. Charles Still identified Ewing King in the courtroom and told how he had followed King on the evening of November 17, 1962, from his home to a restaurant outside of Nashville where King parked his Thunderbird. He said that shortly thereafter, a blue 1959 Ford with Tennessee license number 1C-3705 pulled up next to King's car. He identified the occupant of the Ford as Local 327 Business Agent George Broda. He said that King and Broda went into the restaurant and emerged fifteen minutes later. He said that they looked around and then switched cars, with King heading in the direction of Woodbury, Tennessee, in the Ford and Broda heading in the direction of his residence in King's Thunderbird.

Special Agent Willis S. Turner then testified that he saw a blue 1959 Ford, license number 1C-3705, at the residence of Oscar Pitts near Woodbury at 9:40 that evening. He said he saw the same car at 1:07 the following morning in front of the home of Patrolman James Paschal and that Paschal was standing next to the car in uniform and appeared to be talking to the driver. He said he could not identify the driver of the car because it was an extremely rainy night.

FBI agent Francis W. Norwood said that he was with Special Agent Turner at 1:07 on the morning of November 18, 1962, and also saw a man wearing a uniform, standing in the rain, talking to the driver of a blue 1959 Ford with license number 1C-3705 in front of the Paschal residence. He said that when he drove back by the Paschal home at 1:30 A.M. and again at 1:35 A.M. the blue Ford was not there, but that at 2:12 A.M. Paschal's patrol car was back in the driveway of his home.

The next witness, Special Agent Warren L. Walsh, said that he was seated in his car at an intersection near Ewing King's home on the morning of November 18, 1962, and at 4:12 A.M. saw a blue 1959 Ford with license number 1C-3705 approaching. He said he recognized the driver as Ewing King and followed him to Benson Drive, the street where King lived.

Finally, FBI agent Marvin Eubanks testified that he was parked crossways on Benson Drive with the hood of his car up when a blue 1959 Ford with license number 1C-3705 drove up and stopped. He said that he walked up to the car, observed that the driver and sole occupant was Ewing King, and told him that he would "be out of the way in a minute."

Oscar Pitts was the next witness and was as reluctant as he had been when we talked to him in Nashville. But he told the story of how King had come to his house on October 27, 1962, inquiring about the Paschals and whether he thought Patrolman Paschal would take money. He said he told King he didn't think he would but that he might want a promotion. He said that King said he could help with the promotion if Paschal would talk to his wife, who was on the jury.

Pitts testified about arranging the code with King to call and say his beagle died, which would be a signal to King to come to Woodbury to talk to Paschal. He said he made the call on the evening of November 17, 1962, and that King came to his house driving a blue Ford. He told the court that after failing to locate Paschal earlier, he spotted him in Woodbury when he was getting off duty late that night and followed him home in the blue Ford. He said that when Paschal pulled into his driveway in his patrol car he parked the blue Ford at the foot of the driveway. He related how he called to Paschal, who came down and stood in the rain talking to him through the car window. He said he told Paschal that King wanted to talk to him and they agreed to meet on the river road outside of town. Then, he said, he went back to his house, picked up King and they drove to River Road, where they found Paschal waiting in his patrol car off on a side road by a spring. He said when that they got into the patrol car with Paschal, King told Paschal he could get him a promotion.

Pitts: He said he wanted to know if he could talk to his wife.
Neal: Who said that?
Pitts: Ewing.

Pitts said that Paschal told King he didn't think he could talk to his wife because they were not getting along very well. Pitts said that they then left Paschal to return to his house, and King left in the blue Ford for Nashville about 2:10 A.M.

Patrolman James Paschal then took the stand. He corroborated what Pitts had said about the arrangement of the meeting and the meeting itself. He said that Pitts introduced King as his boss and the head of the Teamsters in Nashville.

Paschal: King said he heard I was wanting a promotion and he said he knew the governor and the incoming governor. I said I'd appreciate any help I can get.
Neal: What was said then?
Paschal: Well, he says, your wife is on the jury.
Neal: Who said that?
Paschal: Mr. King.
Neal: Was he the first one to bring that up?
Paschal: Yes sir . . . and he asked me if I could talk to her . . . and I told him no that I couldn't talk to her— that we weren't getting along too good . . . and King said, you talk to her—said—I will get you the promotion.
Neal: You talk to her and I will give you the promotion?
Paschal: Yes sir . . . Well, after that, I told him—I told Mr. King—that I would talk to her.
Neal: Did you talk to your wife about this?
Paschal: No, sir.

Neal then asked Paschal if it was true that he was not getting along with his wife. Paschal replied that it was not true and that he had only said that because he didn't want to get involved, because "I knew I wasn't suppose to."

On cross-examination, Paschal admitted he had lied to Judge Wilson in the secret session during the Test Fleet case and that he had given false statements earlier to both the FBI and attorney Tommy Osborn. He said he had lied because he didn't want to embarrass his wife or get involved but had finally decided to tell the truth.

The only witnesses we had left were the stationmaster and the others who had been in the train station in Nashville the night Allen Dorfman tried to call Tweel. They would corroborate what Partin had said at the time about Hoffa's conversation about the height of the ceiling. Then, of course, there was Partin himself.

We thought we had built a solid, step-by-step case thus far against Larry Campbell, Tom Parks, Allen Dorfman, Nick Tweel and Ewing King. Every detail that Partin had told me, over one year earlier, had been corroborated by the witnesses who had testified and the records that had been introduced into evidence in the preceding two weeks. Even if Partin were not to testify, the evidence against these defendants was now substantial and the only person who had stood to benefit from efforts to tamper with the Test Fleet jury was James R. Hoffa. But it was now up to Partin to tie Hoffa firmly into the plot.

We decided to put Partin on the stand after the noon recess on the following day, Tuesday, February 4. Hooker and Neal felt that the train station employees would take up the morning session. Everyone would be at lunch during the noon break and it would be possible to bring Partin into the building unnoticed. I told Partin the schedule that night.

While we were plotting our little surprise, Hoffa was engineering one of his own. Bernard Spindel, Hoffa's wiretapper and electronic expert, had flown from New York to Nashville that day. There he was observed by FBI agents renting an automobile at the Nashville airport. He drove directly to Chattanooga, under FBI surveillance, parked at the Patten Hotel and went straight up to the ninth floor. Although all other surveillances had been called off once the jury was empaneled and sequestered, we decided that because of his special talents, Spindel should be kept under observation.

The next morning, after court had been called into session, Frank Grimsley and I left the building and drove out to Lookout Mountain and up to Partin's cabin. He was nervous but ready. At 12:30 we headed down the mountain and into town with Partin in our car and two deputy marshals following behind. When we reached the Federal Building, I drove around to the back door, which was down several steps and led into the basement. Jack Thiede was waiting to take over my car and park it and two other deputy marshals were inside the basement waiting with Bill French. Partin and I got out of the car, went down the steps and through the door. Then we walked through the basement to the front of the building where Tom McKeon had the elevator waiting. We took the elevator to the fifth floor where John Cassidy was waiting. Then Partin and I walked down the stairs to the third floor where the courtroom was located. John Cassidy was in the corridor and gave us the signal that the coast was clear. We walked down the corridor to the United States Attorney's office, directly across from the courtroom, and went in through one of the inner office doors, thus avoiding the reception room. Partin went into Jack Reddy's office and we closed the door. It had all gone very smoothly.

When court resumed for the afternoon, Neal called Joe Rudis, a photographer from the Nashville *Tennessean*, to introduce a photograph into evidence. It was the kind of thing he had done routinely during the trial. It was a photograph taken in Nashville, in front of the courthouse, during the Test Fleet trial. When it was passed to the defense table they looked at it as just another photograph introduced to link them together. In the picture were Hoffa, William Bufalino, Daniel Maher, Chuck O'Brien, Allen Dorfman, Ewing King and John Ivey walking in a group. Also in the group, walking next to Ewing King, was Edward Grady Partin.

While Rudis was testifying, I led Partin across the corridor into the passageway that ran along the side of the courtroom to the witness stand door. When Rudis stepped down, John Hooker called for the next witness.

The door opened and Ed Partin stepped up into the witness box. He raised his hand, took the oath and sat down. He stated that he was the secretary-treasurer and business manager of Local 5 of the Teamsters Union and had held that post for the past twelve years. He said that he had known Hoffa since 1957 and had been in Nashville during the Test Fleet case in 1962 at Hoffa's invitation.

He said that prior to going to Nashville he had met with Department of Justice attorney Frank Grimsley, who had given him my office number in Nashville and told him to report to me if he saw any evidence of jury tampering or other illegal activity. Partin said that he knew defendants King, Dorfman and Tweel as well as Hoffa.

When Hooker asked him if he had seen any of the defendants besides Hoffa in Nashville, Partin told about meeting Dorfman and Tweel in the coffee shop of the Andrew Jackson Hotel the first day of the Test Fleet trial. He said Tweel had introduced himself as Anthony Quinn and said he was in the cigarette vending business. Partin said that he then went to Hoffa's suite and told him of meeting the man. He said that when he described the man, Hoffa said, "He is a friend of Allen Dorfman and he is here to help me."

Partin went on to say that later in the lobby of the hotel Tweel told him that his name was really Nick Tweel rather than Anthony Quinn. He said that at Tweel's invitation he had gone to his room in the Andrew Jackson, where Tweel told him that "Mr. Dorfman had called him and told him it would be a personal favor to him if he would come down to Nashville and help him set up a method to get to the jury."

Up until that point the defense table had sat in stunned silence. Campbell and Parks, who had never seen Partin, obviously did not quickly realize the significance of the testimony. But Hoffa, King, Dorfman and Tweel did know Partin and knew all too well the story he was beginning to tell.

As Partin said the words "get to the jury," Jacques Schiffer leaped to his feet to try to stop the testimony. His voice rising, he demanded a mistrial and asked that his client be severed from the case. Now, suddenly, all of the attorneys shot to their feet, all trying to talk at once. Harvey Silets also called for a mistrial or severance. But James Haggerty kept his composure amid the tumult and asked that the jury be excused so that he might make a motion. When the jury had left and everyone had sat down, Haggerty charged that Partin had obviously been planted by the government in Nashville and had been present when defense strategy was discussed. He said that this was an intrusion on Hoffa's rights and asked for time to study the law before the witness was allowed to continue. "I am taken completely by surprise by this witness,"

Haggerty said. The other defense attorneys followed suit on behalf of their clients with similar arguments. A motion was made to suppress Partin's testimony. Judge Wilson called a recess. When he returned to the bench, he announced that he was granting the defense a hearing on its motion.

The hearing lasted for over four hours. Partin underwent a grueling cross-examination by Harvey Silets as to how he first had contact with the government, the nature of his contacts with Grimsley and me, whether he had been present during discussions of defense strategy and what kind of information he had passed on to me. We had told Partin not to mention the assassination plot as it would be prejudicial to Hoffa and might cause a mistrial. He replied that his original contact with Grimsley had been through William Daniels and had nothing to do with the Test Fleet case. He said that Hoffa had invited him to Nashville and that Grimsley had then told him to be alert for any evidence of jury tampering or other illegal activity. He said he had not been present during discussions of defense strategy. He acknowledged guarding the door to Hoffa's suite on occasions but denied overhearing his discussions with his attorneys. He said that he had furnished information concerning jury tampering to me.

I then took the stand. I testified that Partin had furnished me information throughout the Test Fleet trial and that most of the information pertained to attempts to tamper with the jury. Harvey Silets asked me if the information given to me by Partin had been furnished to the court in Nashville and "led to the removal of the jurors Tippens, Paschal and Fields." I responded, "Mr. Partin furnished me information which I furnished to the FBI. The FBI conducted investigations. As a result of the investigations, certain action was taken by the court. Now, in other words, the information I got was related."

Silets asked me if I had taken notes of my conversations with Partin. I responded that I had taken "cryptic notes" and had them with me. Silets asked Judge Wilson if the notes could be turned over to the defense. Judge Wilson directed me to turn the notes over to him and he would review them overnight and determine whether they should be turned over to the defense.

There was then a parade of defense attorneys who had been in Nashville during the Test Fleet case. They testified that Partin was around all of the time during the trial and had access to defense strategy. Their testimony, designed to show that Partin had violated Hoffa's rights, certainly confirmed that Partin was in a position to hear the conversations he reported about jury tampering.

The following morning Judge Wilson ruled that Partin could testify. He said, "I find the government did not place him in the midst of the defense. He was knowingly and voluntarily placed there by one of the defendants."

Under questioning by Hooker, Partin continued his story. He said that on the first day of the Test Fleet trial he talked to Hoffa in his suite at the Andrew Jackson Hotel. He said Hoffa asked him "to stick around a day or two, that he might have one or two people he wanted me to call." He quoted Hoffa as saying they "were going to get one juror or try to get a few scattered jurors and take their chances."

It was the first direct linking of Hoffa to the jury tampering. Hooker was continuously interrupted by the defense attorneys during almost every question as they fought desperately to somehow stop the testimony. But Hooker and Partin went patiently and quietly forward.

Partin revealed how Hoffa had asked him to call Bill Wade, the former Vanderbilt University quarterback then with the Chicago Bears, and ask him "to come into town and circulate around and see if he knew anyone he could get to on the jury, and to come into the courtroom and shake hands and mix up with the defense." Partin had not called Wade.

Partin said that when on the following day he went to Hoffa's suite to tell him he was leaving town, Hoffa told him that "when I came back he may want me to pass something for him." Partin said that when Hoffa made the statement, he hit the rear pocket of his trousers.

When he returned to Nashville two days later, Partin said, Hoffa told him that "the dirty bastard went in and told the judge that his neighbor had offered him $10,000 and we are going to have to lay low for a few days."

Partin then went into his conversations with King about circulating the jury list to people they could trust and his plans to approach the husband of a juror who was a highway patrolman. He quoted Hoffa as saying, later that day, "I would pay $15,000 or $20,000—whatever it costs—to get to the jury." Partin said that

Hoffa later accused King of "fumbling around" and told him, "King keeps telling me that he can get the patrolman but he don't get to him."

Partin said that on November 7 he had to go to Dallas and stopped in Hoffa's suite before leaving. He said that after Hoffa asked other persons in the room to leave, he told Hoffa he didn't think the trial was going too good and Hoffa replied, "Well, don't worry about it too much because I've got the male colored juror in my hip pocket. One of my business agents, Campbell, came into Nashville prior to the trial and took care of it." Partin said Hoffa mentioned that the juror was a retired railroad worker who went fishing all the time. He said that Hoffa told him, "It looks like our best bet is a hung jury unless we can get to the foreman of the jury. If the jury does deadlock, it will be the same as an acquittal because they will never try it again."

Later in the month, Partin continued, he heard Hoffa again berating King about not getting to the patrolman. He said Hoffa told King "he wanted some insurance."

Partin then described the meeting with King in the courthouse hallway, when King told him about having received the call that "the beagle hound dropped dead at ten o'clock." Partin testified that King also told him about switching cars with a man named Broda and driving to Woodbury to meet with the patrolman. Partin said that King confided that the patrolman would not take any money but wanted a promotion, in exchange for which he agreed to talk to his wife, even though he wasn't getting along very well with her. Partin said that King told him he thought the FBI might have been following him because there was a car with its hood up blocking the road to his house when he returned home. According to Partin, King then said "he was going to get a bunch of people together" the following weekend and ambush the FBI agents.

Then Partin related the conversation he had with Hoffa shortly thereafter: "He said he was disturbed because the highway patrolman would not take the money. He said if he had taken the money it would have pinned him down and he couldn't have backed up."

Partin testified that the next time he returned to Nashville on November 27, 1962, he called Nick Tweel at Dorfman's request to find out if he had heard anything from Dallas Hall. He said that Tweel told him he needed a jury list to pass on to Hall. Partin related how Hoffa had obtained a jury list from Bufalino and described the calls that Dorfman made trying to reach Tweel from the restaurant where they ate, the train station and finally the phone booth across from the Federal Building, where the list of names and addresses were read over the phone.

At this point Jacques Schiffer, who had been up and down with objections throughout the testimony, had an exchange with Judge Wilson.

Schiffer: One need not be a lawyer to understand that he has been shown the entire transcript up to this point and has repeated what he read in the transcript.

Wilson: Will you state your objection, please?

Schiffer: My objection is that this is a well-coached witness and they have no right to do this and give this man the testimony.

Wilson: Ladies and gentlemen of the jury, you will completely disregard that statement. The statement is highly improper, Mr. Schiffer. You will not make such improper statements in front of the jury.

Partin's testimony had been accurate, thorough and devastating. It clearly linked Hoffa with every phase of the activities of the other defendants, and it was corroborated by the testimony of the other witnesses.

Court adjourned for the day and Partin went back up on the mountain to gird himself for the all-out cross-examination he knew he would face in the morning. Judge Wilson decided not to turn over my notes to the defense since they were not substantially verbatum and therefore did not fall under the *Jenks* decision that required such surrender.

Hoffa was in a rage. I was later told by one of his associates that when he entered the defense room down the hall from the courtroom during one of the breaks, he had picked up a heavy desk chair and hurled it across the room.

One of Hoffa's attorneys came up to me in the hallway and said, "I have seen some great coups in my time but that was the greatest coup I have ever seen."

The following morning Harry Berke began the cross-examination of Partin. He probed into his past, starting with his youthful offenses and ending with his indictment by the federal government. Then he turned to Partin's motivation in testifying and tried to get him to admit he had made a deal with the government. Toward the end of the day he began picking away at Partin's testimony, taking events out of order and testing Partin's memory and ability to match dates with events. Partin did not have his hotel bills, which he had been allowed to use to refresh his recollection of the sequence of events in his direct testimony. But when the day was over, he had survived quite well and none of his testimony had been shaken.

Shortly after court adjourned that day Bill Sheets was driving past the Patten Hotel on his way to the office. He was not engaged, at the time, in the surveillance of Spindel. However, he noticed the car Spindel had rented parked near the entrance of the hotel. He also noticed that the occupant was someone other than Spindel. As he passed by he saw the occupant get out and wave to a man with a camera standing by. The man then took a photograph of Sheets driving by.

The tension that had been building daily erupted into pandemonium the next day. It was Friday, February 7, the last day of the third week of the trial. Not only had Hoffa been tied into the jury-tampering activities during his last trial, but the principal witness against him had withstood a full day of strenuous cross-examination. There now began a bizarre series of events—some were obviously designed to cause a mistrial, others appeared to be part of a diversionary offensive—and they were combined with the continued cross-examination of Partin, which was now reduced to pure character assassination.

It started toward the end of the morning session, after the jury had been excused, with an announcement by James Haggerty that the defense was prepared to offer proof that the government had been surveilling defendants and their attorneys: "It's a very difficult thing to prove but we have photographs taken last night and we have photographs of an FBI agent named Sheets. . . ."

At this point Jim Neal sent Jim Durkin out of the courtroom and Cecil Brandstetter arose and suggested that Neal was sending Durkin to tell Sheets. Neal stood up and said, "The purpose I sent that man was to get a subpoena for a well-known wiretapper who was indicted and tried with the defendant Hoffa, who came to town the other day—Bernard Spindel."

Durkin obtained the subpoena and gave it to Marshal Elmer Disspayne to serve and told him that Spindel was probably at the Patten Hotel. I accompanied Disspayne to the Patten Hotel be-

cause I knew what Spindel looked like and he didn't. When we
arrived there, I looked around the lobby while Disspayne went up
to the ninth floor where the Teamsters quarters were. As I was
walking through the lobby I spotted Chuck O'Brien coming in one
of the hotel entrances followed by a man with a camera. I knew
instinctively that we had walked into a trap and I walked on out
the other entrance and back to the Federal Building.

It turned out that Hoffa was right behind O'Brien. He had come
over as soon as court had adjourned for the lunch recess and went
directly to the ninth floor followed by photographers and television cameramen, whom Bufalino had called and invited up "to see
what happens."

Disspayne had gone to the ninth floor where he encountered
Tommy Osborn who told him Spindel was not there. He asked to
use a telephone and went into a room with Osborn that was occupied by Daniel Maher and two clerical employees. He called our
office for further instructions but was unable to reach anyone. He
then started toward the elevator to leave just as Hoffa, the television cameramen and the photographers arrived on the ninth floor.
Disspayne's mission was perfectly legitimate, and he had the subpoena in his pocket, but we had played right into their hands. The
encounter was meant to be an ugly show and it was. Hoffa began
shouting at Disspayne, poking his finger at him. "What are you
doing up here? Are you spying? You have no business being here!"
Then Bufalino chimed in, yelling that Disspayne was trespassing
in the International Union headquarters. "We keep all of our records here. Have you been going through our records?" At one
point Hoffa dropped his briefcase and approached Disspayne
menacingly. "Okay, let's have it out," he challenged.

Disspayne finally managed to push by and escape but they now
had one more thing to distort and use in their desperate effort to
stop the trial. The photographs of the encounter appeared in newspapers throughout the country and there were tapes on local
television.

When court resumed that afternoon the defense played their
next card. Jacques Schiffer arose and complained to Judge Wilson
that when he had returned to his room at the Patten Hotel during
the lunch recess, he found that "all of my original documents, and
the entire file which I have been preparing for these many months
for this trial on behalf of the defendant Parks is missing." Schiffer
said that he had been advised that Disspayne and I had been in the
hotel and that Disspayne had been on the ninth floor. Judge Wil-

son ordered the government to respond in writing to Schiffer's complaint.

Harry Berke and James Haggerty then filed a motion* for a mistrial, accusing the government of surveilling Hoffa and his attorneys. They issued subpoenas for Attorney General Robert Kennedy, FBI Director J. Edgar Hoover, Jack Miller, Bill Sheets, Carl Schultz and me. (They had apparently become convinced that Carl Schultz was some kind of electronics expert because he was always carrying a briefcase with a lock on it. Actually all it contained were the chronologies he was working on.)

Judge Miller took the motion under advisement and ordered the trial to continue, but Jacques Schiffer was just warming up. He now turned his attack on Judge Wilson:

> I advised the court that the government from the inception would try to run a drumhead court-martial case and not the kind of case contemplated by the American laws and rules of justice. What has happened here, your honor, day after day, has proved the point that this is precisely what the government wanted, and they succeeded in obtaining it. . . . This is a drumhead court-martial they wanted and they are getting it. They are getting it to the last vestige of the meaning of a drumhead court-martial and a star chamber proceeding here. . . .

Schiffer was shouting at the top of his voice, pounding on the defense table and flailing his arms. Judge Wilson finally told him to lower his voice, but Schiffer went on in the same decibel, stating that his client could not receive a fair trial "because of this witness and your honor's permissiveness in letting this man violate your order." He claimed that Partin was being evasive and that the government attorneys were giving him hand signals on how to testify.

"Do you have anything further?" Judge Wilson asked. Schiffer shook his head and sat down. Judge Wilson then turned to the clerk of court. "Make a note of this in the record. We will take it up at a later time."

Judge Wilson had kept his composure in the face of Schiffer's defiant outburst. It would not be the last time his patience was deliberately tested.

The jury came back in and the cross-examination continued, but Partin, rather than weakening, was getting stronger. He talked directly to the jury in his soft southern drawl and was becoming a very effective witness. He was more than holding his own in exchanges. When Harry Berke said, "You had your story pretty well rehearsed, didn't you?" Partin retorted, "If I had it rehearsed you would have heard a lot more than you did. I forgot some things!" At one of the recesses Bill French happened to be in the men's room when Hoffa and his attorneys came bursting in. Hoffa was shouting, "He's killing us with those asides to the jury. You've got to get him off that stand."

The third week of trial ended. A grimness and hatefulness had settled in and it would remain that way for the rest of the trial. Hoffa was in a rage. Previously, he had ignored me and directed only occasional barbs at Neal. Now he began hurling obscenities at both of us. I did my best to stay out of his way.

On Sunday afternoon Hoffa attended a rally sponsored by Local 515 at the Tivoli Theater in Chattanooga. The seventeen hundred members of the local and their wives were urged to attend, but only about three hundred persons showed up. Hoffa, with Ewing King beside him on the stage, told the disappointingly small audience that it was too bad that union members had something better to do on a Sunday afternoon such as keeping social commitments and watching television. He departed from his remarks about anti-labor legislation and the need for political involvement to attack the conduct of the trial: "I've had experiences in the courts since I was sixteen years old but I've never seen anything like Nashville and Chattanooga. Marshals and FBI men are here by the hundreds." Newsmen attending the rally said that there was only polite applause and that Hoffa had received a warmer reception at the businessmen's luncheon.

That evening shotgun blasts were fired into the home of Local 5 President Donice Bennett in Baton Rouge, Louisiana.

As the fourth week of trial commenced on Monday morning, Judge Wilson ruled that a hearing would be held on the defense charges of surveillance of defendants and attorneys but not until after the case was submitted to the jury.

The government filed a reply, as directed by Judge Wilson, to Schiffer's motion implying that Elmer Disspayne or I had stolen his file. The reply by the government categorically denied that any employee of the government had anything to do with the disappearance of Schiffer's file—if such a file, in fact, existed. There were attached affidavits by Disspayne and me in which we described what had happened in the hotel.

Harvey Silets, who had taken over the questioning from Harry

Berke on Friday, continued the cross-examination of Partin. When Silets was finished, Harold Brown took up the attack, followed by Henry Grady and finally Jacques Schiffer, each, in turn, trying desperately to wear down Partin and discredit his testimony. If they had quit after the first half-day of cross-examination, they might have been ahead, but now their questions were mostly repetitious and argumentative, while Partin's testimony grew stronger by the day.

They made much of the $1200 which was sent to Partin's wife to offset his expenses and the manner in which it was handled. Partin testified that the amount did not even cover his expenses. Silets charged that the money was in payment for Partin's testimony and was sent through Grimsley "to subvert justice." Neal shot back, "That is an unmitigated lie." He went on to explain that the money was paid from a confidential fund, set up for that purpose by law, and offered to bring Jack Miller down to testify that the procedure was common practice when the welfare of a witness was at stake. Neal said, "We didn't want the terrorism like is going on in Baton Rouge right now," referring to the shooting into the home of Donice Bennett.

Schiffer's cross-examination became more and more acrimonious. At one point Hooker said to the court, "I think it's about time this lawyer be told to observe some courtesy in the courtroom." Schiffer snapped, "I'll show courtesy to lawyers who show me some." After another exchange, Judge Wilson said to Schiffer, "How many times have you heard me tell counsel to quit arguing among themselves?" "At least three times today, your honor," Schiffer replied. The judge stared at Schiffer and said, "All right, I don't want to give the instruction a fourth time."

When court adjourned, Hoffa turned on Schiffer in a rage as they were leaving the courtroom. In the presence of newsmen he castigated Schiffer for not being prepared. He told him to read the transcript and stop talking so much. "I don't care if you have to stay up all night," Hoffa shouted.

Bernard Spindel, whom we had attempted unsuccessfully to subpoena the previous Friday, showed up in the corridor outside the courtroom during the afternoon and was promptly subpoenaed.

With the testimony completed for the day and Partin and the jury excused, the defense fired another salvo in what had become the daily diversionary counterattack. They filed an affidavit by Tommy Osborn in which he swore that after the indictment had been brought against the defendants in May, 1962, he had contacted John Hooker about representing Allen Dorfman and had given Hooker information concerning the defense. He said that Hooker failed to disclose to him at the time that he had already accepted the position as special prosecutor for the government in the case. The affidavit accompanied a motion for a mistrial. Hooker said the affidavit was false and offered to testify under oath.

The next day Jacques Schiffer filed another motion which was the most devious move yet employed in the trial. It again asked for a mistrial based on an attached affidavit by Bernard Spindel which stated that he was an "expert electronics technician" and had been hired by the defense to determine whether or not the government was surveilling the defendants and their attorneys. Attached to the affidavit was a sealed envelope containing over twenty pages of handwritten transcriptions made by Spindel. What he had been doing was listening in on radio communications between FBI radio cars with his electronic equipment, and transcribing the conversations. The FBI radio communications were being made in connection with the surveillance of him. The interception *and disclosure* of such communications was a violation of federal law. Schiffer got around that by submitting the transcripts to the court sealed, thus tricking Judge Wilson into being the one who unsealed and disclosed them.

Judge Wilson again reiterated that he would hold a hearing on the surveillance motions after the case had gone to the jury. He took the Osborn motion under advisement. Hoffa's attorneys told reporters they were going to petition the Court of Appeals to force Judge Wilson to interrupt the trial for the surveillance hearing.

Judge Wilson also rebuked the defense for sending a subpoena to Baton Rouge for Partin's estranged wife, calling for her appearance that morning in court. He said that they knew she couldn't be called as a witness that day since Partin was still on cross-examination and the government had not yet rested its case. He also pointed out that they did not even send funds for her travel expenses, as is the custom. Finally he said that if they wanted to call her as a witness they should first send someone to interview her to determine whether her testimony would be relevant. He noted that six attorneys who were not participating of record had testified for the defense and suggested that one of them might be spared to go interview Mrs. Partin. Harry Berke apologized to the court and said he would see to it that Mrs. Partin was interviewed and provided funds for travel if she was to be called.

It was clear that there were now, and had been for some time, two trials going on at once. One was of Hoffa and his co-defendants—the other was of the government. Having failed to shake Partin's testimony, they were more desperate than ever to somehow stop the trial.

Ed Partin took the witness stand for the sixth time and Schiffer continued his persistent cross-examination. Schiffer asked Partin if he had taken the Fifth Amendment when he appeared before the grand jury in Nashville. Partin answered that he had—at the direction of William Bufalino. He said that Bufalino had told him exactly what to say at a meeting in Washington at the Teamsters headquarters. When Schiffer finally sat down, Cecil Brandstetter rose to continue the round-robin marathon questioning of Partin.

At the end of the day Hoffa held a press conference on the steps of the courthouse. He had with him a number of photographs and a copy of Spindel's transcript. He said that the photographs were of surveilling FBI agents and that the transcript proved the defense's charges that the defendants and their attorneys were being spied upon. Judge Wilson was trying to silence their voices by delaying a hearing on the charges, Hoffa claimed.

Actually the transcript indicated just the opposite—that the agents were surveilling Spindel as they had been instructed and were conscious of both the fact that they had to be careful not to surveil defendants and the possibility that Spindel might be recording their conversations and might so accuse them. Here are some examples:

"Yeah, Billy, he's a big mammoth-looking guy—humped shoulders, heavyset—right at the top of his head, he's got a bald spot." This was a perfect description of Spindel.

Also: "I think you ought to change locations there. They might be trying to set you up so they can say the defendants are being surveilled or something."

At another point: "There is a darn good chance that this fellow is listening to all you said—there is another good chance that he is recording it. You might consider that."

It would also later be demonstrated that in the big stack of photographs Hoffa was waving around, only one was a picture of an FBI agent—the one they took of Bill Sheets as he was passing by the Patten Hotel.

The next morning Partin took the stand for the last time. Affording a glimpse at what was to come, Cecil Brandstetter asked Partin if he had ever had psychiatric treatment, whether he had ever

taken narcotics and whether he had been a gun runner for Fidel
Castro. Partin answered negatively to all three questions. At 11:33
A.M. Partin was excused as a witness after almost five days of
cross-examination.

The defense had issued a subpoena for the records of Local 5 in
Baton Rouge. Donice Bennett, the president of the local whose
home had been shot into three days earlier, appeared with the
records, represented by local attorney William Hutcheson.
Hutcheson claimed that the subpoena represented a "fishing expedition" by the defense and asked the court to quash it. Hutcheson
pointed out that an auditor from the International Teamsters Union had turned up in Baton Rouge during the week with instructions to review the local's records. He had been denied access to
the records. Hutcheson said it appeared that this was the first step
by Hoffa toward placing the local in trusteeship, which Partin had
predicted in his testimony.

Donice Bennett told newsmen that he had not known in advance that Partin was going to testify but that both he and the
members of Local 5 were solidly behind him.

The following morning Judge Wilson quashed the subpoena,
stating that an inquiry into the financial condition of Local 5 was
not relevant to the trial.

Jacques Schiffer jumped to his feet and launched a verbal onslaught at Judge Wilson. He accused him of lending his prestige
and power "to the government." Schiffer shouted, "My client
doesn't need a lawyer here, he needs a pallbearer."

The government then called James C. Tippens, whose appearance as a witness had previously been blocked by defense arguments. Defense attorneys again raised strong objections to his
testimony but Judge Wilson ruled that he could testify. The judge
said, however, that the testimony would be of possible relevance
only to Hoffa and to corroborate Partin's testimony. He said that
Tippens could not testify as to what was said to him by Medlin or
what he reported to Judge Miller about his contact by Medlin.

Tippens stated that on October 22, 1962, he was seated as a
prospective juror in the Test Fleet case after having been accepted
by the government. He said that when he went to his office after
court, his secretary gave him a message to call Lawrence "Red"
Medlin. He said that Medlin asked him to come to his place of
business, which he did, and he had a conversation with Medlin in
his automobile. He said that as a result of the conversation he went
to see Judge William E. Miller the following morning and told him

that he felt that he should be disqualified as a juror because he had been offered a sum of money. Judge Wilson sustained an objection by Harry Berke to the last statement by Tippens.

Hooker then asked Tippens, "Did you say anything to Judge Miller about whether or not any sum of money had been offered to you?" Tippens answered, "Yes." Hooker then asked if he had been disqualified by Judge Miller after he reported the Medlin conversation and Tippens said that he had.

The defense had asked to inspect the telephone toll call records in the possession of the government. When court was adjourned, we turned over all toll call records in our possession to the clerk of court, as directed by Judge Wilson. They were to remain in his possession but could be inspected by the defense. They were piled on the government table in the courtroom and were very voluminous. Hoffa came over to the table as Neal and Hooker were preparing to leave the courtroom. He picked up one of the toll card records and looked at it. He complained that only an expert could read the symbols on the card. Then, assessing the volume of the records, he broke into a rage in frustration. He started shouting at Jim Neal that the government had been afraid to introduce its wiretap evidence. Neal said that the government didn't have any wiretap evidence. Then Hoffa stared at Neal hatefully and yelled, "I'll hound you for the rest of your life, Neal. You won't be in the government forever."

On Friday, February 14, at 11:10 A.M., the government rested its case. After the jury was dismissed for a sequestered weekend, Jim Neal filed a detailed answer to the defense motion charging government surveillance of the defendants and their attorneys. Attached were affidavits from Everett J. Ingram, special agent in charge of the Knoxville FBI office who had jurisdiction over the Chattanooga office. He set forth exactly what surveillances had been conducted and listed the agents who had participated. He said that the only surveillance that had been conducted since the jury was empaneled was that of Spindel and emphasized that all agents were instructed to at no time surveil defendants or their attorneys. He also stated that the surveillances that were conducted "consisted entirely of observations by agents of the Federal Bureau of Investigation of the public comings and goings of the subjects of the surveillances. They did not involve any eavesdropping, wiretapping, microphonic installations, trespasses or any invasions of privacy."

Also attached to the response were affidavits by M. Jay Hawkins, the agent in charge of the Chattanooga office, Bill Sheets and all of the agents who participated in the surveillances, stating, in effect, the same things as Ingram's affidavit. In his affidavit Sheets described how his photograph was taken by the defense photographer.

Relative to the surveillances that were conducted, the government's response noted that "similar lawful investigative activities in the course of the Nashville trial resulted in the cogent evidence of obstruction of justice presented in the course of this trial by agents of the Federal Bureau of Investigation. . . . "

In connection with the only surveillance conducted after the empaneling of the jury—that of Spindel—the response stated that it was conducted because there was reason to believe that he might engage in illegal electronic eavesdropping and had "been shown to have been entirely justified by the very documents which were submitted to the Court" by Schiffer.

After submitting the response, Neal said that of all the photographs submitted by the defense as allegedly depicting FBI agents surveilling, only one—the photograph of Sheets—was of an FBI agent. The others were merely citizens of Chattanooga. Neal went on to say, "The only illegal activity involved in the proceeding is the activity by this man Spindel in violation of Section 605 of the Federal Communications Act."

When Schiffer rose to protest, Neal added, "And perhaps by Mr. Schiffer, in aiding and abetting, counseling, procuring and inducing."

Schiffer screamed back at Neal, "You don't say that again unless you mean to back it up. I will meet you anywhere with anything. We will see who turns yellow first."

Judge Wilson's carefully nurtured patience almost broke at that point. He pointed his finger at Schiffer and said angrily, "Sir, we will not have that sort of conversation in this courtroom. Do you understand me?" Schiffer sat down.

With the government's case completed, all the defendants made the customary motions for directed verdicts of acquittal. Jim Neal said that in view of the fact that Tippens had not been allowed to testify fully, the government was conceding that the count in the indictment charging Hoffa with corruptly influencing Tippens should be dropped. Judge Wilson agreed and dismissed that charge against Hoffa. He denied the motions of all the defendants relative to the other counts in the indictment.

On Monday morning the defendants prepared to put on their

defense, with Nicholas J. Tweel as the first witness on his own behalf. On the witness stand Nick Tweel denied any implication in attempting to tamper with the Test Fleet jury. He said that he had first been introduced to Allen Dorfman by James Kalil, a friend of Dorfman's, sometime before the Test Fleet trial. He said he had discussed the possibility of obtaining a loan from Dorfman to assist in the formation of an insurance company. He said that Dorfman had subsequently called him and asked him to meet him in Nashville on October 22, 1962, to discuss the matter further.

Tweel said that he had met with Dorfman in Nashville for that purpose. He said he talked to Partin only once, in the coffee shop of the Andrew Jackson Hotel. He denied using the name of Anthony Quinn or ever discussing the jury with Partin. He acknowledged meeting Frazier, Paden and Cole in Nashville and accompanying Paden and Cole along with Carol Pettijohn and Helen Rippey to Dallas Hall's bar. He denied that he had any connection with the Huntington trio's visit to Nashville. He said that he did talk to Dallas Hall that evening about racehorses but denied calling him subsequently to ask about the jury. He said that Hall had called him about a season pass to a racetrack. He admitted receiving calls from Dorfman but insisted they concerned strictly business matters.

When the testimony of Tweel and of character witnesses on his behalf was completed, Jacques Schiffer engaged in another attack on the government and the judge:

> How much does this court want the government to be permitted to use against the defendants unconstitutionally? To what point, your honor, are we lawyers supposed to appear here in court and make the pretense of defending according to law, when the government pushes the court to such an untenable position that it cannot do justice in the face of the Partins? If a man is given a license by this court to come in and testify under oath and lie what does you honor want from counsel for the defendants? How can we go on with this farce of a trial now when Partin's testimony is permitted to stand in the face of its provable falsity?

Allen Dorfman testified the following morning. He corroborated Tweel's account of their relationship and their meeting in Nashville. His direct testimony lasted only fifteen minutes. He was then cross-examined by Jim Neal for two hours. He denied having any conversations with Hoffa, Partin or Tweel about the jury. He acknowledged that he was the agent for the Central States

Health and Welfare Fund and that he had been in several business deals with Hoffa. He also acknowledged that his license had been revoked by the state of Michigan but said that Robert Kennedy had caused that to happen. Dorfman admitted attempting to call Tweel one night in Nashville from the railroad station and subsequently reaching him from the phone booth across from the Federal Building, but he denied reading him a jury list and denied that Partin was present. Dorfman associates Sol Schwartz and Myer Breen followed him to the witness stand and corroborated his account of business dealings with Tweel.

Tom Parks was the next witness. He said that he was approached one day in Nashville by James T. "Jack" Walker who told him he had an assignment for him from the government. He said that Walker wanted him to find out from Carl what his father was going to wear every morning and that he would pay him $25 each time he found out. Parks said he gave the $100 to Carl but did not get the information for Walker about what Carl's father was going to wear. Here Parks merely twisted the facts to make Jack Walker a government agent and the instigator of the contact with Fields.

Parks said that when he was subpoenaed before the grand jury in Nashville, he called Walker and asked him what he should do. He said that Walker told him to take the Fifth Amendment. He also said that I tried to make a deal with him. He denied offering Carl Fields $5000 for himself and $5000 for his father to vote for the acquittal of Hoffa.

Defense attorneys had subpoenaed and interviewed Billy Daniels. Daniels told William Bufalino about the first contact between Grimsley and Partin. He also confirmed Partin's testimony about the two calls to Hoffa prior to the Test Fleet trial wherein Hoffa had told Partin to meet him in Nashville. Daniels told Bufalino that the calls had been recorded by Partin with equipment furnished by Daniels. The recordings were, of course, perfectly legal because they were made with Partin's approval. They had been turned over to the court on February 10 at the time of the previous defense motion on surveillances.

The defense now moved to suppress Partin's testimony on the basis of the recorded calls. Judge Wilson said he would hold a hearing on the motion when all testimony was completed.

Tom Parks returned to the stand the next morning for additional cross-examination. He admitted making and receiving phone calls at the residence of Mattie Mix and admitted that some calls were from his nephew Larry Campbell. But he said that all the calls were in connection with family matters. He said that Campbell's sister had been ill and the family was thinking about sending her to Nashville to recuperate. Parks denied that any of the calls had anything to do with the Hoffa trial or the jury. One newsman noted that Jacques Schiffer objected fifty times during the one hour of questioning.

Larry Campbell testified that afternoon. He said that he had been born in Nashville but had lived in Detroit most of his life, and that he had been a business agent for Local 299 for the past twelve years. He admitted making nineteen calls to his uncle Tom Parks during the Hoffa trial but said they were all in connection with his ill sister. He insisted that he was in Louisville on union business. Under cross-examination, he said that Parks had visited him in Louisville "a couple of times" during that period. (In so stating he was admitting something that we had not known.) He denied having anything to do with efforts to influence juror Gratin Fields or any other juror.

Frank Fitzsimmons, vice president of the International Teamsters Union as well as vice president of Local 299, testified that he had sent Campbell to Louisville to assist in an organizing drive at the General Electric Company there. Fitzsimmons conceded under cross-examination that the General Electric Company in Louisville was organized at the time by the International Brotherhood of Electrical Workers, but said that three thousand of the employees had expressed dissatisfaction with their representation by that union. Fitzsimmons also acknowledged that although Louisville was not within the jurisdiction of Local 299, Campbell's expenses while there had been charged to Local 299.

Ewing King was the next witness the following day. He admitted meeting with James Paschal in his patrol car outside of Woodbury in the early morning hours of November 18, 1962, and offering to help Paschal get a promotion. He denied, however, that he had asked Paschal to talk to his wife. He said that Paschal had brought up the trial and the fact that his wife was on the jury but that he had told Paschal, "We better not discuss that." He said that he met with Paschal at the request of Oscar Pitts, who, he said, was interested in helping Paschal get a promotion. He said he had switched cars with George Broda before going to Woodbury because they were thinking of trading cars and wanted to try each other's out.

He denied ever talking to either Hoffa or Partin about efforts to influence the Test Fleet jury.

Under a scathing cross-examination by John Hooker, King maintained that it was "not uncommon for country people to meet at a spring, or aound some hill or someplace by the side of the road."

"What kind of country people do you know who meet by a spring after midnight on a rainy night?" Hooker asked.

King replied, "The best kind of peole I know, country people." Then he said, "Do I look stupid enough to ask a highway patrolman I don't know about his wife on a jury?"

"Don't ask me that question," Hooker said.

King denied discussing the possibility of James Paschal talking to his wife about the trial with Oscar Pitts. He said that at Pitts' house they were discussing buying a rabbit dog.

"But you weren't hunting rabbits that night, were you? You were hunting jurors," Hooker bellowed.

Following King's testimony, the defense called Frank Grimsley to the stand. He testified concerning the manner in which the $1200 had been paid to Partin's wife. He said the payments were made at Partin's request to cover his expenses, which totaled $1,543.47. He said that the remaining $343.47 was still owing to Partin. Grimsley denied that the money was payment for Partin's testimony. An interoffice memorandum from the Department of Justice was turned over to the defense, showing that the money was paid from a confidential fund set up by law for that purpose.

When court adjourned, Hoffa held a press conference in the courtroom and charged that the Attorney General was "operating a $600,000 slush fund for stool pigeons." He accused Kennedy of "absconding" with the money. He and Bufalino lashed out at Tom McKeon and Bill French, who were standing by, shouting that they would get even with them when they got back to Detroit.

In Nashville Henry "Buster" Bell asked Judge Frank Gray to excuse himself in his jury-tampering trial scheduled for April 6. Bell charged Gray with being biased and prejudiced. At the same time, the state bar association filed a petition in Chancery Court asking that Tommy Osborn be permanently disbarred from practicing law in all courts in Tennessee.

The fourth week of trial ended on Friday. Fred Shobe, a black ex-convict from Detroit, testified that James T. "Jack" Walker had told him that he had been a government agent from the beginning of the Test Fleet case and had been promised immunity. He was followed by Otis Tynes, a former business agent of Local 5 in Baton Rouge, who testified that Partin was a dope addict and that he would not believe him under oath. Under cross-examination, he admitted that he had only seen Partin twice since 1960.

The defense then called Dr. Levin F. Magruder, a psychiatrist from Baton Rouge. He said that he had treated Partin for a short period in 1960 for depression. On cross-examination, Dr. Magruder's testimony backfired on the defense when he stated that he had seen no evidence in his treatment of Partin that Partin had ever taken narcotics.

An attempt by the defense to call Partin's attractive estranged wife Norma Jean to the stand was blocked by Judge Wilson when she stated that she did not wish to testify against her husband.

When court adjourned for the weekend, we held our usual strategy session. Hooker and Neal felt that the only testimony in the attempts to discredit Partin that might be damaging in the eyes of the jury was the charge that he was a narcotics addict. Partin assured us that he had never taken narcotics and we were convinced that this was true. Dr. Magruder had testified that he saw no indication of it, but Hooker and Neal thought it would be helpful to have a positive and expert statement to counteract the testimony of Otis Tynes.

I called the Federal Narcotics Center at Lexington, Kentucky, and talked to the director. I explained the situation to him and asked if there was any way they could establish that Partin was not a drug addict. He said there was but it would require that Partin come to Lexington and spend the weekend undergoing simulated tests which would establish unequivocally whether he was addicted. The experience would be an extremely unpleasant one for Partin, he told me, but it could be done.

We explained the situation to Partin and he agreed to go. I went ahead and made the arrangements in Lexington and Partin left that evening. On Sunday afternoon the director of the Lexington Narcotics Center called to notify me that the tests had been completed and that Partin was returning to Chattanooga. He said that both he and the doctor who had administered the tests were prepared to give expert testimony that Partin was not and never had been a narcotics user. I met Partin at the airport when he returned. He said the tests had been an ordeal but he agreed that it was worth it.

On Monday morning Larry Steinberg was the next defense witness. His testimony was neither helpful nor harmful to either side. Partin had testified that on one occasion during the Test Fleet trial, Hoffa had told Steinberg to leave his suite at the Andrew Jackson Hotel and had then talked to him about attempts to influence the jury. When James Haggerty asked Steinberg whether he could remember that happening, he said that he could not. When Hooker on cross-examination asked whether "it didn't happen or you just don't remember it?" Steinberg replied, "I just don't recall the incident." Steinberg did corroborate, however, that Partin had been used by Hoffa to guard the door of his suite.

After the lunch break I was standing in the corridor outside the courtroom when Hoffa and his entourage came down the hall, returning to court. I stepped into the United States Attorney's reception room to avoid the confrontation. On the few occasions when there had been chance encounters Hoffa's remarks had been loud, vicious and obscene. I had never replied. This time he came into the reception room where I was standing and swaggered up to me.

"I understand you've got cancer, Sheridan, is that right?"

"No, that's not right," I said.

"How long does it take to work?" he snarled. Then he turned and strode into the courtroom.

That afternoon Sargent Pitcher, the District Attorney of Baton Rouge Parish, testified. He had been subpoenaed by the defense to bring with him all tape recordings in his possession. He told the court that he had with him the recording and transcript of the original meeting of Partin, Grimsley, Daniels and himself, but that it had nothing whatsoever to do with either the Nashville or Chattanooga proceedings. He said that the two recordings Partin and Daniels had made of the conversations between Partin and Hoffa prior to the Nashville trial had already been turned over to the court by the government. He assured the court he had no other recordings that were in any way connected with the Hoffa cases.

Judge Wilson directed that the recording Pitcher had brought with him should be turned over to the court and he would make a determination as to whether it had any relevance to the trial.

That evening Chuck O'Brien told reporters that Sid Zagri, the Teamsters legislative counsel, had furnished several Congressmen and Senators information concerning government surveillances, including the transcript of FBI communications intercepted by Spindel. He said that the legislators had, in turn, written letters, based on this information, to Senator James Eastland, chairman of the Senate Judiciary Committee, and to Representative Emanuel Celler, chairman of the House Judiciary Committee, requesting a congressional investigation of the government's conduct. O'Brien said that the Congressmen and Senators requesting the investigation were Senators Herman Talmadge (D-Ga.); Ernest Gruening (D-Alaska); Everett Dirksen (R-Ill.); Olin Johnson (D-S.C.); Hugh Scott (R-Pa.); and Representatives Claude Pepper (D-Fla.) and Arch Moore (R-W.Va.). Zagri's letters to the legislators, dated February 18, charged that the government had kept Hoffa, his attorneys and witnesses under surveillance from the beginning of the trial until February 8.

On Friday morning Jimmy Hoffa took the witness stand. With Harry Berke conducting the direct examination, Hoffa told of the difficult early years of his childhood, of losing his father and his family's subsequent move to Detroit. He then told of his thirty-four-year rise up through the ranks of the Teamsters Union to his present position.

Hoffa said that Partin had invited himself to Nashville to plead with Hoffa not to place Local 5 in trusteeship as Murray W. Miller, the head of the Southern Conference of Teamsters, had asked him to do. He said that he was opposed to trusteeships and had been trying to work with Partin to straighten out his local union. But, he said, Partin seemed very nervous and almost incoherent and he asked him if he was ill. Hoffa said that when he told Partin he would have to straighten out or he would put him in trusteeship, Partin blew up and stormed out of the room. He said that he did not remember seeing Partin again during the trial after that one meeting except for an occasional glimpse of him in the coffee shop or lobby of the Andrew Jackson Hotel.

Hoffa admitted assigning Partin to guard the door to his suite for a time after it was ransacked one day, but claimed he later replaced him with Chuck O'Brien. He said that Partin also sometimes brought the newspapers to him in the morning but insisted that they merely exchanged greetings.

Berke then led Hoffa through Partin's testimony, to which Hoffa made strong, point-by-point denials. He denied that he had discussed tampering with the jury with Partin, King, Dorfman or anyone else. He said that Dorfman had spent considerable time in

Nashville during the trial because it was necessary to have frequent discussions about the union's health and welfare program, which Dorfman handled.

The cutting cross-examination by John Hooker brought sharp exchanges between him and Hoffa. At one point Hoffa accused Hooker of shouting at him. "You're not used to being shouted at, are you, Mr. Hoffa?" Hooker responded. At another point Hoffa told Hooker to stop interrupting him.

But Hoffa was not as strong and unequivocal in his answers on cross-examination as he had been in his direct testimony. He appeared to be still convinced that we had some undivulged tape recordings with which to trap him. He was evasive on the question of whether he knew that juror Betty Paschal's husband was a highway patrolman. He also hedged on whether Ewing King had talked to him about Oscar Pitts. Asked whether King had told him about being followed by FBI agents after returning from Woodbury, Hoffa said, "I don't recall any such discussion. He may very well have said that." He qualified other answers and became more and more agitated as the questioning progressed.

When the cross-examination was concluded, Hoffa, aware that he had been edgy and argumentative, said that if he had been too aggressive in his testimony, he apologized. He had been on the witness stand three and a half hours. It had not been one of his better performances.

William Bufalino was the last defense witness. He denied that he had advised Partin to take the Fifth Amendment before the Nashville grand jury. He also challenged Partin's testimony that Hoffa had suggested contacting Bill Wade, the former Vanderbilt football star, to come into the courtroom during the Test Fleet case. Bufalino said that it was Partin who had made that suggestion.

On cross-examination, Neal asked Bufalino if he had been with Hoffa during the 1957 Cheasty trial in Washington. Bufalino said he had.

"Was Mr. Partin the one who suggested that Joe Louis come in and shake his hand?" Neal asked.

Judge Wilson sustained the heated objections to the question by defense attorneys.

Neal also elicited from Bufalino that he did not have a license to practice law in his home state of Michigan, that he was president of Local 985 in Detroit and that he was also employed by the

International Brotherhood of Teamsters. Judge Wilson would not let Neal pursue a question as to whether Bufalino had ever sought to take the bar examination in Michigan.

The following day the government began calling rebuttal witnesses. Neal attempted to call me as a witness but the defense objected on the grounds that my testimony would be corroborative rather than rebuttal. Judge Wilson said he tended to agree with the defense but withheld final judgment.

Jack Walker was then recalled by the government. Fred Shobe was brought into the court and Walker was asked whether he knew him. Walker said that he had never seen Shobe before in his life. He was then asked whether he had given money to Tom Parks to pass on to Carl Fields. He said he had not.

The trial was rapidly moving toward a conclusion. Judge Wilson ruled that I could not testify as a rebuttal witness. Dr. Robert Rasor, the director of the Federal Narcotics Center in Lexington, Kentucky, and his associate, Dr. Harry Isbill, testified that they had examined and tested Partin during the previous weekend and had concluded that he was not, nor had he ever been, a narcotics addict.

FBI agents Bill Sheets and Francis Norwood testified that they had interviewed Tom Parks in late 1962, at which time Parks had told them that he had not seen nor heard from his nephew Larry Campbell in two years.

Frank Jumonville, a Baton Rouge businessman, Donice Bennett, the president of Local 5, and Victor Bussie, the president of the AFL-CIO in Louisiana, then testified that Partin had a good reputation for truthfulness and that they would believe him under oath.

A heated exchange between the defense attorneys and Judge Wilson erupted during the cross-examination of Bussie. When Judge Wilson interrupted questioning by Harry Berke of Bussie about his knowledge of Partin's background, Schiffer moved for a mistrial. Judge Wilson told Schiffer to sit down. Harvey Silets then accused the judge of being "vicious" in his tone. A series of exchanges followed and Judge Wilson finally exclaimed, "Surely the court has a right to speak in court or what is the purpose of having a judge to preside over a trial?" He said he was not biased against any party in the proceeding and had tried to be as fair and impartial as possible.

Jacques Schiffer then launched a loud, vituperative attack

against Judge Wilson, accusing him of allowing the government to put on perjured testimony and of siding with the prosecution.

"I say this," Schiffer shouted, "the net effect to this jury is that all defendants' counsel here are charlatans; that we are tricksters; that we are trying to fool the court. . . . "

It was Schiffer's most raucous and defiant performance in the trial. Spectators in the courtroom gasped and murmured several times during the tirade. When Schiffer finally sat down, Judge Wilson, maintaining his composure with difficulty, quietly overruled the motions for a mistrial.

What had actually been happening was the boldest, most calculated move yet to cause a mistrial. When Schiffer's onslaught approached its crescendo, Frank Ragano left the courtroom and walked quickly to the passageway leading to the jury room. Because he was an attorney, the deputy marshal stationed there let him pass. He proceeded to the jury room and stood at the door listening. He was hoping to hear some expression from a juror indicating that Schiffer's histrionics were audible to the jury and use it as grounds for a mistrial.

The next morning another motion for a mistrial was filed. Attached was an affidavit by Ragano that he had heard a juror make reference to Schiffer's tirade.

The following day, Friday, February 28, Judge Wilson held the promised hearing on the motion to suppress Partin's testimony. The defense was attempting to show that the two conversations between Partin and Hoffa prior to the Test Fleet trial, which Partin had recorded, were illegal testimony. Frank Grimsley, William Daniels of the Baton Rouge District Attorney's office and I testified concerning the original contact between Partin and Grimsley, the subsequent calls to Hoffa and Partin's contacts with me. During the questioning of Grimsley, it did come out that the subject matter of the original conversation between Grimsley and Partin had been "an assassination plot." Judge Wilson would not allow a more detailed explanation. Neal, in questioning Grimsley, brought out the fact that Partin had been given a polygraph test by the FBI in connection with the story he told Grimsley and that the results indicated he was telling the truth. When the hearing was concluded Judge Wilson overruled the motion to suppress Partin's testimony. The sixth week of trial was concluded. All that remained were the arguments to the jury and the charge by the judge.

The arguments to the jury began on Monday morning and lasted all day. The families of all the defendants were in the front rows of the courtroom as one attorney after another rose to make the final pleas for his client. Jim Neal led off for the government, terming the activities in Nashville in 1962 "one of the greatest assaults on the jury system the country has ever known." He reviewed the testimony step by step and reminded the jury that Hoffa was the only defendant in the Nashville trial and the only one who stood to benefit from the jury-tampering activities. "The reason the government says Partin is telling the truth is because it checked and found out that all he said was happening, was happening, and what he said was going to happen, did happen," Neal said.

James Haggerty called the trial a "foul and filthy frame-up," and accused me of being "the architect of the diabolical plot and the servant of his master, Robert Kennedy." Cecil Brandstetter said there wasn't enough evidence against Larry Campbell to win a civil case. He said he felt sorry for Partin because he had a depraved mind. Harvey Silets pointed out that in the entire transcript of the trial, only two persons had mentioned Allen Dorfman's name—Partin and Hazel Fulton, both of whose credibility he attacked. Jacques Schiffer, in his inimitable free-swinging style, directed much of his attack at Robert Kennedy "and his axeman Walter Sheridan." At the end of his oration, Schiffer dramatically hurled coins at the government prosecutors seated at their table.

"I say to the Washington prosecutors, including Mr. Sheridan, take these thirty pieces of silver and share them—you have earned them." Newsmen later picked up the coins and found that there were only twenty-one, totaling $2.50.

The final arguments carried over to the next day and were completed in the morning with Harry Berke as the last spokesman for the defense and John Hooker for the government. Berke, as had the others, leveled an attack against Partin and protested the innocence of his client. Hooker, speaking eloquently, told the jury that being president of the largest union in the world did not give Hoffa "a license to fix a jury." He pointed out that contrary to what the defense attorneys would have the jury think, the prosecution of the case was started by Judge William E. Miller in Nashville, not by the Department of Justice in Washington. As the hushed courtroom listened, Hooker boomed, "Chattanooga, after more than a hundred years, has survived a Chickamauga, and a Missionary

Ridge, but Chattanooga can never survive the acquittal of those who have been proven to be guilty of contaminating, tampering with and fixing a jury in the courts of justice in this state."

That afternoon Judge Wilson made his charge to the jury and the case was finally given over to the jury for its deliberation at 7:30 P.M.

Then he took up the motion for a mistrial and the removal of a juror which had been submitted the previous Thursday as a result of Ragano's listening at the jury room door while Schiffer shouted in the courtroom. The judge sternly overruled the motion and said:

> Now it is an odd procedure, to say the least, when if a defense counsel is thought by another defense counsel to be arguing too loudly that they would resort to this circuitous method of sending another attorney privately to the jury room rather than merely suggesting that defense counsel tone down his remarks. . . . The defendants cannot create such a situation as this and seek to take advantage of their own actions.

The courtroom emptied out and the tense wait for a verdict began. I walked downstairs and stood on the steps of the court-house to breathe in the cold night air. Two figures walked down the sidewalk from the other end of the building. As they came closer, I saw that it was Hoffa and Chuck O'Brien. They stopped at the foot of the steps and Hoffa glared up at me. "You don't have an ounce of guts in your body," he shouted. I turned and walked back into the building.

At 10 P.M. the jury retired for the night without having reached a verdict. The following morning, while the jury continued its deliberations, a hearing on defense charges of government surveillance of defendants and witnesses began.

At 1:55 P.M. Judge Wilson was informed that the jury, after five hours and forty minutes of deliberation, had reached a verdict. The hearing was discontinued and the jurors filed into the court-room and stood in a line in front of the bench facing Judge Wilson. John Hooker, on behalf of the government, waived a poll of the jurors. Judge Wilson then addressed the foreman of the jury, Mr. Hal Bullen:

Wilson: On the third count, what is your verdict with re-
          gard to Thomas Ewing Parks?

Bullen: Guilty.

Wilson: What is your verdict on the defendant James R. Hoffa on the third count?

Bullen: Guilty.

Wilson: What is your verdict on the third count on the defendant Larry Campbell?

Bullen: Guilty.

Wilson: Going to the fourth count of the indictment, what is your verdict upon Nicholas J. Tweel?

Bullen: Not guilty.

Wilson: What is your verdict then with regard to the defendant James R. Hoffa?

Bullen: Not guilty.

Wilson: And the defendant Allen Dorfman?

Bullen: Not guilty.

Wilson: What is your verdict on the fifth count with regards to the defendant Ewing King?

Bullen: Guilty.

Wilson: All right. What is your verdict, ladies and gentlemen, with regard to James R. Hoffa on the fifth count?

Bullen: Guilty.

The anticlimactical hearing on the surveillance charges went on throughout the next day. Bernard Spindel was called to the stand by Jacques Schiffer and offered the court another one of his sealed envelopes. Judge Wilson was not going to be used a second time. He said that he had accepted the similar previous envelope in good faith and had opened it without knowing what it contained. "I had no idea counsel was proceeding by devious means. The court now understands an attempt was made to put something over on the court," he said to Schiffer. Spindel said he would not open the envelope unless ordered to do so by the court. Judge Wilson said he was not going to order him to open it. The envelope remained sealed. When Spindel was cross-examined by Jim Neal, he took the Fifth Amendment.

The hearing wore on with more FBI agents being called and all of them remaining firm in their testimony that there had been no surveillance of defendants or defense counsel. When it was all over, Judge Wilson ruled that the motion was "utterly without merit" and dismissed it. He directed the defendants to appear for

sentencing the following Thursday and instructed all defense attorneys to appear with their clients at that time.

On March 10, two days before the date of sentencing, Hoffa and
his co-defendants filed a motion for a new trial. In addition to
charging Judge Wilson with ninety-four incidents of trial error,
the defendants also alleged that the jurors had been intoxicated
during the trial. Attached to the motion were affidavits from four
bellhops at the Reed House Hotel in which they swore that they
had delivered liquor to the jurors and had observed some of them
intoxicated during the trial. The bellhops had been bribed to give
the affidavits, which were blatantly false. The improvers were still
at work.

When H. E. Bullen, who had been the foreman of the jury, heard
about the motion, he told newsmen, "I am flabbergasted. It is
ridiculous. We were most circumspect, because we realized the
importance of our assignment. That is terrible—just terrible. I am
willing to testify anytime that anyone in authority thinks it should
be done."

The government responded to the charges by filing affidavits
from other bellhops at the Reed House Hotel who had been approached with bribes for false affidavits but had refused to give
them. One bellhop said he was shown an open briefcase full of
cash. He was told that the more information he gave, the more cash
he could have. He was told that it didn't matter if the information
was true or false, so long as it helped Hoffa. The bellhops who
signed the affidavits were fired by the hotel. They immediately
obtained jobs at the Atlanta Cabana Motor Hotel in Atlanta,
Georgia, which had been built with loans from the Teamsters
Pension Fund.

On March 12 Hoffa and the other defendants appeared before
Judge Wilson for sentencing. The judge spoke first to Hoffa and
asked him if he had anything to say before the sentence was pronounced.

Hoffa stood and faced the judge. He protested his innocence and
said that he was confident he would be vindicated on appeal. The
crowded courtroom was quiet and somber as Judge Wilson spoke:

> Mr. Hoffa, it is the opinion of the Court that the verdict of the jury
> in this case is clearly supported by the evidence. It is the opinion
> of the Court that those matters of which you stand convicted, that
> you did knowingly and that you did corruptly after the trial judge

reported to you his information with regard to an alleged attempt to bribe a juror.

Now, it is difficult for the Court to imagine under those circumstances a more willful violation of the law. Most defendants that stand before this Court for sentencing, and certainly sentencing is the most distressing duty that this Court ever has to perform, most defendants that stand before this Court for sentencing have either violated the property rights of other individuals or have violated the personal rights of other individuals.

You stand here convicted of seeking to corrupt the administration of justice itself. You stand here convicted of having tampered, really, with the very soul of this nation. You stand here convicted of having struck at the very foundation upon which everything else in this nation depends, the very basis of civilization itself, and that is the administration of justice, because without a fair, proper and a lawful administration of justice, nothing else would be possible in this country—the administration of labor unions, the administration of business, the carrying on of recreation, the administration of health services, everything that we call civilization depends ultimately upon the proper administration of justice itself.

Now, if a conviction of such an offense were to go unpunished and this type of conduct and this type of offense permitted to pass without action by the Court, it would surely destroy this country more quickly and more surely than any combination of any foreign foes that we could ever possibly have.

Judge Wilson then sentenced Hoffa to eight years in prison and fined him $10,000. Co-defendants Larry Campbell, Thomas Parks and Ewing King were sentenced to three years in prison. Jacques Schiffer, the attorney for Parks, but actually one of Hoffa's lawyers, was cited by Judge Wilson for contempt of court and sentenced to sixty days in prison.

It had been almost eighteen months since that first morning of the trial in Nashville. I had spent most of that time in the state of Tennessee. It had been almost seven years since I first saw Jimmy Hoffa in the caucus room of the old Senate Office Building in Washington. Now I hoped that with the upcoming trial in Chicago, it would finally be over.

But I should have known that it was not the end and that there might never be an end. For even as Judge Wilson was imposing the sentences, Hoffa's agents were moving around Chattanooga offering more bribes for more false affidavits to contest his conviction. They were still "tampering with the very soul of this nation" and would continue to do so.

In Santurce, Puerto Rico, that day, Frank Chavez wrote a letter to Attorney General Robert Kennedy:

> Sir:
> This is for your information.
> The undersigned is going to solicit from the membership of our union that each one donate whatever they can afford to maintain, clean, beautify and supply with flowers the grave of Lee Harvey Oswald.
> You can rest assured contributions will be unanimous.
>
> > Sincerely,
> > Frank Chavez
> > Secretary-Treasurer
> > Teamsters Local 901

On March 18 Judge Wilson filed a reprimand against attorney Frank Ragano for improper conduct during the trial. Referring to the day when Ragano had slipped out of court and gone to the door of the jury room while Jacques Schiffer was shouting in the courtroom, Judge Wilson charged Ragano with "knowingly and intentionally going into the private area reserved by the jury and observing and eavesdropping and conducting surveillance upon the jury . . . a willfull disregard of the orders and instructions of this court."

On March 24 Hoffa presided over a five-hour closed-door meeting of the International Executive Board in Hollywood, Florida. There had been continuing rumors since his conviction that the board would now move to oust him from office. There had been the same kind of secret meetings and jockeying for position and support among some Executive Board members as had preceded the Chattanooga trial. But again, there was little trust or courage among them and the would-be movers of a revolt joined instead in a unanimous vote of confidence in Hoffa when they came face to face with him at the Hollywood meeting.

With his position within the union thus solidified, Hoffa launched his counterattack against the government. While the search for more ammunition for more affidavits went on in Chattanooga, Hoffa again sought a political solution to his problems. He turned to his friends in the Congress of the United States.

On the same day that the Executive Board declared its support of Hoffa in Florida, the House Judiciary Committee in Washington announced that a subcommittee had been authorized to review the transcript of the Chattanooga trial to evaluate Hoffa's charges against the government. The committee had earlier declined to send an observer to the trial as requested in Sid Zagri's mid-trial letter-writing campaign.

On March 30 the trial of Lawrence "Red" Medlin began in Nashville, with Judge Frank Wilson presiding. Medlin was represented by attorney R. B. Parker; John Hooker and Jim Neal prosecuted the case for the government. The courtroom was practically empty as the trial got under way. Medlin testified that he had not attempted to bribe prospective juror James C. Tippens during the Test Fleet case but had merely passed on a conversation he had heard in a restaurant. Tippens testified, however, that Medlin had called him, arranged a meeting and offered him $10,000 in hundred-dollar bills to vote for the acquittal of Hoffa. He quoted Medlin as saying, "We've got a chance to make some big money . . . and no one will have to know where it came from."

Tippens said that after he reported the offer to Judge William E. Miller and was excused as a juror, he went to Medlin and told him what he had done. He quoted Medlin as saying, "That fellow called me last night and wanted to know what you said." Tippens said that he told Medlin he wished that he had not done it and that Medlin replied, "I had no choice." On April 3 the jury found Medlin guilty.

On April 7 Henry "Buster" Bell went on trial in Nashville before Judge Frank Gray, Jr. Two days later the jury found Bell guilty of having offered $30,000 to Nathan Bellamy to attempt to influence the two black members of the Test Fleet jury to vote for the acquittal of Hoffa. So far, six persons had been convicted, including Hoffa, in three separate trials before three different juries and two different judges—all charged with tampering with the jury in Hoffa's trial in Nashville eighteen months earlier. In addition, two attorneys had been disbarred on the same charges. But there was no clamor in the Congress of the United States or elsewhere seeking to vindicate Red Medlin or Buster Bell, or, for that matter, Tom Parks, Larry Campbell or Ewing King. The effort was all on behalf of Jimmy Hoffa—the only person who had originally stood to benefit from the jury tampering, and on whose behalf it was undertaken.

On April 15 Sid Zagri, following up on his mid-trial letters to Congressmen, wrote a letter to Representative Emanuel Celler, chairman of the House Judiciary Committee, asking for an investigation of the government's conduct during the Chattanooga trial. All of the charges leveled by Zagri in the letter had been thoroughly aired in the court hearings in Chattanooga and had been overruled by Judge Wilson. The judge had also overruled the charges of juror intoxication in the motion for a new trial which was now on appeal. Congressman Celler referred Zagri's charges to a special five-man subcommittee for review.

Representative Alvin O'Konski of Wisconsin, who had spoken up in Hoffa's defense in 1962, again came forward with a speech at a DRIVE meeting in his home state in which he castigated the Department of Justice, stating that the trial of Hoffa was "persecution and not prosecution." Hoffa's counterattack was only beginning.

CHAPTER XI

Chicago

ㅡㅡㅡㅡㅡㅡㅡㅡㅡㅡ

ON APRIL 27, 1964, James R. Hoffa and seven co-defendants went on trial in Chicago on the charges that they had conspired to defraud the Teamsters Pension Fund.

On the same day the DRIVE News Service issued a series of releases. One contained excerpts from Representative O'Konski's speech in defense of Hoffa. Another centered on the appointment by Representative Celler of the special subcommittee to look into Zagri's charges. A third was a reprint of a resolution by the Building Trades Council urging its members to write to President Johnson and their Congressmen protesting the persecution of Hoffa and demanding an investigation.

Also on that day *The Nation* published a twenty-four-page article by Fred J. Cook entitled "The Hoffa Trial." It was a scurrilous attack on the judge, the FBI, and the Department of Justice in connection with the Chattanooga case. Cook presented all of Hoffa's and Zagri's charges as fact, and concluded by recommending that Congress examine the record to determine "whether federal law enforcement is becoming a law unto itself." The magazine was mailed to every federal judge in the United States. It was also passed out at subway entrances and street corners in Chicago.

This was followed by a special edition of the *DRIVE Reporter* which announced the formation of the special subcommittee to investigate the Department of Justice, and urged Teamsters members and their wives to write to their Congressmen in support of the investigation. They were also told to send a copy of their letters to President Johnson. "We have a feeling he'd like to add to his stock of expressed opinions on how the American people feel about Bobby Kennedy," the editorial concluded. The special edition also contained a copy of the Building Trades Council resolution in support of Hoffa, an article attacking Partin, copies of the photographs of Chattanooga citizens who were still being depicted as FBI agents, excerpts from the speech by Congressman O'Konski and the Fred Cook article.

In Nashville Henry "Buster" Bell was sentenced to five years in prison by Judge Frank Gray, Jr., for his role in the jury-tampering activities during the Test Fleet trial.

To add to Hoffa's problems as the Chicago case got under way, there were disquieting cracks erupting in the recently announced solid support of the International Executive Board. International Vice President John O'Rourke widened his growing breach with Hoffa by sending a telegram to Secretary-Treasurer John English demanding that no further expenditure of union funds be made for Hoffa's defense in criminal cases. It had been estimated that over $1,000,000 of the union's funds had been spent in the previous year for Hoffa's defense. Following the Chattanooga conviction, there had been scattered rank and file protests about this, which led the Executive Board at the Hollywood meeting to recommend the solicitation of voluntary contributions of $1 per union member throughout the country. This proposal got a mixed reaction from the union membership. The matter was brought to a head when a group of Philadelphia dissidents wrote a letter to each member of the Executive Board threatening to sue and hold them accountable if any more union funds were expended for Hoffa's defense. To quiet the fears of the board members, Hoffa had held a conference call with them in which he claimed that Edward Bennett Williams, the general counsel of the International, had approved continued expenditures. When John O'Rourke called Williams to verify this, Williams told him that he had given no such approval and that in his view such payments were illegal. O'Rourke then sent the telegram to English. English announced that no further legal defense disbursements would be made and Hoffa, in Chicago, reluctantly agreed.

The trial in Chicago began with Judge Richard B. Austin questioning prospective jurors, whose identities had been kept from both the government and the defense until that morning. Judge

Austin announced that the jury would be sequestered for the entire trial.

On May 4 Congressman Roland Libonati from Chicago, a friend of the Chicago mob, introduced the Fred Cook article into the *Congressional Record*, and demanded a full inquiry into the Justice Department's handling of the Hoffa case. He was supported in his demands by Representatives William Brock of Tennessee and Clarence Brown of Ohio. A copy of his statement was sent by Zagri to all Teamsters shop stewards along with a letter-writing kit. Zagri urged that the shop stewards organize letter-writing meetings to generate letters to the President and Congressmen from Teamsters members and their wives.

On the same day Congressmen Torbert Macdonald of Massachusetts and James O'Hara of Michigan made speeches responding to Libonati's charges. They pointed out that all the charges raised had been the subject of thorough hearings by the judge during the trial. Congressman Macdonald outlined the history of efforts to tamper with juries in three of Hoffa's previous trials and said that the Department of Justice would have been derelict in its duty if it had not taken precautions to ensure against such activities in the Chattanooga trial.

On May 6, in Chicago, prospective juror Raymond K. Ryan, Jr., was dismissed for cause when Abe Poretz brought out in questioning that he was an associate of Joey Glimco and had been one of the three cabdrivers who had, represented by Jacques Schiffer, filed suit against Dominic Abata in 1961. (When Ryan's name was called as a prospective juror, Glimco was seated in the courtroom as a spectator and Schiffer was seated at the defense table as counsel for defendant Ben Dranow.) After seven days of trial only seven jurors had been chosen and over three hundred prospective jurors had been excused. Judge Austin was growing increasingly impatient with the slow progress.

Finally, on Monday morning, May 11, a jury of eight men and four women, along with four alternate jurors, was chosen and the government began presenting its case. Charlie Smith, making the opening argument, told the jury that the conspiracy to defraud the Pension Fund began in 1958 in an attempt to extricate Hoffa from the Sun Valley venture. He said that Dranow, George Burris and Herbert Burris had set up a company to buy Sun Valley and that thereafter all of the defendants conspired to obtain loans totaling more than $20,000,000 from the fund through Hoffa's influence, and that they had used $1,700,000 of this money both for their own benefit and for that of Hoffa.

One after another, the defense attorneys then rose to give their opening arguments to the jury. The defense table was even more crowded than the one in Chattanooga, with eight defendants and nine attorneys crowded around it. Only a few of the faces were the same. James Haggerty was there with Hoffa, who, although still exerting command, showed more than usual deference to his Chicago attorneys, Maurice Walsh and Daniel Ahearn, both prestigious defense attorneys. Jacques Schiffer, on appeal from his contempt citation in Chattanooga, was representing Ben Dranow, who had come to the trial from the Sandstone Prison near Minneapolis where he was serving sentences on previous convictions. Frank Ragano sat next to his client, Dranow's alter ego, Abe Weinblatt. The other attorneys were all from Chicago: Charles Bellows representing Calvin Kovens; George Callahan for Zachary "Red" Strate; Richard Gorman representing George and Herbert Burris; and George Costirilos for Sam Hyman.

Judge Richard Austin, in contrast to his calm, patient counterparts in Nashville and Chattanooga, was a feisty, no-nonsense jurist with a dry, cutting wit. During the laborious process of selecting the jury, attorney Maurice Walsh at one point complained that it might be impossible to select a jury. Judge Austin responded, "That will solve our problem, won't it?"

Hoffa himself was grim and edgy. He refused to talk to reporters, ordered photographs taken of all deputy marshals assigned to the trial and pointed out Carl Schultz, sitting as a spectator in the courtroom, prompting Maurice Walsh to accuse Schultz of being the leader of a surveillance team.

With the government ready to proceed with its case, we experienced a severe jolt when Abe Poretz, our chief prosecutor, had to leave suddenly for Washington when his brother died. Charlie Smith took over with Tom McTiernan, Jim Canavan and Bill Ryan backing him up.

The government called Stanton D. Sanson, the real estate investor from Bal Harbour, Florida. He said that he had applied for a loan from the Pension Fund in 1957 for an apartment building project he was trying to put together and that Ben Dranow tried to induce him to take over the Sun Valley project and at one point called him and put Hoffa on the phone. Sanson testified that Hoffa told him Sun Valley was in difficulty and it was a "must" that he take it over, and if he did, his pending loan application would go through. Sanson said that he then had a survey made of Sun Valley and wrote a very critical report of his findings, refusing to modify it as Dranow requested. He said that Dranow also wanted a 10 percent commission if his loan application did go through. Sanson said he did not take over Sun Valley and he did not get his loan.

Our case in Chicago, barely under way, was already beginning to falter. A key witness, James Dioguardi, who had received a $900,000 loan from the Pension Fund, decided, after a private meeting with defendant Herbert Burris, to lose his memory and change testimony he had previously given before the grand jury concerning conversations with Burris and Hoffa about a loan from the Pension Fund. Charlie Smith attempted to have him declared a hostile witness so that he could be cross-examined about the earlier statements but Judge Austin would not allow it. The government suffered another setback when the judge would not allow the admission of documents by Frederick Lower, son of the late Henry Lower, concerning Sun Valley. To complicate matters further, Abe Poretz became ill himself and could not return to Chicago.

Jack Miller flew to Chicago on May 15, and after conferring with United States Attorney Edward Hanrahan, picked Assistant United States Attorney William O. Bittman to replace Abe Poretz as head of the prosecution. Bittman, an aggressive and very able native Chicagoan, though only in his early thirties had an imposing record of success in trying a multitude of varied cases. He now had the monumental task of absorbing almost overnight the intricate facts of an extremely complicated case that had been two years in the making. Fortunately, he was uniquely suited to the challenge.

In Chattanooga an editorial in *The Chattanooga Times* took issue with Fred Cook's article in *The Nation* and Representative Libonati's endorsement of it. The editorial called the article "the most wildly distorted magazine article we have seen this year" and "the definitive propaganda treatment of the Hoffa side, all the way." The *Times*, whose reporter Fred Hixon had covered the trial every day, congratulated Representatives O'Hara and Macdonald for their defense of the Department of Justice. An editorial the next day also noted that according to the *Chicago Sun-Times*, Anthony

Tisci, the son-in-law of Chicago Mafia boss Sam Giancana, was on the payroll of Congressman Libonati. "And so Roland Victor Libonati's background is of interest as he demands an investigation of the Hoffa trial in Chattanooga," the editorial concluded.

On May 18, in Miami, Felix "Milwaukee Phil" Alderisio was indicted for engaging in interstate transportation for the purpose of extortion. Allen Dorfman's friend Irwin S. Weiner was charged with aiding and abetting Alderisio.

Back in Chicago, businessman Vaughn Connelly, who had pointed the way for our farflung investigation of the Pension Fund three years earlier, was recouping the government's lost ground as a very effective witness. Connelly testified that he paid a $300,000 kickback to Cal Kovens and Ben Dranow to obtain a $3,300,000 loan for the Everglades Hotel in Miami. Connelly said that Kovens had first introduced him to Dranow as "Mr. Grossman" and that Dranow told him he would have to pay a 10 percent fee to get a loan from the fund. When he complained to Dranow that he couldn't afford it, Connelly said he was told to make the amount in the loan application big enough to include the kickback.

Connelly said that the first $100,000 of the kickback was paid to Kovens and Dranow in small bills at Kovens' office in Miami. He stated that they counted the money and then placed it in a small overnight bag, and that another unknown man then came in and said he was going to accompany Dranow to take the money to Hoffa. Connelly testified that he had paid the money after being threatened by Kovens and Dranow: "They told me they had to have it immediately, because Hoffa was raising hell and expected it." Then, he said, they told him they hoped no physical harm would come to him but added "these boys play rough."

Connelly said he obtained an additional loan of $1,000,000 from the Pension Fund with the assistance of Burris, Dranow and Hoffa. The additional loan had been approved earlier by the trustees on Hoffa's motion, subject to execution of a mortgage on other property owned by Connelly after it had been inspected and appraised. None of this had been done, but Connelly needed the money immediately, so he appeared personally at a meeting of fund trustees. He said that the trustees were already leaving the room by the time he arrived, but that Hoffa got two of them to sign the check for $1,000,000 and handed it to Connelly. He quoted fund attorney Stanford Clinton, who was standing by, as saying, "Jimmy, this will get you into more trouble than anything you've ever done." Connelly said that George Burris was present at the meeting, but that he had been told in advance to pretend not to recognize Burris.

Then Connelly testified that he had lied to the McClellan Committee investigators when they first asked him about the loans and gave them a false statement. He later showed the statement to Kovens and Dranow and the latter told him he was pleased that he had stood up for him and Hoffa. Connelly said that Hoffa called while they were talking and told him that he appreciated the statement he had given to the Committee. Connelly said that when he was subsequently subpoenaed before the Sun Valley grand jury he had been cautioned by Kovens and Dranow not to implicate them. So again he lied before the grand jury, Connelly said, and told Dranow afterwards that he had done so.

Connelly said that the fund subsequently foreclosed on his loans and took over the hotel. He stated that he had had a net worth of $6,000,000 in 1958 and was now broke and bankrupt.

Connelly also brought Samuel Hyman into his testimony. He said that Dranow had introduced him to Hyman and told him that he had arranged a loan from the Pension Fund which would give Hyman $300,000 in cash and other money to Dranow to help extricate Hoffa from the Sun Valley project.

Connelly stood firmly by his testimony in a long, wearing three-day cross-examination by various defense counsel. He said that he had lied to the McClellan Committee and the grand jury out of fear for his life if he implicated Hoffa. At one point defense attorneys began fighting among themselves while Frank Ragano was questioning Connelly. Kovens' attorney, Charles Bellows, began objecting to Ragano's questions. James Haggerty tried to assist Ragano in his examination, but Bellows continued to object. Hoffa and Ragano engaged in a heated discussion during the recess.

Turning to the loans to the First Berkeley Corporation in Los Angeles, the government called Francis J. Murtha, the executive secretary of the Pension Fund, to the stand. Murtha identified records showing that loans amounting to $3,500,000 were made to the corporation, which was headed by George Burris, even though the trustees had previously rejected a loan for a smaller amount.

In Washington the Department of Labor subpoenaed the records of the International Brotherhood of Teamsters in an investigation to determine the amount of money that had been spent by the union for the defense of union officials in criminal cases. The International refused to honor the subpoena and the department announced that it would go into federal court to enforce it.

On Monday, May 25, the trial of Tommy Osborn began in Nashville before Judge Marion S. Boyd. Osborn was represented by attorney Jack Norman, Sr., while the prosecution was being handled by John Hooker and Jim Neal. The trial lasted five days. Bill Sheets, Bob Vick and I testified about the circumstances leading up to the recorded conversation between Vick and Osborn. The tape recording itself was then played for the judge and the jury. Osborn testified in his own behalf and admitted that it was his voice on the recording and that the transcript was accurate. But he maintained that the idea to approach the prospective juror had been Vick's, not his, and that he had been entrapped.

Jack Norman was brilliant in his defense of Osborn, his white hair tossing about, his arms waving and his voice moving in dramatic sweeps from bellowing indignation to pleading whispers. His cross-examination of Vick was merciless and cutting.

John Hooker was equally masterful in his reluctant task of prosecuting a friend and fellow member of the bar. Neither he nor Neal took any pleasure in the unpleasant duty they had. In his summation Hooker roared, "I wouldn't have to be here today if Z. T. Osborn hadn't gotten mixed up with James Riddle Hoffa. . . . This is a sad, dark day, but there was a sad, dark day before this—and that was the day that Tommy Osborn got mixed up with Hoffa. Ever since he came into the courts of Tennessee, there has been a trail of jury fixing across this state."

In the end it was Tommy Osborn's own voice that convicted him. On May 29 the jury found him guilty on one count of jury tampering.

In Washington Sid Zagri's letter-writing campaign was bearing fruit as correspondence flowed into the White House, the Congress and the Department of Justice. In a memorandum dated May 28, 1964, the chief of the Records Administration Office of the Department of Justice described the influx as an "organized, nationwide effort . . . several identical types of letters are used. Samples: Bobby Kennedy's Justice Department framed James R.

Hoffa; The courts of our land have been misused; Unless you remove Bobby Kennedy from being Attorney General, I will certainly vote Republican in November." Zagri's effort was also obviously playing on President Johnson's undisguised apprehension about the growing support for Robert Kennedy as the Vice Presidential candidate in the approaching campaign.

At the Chicago trial Morris A. Lieberman, director of appraisals for the Real Estate Research Corporation, testified as a government witness. He and his companies had been doing all appraisals for the Pension Fund for some time. He told of a heated exchange with Ben Dranow in a Miami hotel room, wherein Dranow berated him for making too low an appraisal of property owned by Sam Hyman's Key West Foundation relative to an application for a Pension Fund loan. He also testified, under questioning by Bill Bittman, about two telephone calls from Hoffa concerning a loan application by Cal Kovens for the Good Samaritan Hospital in North Miami, and another loan application by Zachary Strate in connection with the loan application of the Fontainebleau Hotel in New Orleans.

FBI agent Stuart Godwin then testified that Sam Hyman had admitted in an interview in 1961 that after receiving a loan from the Pension Fund through the efforts of Dranow and Burris, he had, at their suggestion, issued a check for $100,000 from the proceeds of the loan payable to one of their corporations. He told Godwin that in return he was given a one-half interest in their Union Land and Home Company, which they were using to buy Sun Valley and bail out Hoffa.

There followed testimony by Cecil R. Black, a Key West, Florida, masonry worker who stated that he had signed receipts for $650,000 at the request of Sam Hyman for work he supposedly did on Hyman's Poinciana Apartment project. He said he signed the receipts as the "Black Construction Company," but actually there was no such company, he did not do the work he was represented as having done and he never received any of the $650,000. The money had been received from the Pension Fund by Hyman and was represented to have been paid to the "Black Construction Company" for work done. Black said that he had received $125 a week from Hyman for a period of time.

Another construction worker, George English, testified that he was paid $10,000 or $12,000 for work he did on the Poinciana Apartment project. When he was shown a receipt supposedly signed by him for $50,400 he said that he could not remember signing it. An FBI handwriting expert then testified that the signature was a forgery.

The prosecution next zeroed in on the loans from the Pension Fund to the Fontainebleau Hotel in New Orleans. Warren A. Rose, a former partner of Zachary Strate's in the hotel venture, related how he, Strate and two others set up the Pelican State Hotels Corporation to build the Fontainebleau. He said they were approached by Ben Dranow, who told them he could obtain a $1,350,000 loan for them from the Pension Fund if they would pay him $165,000 in cash. Rose said that the loan was obtained and Dranow received his money in two payments: the first, in the amount of $50,000 in small, old bills, was given to Dranow in New Orleans; the second, $115,000 in cash, was taken to Dranow in Miami by Strate.

Dranow also attempted to get him to invest in the Sun Valley project, Rose told the court. He said he went to look at the project and found that it consisted of only five houses on one street. Shortly after they obtained their loan, he said, he made out a check for $20,000 to George Burris at the direction of Dranow.

Rose said that they applied for a second loan from the Pension Fund in the amount of $2,325,000, and that Zachary Strate told him to place the required equity money in a New Orleans bank. He deposited $300,000 in the bank but withdrew it at the direction of Strate before the loan was obtained.

Restauranteur William Sherman testified that he was approached by Strate and Dranow, who said they owned the Fontainebleau Hotel and asked him to manage it for them. He said that part of the deal required him to loan the hotel $100,000 a year in return for stock options. At the direction of George Burris, who had been Sherman's accountant for years, he made out a check for $100,000 to an oil company of Strate's. He said he thought this was peculiar but Burris, whom he trusted, told him it was all right. Sherman managed the hotel for five months while it was being constructed and decorated, but became upset when he discovered $90,000 in unpaid bills. When he asked Strate about this, he said Strate told him not to worry because they were getting another $2,300,000 loan from the Pension Fund. He said that Strate told him they could finish the hotel for $1,300,000 and "cut up a million dollars" among them. At that point, Sherman said, he asked for and received his $100,000 loan back and pulled out of the venture.

Harry Kadis, a New York City accountant who was secretary of the Burrises' First Berkeley Corporation which received a $3,350,000 loan from the Pension Fund, testified that he had never taken an active part in the corporation, knew nothing about its operation or the Pension Fund loan and had given George Burris permission to sign his name to documents.

Another official of the corporation, Irving V. Link, a dapper Beverly Hills real estate man, said that at the direction of Ben Dranow, he had obtained a $125,000 loan from John "Jake the Barber" Factor, who had been the victim of a gangland kidnapping in Chicago in the early thirties. Link was acquainted with Factor, who was also in the real estate business and had an office next to his. Dranow told Link he needed the money for "a problem he had in Sun Valley, Florida."

On June 10, in Kansas City, Missouri, while the Chicago trial was in progress, Floyd Hayes, a former Teamsters official who had testified for the government and who had been furnishing valuable information concerning Teamsters officials and underworld figures there, was murdered. Hayes and his wife were sitting in their car in a parking lot when he was hit by a shotgun blast from a car that pulled in beside them. His wife was wounded.

At the trial the government moved on to testimony concerning a $2,300,000 loan to Cal Kovens for the construction of the North Miami General Hospital. Bill Bittman introduced the minutes of meetings of the Pension Fund trustees, wherein Hoffa urged the loan be approved and stated that Dade County, Florida, was investing as much money as the fund in the hospital and that the county was going to lease and operate it. The loan was approved as a result of these representations by Hoffa.

Dr. Kermit H. Gates, the director of the Dade County Department of Hospitals, then testified that Dade County never invested in, leased or operated the hospital, and never had any intention of doing so.

One of the conditions of the loan to Kovens for the hospital was that he obtain a construction bond. In order to do so, he had to demonstrate to the bonding company that he had $250,000 available in addition to the money derived from the loan. According to testimony by Spencer Brewer, vice president of the Continental Casualty Company, which provided the bond, Kovens placed

$250,000 in an escrow account but removed it before the construction was completed, in violation of the bonding agreement.

The minutes of the trustee meetings also showed that an additional loan of $500,000 was subsequently made for an addition to the hospital. According to the minutes of a subsequent meeting, Hoffa told the trustees that the $500,000 "went into the hospital to add another floor." As the original loan had been made to build a three-floor structure, an additional floor should have resulted in a four-floor building.

Bill Bittman showed a recent photograph of the hospital to witness Bert Sager, a former partner of Kovens' in the construction of the hospital. The picture of the hospital showed only three floors.

"Is not that fourth floor a roof?" Bittman asked.

"The fourth floor of the building is also the ceiling of the third floor," Sager replied. He complicated things further by adding, "It is not the roof in the usual sense but it is acting as a roof."

The government next called witnesses concerning an $840,000 loan to the 4306 Duncan Corporation in St. Louis, which was owned by Fred W. Strecker, Jr., one of the Pension Fund trustees. Ben Hagan, an executive from Ballwin, Missouri, who was named as an officer and director of the corporation in the loan application, testified that he was never either an officer or a director and knew nothing about the loan application. The person who signed the application for the loan as president of the corporation was Max Federbush.

Federbush, who had a criminal record, testified that he had been approached by George Burris, who told him that a man named Fred Strecker in St. Louis was in financial difficulty and had some property Federbush could buy. Burris said that he could obtain a Teamsters Pension Fund loan for Federbush to purchase the property. So, Federbush said, he borrowed $15,000 for a down payment on the property and signed many papers given to him by Burris without reading them. One of the papers was the loan application. Federbush said that Burris later told him that the loan application had been rejected and he signed a paper resigning from the corporation. (Actually, the loan application had not even been presented at that time.) His $15,000 was subsequently returned to him by Abe Weinblatt.

Minutes of the meetings of the Pension Fund trustees showed that the loan application was subsequently submitted, still as signed by Max Federbush, recommended by Hoffa and approved by the trustees. Strecker, who attended the meeting as a trustee, was told beforehand by Ben Dranow and George Burris that the loan application would be considered at the meeting.

Irving Kipnis, a Miami Beach businessman, testified about another loan. He had tried unsuccessfully to obtain a loan from the Pension Fund. Then, he said, he met George Burris who told him he was going about it the wrong way. Burris subsequently prepared an application for him for a loan of $1,500,000 to be used to construct the Causeway Inn in Tampa. While the loan application was pending, Burris asked Kipnis for some money which he said he needed to close a deal on Sun Valley. Kipnis gave him $57,000 for an option on 10 percent of Sun Valley. This money was used as part of the bail-out funds.

Kipnis said that Ben Dranow then entered the picture and he agreed to give Dranow and Burris $115,000 for obtaining his loan from the Pension Fund. He also agreed to retain Burris as the accountant for the Causeway Inn. Kipnis then obtained the loan for $1,500,000 from the fund. The construction contract to build the inn went to Cal Kovens. The following year, in financial difficulty, Kipnis told Burris he needed another $350,000 from the fund. Kipnis got the loan, and when Burris complained that he needed an additional fee, Kipnis gave Burris half of the Causeway Inn.

Two years later Kipnis was losing money on the Causeway Inn and appeared before the Pension Fund trustees to ask for another loan of $1,000,000 and the deferment of payments for eighteen months. On Hoffa's motion the loan was granted and the payments deferred.

Carl Langford, an Orlando, Florida, builder, testified that he had been appointed as the trustee for Sun Valley by the court when it went bankrupt. He recounted how the Dranow group had finally come up with $500,000 to pay the Sun Valley debts. This enabled Hoffa to finally withdraw the $400,000 in Local 299 funds from the noninterest-bearing account at the Florida National Bank. A former secretary of Cal Kovens' then testified that Dranow, Weinblatt and the Burrises frequently used Kovens' office to conduct their business and make and receive phone calls.

Next an FBI handwriting expert testified that the signature on a previously undisclosed trust agreement was that of Hoffa. The agreement, also signed by Henry Lower and Bert Brennan, certified that Lower held 45 percent of Sun Valley for Hoffa and Brennan. This meant that Hoffa actually owned 22 1/2 percent of the project. Bill Bittman read McClellan Committee testimony in which Hoffa admitted having an option to buy 45 percent of the stock but said nothing about actually owning 22 1/2 percent.

On June 19, in Nashville, Tommy Osborn was sentenced to serve three and one-half years in prison for jury tampering.

In Chicago the government moved toward concluding its case by calling FBI accountants as witnesses to trace the various loans to show how much money was diverted for what purposes and whose benefit. Their testimony (interrupted continually by objections from defense attorneys) showed the complex pattern of widespread diversion, misrepresentation and fraud.

Altogether the Pension Fund made four loans to the Fontainebleau Hotel totaling $4,675,000. Of this $1,837,556.35 was shown to have been diverted by Zachary "Red" Strate. According to the testimony, almost half a million dollars went to Strate himself and $168,000 went to Dranow, Weinblatt and a Florida corporation, Bene Originals, owned by Dranow and Weinblatt. Of this amount, $50,000 went from Dranow and Weinblatt toward the Sun Valley bail-out. In addition, there was the original cash payment of $165,000 to Dranow to obtain the loans, and another $139,500 that flowed from Strate to Dranow and Weinblatt which could not be traced back to the proceeds of the Pension Fund loans.

Of the $875,000 loan to Sam Hyman for the construction of a shopping center, $200,000 went to Hyman himself; $125,000 was used by Hyman to buy out the other stockholders in a corporation in which he had an interest; $75,000 went to another corporation owned by Hyman and his wife; and $100,000 was passed through two corporations to Dranow, Weinblatt and Burris and became part of the Sun Valley bail-out.

A second loan of $400,000 was obtained by Hyman to remodel apartments owned by one of his corporations. The loan was made after Hoffa told the trustees that Sears, Roebuck was building a $55,000,000 shopping center complex near Hyman's apartments and that the government was moving fifteen thousand people to Key West, where the apartments were located. Neither of these statements was true. After obtaining the loan, Hyman showed on his books remodeling expenses of $706,000. The expenditures were backed up by receipts showing $50,000 paid to the Mid-Florida Paving Company and $650,000 to the Black Construction Company. Previous testimony had shown that only $12,000 was paid to Mid-Florida, and Cecil Black of the "Black Construction Company" was paid $125 a week. The remainder of the receipts in both instances were forgeries. Here, $50,000 of the loan proceeds went toward the Sun Valley bail-out.

The first loan of $2,996,000 to the First Berkeley Corporation, owned by Burris, was for the purchase of buildings in Los Angeles. The loan was made on a representation by Burris that First Berkeley had a net worth of $3,673,000, when its actual net worth was $634.17 and it was necessary to borrow $200 to open a bank account in which to deposit the proceeds of the loan. The application also claimed that First Berkeley owned stock in a Florida corporation, whereas the stock was actually owned by Cal Kovens and was loaned by Kovens to Burris for purposes of the loan application.

Four days after the loan was obtained, Irving Link, who had been brought into the First Berkeley venture, was approached by Dranow who said he needed money immediately for the "Sun Valley problem." Link then obtained the $125,000 from John Factor, which was given to Dranow. Of this money, $40,500 was used to pay off Sun Valley creditors. First Berkeley then borrowed money from third parties to give to Link to repay Factor, and then borrowed $300,000 more from the Pension Fund to repay the third parties and other creditors.

The $2,300,000 loan application for the Good Samaritan Hospital was approved by the trustees on the condition that $950,000 be placed in escrow by the borrower—the same type of condition that had been placed on the approval of the loan to the Fontainebleau Hotel. Four months later Hoffa told the trustees that escrow requirements had been met and the loan was made. Actually, when Hoffa made that statement, there were no funds in escrow nor were there at any time thereafter. This was just another misrepresentation, along with the previous testimony concerning the available funds for the construction bond and the additional loan for construction of the invisible "fourth floor" of the hospital.

Cal Kovens received $200,000 for building the hospital; $28,000 was paid by Kovens and the Cal Kovens Construction Company to George Burris and Ben Dranow for the Sun Valley bail-out.

As a result of all these manipulations, Hoffa and his co-defendants were able to pay off the Sun Valley creditors, including the payment to Local 299 of $42,000, representing the interest that would have accrued to the local if the funds deposited in the Florida National Bank had not been in an interest-free account. Dranow then prevailed upon Ed Levinson, a Las Vegas gambling casino operator, Ben Sigelbaum, an associate of Levinson's, and Edwin Willis, a Florida orange grower, to put up $250,000 for a share of Sun Valley. Then Dranow put up the remaining money necessary to pay off the debt to the Florida National Bank, thus allowing Hoffa in the summer of 1960 to finally withdraw the $400,000 in Local 299 funds from the interest-free account. A substantial part of the money put up by Dranow in this final settlement was derived from funds furnished to George Burris by Irving Kipnis when he was obtaining his loan from the Pension Fund.

When Hoffa took the witness stand, he denied the signature on the secret trust agreement concerning his interest in Sun Valley was his. In spite of the testimony of the FBI handwriting experts to the contrary, Hoffa maintained that he never used the signature "J. R. Hoffa," which appeared on the trust agreement, in signing legal documents but always used his full name, James R. Hoffa. Between court sessions, Bill Bittman and the other attorneys searched frantically through all their records for any document bearing the signature "J. R. Hoffa" without success. Then, while Bittman was routinely going through documents which he had gathered together for the cross-examination of Hoffa, he came upon a lease agreement between Hoffa and Cal Kovens in connection with Hoffa's rental of an apartment at the Blair House in Miami Beach. Jim Canavan had given the document to Bittman earlier as one of the pieces of evidence linking Hoffa to Covens. Bittman was astonished when he looked at the signature at the bottom. It was "J. R. Hoffa."

The document was a Thermofax copy of the original, and as such, did not lend itself to successful examination by FBI handwriting experts. Bittman decided that he had to somehow get Hoffa to admit that it was his signature.

When he resumed the cross-examination, Bittman asked Hoffa about his relationship with Kovens and then about his apartment at the Blair House which was owned by Kovens. Hoffa, suspecting that the questions were designed to show some impropriety about his having the apartment, took the offensive and leaped into the trap. He said that there was nothing wrong with the arrangement and that he had signed a lease and paid his rent. Bittman then casually showed Hoffa the copy of the lease and asked if that was the agreement that he had signed with Kovens. Hoffa instinctively hesitated but then acknowledged that it was.

"Isn't it a fact that the document is signed 'J. R. Hoffa?' " Bittman bellowed.

Hoffa tried to recover by claiming that it was not a legal document but it was obvious that Bittman had scored a devastating blow.

Aside from the gross misrepresentations, diversion of funds and kickbacks, the actual callousness of the fraud can best be seen in retrospect. All of the transactions leading up to the Sun Valley bail-out took place between the summer of 1958 and the summer of 1960. This was the very time Hoffa was under investigation by the McClellan Committee, the Board of Monitors and, in the latter period, by Jim Dowd's grand jury. While George Burris and Hoffa were giving evasive answers before the McClellan Committee and praising Vaughn Connelly for lying to the Committee; while Hoffa and his attorneys were desperately fighting the attempts by the Board of Monitors to delve into the situation; while Jimmy Hoffa was telling Vice President Nixon's friend Allan Oakley Hunter that the investigation by Dowd was nothing but harassment; and when Dowd was called out of the grand jury and told not to bring an indictment—Hoffa was using funds reserved for the pensions of Teamsters members to extricate himself from a situation where he had misused funds belonging to Teamsters members for his own benefit. This is what the Chicago case was all about.

In a five-and-one-half-hour summation to the jury, Bill Bittman pulled all of the threads forming the complicated fabric of fraud together. Using charts prepared by FBI agents he traced the flow of funds to the intricate and devious channels through which the scheme was executed. It was a masterful condensation of the thirteen weeks of testimony and the fifteen thousand documents which the government had introduced in evidence.

As part of the rebutal which followed, defense attorney Charles Bellows presented his own charts containing facts and figures at variance with those introduced by Bittman. While Bellows was addressing the jury, Bittman asked one of the government attorneys to make note of the exhibit numbers on the Bellows charts, which were supposed to represent the supporting evidence from the trial record.

When court adjourned for the day, Bittman asked to inspect the charts but Bellows would not let him. When Bittman reached to pick up one of the charts, a shouting and shoving fracas erupted and the deputy marshalls intervened. The charts remained in the custody of the defense attorneys. That evening Bittman checked the exhibit numbers from the charts and found that none of the exhibits cited had been introduced during the trial. He called Bellows' accountant who had prepared the charts and asked him where he got the information and exhibit number for the charts. The accountant said they had been furnished by Bellows.

The following morning, Bellows, now aware of Bittman's discovery, asked Judge Austin for a conference in chambers in an attempt to quietly explain it away. Bittman protested and charged in open court that Bellows' charts were fraudulent. When Judge Austin questioned Bellows about the exhibits in support of the charts, Bellows acknowledged that they had not been introduced in the trial. He then claimed that they were being flown in from New York City that day. Judge Austin was furious. When the jury was brought in, he told its members to disregard the charts presented by Bellows and anything that Bellows said in reference to them. He then ordered a deputy marshal to remove the charts from the courtroom.

On Sunday, July 26, after seventeen and a half hours of deliberation, the jury found Hoffa guilty on four counts and all of the remaining co-defendants guilty on from two to nine counts. It was a great tribute to all the attorneys and FBI agents who had worked for three years putting all of the intricate pieces together, but especially, it was a tribute to Bill Bittman, who had moved in without hesitation to take over a major complicated case which he knew nothing about, with the trial already in progress, and carried it to a successful conclusion.

Meanwhile, Hoffa's political efforts against Robert Kennedy and the Justice Department went on. Sid Zagri attended both the Democratic and Republican conventions peddling his story of the persecution of Hoffa to whoever would listen. He finally succeeded in getting a plank inserted in the Republican Party platform stating that the Department of Justice should be investigated. Members of the academic community, including Professor Daniel M. Berman of American University and Professor Philip Kurland of the University of Chicago Law School, were also recruited in support of the Hoffa cause. Their letters to Congressman Celler were widely distributed by Zagri.

The nationwide letter-writing campaign by Teamsters and their wives was pressed. Teamster Local 968 in Texas had a "Win a Watch and Help Hoffa" contest. "For the Teamster who turns in the largest number of letters to President Johnson, there will be a beautiful $70 watch. Most of the work has been done for you already. There are helpful suggestions contained in a handy form ... letters must be turned in by Wednesday, July 29th. We will pay postage, address the envelopes and mail them. All you have to do is GET LETTERS. Use the helpful form provided. . . ." Attached were a number of suggested phrases for use in different sections of the letters: "We Texans are proud of you . . . We in the Teamsters feel Jimmy Hoffa got a raw deal . . . That mess in Chattanooga needs a public airing . . ."

On August 17 Judge Richard B. Austin sentenced Hoffa to serve five years in prison, to run consecutively to the eight-year jury-tampering sentence. Ben Dranow also received a five-year sentence. Zachary Strate and Cal Kovens each received three years, and George Burris got eighteen months. Sam Hyman was sentenced to one year and one day and Abe Weinblatt to one hour in the custody of the United States marshal.

On August 25, 1964, Robert Kennedy announced his intention to seek the nomination as the Democratic candidate for the United States Senate in New York State against the incumbent Senator Kenneth Keating. He asked me to join the campaign. I resigned from the Department of Justice and became the coordinator for thirteen upstate counties.

On the House Judiciary Committee the forces led by Congressman Libonati now gained new support from Republicans and anti-Kennedy Democrats, who recognized the advantage of possible embarrassment to Kennedy that might result from an investigation of the Department of Justice. Libonati introduced a resolution calling for an in-depth investigation of the violation of individual rights by the Department of Justice.

A substitute resolution was presented by Representative William C. McCulloch of Ohio, the ranking Republican on the committee. It called for an investigation to determine whether the Department of Justice had infringed upon the constitutional rights of any individual, but it did not make specific reference to Hoffa or any particular person. On September 22 the resolution passed by a vote of 20 to 13. An attempt by Representative Mathias of Maryland to amend the resolution to exclude cases pending before the courts from the investigation was defeated by a vote of 17 to 16.

Chairman Celler commented, "This all grows out of the Hoffa agitation. The resolution does not mention names, but this undoubtedly will be called the Hoffa resolution." He described the forces who supported the resolution as an "unholy coalition."

On the *Huntley-Brinkley Report* that evening David Brinkley said:

> Jimmy Hoffa of the Teamster Union was convicted of two crimes by juries in two states—in Chattanooga of trying to rig a jury and Chicago of defrauding his union's pension fund.
>
> Both convictions are on appeal and so are still in the courts.
>
> When he was convicted, Hoffa then had his head lobbyist looking to Congress for help. He's been all over the Capitol and at both party conventions claiming Hoffa's civil rights were violated.
>
> What follows is opinion:
>
> After all these years, when Hoffa finally lost in the courts, he's now trying to get bailed out by some political means.
>
> Today, surprisingly, the House Judiciary Committee voted to do what the Teamster lobbyist asked them to do—to investigate the Justice Department. The Committee Chairman, Emanuel Celler, opposed it, but he was out-voted, mainly by Republicans and southern Democrats, some of whom have old scores they would like to settle with the Justice Department and some of whom hope for political advantage.
>
> One member, Mathias of Maryland, asked they not investigate any cases now before the courts. That would have avoided the gross impropriety of seeming to influence or tamper with the courts. But the Republican and southern Democratic zeal for Hoffa's civil rights was so great they voted him down.
>
> Now there will be a lot of pious mouthing about civil rights, but the spectacle here is that a committee of Congress is dancing to Jimmy Hoffa's tune, investigating criminal cases now in the courts—a kind of political help that convicted criminals are usually not able to command.

Hoffa realized that even though the resolution had passed, there was little likelihood that anything would be done while the campaigns were in full swing throughout the country. Therefore he decided to do his best to defeat Kennedy in New York. Another special edition of the *DRIVE Reporter* was printed for mass distribution in New York State. It contained the same material as the earlier edition with the new title "Why Bobby Kennedy Must Be Defeated." It also carried updated captions: "Vote for Freedom—

Vote for Keating"; "New York Does Not Need a Kennedy Dynasty"; "Bobby Kennedy Slogan: Ask Not What I Can Do for New York, but What New York Can Do for Me." *International Teamster* magazine, the official organ of the union, also endorsed Keating.

Then scurrilous pamphlets attacking Kennedy began turning up in New York City. He called me in upstate New York and asked me to come down and try to find out who was behind it. I discovered that Zagri had set up a phony organization in New York City called "Committee of Democrats for Keating-Johnson-Humphrey." Using the committee as a front, Zagri was grinding out anti-Kennedy literature. Five hundred thousand fliers attacking Kennedy's civil rights record were distributed in Harlem. Other pamphlets in equal volume, depicting Kennedy as anti-Italian, antilabor and anti-Semetic, were printed and forwarded to Teamsters locals throughout the state for distribution. The literature also contained sample ballots with instructions on how to split one's ticket to vote for Johnson, Humphrey and Keating.

Some, and perhaps most, Teamsters locals refused to distribute the literature. Others did. Joint Council 16 in New York City, the largest Teamsters organization in the state, publicly endorsed Kennedy. It was a courageous stand for John O'Rourke, the president of the Council, who, seven years earlier, had openly wept after taking the Fifth Amendment in response to Kennedy's questions before the McClellan Committee to protect Hoffa. Now he publicly defied Hoffa.

On the morning that Vice President Humphrey was to come to New York City to campaign jointly with Kennedy in the garment district, *The New York Times* carried an article about the Keating-Johnson-Humphrey Committee and its literature and indicated that Hoffa was behind it. Robert Kennedy thereupon issued the following statement:

> In my judgment, the story this morning in *The New York Times* merely confirms what a lot of people have known for a long time. James Hoffa is putting money, men and scurrilous literature into New York State in an effort to defeat me and elect my Republican opponent.
> It is the responsibility of Mr. Keating to disavow the support of Mr. Hoffa. I call upon my Republican opponent to do this now. He has already delayed much too long. Obviously, he has known for a long time that Mr. Hoffa was supporting him. Up to now, he has ac-

cepted this support. I do not see how he can in conscience continue
to do so.

I am grateful for the support of John O'Rourke of The Teamsters
Union of New york City. I know that the vast majority of Teamster
members resent this activity of Mr. Hoffa.

When *Air Force One* landed later that morning at La Guardia
Airport, Robert Kennedy and I went aboard to talk to the Vice
President before he emerged. We had with us samples of the litera-
ture, *The New York Times* article and a proposed statement which
Kennedy hoped that the Vice President would make disavowing
Hoffa's support.

Humphrey looked over the article and the literature. Shaking
his head, he commented, as he read, how scurrilous and unfair it
was. He then looked at the proposed statement and finally said,
"Bob, I'll be glad to denounce this material—but Hoffa— Well,
you know I just can't be sure where all of the President's support
is coming from, and I don't know if it would be wise."

Perhaps the reluctance of Hubert Humphrey to denounce
Hoffa's role in the Keating campaign can be explained by other
events that happened about the same time in Washington, D.C.,
according to statements subsequently given under oath by Jack
Sullivan, the former administrative assistant to former Senator
Daniel Brewster of Maryland.

When George Wallace was seeking the Presidential nomination
in the 1964 primary campaign, one of the primary contests he
entered was in the state of Maryland. President Johnson prevailed
upon Senator Brewster to run in the primary against Wallace as
a stand-in for him. Brewster did so and received considerable
national publicity.

During the general election that followed, Brewster was approached by Paul Demos, the administrative assistant to Senator
Joseph Montoya of New Mexico. Demos suggested that Brewster
meet with representatives of the Teamsters Union, who, he said,
could be of assistance in further enhancing the Senator's national
image. At a subsequent meeting between Montoya and Brewster,
the latter was asked if he would be willing to help Jimmy Hoffa.
Brewster said that he would. Shortly thereafter, Brewster was
invited to a cocktail party in the penthouse atop the Teamsters
Union headquarters in Washington. Sullivan went with Brewster
and they were greeted by Demos and Sid Zagri. While they were

talking, Hoffa came over to join them, and was introduced. He asked Brewster if he could talk to him privately and the two walked off onto the terrace overlooking Capitol Hill. After the party Brewster told Sullivan that Hoffa had asked him if he would serve as a middleman to pass $100,000 in cash from Hoffa to Cliff Carter for President Johnson. Brewster told Sullivan that he had agreed to do so.

A few days later Zagri appeared in Senator Brewster's office carrying a tan suitcase full of money. He gave the suitcase to Brewster. Sullivan then drove Brewster to Cliff Carter's office at the Democratic National Committee. Sullivan waited in the car while Brewster carried the suitcase into the office. When Brewster came out without the suitcase, he got into the car and said to Sullivan, "Well, I did it."

As a result of Lyndon Johnson's landslide victory in November the complexion of the House Judiciary Committee was considerably changed. Kennedy had been elected to the Senate in New York and there was now little interest on the committee in pursuing the resolution to investigate the Justice Department.

After the New York campaign I returned home completely exhausted. I was looking forward to a little relaxation and the holidays. Then Bob Vick called. He said that he had been unable to get a job since testifying in the Osborn case. He was $3000 in debt and in desperate financial condition. With a family and Christmas coming, he did not know what to do. I knew that there was considerable ill-feeling toward him in Nashville, particularly among some members of the bar because of his role in the Osborn case.

I was no longer in the Department of Justice. Technically and officially it was no longer my concern. But it doesn't work that way. Bob Vick called me because I was the one with whom he had dealt and he knew and trusted me. I felt an obligation because I was somewhat responsible for the position he was in. I did not have any money myself, so I finally called Steve Smith, Senator Kennedy's brother-in-law, and asked him if I could borrow $3000. I did not tell him why I wanted it and did not say anything to the Senator. Smith gave me the money, which I, in turn, gave to Vick at my home. I immediately questioned my own judgment and asked Vick to go with me the following morning to see an attorney. I told him that I wanted the transaction to be formal and above board and he agreed. I also questioned whether it was wise or proper. That evening I called Martin O'Donoghue, a lawyer whose judgment and integrity I trusted implicitly, and asked to see him the next morning.

Vick accompanied me to O'Donoghue's office. I explained the entire situation to Mr. O'Donoghue and his son Pat, who was also an attorney. They both said that, under the circumstances, the transaction might be misconstrued and could indeed be improper. They agreed that I should ask Vick to return the money. I was not surprised and was greatly relieved, because I knew by then that I had used poor judgment. They tried to explain it to Vick but he was desperate, confused and angry. He gave me the money and I returned it to Smith the following day.

Vick went back to Nashville very upset. I told him I was sorry, but I knew he did not understand. Then shortly after Christmas, he called me. He said that he had called his family together and explained to them that they just didn't have any money for Christmas. He said that he respected what I had done and was sorry he had been angry.

On December 24 in Miami attorney Ben Cohen, who had arranged, for cash fees, the loans from the Teamsters Pension Fund for Maryland hotel builders Samuel Eig and John McKeever and for the Whitcomb Hotel in San Francisco, was found guilty of having evaded $34,500 in income taxes. Charlie Shaffer and John Cassidy prosecuted the case. Cohen, an old friend of Hoffa's, had served the same middleman role in these loans as Ben Dranow had played in the loans involved in the Chicago case. The outcome of this case merely reinforced what had already been proven in Chicago—that the Pension Fund was fair game for exploitation by Hoffa and his friends.

It had taken four years of concerted effort, but during that period, 201 Teamsters officials and their associates had been indicted and there had been 126 convictions.

PART III

THE FIXING

CHAPTER XII

Prostitutes and Politicians

═ ═ ═ ═ ═ ═ ═ ═ ═

On January 4, 1965, Robert F. Kennedy was sworn in as the junior Senator from the state of New York.

On the same day Herman Frazier, Nelson Paden and Albert Cole, who were charged with making the calls to prospective jurors in the Test Fleet case, went on trial in Columbia, Tennessee. Their previous trial in late 1964 had ended in a mistrial when it was discovered that one of the jurors had also been a prospective juror in the Test Fleet case. Charlie Shaffer and John Cassidy, who had prosecuted the previous trial, represented the government again in the retrial. On January 7 the three men were acquitted by the jury.

Bob Kennedy asked me to stay on his Senate staff as his upstate representative. At first I said I would but shortly thereafter I told him I would like to get into some type of investigative reporting. He told me to go ahead and on February 23 I began employment as a special correspondent with the National Broadcasting Company. I was aware that from time to time I would necessarily be involved in Hoffa's appeals and other follow-up matters. William McAndrew, the president of NBC News, hired me with that understanding. I did not realize, however, that the involvement would continue for the next seven years and would not, even then, be finished.

Hoffa now stood twice convicted and faced an aggregate thirteen-year sentence, but the appellate process guaranteed him a long reprieve before he would actually have to start serving either part of that sentence. It was soon apparent that he was going to do everything in his power to avoid it altogether. The ways he and his friends would go about it were, I suppose, predictable, but the lengths to which they would go could not have been foreseen.

Their activities were focused on three areas. The first was political—to keep pressure on Senators, Congressmen and the President and to find another congressional committee to do their bidding. The second was to obtain additional affidavits, whether true or not, for additional motions for a new trial while the first motion was being appealed. The third was to induce witnesses who had testified for the government against Hoffa to recant or to amend their testimony.

In the first area, it did not take Sid Zagri long to find a congressional committee that might be helpful.

Senator Edward Long of Missouri had taken over the chairmanship of the Senate Subcommittee on Administrative Practices and Procedures. In early 1965 he launched an investigation into what he termed unwarranted surveillances by the government. Persons close to the committee were aware at the time that Zagri was feeding information to the committee and hoped to use it to get at Kennedy and help Hoffa.

Meanwhile, in Chattanooga, Hoffa had filed a second motion for a new trial, claiming that Bob Vick had, through his relationship with the government, violated Hoffa's rights under the Sixth Amendment by depriving him of the services of his attorney, Tommy Osborn, in the Chattanooga case. The motion contended that Vick had furnished information concerning defense strategy to me while he was working for Osborn. The government filed a reply on February 26 contesting the motion and attaching an affidavit by me denying that Vick had furnished me any such information.

On March 3 Local 327 in Nashville called a strike in Lawrenceburg, Pennsylvania, against the Murray Ohio Manufacturing Company. The company had moved from Cleveland, Ohio, to Lawrenceburg in 1955. In Cleveland the company had a labor contract with the United Auto Workers. When they moved to Lawrenceburg, the UAW tried to organize the new plant, without success. Finally, in late 1964, the UAW gave up. Local 327, under Don Vestal, moved in at the request of some of the employees and took over the attempts to organize the plant.

Don Vestal hired Bob Vick to assist in the organizing drive and strike in Lawrenceburg. When Vestal applied to the International Union for strike benefits, Hoffa turned him down.

Vestal then sent James Craighead, one of his business agents, to Washington to press for the strike benefits. Hoffa told Craighead that he could not give strike benefits but that he could grant equivalent donations. Hoffa said that he would do that and even better if he could get some help from "the little guy in Nashville," meaning Vick.

When the donations had not arrived about ten days later, Craighead called Hoffa. Hoffa told him that he would send $20,000 immediately and would ensure enough money to win the strike, if he got some help from "the little fellow."

The Lawrenceburg strike went on without help from the International. Vestal went to Washington himself, taking local union official Red Vaughn with him, to see Hoffa. Hoffa promised him $11,000 but after the meeting Vaughn told Vestal he could get anything he wanted if he would help Hoffa with Vick. The $11,000 never came. Shortly thereafter, Vestal was approached in Nashville by George Broda, the Teamsters official who had switched cars with Ewing King during the approach to Patrolman Paschal during the Nashville trial. Broda told Vestal that he could "write your own ticket" if he would help Hoffa.

At about the same time, James Harding, Hoffa's executive assistant, contacted Earl Wingo, a business agent for Local 327, on several occasions, asking Wingo to contact Vick. Harding told Wingo that if he could get Vick to recant his testimony in the Osborn case or show that the government had entrapped Osborn, "we could overturn Mr. Hoffa's conviction."

Vestal then sent Wingo to Washington to see Hoffa about strike benefits. When Wingo arrived, he was told that Hoffa was busy and that he should talk to James Harding. Harding told Wingo that he was authorized by Hoffa to offer Vick $25,000 if he would sign a statement saying that the government had entrapped Hoffa. In addition, Harding said, they would arrange for a $10,000-a-year job for Vick outside of the country and would subsidize him for another $8000. Harding also told Wingo that if Vick cooperated, the strike benefits could be quickly worked out and Vestal would have "a place in the sun." Harding wrote the amounts offered to Vick on a sheet of paper rather than saying them. He also wrote on the paper, "This office is bugged." He then burned the paper in an ash tray.

Several days later Wingo told Vick that Harding wanted Vick to call him. He gave Vick Harding's number and Vick placed the call. They discussed strike benefits for Lawrenceburg and Harding told Vick that if they could reach an understanding the benefits would be forthcoming. Vick told Harding that he thought they were all a bunch of s.o.b.s and he was not interested in their offers.

The next time Wingo saw Harding in Washington, Harding asked more questions about Vick and suggested to Wingo that henceforth they refer to Vick as "Wingo's uncle."

During early 1965 forces loyal to Ewing King and Hoffa in Local 327 began agitating for a separate local and circulated petitions among the membership. Vestal viewed this as further harassment to get them to persuade Vick to help Hoffa.

On March 23, 1965, Harding called Vestal and invited him to come to the Eden Rock Hotel in Miami, where the International Executive Board was meeting, to talk to Hoffa about strike benefits and the separate charter petition. Vestal arrived at the Eden Rock on the afternoon of March 26 and was greeted by Hoffa. Hoffa told Vestal not to worry about the separate charter because he had no intention of splitting the local. He said that the strike benefits for Lawrenceburg had been authorized by the Executive Board and that Harding would work it out with Vestal. Then Hoffa said they were in the business of scratching each other's backs—that Vestal was in a position to help Hoffa and he expected him to do so. Hoffa asked Vestal if he had brought the man that Harding was waiting for. Vestal knew that Hoffa was referring to Vick, and said that he had not. Hoffa then told Vestal where to find Harding.

After some discussion about the Lawrenceburg strike, Harding asked Vestal whether Vick was coming. When Vestal said no, Harding prevailed upon him to call Vick, which he did. Vick told Vestal he was not coming. Then Harding again told Vestal he was convinced Vestal could get Vick to help Hoffa, and that anyone who helped Hoffa would be set for life. Harding said that if Vick stuck to his position the CIA or the FBI would probably kill him. But if Vick would help Hoffa, Harding said, they knew a man who owned a South American country where Vick could go and be protected.

On March 19 in Miami attorney Ben Cohen was sentenced to eighteen months in prison following his conviction for income tax evasion growing out of his role as middleman in obtaining loans from the Teamsters Pension Fund.

On April 15 Judge Wilson in Chattanooga denied Hoffa's second motion for a new trial, which had been based on the claim that Bob Vick had violated Hoffa's right to counsel.

On May 3, 1965, an antitrust lawsuit against the *Manchester Union*

Leader resulted in a judgment against the newspaper in the amount of $1,250,000. Three days later William Loeb wrote a letter to the Teamsters Pension Fund applying for an additional loan of $1,500,000.

In June, 1965, still having received no strike benefits, Don Vestal again went to see Hoffa in Washington. After a heated discussion Vestal and Hoffa almost came to blows when Vestal accused Hoffa of blackmailing him by holding up strike benefits until Vick helped Hoffa.

In Baton Rouge William Daniels, now a judge, was contacted by Pete Rotolla, a friend of Carlos Marcello, the head of the Mafia in Louisiana, and later by G. Wray Gill, Marcello's attorney. Daniels met with Gill at the Forest Restaurant, which was owned by Rotolla. Gill was seeking anything that would help Hoffa. He met subsequently with both Daniels and Baton Rouge District Attorney Pitcher, who, along with Daniels, had been a government witness. He made it clear that money was no object if tape recordings or other information helpful to Hoffa could be produced.

Later Sargent Pitcher was approached by Baton Rouge attorney Jimmy Major, who offered Pitcher a substantial campaign contribution for the upcoming election if Pitcher could furnish information to help Hoffa. When this attempt was unsuccessful, another attorney, Jerry Millican, was offered $50,000 by Hoffa and Morris Shenker to finance a campaign to run against Pitcher for District Attorney.

On June 23 a commitment was made by the Teamsters Pension Fund to the *Manchester Union Leader* for a loan in the amount of $1,500,000. The loan was made one week later.

On July 13, after six months of investigations and hearings concerning "invasions of privacy" on the part of such agencies as the Post Office Department and the Food and Drug Administration, Senator Edward Long announced a new series of hearings and investigations on electronic eavesdropping, wiretapping and other surveillance practices by the Internal Revenue Service.

On July 19 Jacques Schiffer was ejected from another federal courtroom. He was in San Juan, Puerto Rico, assisting Frank Ragano in the defense of Frank Chavez and others. When the exasperated judge evicted Schiffer, he admonished him, "If I ever see you on this island again, I'll have you arrested for practicing law without a license."

On July 29 the Court of Appeals affirmed Hoffa's conviction in Chattanooga and also affirmed Judge Wilson's denial of Hoffa's

first motion for a new trial. Chief Judge Paul C. Weick, speaking
for the court, said that Hoffa was the only person who could
possibly benefit from the jury-tampering activities. He added:

> We think that the jury could reasonably have concluded from the
> evidence that the large scale endeavors at jury tampering were not
> brought about by spontaneous action of the other participants, who
> derived no benefit therefrom and were risking criminal prosecu-
> tion; and that the endeavors resulted from the instigation, careful
> planning and agreement in which Hoffa was an active participant.

Relative to the claim by Hoffa's attorneys that they had been
limited in their cross-examination of witnesses, Judge Weick said,
"Almost every question which the ingenuity of counsel could
think of was raised in the trial court."

Hoffa's agents immediately went back to work in Chattanooga.
With the help of a pimp and a bellhop, they lined up prostitutes
who were willing to swear, for a price, they had slept with members of the jury. The girls were carefully screened and indoc-
trinated as to what was expected of them. They would
subsequently pick out from photographs the juror with whom
they supposedly had relations during the trial. They would also
pick out the photograph of the deputy marshal who had supposedly arranged the liaison. One girl even swore she had had
relations with the judge.

In September, 1965, Hoffa filed his third motion for a new trial
supported by affidavits of four of the prostitutes swearing they had
had relations with specific jurors, arranged by specific marshals.
One of them, Marie Monday, swore she had met with Judge Wilson at the Reed House Hotel during the trial and that he had told
her he was going to "get Hoffa." The motion also demanded that
Judge Wilson recuse himself. When the filing of the motion did not
create sufficient publicity, Hoffa's attorney, Daniel Maher, and
Hoffa associate I. Irving Davidson went to see the editors of the
Washington Post. During the conversation with the editors, in an
attempt to create more enthusiasm for the story the attorney and
his associate mentioned that they had a tape of Marie Monday's
statement about Judge Wilson which was more salacious than the
affidavit. The *Post* editors were disgusted and declined to listen to
the tape.

In his denial of the third motion on September 12, 1965, Judge
Wilson labeled Marie Monday's affidavit "a complete and total

fabrication and fraud," and said that "patent perjury" had been committed. Judge Wilson added that the government's affidavits from the jurors and marshals "are not refuted by the signatures upon the affidavits of four women who admit selling their bodies, if not their signature, for immoral purposes for twenty dollars." One of the girls was subsequently convicted of perjury, and Marie Monday recanted her affidavit.

Meanwhile, the pressure on Don Vestal to use his influence to get Bob Vick to change his testimony continued. Plans were set in motion to split Vestal's local. Jim Harding told Jim Craighead that the local would be split unless Vestal helped Hoffa. He also urged Craighead to run against Vestal or to back someone else to do it. The strike at Lawrenceburg continued without strike benefits. Hoffa told Craighead that if he could talk to "the little man" and get some help from him, there would be no further problem about strike benefits.

On October 20 the Department of Labor issued a news release which stated that an audit of the records of the International Brotherhood of Teamsters showed that union funds in the amount of $570,396.84 had been spent for Hoffa's defense in the three trials in Nashville, Chattanooga and Chicago. The department had finally gained access to the records when the Court of Appeals ruled earlier in the year that under the Landrum-Griffin Act the Secretary of Labor had the authority to review such records.

On October 23 in New York City sixteen hundred persons turned out in the ballroom of the Americana Hotel for a $100-a-plate testimonial dinner for Hoffa. One speaker, C. B. Moore, the head of the Philadelphia chapter of the NAACP, praised Hoffa and said, "He's just about like Jesus Christ who died on the cross. Bobby Kennedy was on one side, some informers from the Teamsters on the other." Tony Provenzano also spoke. The dinner was held to raise funds for Hoffa's defense.

In November rumors again began circulating about various members of the Executive Board making moves to run for Hoffa's job at the next Teamsters Convention the following July. Newspaper articles reported that Harold Gibbons and Einar Mohn, the head of the Western Conference of Teamsters, were the two potential front runners. Both men disclaimed any intention of running if Hoffa were still in office, i.e., not in prison. Finally Mohn issued a statement in which he said that since no vacancy existed in the office of general president, any discussion about his running at that time was academic. He went on to say, however, "Should the present General President not seek re-election or should a vacancy occur, I will be a candidate for the office."

Those Executive Board members who had talked secretly of ousting Hoffa from office if he was convicted in Chattanooga had decided after the Chattanooga conviction that they would take action if he was convicted in Chicago. After the Chicago conviction they decided they should wait until the Court of Appeals had acted. Now that the Court of Appeals had acted, they decided to wait until Hoffa took his appeals to the Supreme Court. Mohn's statement—the only forthright one that had been made—was also to become meaningless, because Hoffa would still be very much on the scene when the next convention was held in July, 1966.

On November 16 the Tennessee and Chattanooga bar associations moved to disbar Harry Berke, Hoffa's attorney at the Chattanooga trial, charging that Berke had charged usurious interest on a loan to a client.

In November, 1965, Red Vaughn, a former business agent for Local 327, asked Bob Vick how much money it would take for Vick to help Hoffa. Vick told Vaughn that there was no way he could help Hoffa and that Vaughn could get himself in legal difficulties by what he was doing. Vaughn then told Vick that some cold night they might drag Vick's body out of the river.

On January 5, 1966, Robert G. "Bobby" Baker, the former majority secretary of the United States Senate, was indicted by a federal grand jury in the District of Columbia for tax evasion and fraud. The indictment climaxed a year-long grand jury investigation under the direction of Bill Bittman, assisted by departmental attorneys Donald Page Moore and Austin Mitler. The Baker case, which first surfaced in the fall of 1963, had dragged through almost two years of investigation by Senate subcommittees, the Internal Revenue Service and the FBI. Finally Jack Miller had appointed Bittman to take over the investigation and conduct the grand jury inquiry. There was considerable speculation that Baker, who had been President Johnson's protégé and close confidant, would somehow escape prosecution. It turned out that the speculation was well founded. Several efforts were made to get Bittman off the case and an eleventh-hour effort was made within the administration to water down the indictment drastically. Only Bittman's perseverance and his threat to resign and publicly denounce the fix efforts kept the case intact.

During the investigation Bittman discovered that the FBI had installed and monitored a listening device in the suite of businessman Fred Black in the Sheraton-Carlton Hotel in Washington, D.C. Black, who had been convicted of income tax evasion, was a close friend and associate of Baker's. As a result of Bittman's discovery, the Department of Justice advised the Supreme Court, which was considering Black's appeal, of the existence of the listening device and the fact that conversations between Black and his attorney had been overheard. The Supreme Court set aside Black's conviction and ordered that he be given a new trial. The Department of Justice then advised the court that it would review its files to determine whether electronic eavesdropping had occurred in other pending cases.

The department instructed the FBI and other investigative agencies to search their records and furnish the department information concerning all instances wherein electronic eavesdropping had been employed in pending cases. An ad hoc committee was established within the department to review these cases and advise the appropriate court of the facts for its determination. As the results came in, it was apparent that both the FBI and the Internal Revenue Service had installed numerous listening devices in their pursuit of organized crimes cases. Consequently, some prosecutions were abandoned, and as the year went on, hearings were held in a number of cases before the courts to determine whether the evidence was tainted by electronic eavesdropping.

These revelations tended to corroborate and lend further credence to Senator Edward Long's findings and proclamations of extensive "big brother" activities by law enforcement agencies. The Internal Revenue Service, never a popular agency with the public because of its role as tax collector, had continued to be the target of investigations and hearings by Senator Long's committee since the previous July.

On January 31, 1966, the Supreme Court agreed to review Hoffa's appeal from the Chattanooga conviction. In so doing, the court limited its review to only one point in Hoffa's appeal—the question of whether evidence obtained from Partin was admissible in the Chattanooga trial. Justices Byron White and Abe Fortas disqualified themselves from hearing the case—White because he had been in the Justice Department during the Hoffa investigations, and Fortas because he reportedly had represented a Teamsters dissident group in a suit against the International.

In February, 1966, Don Vestal was approached by George Broda and Ewing King, who suggested they could be of mutual benefit to each other if Vestal could get Vick to help Hoffa. At King's request, Vestal went to Washington, where he was told that if Vick would give a statement for Hoffa, all the legal fees in connection with the Lawrenceburg strike would be paid. In addition, Vestal was told that he could then go to a hotel in Chicago where he would be handed $10,000 in cash.

Other activities on Hoffa's behalf continued elsewhere. In Detroit another benefit dinner was held to raise more funds for his defense. In attendance, along with other notables, was the police commissioner, Ray Giardin. According to labor columnist John Herling, C. B. Moore, the head of the Philadelphia chapter of the NAACP, conveyed an offer of substantial contributions to the NAACP in an effort to enlist the Legal Defense Fund of that organization to file an amicus curiae brief in the Supreme Court on Hoffa's behalf. This apparent attempt to influence recently appointed Justice Thurgood Marshall was rejected by the NAACP, whose officials stated that if they thought there was a civil liberties issue involved in the Hoffa case, they would have intervened on their own and would neither seek nor accept contributions to do so.

This was not the only activity which appeared designed to influence Justice Marshall. While he was still Solicitor General of the United States, Martha Louis, the wife of Joe Louis, had attempted to approach him on Hoffa's behalf. At about the same time, one Martha *Lewis* was listed in records of the Teamsters Pension Fund as sharing in a fee of $30,000 on a loan to a Detroit hospital. The application for the loan was submitted by Cal Kovens. Two years later Cal Kovens and Martha Louis were successful applicants for a $1,470,333 loan for a hospital in Los Angeles.

On April 7 a civil trial got under way in the Court of General Sessions in Washington, D.C. A Los Angeles firm was suing Hoffa's attorney Daniel Maher to recover a $7500 fee it claimed to have paid Maher in an unsuccessful attempt to obtain a loan from the Teamsters Pension Fund. The firm charged that Maher was to have been paid $30,000 to obtain the loan.

In April, 1966, a contractor from Gonzales, Louisiana, was contacted by James Harding and offered a loan from the Teamsters Pension Fund. The contractor was in dire need of the loan and went to Washington to work out the details. He was told that in order to get the loan he would first have to sign an affidavit stating that he had paid off one of Partin's business agents as a result of extortion threats. The contractor signed the affidavit, which he knew was not true and which he told them was not true. When he returned to Louisiana he had second thoughts and went to Partin and revealed what had happened. He gave Partin an affidavit relating the story and he did not get the loan.

On June 14, at the quarterly meeting of the Central States Drivers Council in Chicago, Hoffa announced an immediate and intensive organizing drive to bring professional football players into the Teamsters Union. Hoffa said the drive would be under the direction of Harold Gibbons, the head of the Professional Athletic Division of the union, and would eventually extend to the organization of all professional athletes.

On June 15 Hoffa's appeal from his conviction for defrauding the Pension Fund was argued before Judge Austin in Chicago by attorneys for the defense and the government. Judge Austin affirmed the conviction and denied Hoffa's motion for a new trial.

In Nashville Jim Craighead met Sid Zagri at a Teamsters meeting. Zagri told Craighead that the Lawrenceburg strike, which was now over, could have been won if Vick had "helped the boss." Zagri urged Craighead to help Hoffa with Vick even if Vestal would not. Zagri said that if they helped Hoffa they would be "sitting on top," and if they did not the local would be taken away from them. Subsequently Zagri called Craighead and told him to "hurry up and get Vestal and Vick together and get them to come up here so that the local can be saved and there will be extra money for everything." Zagri said that if they did not comply soon, the local would be taken away.

On July 4, 1966, the convention of the International Brotherhood of Teamsters opened in Miami Beach. Hoffa had announced beforehand his intention to rewrite the constitution again, this time to provide for the establishment of a new office—general vice president—the occupant of which would run the union in the event Hoffa went to prison. Hoffa had also made it quite clear that if he did go to prison, he would reclaim the vacant office of general president when he got out. He also told newsmen he intended to see to it that Frank Fitzsimmons became the new general vice president. He denied that Fitzsimmons would be merely a "caretaker" leader so that Hoffa could run the union from prison.

Harold Gibbons had expressed his intention to oppose Hoffa's plan and, if necessary, to run against Fitzsimmons for the new office. Hoffa told Associated Press reporter Neil Gilbride that he didn't think Gibbons would run against Fitzsimmons, and if he did, he would not only lose the election, but would also probably lose his seat on the Executive Board because Teamsters official Roy Williams from Kansas City would then run for that seat with Hoffa's support.

By the time the convention got under way Gibbons had seen the error of his ways and decided not to oppose Hoffa in any way. In fact, he agreed to give a speech seconding Hoffa's nomination. The seventeen hundred delegates roared their approval as Hoffa pushed through not only the new office of general vice president, but also other changes in the constitution to give himself an even greater dictatorial control over the union than he had obtained at the convention in the same city five years earlier. His salary was increased another $25,000 to $100,000 a year with the provision that he would continue to receive it if he went to prison. The delegates approved a resolution authorizing the past payment of $1,277,680 by the union for legal fees for Teamsters officials in criminal cases, and also authorized "further expenditure of any sums necessary for the defense of these or further similar criminal prosecutions that may be brought against the union." Only one delegate, Larry Thomas, the black president of Local 596 in Philadelphia, rose and voted in opposition to this resolution. The only other resistance to Hoffa's new program came from a scattering of delegates who voiced opposition to the amendment raising the members' dues from $5 to $6 a month. Another amendment was passed centralizing authority in Hoffa's hands to appoint negotiating committees and establish procedures for areawide, industrywide or national contracts. Hoffa was also given the power to submit an employer's settlement offer directly to a local if the local leaders did not do so.

When reporters tried to interview Larry Thomas, who had voted against the payment of legal fees, they were barred by the sergeants at arms, and Hoffa directed a verbal attack on the press in general and reporter Clark Mollenhoff in particular.

Two of the speakers at the convention were Senator Eugene McCarthy of Minnesota and Senator Edward Long of Missouri. Senator McCarthy spoke of the need on the part of the press to "give as much protection as it can to those who are accused." Senator Long recalled attending a Teamsters meeting in Missouri at which Hoffa spoke several years earlier. Turning to Hoffa, Long said, "After hearing you speak, I told that crowd and told you that you delight your friends, and you amaze your enemies, and to keep on fighting them, Jimmy."

The convention unanimously elected Frank Fitzsimmons as the new general vice president and reelected Jimmy Hoffa as the general president.

Taking advantage of the climate created through the revelations by both Senator Long's committee and the Justice Department of electronic eavesdropping by government agencies, the Hoffa forces began a campaign to demonstrate, one way or another, that Hoffa, too, had been the victim of illegal wiretapping or bugging. In August Hoffa placed an ad in the Tennessee newspapers offering a $25,000 reward for anyone who could furnish information about electronic eavesdropping in his case.

In Nashville Don Vestal filed a suit in the state court asking for a restraining order against Hoffa and the International Union to stop them from interfering in the operation of Local 327. The petition set forth the efforts by Hoffa and others to pressure Vestal into influencing Vick to help Hoffa, and the harassment that had resulted when he refused.

In Chattanooga Jacques Schiffer surrendered to start serving his sentence for contempt of court. A last-minute plea by his attorney, Harvey Silets, was rejected by Judge Wilson who said, "The court is of the opinion that Mr. Schiffer purposely set about not to avoid error but rather to create error in the proceedings of the trial . . . he deliberately set about to disrupt proceedings of the court."

On August 8 Harry Berke, another defense attorney in the Chattanooga trial, was disbarred from the practice of law in the courts of Tennessee for a period of two years for charging usurious interest on loans to a client and for misleading the court in a prior disbarment proceeding.

On September 22 a group of well-dressed and well-manicured men, preparing to have lunch at the La Stella Restaurant in Forest Hills, New York, were arrested by police in what was described as a "little Apalachin meeting." They were all Mafia leaders or lieutenants, including New York Mafia chieftains Joseph Colombo, Thomas Eboli, Joseph Gallo, Carlo Gambino and Michele Miranda. Also in attendance were Tampa, Florida, boss Santos Trafficante and New Orleans Mafia leader Carlos Marcello. In addition to the Mafia figures, two attorneys were present, including sometime Hoffa lawyer Frank Ragano, whose most recent tour of duty had been the representation of Frank Chavez, the head of the Teamsters in Puerto Rico.

On October 4 the Court of Appeals upheld the conviction of Hoffa and his co-defendants in the Chicago Pension Fund case. The following day reporter Robert M. Lewin, in an article in the Chicago *Daily News,* quoted Teamsters sources as stating that the Executive Board had the authority to continue to pay Hoffa his $100,000-a-year salary if he went to prison. The sources told Lewin that a prison term could be construed as traveling for a rest period to conserve one's health.

The limited hearing before the Supreme Court on the appeal from the tampering conviction was held on October 13. Washington attorney Joseph A. Fanelli, a newcomer to the Teamsters legal scene, argued the case for Hoffa. The government was represented by Fred Vinson, the Assistant Attorney General in charge of the Criminal Division who had replaced Jack Miller, accompanied by Nat Lewin. Fanelli referred to me in his arguments as a "nonlawyer layman." He argued that the government had deprived Hoffa of his rights under the Constitution by planting Partin in the defense camp in Nashville. In spite of a brilliant summation by Nat Lewin, following Vinson's arguments for the government, we were not at all certain when it was over how the Justices would rule.

During the weeks that followed, while the Supreme Court was considering the case, the improvers made a move that reached a new plateau of arrogance, even for them. A Teamsters official approached the brother of Supreme Court Justice William Brennan. The Justice's brother, who owned a brewery, was told that if his brother did not vote right on the Hoffa case, the brewery would be closed down and would never reopen.

On November 21 the Supreme Court refused to review an appeal by Miami attorney Ben Cohen from his conviction for income tax evasion. Nine days later he surrendered in Miami and pleaded for mercy before Judge Charles B. Fulton. Judge Fulton said, "I am moved and shaken by the responsibility I have in this matter." He added, however, "I can't believe now that I should change my mind or recede from my sentence of some months ago. I just couldn't live with myself if I did anything different from what I have done." Cohen, once one of the most powerful men in Miami, was committed to begin serving his eighteen-month sentence.

On December 12 the Supreme Court affirmed the conviction of

Hoffa and his co-defendants in the Chattanooga trial. This would ordinarily have been the end of the line. But Hoffa was not ready to give up.

Two days earlier, on a Saturday afternoon, the whole question of who had authorized widespread electronic bugging by the FBI in organized crime cases had broken out in the open. In a letter to Representative H. R. Gross of Iowa, which was released to the press, FBI Director J. Edgar Hoover said that Robert Kennedy, while Attorney General, had authorized the eavesdropping. Kennedy denied it and countered with a letter he had received from former FBI Assistant Director Courtney A. Evans in which he stated that he had never discussed the use by the bureau of these devices with Kennedy. The feud continued over the weekend with further exchanges between Kennedy and Hoover.

On Monday evening, the day the Supreme Court turned down Hoffa's appeal, Senator Edward Long announced that he would invite Hoover and Kennedy to testify before his committee concerning the matter. Up until this point, Senator Long had not once delved into the subject of electronic eavesdropping by the FBI. He now explained this way: "We had been extremely reluctant to call officials from the F.B.I. and the Justice Department because we did not want to do any possible harm to national security or the drive against organized crime. Now that some of the principal participants have opened up these matters, we feel that an on-the-record airing is necessary."

Senator Long had not been concerned about the drive against organized crime during his investigations and hearings over the past year and a half concerning the use of electronic eavesdropping by the Internal Revenue Service in organized crime cases. In fact, he had ridiculed the organized crime program and effectively destroyed it in the Internal Revenue Service. His reluctance to investigate the FBI earlier and his eagerness to exploit the Hoover-Kennedy feud appeared to be motivated by other considerations.

Kennedy agreed to appear before the committee if Senator Long would also call as witnesses previous and subsequent Attorneys General and if Hoover would produce all of his files relating to the matter. Senator Long did not pursue the matter further and neither Hoover nor Kennedy appeared. It is of interest that Hoover had told President Johnson earlier that Robert Kennedy was not aware of the bureau's electronic eavesdropping activities.

Time was now running out for Jimmy Hoffa. He had until

February 11, 1967, to file a petition for a rehearing before the Supreme Court. Such petitions are routinely filed and rarely granted. The actions of the Hoffa forces now became concerted, desperate and bold.

In Chicago four trucking company executives went on a nationally televised news program and protested that if Hoffa went to prison before the completion of the upcoming negotiations on the national agreement (scheduled to begin January 17, 1967), the stability of the trucking industry would be dangerously threatened.

In Detroit a "Friends of Hoffa Committee," headed by William Bufalino, was set up. The committee offered a $100,000 reward to anyone furnishing information about bugging or wiretapping of Hoffa.

In Manchester, New Hampshire, William Loeb announced that the *Manchester Union Leader* was offering a $100,000 reward for information about electronic eavesdropping in connection with the Hoffa cases. One week earlier Loeb had written to the Teamsters Pension Fund with a request that he be allowed to use money for "operating expenses" from the proceeds of the last loan. Loeb placed advertisements about his reward offer in newspapers around the country. Including Hoffa's earlier reward offer, there was now the sum of $225,000 being dangled for information to help Hoffa.

In Houston, Texas, a housepainter named James D. East, formerly from Chattanooga, read the advertisement and decided to try to collect the money. He called Loeb, who put him in touch with his attorney, James Malloy. East told them that he knew two bellhops at the Patten Hotel (where Hoffa had stayed during the Chattanooga trial) who had information about Hoffa's phone being tapped. Malloy and reporter Arthur Egan met East in Chattanooga. East was given $2150 but was not able to deliver affidavits from the two bellhops he had talked to. When Malloy became angry and wanted the money back, East became frightened and called *Chattanooga Times* reporter Fred Hixon and told him the story. Hixon printed the story, East returned to Houston and Egan and Malloy went back to Manchester.

On December 20, 1966, Loeb went to see Walter Trohan, Washington bureau chief of the *Chicago Tribune.* He offered Trohan a portion of the $100,000 if he could furnish information about eavesdropping in the Hoffa case. Trohan said that he did not know whether there had been such activity in the Hoffa case. Loeb told

Trohan that I. Irving Davidson, a Hoffa associate, had given him the name of Eddie Jones as a likely wiretapper for Robert Kennedy. Jones had worked for Kennedy on the McClellan Committee and was then employed by the Immigration and Naturalization Service. Loeb asked who else would have engaged in such activity for Kennedy. Trohan suggested Carmine Bellino and me. Trohan then arranged for an appointment for Loeb with FBI Assistant Director Cartha DeLoach for later that day.

Loeb and DeLoach later gave conflicting versions of their meeting. According to DeLoach, Loeb told him that Trohan had said that Carmine Bellino, Eddie Jones and I had engaged in wiretapping activities for Robert Kennedy. DeLoach said he did not know. DeLoach said that Loeb asked whether any of us would furnish information if paid a sufficient amount of money. Again, DeLoach said he did not know. Loeb then asked DeLoach if he thought he should obtain an order from the Supreme Court to take our depositions. DeLoach said that was up to him. According to Loeb, DeLoach acknowledged that Bellino, Jones and I were the wiretappers in the Hoffa case.

The following day Loeb called DeLoach. He said that he was calling long distance from a pay phone, and that his call might be out of line. Then he asked DeLoach if J. Edgar Hoover would send a telegram stating that Robert Kennedy had engaged in electronic surveillance of Hoffa. He said that if he would, $100,000 would be paid to Hoover or the Hoover's favorite charity. According to DeLoach, he told Loeb that Hoover would never stoop to such tactics. He said that Loeb then asked if DeLoach had personal knowledge of such activity. DeLoach says he told Loeb that he should talk to the Department of Justice for any such information. Loeb's version is that DeLoach indicated he would like to help but could not get involved.

On the same day Loeb sent a letter to Supreme Court Justice Potter Stewart, a former college classmate. In the letter Loeb indicated that there was a matter relating to the Hoffa case that he wished to bring to the attention of the court. He said that he had had a meeting with "one of the top officials of the highest investigatory organization in our country" and, according to Loeb, the official with whom he was speaking said, "Of course Attorney General Kennedy had used wire taps on Hoffa. . . . There is no question about it." Loeb said that the same official then gave him the names of the three people involved in the wiretap operations.

Loeb then told Mr. Justice Stewart that he had suggested to the official that his statement be made formally and, according to Loeb, the man had responded: "If there is anything I can do to help, I want to do it, but I cannot become personally involved and if you say I ever said this to you I will deny that I've even seen you." Loeb ended his letter by stating that he presumed the unnamed official would have to respond to a court subpoena and would in that case have to tell the truth.

During late December and early January contacts were made with a number of people by representatives of Loeb and Hoffa, using the $225,000 as bait, in attempts to get information about wiretapping. Arthur Egan contacted a secretary at the Democratic National Committee. He told her that the lawyer who had been hired by the Justice Department to try the Chattanooga case did not even have a law degree; that President Kennedy knew that illegal means were used to "get Hoffa"; that reports concerning Hoffa were typed at the Democratic National Committee; and that he had offered me $200,000 but that I wouldn't tell him anything. The girl didn't know what he was talking about and told him so. Approaches were made by others to Carmine Bellino, Charlie Shaffer, newsman Clark Mollenhoff, a deputy United States marshal and the owner of a restaurant in Washington where my wife and I sometimes had dinner.

In early 1967 Hoffa admitted to Vestal that he had arranged for information to be furnished to the Department of Labor about Local 327 to harass Vestal. Hoffa told Vestal that if he could get Vick to help him, he would give Vestal $50,000 and put him on the International payroll as a general organizer at $25,000 a year with a $100,000 bonus. Hoffa said that after one year, Vestal could retire at $25,000 a year. Vestal told Hoffa that there was nothing he could do.

On January 24, 1967, I was at my office at NBC when I received a phone call from Jerry Landauer of the *Wall Street Journal.* He asked me if I knew a man named Bud Nichols. When I told him I did not, he said that a man by that name had given an affidavit to Hoffa in which he swore that I had paid him to bug the phones and mattresses of the jurors in Chattanooga as well as the rooms of Hoffa and his attorneys. Landauer said that according to the affidavit, Nichols had picked out my picture from a group of photographs and claimed I had been to his home and met his wife and children. I told Landauer that I had never met the man and that the affidavit was false. But it was an eerie feeling, having a man

I did not know and had never met describing in detail what he alleged our relationship to be.

The following day a front-page story in the *Wall Street Journal* told Nichols' story:

> Bud Nichols swears that Walter Sheridan, former head of the Justice Department's special "Hoffa squad," instructed him to slip tiny transmitters under the mattresses of the Chattanooga jurors when they were sequestered in the Reed House hostelry there. Moreover Mr. Nichols is prepared to swear that he placed four microphone "bugs" and tapped six telephone lines leading to rooms in the Patten Hotel which were occupied during the trial by Mr. Hoffa and his legal counselors.

On January 27 Hoffa filed with the Supreme Court a "Motion for Relief Because of Government Wiretapping, Electronic Eavesdropping and Other Intrusions." There were twenty-one affidavits attached to the motion. One of these was by Benjamin "Bud" Nichols. There were some significant differences between the Nichols affidavit that was filed and the one Landauer had seen earlier. This affidavit said nothing about bugging the jurors' mattresses or about my having been in Nichols' home. It did state that he had bugged the phones in the jurors' rooms at my direction. (There were no phones in the jurors' rooms.) It also described in detail my meetings with him and his bugging and tapping of Hoffa's and his attorneys' rooms following sketches I allegedly had furnished him. A number of the other affidavits were by Hoffa and his attorneys stating that they did in fact use those rooms and those phones described in Nichols' affidavit. There was also an affidavit by Bernard Spindel, Hoffa's own wiretapper, attesting to Nichols' electronic competence and knowledge of the structure of the Patten Hotel in Chattanooga.

But that was not all. There were affidavits by Herman A. Frazier, Nelson Paden and Albert Cole, the three Huntington, West Virginia, men who had been indicted and acquitted of jury tampering in the Nashville Test Fleet case. They all swore that I had played tape recordings for them of conversations between Hoffa and his attorneys during the grand jury investigation four years earlier. Frazier said that when he had read in the paper that Hoffa might be going to jail soon, he decided to tell him, as he almost had on several occasions over the years, what he knew about his phone being tapped. He said that Paden and Cole had promised to back him up, and he then sent telegrams to Hoffa and Bufalino. It was a remarkable story, as were the affidavits.

They described in great detail the contents of the conversations I was supposed to have played for them, and actually quoted from them. (It would have been an amazing display of memory—except that it was completely false.) Again, there were affidavits from Hoffa and his attorneys stating that the conversations the affidavits described had, in fact, taken place.

There was also an affidavit by a Detroit policeman, Paul Quaglia, stating that he had once tapped the telephone of William Bufalino at the direction of police sergeant William De Pugh.

Bufalino had filed a lawsuit against the Michigan Bell Telephone Company in 1965 charging that his phone had been tapped. At a subsequent hearing on a motion by the telephone company for a summary judgment, Officer Quaglia had testified that he had placed a tap on Bufalino's phone on instructions from De Pugh. De Pugh, who had since left the police department to become an intelligence agent with the Internal Revenue Service in Detroit, also testified and denied that he had directed Quaglia to place such a tap. A Long Committee investigator, Gordon Homme, was present at the hearing.

There were other affidavits from Hoffa's friend I. Irving Davidson stating that John Hooker had once told him that we had tapped Hoffa's phone in Nashville and Chattanooga, and an affidavit giving William Loeb's account of his conversations with DeLoach. A supplemental motion was filed, attached to which was an affidavit by Hazel Fulton of Huntington, West Virginia, who had been a government witness in the Chattanooga trial. Her statement was very similar to those furnished by Frazier, Paden and Cole. She also swore that I had played tape recordings of conversations between Hoffa and his attorneys.

While we were digesting all this, the campaign went on. On February 1 Gordon Homme of Senator Long's committee visited Frank Grimsley in Atlanta. He told Grimsley he had a subpoena for him but never did serve it. He had a drink with Grimsley and during their conversation let Frank know that he had a detailed knowledge of his financial condition, which at the time was poor. Homme asked Grimsley what he would do if anyone ever offered him money for information. Grimsley said that he would punch anyone making such an offer in the jaw. I had received a telephone call from committee counsel Bernard Fensterwald three weeks earlier. He said that he might want me to testify before the committee, but I had heard nothing further from him.

On February 2, 1967, Senators Wayne Morse, Ernest Gruening, Bob Bartlett and Mark Hatfield made speeches on the Senate floor calling for an in-depth investigation into bugging and wiretapping by the government.

On February 4, 1967, the Committee to Preserve American Freedom held its first meeting in Detroit. The Committee had been formed by friends of Hoffa's in Detroit to protest against government eavesdropping. The principal speaker at the meeting was Senator Edward Long.

On February 7, 1967, Sid Zagri was trapped and burned to death in a penthouse restaurant fire in Montgomery, Alabama. William Loeb immediately sent a telegram to Governor Lurleen Wallace of Alabama in which he said that Zagri had been in Alabama following a very strong lead that might have led to overturning Hoffa's conviction. He said, "Since the agents of that sinister conspiracy against Mr. Hoffa, in my estimation, will stop at nothing, including murder, and since it seems incredible to me that a fire should have soared so quickly without artificial stimulation, I would suggest very careful consideration of this aspect of the tragedy." In an accompanying statement, Loeb said, "I most sincerely hope the Alabama authorities will get to the very bottom of this tragedy. Only about two weeks ago, Zagri cautioned me against revealing the names of certain individuals who were attempting to help Hoffa in the face of powerful forces arrayed against him and said, 'Don't forget our opponents will stop at nothing, including murder.'" I have been told that Sid Zagri's daughter still believes we may have been responsible for her father's death.

On February 9 an article appeared in *The Chattanooga Times* stating that Bud Nichols had been observed back in Knoxville, Tennessee, driving a new white Cadillac.

On February 15 Senator Edward Long announced that he hoped to resume hearings on electronic eavesdropping on March 16. However, on Friday, February 17, the Internal Revenue Service was asked to produce William DePugh, who had allegedly supervised Quaglia's tapping of Bufalino, before an executive session of the committee on *Sunday* morning, February 19, at 10 A.M.! It was a highly unusual time for a Senate committee to be meeting. When DePugh arrived for the hearing there were no Senators present—

only committee counsel Bernard Fensterwald and staff member
Gordon Homme—who questioned DePugh about his knowledge
of bugging and wiretapping in Detroit and about Quaglia in particular. It was becoming very obvious that Senator Long's committee was being used in a last-ditch effort to bail out Hoffa. It had
been anticipated that the Supreme Court would rule on Hoffa's
motion for relief within the next week.

The February 20 issue of *The Nation* featured another article by
Fred Cook entitled "Anything to Get Hoffa." Again, Cook took
Hoffa's allegations and printed them as facts. The contents of the
affidavits submitted to the Supreme Court with the motion for
relief were laid out in a seven-page narrative. Cook made passing
reference to the fact that Solicitor General Thurgood Marshall had
submitted a denial of the allegations to the Supreme Court and
commented, ". . . it is not necessary to interpret the evidence
detailed above as casting doubt on Mr. Marshall's word. More
likely, he is only one of many Americans who have not yet grasped
the extreme sophistication with which certain government agencies cut the corners of veracity."

In fact, it was Mr. Cook who was again participating in the truly
sophisticated prostitution of veracity in which Hoffa's agents and
apologists had been engaged for some time. The filing of blatantly
false affidavits in courts—now even in the Supreme Court of the
United States—and the peddling of lies in the Congress and in the
press to influence the courts was almost incredible in its arrogance.
That was the real sophistication.

On February 22 a man named David Ferrie was found dead in
bed in his apartment in New Orleans. Jim Garrison, the District
Attorney of New Orleans, who had received scant public attention
thus far in his announced investigation into the assassination of
President Kennedy, now proclaimed that Ferrie had been the key
person in the plot to kill Kennedy. The press and the media around
the world took notice of the startling disclosure and NBC sent me
to New Orleans to look into it.

On February 27 Hoffa's motion for relief was denied by the
Supreme Court which ruled, in effect, that it was properly a mo
tion for a new trial and should, as such, be filed in the District
Court in Chattanooga. On March 1 the Supreme Court denied
Hoffa's petition for rehearing.

That same day Frank Chavez, the head of the Teamsters Union

in Puerto Rico, left San Juan for Washington, D.C. Chavez had recently sworn to kill Robert Kennedy, Ed Partin and me if Hoffa went to prison. Chavez was a cocky, rough Teamster who carried a gun and traveled with two armed bodyguards. He went frequently to New York City, where he always stayed at the same hotel. He had the hotel management so intimidated that he never paid the bill and they never tried to collect it. During the Chattanooga trial he had called an associate in Puerto Rico and reported that things looked bad because the jury was being watched so closely by the government that "they had not been able to get to them."

During the 1964 New York Senate race Chavez had traveled to New York for the ostensible purpose of agitating among Puerto Ricans in that city against Robert Kennedy's candidacy. Chavez's real purpose was to kill Robert Kennedy. Someone dissuaded him at that time from going through with it.

The FBI had advised the Department of Justice of Chavez's threats, and accordingly the department asked the FBI in late February to make contact with airlines so that they might be notified in the event Chavez left Puerto Rico. The FBI replied that it did not have jurisdiction to do so. Tom Kennelly thereupon called his own sources in Puerto Rico and asked them to be alert for a departure by Chavez.

On March 1 Kennelly was called by one of his sources, who told him that Chavez had left Puerto Rico for Washington, accompanied by his usual two bodyguards. The source said that all of them were armed. It was known that when in Washington, Chavez usually stayed at the Continental Hotel. The former chief of U.S. marshals, James P. McShane, enlisted the cooperation of the Washington Police Department to locate Chavez. The police ascertained that he was at the Continental Hotel and agreed to maintain a surveillance. Senator Kennedy was in New York and his office was alerted. McShane also arranged for police protection in the vicinity of the Senator's home in McLean. He called me in New Orleans and told me what had transpired and said that he had arranged for the police in Montgomery County, Maryland, where I lived, to maintain a twenty-four-hour surveillance of my home.

I later learned that Chavez did, in fact, intend to do exactly what he had threatened. Hoffa pleaded with him not to do it and told him that anything like that would destroy any chance he had to either stay out of prison or to get out if he had to go. Chavez finally surrendered his gun to Hoffa and returned to Puerto Rico. Several months later he was murdered by one of his bodyguards.

In Baton Rouge Aubrey Young, who at that time was an administrative assistant to Governor John McKeithen of Louisiana, came to Partin and told him that it would be worth $25,000 to Young to set up a meeting between Partin and D'Alton Smith. Smith was a close associate of Louisiana Mafia boss Carlos Marcello. The meeting took place at Smith's house with Young present. Smith told Partin that if he could furnish information about wiretapping in the Hoffa case, "the sky's the limit. It's worth at least a million bucks. You'll be put in charge of all loans in the south." Smith told Partin that whatever information he furnished would have to be backed up by "strong people, like your brother." (Partin's brother had been in Chattanooga during the trial.) When Partin asked Smith what "they" wanted him to say, Smith said, "We'll come up with something. Schiffer's going to write up something—a statement to be signed by you and two or three others, preferably including your brother." Smith then called Allen Dorfman. While he was telephoning he said, "You know, Dorfman's controlling this thing—he's running it. The 'little man' is holding the money." Smith later told Partin that the "little man" was Carlos Marcello. On the phone Smith told Dorfman that he and Partin had had a friendly conversation and asked Dorfman when he could see him.

Smith told Partin that "they" had helped Senator Russell Long get elected whip, that he had carried money to Long from New Orleans and that he and Allen Dorfman had bought seven votes for Long in the whip election. Smith told Partin that he had been promised a Pension Fund loan for an apartment complex in Los Angeles and would share control with Partin of all Pension Fund loans in the area.

Later, while driving Partin home, Smith said that "they" could protect him and mentioned that there were "contracts" out on Partin.

Young called Partin several times during the next two days. During one of these calls he asked Partin to pick a Hoffa attorney whom he would talk to. Partin replied he would talk to Jacques Schiffer. Young also told Partin that Carlos Marcello was supposed to have been holding the $25,000 for Young for arranging the meeting between Smith and Partin. He told Partin that he had called Marcello about the money but was told he didn't know anything about it. He said that he was going to have to go to see Marcello personally about it.

Shortly thereafter Smith called Partin and told him that Schiffer was coming to town. He said that he would pick Partin up at the Pancake House and take him to meet Schiffer. Smith did so and they drove to nearby Gramercy, where they found Schiffer and Jim Harding parked in a car on the shoulder of the road. Schiffer and Harding got out of the car and shook hands with Partin. Then Schiffer asked Partin to strip down so he could be sure he was not wearing a recording device. Partin said, "All I'm wearing is a gun, which I intend to use if I have to." Schiffer became frightened and said, "I ain't done nothing to you. Let's get a room and strip down and talk." Partin said, "As long as I can hold the gun, I'll strip down as much as you like." Schiffer then said that there was no need for that and that they might as well just talk there.

Smith complained to Schiffer that he didn't have money for expenses for all the running around he was doing. Schiffer told him the money was in New Orleans and that they would go there and pick it up as soon as they finished their meeting with Partin. Partin then asked about Young's money and Schiffer said that it was in New Orleans too.

Harding said that he had not been involved in the deals and was only there to see that everything was on the up and up. Schiffer asked Partin what his brother could say. Partin said, "There was no wiretapping. If there was any I would have known. You want me to say that taped conversations were played for me or read to me to rehearse my testimony?"

Schiffer answered, "We can prove that you did, if you will come on through."

Then Schiffer said, "We'll go to New Orleans, get the money, and I'll call D'Alton and also get Aubrey Young shut up. He could hurt us."

After Schiffer and Harding left, Smith told Partin that he would call him after he heard from them. He asked Partin how much was in the trust fund that "they got set up for your kids, that Kennedy gave you." Smith said that it couldn't be more than $60,000 and promised they would deposit the money any way Partin wanted it.

Later that day Smith called Partin at the Bellmont Hotel in Baton Rouge to tell him that he had not heard from Schiffer and that he was going to call Dorfman to find out what had happened. When Smith called back, he told Partin that Schiffer and Harding had left town because they thought they were being followed, but they would be back in touch with him.

Several days later Smith called Partin and told him that Schiffer was coming back to town and asked Partin to meet with them at Aubrey Young's house. When Partin arrived, Smith, Schiffer and Young were present. Schiffer handed Partin a four-page typewritten statement and said they had the cash. Smith commented that the supply of cash was unlimited. The statement contained details of how I had read Partin transcripts which he said had come "off the wires." It also contained comments by me to Partin that as a result of tapes, I knew that on a particular Monday Partin would be questioned about narcotics and that I had talked to Kennedy and arranged for Partin to go to Louisville for narcotics tests before Monday. Schiffer said, "This is a cinch because no one knows how we know that." Schiffer said that the other people, including Partin's brother, would have to swear that they were present when I read the transcripts to Partin.

After reading the statement, Partin said, "These are nothing but lies."

Schiffer said, "It will get us what we want. What will it take to get this?"

Partin said, "You're the one doing the buying."

Schiffer said, "How about $5000 apiece for the others."

Smith interjected, "You better make it $10,000 because you're asking for some good boys."

Partin said, "Don't tell me. You're doing the buying. Go talk to them."

The statement also had Partin making derogatory remarks about Hoffa, but declaring he was making the statement as a matter of conscience since Hoffa had been persecuted.

Partin told Schiffer that he would have to take the statement and study it, but Schiffer refused to give it to him. He said that he would leave the statement with Smith and handed it to Smith in everyone's presence. Schiffer said, "If anyone checks, we have business in New Orleans with a client." He then asked Partin, "If I get Hoffa on the phone, will you tell him you will cooperate?"

Partin said, "I'll tell Hoffa if I know anything legal that will help, I'll help if it's not perjury. But this statement is a lie. There was no wiretapping."

Smith then went to the kitchen and placed a call and Partin spoke on the phone to a man he did not think was Hoffa. The man did, however, have the same tone of voice and did close the conversation with Hoffa's familiar "Take care." The man on the phone asked Partin if he would help. Did Partin want to see him go to jail, he asked, after all he had done for him. He said, "All we want is the truth." Partin replied, "I can tell that from the affidavit. If you're hunting for wiretapping, you are wasting your time in my opinion. From what I saw, they were trying to protect themselves from your wiretapper Spindel—watching not tapping."

Shortly thereafter Smith told Partin that they had talked to Dorfman and had met with the "Syndicate crowd" in Chicago, who had put Smith in complete charge. He said there was no longer any worry about money because the man in charge of the whole Syndicate was there, and that if Hoffa double-crossed them, he'd never live to go to prison. The man he spoke to, Smith confided, was even Carlos Marcello's boss.

On March 2, 1967, attorney Harold Brown, who had represented Ewing King during the 1964 jury-tampering trial, left Chattanooga and flew to New Orleans. Brown had now become one of the key attorneys in the efforts to obtain information to help Hoffa. He went to the apartment of Zachary "Red" Strate, one of the former owners of the Fontainebleau Hotel in New Orleans, who had been convicted along with Hoffa in the Chicago trial. Waiting there with Strate were New Orleans Parish Judge Malcolm O'Hara and his court reporter, Julian Levy. Brown dictated a two-page statement to Levy to the effect that during Partin's testimony in the Chattanooga trial, I had gone over with him each evening the transcripts of recordings of conversations between Hoffa and his attorneys.

The following morning the four men journeyed to Baton Rouge in Strate's car with O'Hara driving. They went to the office of James "Buddy" Gill, former administrative assistant and close associate of Senator Russell Long. Prior to their arrival, Gill had called Partin and asked him if he would come over to his office to meet someone. When Partin arrived, he found Gill and Judge O'Hara waiting. Strate and Levy remained in another room. Gill introduced O'Hara to Partin. Gill mentioned that he had heard that Jim Garrison was going to subpoena Partin in connection with his assassination probe. He asked O'Hara whether he could look into it and O'Hara said he thought he could take care of it. The judge then handed Partin the statement prepared by Brown. He asked Partin if he would sign it. Partin read the statement and handed it back to Judge O'Hara, saying he could not sign it because it wasn't true. Judge O'Hara then left the room and Gill asked Partin to reconsider. He told him it would be worth a million dollars in cash. He then asked Partin whether he thought either Judge Daniels or Sargent Pitcher would help them. Partin told him he would have to ask them that.

When Partin left, Gill accompanied the four men to Sabin's Restaurant in Baton Rouge. During lunch Gill left the table, saying he was going to call Pitcher. When he returned to the table he announced that he was going to meet with Pitcher. Sargent Pitcher later described the meeting with Gill. He said Gill came to his farm and asked if they could talk privately. Pitcher said that they were talking on the porch of the cabin, which was secluded and remote, but Gill suggested they go for a walk. They walked to a tree where, according to Pitcher, Gill said, "If you ever repeat what I'm telling you, I will have to deny it . . . I am out here to see you on the Hoffa case. There is a lot of politically prominent people interested in getting Hoffa out of his trouble . . . these political friends of mine want to help him. . . ." Pitcher said that Gill then mentioned Judge O'Hara and said, "We have an affidavit that we want to get Partin to sign . . . we would like you to call Partin and ask him to sign that affidavit." Pitcher said he told Gill he didn't want to have anything to do with it. Gill then returned to the restaurant where the others were waiting and reported that he had not been successful.

At about the same time in a hotel room in New York City, Vaughn Connelly, who had been one of the key witnesses in the conviction of Hoffa in Chicago, was approached by a man who claimed to represent Allen Dorfman. Connelly had been kept in a state of bankruptcy since the foreclosure on his loans from the Pension Fund and was in dire need of financial relief. The man gave Connelly a prepared affidavit recanting his testimony and asked him if he would sign it. Connelly felt certain that if he did sign the false affidavit he would get the relief he sought but he declined to do so.

On March 6 Hoffa's attorneys made a final appeal to Judge Wilson in Chattanooga to allow Hoffa to remain free on bond until his other appeals had been decided. Representatives of the trucking industry appeared with the attorneys as supplicants for their supposed bargaining-table enemy. They asked that Hoffa be given a thirty-day reprieve so that the nationwide contract negotiations could be completed, raising the specter of a possible strike resulting otherwise. Judge Wilson turned them down.

At 8:58 A.M. on March 7, 1967, Jimmy Hoffa led his entourage into the office of Luke Moore, the United States marshal for the District of Columbia, to surrender. Now, in his final moments of freedom, Hoffa was still in command and still fighting. He asked Moore if they could use his phone. He directed one of his attorneys to make a call to check on a last-minute appeal being made to Judge Wilson. The attorney was having trouble with the call and Hoffa jerked the phone away from him to place the call himself. As he did, the bottom of the phone fell out.

"See, what did I tell you," Hoffa quipped, "even this phone is bugged." He completed the call on another phone and then addressed Luke Moore, "Okay, let's go."

At 3:30 that afternoon, three years and three days after conviction, Hoffa, accompanied by two deputy marshals, arrived by automobile at the federal penitentiary at Lewisburg, Pennsylvania.

I felt no elation. My only consolation was the thought that, finally, it might be all over. Again, I should have known better. Three weeks after Hoffa went to prison, Allen Dorfman became a "consultant" to the Teamsters Pension Fund and took over Hoffa's role as the ultimate dispenser of the coveted funds.

CHAPTER XIII

Louisiana Hayride

━━━━━━━━━

Hoffa had lost his long battle to stay out of prison. Now the efforts began to gain his freedom.

Two weeks after he entered Lewisburg Penitentiary an official of the prison was offered a bribe by a local Teamsters official to give preferential treatment to his new inmate. The official rejected the offer.

The affidavits that had been filed with the Supreme Court with the motion for relief were now filed in the District Court in Chattanooga. On March 20 Judge Wilson set a hearing on the motion for May 9, 1967. The FBI had already begun an investigation into the circumstances surrounding the obtaining of the affidavits. The Department of Justice submitted counteraffidavits in which all of the allegations were unequivocally denied.

On April 4, 1967, Senator Edward Long's committee began three days of public hearings on the possible use of electronic eavesdropping on the part of the Detroit Police Department and the Intelligence Division of the Internal Revenue Service in that city. William DePugh, who had previously been subpoenaed to the unusual Sunday morning executive session of the committee, was called to testify, along with the key personnel from both Detroit police intelligence and IRS intelligence. These men had formed the backbone of investigations into not only organized crime but Hoffa and his empire as well. After the second day of hearings a Washington newspaper story speculated that the hearings appeared to be designed to help Hoffa. On the morning of April 6

Senator Long, taking note of the article, made a statement saying that he wanted to make it clear he had no purpose or intention of using the hearings to influence any pending case.

William Bufalino attended the hearings and subsequently attempted to file the transcript of the hearings in support of his lawsuit against the Michigan Bell Telephone Company. The judge, however, refused to allow this and eventually dismissed the suit.

While the hearings were in progress, Judge Malcolm O'Hara, Zachary Strate and Buddy Gill attended a meeting at Teamsters headquarters in Washington with Frank Fitzsimmons and others. One of the matters discussed was the possibility of arranging for a transfer of Hoffa to some other prison.

Shortly before the hearing scheduled for May 9, in Chattanooga, Buddy Gill again approached Partin. He said that a friend had asked him to see if he could help Hoffa and he only had two weeks to do it in. He told Partin that he could name his own price if he would agree to help Hoffa. "We can both be rich," Gill said. Partin asked Gill what protection he would have from the government if he changed his testimony. Gill said, "We've got that fixed. Senator [Russell] Long is the most powerful man in the United States today. Don't you worry about it. You will be protected."

Partin asked Gill what would happen if the government decided to go ahead with the original indictment still pending against him and bring him to trial. Gill said, "We've checked it. First of all, the Supreme Court says you must get a speedy trial. Second, you don't have witnesses against you. Third, LBJ has got to have Russell."

Gill told Partin that if he didn't cooperate and help Hoffa, the International would put his local in trusteeship. He implied that he had recently talked to Frank Fitzsimmons, who was now the acting head of the Teamsters Union. Partin refused the offer.

On May 9, 1967, the hearing on the motion for relief convened in Judge Wilson's courtroom in Chattanooga. During the months since Hoffa's affidavits had been filed, it had been established that money had been paid to some of the persons who signed the affidavits. Hoffa's attorneys knew that the government knew this. When Judge Wilson directed Hoffa and his attorneys to proceed with their showing of proof, Morris Shenker, who had become Hoffa's chief attorney, stood up and said that because of information that had just come to their attention they were not going to offer any proof at this time. He asked that the proceedings be postponed for

ninety days to give them time to check out what they had just
learned. Judge Wilson's answer was that they had had several
months to prepare for the hearing, and if they had anything to
offer, they would have to present it now. Shenker declined to do
so and Judge Wilson thereafter dismissed their motion with prejudice. Bud Nichols subsequently admitted that his entire affidavit
had been false.

Shortly after the hearing *Life* magazine published an article
charging that Senator Edward Long had been using his committee
in an attempt to help Hoffa. The article stated that Long had
received thousands of dollars from Hoffa's chief counsel, Morris
Shenker, in "referral fees." It later developed that the figure was
well over $100,000 and that Edward Long had not practiced law
during the entire time the payments were being made.

The hearing in Chattanooga had been a disaster for Hoffa. His
much-publicized evidence of wiretapping, which had been submitted as true not only to the District Court, but also to the Supreme
Court of the United States, was held back from the test of a hearing
under oath. The attempts to bribe Partin had failed. But Partin had
been warned what would happen if he did not come forward to
help Hoffa. He would now learn that these were not hollow
threats. And there was another hearing coming up in Chicago
which would give the Hoffa forces another chance.

When Hoffa had petitioned the Supreme Court to review the
Chicago case, the Solicitor General of the United States had, in
responding to the petition, advised the court that the Department
of Justice had discovered that in monitoring an electronic surveillance of the Miami office of one Benjamin Sigelbaum, the FBI had
overheard a conversation by George Burris, one of Hoffa's co-
defendants. The Supreme Court had, thereupon, remanded the
case back to the District Court in Chicago for a hearing, which was
scheduled for August, 1967.

There was still another factor. Both Partin and I were now in
Louisiana. I had been in New Orleans the better part of the time
since late February pursuing an inquiry on behalf of NBC into
Garrison's assassination probe. Clay Shaw, a reputable businessman, had been arrested by Garrison on March 1, charged with
conspiring to assassinate President Kennedy. It had become increasingly apparent to me and my NBC associates that Garrison
and his staff were engaged in an enormous fraud involving bribery
and intimidation of witnesses, and that there was no basis in fact
for the charge against Shaw or any of Garrison's numerous other

theories. It was inevitable, I suppose, that the two webs of intrigue —Garrison's investigation and the efforts of the Hoffa forces— would become intertwined. A bit of background information will indicate why.

Jim Garrison had come into office originally as a reform candidate. One of his first official acts was to appoint as his chief investigator a man named Pershing Gervais, whose qualifications included having been fired by the New Orleans Police Department. Gervais had—not once, but twice—stolen the payoff money that had been collected and was awaiting distribution to other police officers and used the money to finance free-spending trips to New York City. Garrison then conducted a sweeping cleanup of Bourbon Street which received wide acclaim. What was not apparent to the casual observer was that the Bourbon Street raids were selective and did not interfere with those night spots controlled by associates of New Orleans Mafia boss Carlos Marcello.

In 1966 Garrison had gone on record as stating that there was no organized crime in New Orleans and that Carlos Marcello was a respectable businessman. It was understandable, therefore, that Garrison, while claiming that former Eastern Airlines pilot David Ferrie was the key to the plot to assassinate President Kennedy, never mentioned the fact that when the President was killed, Ferrie was employed by G. Wray Gill, the attorney for Carlos Marcello. Garrison chose to investigate Ferrie's connections with Cuban nationals but never pursued his connection with Marcello.

By the time Garrison was running for reelection, Pershing Gervais had become a political liability. He resigned and set up headquarters in the lobby of the Fontainebleau Hotel, which had been built with funds from the Teamsters Pension Fund. The loans in question had been part of those involved in the defrauding of the fund for which Hoffa had been convicted in Chicago. Both he and Zachary "Red" Strate made their headquarters at the hotel. They were close friends and in 1967 had gone into business together in a New Orleans nightclub. Both were friendly with Judge Malcolm O'Hara.

I had gone to the Fontainebleau to see Gervais when I first arrived in New Orleans on the Garrison story. I had been told that Gervais was very close to Garrison, had been in the Army with him, and exerted considerable influence over him, so I thought he might be able to give me some insights into Garrison and his investigation. I sat in the lobby and waited and before long there was a page for Mr. Gervais. I watched to see who answered the

page and then approached him and introduced myself. He invited
me to have a cup of coffee in the coffee shop. He said that he had
stayed away from the Garrison investigation because he didn't
want to get involved, and that his only aim in life was to make a
buck. While we sat there, just about everyone who came in or out
spoke to him. Two men stopped and talked to him, then sat down
at a table in front of us. Gervais identified them as New Orleans
judges.

"Where is your office?" I asked.

"This is my office," Gervais said, waving his arm to indicate the
coffee shop. "And these are my desks"—motioning to the tables.

"And are these your employees?" I asked, alluding to the judges.

"In a manner of speaking," Gervais nodded.

NBC's affiliate station in New Orleans is WDSU. It was until
recently owned by Edgar Stern, a courageous, liberal man who
shared our views concerning Garrison and his probe. The news
director, Ed Planer, did also, and we worked very closely together
in an atmosphere of absolute mutual trust. WDSU was the only
voice in the Louisiana wilderness speaking out against what Garrison was doing. During the entire Garrison caper the New Orleans
newspapers did not print one editorial word about an investigation that was capturing headlines all over the world. In fact, two
reporters for the *States Item* were, in effect, working for Garrison,
exchanging memoranda with him, and continually slanting their
stories in his favor. The other local television stations merely reported what he said or asked only soft questions.

Ed Planer had assigned Rick Townley, an investigative reporter,
to work full time on the Garrison case, and he and I worked closely
together. A man named George Wyatt had been calling Townley
asking to meet with him and me to furnish information about the
investigation. I agreed to go with Townley to see him. We drove
out to a shopping center designated by Wyatt and waited for him.
After a while he walked down the street toward our car. Townley
had met with him previously and recognized him. Wyatt got into
the car and we began to talk. As the conversation wore on, it
became obvious to me, because of his leading questions, that what
we were saying was probably being recorded. I later learned from
Bill Gurvich, Garrison's chief investigator who finally quit in
disgust, that my suspicions were well founded. Garrison had set
up the meeting and recorded it. He had given orders that if we said
anything out of line, his men, who were nearby, were to move in
and arrest us, beat us up, handcuff us and put us in jail.

In Garrison's bid for a second term as District Attorney he had been opposed by Malcolm O'Hara. During the campaign O'Hara had produced a copy of Garrison's discharge papers which showed that Garrison had received a medical discharge for psychiatric reasons. O'Hara's campaign manager had been a local attorney, Ed Baldwin. I went to see Baldwin. In discussing O'Hara, who was now a judge, I mentioned that he and Red Strate had approached Ed Partin in an attempt to get him to sign an affidavit stating that we had bugged Hoffa and his attorneys.

On June 7 our producer Fred Freed and I went to see Louisiana Governor John McKeithen to find out if he would be willing to appear on film concerning the Garrison investigation. Because of the facts we had uncovered concerning the investigation, NBC had decided that we would present a white paper on the entire matter on June 19. The governor talked about many things but declined to give a statement on Garrison. That afternoon, back in New Orleans, Ed Baldwin came to see me. He said that he had spent an evening with Judge O'Hara, who claimed that he had some information about the Garrison investigation that would really wrap up our program and wanted to know if I would meet with him. I said I would. Baldwin then said that there could be a quid pro quo involved. I asked him why. He said that O'Hara had confirmed to him that he had gone with Strate to see Partin to attempt to get him to sign an affidavit about wiretapping. Actually, he told Baldwin, he had been traveling all over the country for Hoffa and had become a messenger boy in attempts to help Hoffa. In discussing me, O'Hara had said, "I can have a million dollars in cash down here tomorrow." Baldwin said he had cautioned O'Hara not to offer me any money.

On June 12 Baldwin called and said that Judge O'Hara would meet us in the cocktail lounge of the Bourbon Orleans Hotel at five o'clock that evening, and that he might bring someone with him. I was now very curious not only as to what O'Hara had to offer by way of information, but also what he might want in return, so I told Baldwin I would meet him in the lounge. Then I told Fred Freed about it. He agreed that it was probably going to be a waste of time but thought I should see what it was all about.

I arrived at the lounge first and went to the bar and ordered a drink. Baldwin came in shortly after and joined me. A few minutes later two men entered and sat at a table in the rear. We walked over to the table and I immediately recognized one of the men as Red Strate. Then the judge got up and he and Baldwin went to another table across the room, leaving me with Strate.

Strate said, "I have a good friend, Pershing Gervais, who can be a lot of help to you." He· added that he and Gervais were also business associates, having just bought a New Orleans night spot called the Emerald Door.

"Before you go any further," I said, "what do you want from me?"

"That's easy," responded Strate. "Hoffa out of prison. You two won the war—now, why don't you let him go?"

Strate continued, "You just tell me something about wiretapping in Chattanooga and Gervais will help you."

"There was no wiretapping," I replied. Then I asked, "Why are you so interested in helping Hoffa instead of worrying about your own conviction in Chicago?"

Strate said that he thought Partin was a son of a bitch and Hoffa was a good man. He had spent a lot of time with Hoffa and admired him very much. He said that they thought the Chicago case was going to turn out all right anyway.

"What is the judge doing in this?" I asked, referring to Judge O'Hara.

"He's in it for what he can get out of it," Strate said.

I said, "Well, there wasn't any wiretapping and I guess there is no point in going any further."

I motioned to Ed Baldwin and he and O'Hara returned to the table and sat down. There was some general discussion of Garrison and his investigation and we shook hands and left.

NBC's special program entitled "The JFK Conspiracy: The case of Jim Garrison" appeared on the evening of June 19. It was extremely critical of Garrison's case against Clay Shaw and of the methods employed by him and his staff.

On July 7 Garrison issued a warrant for my arrest, charging me with bribery. The information he filed in support of the warrant alleged that I had offered Perry Russo, his chief witness against Clay Shaw, a job and residence in California and payment of legal fees for an attorney. I had talked to Russo on three occasions but had never offered him anything.

In Baton Rouge the stage was set for what was to become an all-out effort to destroy Ed Partin. He had been told in no uncertain terms what would happen if he did not come to the aid of Hoffa in the Chattanooga hearing. Almost immediately thereafter forces were unleashed that would, in the next four years, focus an incredible array of power in the singular pursuit of grinding Partin into the ground and finally attempting to send him to prison. As the vise was continually tightened, he would occasionally be offered an easing of his pain and perhaps an end to his troubles—if he would surrender and help Jimmy Hoffa.

There is no question that Edward Grady Partin was and is a controversial figure. Perhaps he brought some of his problems on himself. He is a proud, tough and cunning man operating in a section of this country with its own unique tradition of justice and an unusual tolerance for corruption. It does appear, however, that the only labor leader in the United States who has received such concentrated attention since May 9, 1967, is Ed Partin, the man whose testimony for the United States government helped put Jimmy Hoffa in prison and the only logical person, other than the President or the parole board, who might have been able to get him out. What follows is a recounting of what has happened to that man since he said "no" to the bribes and the ultimatum.

The climate was right in Baton Rouge in June, 1967, to begin the discrediting of Ed Partin. There are those who say he helped to create it.

In the early 1960s Baton Rouge became a bustling center of new plant construction for the oil and chemical industries. When Governor John McKeithen was elected in 1964, he proceeded to encourage this industrial growth through tax incentives and public relations efforts. By 1966, when he was reelected, this expansion had more than doubled. The competitive eagerness of industry, the shortage of the labor supply and the moral climate were conducive to bribery, shakedowns and political corruption. Jurisdictional disputes and rivalries among labor unions and aggressive struggles among companies were rife.

Most construction companies in the United States belong to the General Contractors Association with headquarters in Washington, D.C. The association, in turn, maintains offices in every major city to service the contractors. The function of the local offices is to assist the industry with public relations, information, political influence and labor relations. There is such an office in Baton Rouge. Contractors coming into the Baton Rouge area, however, found it advantageous to retain the services of another organization, called the Baton Rouge Industrial Contractors Association (BRICA), operated by James "Buddy" Gill, the former administrative assistant to Senator Russell Long. BRICA was paid a fee of 1 percent of the amount of the contract.

In the construction of new plants, the industries and their contractors would turn to local ready mix companies for cement and concrete and sometimes to local pipeline companies for their products. There were several ready mix companies in the Baton Rouge area.

One of these, the Altex Company, was owned in 1966 by Roland Stevens and Wallace Heck. Stevens also owned the Stevens Concrete Pipe Company. On August 10, 1966, the labor contract between the ready mix companies and Local 5 of the Teamsters Union expired. A ten-day extension period was granted to complete negotiations for the renewal of the contract. At the end of the extension period all of the companies except Altex had signed the new contract. Altex was willing to pay a higher wage scale but was not willing to accept the fringe benefits agreed to by the other companies. As a result, Local 5 called a strike against Altex, which lasted until Altex agreed to sign the contract on September 12.

One of the other companies was the Louisiana Ready Mix Company. On October 7, 1966, Baton Rouge businessman Ted Dunham, Sr., and his son, Ted Dunham, Jr., who had previously been in the ready mix business, acquired control of Louisiana Ready Mix.

During December there was another strike of Altex by Local 5 over payment of back wages which lasted for three days. On January 25, 1967, Wallace Heck bought out Roland Stevens' interest in Altex. On March 21, 1967, the Altex Company brought a $3,150,000 lawsuit against Partin, Louisiana Ready Mix, the Dunhams and another company, charging that they had conspired in restraint of trade to the benefit of Louisiana Ready Mix and to the detriment of Altex. The suit charged that the Dunhams had acquired Louisiana Ready Mix in the summer of 1966 and that the strikes by Local 5 at that time and since had been designed to help the Dunhams while harming Altex.

On April 24, 1967, two weeks before the Chattanooga hearing, Partin's deposition was taken by Altex attorneys. Partin answered all of the questions except two, which he claimed had nothing to do with Altex but were designed instead to elicit information concerning the then pending contract negotiations between Local 5 and the Stevens Concrete Pipe Company. During the questioning, Partin was asked whether he was paying per capita taxes to the International Union and whether Local 5 was affiliated with the International. In the deposition Partin charged that Chuck Winters of Local 270 in New Orleans had been meeting with Altex.

Following the hearing in Chattanooga, Partin was notified by the International Teamsters Union that Local 5's per capita taxes were far in arrears and would have to be paid immediately or the local would be placed in trusteeship. Partin said that Hoffa had told him during an earlier organizational drive against one of the oil companies to defer paying per capita taxes in lieu of receiving strike benefits from the International. Partin had nothing on paper to back up this oral authorization by Hoffa, but submitted affidavits from witnesses to the conversation to corroborate his position. He was instructed to appear at the next meeting of the International Executive Board on July 12.

On June 20 two thousand members of Local 995 of the Electrical Workers Union walked off their jobs. Within forty-eight hours the work stoppage created a shutdown of virtually all construction in the Baton Rouge area. Governor McKeithen, who had since his election in 1964, more than doubled the industrial growth of the area, was obviously very upset. The Chamber of Commerce said that $250,000,000 worth of industry was affected by the shutdown.

On June 23, four days after our program on Garrison, station WJBO in Baton Rouge did an in-depth story in which it blamed Partin for the labor difficulties:

> We can report that Edward G. Partin has been under investigation by the New Orleans District Attorney's Office in connection with the Kennedy Assassination investigation . . . based on an exclusive interview with an Assistant District Attorney in Jim Garrison's office. We can report that Partin's activities have been under scrutiny. In his words: "We know that Jack Ruby and Lee Harvey Oswald were here in New Orleans several times . . . there was a third man driving them and we are checking the possibility it was Partin."

On the same day Charles D. Winters, president of Local 270 of the Teamsters Union in New Orleans, made a television statement in which he said that Local 5 in Baton Rouge was not presently a member of the International Teamsters Union but had applied for readmission.

On June 26 Partin made a plea for arbitration of the labor dispute and agreed to be bound by the result. He sent a telegram to the Department of Justice asking for an investigation and said that his union was becoming the whipping boy. The Baton Rouge television station took note of the telegram and then went on to quote in detail remarks attacking Partin that had been made on the floor of the House two years earlier by Congressman Gray. (This was the same statement that had been incorporated in Sid Zagri's publicity releases during the operation to keep Hoffa from going to prison.)

Chuck Winters in New Orleans sent Partin's old enemy J. D. Albin to Baton Rouge to start raiding Partin's jurisdiction. Members of Local 5 were told that if they remained in the local they would lose their benefits under the Teamsters Pension Fund. One of the companies to which Albin directed his efforts was the Stevens Concrete Pipe Company. Partin filed a complaint with the National Labor Relations Board, which ultimately issued an order directing the Stevens Company and Albin to cease and desist their activities.

With the pressures on him mounting, Partin now received a call from his former attorney, Osie Brown, who asked him to drop by his house. When Partin arrived, he found two other men there with Brown: Frank Ragano and Wilson Abraham, a wealthy Baton Rouge contractor and owner of the Statler Lakeshore Hotel in that city.

Abraham mentioned that he had applied for a loan from the Teamsters Pension Fund for $32,000,000 to build a hotel in Las Vegas. He said that he had already paid Jacques Schiffer $87,000 to help get the loan but indicated that his success might be contingent on obtaining help from Partin for Hoffa. Ragano told Partin that Hoffa had sent him and realized that Partin was his last hope. He said that Hoffa would arrange to have J. D. Albin and Chuck Winters stop interfering in the Baton Rouge area and that no one else would bother him. In return, Ragano said, he needed an affidavit from Partin about wiretapping. Partin refused.

Shortly thereafter Partin was again contacted by Abraham. He told Partin that Senator Russell Long had talked to Attorney General Ramsey Clark within the past several days about the department's original twenty-six-count indictment of Partin. He said that Long told the Attorney General that if the Department of Justice tried to dismiss the indictment, he had twenty-five Senators who would raise strong objections. Abraham said that Hoffa was going to be transferred to a prison in Florida where he would be closer to Ragano. Abraham said further that if the Department of

Justice should start an investigation of efforts to bribe Partin, Buddy Gill would be the scapegoat. Then Abraham reminded Partin that Baton Rouge federal Judge E. Gordon West was a former law partner of Senator Russell Long, and that other federal judges in Louisiana had also been appointed through Long. "They'll burn your ass," Abraham said. Abraham also mentioned that he had heard that Jim Garrison was going to subpoena Partin in his assassination probe.

All of the heat would be taken off him, Abraham said, if Partin would help Hoffa. He then attempted, unsuccessfully, in Partin's presence to call Frank Ragano in Room 767 of the Royal Orleans Hotel, assuring Partin that Ragano could take care of the pressures. Abraham said that Senator Long was coming to Baton Rouge on June 30 and that he wanted to set up a meeting between Partin and Long.

Senator Long did come to Baton Rouge and Partin called him. When Partin mentioned their getting together, Senator Long immediately said that he had not seen Buddy Gill in several weeks. (Partin had not even mentioned Gill.) The conversation developed into a shouting match and Partin hung up.

Wilson Abraham subsequently talked to Judge William Daniels along the same lines as he had to Partin, and also mentioned that he was attempting to get a Pension Fund loan from the Teamsters.

On June 27 Chuck Winters announced in a television interview that the employees of the Union Tank Car Company in Baton Rouge had asked his local rather than Local 5 to represent them. Partin made another plea for forced arbitration and suggested a fifteen-day truce with all workers returning to their jobs in an effort to settle the labor strife.

On the following day Winters repeated his claims about the Union Tank Car Company employees and said that he was petitioning the NLRB for an election.

On July 13 the Executive Board of the International Brotherhood of Teamsters, meeting at a country club in Seaview, New Jersey, passed a resolution to place Local 5 in trusteeship if the per capita dues in arrears were not paid.

On July 17 Governor McKeithen called a special session of the Louisiana state legislature to ask for the enactment of legislation creating a Labor-Management Commission of Inquiry to look into the problems of labor strife in the Baton Rouge area.

The next day I went to New Orleans to surrender and post

bail in connection with Garrison's charges against me. I had received the complete backing of NBC and had held a press conference in Washington the prior week at which I accused Garrison of attempting to intimidate the press. I brought with me to New Orleans a $5000 certified check drawn on NBC's account at the Chase Manhattan Bank in New York. The clerk of the court said he could not accept it. He produced a letter written one week earlier by the attorney for the court which set forth the "new" policy covering payment of bail. Only checks on local banks were acceptable. It was now four o'clock in the afternoon and the banks were closed. My local attorney, Milton Brenner, hurried off to his bank to try and get cash. In the meantime I was left standing there under the watchful eye of the sheriff. It was obvious that Garrison wanted me in jail. After pounding on the closed bank door for a while, Brenner finally was allowed in and obtained $5000 in cash. We turned it over to the clerk and started to leave. I was then served with a subpoena directing me to appear before Garrison's grand jury the following morning. Jack Miller, Milton Brenner and Ed Baldwin stayed up all night preparing a petition to the State Court of Appeals claiming that it would be a violation of due process to force me to go before the grand jury after I had already been charged. The judge in charge of the grand jury was Malcolm O'Hara! Both the Court of Appeals and the state Supreme Court denied the motion. We then went into federal court for an injunction against Garrison, asking that he be prevented not only from forcing me to appear before the grand jury but also from prosecuting me—on the basis that it was a malicious prosecution. The judge granted our request pending a hearing in federal court.

On the day I surrendered, Senator Robert Kennedy issued the following statement:

> I have been fortunate to know and work with Walter Sheridan for many years. Like all those who have known him and his work, I have the utmost confidence in his integrity, both personal and professional.
> This view was shared by President Kennedy himself, with whom Mr. Sheridan was associated for many years in a relationship of utmost trust, confidence and affection.
> His personal ties to President Kennedy, as well as his own integrity, insure that he would want as much as, or more than, any other

man to ascertain the truth about the events of November, 1963. It is not possible that Mr. Sheridan would do anything which would in the slightest degree compromise the truth in regard to the investigation in New Orleans.

In reply, Garrison said:

Whether Mr. Sheridan—a known intimate of Senator Robert F. Kennedy—is innocent of the crime of attempted bribery will be determined by a jury of citizens. It still remains to be determined what motives lie behind Mr. Sheridan's efforts to interfere with law enforcement in New Orleans.

If he actually represents the interests of Senator Kennedy, then he has been unfair to his employer, the National Broadcasting Company. If he really represents only NBC, then Senator Kennedy should pick his associates more carefully. In either case, justice in Louisiana is our problem and not theirs.

Back in Washington at the Department of Justice, only Mike Epstein was now left to cope with the continuing machinations of the Hoffa forces. Bill Bittman and Charlie Shaffer had both gone off into private practice. The career employees who had worked with us at the department had been reassigned to other areas. The Johnson Administration had no real desire to pursue these matters. The nature of the system does not provide for the continuity of purpose and persistence required for such an effort. Consequently Ed Partin and others who had gone the whole way for the government would be subjected to endless pressures because they did, while the support and protection of the government would become more and more illusive and finally nonexistent.

On August 3, 1967, the Criminal Division of the Department of Justice convened a grand jury in New Orleans under the direction of Mike Epstein to investigate the continuing efforts to bribe and intimidate Partin. One of the subpoenas for the grand jury went to James "Buddy" Gill, Senator Russell Long's friend and former aide.

When Senator Long learned of this he was furious. He called Epstein at the Department of Justice in a tirade. He wanted to know who Epstein thought he was starting a grand jury in his state. He went on for several minutes in a diatribe against Ed Partin and the Department of Justice. Senator Long then called Fred Vinson, who had replaced Jack Miller as Assistant Attorney

General in charge of the Criminal Division, and carried on with him in much the same manner. A meeting followed between Long, Epstein and Vinson. Senator Long was again vituperative and subsequently threatened to have both Epstein and Vinson indicted by the state of Louisiana if they went forward with the grand jury. He said that Partin was the one they should be investigating. Vinson told Long that if he learned of any evidence of criminal activity on the part of Partin, the Criminal Division would certainly pursue it, but that the grand jury investigation would proceed.After personally reviewing the entire Hoffa case, Vinson said, he was morally certain that Partin had told the truth and that Hoffa had been guilty. Senator Long insisted that Partin and Ted Dunham were driving other people out of business in Baton Rouge. Vinson told him that if he had evidence of this it should be furnished to the Antitrust Division of the department.

The Labor-Management Commission of Inquiry was established on July 22, 1967, by what was known as Act No. 2 of the special session of the Louisiana legislature. The act provided for a commission of members under a chairman who was empowered to appoint a chief counsel and staff. The function of the commission would be to investigate and make findings of fact relative to possible criminal violations in the labor-management field.

Governor McKeithen appointed Cecil Morgan, dean of the Tulane University Law School, as the chairman of the commission. The first chief counsel, attorney Camille Gravel, resigned after a short period after a dispute with Victor Bussie, the president of the AFL-CIO in Louisiana, and was replaced by A. Harry Roberts, an ex-FBI agent who owned a private investigation agency called Southern Research, Inc., in Shreveport. Prior to accepting the position, Roberts and his agency had derived a substantial part of their income from investigations performed for management in labor relations matters. Roberts, in turn, hired Joseph Oster as a member of the investigative staff. Oster also had a private investigation agency in New Orleans called Joseph A. Oster & Associates, Inc. But it later developed that Oster owned only 50 percent of his agency; the other half was owned by A. Harry Roberts. Oster had previously served with the New Orleans Police Department. Another member of the staff was Raymond Ruiz, who had also been a member of the New Orleans Police Department.

A. Harry Roberts and his staff, in pursuit of their inquiry, showed little interest in anything except Edward Grady Partin and Local 5. Their entire investigative efforts were pointed in that direction.

On August 17 I was subpoenaed by Hoffa to appear as a witness in the hearing in Chicago that had been ordered by the Supreme Court to determine whether electronic eavesdropping by the FBI had, in any way, tainted the conviction in the Pension Fund case.

On August 18 and 21 Red Strate and Judge Malcolm O'Hara testified at the hearing. They merely turned the true story around, saying that I had requested to meet with them and had offered to furnish information about bugging and wiretapping in the Hoffa case if they would, in turn, give me information to discredit Garrison's investigation of the assassination.

During their cross-examination, they admitted that they were intimate friends, saw each other daily, and played golf and went to the racetrack together. They also admitted making trips together to Las Vegas and Washington, D.C. Judge O'Hara testified that his transportation and hotel bills on these trips were paid for by Strate, and that whenever they went to Washington together, they had visited the headquarters of the International Brotherhood of Teamsters. O'Hara acknowledged having met Frank Fitzsimmons, Cal Kovens and Buddy Gill there and recalled a conversation on one occasion about attempts being made to get Hoffa transferred to another prison.

Strate and O'Hara also admitted traveling to Baton Rouge, where the latter met with Ed Partin at the office of Buddy Gill. O'Hara testified that he asked Partin to sign an affidavit dictated by attorney Harold Brown from Chattanooga concerning wiretapping in the Hoffa case because Strate had asked him to do so, knowing that Partin had not been interviewed about the subject matter of the affidavit. O'Hara stated that he was merely acting as a messenger boy for Strate.

Relative to the meeting with me in New Orleans, Strate admitted that he was attempting to obtain information about wiretapping in the Hoffa case and that I had told him that there was none.

At the conclusion of the hearing, Judge Richard Austin had this to say about their testimony:

> Because of the many conflicts and contradictions in the testimony given by these two close friends, the unquestioned obedience imposed by this friendship, the contradictions in Strate's testimony alone, his declared personal concern for Mr. Hoffa's predicament,

all indicate an interest and motivation which casts such doubt upon the credibility of their testimony and this Court refuses to place any credence on it.

Judge Austin, on September 22, 1967, ruled "that the convictions of none of the defendants were tainted by the use of evidence improperly obtained." He denied their motion for a new trial and reimposed the same sentences as before.

On September 1, 1967, *Life* magazine published the first in a series of articles entitled "The Mob." In the section dealing with Louisiana, it said, "*Life* has found conclusive evidence that Hoffa's pals—some in the union, some in the Mob, some in both—dropped $2 million into a spring-Hoffa fund late last year. The money was placed at the disposal of Cosa Nostra mobsters, and it was to be made payable to anyone who could wreck the government's jury-tampering case on which Hoffa had been convicted. In due course the money was made available to Marcello to do the job." The article went on to describe how Aubrey Young, then an aide to Governor McKeithen, had set up the meeting between Ed Partin and D'Alton Smith at which Partin claimed to have been offered $25,000 a year for ten years, and finally $1,000,000, if he would change his testimony against Hoffa or furnish information about wiretapping or bugging.

One week later *Life*, in its second article in the series, included a section captioned "Carlos Marcello: King Thug of Louisiana": "State authorities, for the most part, take the view that Marcello and his gang aren't there. 'I'm thankful we haven't had any racketeering to speak of in this state,' says Governor John McKeithen." Then the article quoted New Orleans District Attorney Jim Garrison as saying, "I don't have to worry about things like that. I've cleaned up the rackets in this town." The article went on to point out that three times since 1963 Garrison had had his hotel bill at the Sands Hotel in Las Vegas paid for by Marcello's lieutenant Mario Marino, who had moved from New Orleans to Las Vegas ten years earlier. *Life* said that on his last trip to Vegas in March of that year, Garrison had also been granted $5000 credit at the cashier's cage. Garrison told the *Life* reporters that he believed it was customary for casinos to pick up the hotel tabs of public officials. "I may be naive—this is my first public office—but I don't see what's wrong with it," he said.

Life also said that Pershing Gervais admitted frequent meetings with Marcello and "now calls himself 'counselor for people who get arrested.' He arranges settlements for a fee."

Aaron Kohn is the director of the Metropolitan Crime Commission and has held that post for almost twenty years. The commission is supported by public donations to serve as a watchdog for the community to feret out and publicize public corruption and organized crime activities. For most of those years Kohn has been the only voice speaking out against the extent of organized crime in New Orleans, the nature of its activities and its dominance by Carlos Marcello. He had recently been extremely critical of the governor and his investigation and asked the governor to resign from office.

Kohn now made a public appeal to Governor McKeithen to investigate the *Life* charges and to take action to remove Judge O'Hara from the bench. McKeithen said he would investigate but later told reporters at the Southern Governors' Conference at Asheville, North Carolina, that there was no organized racketeering in Louisiana—with the possible exception of some illegal union activities. He declined to remove Judge O'Hara but suggested that Kohn could petition the attorney general of the state to do so.

In a third article two weeks later *Life* quoted both McKeithen and Garrison as stating that they would resign if it could be shown that organized crime was flourishing in Louisiana and New Orleans, respectively. *Life* then went on to charge that during the period June, 1966, to March, 1967, many calls were made from Carlos Marcello to Aubrey Young's direct line at the governor's offices in the state capital, and noted that this covered the same period during which Young was involved as an "intermediary in the efforts to bribe Edward G. Partin." During the same period, the article continued, Marcello made calls to at least six Mafia leaders throughout the country, including Santos Trafficante in Florida.

Relative to Jim Garrison, the article said that Mario Marino, whom they had previously identified as the Las Vegas pal of Marcello's who had arranged for Garrison's free-loading trips to Vegas, had appeared before the federal grand jury in New Orleans on August 15 and had reportedly taken the Fifth Amendment after consulting with Marcello. *Life* then named the bosses of the Marcello-backed bookie operations in New Orleans, including Marcello's brother Sammy and Frank Timphony. According to *Life*, Garrison had denied in an interview on August 16 ever having heard

of Timphony. Yet, when he placed a call to Pershing Gervais in
the presence of the *Life* reporters, Gervais "promptly assured him
that Timphony was and still is one of the biggest bookies in New
Orleans."

After the article appeared, Governor McKeithen left for New
York City, stating that *Life* had offered to furnish him with further
information to document its charges. When he returned he called
a press conference and announced that *Life* had been right and said
the magazine had actually been "light on Louisiana" in view of the
evidence they had presented to him in New York. The governor
said he was going to put Marcello out of business in the state of
Louisiana and that Aubrey Young would be given an opportunity
to turn state's witness against Marcello. He said that *Life* had
agreed to assign David Chandler, one of the reporters who had
worked on the probe, to him to assist in the investigation. A grand
jury was convened in Baton Rouge and Aubrey Young testified
before it on September 28.

In New Orleans Garrison criticized the governor for conceding
anything to *Life* and convened his own grand jury to investigate
the charges. He said he would resign from office if they found any
organized crime in New Orleans.

Garrison's first move was to subpoena Aaron Kohn, who that
same day formally presented Louisiana Attorney General Jack
Gremillion with a petition containing the signatures of forty-five
attorneys—twenty more than necessary—demanding the removal
of Judge O'Hara from the bench. Kohn was ordered to produce the
membership and contribution lists of the Crime Commission as
well as the names of its confidential informants. The judge who
was supervising the grand jury was Judge Malcolm O'Hara!

In an editorial on September 27 WDSU said, "The Grand Jury
is investigating the allegations about organized crime. The Metropolitan Crime Commission has charged that organized crime
does exist in this area. So now the Grand Jury is investigating the
Metropolitan Crime Commission."

The next day I went to see Governor McKeithen in Baton
Rouge. I had arranged the appointment through General Tom
Burbank, the head of the Louisiana State Police, who had been
very helpful to us earlier. I told the governor that organized crime
did flourish in Louisiana under Marcello and that Marcello and
others had been involved earlier in the year in attempts to bribe
and intimidate Partin. I also told him about Buddy Gill's efforts

in the same direction and of Senator Russell Long's actions. I went on to say that efforts to help Hoffa both in Louisiana and elsewhere had been continuous and intensive and were not likely to let up. Then I pointed out that the Labor-Management Commission, which he had initiated to look into the problems of labor strife in the area, appeared to be devoting its activities exclusively to investigations of Partin and his local. I told him I was not implying that he was in any way involved in any effort to help Hoffa but cautioned that persons on the commission could be knowingly or unknowingly being used to that end.

Governor McKeithen assured me that he had no brief for Hoffa nor any desire to see him assisted in any way, and would never be a party to such an effort. He said that he was determined to get to the bottom of the organized crime question and was going to do everything in his power to clean up whatever crime there was in the state. He even offered to give me the job of heading the investigation. I told him that I was in no position to do so. I don't know what he would have done if I had said yes.

On October 11 a recommendation was made within the Federal Trade Commission that the case involving alleged conspiracy in restraint of trade by Ed Partin and Ted Dunham, Jr., against the Altex Company in Baton Rouge be referred to the Antitrust Division of the Department of Justice for possible criminal prosecution. When the chairman of the FTC was later asked by a reporter whether Senator Russell Long had been influential in the matter, he refused to comment.

The investigation of Partin and Local 5 by the Labor-Management Commission continued throughout October and November. In mid-December Partin called me and said that two men had been to the local looking for work. They told him they had been working for a company with whom Local 5 had recently had labor difficulties but were going to quit because the company's equipment was obsolete. They suggested that perhaps some of the company's equipment might be blown up. Partin had told them to check back later and then called me. He said their names were George Wyatt and Morris Bromlee. I described how Wyatt had tried to set me up earlier for Jim Garrison and that Bromlee was a friend of his who had also done some work for Garrison. I told him to be very careful of them.

When they returned to Local 5 the next day Partin noticed that there were out-of-state license plates wired on over the regular plates on their automobile. He avoided them and called Sargant Pitcher, who had them arrested for driving with stolen license plates.

Soon after Wyatt and Bromlee went off the commission payroll they came to Partin and told him they had been hired by the Labor-Management Commission to frame him. They said the Labor-Management Commission had arranged for them to obtain employment with the company that Local 5 was striking, and the plan was for them to sabotage company equipment (with the consent of the company) and blame it on Partin. They said that they had been promised immunity from prosecution if they became implicated in any way.

Wyatt told Partin that after they had been arrested on the license plate charge, Jack Martin, a private investigator who had also done work for Garrison and who Wyatt said had originally approached him on behalf of the Labor-Management Commission, called and asked him if he needed an attorney. Martin said that F. Lee Bailey would represent him without charge, and they could file a charge against Partin for kidnapping and false arrest. If he was interested, Martin told Wyatt, he should call a television newsman in New Orleans who could put Wyatt in touch with an intermediary to Bailey.

Wyatt called the newsman, who instructed him to go to the Fontainebleau Hotel in New Orleans and page Pershing Gervais. Wyatt went to the Fontainebleau that night and asked at the front desk that they page Gervais. Gervais, paged under the name of Sam Maxwell, appeared and introduced himself to Wyatt. They then went to the coffee shop and talked.

Gervais already knew about everything Wyatt had been doing for the Labor-Management Commission, and in fact, maintained that he had told the commission people they were not going about it the right way. Gervais said that the evening Wyatt and Bromlee had been arrested, Sargent Pitcher had called Garrison's office and asked who they were. Pitcher had talked to one of Garrison's assistants, who in turn, had called Gervais. Gervais said that he had instructed the assistant to tell Pitcher they were just a couple of narcotics users. (Harold Weisberg, JFK assassination buff and author, later told Bromlee that he had been in Garrison's office at the time and could confirm that Pitcher had called Assistant District Attorney Sciambra, who in turn, called Gervais.)

Gervais told Wyatt that the only way to get Hoffa out of jail was to put Partin in jail. When Wyatt asked about the idea of filing kidnapping or false arrest charges and obtaining F. Lee Bailey's services, Gervais left the table and said he was going to call "the people up north." When he returned about one-half hour later he said that filing the charge wasn't good enough and that they should hold that in abeyance. What they really wanted, he said, was to get several charges and file them against Partin all at once. They discussed the possibility of planting narcotics on Partin and Gervais said, "Do anything but kill him. He has to be alive to testify that he committed perjury in Chattanooga." Gervais told Wyatt to have Raymond Ruiz, of the Labor-Management Commission staff, get in touch with him.

After Wyatt and Bromlee went to Partin and told him what had been transpiring, Wyatt called Ruiz and told him that he had gotten close to Partin and might be able to help them. (Of course, Wyatt was now actually working on behalf of Partin.) Immunity for Wyatt was again discussed. Wyatt also called Gervais from the Shady Oaks Motel in Baton Rouge and told him that he was getting close to Partin. Gervais asked Wyatt to have Ruiz call him, and Wyatt went to see Ruiz with this message. Ruiz told him he was going to see Gervais the following day.

The next day Wyatt called Gervais, who claimed that he had not heard from Ruiz. Gervais then said that he no longer wanted to be involved and that Wyatt should work directly with Ruiz. Wyatt immediately called Ruiz, who said that he had just come back from seeing Gervais and Gervais had told him that "the best 'they' can do is five figures, but first you have to produce the evidence." Ruiz said that the evidence had to show that Partin had committed perjury. When Wyatt asked Ruiz when he could meet with someone to present the evidence and expressed concern about being double-crossed out of the money, Ruiz assured him, "You won't be double-crossed. These people have a reputation to keep up. They have been skinned pretty good before." Ruiz said that he would try to get in touch with Gervais so that Wyatt could present his evidence to him and get his money. Ruiz called back a few minutes later and said that he had just talked to Gervais and now "it is up to me to decide what you have got."

It was becoming apparent that not only was the Labor-Management Commission out to nail Partin but also that some of its staff members were in contact with persons whose motive was to help Hoffa by getting at Partin.

CHAPTER XIV

"Why Richard Nixon?"

═ ═ ═ ═ ═ ═ ═ ═ ═

THE PRESIDENTIAL CAMPAIGN OF 1968 started, as all such campaigns do, in the January snow of New Hampshire. Richard Nixon had already committed himself to the Presidential race and knew that if he was going to be President of the United States he had to win and win big in New Hampshire.

The *Manchester Union Leader* is the only newspaper in New Hampshire with a statewide circulation. Its position of influence is even more pronounced because there is only one television station in the entire state. All other television news is generated from outside its boundaries.

On January 4, 1968, in his paper's editorial, William Loeb called Nixon the "GOP Catalyst." The editorial page also carried an article by Ralph De Toledano captioned "Hoffa's Special Treatment." The article said that a monsignor had not been allowed in to see Hoffa and that *Manchester Union Leader* reporter Arthur Egan had not been permitted to examine the register of visitors. The January 7 issue of the paper contained a cartoon showing Robert Kennedy standing on the shoulders of Senator McCarthy and President Johnson.

The front-page editorial on January 12 was an attack on Senators McCarthy and Kennedy. On January 15 Vice President Humphrey was attacked in the front-page editorial for his visit to South Africa. The editorial for January 16 was an attack on Jacqueline Kennedy for her trip to Cambodia. The front-page editorial attack on January 27 was directed at Governor George Romney. Loeb

closed out the month with an editorial attack on January 31 on the
late President John Kennedy for sending the destroyer *Joseph
Kennedy* as part of the intercept force during the Cuban missile
crisis.

In a front-page editorial on February 2 entitled "Why Richard
Nixon?" Loeb wrote:

> Richard Nixon merits the Republican presidential nomination be-
> cause, at this crucial time in our nation's history, he alone, of all the
> Republican Candidates, has had extensive experience in foreign
> affairs. . . . Next, Mr. Nixon deserves the Republican nomination
> for the presidency because none of the other candidates have
> given the unstinting, unwavering devotion to the Republican Party
> and its interests that Mr. Nixon has done over a number of
> years.

In the weeks that followed, the *Manchester Union Leader* gave
extensive, favorable coverage to the Nixon campaign. During the
same period there were unfavorable cartoons and editorials concerning Robert Kennedy, Edward Kennedy, Eugene McCarthy,
President Johnson, Nelson Rockefeller, George Romney and Ronald Reagan. On February 28 George Romney withdrew from the
contest. Rockefeller and Reagan never entered the primary, and
Nixon won handily on March 12.

There was a quid pro quo in Nixon's first and vital step toward
the Presidential nomination. In return for his support, Loeb extracted a commitment from the Nixon forces that if Nixon were
elected President, the Nixon Administration would do what it
could to help James R. Hoffa.

On the other side of the political fence, Senator Eugene
McCarthy had successfully challenged President Johnson and his
policies, gaining 42 percent of the vote and twenty of the twenty-
four New Hampshire delegates. On the following day Senator
Robert Kennedy said that he was "actively reconsidering"
whether or not to run. Kennedy realized that his fears of tearing
the party apart were no longer valid since the primary results
demonstrated that deep discontent already existed within the
party. So on March 16, 1968, Senator Kennedy announced his candidacy for the nomination in the Caucus Room of the old Senate
Office building in Washington—the same room where his struggle

with Jimmy Hoffa had begun—and the same room in which his brother had made his announcement eight years earlier.

Five days later I took a leave of absence from NBC and joined the campaign. At first, Bob Kennedy wanted me to go to Michigan and be the coordinator for that state. Then someone decided that would not be a good idea because it was Hoffa's home state. I finally ended up in Indiana working as a coordinator for the primary in Indianapolis.

Meanwhile, in Louisiana, some members of Local 5 had played right into the hands of Governor John McKeithen and forces moving against Ed Partin by becoming involved in a shooting incident on a picket line at the W. O. Bergeron Company in Plaquemine, Louisiana. It mattered little that Partin was not there and had cautioned the men, with his attorney and other witnesses present, to avoid violence at all costs. It also was not enough that the management personnel involved had guns, that there was shooting from both sides and that there were conflicting reports about who fired the first shot. W. O. Bergeron himself was quoted by Plaquemine Chief of Police Dennis Songy as saying he did not know who fired first.

Governor McKeithen, whose promised war against organized crime had produced meager results, seized the incident and ran with it. He called a press conference and placed the blame for the fracas squarely on the Teamsters. He said the whole state was being challenged by a "small group of hoodlums." "These hoodlums make Marcello and the Mafia look pretty good," the governor said. At a subsequent news conference Governor McKeithen said that he was going to arrest Partin "as soon as we get the evidence on him."

Shortly thereafter the governor called me. He said that he knew I had some misgivings about the Labor-Management Commission but that he had to do something about Partin. He said that he was going to be in Washington for the annual Mardi Gras Ball and would like to see me then. We agreed to meet at his suite at the Sheraton Park Hotel. At the meeting Governor McKeithen said that Partin had become a real problem for him. He told me that he personally liked and respected Partin but that he was driving him crazy. In all honesty, he said, he did not have any evidence against Partin for anything but he was going to keep going until he got some.

Finally he said, "Walter, get him out of my state. Now listen to what I am saying to you. Just get him out of my state. I'll help you do it and I'll give him immunity. You write it up and I'll sign it. Just please get him across that state line."

I told the governor that I had suggested to Partin much earlier that he get out of the labor movement and out of Louisiana because he was too vulnerable in either. But, I said, Partin had children in Baton Rouge, in the custody of his estranged wife, and was reluctant to leave them. I also told him that Partin was a proud man who did not think he had done anything wrong and was unlikely to run under pressure. Besides, I said, there seemed to be two sides to the shoot-out incident, and though I didn't know which was correct, as far as I knew, Partin had nothing to do with it.

I showed him affidavits executed by George Wyatt and Morris Bromlee in which they stated under oath that they had been recruited by the Labor-Management Commission to frame Partin. I told the governor that Mike Epstein at the Department of Justice had further evidence which raised questions about the motivation of some staff members of the Labor-Management Commission. Governor McKeithen said that he would like Epstein to discuss the matter with Dean Morgan, the chairman of the commission.

Shortly thereafter the governor called Epstein and arranged an appointment for him with Dean Morgan. With the approval of Fred Vinson, the head of the Criminal Division, Epstein met with Dean Morgan and told him that it appeared that members of his staff might be working for Hoffa's interests. Dean Morgan replied, "What if they are, as long as the facts come out?"

Both my meeting with Governor McKeithen and Epstein's meeting with Dean Morgan were later leaked to the press in Louisiana, in a light favorable to them. Governor McKeithen denied to me that he had been the source of the leak.

The Labor-Management Commission brought charges against a number of officials of Local 5 and their associates in the effort to get at Partin. One of these was Wade "Slim" McClanahan, a big, rangy man from Texas who had recently joined the local. McClanahan was just the type of person Ed Partin did not need around him, but that was one of Partin's weaknesses. McClanahan was a troublemaker who liked to throw his weight around. He had been one of the leaders of the picket line involved in the shooting incident and multiple charges were subsequently brought against him.

In late March McClanahan called Partin from Texas and told him that representatives of the Labor-Management Commission were en route to Texas and were going to offer him $100,000 to furnish information about Partin. McClanahan said that they had approached him through a man named Billy D. Miller, a friend of his. McClanahan said that he had called Sheriff Bill Decker of Dallas and told him. Partin told McClanahan that he might be walking into a trap and suggested he come back to Louisiana. McClanahan did as Partin suggested. Billy Miller and McClanahan subsequently furnished affidavits in which they related what had happened.

Miller said that on March 24 he was at his brother's home in Starkville, Mississippi, when he received a call from Tom McFerrin who had replaced A. Harry Roberts as chief counsel for the Labor-Management Commission. McFerrin told Miller that it was important that he see him right away and Miller agreed to meet with him the following day at the police station in Woodville, Mississippi. The next morning Miller drove with his brother to Woodville and met with McFerrin and Joe Oster. They told Miller that they wanted him to approach Wade McClanahan, whom he had known in Baton Rouge, to furnish an affidavit for which they were prepared to offer as much as $100,000. They told Miller they would pay him $200 a week for expenses and would give him a $10,000 bonus if he obtained the affidavit. They knew about Miller's difficulties in Texas (where he was wanted for a burglary), and said if he went along with them, he would not have to worry about the Texas charges. But if he did not cooperate, they threatened to turn him over to Texas authorities.

Miller confirmed that he had met with McClanahan in Grapevine, Texas, and relayed the proposition to McClanahan that McFerrin and Oster were willing to pay him $100,000 for an affidavit against Ed Partin. He told McClanahan that they had said the affidavit did not have to be true. McClanahan agreed to give them the affidavit. A few minutes later Oster called. Miller told him he had what he wanted and asked Oster how soon he could come to Texas. Oster said they would be there as soon as possible, even if they had to use the governor's plane, and that they would call him as soon as they arrived. When Miller hung up, McClanahan picked up the phone and called Sheriff Bill Decker of Dallas and told him

that Oster and McFerrin were en route to Dallas to offer him a
$100,000 bribe. Then he called Ed Partin and told him what had
happened. That's when Partin told McClanahan he thought he
might be walking into a trap and McClanahan decided to leave
Texas and return to Baton Rouge.

Miller was upset and afraid because he felt he was now in the
middle. He again met with McFerrin and Oster, this time in Dallas. They were upset that McClanahan had left but told Miller they
wanted him to go to Louisiana and talk to Governor McKeithen.
They wanted him to tell the governor that he was a good friend
of McClanahan's, that he knew what was going on in Local 5 and
that Ed Partin and Local 5 were responsible for all the labor difficulties in Baton Rouge. They said that if he could convince the
governor of this, he would give them free reign and funds and they
would pay Miller $1000.

That night Wade McClanahan called Miller and told him he
wanted him to come to Louisiana and give an affidavit that he had
tried to bribe him for Oster and McFerrin. Miller, now quite
frightened, refused to do so. When Oster called him the next morning he told him about McClanahan's demand. Oster told him to ask
McClanahan to wire him the travel money but not to cash the
wire. Oster said that they could then charge McClanahan for trying to bribe Miller to give an affidavit.

Miller called McClanahan that night and again refused to give
the affidavit. McClanahan became angry and the conversation was
terminated.

The following Monday, in New Orleans, Oster introduced
Miller to a man named Jack Oliphant, another staff member of the
Labor-Management Commission, and the three men drove to Baton Rouge and went to the governor's mansion. Tom McFerrin
and Dr. J. Taylor, a member of the commission, were with the
governor. Miller told the governor what McFerrin and Oster had
instructed him to say. When he was finished, McKeithen told
McFerrin to do whatever he had to do to break up Local 5. He said
that if the commission were declared unconstitutional, he would
move everything over to the state police. Then the governor assured Miller that he did not have to worry about any difficulties
in Louisiana since he would have immunity.

Miller then accompanied Oster and McFerrin in McFerrin's car
to the Labor-Management Commission headquarters, where he
told them that he had done what he was supposed to do and now

wanted out. But they said they wanted him to meet the attorney general. The next day Miller went to meet Attorney General Jack Gremillion, who promised Miller immunity and said they were after Ed Partin and that Miller should do everything he could to influence Wade McClanahan to help them.

Miller stayed in New Orleans for a time and received $200 a week although he was not actually doing anything. Oster told him that the attorney general's office had a fund of $5000 for which no accounting was required. Checks were drawn on this account to McFerrin, who cashed them and gave the money to Miller. Miller usually received the money at Oster's office and was paid on different occasions by Raymond Ruiz, Nick Ross and Tom McFerrin.

On April 22, in Washington, D.C., the Assistant Attorney General in charge of the Antitrust Division of the Department of Justice wrote a memorandum to Attorney General Ramsey Clark recommending that a grand jury investigation be authorized concerning the alleged conspiracy by Ed Partin and Ted Dunham, Jr., to restrain trade in the Baton Rouge concrete industry.

Both Senator Russell Long and Governor McKeithen made arrangements for Wallace Heck and others to go to Washington and meet with the Attorney General and other officials of the Justice Department to complain about Partin.

On April 28 Billy Miller signed an affidavit stating that he had seen a machine gun in the possession of Wade McClanahan.

On April 29, 1968, a law enforcement official in Baton Rouge told Ed Partin that he should be careful because the Labor-Management Commission people were going to try to plant a machine gun on him. That afternoon Wade McClanahan was arrested for possession of a machine gun. Simultaneous raids were made by a combined force of Labor-Management investigators and state police on the homes of other Teamsters members and the Local 5 offices. At the same time Ed Partin was arrested by Joe Oster on a complaint by Irby Aucoin, a former photographer for Channel 12 in New Orleans. In the complaint Aucoin charged that twenty months earlier he had been threatened with a gun by Partin when he was attempting to take photographs.

At the Department of Justice the antitrust investigation of Partin had been assigned to Wilford Whitley, a career attorney in the Antitrust Division. Mike Epstein had several meetings with him and other members of the division to acquaint them with Partin's role in the Hoffa case and the various efforts that had been made and were in progress to influence Partin to change his testimony. Whitley tended to treat Epstein with suspicion, and a tension developed between the two divisions within the department. Personnel in the Antitrust Division acknowledged that there had been pressure from Senator Long to push the investigation. But Whitley's position stiffened and it became more and more obvious that he was keenly intent on prosecuting Partin.

It had been the policy of the Department of Justice during the past five Administrations not to prosecute labor officials for violation of the antitrust laws. I did not know whether Partin had violated these laws or not. He said that so far as he knew, he hadn't. But neither he nor I understood the laws or the facts of the case that well. It was clear, however, that the same laws were not being applied to any other labor official in the country. It appeared that, at best, the Department of Justice, under political pressure, was reaching out to prosecute one of its own witnesses in a major criminal case on an issue it would not ordinarily apply, and was not applying, to any other labor official.

The stop-Kennedy forces began coming together. On May 2, a Big Brother Testimonial Dinner for Drew Pearson was held in Washington, D.C. Vice President Humphrey was the main speaker and Frank Sinatra was the featured entertainer. The night before the dinner a party was held at Pearson's home. At the party Sinatra came out for Humphrey stating that he didn't think "Bobby Kennedy is qualified to be President of the United States." (Sinatra had worked for the election of President Kennedy but a rift had developed after Kennedy's election because of Sinatra's close association with Chicago Mafia leader Sam Giancana.) Also present at the Pearson party were Hoffa friends Allen Dorfman and I. Irving Davidson. Washington society reporter Maxine Cheshire, who attended the party, wrote in the following morning's *Washington Post*, "The group also included dapper, sun-tanned Allen Dorfman of Chicago, whose green-suited sartorial splendor had been attracting attention at the Pearson party." The columnist later told me that the people at the party had wondered who Dorfman was. Some thought that he was Sinatra's manager. She knew who he was and approached him.

"You're Allen Dorfman aren't you?" Maxine asked.

"That's right," responded Dorfman.

"I've heard you are here to try to get Jimmy Hoffa out of jail," Maxine said.

"That's right, baby," said Dorfman, "I'm here to buy anyone who can be bought. Are you for sale?"

After the party there was a gathering at a table at the plush Rive Gauche Restaurant which included Dorfman, Sinatra, Davidson and Mrs. James R. Hoffa.

On May 3, at the direction of Fred Vinson, United States Attorney Louis La Cour from New Orleans and Mike Epstein went before Senator Russell Long's former law partner Judge E. Gordon West in Baton Rouge to ask for the dismissal of the original 1962 indictment of Partin. Judge West had been publicly outspoken against Partin.

In the petition to dismiss, filed several months earlier with Judge West, the Department of Justice said that "the interests of justice would best be served" by dismissing an indictment. The petition noted that there was an obvious bias on the part of certain government witnesses and that one key witness had died. "The Justice Department feels although no bargain was made, we cannot be oblivious to the fact that the defendant aided the government in testifying."

Judge West was caustic in his remarks. He said, "In other words, this is a payoff for testimony in the Hoffa case." When Epstein denied it, he said, "If that isn't a payoff, I don't know what is." Later Judge West said, "Are the interests of justice to be served by the granting of lifetime immunity to someone because of the wishes of a previous attorney general?" "No, sir," Epstein replied, "no such immunity is in existence today." Judge West denied the motion to dismiss.

Meanwhile, the Presidential primary campaigns were going forward, and the Teamsters were actively involved in a stop-Kennedy movement. In Indiana the Teamsters backed Governor Roger Branigan, who was considered to be a stand-in for Vice President Hubert Humphrey. There were subsequent meetings between Teamsters representatives and Vice President Humphrey and his staff. Offers were made to support Humphrey if he would agree to let Hoffa out of prison.

On June 6 Senator Kennedy won the South Dakota primary with 50 percent of the vote and the California contest with 46 percent. Late that night Robert Kennedy's campaign came to a sudden and tragic end on the floor of the kitchen in the Ambassador Hotel in Los Angeles.

One week later, on June 13, Ed Partin and Billy Daniels met in Room 168 at the Hilton Airport Hotel in New Orleans with attorney F. Lee Bailey. The meeting had been arranged by a private investigator named Don George who was working for Bailey. At the meeting Bailey said that he was considering representing Hoffa but had not yet taken the case. He said his only contact so far had been through Allen Dorfman, and that contact with Hoffa was through Hoffa's son James. Bailey told Partin that he was only interested in the truth. Partin replied that the truth would keep Hoffa in prison. Bailey said that he had read the trial transcript and that the jury had not been given all the facts. He said he wanted to obtain a new trial so that all of the facts would come out. Partin asked him if he was referring to wiretapping and Bailey replied that he was. Partin told him that there had been no wiretapping. As Bailey prepared to leave, Partin asked him how he hoped to spring Hoffa. Bailey said that Robert Kennedy was dead and that the public soon forgets. He said he was going to file a motion after the Democratic Convention in August on Hoffa's behalf. The meeting broke up at that point.

Bailey later told Don George that if Robert Kennedy had not been killed, he had intended to file a suit just prior to the Democratic Convention, charging that Kennedy had paid Partin and Daniels $200,000 in cash to testify against Hoffa. Bailey had previously told George that the $200,000 had been sent to Partin and Daniels in small denominations from a bank in Hyannis Port, Massachusetts. He had hired George to obtain evidence of this, but to George's knowledge there was no such evidence. George said that Bailey promised him $200 a week and a bonus of $10,000 "the day Jimmy Hoffa hit the street."

George later told Bill Daniels that Jim Garrison had told him that it was he who had been instrumental in getting F. Lee Bailey interested in the Hoffa case. George also said that during the course of his investigation for Bailey he had met a New Orleans attorney, Guy Johnson, who claimed to be a former officer with the

Office of Naval Intelligence. He said that Johnson had given him the name of H. Gordon Homme, of the staff of Senator Edward Long's committee, as a good contact in Washington.

Homme and Bernard Fensterwald had made several trips to New Orleans and had paid visits to Jim Garrison's office. According to one of Garrison's former staff members, Fensterwald was interested in Garrison's assassination probe, but seemed to be more interested in what his staff knew about me and Mike Epstein.

On June 14, when Wade McClanahan had a preliminary hearing on the charge of possessing a machine gun, both Billy Miller and Lawrence Samuels testified for the state that they had seen a machine gun in McClanahan's possession. Both later admitted in statements furnished to the Department of Justice that they had lied in their testimony and that Ken Scullen, a staff member of the Labor-Management Commission who was representing the state at the hearing, knew they were lying. Both men said that they testified as they did because of intimidation by staff members of the commission. Miller said that the commission investigators did not expect to convict McClanahan on the charge, but kept filing charges against him to harass him into cooperating against Partin. According to Miller, the investigators bragged about what they were doing. He said that on one occasion a state policeman named Herbert Hamilton said that he would shoot Partin if given any excuse and had tightened handcuffs on McClanahan in such a way that they left marks on his wrists for three or four days. On another occasion, according to Miller, A. Harry Roberts, after an argument with Bill Daniels, said that he was going to kill Daniels. Miller said that they also discussed ways of framing General Tom Burbank of the state police and George Wyatt and Morris Bromlee.

Miller stated that the preliminary hearing on McClanahan had originally been set for May 10. On the previous day Miller was given $200 and left for Grapevine, Texas, with the consent of the commission investigators. Miller said that about one week later he was called by Oster, who told him that McClanahan had blown the whistle on him in Texas and that he had better come to New Orleans and surrender to Oster. Oster wired another $200 to Miller in Fort Worth in Samuels' name. Miller went with Samuels to the Western Union office to pick up the money. Oster also sent prepaid airline tickets on Eastern Airlines in the name of H. Hudson.

Miller said that he flew to New Orleans and was met at the airport by Oster and Raymond Ruiz, who took him directly to the office of Jim Garrison. Miller said that he was taken before Judge Matthew Braniff, who commented, "So this is the fellow who is helping you get Ed Partin." Miller said that the judge set bail at $500 and he was released on his own recognizance.

Miller also said that he met Billy Simpson at the Labor-Management headquarters and that Simpson introduced him to J. D. Albin. Simpson had furnished one of the affidavits for Hoffa's appeal. Simpson said they were also paying him $200 a week. Miller said that Simpson and Albin discussed Ed Partin and claimed he had lied at the Hoffa trial.

Now, Miller said, there came a time when for some reason the funds for payment of informants were cut off. Joe Oster suggested that they go see Chuck Winters, head of the Teamsters Union in New Orleans, so Miller drove to Winters' office with Billy Simpson. They were joined there by Joe Oster and J. D. Albin. Oster explained to Winters that Simpson and Miller needed money since the state funds had been cut off. Winters said that he would have to call Frank Fitzsimmons and asked them to leave the room. When they returned, Winters told them that when Hoffa hit the street they would be well taken care of. In the meantime, Winters said, he would try to work something out to get them jobs. They were later offered jobs at the Viking Dock of the Specter Freight Lines and were told they would make $300 a week although they would not have to work.

Miller said that on another occasion Ken Scullen told Miller to go to the Baton Rouge jail and visit Edgar Coleman. Coleman had been originally charged with aggravated battery in connection with the Plaquemine incident; the charge was later reduced to simple battery, and Coleman was found guilty. Miller said that Scullen instructed him to offer Coleman $200 a week, a promise of protection and removal to any place in the country if he would sign an affidavit against Partin. He was told to tell Coleman that if he didn't cooperate he would spend forty years in prison. Miller said that he went to the jail with staff member Pete Brandon and state police officer Herbert Hamilton. Scullen had told him that there would be a judge standing by to release Coleman if he gave the affidavit. Coleman refused.

On May 16, 1968, Edgar Coleman furnished an affidavit in which he stated that on May 7, 1968, Billy Miller came to visit him about

9:30 in the evening. He said that Miller was accompanied by Mr.
Hamilton, a state policeman, and a man called Pete. He said that
he had not asked Miller to come to see him. He said that Miller
came into his cell and the others remained outside. According to
Coleman, Miller told him that he could get him out of jail if he
would go with him to the Labor-Management Commission and
give a statement about Partin. He said that Miller mentioned his
family and having to do forty years in prison, and suggested that
maybe he had to choose between his family and Partin.

Donald Lloyd Howell, who was Coleman's cellmate at the time,
also gave an affidavit in which he said that Miller, Hamilton and
another man came to see Coleman. Howell said that he was standing outside the cell in the jail during the conversation between
Miller and Coleman and that he overheard Miller tell Coleman
that the judge would let him out of jail if he would talk to some
people. He said that he also heard Miller ask Coleman if he wanted
to trade his family for Ed Partin.

The antitrust grand jury was convened in New Orleans and
Wallace Heck and Roland Stevens testified before it on June 18,
1968. Other witnesses were called during July and August. On
August 11, 1968, Ted Dunham, Jr., told Partin that Senator Long
had called his father that day and apologized for starting the investigation and involving the Dunhams.

The situation was awkward, to say the least. One grand jury in
New Orleans was attempting to protect a government witness
from attempts to bribe and intimidate him, while another grand
jury was trying to indict the same witness.

On July 30, 1968, George Wyatt, Morris Bromlee and a friend,
Kenneth Harris, were arrested at the Bellmont Motel in Baton
Rouge. A heavily armed raiding party made up of former commission investigators assigned to the attorney general's office, state
police and East Baton Rouge sheriff's deputies made the arrests
and led the trio away in handcuffs. Wyatt was charged with perjury for filing an affidavit in federal court about having been hired
to frame Partin. His bond was set at $15,000. Bromlee and Harris
were charged with vagrancy and their bonds were set at $50,000
each. A newspaper account of the raid quoted one of the arresting
officers as saying:

Have you ever read Hitler's *Mein Kampf*? If you write this up, you can count on the Labor-Management Commission denying everything. I don't give a damn about Ed Partin—I don't even know him —but I don't like being a part of this sort of thing.

On August 19, 1968, a hearing was held in federal court in Nashville on Tommy Osborn's motion for a new trial. Osborn had already begun serving his sentence. Both Bob Vick and I testified about the $3000 I had lent him and then retracted the following day. I took the opportunity during my testimony to outline all of the activities that had been transpiring in relation to Don Vestal, Vick and Partin in efforts to get them to change their testimony. Earl Wingo and James Craighead, though called as defense witnesses, on cross-examination by United States Attorney Gil Merritt, related the various efforts by Hoffa's agents to bribe Vick to help Hoffa.

Tommy Osborn then took the stand. The government had recently learned that a loan had been made by the Teamsters Pension Fund to a company in Texas. Of the loan, $127,500 had been diverted and given in cash to Osborn in Atlanta, Georgia, in January, 1964—after Osborn had been disbarred by Judges Miller and Gray but before both the Hoffa trial in Chattanooga and the subsequent trial of Osborn. When Gil Merritt asked Osborn about the transaction he at first claimed it was irrelevant. But when pressed by Merritt and the judge, he took the Fifth Amendment and declined to answer.

As a result of the testimony in the hearing, Judges Miller and Gray ordered that a grand jury be convened to investigate the charges that had been made during the hearing about the widespread and concerted efforts on Hoffa's behalf.

In early September while walking through the corridor of the old Senate Office Building I encountered reporter Clark Mollenhoff.

"Is there anything to that story in the *Government Employees Exchange*?" Clark asked.

"What is the *Government Employees Exchange* and what are you talking about?" I asked back.

"It's a paper that circulates up here on the Hill. There's a big story in it about you and Otepka."

Otto Otepka had been a high official in the Security Division of the State Department. When the Kennedy Administration came into office in 1961, Otepka had begun furnishing information about some of the Kennedy appointees, whom he considered too liberal, to Jay Sourwine, chief counsel of the Senate Internal Security Committee. He had been caught in the act by other members of the Security Division and had been transferred to another position and subsequently fired by Secretary of State Dean Rusk. One of the men involved in catching Otepka was David Belisle, a friend of mine, with whom I had once worked at the National Security Agency. In the process of catching Otepka, the Security Division personnel had made the mistake of placing a bug on his telephone. When Jay Sourwine learned of this, he summoned these men before the Internal Security Committee to testify about it. Belisle had not been involved in the bugging operation, as he was out of the country at the time.

I told Mollenhoff I did not know what he was talking about but that I would pick up a copy of the paper and call him. I found the *Exchange* at one of the newstands and was astounded to read a front-page article captioned "5 Eyes and Doodlegrams Used by Department for Tapping." A box on the front page said, "Sheridan Was Alleged Contact at WH." The article itself was absolutely incredible. It started out:

> Walter Sheridan, the closest collaborator of the late Senator Robert F. Kennedy in the surveillance and prosecution of James Hoffa, the leader of the Teamsters Union, has been identified by a knowledgeable source as the "mysterious person" to whom the tapes prepared by Clarence Jerome Schneider from the tapped telephone of Otto F. Otepka were delivered, it was authoritatively reported last week. . . . Currently an "investigative reporter" for NBC News, Mr. Sheridan was also identified by the source as one of the chief contacts for Robert F. Kennedy with "International Investigators Incorporated, Indianapolis, Indiana," a "hush hush" organization.

The article went on to say that the Indiana corporation was known both as "The Three Eyes" and "The Five Eyes" and that its employees were contracted out to the government for wiretapping and used "doodlegrams" to identify themselves and their projects. The article said that the Kennedy Administration had used these services and paid for them through unvouchered funds in the White House, thus leaving no trace in the records of the Justice Department.

> Although on the payroll of the Justice Department and nominally with an office there, Mr. Sheridan actually was physically located at the White House, the source said. Through a series of interconnected transfers of funds, he disposed over the personnel and currency of whole units of the Central Intelligence Agency. In addition, wire tap tapes, including the "voice profiles" made at the White House by the Secret Service and at the Department of State through the "electronics laboratory," were passed on to him and maintained in a separate facility outwardly appearing as a weather station, the source claimed. In addition to its illegal intelligence operations, the "wire tapping" was used to provide Robert Kennedy and Walter Sheridan material for "plants with the press," the source said. In explanation he asserted that a special relationship existed between Mr. Kennedy and Time-Life, Inc. and between Mr. Sheridan and the Huntley-Brinkley Report.

The article concluded by stating that I had protected Dave Belisle from perjury charges before the Senate Committee because "Mr. Sheridan and Mr. Belisle had worked together at the National Security Agency."

I had, of course, by this time become immune to surprise at almost anything, but this article did set a new mark in the realm of the absurd. I took the newspaper and went directly to the *Government Employees Exchange,* which turned out to occupy a small two-room office on the second floor of 1913 I Street, N.W., in Washington. Sidney Goldberg, who was listed on the masthead of the paper as publisher and executive director, appeared to be the only employee of the paper other than the receptionist. I introduced myself to Goldberg and told him that the article was completely untrue and outlandish and asked him why he had not checked with me before printing it.

"Mr. Maher said that you were in Tennessee," he replied.

"Which Mr. Maher—Danny Maher?" I asked.

He nodded.

"Why would you check with Jimmy Hoffa's lawyer to try to locate me?"

He did not answer.

I told Goldberg that I wanted him to retract the article. He said that he would check back with his sources and that if it was not true, he would retract it. I asked him who his sources were. He wouldn't tell me but said, "One of them was a delegate to the Democratic Convention." I told Goldberg I would be back in touch with him and left. He had also mentioned the name Fensterwald.

The following night I called him and asked him what he was going to do about the article. He said that "they" had some questions "they" wanted to ask me. I asked him who "they" were and he replied that he could not tell me. I told him to send the questions to my attorney, Jack Miller, and I would look them over.

On September 9 Goldberg sent a letter to Jack Miller enclosing a list of thirty-eight questions which he said I had agreed to answer. The first fifteen questions related to my relationship with Dave Belisle. The next two, under the caption "Unvouchered Funds," related to whether I had received funds from Robert Kennedy or a relative. The rest dealt with my relationship with "The Five Eyes," Robert Kennedy, NBC, the State Department and the "Otepka tapes." I decided not to waste any more time with this questionnaire.

In the September 18 issue of the *Exchange* there was a detailed rundown on the history of "The Five Eyes," which had, according to the article, been formed by a group of ex-FBI agents as a private investigating agency and had changed its name to the 904 Realty Corporation of Indianapolis. The source for the entire article was "statements obtained from the Senate Subcommittee on Administrative Practices." This was Senator Edward Long's committee and explained Goldberg's prior reference to Bernard Fensterwald.

I had, of course, never heard of "The Five Eyes" or "The Three Eyes"; I did not know anyone associated with it; I did not receive any "Otepka tapes"; I did not have an office in the White House, nor an office disguised as a weather station; I did not receive any Secret Service tapes or "voice profiles"; and I had never had any relationship with the CIA.

I later learned that Goldberg had been in dire financial straits at the time and had been seeking to obtain funds from either the

Teamsters Pension Fund or the *Manchester Union Leader*. He was subsequently charged by the Federal Trade Commission with publishing unauthorized advertisements and then demanding payments for the nonexistent debts.

The grand jury in Nashville, conducted by Mike Epstein and Gil Merritt, began hearing testimony on October 3. Ed Partin and Bill Daniels again testified about the many approaches on behalf of Hoffa, as did George Wyatt, Morris Bromlee and others. There was a new feeling of security in being outside of the state of Louisiana, where some witnesses had been reluctant to testify candidly because of repeated indications of leaks from the grand jury. But time was running out. The Presidential campaign between Vice President Humphrey and Richard Nixon was in full swing, and one month later Nixon was elected President of the United States.

In Missouri Senator Edward Long, tarnished by the publicity concerning his receipt of over $100,000 in "referral fees" from Morris Shenker and the charges that he had used his Senate subcommittee to attempt to assist Hoffa, was defeated in his bid for reelection.

In Detroit Local 299 a slate of officers for reelection was chosen. It was headed by Jimmy Hoffa, seeking to renew his tenure as president of the local from his prison call in Lewisburg. On November 12 newspapers across the country carried a photograph of one Bernard Jacubus sprawled on the sidewalk trying to protect his face with his arms while a huge man stood over him, kicking him. He had been beaten up for passing out literature in front of the Teamsters Hall in Detroit, protesting the slate of nominees headed by Hoffa.

With the change of Administrations came the appointment of a new United States Attorney in Nashville who knew nothing about what had transpired. There were also jurisdictional problems, since most of the activity had been in Louisiana. The grand jury finally went out of existence with no action being taken.

In December Jimmy Hoffa, running from prison, was reelected president of Local 299 in Detroit by an overwhelming majority.

CHAPTER XV

The Witness Becomes the Defendant

▭ ▭ ▭ ▭ ▭ ▭ ▭ ▭ ▭

THE NIGHT THAT President-elect Nixon announced his new Cabinet at the Shoreham Hotel in Washington, there was a cocktail party in their honor. The host was William Loeb of the *Manchester Union Leader*. The President-elect stopped by to pay his respects. As the new Administration settled into position, the men who would control the government began to take their places. John Mitchell, the new Attorney General, appointed Will Wilson, a craggy Texas judge and former prosecutor, to replace Fred Vinson as head of the Criminal Division. Shortly after taking office, Wilson was visited by William Loeb. Wilson had agreed to see Loeb in spite of having been advised by representatives of the Criminal Division of Loeb's past activities on behalf of Hoffa and the fact that he had received loans from the Teamsters Pension Fund. Loeb had previously written letters to Fred Vinson on behalf of Hoffa, and Vinson had finally adopted a policy of not even replying to the letters. Wilson was also aware of this.

On March 10, 1969, Hoffa attorney Daniel Maher sent a letter to Loeb in which he said that he had met with Hoffa the previous Friday to discuss "pending matters" and they agreed that "the tack which should be taken in the discussions is a plea for unconditional pardons in both cases." Maher said that this line would be taken because a pardon in the Chattanooga case would be useless if the appeal of the Chicago case were lost.

Maher also suggested that "it would be best" not to raise the question of commutation or parole in early conversations, saying that if "we have to raise these questions, it can be done later."

Maher also told Loeb that Attorney General John Mitchell was "convinced that there was something wrong with the Hoffa cases [Brock quote]," and that "it would be helpful" if the Attorney General were to direct his attention to "the expenditures made from the confidential fund at Justice Department (to which knowledge only he has access), made to Partin and Vick," as well as to wiretapping and surveillance of Hoffa's counsel.

Maher went on to say that Hoffa had learned from Dick Holtzmann, a deputy U.S. marshal from Harrisburg, Pennsylvania, that payments of $500 each had been made to deputies assigned to the trial in Chattanooga and Maher suggested to Loeb that "this may be the source of funds for the prostitutes and booze."

Maher then moved on to the subject of Ed Partin by suggesting to Loeb that if Attorney General Mitchell "indicates that he is willing to pursue the inquiry, you could inquire why Partin has not been prosecuted." Maher indicated that it would also be of help if Mitchell would follow up on Arthur Egan's investigation of "The Three Eyes" and any government assignments given to them, saying that Mitchell should be able to learn if "a facility disguised as a weather station was used as an operation and storage center for the wiretapper."

Loeb was reminded in the letter that Gordon Homme was employed by Long's wiretapping subcommittee of the Judiciary Committee. And Maher suggested that before Egan interviewed Homme "it might be better if the proper entree is prepared by a preliminary call to Homme by Long or Shenker," which Maher would arrange.

Maher then asked Loeb if Egan was "still in touch with the New Orleans people" and said that if he was, Loeb should ask him to find out the current status of the indictment against me and when it was scheduled to go to trial.

Maher ended his letter by saying that Hoffa had asked him to express his thanks to Loeb for his help. In a postscript he mentioned that Tommy Osborn would be paroled in April, noting that "Persistence plus a bit of Congressional Intervention pays off."

Loeb sent a copy of the letter, along with some other material, to Will Wilson.

It was an interesting letter in many respects. It was obvious that

Maher and Hoffa had information that Loeb had already made arrangements to intercede with Attorney General Mitchell for Hoffa. They also had information that Mitchell was "convinced that there was something wrong with the Hoffa cases," and was going to take a good look at them. This information was attributed to "Brock"—presumably Senator William Brock (then Congressman from Tennessee), who had previously spoken up on Hoffa's behalf on the floor of the House during one of Sid Zagri's productions.

The information concerning the payment of Partin's and Vick's expenses had already been the subject of extensive hearings in court. The information attributed to Deputy Marshal Holtzmann was false and Holtzmann subsequently flatly denied that he had made such a statement.

The question to be directed to the Attorney General as to why Partin had not been prosecuted was well on its way to being corrected by the activities of the Antitrust Division, whose investigation of Partin was now gaining new momentum.

The information about "The Three Eyes" related, of course, to the article in the *Government Employees Exchange*, which now appeared to have been originated by Loeb reporter Arthur Egan.

The relationship between Hoffa's attorney Morris Shenker and Senator Edward Long was nicely capsulated by the suggestion that Long or Shenker could pave the way for Arthur Egan to talk to Long Committee investigator Gordon Homme.

Then there was the verification that the network also included "the New Orleans people" who would be in a position to know the status of Garrison's charges against me and when I was expected to go to trial.

Finally, there was the assurance that Tommy Osborn would be paroled five weeks hence and the boast that "persistence plus a bit of Congressional Intervention pays off." Tommy Osborn was paroled after the Parole Board was falsely advised that he had been disbarred by the state of Tennessee.

That letter told it all. It was not only a synopsis of what had been but also a blueprint of what was to come.

On Easter Sunday, April 6, a note was left at Ed Partin's home with a Detroit phone number on it. Partin called the number and the man answering said that he was Jimmy Hoffa, Jr. The man said, "You don't sound like Ed Partin." Partin replied, "You don't sound like Jimmy Hoffa, Jr."

Hoffa, Jr., then asked for Partin's number and said that he would call him back. He did so shortly afterward and asked Partin if he would give him information concerning wiretapping. Partin told him that there hadn't been any wiretapping and that he was wasting his time.

On April 15 Buddy Gill told Partin that they "were going to get that Jew bastard Epstein fired or transferred to Siberia." He said that the Kennedys were gone now and the Justice Department was going to bring an eleven-count indictment against Partin.

On May 20 A. T. "Apple" Sanders furnished an affidavit to Ted Dunham, Jr.'s attorney in Baton Rouge which stated in part:

> About the end of March 1969 Wallace Heck invited Sanders to have lunch with him at Bellmont on Friday about noon. He asked Sanders to come to work for him as sales manager, and told him that he, Heck, was going to get Ted Dunham, Jr., and Ed Partin indicted by a Federal Grand Jury. Sanders questioned this, saying that this was a function of the Grand Jury and that it was nothing Heck could direct. Heck answered by saying that his efforts against Dunham had cost him Three Hundred Thousand Dollars, that he had been "living" in Washington seeing a Mr. Whitley, and that he would get the indictment in about three or four weeks. Mr. Heck added that when he got the indictment against Dunham this would ruin Dunham's business and this is what he had set out to do. He added that when the Federal Grand Jury indicted Dunham, it would win his civil anti-trust suit for him against Dunham.

The affidavit was turned over to the Antitrust Division.

On June 13 a front-page article appeared in the *Wall Street Journal*: "A Special Case? A Louisiana Teamster Eludes Courts Since Hoffa Trial Testimony." The two reporters who wrote the article worked out of the Houston bureau and had talked to me two weeks earlier. I asked them what had raised their interest in Partin and they told me that some pipeline people in Houston had suggested the case to them. It was obvious talking to them that their minds were made up. The article quoted me as saying, "It's natural for people to think I'm paranoic and see Hoffa behind every bush. But Hoffa is behind a lot of bushes." The article also quoted Governor

John McKeithen: "We have been harassed by people representing the Justice Department who we hoped were here to help us, but instead insisted we were tools of some sinister force to free Hoffa from the penitentiary." The article went on to say:

> One persistent, though unconfirmed report is that Mr. Partin has a letter signed by Robert Kennedy making certain commitments in return for his testimony. Public disclosure of such a letter—whose existence Mr. Partin denies—would be highly embarrassing. . . . Under pressure from Louisiana Congressmen and business leaders, Attorney General Mitchell is said to have ordered a full review of Mr. Partin's treatment by the Justice Department in recent years. The outcome of that review isn't clear but there are hints that Mr. Partin's luck may be running out.

On June 20 Ed Partin and Ted Dunham, Jr., were indicted by the antitrust federal grand jury in New Orleans for conspiracy to commit extortion and to restrain trade. Later that day Frank "Tickie" Saia picked up Dunham and drove him to Russell Long's home outside Baton Rouge. Saia, an old friend of Senator Long's, ran an electrical business in Baton Rouge. He had recently been named "Small Businessman of the Year" in Louisiana and served, through Senator Long's influence, as a member of the advisory council of the Small Business Administration (SBA) in Baton Rouge. He was subsequently eased out of his position on the advisory council by SBA administrator Hillary Sandoval after he was arrested in Houston along with underworld figures in a gambling raid.

At the poolside meeting at Senator Long's home the Senator told Dunham, who had been a political supporter in the past, that he was sorry about his indictment. He asked if there was anything he could do and suggested that Dunham could best help himself by furnishing information on Partin. Dunham told Senator Long that he did not have any information on Partin and the brief meeting ended shortly thereafter.

Later that month Ted Dunham, Sr., met with Senator Long at the latter's apartment in the Watergate East in Washington. Dunham was interested in obtaining a $20,000,000 loan to take advantage of a revolutionary new cement-making process for which he was negotiating and the construction of a huge new plant that it would entail. Dunham offered Senator Long a piece of the action if the loan could be obtained. He stayed at Senator Long's apartment for the night and the Senator made an unsuccessful effort to call Frank Fitzsimmons of the Teamsters Union.

Senator Long subsequently introduced Dunham to Harold S. Geneen, the president and chairman of the board of the International Telephone and Telegraph Corporation, at a private luncheon in the Senate Dining Room. Geneen expressed an interest in Dunham's proposition and sent a representative of ITT to Louisiana to explore it but it did not work out.

On July 10 I testified at the hearing in Chicago which had been ordered by the Supreme Court to determine whether the overhearing of the conversation of George Burris on the FBI bug in Ben Sigelbaum's Miami office had in any way tainted the evidence in the Pension Fund case. There had also been a more recent Supreme Court decision holding that the previously accepted policy of the Department of Justice of turning over to the courts only those electronic overhearings that were considered in any way relevant to the case in question was no longer sufficient. The court now held that all overhearings, whether considered relevant or not, must be turned over.

After a thorough review of all records, the department had found that in the entire investigation in connection with the Hoffa cases there had not been one instance of wiretapping or bugging of Hoffa. There had been a recording of a conversation between Morris "Moe" Dalitz, one of the owners of the Desert Inn in Las Vegas, and Hoffa in 1962. The overhearing was accomplished by a bug planted by the FBI in Dalitz's office and recorded only Dalitz's end of the conversation. It also turned out that, unbeknownst to any of us, the FBI had monitored the Teamsters radio cars in Detroit for a period of time and had on several occasions overheard both Larry Campbell and Hoffa.

After a careful study of the transcripts of these overhearings, the department had previously decided they were in no way relevant to either the Chicago or the Chattanooga cases and had therefore not submitted them. But they, along with the Sigelbaum transcripts, were now turned over to Judge Richard Austin. I had not known about any of these overhearings until long after I left the Department of Justice.

There was no other overhearing of any kind of Hoffa or his

co-defendants except one perfectly legal one of Ewing King. Shortly before Hoffa and the others were indicted for jury tampering in Nashville, Ed Partin had driven to Nashville to meet with Ewing King, who subsequently became a defendant. At our request, and with Partin's permission, the FBI bugged Partin's car. Partin picked up King and they went for a short drive. It was hoped that King might make additional admissions which would have been legally admissible in court. The fact that the conversation occurred prior to the indictment and in Partin's car, with his permission, made it a perfectly legal investigative effort by all judicial precedents—as it still is. Because of noise interference the resulting recording of the conversation was absolutely worthless. According to Partin, King did not say anything of significance anyway, and what he said was, for the most part, unintelligible. Therefore it was not used at the trial and the fact of its existence never came up. Since it was not illegally obtained, it was not subject to disclosure, and hence it was not submitted for the Chicago hearing.

When I was called to testify in Chicago, Hoffa's attorney asked me whether I had ever heard of an organization called "The Five Eyes" or "The Three Eyes." I replied that I had never heard of the organization until I read about it in the *Government Employees Exchange.* I said that the article was completely false. I was also asked whether I knew Eddie Jones and Carmine Bellino and whether we three had been Robert Kennedy's wiretap squad—the same question that William Loeb had asked Cartha DeLoach. I said that I did know both Jones and Bellino but that none of us had ever engaged in any wiretapping in the Hoffa investigations.

When the hearing was over, Judge Austin ruled that the defense had failed to show any material relevancy between the overhearings submitted by the government and the case, and had also failed to prove any additional evidence of electronic eavesdropping. Judge Austin again affirmed the conviction of Hoffa and his co-defendants.

In view of the recent Supreme Court decision, it was now also necessary to have another hearing in Chattanooga to determine if any of these overhearings might have had an effect on the jury-tampering case. That was held the following month. Bob Rosthal, a veteran career attorney in the Criminal Division who had participated in the last two Chicago hearings, and Mike Epstein handled the hearing for the government.

Rosthal and Epstein decided that they were tired of being on the defensive. Hoffa and his agents had been proclaiming for years to anyone who would listen that the Department of Justice had engaged in widespread wiretapping and bugging of their homes and offices. Rosthal and Epstein knew now with certainty that there had never been any wiretapping, and that aside from the isolated four instances of FBI bugging already submitted in Chicago, there had been nothing else of this nature other than the perfectly legitimate placing of a bug in Partin's car.

They decided to take the offensive and call me as their first witness, to be followed by Jack Miller, Bill Sheets, who had since retired from the FBI, and Jim Neal. They knew that the bugging of Partin's car would undoubtedly come out in my testimony but they welcomed that. They not only considered it perfectly proper but they also felt that everything would then be out on the table and that this might finally be the last Hoffa hearing. As Rosthal put it, "We're going to put you guys up there and say to them: There they are—have at them—and let's put this thing to rest once and for all."

When asked by defense attorneys whether I knew of any electronic overhearing of any of the defendants, I testified to the fact of the bugging of Partin's car and the conversation with King. I also said that the recording had not been used in either the indictment or the trial. Bill Sheets then testified that the recording was "utterly useless, it was of no value whatever from an evidentiary standpoint, nor was it of any value for any purpose." Jack Miller testified that he had, as head of the Criminal Division, authorized the recording and considered it legal in every respect. Jim Neal explained why he had not used or introduced it in the trial. I had testified for two and one-half hours. The cross-examination of me and the other government witnesses by all of the defense attorneys failed to elicit any other new or pertinent information.

While the hearings were in progress, the improvers were at work in Baton Rouge, again trying to get Ed Partin and Bill Daniels to bail Hoffa out. It had become predictable that as a hearing approached, somebody would offer somebody something to come to the rescue.

Osie Brown, the Baton Rouge attorney who had once represented Partin and now represented Ted Dunham, and who had arranged the meeting between Partin, Wilson Abraham and Frank

Ragano following the 1967 Chattanooga hearing, approached Partin again.

Shortly after Partin and Dunham were indicted, Brown indicated to Partin that he thought he could be helpful if Partin were willing to help Hoffa. Although Brown was officially representing Dunham, Partin was aware that his true role in the case was to somehow obtain Partin's cooperation with Hoffa. Brown made it quite clear as time went on that he was acting on behalf of Carlos Marcello in this effort. Brown was also in contact with Jimmy Hoffa, Jr.

Brown first talked in terms of delaying the Partin-Dunham case. He said that United States Attorney Louis La Cour was going to be replaced soon by the Nixon Administration and that his replacement would be either a man named Ethridge from Marcello's parish, outside New Orleans, or a man named Gallinghouse from New Orleans. He said that Ethridge was preferable, "but it doesn't matter. Either one is okay." He said that the new United States Attorney would have a lot to say about when Partin's case came up. Brown suggested that Partin and Judge Daniels together might be able to help Hoffa.

At one point, relative to a conversation with Marcello, Brown said, "Wait until we get together for this, but this is solid, it's no bull. But I met yesterday about that."

Partin said, "In other words, he can talk to RL [Russell Long]?"

"Oh yeah, oh yes, oh yes," Brown replied.

Partin asked, "He's got some people to talk to the top man?"

Brown answered, "Yes. That's where the good can be done—at the top."

Now Brown was urging Partin to testify on Hoffa's behalf in the Chattanooga hearing. He said it would also be helpful to get other witnesses to corroborate his testimony, such as Judge Bill Daniels, his brother Douglas and Emmett Tucker, all of whom had been in Chattanooga with Partin during the trial.

Emmett Tucker had recently had a serious heart attack and was a patient in a Baton Rouge hospital. One day a man whom he had never seen walked into his hospital room. The man said that he would give Tucker $25,000 in cash if he would sign an affidavit about wiretapping in the Chattanooga trial. Tucker told him to go away.

I had testified in Chattanooga on August 18 and returned to Washington, but the hearing continued for several days. On the morning of August 20 Partin called me. He said that Osie Brown told him that Frank Ragano was at the Royal Orleans Hotel in New Orleans and had six blank subpoenas with him. Brown was going that evening to meet with Ragano and Marcello. Brown was pressing Partin about going to Chattanooga.

On August 21 Brown was desperately trying to locate Judge Bill Daniels. Meanwhile, A. T. "Apple" Sanders, a friend of Carlos Marcello's, approached Judge Daniels and offered him $150,000 to testify for Hoffa. When Osie Brown learned of this he was very upset that Sanders had injected himself into the transaction. He told Partin that Sanders was only supposed to locate Daniels but that he, Brown, was the one who was to carry on any negotiations. He said that Sanders had reported back that the money had to be in cash and that this was impossible. He thought Sanders was trying to make money on the deal. Brown said that a thing like that should be handled by a lawyer.

Brown said, " 'Cause I'm a lawyer—hell, anything I do . . . what I do with you, what I give you, or anyone else—I'm a lawyer, that's my business—see? You are my client."

Another Marcello associate, Tommy Wells, also approached Partin and wanted to discuss the offer of money to Daniels. Partin said that he would not discuss it with him. He then contacted Osie Brown and told him about the visit from Wells. Brown was again highly agitated and complained that there were too many people involved. He said he would call Marcello and get it straightened out. Brown later assured Partin that Wells had been told to keep out of the situation. Partin called Wells to confirm this.

Wells said, "I went down and talked to him a little bit. And he said he's really kinda scared that he might, you know, get caught or something. And he told me that he was going to just sit on it because the way things are now somebody would get caught. He said . . . let Osie handle it. This is his work. Let him handle it."

Brown continued to complain to Partin that Daniels was still dealing with Sanders and that Sanders still maintained that the money had to be in cash and that he was to hold it. Brown said that he had talked to Daniels and that Daniels was supposed to call him back but hadn't.

Finally, in a rare outpouring, stripped of much of the usual double-talk with which he ordinarily camouflages his conversation, Osie Brown laid it on the line. In a mixture of quotes and interpolations, he told of the inhibitions that prevented

Carlos Marcello from coming up with a large chunk of cash in a hurry:

> The man said they're watching every move he does and if he goes and draws anything out of his bank—he said they're checking him like a hawk. So he said, now with time this other outfit could take some out of various accounts and it wouldn't be noticeable. He said, "So what I'm willing to do is this, and if they don't trust me this much, hell, there's no point in doing anything." He said, "I'll give you, talking to me, my note on demand for the one hundred and fifty . . ." he said, "that can be attorney fees." He said, "Then I will call . . . Jack . . . my banker at Merchants' Bank is Johnny Matassa." He gave the number and said, "He is waiting for you to call him. He'll give you a letter guaranteeing that it will be paid upon pre-sentment. He'll write you a letter to that effect—make it in the form of a contract. You can hold that and show it to them and if they don't believe that—get them on a phone away from anybody's office, on a pay phone and call me at this number and I'll tell them exactly. If they can't trust me," he said, "there's nothing I can do."
> He said, "There's no way I can come up with that much stuff. . . ." He said, "What more would they want? I'm not going to lie. I've never reneged on a deal yet. . . ." He said they watch—the Revenue people—watch every nickel he puts in and every nickel he draws. He said for me to go and draw out something like that at this time. He said, "They're going to know what I've been doing. . . ." He said he would give me this letter—note on demand, payable on demand for the full amount . . . and this guy can give me a letter and he said he'd be standing by for you to call him—will guarantee it—it will be in the form of a contract, he said, you can have that and show it to them—and let them keep it, he said. "I'll even do that. But," he said, "I can't do more than that." He said, "I cannot." He said, "There's no way." He said, "Look, I'm trying to stay out of this thing." He said, "I cannot." He said, "We'll all be in the peniten-tiary. . . ." But Apple says no deal—he says they got to have the green. . . . Apple says, "Well, he can do it by Tuesday or Wednes-day." I said, "No sir, he can't. . . ." I said, "Just stop and think—that's something you're not paying taxes on . . . you got to stop and think where it's coming from."

The following day Judge Daniels went to Florida on vacation. Osie Brown continued to hope that Daniels would contact him but he didn't. Brown assured Partin that if everything could be worked out, Emmett Tucker would also be paid, and that in the event his heart attack should prove fatal, his wife and children would be taken care of.

Both Partin and Daniels had been leading them along, as they had in the past, hoping thereby to gather enough evidence to somehow put an end to it all. But they were growing increasingly aware that there was really no one to go to with their evidence. Partin was now a defendant first, and a former government witness as a very poor second. He still told me everything that happened and I passed it on to Epstein, but other than Epstein and a couple of others, no one in the government was really interested anymore in what happened to Ed Partin. He was now just another defendant.

Osie Brown had kept in touch with Hoffa representatives in Chattanooga during the hearing and had kept Partin informed of its progress. However, like others before him, he had failed in his attempt to buy the testimony of Partin and the necessary corroborating witnesses to falsely swear that we had bugged Hoffa and his attorneys during the Chattanooga trial. The hearing ended and Judge Wilson subsequently ruled that evidence produced failed to show that the rights of Hoffa or his co-defendants had been violated and again affirmed their conviction.

From the time Ed Partin testified against Hoffa in Chattanooga in early 1964 until the time he refused to testify for Hoffa in Chattanooga in May, 1967, he had experienced no difficulties or consequences. Since May, 1967, he had been beset by nothing but difficulties. Now he had been given one more chance and had again turned it down. He had been told by Osie Brown that if he helped Hoffa, his problems, not only with the International Union but also with the United States government, could be settled. At one point Brown had told him that Murray Chotiner, one of President Nixon's closest political advisors, was a friend of D'Alton Smith's and could come to Partin's aid. Brown had also talked about Senator Russell Long using his influence to help Partin. It was understandable therefore that when, in the months to come, the United States government became his principal tormentor, Ed Partin might conclude that the government for which he had testified was now a party to the conspiracy to force him to help Hoffa. When the antitrust investigation had been suddenly triggered two years earlier after his failure to testify for Hoffa, and he saw Senator Russell Long's violent reaction to the investigation of those who attempted to induce him to, he had suspected a cause-and-effect relationship. Now he would suspect even more, and as events unfolded they would tend to confirm his worst fears. The letter from Danny Maher to William Loeb, which Partin knew nothing about, certainly pointed toward that possibility.

After Partin and Ted Dunham, Jr., were indicted, Judge E. Gordon West, the former law partner of Senator Russell Long who had been publicly critical of Partin, disqualified himself from the case. Soon it was announced that the case had been reassigned to Judge William D. Murray, the retired chief federal judge from Butte, Montana. It seemed curious that with all the federal judges in Louisiana, a judge would have to be imported all the way from Butte, Montana, to hear the case. It was somewhat disquieting, therefore, when Partin learned that Judge Murray's son was married to the daughter of the mayor of Independence, Louisiana, Charles Sinagra, a former campaign manager for Senator Russell Long.

Judge Murray would later tell newsmen that he had offered his services to Judge West on a prior visit to Louisiana, and it was understandable why he would rather spend some of the winter months in Louisiana than in Montana, but it was, nevertheless, disquieting. Also, Judge West had bypassed the normal channels in arranging for his replacement.

The problem of allocating federal judges to try cases and to replace other judges who might be unavailable because of sickness, prejudice or other reasons has existed for a long time. When the occasion arises, the chief judge in the circuit can ordinarily find another judge in the same circuit to handle the case. It is, however, sometimes necessary to go outside of the circuit. Over the years abuses of the system increased. A judge in the North who wanted to spend the winter in the South could arrange privately with a judge there to take over a case. The convenience of a judge rather than the requirements of justice too often prevailed.

To remedy the situation there was established as a clearing house the Inter-Circuit Assignment Committee in St. Louis, Missouri. A system was established whereby a judge seeking help or replacement would address his request to the chief judge of his circuit. If the chief judge could not assign the case to a judge in his circuit, he was to write to the judge in charge of the Assignment in Committee in St. Louis, who would be in a position to know what judges outside the circuit might be available.

In the selection of Judge Murray the system was circumvented.

Judge West contacted Judge Murray directly and the latter agreed to handle the case. Judge West then contacted Judge John Brown, chief judge of the Fifth Circuit, who in turn contacted Judge Roy Harper of the Assignment Committee in St. Louis.

The trial and possible conviction of Ed Partin would take a long time. It would keep the pressure on Partin, but in the meantime Hoffa would still be in prison. Again, alternative courses needed to be pursued, and again, political muscles needed to be flexed.

Hoffa's case was scheduled to come up before the United States Board of Parole in October. By then he would have served the minimum one-third of his eight-year jury-tampering sentence. The Chicago conviction was still on appeal. In the weeks prior to the parole consideration, William Loeb again interceded with Assistant Attorney General Will Wilson on Hoffa's behalf.

On October 2 the Parole Board considered Hoffa's case. As the day wore on there was no communication between the board and the Department of Justice. Finally, late in the afternoon, the board sent an inquiry to the department asking whether Hoffa had anything to do with organized crime! Henry Peterson, Wilson's deputy, who had previously served as head of the Organized Crime Section in the department, took a strong position that Hoffa was intimately connected with organized crime. They were still discussing the matter when word was received that the parole had been denied. The board had acted without the information requested from the department and its question went unanswered. The board directed that Hoffa would not again be eligible for parole until March, 1971.

Now the only avenue open for Hoffa's release before that time was a commutation of his sentence by the President of the United States. The exploration of this possibility had already begun at the White House. In mid-September, before leaving for a weekend at Camp David, Presidential Assistant John Ehrlichman had left word at the White House to go easy on the Hoffa matter because consideration was being given to possible executive clemency action. Ehrlichman termed the matter "very sensitive." Further inquiries were made at about the same time by the liaison man between the White House and the Department of Justice. At one point, when he asked White House staff members about the desirability of commuting Hoffa's sentence, he said that he had Attorney General John Mitchell on the other line. Clark Mollenhoff, who had been appointed a special assistant by President Nixon to keep the Administration free from corruption, cautioned against any precipitous action. He cited his fifteen years of experience in covering the investigations of Hoffa and his associates and warned against "other than arms-length dealings with William Loeb."

As Christmas drew near, the pressure mounted. A delegation of Teamsters visited the White House and promised Hoffa's cooperation before a grand jury in return for his release from prison. Then there were reports that Morris Shenker had filed a commutation petition with the Department of Justice. When contacted by newsmen, Shenker acknowledged that he had submitted such a petition to the department three weeks earlier. Yet, when reporters contacted the Justice Department, they were told that no such petition was on record as having been filed. The only explanation was that the petition had been secretly hand-delivered by Shenker or one of Hoffa's representatives to a high official of the department. The public disclosure apparently terminated whatever consideration was being given to the commutation of Hoffa's sentence at that time.

As the year ended, there were two other developments. Gerald Gallinghouse was appointed the new United States Attorney for New Orleans. He had been one of the persons whom Osie Brown had predicted would get the job. At about the same time, Wade McClanahan, who had fled to Texas under multiple indictments resulting from the charges by the Labor-Management Commission, weary of running, decided to return to Louisiana and make the best deal he could.

CHAPTER XVI

"*The Umbrella Is Folded*"

IN JANUARY, 1970, Hoffa's attorney Morris Shenker was appointed by Mayor A. J. Cervantes of St. Louis to serve as chairman of that city's new Commission on Crime and Law Enforcement.

At about the same time, Gerald J. Gallinghouse took office in New Orleans as the new United States Attorney for the Eastern District of Louisiana. A former Democrat, who had been appointed as chairman of the Levy Board during the administration of former Governor Jimmy Davis, Gallinghouse had changed his registration to Republican when President Nixon was elected President of the United States. To receive his new appointment as United States Attorney, Gallinghouse had to first be approved by the Republican leadership in Louisiana and then receive at least the tacit approval of Senators Russell Long and Allen Ellender. One of the unsuccessful candidates for the appointment told of his meeting with the Republican leaders. One of the questions he was asked was whether he would be willing to prosecute Edward Grady Partin. In at least this respect, both they and Senator Long seemed to be of one mind.

For Wade McClanahan, things had not gone as he had anticipated when he agreed to come back to Louisiana. He was tried and convicted of aggravated battery and sentenced to two years in prison. He faced another trial for larceny as well as other charges.

On the morning of January 16 Osie Brown called Partin and told him that he had been informed by a bondsman that McClanahan would like to see him. Partin called the jailer, told him of

McClanahan's request and asked if it would be all right to visit the jail. The jailer gave his permission. Partin went to the jail, taking with him two members of the local, Hugh Marinioux and Earl Jones, as witnesses. McClanahan was allowed out of the cell block and talked to Partin in the booking room. Partin told me about the meeting the following day.

He said that McClanahan told him that "they" were trying to get him to testify against Partin but that he had told them he did not know anything against him and had given an affidavit to that effect in Washington, D.C. Partin said that the entire conversation had been friendly and that he had given McClanahan some money for cigarettes and left.

In Nashville the tragic story of Tommy Osborn came to a shattering climax. On February 2, despondent over the wreckage of his career, Osborn shot himself.

On February 4 I flew to New Orleans to testify in Partin's pretrial hearing before Judge Murray. One of the key points that had been raised by Partin's attorneys was the contention that, in testifying before the Nashville grand jury about matters involved in the antitrust indictment, Partin had been granted immunity from prosecution concerning these matters. It was a very good and very close legal question. I testified as to Partin's concern about testifying in Nashville because of the then uncertain political climate. Gil Merritt, the former United States Attorney in Nashville, testified that he had discussed the matter with Partin at the time and had, in his judgment, granted Partin immunity relative to his testimony. Mike Epstein testified that he had not discussed immunity with Partin.

Both Partin and Dunham had also asked for a change of venue, claiming that they could not be afforded a fair trial in Louisiana because of the climate that had been created by widespread publicity. Judge Murray said that he might be inclined to give favorable consideration to their request and asked the attorneys and their clients to get together and suggest possible alternative sites for the trial.

When I met with Partin that evening after the hearing, he was depressed and agitated. He told me why. A week earlier Ted Dunham had told him that he had met with former Congressman Jimmy Morrison, who had indicated that he might be able to help them. Dunham suggested that Partin contact Morrison. Partin told me that he had gone to see Morrison at his home in Albany, Louisiana, and had a long conversation with him in his front yard. He said that Morrison had told him that he had talked to Mayor Charles Sinagra of Independence, Louisiana, whose daughter was married to Judge Murray's son. Morrison told Partin that if he and Dunham would pay $50,000, and if Partin would furnish an affidavit about wiretapping in the Hoffa case, Judge Murray would rule Partin had been granted immunity by testifying before the Nashville grand jury. Partin said that Morrison had told him that, as a token of good faith, he should mail $3500 in hundred-dollar bills to Sinagra. He said the Sinagra had an overdue loan payment in that amount. Morrison told Partin that he knew he could trust Sinagra because he had once saved him from going to the penitentiary for five years in connection with an investigation of an SBA loan involving a factory Sinagra owned. Partin gave me two pieces of paper which he said were both in Morrison's handwriting. One contained the name and address of Sinagra and the amount of postage required to send the package. The other contained Morrison's itinerary for the following week. Partin said that Morrison had given him the latter so that he might be able to contact Morrison if he needed him. Partin said that to protect himself, he had recorded the entire conversation.

I should not have been surprised after all that had transpired before, but still I was somewhat shocked at the boldness of the newest overture. The hearing before Judge Murray was due to conclude the following day. Partin dropped off the tape of his conversation with Morrison in the morning on his way to the courtroom. I sat in my hotel room and listened:

Morrison: Well, look I know they're good for it. I mean there's no question about it. . . . If we were dealing with a suspicious guy, I can understand, but look, I saved that guy from going to the federal penitentiary for five years.

Partin: Then he didn't hesitate—he said it would be all right—he could take care of it? He didn't say he'd try—he said he knew he could? In other words, there isn't any gamble in it as far as you can see?

Morrison: Really don't—and if I did, I'd be the first one to tell you. . . . Look, we don't want to let those

	lawyers know about it. No, let those lawyers get up there and make their eloquent arguments and all that, see?
Partin:	Did you tell me thirty-five—or what?
Morrison:	Well, uh, thirty-five hundred.
Partin:	That's what I thought.
Morrison:	The other was, un—
Partin:	I know what it was.
Morrison:	You put up twenty-five and Ted puts up twenty-five.
Partin:	Fifty altogether—fifty total.
Morrison:	Look, you ain't going to have a bit of trouble from that guy going for that. You ain't going to have a bit of trouble.
Partin:	But I tell you something—I don't want no bull-shit if he can't.
Morrison:	Now look, listen, now, uh, I think you know me well enough to know that if I dreamed that there was any chance of him doing that—I think that you know I'm man enough and close enough to you that I'd tell you. And let me tell you another thing—I think a lot of Ted and Ted's been good to me.
Partin:	He may be leaving the next day.
Morrison:	No. He's going to stay around two or three days. He's going to take it under advisement. Hundreds are acceptable. . . . Why don't you do this. Thing to do—I'll tell you what to do,—thing to do—put it in an envelope and put a dollar's worth of stamps on it—special delivery—and he'll get it tomorrow afternoon.

I looked at one of the pieces of paper that Partin had given me the night before. It said: "Mayor Charles Sinagra—Independence, La.—$1.00 Postage—.30 Special Delivery—$1.30."

Morrison:	All right, now I want to give you—where I'll be. Piece of paper. All night tomorrow and Wednesday—King's Inn. That's a hotel—Freeport, Bahamas.

I looked at the other piece of paper I had received from Partin. It said: "Tomorrow, Wed—Kings Inn—Freeport—Bahamas." Morrison's voice went on, giving the rest of his itinerary. I followed it word for word on the piece of paper.

Morrison then went on to describe how Partin could even get his money back. Employers would be told to retain Morrison in labor negotiations with Partin. Morrison would be paid a fee—half in check and half in cash—and would split it with Partin. Then Morrison told Partin how to pay the balance of the $50,000.

Morrison:	Sitting in your car. Look, I'll come right to your car and pick it up.
Partin:	Good.
Morrison:	I'll go put it in my car and head up the road. See, now, and the other—you just subtract it from that.
Partin:	That's right.
Morrison:	And bring it over in a paper bag—just blow your horn and I'll come out . . . just have it on the front seat and I'll come and take it off the front seat.

So there it was. But what were we to do with it? Morrison could be merely playing a con game and Sinagra and Judge Murray might know nothing about it. Or, Morrison and Sinagra might be plotting without the judge's knowledge. Then again, they could all be in on it. In any event, it would do no good, at this point, to expose only Morrison. Partin had not sent the $3500 to Sinagra as he was supposed to do. We decided to wait and see what happened next.

Judge Murray stayed on for a few days for Mardi Gras and took the motions under advisement, as Morrison had said he would. I returned to Washington. I decided to do a little checking. I found out that Mayor Charles Sinagra had indeed been the subject of an investigation as a result of a loan he had obtained from the Small Business Administration, and that a decision had been made not to prosecute him. Judge Murray, I learned, was the son of the late Senator James E. Murray of Montana. He had served as the United States Attorney in Butte during the late thirties and early forties and had been appointed a federal judge by President Truman in 1949. He had served as the chief judge of the Montana District from 1958 until his retirement in 1966. Since his retirement, he had been designated senior judge of the district. As is customary with retired federal judges, he continued to preside over cases as the need arose.

Following the hearing in New Orleans, Osie Brown, on several occasions, suggested to Partin that he go back to see Jimmy Morrison, whom he called "the strawberry man." On one occasion Brown said, "Check if you can with that strawberry fellow over there. If he could, if that could be done, I'd give him $7500 a crate."

Meanwhile Wade McClanahan was convicted of larceny in Baton Rouge. Shortly thereafter a friend of Partin's told him that there was a man named Claude Roberson in jail with McClanahan who wanted to furnish information to Partin. Partin asked Osie Brown if he would go to see Roberson. Brown reported back to Partin that he had checked and learned that Roberson was a very disreputable person and he didn't think it was worthwhile going see him. Within a few days Roberson appeared at the Local 5 headquarters in a taxi. He said that he had just been released from jail on his own recognizance. But since he also said that he had been in jail for possession of a gun while on parole and that he was a three-time loser, Partin was very suspicious of his release. Roberson said there was talk that McClanahan was saying Partin had threatened him. He told Partin that he did not like McClanahan and said, "Just get me put back in that jail and I'll cut his throat." Partin told Roberson that the last thing in the world he wanted was for anything to happen to McClanahan. Partin gave Roberson $20 and told him to go get something to eat.

The following day Roberson called Partin from the hospital. He said that he had gotten drunk the previous night, became involved in a fight and been taken to the hospital. He wanted Partin to come to see him. Partin, still suspicious, sent Earl Jones and another Teamster, J. D. Arnold, to see Roberson. Roberson told them that an FBI agent had been to see him in the hospital asking if he had heard Partin threaten Wade McClanahan in jail. He said that he had told the agent that he had not heard any such threat.

On February 6 Wade McClanahan testified before the federal grand jury in New Orleans and was placed in the protective custody of U.S. marshals. On February 16 Earl Jones and Hugh Marinioux were subpoenaed before the grand jury. They were questioned about their visit to the jail with Partin and asked whether Partin had threatened McClanahan. They both testified that he had not. On the following day Partin told me that he had been tipped off by a gambler in Baton Rouge that he was going to be indicted on February 20 for allegedly threatening McClanahan. Partin assured me that he had in no way threatened McClanahan. He said that there were three deputies, the coroner and the deputy coroner in the vicinity while he was talking to McClanahan and he was sure they would verify that the conversation was an amiable one. He said that McClanahan was laughing and joking and had patted him on the back when he left.

I called Henry Peterson at the Department of Justice and told him what Partin had heard about the fact that he was about to be indicted. I said that from what Partin said, it appeared that such an indictment might be terribly unjust.

On the morning of February 20 Peterson told me that it looked like my information was accurate. He said that it was in the hands of the United States Attorney and there was nothing he could do. Ed Partin was indicted that afternoon for allegedly threatening Wade McClanahan, who had now been designated as a government witness. In a press conference on that day United States Attorney Gallinghouse said, "We are not going to quit until we clean up that mess in Baton Rouge."

The following week William Loeb contacted Will Wilson. He noted that Partin had been indicted for the second time and asked permission for his reporter Arthur Egan to interview Wade McClanahan. Loeb had the mistaken notion that McClanahan had been closely associated with Partin at the time of the Chattanooga trial and thought that he might be able to furnish information to Egan about Partin's testimony in the Hoffa case. Loeb indicated that Egan had been calling the United States Attorney in New Orleans over the past several days but he would not answer his calls. Wilson referred the matter to Richard McLaren, the head of the Antitrust Division, who declined Loeb's request.

On March 2 a front-page article in the New Orleans *States-Item* was captioned "Teamster Partin's Federal Umbrella Is Folded":

> The federal umbrella that once protected Baton Rouge Teamster boss Edward Grady Partin has been removed officially by U. S. Attorney General John Mitchell, the *States-Item* has learned. In a letter to the antitrust division of the Justice Department, Mitchell has ordered an all-out cleanup and investigation of the labor-management problems that engulfed the Baton Rouge area. Partin is the business agent of Teamster Local 5 in Baton Rouge and has been a

prime target of state and local probes involving labor racketeering
in the area. Gerald J. Gallinghouse, recently-appointed U. S. Attorney for the eastern district of Louisiana which includes Baton
Rouge, is using the Mitchell edict as a vehicle for launching a
determined investigation of the situation. . . . The latest evidence the
federal umbrella has been lifted from Partin is the recent indictment of the union official for alleged intimidation of a witness—one
Wade McLanahan, his former strong arm man and close associate.

The following day an article in the Baton Rouge *Morning Advocate* quoted Governor McKeithen as saying that the "new U.S.
Department attitudes" were something "he had actively sought for
months." "The Governor said he held several talks with the Chief
of the Justice Department's criminal division, once even calling
him to Baton Rouge." Two days later McKeithen was quoted as
saying, "You are indeed correct that the Republican Party must
receive full credit for the continued investigation and prosecution
at the federal level of the labor situation here in Baton Rouge."
McKeithen's statement was in a letter to Republican leader
Charles De Gravelles of Lafayette, Louisiana, who had complained
that McKeithen was wrongfully taking credit for the federal action.

On March 5 Jack Miller and I went to see Will Wilson at the
Department of Justice. We outlined the history of the efforts over
the past several years to bribe and harass Partin. When we brought
up the recent indictment for allegedly threatening McClanahan,
Wilson professed complete ignorance and said that he had not
known anything about it until we told him. It was inconceivable
that the head of the Criminal Division would not be aware of such
an indictment—if for no other reason than, it turned out, that
William Loeb had contacted him about it less than two weeks
before. Wilson said he would look into the situation but I left the
meeting with the distinct feeling that I was being put on.

On March 10 Gallinghouse announced that he was assigning
four attorneys and clerical assistants to work full time for the next
two weeks reviewing the records of the now defunct Labor-Management Commisssion. Governor McKeithen said that he would
make the records available and said the activity had his "enthusiastic support." There was no mention of the fact that the United
States Supreme Court had ruled that the constitutionality of the
commission was questionable and that it should not continue to

function unless or until a hearing were held in federal court to resolve that issue. Three days later Gallinghouse was quoted as saying that the commission records had been "extremely helpful." But he went on, "According to all information available to us there may now be only isolated instances of wrongdoing ... whether the racketeering is just in suspense, or whether the people responsible have stopped, and put it behind them, we just don't know." Yet two days later, in a speech in Baton Rouge on March 16, Gallinghouse said that the same conditions still prevailed in the Baton Rouge area as had existed at the height of the labor-management controversy. In the same speech Gallinghouse said that he was reviewing the original twenty-six-count indictment of Partin, "and if we can breathe life into it, we'll prosecute."

While Gallinghouse was generating daily headlines, Partin received a collect call from Austin, Texas. It was Claude Roberson. He told Partin that he had testified before the grand jury against Partin and had been told what to say by Gallinghouse. He said that he had been driven to New Orleans from Baton Rouge and lodged overnight in jail "for his own protection." He said he had been furnished a new pair of trousers, shirt and tie and had been rehearsed on what to tell the grand jury. He claimed to Partin that he had not said everything they had wanted him to say but was not clear on just what he had said. What they wanted him to say, he told Partin, was that he had heard Partin tell McClanahan in jail that "he would not live to see the light of day." Roberson told Partin that actually he had not heard anything that Partin or McClanahan had said, but had agreed to testify to get out from under the charge of possessing a gun, which they told him would be dropped. He said that after he testified he was given $89 for a bus ticket to Texas. He promised Partin that when the time came he would testify truthfully, and he offered to furnish an affidavit to Partin if he would send him a plane ticket to Baton Rouge.

Partin sent the ticket to Roberson. The following day he called me. Roberson was with him and he put him on the line. Roberson repeated to me the story he had told Partin. He told me that he had testified the way they wanted him to before the grand jury and had said what they told him to say.

It was obvious just talking to him that Roberson was not going to be a credible witness for anyone—but it was on testimony such as his that they had indicted and hoped to convict Partin! From talking to the other witnesses before the grand jury, Partin and his attorneys felt they had a good idea of what the testimony had been. Marinioux and Jones, who accompanied Partin to the jail, had testified that Partin had not threatened McClanahan. The deputies and the jailer had testified that Partin had visited the jail but that they had not heard his conversation with McClanahan. It was reasonably certain, therefore, that Partin had been indicted solely on the testimony of McClanahan and Roberson.

On March 20 Partin entered a plea of not guilty to the charge before Judge E. Gordon West in Baton Rouge. Partin's attorney, Lou Merhige, asked for forty-five days to prepare preliminary motions. Judge West told him he could have only twenty days. Gerald Gallinghouse sat in the courtroom throughout the proceedings. Judge West gave no indication that he would disqualify himself in this case as he had in the antitrust case.

On April 13 Partin's attorney filed pretrial motions with Judge West in the McClanahan case. They included motions for a change of venue and a request that Judge West disqualify himself from the case as he had done in the antitrust case. The latter motion cited several public statements by Judge West against Partin and attached a statement by Baton Rouge contractor Bruce Hunt that West had told him on two occasions that he was going to use his position as a federal judge to "get Partin."

A federal grand jury in Baltimore had been investigating allegations of bribery of public officials for over a year. The jury had already indicted former Senator Daniel Brewster and others. On May 1, 1970, Attorney General Mitchell rejected the recommendation of Baltimore United States Attorney Stephen Sachs that Senator Russell Long be indicted. On the same day Senator Long's former law partner, Judge West, refused to disqualify himself from the McClanahan case. He set June 22 for hearings on the other Partin motions.

On May 22 Gallinghouse announced that he was reactivating the original twenty-six-count indictment against Partin and intended to prosecute. This was finally too much for Henry Peterson at the Justice Department. He had apparently felt, up until then, for whatever reason, that there was nothing he could do. He now told Will Wilson that he did not think Gallinghouse should be allowed to proceed on the old case. Others in the Criminal Division, who had also been too long silent, also protested. Wilson finally agreed and summoned Gallinghouse to Washington to so inform him.

In Albany, New York, Hoffa biographer Ralph C. James, now

an associate professor of economics there at the State University of New York, published a paper entitled "Why Bobby Kennedy Went after Jimmy Hoffa: Looking Back on It All and Looking Ahead." James' theory was that it had all started accidentally but then became politically expedient, and later politically necessary, for President Kennedy and Robert Kennedy to put Hoffa in jail. Professor James did not allow the facts to interfere with his thesis. He stated that Robert Kennedy had "lined up" Cye Cheasty to "con" Hoffa. Actually Hoffa "lined up" Cye Cheasty to "con" Kennedy. He stated that Kennedy "had been beaten" in the two 1957 wiretap trials of Hoffa in New York. These prosecutions were brought by the Eisenhower Administration and Kennedy had nothing to do with them. He stated that between 1957 and 1960, "Twice, Bobby tried to get President Eisenhower's Attorney General to indict Hoffa and twice he refused." It was Eisenhower's Attorney General, William Rogers, who decided to indict Hoffa in the Sun Valley case in 1960, then decided not to—just before the election—and then decided to indict right after the election. In connection with Hoffa's conviction for jury tampering, James stated that the government had not alleged that Hoffa had attempted to bribe jurors nor that those who did were his agents. The facts are that the government alleged precisely that and it was for conspiring in that effort that Hoffa was convicted. He stated that the government's case against Hoffa rested entirely on the testimony of one man, Edward G. Partin. Actually, Partin's testimony merely linked Hoffa directly to a plot whose only benefactor could have been Hoffa, and the existence of which was corroborated by the testimony of numerous witnesses. James stated, "Partin had been in Hoffa's company during the days preceding the Nashville trial and purportedly reported each evening to the FBI on what Hoffa was saying about attempts to influence the jury prior to the selection of the jury." Partin was in Hoffa's company throughout the trial and reported on the activities of Hoffa and others in connection with attempts to influence the jury during the entire period. James stated that "the FBI set up Partin to entrap Hoffa. There seems no question about this." This allegation was the subject of extensive court hearings and was rejected by the trial judge, the Court of Appeals and the Supreme Court. James stated that Hoffa's allegation that prostitutes had relations with the jurors during the trial "has considerable foundations and certainly extensive documentation." Again, these allegations were rejected by the courts and one of the prostitutes recanted her testimony. In connection with the Chicago case, Professor James said, "After seven weeks of hearings, the presiding judge, the Honorable Richard Austin of Chicago, almost threw the case against Hoffa out of court." To the contrary, after each of two hearings Judge Austin affirmed Hoffa's conviction without equivocation.

Then Professor James says:

> What happens, and what is relevant, for both pragmatic politics and the State of the Nation is what President Nixon does. There is an easy solution. He could pardon Hoffa by Executive Order.
>
> Nixon could justifiably do this. Maybe he does not know (but probably he does) whether Hoffa was really guilty of his Chattanooga conviction. However, as a lawyer, Nixon *does* know of a basic simple legal concept in this country, namely, "Let the Punishment Fit the Crime." *He knows* that eight years in maximum federal detention for the flimsy charges against Hoffa do not fit this legal concept.
>
> With respect to a pardon, President Nixon could reasonably explain, "This man has suffered enough" without passing on the uninformed judgment (possibly prejudiced) of the jury. He could add, "Hoffa has been in jail for almost three years on charges, even if completely true, would ordinarily only involve one year of imprisonment." Concerning Hoffa's second conviction (still under appeal), any reasonable autopsy of the evidence would be sufficient to merit a full pardon.

Professor James does not say how President Nixon should know —his inference—that Hoffa was not guilty as convicted in Chattanooga. He repeats that the charges of jury tampering were "flimsy" and imposes himself as a better judge than Judge Wilson in determining that the sentence for the charges, "even if completely true," should only have been one-year imprisonment. He then challenges both judge and jury in the Chicago case and decides that for defrauding the Pension Fund of over $1,000,000, Hoffa should "merit a full pardon," rather than the five-year sentence he received.

After listing the political advantages to President Nixon for pardoning Hoffa—support from the Teamsters, labor, blacks and Jews—and the disadvantages—charges of a deal and being soft on the Mafia—he then concludes that such a decision by the President "would require guts and have to be decided almost exclusively on moral and ethical (if not religious) grounds. . . ." Professor James has come a long way from the "objective" biographer of *Hoffa and the Teamsters*.

On May 26 a dinner was held at the White House in honor of visiting President Suharto of Indonesia. Among the guests were Mr. and Mrs. William Loeb of Manchester, New Hampshire. In the afternoon prior to the dinner William Loeb and his wife paid a visit to Will Wilson at the Department of Justice.

In late May a new "Free Hoffa" campaign was launched, emanating from Local 676 in Vineland, New Jersey. John Greeley, the president of the local, was also an official of the International Union. Letters were again sent to local unions and to Congressmen and Senators:

> One of the greatest Labor Leaders of this country of ours is presently confined at Lewisburg Prison; because of a personal vendetta by some very small minority of people who could not stand the virtues of James Hoffa proudly representing the men and women, and developing a great International Union with better than two million members. . . . You know and I know that James Hoffa is one of America's smartest and [most] understanding men of our times. . . . Therefore, some recognition and consideration should be given for the release of James Hoffa. . . ."

Each letter enclosed a "Free Hoffa" bumper sticker.

An article in the May 29 issue of *Life* magazine by former St. Louis newsman Denny Walsh charged that St. Louis' new Crime Commissioner Morris Shenker, in addition to having represented leading mobsters both in St. Louis and throughout the country, had also had business dealings with underworld figures and had obtained enormous fees for his role in obtaining millions of dollars in loans from the Teamsters Pension Fund. The article suggested that some of these fees were in payment for Hoffa's legal fees since the 1964 prohibition by the courts against the payment of such fees with union funds.

Back in Louisiana, the National Labor Relations Board reactivated a dormant case against Partin and demanded that he pay $15,000 to a former union member named Calvin Cleary, who had filed a claim in 1964 charging Partin with depriving him of employment. Next, at the request of Gallinghouse, the Department of Labor subpoenaed the books and records of Local 5 in what was described as a "routine investigation."

On June 9 the federal grand jury in New Orleans indicted seventeen members of Local 5 and Sheriff Jesse Ourso, charging them with violation of the antitrust and Hobbs Act statutes in connection with the Plaquemine shoot-out. Partin and Dunham were named as co-conspirators.

Osie Brown had been urging both Partin and Dunham to withdraw their requests to be tried outside of the state of Louisiana and to agree to a trial in New Orleans. The message was that Carlos Marcello would help, and that it only took one juror to avoid conviction. Partin said to me, "That's all I need now—is to be charged with jury tampering."

Dunham finally took Brown's advice and wrote a letter to Judge Murray requesting that he be tried in New Orleans. He pressed Partin to do likewise. Partin declined to go along. On June 12 Judge Murray severed Dunham from the case and agreed to a New Orleans trial.

On July 27 busloads of Teamsters wives descended on Washington to visit their Congressmen and Senators to plead for Hoffa's freedom.

The same day in Baton Rouge Victo Sachse, one of Dunham's attorneys, called Partin and asked if he would come to see him the next morning. Partin parked his car near Sachse's office the following morning and was preparing to get out of the car when Sachse got in. He asked Partin if he would drive him to the courthouse as he had to sign a paper. Partin did so and waited for him in the car. They then drove to Sachse's office. Sachse's secretary was there and took notes of their conversation. Sachse said that he had been approached by both Senator Long and Wilford Whitley and offered a deal on behalf of his client, Ted Dunham, Jr. He said they had told him that Dunham would receive only a suspended sentence and a fine if he would testify against Partin. Sachse said that Senator Long had told him that he would merely have to take Sachse to see Attorney General Mitchell to make the deal. Sachse said that he had talked to Dunham about it but that Dunham had said that he did not have any information that could be used against Partin. Sachse said that when he had called Senator Long and told him that and asked to see him, Senator Long had replied that there was no point in their meeting unless Dunham would furnish information against Partin. Sachse said that Senator Long had said that Dunham might change his mind if there was enough heat put on him. Sachse then asked Partin if he had once told someone that he would be sympathetic to Hoffa's release from prison. Partin replied that he had, on one occasion, been asked if he wouldn't be sympathetic to Hoffa's release if Hoffa was being kept in prison for political reasons. He said that he had responded he would be sympathetic—if it was purely political, but that he didn't think that it was. Sachse said that he guessed Partin knew that Hoffa was right in the middle of everything. Partin said that he should certainly know it better than anyone.

Sachse then said that Senator Long and Judge West had arranged to bring Judge Murray into the case. He then picked up a book and began to read to Partin biographical facts about Judge Murray—where he went to school, that his father was a Senator. Sachse then said that he knew Will Wilson of the Justice Department very well and had known him in Texas. Sachse also mentioned that he had talked to the Solicitor General of the United States. He finished by saying that he was going to call Senator Long and tell him that Partin was sympathetic with Hoffa's release from prison. Partin did not respond. Sachse said that he would be back in touch with Partin.

About a week later Partin ran into Sachse at the courthouse. Sachse said that he wanted to get together with him but that he wanted to talk to Osie Brown and Ted Dunham first. Then he said, "You won't come wired for sound will you?"

When Partin inquired about getting affidavits from the deputies who had been present when he visited Wade McClanahan in jail, he was told that if he would give Sheriff Bryan Clemons, who was their superior, $5000, the affidavits could be obtained. It was explained that the sheriff had lost $30,000 gambling in Las Vegas and he was being pressured to pay up. On August 3 Sheriff Clemons called the Local 5 office and left word for Partin to call him. When Partin did not respond, he began noticing marked cars from the sheriff's office in the vicinity of the local office and his home.

On August 31, in response to a press inquiry, Sheriff Clemons acknowledged having lost $18,000 gambling in Las Vegas. He said that the previous week he had paid back the last $11,000 of the debt. He said that he had incurred the debt when he was "weathered in" in Las Vegas for five days while returning from a West Coast vacation trip. The paper quoted Clemons as saying, "They extended me credit at the casino and over that five-day period I wound up owing the $18,000." He said that he had paid the last installment by borrowing $5000 on some "building and loan stock which my mother left me when she died, and my good friend, A. T. ["Apple"] Sanders co-signed a note with me for the remaining $6000."

On October 13 Jimmy Morrison called Local 5 asking for Partin. He finally talked to Earl Jones. He told Jones to find Partin and tell him that Mayor Charles Sinagra would meet him at The Village restaurant at three o'clock. Jones found Partin at the Bellmont Hotel and they called Morrison. He said he was glad they had called because he realized after talking to Jones, that The Village did not open until five o'clock. Morrison said that Sinagra would come to the Bellmont Coffee Shop in a few minutes to see Partin. Partin took Jones with him and went to the coffee shop to wait. After a few minutes a man came in and sat down alone. He was sixtyish, dressed in a business suit, and had graying black hair combed straight back. Partin walked over to his table.

"Are you Charlie?" Partin asked.

"Yes, are you Ed Partin?" Sinagra said.

"Let's go out in the lobby and talk," said Partin.

They walked out into the lobby and sat down on a bench. Earl Jones was nearby. Sinagra asked Partin how things were going. Partin replied that things were not going very well at all. Then Sinagra said that things could be worked out. He told Partin that his son-in-law—the judge's son—was going to get a job with the state of Louisiana and would be coming in to look things over on the weekend. He said he would then return to Butte, Montana, for a short while before coming back to Louisiana to stay. Sinagra then confided that the judge had been worried that he might be walking into a trap. He said that there were people who could help but there were some things they needed to know. He told Partin he would be in touch with him again. Sinagra was quite nervous throughout the conversation.

Two days later Jimmy Morrison again called Local 5 and left word for Earl Jones to call him. Partin used this as an excuse to call Sinagra, whom he reached in his office at City Hall in Independence. He told Sinagra that Morrison had called and he thought that Sinagra might have a message for him. Sinagra was very guarded.

"There won't be anything until Tuesday," he said.

Partin asked whether his son-in-law was still coming in on the weekend. Sinagra said that he wouldn't be in until Monday and that he would get back in touch.

The trial of Ted Dunham, Jr., had been set for November 29 in New Orleans. On Friday, the 20th, Dunham's attorneys went before Judge Murray, who had returned from Montana for the trial, and asked for a delay until December 15. They said Osie Brown, one of Dunham's attorneys, had been tied up for many weeks defending Sergeant Mitchell in the My Lai atrocity trial in Houston and had been unable to properly prepare for the Dunham trial. Judge Murray ruled that they could have a one-week delay but cautioned that there would be no further delays. Wilford Whitley, on behalf of the government, had strongly opposed any delay, claiming that Dunham had been telling people that the trial would be delayed indefinitely.

On the following afternoon Partin was standing with a group of men in the lobby of the Belmont Hotel. A man he had never seen before tapped him on the arm and said that he was wanted on the phone. When Partin picked up the phone, it was Mayor Sinagra.

"Things are looking better," Sinagra said. "I have the judge here with me now. Things are looking better. Get in touch with me the first of the week." Partin said he would and hung up.

The next day Judge Murray sent a telegram to the United States Attorney's office in New Orleans, postponing the Dunham trial until January 17, 1971. None of this made much sense—but then things hadn't for some time.

In late October a book entitled *The Trials of Jimmy Hoffa: An Autobiography of James R. Hoffa—As Told to Donald I. Rodgers* was published. The flyleaf gave the impression that this was Jimmy Hoffa's story as told from prison. The first half of the book deals with Hoffa's life from his birth to his first encounter with Robert Kennedy and the McClellan Committee. The last half tells the story of his rise to the presidency of the union and his battles with Kennedy and the government, concluding with the conviction in Chattanooga. The book, particularly the last half, is replete with half-truths, distortions and misstatements of fact. It is also notable for what it omits. There is nothing recounted after March, 1964. The Chicago trial is not even mentioned—as if it had never happened. It is obviously not a book written in prison—federal regulations prohibit that. But the three-year period between Chattanooga and Lewisburg is completely ignored. And why had they waited almost seven years to publish it?

The lessons of the past indicated that it was the opening gun in a new propaganda effort to obtain Hoffa's release from prison. Almost simultaneously, across the country, there commenced a circulation of petitions among Teamsters members—"Bring Jimmy Home for Christmas." The petitions were tacked up in terminals and union halls and offered for signature to union members by their stewards.

On November 4, 1970, a column by Holmes Alexander appeared in the Chattanooga *News-Free Press* with the heading: "Pardoning of Jimmy Hoffa Could Be Political Windfall." Alexander adopted the views expressed by Professor James in his paper and suggested that President Nixon might gain Negro, Jewish and labor support by pardoning Hoffa. To these quoted and paraphrased conclusions of Professor James, Alexander added his own suggestion of an additional political advantage:

> Finally, it would be advantageous for the Republican chief of party to land a blow against the Kennedy myth under any circumstances. As I wrote here recently, Ted Kennedy isn't the only "Kennedy" who is running this year. Tydings of Maryland and Tunney of California are JFK proteges. Sargent Shriver, an in-law, is slavering for public office, and is raising funds for Democratic candidates. . . . This paper by Professor James would make interesting reading at the White House, the Republican National Committee and John Mitchell's Justice Department. Republican candidates ought to make sure that copies are mailed to those places.

In early December Mayor Sinagra phoned Partin at the local and left word for him to call. When Partin finally reached him at the City Café in Independence, Sinagra told him to get in touch with Jimmy Morrison. Partin called Morrison, who said he would talk to Sinagra and call Partin back. On December 4 Morrison again called Local 5 and left word for Partin to call him. Morrison said he had seen "that fellow" and now needed to see Partin. They agreed to meet at Morrison's office in Baton Rouge that afternoon.

At the meeting Morrison said that it would be helpful if Partin called off a threatened strike at a certain company. Morrison said that he could then take credit for it and would be able to secure a job there for Judge Murray's son.

As the seventh year after the Chattanooga trial drew to a close, the same pattern of activity on Hoffa's behalf, which had endured year after year, continued in full swing—the attempts to bribe and pressure Partin, the propaganda, the political pressure and the latest corrupt plot to buy political clout, which was just unfolding. An ex-convict recently released from federal prison and a friend approached Hoffa attorney Harold Brown in Chattanooga. They said that for $1,000,000 in cash they could arrange for Senator McClellan to intercede with the United States Parole Board on Hoffa's behalf. They claimed that they could achieve this improbable feat through a friend of the Senator's. Shortly thereafter Brown made one of his infrequent visits to Hoffa at Lewisburg Penitentiary. Brown then reported back that the price was too high. After much negotiating and another trip by Brown to Lewisburg, a price of $250,000 was agreed upon. The plotters then asked that the money be placed in escrow with another attorney in Alabama. This required another trip to Lewisburg by Brown, who came back and said that Hoffa would not agree to the escrow arrangement and that they would have to take his word.

On December 23 Frank Fitzsimmons, the general vice president of the Teamsters Union, met in the White House with the President of the United States. Also present were Assistant Secretary of Labor William Usery and Presidential Assistant Charles Colson, who had arranged the meeting. Although Fitzsimmons had previously had a number of meetings with Attorney General John Mitchell, whom he had known for some time, this was the first entree to the White House for such a high-ranking official of the Teamsters Union since Dave Beck's heyday during the Eisenhower Administration. It was an amiable conversation, with President Nixon offering strong assurances that his Administration had nothing against the Teamsters Union and would see that it was treated fairly.

On December 29 Senator Norris Cotton of New Hampshire delivered to the White House, on behalf of William Loeb, a petition containing 300,000 signatures asking for the release of Jimmy Hoffa.

CHAPTER XVII

If at First You Don't Succeed

━━━━━━━━━━━━

ON JANUARY 11, 1971, the United States Supreme Court denied the petition for review by Hoffa and his co-defendants of their conviction in the Chicago Pension Fund fraud trial. It had taken almost seven years to exhaust the appelate process. For the others, it meant they would soon go to prison. For Hoffa, it established that he was now serving a thirteen-year sentence. This offered both advantages and disadvantages to Hoffa. When Hoffa had applied for parole earlier, it had been on the basis that he had served one-third of the eight-year sentence for jury tampering. The fact that the Pension Fund fraud conviction, with the additional five-year sentence, was still under appeal at the time, undoubtedly had an influence on the Parole Board and he was told to reapply in March, 1971. Now that the aggregate thirteen-year sentence was final, the Parole Board might be reluctant to release him so soon after the second conviction had been affirmed. On the other hand, by March, 1971, he would have served almost one-third of the thirteen-year sentence, and with both sentences now joined, the board might grant the parole.

The next convention of the International Brotherhood of Teamsters was scheduled for the coming July in Miami Beach. General Vice President Frank Fitzsimmons, who had been selected by Hoffa to run the union in his absence, announced that he would not be a candidate for general president at the convention if Hoffa were paroled before then and sought reelection. Fitzsimmons said, however, that if Hoffa were still in prison at the time of the convention, he would be a candidate for Hoffa's position.

Considerable attention was therefore focused on the upcoming meeting of the Parole Board in March. There were those who felt that Hoffa would run for reelection whether he was out of prison or not. There were few who doubted that Hoffa would be reelected if he were free and eligible, but there were also many who were convinced that he could run successfully from prison!

Indicative of the general feeling of uncertainty was the rejection by the General Executive Board of the union, meeting in Palm Springs, California, in mid-January, of a bid by Fitzsimmons for its support of his candidacy in the event Hoffa was not paroled.

Behind the scenes there were quiet discussions and feelers were floated by others in the hierarchy who craved the top spot, but one thing was certain: no one was going to make any overt moves until the March ruling by the Parole Board—and maybe not even then.

Another factor was speculation among some of the inner circle in the union concerning the true motives of Fitzsimmons. There were those who wondered whether Fitzsimmons really wanted Hoffa out of prison. Outwardly, Fitzsimmons was doing everything he could to obtain Hoffa's release. His visits to Attorney General Mitchell and his recent audience with the President seemed to support that view. But some wondered what he actually said to the Attorney General and what his private feelings were.

On January 18 Ted Dunham, Jr., went on trial in New Orleans before Judge William Murray on the charges of having conspired with Ed Partin in violation of the Sherman Anti-Trust Act and the Hobbs Act. Partin had obtained a severance and change of venue and would be tried later in Butte, Montana. Wade McClanahan would be the government's key witness in both trials. The day the Dunham trial started, a New Orleans attorney informed Partin that it could be arranged for McClanahan to take the Fifth Amendment rather than testify, if Partin would sign an affidavit that he had wiretapped Louisiana Attorney General Jack Gremillion's telephone for the government. Gremillion had been indicted for fraud by a federal grand jury and his trial was coming up. Partin turned down the offer.

On January 21 the Court of Appeals affirmed Judge Wilson's denial of Hoffa's fourth and last motion in the Chattanooga case.

The appeal centered on the legality of the recording of the conversation between Ewing King and Ed Partin, in the latter's automobile, just prior to the jury-tampering indictment in 1963.

On the same day the government asked that Partin's trial in Houston, scheduled for late February, be postponed for thirty days. This was the obstruction of justice case alleging that Partin had threatened Wade McClanahan in jail. The government based its request on the contention that they had not been able to locate Claude Roberson, whom they termed a key witness.

On January 25 Arthur Egan, the reporter for William Loeb's *Manchester Union Leader*, called Ed Partin from New Hampshire. Egan said that he understood that Partin had a trial coming up and asked whether it wasn't true that he had received a letter of immunity from Robert Kennedy. When Partin replied that he had not received any immunity, Egan asked if there was any way he could help Partin with his case. Partin suggested that he talk to his attorney, Ed Baldwin, in New Orleans.

On February 2, 1971, Arthur Egan showed up in Baton Rouge and paid a visit to Ed Partin at the Local 5 union hall in Baton Rouge. He got right to the point. He told Partin that he and his newspaper were interested in helping Jimmy Hoffa and wondered if Partin might have any ideas how that could be accomplished. He told Partin that they had something in common because his father had been a telephone man for fifty years and his younger brother had been the representative for the Telephone Workers Union.

Egan said he couldn't understand why his newspaper hadn't received any response for the reward it was offering for information about wiretapping in the Hoffa case. He said they had put ads in fifteen of the biggest papers in the country for a week and had not received one phone call. "I can't understand why nobody will go for that hundred thousand dollars," Egan said.

Egan told Partin that he was inviting him to come up to New Hampshire any time he wanted to take a vacation. He said that he would pick Partin up at the airport and he could go through the newspaper plant and meet Mr. Loeb.

Then Egan told Partin that his boss had good political connections, and that since President Nixon came to office, Loeb had been to five White House dinners. Egan said their newspaper was the first one in the country to come out and support Nixon for reelection and in the New Hampshire primary. He said that David Eisenhower and his wife Julie had spent several weeks with the

Loebs, and that Loeb owned a ranch in Reno, Nevada, where some of the important people from Washington went when they wanted to get away for a vacation. "They scoot out there to the ranch and nobody knows they are there except one or two of us," Egan said. "They go out there and hide."

Egan gave Partin his telephone numbers in Manchester and told him to call him. Partin again suggested that Egan talk to his attorney.

On February 2, 1971, Wade McClanahan testified in the Dunham trial. He repudiated two affidavits he had given in Washington, D.C., about being offered money by the Labor-Management Commission to furnish information about Partin. He said that he had given both affidavits under duress from Partin, and that the second one had been made out before he got to Washington and that he had signed it without reading it. (McClanahan had stated in the affidavits he repudiated that he knew of no wrongdoing on Partin's part.) He then testified that Partin and Dunham had conspired in restraint of trade and that Partin had ordered the shooting at the Plaquemine incident. It was very damaging testimony against Dunham, and obviously would be just as damaging against Partin in the upcoming Butte trial.

Epstein and I both testified in the trial later in the week. I stated that McClanahan had given the first statement in Washington freely and with no apparent indication of duress. I also testified that the statement had been read and signed by McClanahan and sworn to before a notary public. (McClanahan had testified that he had not sworn to the statement.) Epstein testified that McClanahan had talked to him freely; that he did not have the affidavit prepared in advance; that he had interviewed McClanahan in-depth and then prepared an affidavit; and that McClanahan, after initialing corrections, had sworn to the truthfulness of it before a notary public at the Department of Justice.

On February 19 Ted Dunham, Jr., was convicted of having violated one count each of the Sherman Anti-Trust and Hobbs acts.

Ed Partin now faced two imminent trials in federal court, and his co-defendant in one of the charges against him stood convicted. Partin firmly believed that all of his problems of the past four years were the direct result of his testimony against Hoffa and his continued refusal to recant that testimony or to otherwise testify falsely to help Hoffa. When he rejected the bribe offers in early 1967 he had been told in no uncertain terms that if he did not help Hoffa he would be destroyed. He had experienced nothing but trouble since and had a healthy respect for the power of those who might attempt to crush him into submission.

He was also convinced that the Nixon Administration and other powerful political forces, such as Senator Russell Long, had become collaborators in the endeavor to assist Hoffa, and that continual pressure on him was one of the means.

One of the first persons to approach Partin in 1967 on Hoffa's behalf had been D'Alton Smith, a friend of New Orleans Mafia boss Carlos Marcello. Smith was a sort of in-law to the Marcello empire. His eldest sister had married Joseph Poretti, who managed the restaurant in Marcello's Town and Country Motel, which served as Marcello's headquarters in Jefferson Parish, adjacent to New Orleans. Another sister married Nofio Pecorra, one of Marcello's associates, and she served for a while as a secretary to Marcello. She was later appointed to the Louisiana Insurance Rating Commission and became chairman of its Fire and Casualty Division, a position she still holds.

In the late 1960s Smith began dealing in stolen and worthless securities. The latter involved companies such as Comutrex, a Shell corporation with no meaningful assets. In 1970 he was indicted by a federal grand jury in Los Angeles for the interstate transporation of stolen securities. He was also indicted by the state of California for his alleged part in the theft of securities there, in a separate transaction.

Smith moved to Denver, where he bought a huge home near a country club, using Comutrex stock instead of money to purchase it. When the previous owner, a businessman who had been in financial difficulty at the time of the sale, realized that the worth of the stock had been misrepresented, he instituted a suit against Smith. Smith threatened to have him killed. In the meantime, Smith had acquired a plastics company and an airplane and began looking for other investment opportunities to expand his paper empire. In early 1971 he was convicted on the federal charge of transporting stolen securities.

Somewhere along the line, Smith met Audie Murphy, the most decorated hero of World War II and a former movie star. Murphy's career in motion pictures and later in television had gradually faded and, following some abortive investments, he declared bankruptcy in 1968. In 1970 he had been acquitted on a charge of assault with intent to murder arising out of a dispute with his wife's dog trainer. Now, still in poor financial condition, Murphy was attempting to finish a movie he was producing. While Smith was trying to assist him by raising some money to tide him over, Murphy became interested in Smith's growing business ventures.

Ed Partin had been in infrequent contact with D'Alton Smith since he moved to Denver and was aware of his friendship with Murphy. When the Department of Justice had moved to indict Partin in 1969 after the Nixon Administration took office, it was Smith who conveyed to Partin, through Baton Rouge attorney Osie Brown, the information that he was close to Presidential Assistant Murray Chotiner, who might be able to help.

In early March, 1971, Smith told Partin he had some important information for him and asked him to meet him in Los Angeles. Partin flew to Los Angeles on March 6, accompanied by Jerry Millican, a Baton Rouge attorney, who had become acquainted with Smith two years earlier during one of the latter's early stock manipulations and had been a government witness against Smith at his trial. Millican had recently begun representing Local 5.

Partin and Millican were met at the Los Angeles airport by a man who introduced himself as Mike Benedict and said that he was a former photographer for *Life* magazine. When they got into the car, Benedict suggested that they drive to Palm Springs to see Frank Matula, the Teamsters official who had been given a furlough from prison in 1959 to attend a meeting of Teamsters International trustees in Washington. Benedict said that Matula would like to talk to Partin. Partin declined and said he would rather go to a hotel. They were then driven to the Beverly Hilton Hotel where Smith had arranged accommodations.

Smith subsequently met with Partin. In a long, rambling conversation, Smith told Partin that he was now in the plastics business in Denver; that he was not worried about his upcoming state trial on the stolen securities charges; that he was also not worried about his conviction in federal court for which he had just been sentenced to twenty-five years in prison; that Osie Brown had received $25,000 from Hoffa, through Frank Ragano, to influence Partin to help Hoffa; and that some of Hoffa's former associates didn't really want him out of prison. Smith said that President Nixon was supposed to let Hoffa out of prison two years earlier but that something had gone wrong. Smith ended up with the pitch that they could use the $200,000 that was being offered by "that newspaper" and asked Partin if he would furnish an affidavit that he lied in the jury-tampering trial. Smith said that if he did, Hoffa would forgive him for testifying. Partin said he would have to think about it.

While they were talking, a young man came into the room and handed some papers to Smith. Smith introduced him as Mike Fitzgerald and later told Partin that he was a part-time District Attorney in Aspen, Colorado. Smith said that he had been using Fitzgerald as a courier and that he had brought some securities to him. He said that one of Robert Kennedy's former secretaries worked for Fitzgerald in Aspen.

I knew that Diane White, who had worked in Bob Kennedy's Senate office and on the 1968 campaign, had moved to Aspen the previous year. Joe Dolan, who had been one of the top officials in the Department of Justice when we were there and who had served as Bob Kennedy's administrative assistant in his Senate office, had moved back to Denver. Dolan and his wife and family were very fond of Diane and had been instrumental in her decision to move to Aspen. I called Joe and he confirmed that Mike Fitzgerald was a part-time District Attorney in Aspen and that Diane worked for the law firm with which he was associated. I then called Diane and she said that Fitzgerald was with the firm but was spending more and more time in Denver with a man named D'Alton Smith and was thinking of leaving the firm to go into business with Smith. He subsequently did.

Mike Epstein had left the Justice Department in February to accept a position on the staff of the Subcommittee on Administrative Practices and Procedures of the Senate Judiciary Committee. Before he left, he prepared a lengthy memorandum. Epstein's memorandum set forth the efforts that had been made during the previous seven years to keep Hoffa from going to prison and subsequently to obtain his release. He cited only those that were public record, either from court records or otherwise. He attached another memorandum suggesting that it be referred to the Parole Board for its consideration. The memorandum went to Will Wilson but it was never sent to the Parole Board. It was sent instead to the files.

Hoffa's parole hearing was scheduled for March 31. The policy of the Department of Justice over the years had been flexible concerning Parole Board hearings. In some instances, recommendations were made to the board, either in favor of or in opposition to parole. In other instances, no recommendations were made. The department had never answered the question asked by the Parole Board in the fall of 1969 as to whether Hoffa had connections with organized crime.

Now, with the hearing before the board on Hoffa's second application only two weeks away, Wilson was not, from all indications, going to furnish the board Epstein's memorandum or any other information and was not going to make any recommendation. During the interim, the periodic visits of Frank Fitzsimmons to the Attorney General and of William Loeb to Will Wilson continued. A copy of Hoffa's "autobiography" had found its way to Wilson's desk.

This time, however, the Parole Board took the initiative. Representatives of the board contacted the Labor Racketeering Section of the Criminal Division for an up-to-date summary on Hoffa. Coincidentally, representatives of the Organized Crime Section of the Criminal Division had just recently, at the board's request, made an oral representation to the board members on the nature and extent of the organized crime problem in the country. A working agreement had resulted whereby the board would routinely query the Organized Crime Section as to the organized crime connections, if any, of prospective parolees. As a result, the Organized Crime Section was now also asked by a Parole Board representative whether Hoffa had any such connections.

A memorandum was prepared by the Labor Racketeering Section and was sent to the board. In addition, a lengthy memorandum containing information concerning the numerous connections of Hoffa to organized crime was prepared by the Organized Crime Section, but a decision was made up the line not to send it to the board. Tom Kennelly, then a deputy in the Organized Crime Section, thereupon asked permission of Will Wilson for himself and Jim Featherstone, another veteran lawyer, to appear before the board and summarize the information orally. Wilson finally agreed.

On March 11, in Nashville, Local 327 was placed in trusteeship by Frank Fitzsimmons and the International Executive Board. Don Vestal filed a petition in federal court in an attempt to block the trusteeship.

On March 14 an announcement was made that the Administration had forwarded to the House and Senate labor committees an amendment to the Landrum-Griffin Act which would substantially broaden the list of specified crimes, the conviction for which would preclude a person's holding union office for a five-year period. Ever since the Landrum-Griffin Act had been passed, there had been almost annual attempts to do this by each of the succeeding Administrations since it was obvious that many offenses that should have been specified in the original legislation were not. These included illegal payments from employers (still only a misdemeanor under the Taft-Hartley Act), perjury, loan sharking, obstruction of justice and mail fraud. The last two, the crimes for which Hoffa had been convicted, were not included in the original act and he was not, therefore, precluded from holding office under its provisions.

At first glance, it appeared that the Administration was proposing legislation that would keep Hoffa out of office, since the new amendment would be retroactive. However, each time such legislation had been proposed in the past, it had died in the Senate Labor Committee. This latest attempt would also fail unless the Administration pushed it vigorously, which it did not do. Thus it appeared that the announcement of the proposed amendment one week before Hoffa's parole hearing might be designed to blunt public criticism in the event he was paroled.

On March 17, in New Orleans, the government again asked for a delay in the obstruction of justice trial of Partin, now scheduled for March 22 in Houston. The government again gave as the reason the inability to locate Claude Roberson.

On March 22 Thomas Flynn, the new general secretary-treasurer of the International Teamsters Union who had replaced the retired John English, wrote a letter to Ed Partin telling him that he was not being sent material for the upcoming convention and that Local 5 would not be allowed to participate because it was still behind in its per capita payments to the International.

On March 25 Ed Partin phoned me and said that he had just returned from Denver. He said that D'Alton Smith had again called him and told him it was urgent that he come out to Denver. He had taken his brother-in-law, J. M. Walters, with him as a witness. He said they had gone to Smith's house, which he said appeared to be worth over $100,000. They had then accompanied Smith to the airport where he was to meet a man arriving on a flight from Los Angeles. Partin said that Smith had the man paged under several names, including Tom Jordan, Ray Oliver, Oliver Holmes and Pat Wilson. They finally made contact with the man who was introduced to Partin merely as "Pat." According to Partin, the following conversation ensued.

Pat told Partin that he should realize that he had been "sacked" and was in the bag. He said that Partin had no choice but to cooperate with Hoffa and give an affidavit to help him. He told Partin that President Nixon wanted to pardon Hoffa but so far had not been able to do so. He said that if Partin would furnish an affidavit that he committed perjury in Chattanooga, it would give the President a reason for granting the pardon and would gain him the financial and political support of the Teamsters Union in 1972. Pat said that Hoffa was going to be paroled soon anyway, but also needed the pardon.

He told Partin that he had excellent access to the President through a San Diego banker named Smith and through Secretary of the Treasury John Connally, whom he claimed to know from his days on the Houston Police Department.

Pat told Partin that he did not have to worry about being charged with perjury and that he would obtain Presidential immunity for him in all of his cases. He said that he would let Partin sit in a hotel room across from the White House while he went in to see the President. Partin would not have to sign the affidavit until Pat came back with written immunity from the President.

Pat said that "they" had Partin right where they wanted him— that the Dunham case had come out the way it was supposed to and that he didn't have a chance in his upcoming case in Butte.

Pat asked Partin if he knew William Loeb. Partin said he didn't but had met his reporter, Arthur Egan. Pat asked Partin if he would call Egan and have him send a transcript of the Chattanooga trial to Pat. He said he would give Partin the address the next time they talked. He said that he had a court reporter standing by and suggested that Partin come back out to the West Coast in the near future and bring two other persons with him to corroborate what he would say in the affidavit.

Partin told Pat that if he gave such an affidavit it would be perjury. Pat again told him not to worry about that since he would be given immunity.

Pat also told Partin that the President had been wanting for some time to get rid of J. Edgar Hoover. He said that Partin's affidavit would give him a vehicle to force Hoover out because he could blame what went on in Chattanooga on Hoover, based on the affidavit.

Pat said that he was a good friend of Audie Murphy's and was involved in a business deal with Murphy in the Philippines. (D'Alton Smith had previously told Partin of his own association with Murphy.)

Partin said that Pat was carrying a briefcase which contained a gun and handcuffs. He described himself as an international investigator and claimed that he did work overseas for the FBI, the State Department and business concerns.

D'Alton Smith told Partin about his new plastics company and said that Gordon Cooper, the astronaut, was on his board of directors.

I told Partin I thought that Pat sounded like a con man but that I would try to check on him.

Later that day Pat called Partin in Baton Rouge. He said that he had talked to Richard Helms, the director of the Central Intelligence Agency, the previous evening. He claimed that Helms was a friend of his and that he had worked closely with his agency. He said that Helms was eager to be of assistance, and was also interested in getting rid of Hoover.

Pat said that he had called Arthur Egan himself and that the transcript of the Chattanooga trial was being shipped to him by Egan via Emory Freight.

He again told Partin that he did not have to worry about perjury and that there would be no problem in obtaining immunity. He wanted to know what Partin was going to do. Partin told him he had to think about it.

In still another call that day Pat continued to pressure Partin to give an affidavit. He reiterated his contention that Partin did not have to worry about perjury and again promised Presidential immunity. He said that in setting everything up, he had intentionally bypassed Attorney General Mitchell because he was "wishy-washy."

Pat told Partin that if he came out, he should stay at the Rodeo Hotel in Beverly Hills, California. He said that he still had a court reporter and another person standing by and needed to know soon whether Partin was coming. Partin then talked to D'Alton Smith. Smith told him that he thought he ought to go along with Pat. He said that Pat would be at Audie Murphy's home that evening and gave Partin the number.

Partin later called the number and asked for Pat. The woman who answered said she did not know Pat but gave Partin another number where Murphy could be reached. When Partin called that number Audie Murphy answered. Murphy asked Partin if he was coming out. He said that he had made reservations at the University Sheraton Hotel for Partin and had called the White House and "made arrangements for the deal there for us."

Partin then asked Murphy how well he knew Pat. Murphy said that he had known him about one year and had checked him out through a friend with the Internal Revenue Service. He said that he was satisfied that he was all right. Murphy told Partin that he had set Pat up in a deal in the Philippines and added, "I don't do those kind of favors for many people."

Murphy said he had made the reservations at the University Sheraton for a three-bedroom suite in D'Alton Smith's name, and he hoped to see Partin the following day.

The next day Partin had another conversation with Pat. Pat told him that the President was coming to the Western White House that day so they would work everything out there instead of having to go through Washington. He said that they were really better off because "you get in there [Washington] and you get messed up with front people. Down here it's a relatively simple matter."

Pat kept pressing Partin as to when he was coming. He reiterated that he had the court reporter standing by as well as "an attorney that will do exactly what I tell him to do." Partin said he had to talk to D'Alton Smith because he was supposed to come with him.

I had been able to establish that Pat was Pat Willis, a former police officer who now worked as a private investigator, professional informant and con man. I told Partin what I had learned. I told him that he should not under any circumstances go out to California to meet with them. Up to now I had always encouraged him to play along somewhat with these kinds of approaches because it was the only way to obtain evidence of what these people were really up to. But this time I said he should not go any further. I told him if he tried to trap them, they would trap him. I said that Willis was a con man and Smith was in it for what he could get out of it, as he always had been. I added that Audie Murphy was also obviously in need of money. I thought Partin agreed with me and had no intention of going to California. But the next day he was missing from his usual haunts in Baton Rouge.

It turned out that Partin had gone to Los Angeles, again accompanied by his brother-in-law. When he returned he told me that they had met with Pat Willis and D'Alton Smith and had accompanied them to a hotel. He had been shown a letter on White House stationery which began "Dear Mr. Partin." He said that the letter went on to say that Partin was courageous for coming forward. It did not say anything about immunity but, according to Partin, it was signed "Richard M. Nixon." He said that there was an attorney there named Irving Kramer who then proceeded to ask him a lot of questions. A court reporter took down the questions and answers. Partin said, and his brother-in-law confirmed, that Partin told them that the statement was not true. Partin said that the attorney who asked the questions was using an article in the *Wall Street Journal* and other newspaper clippings as a guide in the questioning, and he obviously didn't know much about the case.

The transcript of the session reflects a rambling series of questions and answers. In effect, Partin stated that he had been coached each evening during the Chattanooga trial about his testimony for the following day, that he had been planted in Hoffa's camp in Nashville to obtain defense strategy and reported everything to Frank Grimsley daily. He also said he had deputy marshals assigned to him throughout the Test Fleet case in Nashville. He said that the government had pressured him into testifying against Hoffa and had told him what to say. He intentionally garbled everything. (For example, Grimsley was never in Nashville during the Test Fleet case.) He never mentioned my name until they asked who I was—then he gave a nebulous answer. It was a worthless document from an evidentiary standpoint. Besides being a total fabrication, it was neither signed nor notarized.

At the same time, it was a statement before witnesses which, however much fabricated, did represent a sort of recantation. It was the kind of thing they could play with. It was a stupid thing to do and Partin knew it. He did not want me to know that he had done it.

Partin did not get his promised Presidential immunity, written or otherwise. He did get an affidavit signed by Pat Willis and witnessed by his brother-in-law and D'Alton Smith which stated:

The affidavit being given 27th day of March, 1971, by Edward G. Partin in the office of Irving Kramer Attorney at Law located at 13044 Hartsook Street, Sherman Oaks, California, County of Los Angeles, will not be used under any conditions or for any purpose whatsoever until Edward G. Partin has placed his signature on the affidavit being given before notary public David Newman and attorney Irving Kramer and the understanding between Pat Willis and Edward G. Partin has been fulfilled.

When I told Partin on the evening of March 30 that I had heard about the statement he had given and that I understood that Arthur Egan was flying out to the West Coast to pick it up and bring it to Washington in time for Hoffa's parole hearing the next day, he was very upset. I told him I understood it was thirty-one pages long. Partin had left California before it was transcribed, so he did not know how long it was.

He called D'Alton Smith who said that he understood the statement was thirty-one pages long and had been sent East. Smith said that he also understood that the President had given Partin immunity. He said that Willis would call Partin shortly from a pay phone. Willis did call and said a copy of the statement had been sent on a plane the previous evening with Senator George Murphy to the Attorney General "at the direction of the man down at San Clemente." Willis said that he had spent a half-hour with "the man."

Partin reminded Willis that they had an agreement and that Willis was not supposed to use the statement until Partin had signed it. Willis replied, "Am I gonna tell this man that I have to wait? He's the one that told me what to do—that was the man that I went in to get the concessions from."

Partin then told Willis that he had no right to send the statement to Washington and if necessary he would appear before the Parole Board the following day and repudiate it. "I'll call everything that's in there a bunch of goddamn lies," he said.

"Well, Ed, if you want to do that, well that's fine. The only thing you do is hurt and embarrass a lot of people," Willis replied nervously.

Willis kept insisting that he had obtained the concessions Partin wanted from "the man."

"In other words, the charges I got hanging over my head supposed to be dropped?" Partin asked.

"I'm not going to talk on the phone, Ed," Willis stammered.

Willis kept trying desperately to cut the conversation off. He said he was out of change but Partin told him to charge the call to him.

Partin said that he guessed what he'd better do was talk to his attorney for advice. Willis tried to discourage him from doing that.

Partin took his parting shot: "I want you to remember this well, Pat, in that car, me, you and D'Alton and J. M. Walters—and I told you that what I gave you was perjury."

Willis was beside himself. "I don't want—I don't want—I don't want to hear it on the phone! I don't want to hear it on the phone! I would rather—I don't want to hear any more about anything."

Partin then talked to Audie Murphy. Murphy told him that Willis had told him he had obtained the concessions they wanted and that the statement had gone out on a four o'clock plane. Partin told Murphy that the statement was false and that he had a commitment from Willis not to use it in anyway.

Murphy said that he had arranged through Senator George Murphy to get Willis into the Western White House and that someone from there must have leaked out the information about the statement.

In the early morning hours of March 31, the day of the parole hearing, Arthur Egan arrived in Washington on a flight from Los Angeles with a copy of the thirty-one-page document. Later that morning he delivered the document to Hoffa's attorney Morris Shenker and Hoffa's son James P. and daughter Barbara, who were going to appear before the Parole Board. Shenker, realizing that the document was garbled and unsigned, decided not to use it in the parole hearing.

Hoffa's petition for parole was considered that day. William Loeb had sent each Parole Board member a packet of pro-Hoffa material. Morris Shenker and his associate Bernard Mellman appeared before the board along with Washington attorney Rufus King. They were followed by Hoffa's son and daughter, who said that their mother had entered a San Francisco hospital on March 19 with a critical heart ailment.

A Parole Board examiner had interviewed Hoffa in the Lewisburg Prison the previous week, as was the customary practice. When Hoffa was asked what employment he hoped to obtain if he were paroled, he answered without hesitation that he intended to take over the reins again as general president of the Teamsters Union. The Parole Board rejected Hoffa's petition and ruled that he would not be eligible to reapply until June, 1972. In announcing the decision, George R. Reed, chairman of the Parole Board, said only that "the Board reviewed Mr. Hoffa's application for parole for the first time under the recently aggregated 13 year sentence."

On April 1 reporter Ken W. Clawson, writing in the *Washington Post*, quoted a high Teamsters official as stating that he still anticipated Hoffa would run for reelection from prison and expected him to announce his candidacy within the next few days.

The first week in April D'Alton Smith and Audie Murphy renewed their contacts with Partin. They both blamed Pat Willis for the manner in which things had been handled and said that they were not going to have anything further to do with him.

They told Partin that they had lined up a man in Dallas to help them by the name of Gordon McClendon. He was very well to do and had radio stations all over the country. They wanted Partin to meet them in Dallas and give another affidavit. Smith told Partin that he had arranged a $15,000 loan for Murphy but that he needed $150,000 more to finish the movie.

On April 6, 1971, Audie Murphy called Partin from Dallas. He said that D'Alton Smith had not been able to get in from Denver because of the storm but that Arthur Egan and Dallas attorney Lester May were there. Murphy said that they were still having difficulty getting a transcript of the trial but that Egan was calling Harold Brown to try to obtain one. He said that once they obtained a transcript, it would only take Mr. May about three days to review it "and pull out the things that are pertinent." Murphy said, "We don't want another piece of junk around . . . because we got one more shot at this and that's all."

Arthur Egan then spoke to Partin. He told them that he had talked to Harold Brown the previous evening about getting a copy of the transcript and that Brown was working on it. He asked Partin how long he had been on the witness stand. Partin said he was on direct testimony for about one week. Egan said he would call Brown back and tell him to just send the direct testimony.

On April 7 Jimmy Hoffa walked out of the Lewisburg Prison unescorted and boarded a plane for San Francisco. He had been given an "emergency furlough" to spend the Easter weekend with his wife at the University of California Medical Center in San Francisco. A Bureau of Prisons spokesman said that such temporary furloughs were not unusual for prisoners who were not considered escape risks.

Hoffa moved into the San Francisco Hilton Hotel and Teamsters leaders began coverging quietly from all over the country for what appeared to be a summit meeting. One of the conditions of Hoffa's temporary release was that he was not to discuss union business while he was out.

On April 9 Senator George Murphy acknowledged to a reporter from the *Los Angeles Times* that he had been contacted by Audie Murphy about ten days earlier. He said that Murphy had a letter he wanted to send to the San Clemente White House and wanted to be sure that it got through. Senator Murphy said that he had called the White House and asked for Robert Finch, but he was not in. He said that he had then told some girl there that a letter would be coming in. He said he did not know anything about the contents of the letter.

On April 10, D'Alton Smith and Audie Murphy flew to Baton Rouge and met with Partin. Murphy told Partin that Lester May, the attorney in Dallas, was the brother-in-law of Gordon McClendon and had at one time been in the United States Attorney's office. Murphy said that they had to reopen the parole hearing. He mentioned that Clint Murchison of Texas might be able to help.

Partin asked Murphy whether the letter he had been shown with the signature of Richard M. Nixon on it had really been the President's. Murphy said that he was not sure. He said he had seen a draft of the letter beforehand.

Murphy told Partin that Senator George Murphy had been called by a reporter from the *Los Angeles Times*. He said Senator Murphy had told the reporter that he had been asked by Audie Murphy to deliver an urgent package to the White House, and had done so, but did not know what was in the package. But the Senator did, of course, know what was in the package, according to Murphy.

D'Alton Smith then said that Murray Chotiner would help. He said that Chotiner had left the White House because of pressure from his wife but would be collecting money for the upcoming campaign. Smith said that he had had a deal all worked out for Carlos Marcello during the Eisenhower Administration but that Chotiner had wanted $200,000. By the time they were through bickering about it, he said, it was too late.

Murphy told Partin that they were planning a campaign, coordinated by the White House, to create an atmosphere like the Calley case so that the President could act in the Hoffa case.

On April 13 Arthur Egan called Partin. He said that Will Wilson was still the boss and he and his boss were great friends and went hunting and fishing together. Egan began knocking Willis and said he was just an opportunist. He said that they had told Willis they were not going to pay him a dime. Egan then offered to pay for Partin's expenses for his trips to Denver and Los Angeles.

Partin then told Egan that he thought that Senator Russell Long was the one who was pushing the actions against him.

Egan said, ". . . Well, I think we can take care of Senator Long, because his qualifications are a little questionable . . . Yep, damn questionable. In fact, Congressman Rarick told me that. Rarick said that, Jesus Christ, Long would skin a cat for a dime and want nine cents change. And Rarick said anything he can do to help skin Long, he'll help us. So I took some heart from that and I know this one Senator I talked to—has access to the White House, he's an older Senator—he's been down there four terms and he's on our side of the fence. In fact, when my boss goes down there, this Senator meets him at the airport, brings him in and everything— and this all adds up in the long run, you know?"

Then Egan told Partin that he could have used Partin's statement in his newspaper "but I told you I wouldn't do it and I won't do it." Egan said that his main aim was to help Jimmy Hoffa and "break that element that we got down there in Justice."

Egan told Partin that he wasn't dealing with Willis any longer and that Audie Murphy was a better type of person. "Just like my boss was saying, how can the general public or anybody question Audie Murphy. He's the biggest hero of World War II. He's a movie star and everything else. They couldn't get away with this. Let's face it—the guy's a Congressional Medal of Honor winner and you know that still carries a hell of a lot of weight when this guy is on your side."

On April 11 Hoffa returned to the Lewisburg Prison. According to the *Los Angeles Times*, Hoffa, while in San Francisco, had conferred with numerous Teamsters officials, including Frank Fitzsimmons, Harold Gibbons, Murray "Dusty" Miller, Robert Holmes from Detroit, International Vice President Joseph Diviney, Jack Goldberger of San Francisco and Frank Matula, as well as Harry Bridges, the president of the West Coast Longshoremen's Union.

On April 14 there was another conversation between Partin and Audie Murphy. Murphy said that he had had a long talk with Senator George Murphy. He said that the Senator had told him that he'd be back on the Hill Monday and would call him Tuesday.

He said that according to the Senator, "This thing's hot as a deep-bowled stove and nobody wants to touch it."

Murphy said, "I told him somebody better touch it . . . he agrees, he says—hell, that means like six million for the man—you know . . . they count them, you see."

Murphy told Partin that if things worked out, he wanted to have Senator Murphy come to Dallas to meet Partin and they could meet Clint Murchison, Jr., too who was a big benefactor to "the man." Murphy said that he told the Senator that the thing he read wasn't finished and never should have been submitted. Audie Murphy said that he would get together with Partin soon and "nail things down."

As the by-play with Egan, Murphy and Smith continued, the pressure on Partin from the government also went on. In addition to the fast-approaching trial in Butte and the Houston trial, which the government kept postponing, pressures by the Internal Revenue Service, the Labor Department and the National Labor Relations Board mounted. The IRS sought immediate collection of Partin's back taxes, the NLRB subpoenaed him to a hearing on the Cleary case, and the Labor Department investigation continued.

On April 16 Jimmy Hoffa was transported from the Lewisburg Prison to Foley Square in New York City where he had been subpoenaed to appear and testify before a federal grand jury investigating kickbacks from the Teamsters Pension Fund. The case involved a kickback by a Florida banker to Allen Dorfman. This particular transaction had occurred after Hoffa went to prison. There had been prior kickback payments by the same banker, in cash, to both Dorfman and Hoffa. The payment to Hoffa, amounting to over $100,000 in cash, was made after Hoffa's conviction in Chattanooga for jury tampering and prior to the trial in Chicago for defrauding that very fund.

On April 17 Judge William Daniels called Partin. He said that Arthur Egan and Ralph Sullivan, an attorney for the *Manchester Union Leader*, had been to see him the previous evening. Daniels said that they wanted to know whether Partin had received any money. Daniels said he told them he had not.

On April 27 Arthur Egan again contacted Partin. He said that he had talked to some people and that anything Partin did "that freed Jimmy" would be rewarded. "They're afraid to approach directly anybody outside of Nixon himself, and you know Nixon is not going to put anything in writing. He'll make an oral commitment—they're pretty sure of that—and they won't guarantee it until somebody talks to him, but they believe they can get an oral agreement," Egan said.

Egan continued, "Now, I can arrange for Mr. Loeb to visit the White House on some—just on visit—and he'll talk to Nixon. He's talked to him many times before. It won't be strange to visit the White House, so that won't raise any speculation . . . But if the affidavit you give frees Jimmy, you get the hundred thousand dollars we have in escrow for this. I showed you that letter I carry from my company's lawyer—and this reward is offered for it—it doesn't matter who it is. They get the hundred thousand and what they do with the money is up to them. We just deliver it to who furnishes the information and gets him out—they get the hundred grand."

Partin said he thought he would just pass it up. He said that the last time he had fooled around with an affidavit, he saw what happened to it. Egan said he hated to see him do it.

Egan said, "Well, we know we can get an oral commitment from the man in the White House."

Partin said that his case in Butte was coming up in another month. Egan said that Partin would find the government would move for a continuance in Butte and that the Houston case "is just going to sit there and die a natural death." He said he couldn't tell Partin how he knew that. The government's move to continue the Butte case, according to Egan, would occur in about three weeks.

Partin asked if that couldn't be speeded up a little. Egan replied, "As soon as my boss comes back from fishing, I'll talk to him and speed it up. I know what I'm talking about there in Montana . . . I'll do everything I can tomorrow to talk to him and have him get his fanny down there to Washington and see what he can do to speed it up."

On May 5 Egan called Partin again. He said that he had just returned from Washington where he had talked to four United States Senators, a United States District Attorney and three lawyers. He said that William Loeb had sent a telegram to President Nixon which was going to be made public in the morning, asking that Partin be placed in protective custody and that the Attorney General investigate "the conduct of Mr. Sheridan, and Mr. Grimsley and everybody else connected with the Kennedy Justice Department."

He said that he and the attorney for the newspaper had talked to Senator Norris Cotton and another Senator from out West "who was a Vice President—or Presidential candidate," and that the following Monday they were going to ask, on the floor of the Senate, "that the Senate Administrative Practices Committee conduct a thorough investigation of the whole procedure."

Egan said, "That will stop Butte right in its tracks, because with John Mitchell conducting an investigation, Butte, Montana, can't go on."

Partin asked whether Mitchell knew what they were doing. Egan said they had talked to Will Wilson and he said to go ahead and send the telegram and he would take it from there.

Egan said that Senator Cotton was very close to the President because he was one of the few Republican Senators who had stuck with him when he was down. "Norris Cotton gets invited to the White House many times when the rest of them are on the outside looking in," Egan added.

Partin then talked to Audie Murphy. Murphy knew all about what Egan was doing. He said they were evidently doing it because time was getting short. Murphy said that if they went ahead with it, "It's just going to be a battle between which one's got the biggest dogs. . . . After they run that Epstein out of there—then Walter Sheridan is the only one they got to worry about it looks like. I told them to get a hold of Murray Chotiner and George Murphy and make sure we have them on our side—you know? . . . He said he would. I said if they're going forward with this thing, be sure and get Murray Chotiner because he's the one that made Nixon—you know? Took him from nothing to the Presidency—so the man has to listen to him. And I asked George the other day if he wouldn't talk to him and he said he doesn't particularly like him because he's greedy . . . which he is."

Partin told Murphy to be sure that everyone understood that any statement he gave now would be perjury and that he had to be protected.

On the following morning the *Manchester Union Leader* ran a front-page copyrighted story by Arthur Egan. Egan led off by claiming that Billy Daniels, in an interview with the reporter and attorney Ralph Sullivan, had told them he had many tape recordings he had made in connection with the Hoffa case and would turn them over to the *Manchester Union Leader* as soon as he could sort them out. This was, of course, at variance with what Daniels had told Partin about his conversation with Egan and Sullivan.

Egan then went on to report that Partin had made a thirty-one-page deposition on March 27 in Sherman Oaks, California. In the long article, Egan made only two references to the contents of the so-called deposition. In one of them Egan quoted Partin as stating in it that representatives of the Department of Justice had coerced him into being an informant by threatening him with a "hundred years in jail." The phrase "hundred years in jail" did not appear anywhere in the document from which he was supposedly quoting.

Egan then went on with a series of "quotes" attributed to Partin which he claimed to have obtained "in a later interview" with him. "I have received protection and free legal advice from both Sheridan and Epstein since Hoffa was convicted. Every time some government official tries to prosecute me, these two, Sheridan and Epstein, come to my rescue and stop the prosecution," Egan quotes Partin as saying. Egan said that Partin told him, "Hoffa shouldn't really be in prison. I know I committed perjury, but I was forced into it by Kennedy's people."

Egan then quoted United States Attorney Charles H. Anderson of Nashville as having told him in an interview "that he was 'horrified and shocked' at some of the methods employed by the Kennedy Justice Department in the Nashville area during the Hoffa investigation."

Egan went on to tell of the involvement of Pat Willis and Audie Murphy and that the latter had arranged for a copy of the deposition to be delivered to President Nixon in San Clemente on April 7. Egan said that Murphy had also arranged for former Senator George Murphy to hand-deliver a copy of the deposition to Attorney General John Mitchell, and that a third copy of the document had been turned over to Egan by Murphy and Willis in Los Angeles.

Egan said that he had subsequently met with Murphy and attorney Lester L. May in Dallas on April 22 and that May had agreed to obtain a more thorough affidavit from Partin. Egan claimed that they had not been able to go forward, however, "because of the threats being made against him by Sheridan and other former Kennedy people . . ."

When I read the article to Partin, he said that he had not made any of the statements that Egan quoted in the article. He said the quotes were absolute fabrications.

United States Attorney Anderson of Nashville also denied to

representatives of the Department of Justice that he had made the statements attributed to him by Egan.

Time was running out. On May 10 the Teamsters International Executive Board began its quarterly meeting at the Diplomat Hotel in Hollywood, Florida. On the agenda were preparations for the convention in July and the troublesome question of who was going to be the candidate for general president at the convention.

The abortive efforts to parley the machinations with Partin into a parole vehicle had failed. The continuing attempts to get an affidavit from Partin were foundering. Egan's "exclusive" story had bombed when the wire services chose not to carry it. In an apparently parallel move, Hoffa had petitioned Judge Austin in Chicago to change the five-year sentence in the Pension Fund case so that it would run concurrent with, instead of consecutive to, the eight-year jury-tampering sentence. The Executive Board meeting had originally been scheduled for April 29 but had been postponed to allow more time for Judge Austin to act on the petition. On May 11, while the Executive Board bided its time in Hollywood, Florida, delaying a decision on the candidate for general president, Judge Austin denied Hoffa's petition.

Ken W. Clawson, covering the Executive Board meeting for the *Washington Post*, reported that Teamsters officials there told him that during his furlough in San Francisco to visit his wife, Hoffa had agreed to resign and not be a candidate if the petition to Judge Austin were turned down. Clawson quoted another Teamsters official as saying, "The only way that Jimmy is not going to be reelected is for him to resign in advance and endorse Fitz. Even then I'm not sure his friends—I think you call them organized crime figures—won't still try to ram through his reelection."

Attorney Morris Shenker went to visit Hoffa at the Lewisburg Prison while the Executive Board awaited his decision. As one Teamsters official told Clawson, "Jimmy holds all the cards."

That evening Egan called Partin and told him that he had received a call from Judge Frank Wilson in Chattanooga and that the judge wanted him, Harold Brown and a Justice Department attorney to meet with him two days hence. According to Egan, Judge Wilson had told him that he wanted to find out whether he had been lied to. Actually, Egan had called Judge Wilson and said he would like to talk to him. The judge had told him that he would only see him if attorneys for both Hoffa and the government were present. Judge Wilson agreed to see Egan on May 14 at 4 P.M. He then asked Harold Brown and United States Attorney John L. Bowers, Jr., to be present as attorneys for Hoffa and the government, respectively.

Egan also told Partin that William Loeb had called Herb Klein, the President's director of communications, and told him that if he wanted any help in New Hampshire, he had better help Hoffa.

Egan said that the Teamsters Joint Council in Boston, under Nicholas Morrissey, had passed a resolution in support of Hoffa and that Morrissey had held a press conference to announce the resolution. Egan said that twenty-six other locals throughout the country were going to do the same thing. Egan's story to that effect appeared on the front page of the *Manchester Union Leader* the following morning.

Egan told Partin that arrangements could be made for the $100,-000 he had previously mentioned to be placed in any bank that Partin might choose.

The following day Hoffa sent word to the Executive Board in Florida that he wanted more time to make a decision. This made it awkward for Frank Fitzsimmons, who had told reporters that he would have an announcement on his candidacy for union president by the end of the week. He had no choice now but to wait.

On the same day Audie Murphy called Partin and invited him to come to Las Vegas the following week to see a fighter he had acquired perform in a boxing match to be held at the Silver Slipper. Murphy said that he would arrange for a room for Partin at the Desert Inn. He said that D'Alton Smith would also be there. Partin suspected, correctly, that the real reason he was being invited to Las Vegas was that they again wanted to attempt to obtain an affidavit from him. He told me he had no intention of going. The invitation must have also been extended to Billy Daniels because he called Partin the next morning and asked him if he was going. Partin said no.

On May 14 Arthur Egan went to Chattanooga and presented the Partin "deposition" to Judge Wilson in the presence of Harold Brown and United States Attorney John Bowers. After reviewing the document that evening, Judge Wilson again met with Egan, Brown and Bowers the following day. The judge said that most of the matters contained in the document had been gone into quite thoroughly at the trial and had been the subject of extensive cross-examination. He concluded that if either Hoffa or the government wanted to submit anything further in connection with the document, they could, but that he didn't think that any further action was warranted on his part at this time.

While Egan was submitting his "new evidence" to Judge Wilson, the International Executive Board gave Hoffa twenty days to come up with "new evidence" that might gain him a rehearing before the Parole Board. (Parole Board regulations provide that a petition for rehearing may be made ninety days after a hearing if "new evidence" is produced.)

On May 19 James Hoffa, Jr., went to see Will Wilson at the Department of Justice on his father's behalf. Young Hoffa told Wilson that his father would resign as general president of the Teamsters Union if he could thereby obtain his release from prison. Wilson told Hoffa to recontact him at a subsequent time.

On the same day Arthur Egan called Partin. Partin mentioned that Egan had previously said that the government would move for a continuance of the case in Butte within twenty days. He said that the twenty days had passed. Egan told him not to worry. "It's not going to go to trial—now this we know." Egan said that the Houston case against Partin was "out the window" and that the Butte case would be "out the window" too because Judge Murray, who was supposed to preside over it, had been assigned to Boston for the next 180 days. This was not true. Judge Murray was still in Butte.

"Now we've got people working on this like crazy down in Washington. The boss was down in Washington yesterday—he's going back down again Friday morning," Egan said.

Egan told Partin that Audie Murphy was at the Desert Inn in Las Vegas and was looking for Partin. He said that Murphy had a couple of fighters who were going to be in bouts there that evening.

Egan said that he had called an Assistant United States Attorney in New Orleans about the status of Partin's case but the government attorney was reluctant to talk to him. Egan said that he told him the government hadn't been able to protect Partin "against Sheridan and Epstein, so I said we had to take the steps . . . I said we went to the President of the United States, now you take your orders from him . . . but they are really bullshit because we went to Nixon and asked for it."

Egan said, ". . . We're not letting any grass grow under our feet. I mean, you'll be surprised how much—you can't imagine how much work has been done on this thing. Pressure on everybody and I mean pressure, too—because the boss sent a flat-ass letter to John Mitchell and told him that Nixon, politically, is in trouble and he needs support—and he says—I own the biggest newspaper in the state and we have the first Presidential primary. Now, he said, if you expect me to support Nixon, by God, he said, I expect something in return, . . . I've never seen the boss lay it on the line like that to anybody. . . ."

On May 19 Hoffa filed a motion in federal court in Chattanooga to vacate and set aside his sentence, claiming that the government had knowingly allowed Partin to commit perjury in the trial when he testified that he had not recorded conversations of any defendants, whereas, in fact, he had recorded his conversation with Ewing King in his automobile just prior to the indictment. The part of Partin's testimony to which the motion referred was his conversations with King during the Test Fleet trial and had no relation to his single recorded conversation with King the following year. The testimony was being taken completely out of context in this newest motion. The motion also asked that Judge Wilson remove himself from the case since he might be a witness in the event of a hearing on the merits of the motion.

On May 21 Egan wrote an article in the *Manchester Union Leader* in which he quoted Teamsters official William Joyce of Local 710 in Chicago as stating that he was going to place Hoffa's name in nomination at the July convention. Egan also wrote that John P. Greeley, the president of Local 676 in Camden, New Jersey, had sponsored a resolution calling upon President Nixon to grant Hoffa executive clemency. Egan also noted the previous resolution by Joint Council 10 in Boston in support of Hoffa's candidacy "in or out of prison."

On May 25 James Hoffa, Jr., called Partin and told him that he was coming to Baton Rouge the following week to take Partin's deposition. In the meantime, Egan was attempting to set up a meeting in New Orleans for Friday, May 28, with himself, Partin and Harold Brown. Egan was in Chattanooga on May 26 and flew that evening to New Orleans where he checked into the Hilton Hotel at the airport. The following morning he left New Orleans and took a plane to Atlanta.

On May 28 Audie Murphy, accompanied by three other men, left Atlanta in D'Alton Smith's private plane, piloted by Smith's pilot, Herman Butler. Murphy had recently expressed concern to Partin about both the condition of the plane and the ability of the pilot. Murphy and the others were en route to Martinsville, Virginia, to inspect a plant of Modular Properties, Inc., of Atlanta, which they were considering as a possible investment. The plane overflew Martinsville during a violent thunderstorm and crashed into the side of a mountain. Murphy and the others were all killed. D'Alton Smith later acknowledged to the *Los Angeles Times* that Murphy was representing him and his business associate, Michael Fitzgerald, and other investors who had expressed an interest in the Atlanta-based company.

On May 31 James Hoffa, Jr., again visited Will Wilson at the Department of Justice and conferred with him for over an hour.

That evening Egan called Partin. He said that Herb Klein had called William Loeb and told him that he had an appointment with the President at the White House on June 2 at 10:30 A.M. and an appointment with Attorney General John Mitchell that afternoon. Egan said that Klein told Loeb to come alone.

On June 2 William Loeb met with Attorney General John Mitchell. John W. Hushen, the public information officer for the Department of Justice, told reporters that Loeb had conferred with the Attorney General but declined to say what the subject matter of the meeting was. He said that Hoffa was discussed only in passing. Loeb would not comment on the hour-long meeting.

On June 3 Frank Fitzsimmons, accompanied by Hoffa's son James, announced that the International Executive Board had received a letter from James R. Hoffa stating that he would not be a candidate for reelection and endorsing Fitzsimmons to succeed him as general president of the union. Fitzsimmons said that he would therefore be a candidate and had been endorsed by the Executive Board.

On the following day Nick Morrissey, the top Boston Teamsters official, called Partin. He said that he knew an attorney in Washington to whom Judge William Murray was indebted because of past services. He said that if Partin would give an affidavit to help Hoffa, the attorney would call Judge Murray on Partin's behalf. Morrissey gave Partin his office and residence telephone numbers and told him to think it over and call him back

On June 11, in Nashville, Judge L. Clure Morton ruled that the trusteeship imposed on Local 327 was illegal under the Teamsters constitution and ordered it removed. The judge acted on a motion by Don Vestal which claimed that under the constitution Frank

Fitzsimmons, as general vice president, did not have the authority to place the local in trusteeship.

On June 14 Partin went on trial in Butte, Montana, before Judge William Murray on the charges that he had conspired with Ted Dunham, Jr., in restraint of trade and for extortion.

On the morning of June 21 Don Vestal filed a petition in federal court in Washington, D.C., seeking to enjoin the International Brotherhood of Teamsters from holding the convention scheduled for July 5 in Miami Beach. In his petition, Vestal claimed that Hoffa did not have the right under the Teamsters constitution to delegate his authority to Frank Fitzsimmons, and that even if he did have the right, he had not in fact done so. Vestal claimed that official acts by Fitzsimmons, including the calling of the convention, were therefore invalid.

Later that morning, at the Playboy Plaza Hotel in Miami Beach, Frank Fitzsimmons announced that Hoffa had resigned his position as general president. Fitzsimmons was immediately chosen by the Executive Board to replace Hoffa, on an interim basis, until the convention.

Within minutes of the announcement, President Nixon walked into the Executive Board meeting and sat down next to Fitzsimmons. It was the first time a President of the United States had attended a Teamsters meeting since President Franklin D. Roosevelt addressed a Teamsters gathering in Constitution Hall in Washington, D.C., to kick off his 1944 Presidential campaign.

The Miami Beach Executive Board meeting was closed to reporters but photographers were allowed to take pictures of the President seated at the meeting next to Fitzsimmons. Ronald Ziegler, the White House press secretary, quoted President Nixon as saying, "My door is always open to President Fitzsimmons and that is the way it should be." The President noted, according to Ziegler, that he also met with other business, labor and church groups.

Two days later James P. Hoffa wrote a letter to the Parole Board on behalf of his father, asking for a rehearing. In the letter Hoffa's son said that his father had resigned not only as general president of the International, but also as president of Local 299, Joint Council 43 and the Michigan Conference of Teamsters, and as chairman of the Central States Conference of Teamsters. The letter said that if Hoffa were released from prison, he planned to teach and lecture on a limited basis and live on his pension. Young Hoffa said that his mother had suffered a relapse on May 10 and was under the careful observation of doctors. On June 25 the Parole Board set July 7 as the date for a preliminary hearing on the new petition.

On July 5 the International Brotherhood of Teamsters Convention opened in Miami Beach. President Nixon had been invited by Frank Fitzsimmons to address the convention but had declined because of prior commitments. However, he sent a delegation of high-ranking government officials led by Secretary of Labor James D. Hodgson, who praised the Teamsters Union as being "strong without being strident, effective without being flamboyant and self-serving without being selfish." Hodgson continued, "I know you may have felt a little isolated from some of the mainstream in the past, but I think this is changing. Doors are opening in the Labor Department and other agencies and the White House, and we in the Labor Department mean to do our best to keep them open."

The President also sent a letter to Fitzsimmons which began, "Dear Frank," and which lauded the Teamsters Union as a "cornerstone of the American economic structure" and made reference to the earlier meeting with Fitzsimmons and the Executive Board as "gratifying."

Also in prominence at the convention was the former general president of the Teamsters Union—Dave Beck. Mrs. James R. Hoffa was also on hand and spoke to the delegates, conveying her husband's best wishes. They both received standing ovations. Also appearing as a speaker at the convention, in what appeared to be an out-of-character role, was Leonard Woodcock, the president of the United Auto Workers. He called for Hoffa's release from prison, terming him a "political prisoner." The UAW had, during the previous year, received $50,000,000 in loans from the Teamsters Union.

On July 7 the Parole Board announced that Hoffa would be granted a rehearing on August 20 based on "new and substantial information" presented to the board by his son James. According to Parole Board regulations, the vote of only two of the eight members of the board is required to grant such a rehearing.

On the following day a mistrial was declared in the trial of Ed Partin in Butte, Montana, when the jury was unable to reach a verdict.

On July 9 *The New York Times* carried an editorial headed "What Price Teamster Support," which stated in part:

> The budding love affair between the Nixon Administration and the International Brotherhood of Teamsters has some ugly overtones. The ardor with which the President and Secretary of Labor Hodgson have been wooing the two million member union, exiled from the rest of the labor movement in 1957 for hoodlum domination, would be questionable enough if it were regarded solely as a bid for political and financial support in next year's Presidential election. But in the cynical environment that enshrouds this rich union, no amount of official denials can erase suspicion of a deal to free Teamsters boss James R. Hoffa, now one third of the way through a total sentence of thirteen years for jury-fixing and pension fraud.
>
> Just three months have gone by since the United States Board of Parole rejected a plea to let Hoffa out of jail. Since then, the former Teamsters president has resigned from all his union posts, thus clearing the way for the election at the union's convention in Miami Beach yesterday of his hand picked successor, Frank E. Fitzsimmons, whose only discernible distinction in his union career has been absolute subservience to Mr. Hoffa. . . .
>
> The convention brought no slightest hint of resolve on the Teamsters' part to clean up the corruption disclosed by the McClellan Committee more than a decade ago. On the contrary, the convention re-elected a vice president who pleaded guilty to taking illegal payments from employers only a few months ago, and who was spared imprisonment only because his physician told a Federal judge he was too ill to serve. Also re-elected was another vice president awaiting trial on Federal charges of counterfeiting. . . .
>
> All in all, it is a sorry aggregation that the Administration is clutching to its bosom. . . . Before going to the penitentiary, the ex-Teamster chief often boasted that every man—and especially every politician—could be bought. That suspicion must not cloud the ultimate decision on his plea for freedom.

On July 14 Allen Dorfman was indicted by a federal grand jury in New York City on charges of conspiring to receive an illegal kickback of $55,000 in 1967 in return for using his influence on a loan application to the Teamsters Pension Fund by a North Carolina textile company. Dorfman was identified in the indictment as a special consultant to the Central States Southeast-Southwest Areas Pension Fund and the president of the American Overseas Insurance Company of Chicago.

In Nashville Local 327 was again placed in trusteeship and Don Vestal was removed from office. Frank Fitzsimmons was now general president of the Teamsters Union, and so did have the authority, under the union constitution, to impose the trusteeship.

On August 2 the government filed a motion in Butte, Montana, asking Judge William D. Murray to recuse himself from presiding in the retrial of Ed Partin scheduled for November 1 in Butte. The motion cited a 1968 Second Circuit Court of Appeals decision which held that in the retrial of a lengthy case it was wiser for a new judge to be assigned, unless both the government and defense request that the same judge retry it. On the following day Judge Murray recused himself and the case was reassigned to Judge James F. Batton, a recently appointed former United States Congressman from Billings, Montana.

On August 19 Frank Fitzsimmons announced that the Teamsters Union would support President Nixon's new economic policies. George Meany and most other labor leaders had been outspoken in their opposition to the President's program.

On August 20 James P. Hoffa appeared before the Parole Board on behalf of his father. He was confident, as a result of his conversations with Will Wilson, that the parole would be granted. His father had resigned from all of his positions within the Teamsters Union, as had been suggested, and there was a general feeling in the Hoffa camp that an understanding had been reached. At the hearing young Hoffa was questioned closely about the continued employment of himself and his mother by the International and the fact that his father had recently received a $1,700,000 lump-sum pension settlement. He was also questioned about his father's connections with organized crime.

Late that afternoon the board announced that Hoffa's new petition for parole had been denied. The vote by the board members was unanimous, as had been the case in all of the previous hearings. The board said that Hoffa could reapply for parole in June, 1972. The Hoffa forces were indignant and felt they had been double-crossed by the Administration. One Hoffa attorney stated, "At least when Bob Kennedy gave his word he kept it."

Will Wilson, who had made what was considered a commitment by Hoffa's attorneys, now came under fire himself, when it was disclosed that he had obtained substantial loans from Texas real estate developer Frank Sharp, who was under investigation by federal authorities for alleged stock fraud. He canceled an appointment with a Hoffa representative on August 27 after a *New York Times* editorial that morning called for his resignation.

Frank Fitzsimmons met with Attorney General Mitchell to express his displeasure over the failure of the Parole Board to act favorably.

In a front-page article in the *Manchester Union Leader* on August 25, it was reported that William Loeb had sent a telegram to President Nixon at the San Clemente White House asking the President to pardon Hoffa. The telegram concluded, "By a stroke of your pen, you can give him that freedom to which he is entitled. I urge you to do so now."

Loeb also wrote a front-page editorial in the same issue of his newspaper in which he charged that Hoffa was a political prisoner, criticized the reputation of Parole Board Chairman George Reed, defended the salaries being paid to Hoffa's wife and son by the International Union and called for the formation of a "National Committee to Free James Riddle Hoffa."

The August 27 issue of the *Manchester Union Leader* carried a front-page article stating that Herbert Klein, the President's director of communications, had refused to comment on Loeb's telegram. The article noted that "a short time ago Mr. Klein met in Manchester with top executives of the *Manchester Union Leader.* . . ."

On August 30 Judge James F. Batton reset the trial of Partin to January 31, 1972, in Billings, Montana. The following day, Ted Dunham, Jr., was sentenced to one year in prison by Judge William D. Murray in New Orleans.

In a Labor Day speech in Detroit, Frank Fitzsimmons deplored the failure of the Parole Board to free Hoffa and publicly called upon President Nixon to grant Hoffa a pardon.

On September 10 Don Vestal filed suit in federal court in Washington, D.C., asking that the $1,700,000 lump-sum pension payment to Hoffa be declared invalid. The suit charged that Hoffa conspired with Executive Board members to obtain the payment and claimed that it had been made in July in anticipation of Hoffa's release from prison. The suit charged that the fund from which the payment had been made had contained only $2,000,000 and that the payment to Hoffa had "drastically depleted" the fund.

On September 13 Arthur Egan wrote a front-page story in the *Manchester Union Leader* in which he charged that Will Wilson, with the knowledge of Attorney General Mitchell, had made a deal with James P. Hoffa that if his father resigned all of his positions with the Teamsters Union, he would be paroled. Egan charged that Hoffa had been double-crossed.

In early October Ed Partin asked Jim Neal, who had been in private practice in Nashville since leaving the government, to represent him in the upcoming retrial of his case in Butte. Neal agreed. He met with government attorneys and both agreed to request a change of venue to a more convenient location. There was a mutual agreement on Atlanta, Georgia, as an alternate site for the trial and the proposal was accepted by Judge Batton.

On October 21 Partin was served with a subpoena from Morris Shenker directing him to be in the Federal Building in Baton Rouge on October 26 for a deposition in connection with the motion pending in the Chattanooga court. On the following day the government moved to quash the subpoena on the grounds that under existing law, Hoffa did not have the right to obtain Partin's testimony in this manner, rather than in a hearing in court. Judge Frank Wilson granted the government's motion and quashed the subpoena.

In Washington President Nixon named Frank Fitzsimmons as one of the five labor representatives to serve on the newly created Pay Board to participate in administering phase two of the President's economic program.

On November 2 D'Alton Smith, having lost his appeal, was again sentenced by federal Judge Manuel Real to twenty-five years in prison. However, he was sent to the federal detention center at San Pedro, California, for a ninety-day review period, after which time the judge would make a reevaluation and pronounce the final sentence. Smith told Partin that he had it taken care of and would only serve the ninety days. I told Partin that Judge Manuel Real had a reputation as a tough judge and that there was no way Smith would get off that easy.

During November and early December rumors were circulating in Teamsters circles that the President might soon commute Hoffa's sentence and release him from prison. On December 19 Morris Shenker acknowledged to a *Los Angeles Times* reporter that an application for commutation of Hoffa's sentence had been made but refused to discuss it any further. Department of Justice officials would neither confirm nor deny that an application had been made. Lawrence M. Traylor, the pardon attorney at the Department of Justice, told a *Times* reporter that a large number of clemency petitions had been forwarded to Attorney General Mitchell but would not state whether a petition on behalf of Hoffa was included.

On December 23 President Nixon signed an Executive Grant of Clemency for forty-nine persons. Included in the list was James R. Hoffa. The President commuted Hoffa's thirteen-year sentence to six and one-half years, making him eligible for immediate release. The commutation attached the condition that "the said James R. Hoffa not engage in direct or indirect management of any labor organization prior to March sixth, 1980, and if the aforesaid condition is not fulfilled this commutation will be null and void in its entirety. . . ."

The petition for commutation had actually been filed on December 16, one week earlier. The usual procedure, which takes weeks, of contacting the sentencing judge, the United States Attorney and the government prosecutors, had been dispensed with. Will Wilson had quietly resigned under the shadow of the growing scandal in Texas, but in his absence, the Criminal Division of the Department of Justice was not consulted.

That afternoon Hoffa walked out of the Lewisburg prison a free man. He flew immediately to St. Louis, Missouri, to join his wife and family at the home of his daughter, Mrs. Robert Crancer. He told newsmen he was grateful to President Nixon for his release.

In an editorial the following day, *The New York Times* stated:

> It would be nice, but naive, to believe that the spirit of Christmas and James R. Hoffa's unblemished record as a prisoner were the only factors that influenced yesterday's decision by President Nixon to let the former leader of the Teamsters Union out of jail. However, the evidence has been mounting in recent months that Hoffa's release has been a pivotal element in the strange love affair between the Administration and the two-million member truck union, ousted from the rest of the labor movement in 1957 for racketeer domination. . . .
>
> The terms of the Hoffa commutation bar him from engaging in the "direct or indirect management" of the Teamsters or any other union until March, 1980. But, even if that restriction is rigorously enforced, it is a bit difficult to avoid the suspicion that imminence of the 1972 election was a factor in Mr. Nixon's decision to release him—only four months after the United States Parole Board had refused for the third time to let Hoffa out.

An editorial in the *Philadelphia Inquirer* stated, "At best, the clemency was woefully misplaced; at worst, it was an act of crass political opportunism."

William Loeb's reaction was somewhat different. In a telephone interview with *The New York Times*, he said that consideration was being given to legal action to lift the restrictions placed on Hoffa. "If we can clear up some of the restrictions on his release, he'd be back in control of the Teamsters in short order," Loeb said.

On December 27 Hoffa went to Detroit to confer with Charles T. Hosner, chief of the parole and probation office there. After a one-and-a-half-hour conference, both Hoffa and Hosner said that there was still some question in both of their minds what the phrase "indirect management" in the commutation conditions actually meant. Hosner said that he would seek advice from Lawrence Traylor, the pardon attorney at the Department of Justice, in an attempt ot clarify it. Traylor told newsmen that the word "indirect" was not intended to interfere with Hoffa's right to express his opinions. He said that Hoffa could associate with Teamsters friends, attend union functions and speak out on issues, such as the support by the Teamsters Union of the President's economic program. Hoffa asked for and received permission to go to Florida the following week to join his wife.

Morris Shenker told reporters that if Hoffa's appeal of the Chattanooga case were successful, there would be a good chance that the restrictions would be lifted, inasmuch as Hoffa had already served almost five years, which was the sentence in the Chicago case.

Hoffa said that after a ninety-day stay in Florida, he intended to start speaking out on issues, particularly prison reform, and would use national talk shows and other vehicles to do this.

In Washington, D.C., Gerald Vestal, the son of Don Vestal, whose local in Nashville had been placed in trusteeship, filed suit in federal court against Frank Fitzsimmons and the other trustees of the Pension Fund charging them with misuse of funds and asking that the fund be placed in receivership. The law firm of Rhyne and Rhyne in Washington was retained by Fitzsimmons and the fund to defend against the suit. Charles Rhyne of that firm is a close personal friend of President Nixon's, having attended law school with him at Duke University.

CHAPTER XVIII

The Waiting Game

On January 5, 1972, Jimmy Hoffa flew to Florida and moved into his apartment in the Blair House, an apartment building in Miami Beach built in 1961 with loans from the Teamsters Pension Fund. Hoffa had announced that he intended to vacation there with his wife, who was convalescing from her recent illness.

The retrial of Ed Partin had, on mutual recommendations by the defense and the government, for the convenience of both, been transferred by Judge Batten from Butte, Montana, to Atlanta, Georgia. Partin had retained Jim Neal to represent him. On January 11 Nick Morrissey, the Boston Teamsters official who had contacted Partin prior to the trial in Butte offering to intercede on his behalf in return for an affidavit from Partin to help Hoffa, called attorney Jerry Millican, who represented Partin's Local 5. He told Millican that he was going to somehow get Hoffa back in office, but he needed Partin's help to do it. Again he offered to help Partin in his upcoming trial and asked Millican to meet him in Washington. Millican went to Washington that night and met with Morrissey the following morning at the Shoreham Hotel. Morrissey was accompanied by Chattanooga attorney Harold Brown. They told Millican that there was now an open rift between Hoffa and Frank Fitzsimmons and that they wanted to help Hoffa get back in office. If Partin would sign an affidavit for Hoffa, they said, they would intervene on Partin's behalf to delay his trial or obtain immunity for him. Morrissey said that there was $225,000 available if the Hoffa conviction in Chattanooga could be reversed. At one point, Morrissey said he was going to call Hoffa and wanted Millican to talk to him, but Millican declined. Millican was noncommittal and the meeting finally broke up.

On January 18 William Loeb sent telegrams to Secretary of Labor James Hodgson and Secretary of Agriculture Earl Butz urging them to recommend to President Nixon that he enlist the help of James R. Hoffa in settling the West Coast strike, which involved a jurisdictional dispute between the Longshoremen and the Teamsters. If the President had hoped to placate Loeb by releasing Hoffa, apparently the move had little effect. Loeb had been highly critical of Nixon's approaching trip to China and was supporting conservative Congressman John Ashbrook against the President in the New Hampshire primary campaign. He was, however, continuing in his support of Hoffa with his new indirect approaches to the President on his behalf.

On January 27 Morris Shenker resigned as head of the St. Louis Commission on Crime and Law Enforcement. An article in the *St. Louis Post Dispatch* the following day stated that Shenker was pressured into resigning when a Department of Justice official objected to the fact that part of a $20,000,000 federal grant to fight crime was going to the commission. Shenker denied it.

On January 31 Ed Partin went on trial as scheduled in federal court in Atlanta.

On February 11 Judge Frank Wilson denied Hoffa's motion for a new trial on the claim that Ed Partin had committed perjury.

On February 13 Jimmy Hoffa was the guest on the ABC program *Issues and Answers.* Most of the discussion was concerned with Hoffa's ideas on the need for prison reform. When asked about his choice of Presidential candidates, Hoffa replied, "I would say President Nixon is the best qualified man at the present time for the Presidency of the United States in my own personal opinion."

The following day Hoffa showed up in the lobby of the Americana Hotel in Miami Beach where the AFL-CIO Executive Council was meeting. When George Meany heard of Hoffa's presence he said, "What's that guy doing around here?" Hoffa told newsmen that he was active in the real estate business in Florida.

On February 29 Allen Dorfman was convicted in federal court in New York City of conspiring to obtain a $55,000 kickback on a $1,500,000 loan from the Teamsters Pension Fund. Some of the Pension Fund trustees had dutifully showed up to testify on Dorfman's behalf. Two days later Ed Partin was convicted in Atlanta of violation of the antitrust laws and extortion. Nick Morrissey, the Boston Teamsters official, immediately began passing the word to Partin's friends, and even to his son, that Jim Neal had thrown the case. Neal's defense of Partin had been outstanding and prompted one Baton Rouge newsman who covered the trial and who had previously been critical of Partin to state that it was the best performance by a defense attorney he had ever seen.

On March 10 Tom Flynn, the secretary-treasurer of the International Brotherhood of Teamsters, died of a heart attack. Jimmy Hoffa attended the funeral in Washington and engaged in a bitter exchange with Frank Fitzsimmons as to who was going to replace Flynn. When Fitzsimmons said that he had not yet decided, Hoffa snapped, "What do you mean *you* haven't decided? The Executive Board makes that decision."

On March 20 Nick Morrissey called Jerry Millican and told him he wanted to set up a meeting for him with Edward Nunn, whom he described as the number two man in the campaign to reelect President Nixon. Morrissey said that he was sure Hoffa would receive a pardon if the President was reelected. On the same day Millican received a copy of the transcript of Partin's testimony in Chattanooga from Harold Brown. Brown and Morrissey had suggested that it would be helpful in preparing an affidavit for Partin to sign.

On March 22 George Meany called an emergency session of the AFL-CIO Executive Council and thereafter announced that the three AFL-CIO representatives on the President's Pay Board were withdrawing. Leonard Woodcock, the president of the UAW, followed suit. Frank Fitzsimmons of the Teamsters Union, who was invited to the AFL-CIO meeting but did not attend, announced that he would stay on the Pay Board as the sole remaining representative of labor. The quid pro quo between the Teamsters Union and the Administration was obviously a continuing arrangement.

On March 27 Judge James Batton granted Jim Neal's motion for a mistrial, and acquitted Partin on three of the four remaining counts in the indictment and ordered a new trial on one count. (The original indictment had contained five counts but Neal had succeeded in getting one count dismissed during the trial.) On the same day D'Alton Smith again came up for sentencing before Judge Manuel Real in Los Angeles. In spite of the fact that the pre-sentence investigation had recommended that Smith be given the maximum sentence, and in spite of the fact that Smith was under investigation by the FBI in Denver for allegedly bribing an SBA official, Judge Real gave Smith a five-year suspended sentence and five years probation. Smith was back on the street that day, just as he had predicted to Partin.

On April 8 Harold Brown went to Baton Rouge and dropped in at Jerry Millican's house. He gave Millican a list of questions that he wanted Partin to answer as the basis for an affidavit. The following morning Nick Morrissey called Millican and said that he had talked to Murray Chotiner, whom he referred to as the "pajama man," and that Chotiner would set up an appointment with someone in the Administration but first they needed the affidavit from Partin. Morrissey said they would not use the affidavit unless they could first obtain immunity for Partin. It was a renewal of the Pat Willis-Audie Murphy ploy. He said that they were anxious to get the ITT matter off the front pages and try to somehow turn a Partin affidavit against Senator Edward Kennedy.

And so it goes on. It will continue to go on so long as Jimmy Hoffa continues in his quest to reclaim the office of general president of the International Brotherhood of Teamsters.

Meanwhile, nothing has really changed. In New York City Abe Gordon is still running Local 805 and his friend from the paper local days, Harry Davidoff, was, until a year ago, still running Local 295. According to a *Life* magazine article by Denny Walsh, in February, 1971, Davidoff and Gordon had a stranglehold on all trucking at Kennedy Airport in New York through a mob-dominated trucking association. The association was seeking to become the nationwide bargaining agent with the Teamsters Union for the entire air freight industry. Companies found that it was easier to ensure labor peace if they retained the services of a labor relations consultant who was none other than Abe Gordon's old friend Milton Holt. There was also added behind-the-scenes muscle in the person of Johnny Dio. According to the article, when the heat from federal investigators got too close, Frank Fitzsimmons moved Davidoff into a new Teamsters local after a secret meeting with Abe Gordon and Johnny Dio. Milton Holt was indicted in April, 1971, for extortion.

In Ohio William Presser is still the head of the Teamsters organization and still serves as an International vice president and trustee of the Pension Fund, despite the fact that he has been indicted twice in the past two years for taking payoffs and for embezzlement of union funds. He pleaded guilty to one charge just before he was reelected as an International vice president at the last Teamsters Convention, to which President Nixon sent his Secretary of Labor and his best wishes.

Louis "Babe" Triscaro still heads Local 436 in Cleveland and remains the number two Teamster in the state of Ohio. In Youngstown Joe Blumetti remains in office in Local 410 even though he was indicted in July, 1970, for embezzlement.

In New Jersey Tony Provenzano, now out of prison, is no longer head of the Teamsters, nor an International vice president, but his brother, Salvatore, is. Salvatore Provenzano was indicted last year for counterfeiting but the indictment was dismissed when it was discovered that there was a case of mistaken identity. Another Teamsters official was thereupon indicted. Joseph Pecora, who was indicted back in 1962 with Phil Weiss in a Newark extortion case, was recently indicted for embezzlement but is still the president of Local 831.

In Chicago Gus Zapas carries on as secretary-treasurer of Local 46 of the Laundry Workers Union. In addition to his $42,000 salary, Zapas receives $200 a week from the International Union, and as of recently, a $9600 a year fee as a trustee for the local's pension fund. His brother, William, who appears to spend most of his time operating a restaurant, is also on the payroll of the local as an organizer for $100 a week. In 1969 Zapas' brother-in-law was paid $8000 by the local for maintenance work. In addition, two members of the Chicago syndicate, Leonard Gianola and Albert De-Fiore, are on the payroll as business agent and organizer, respectively, for a total of $375 a week.

Over on La Salle Street in Chicago Allen Dorfman still handles the insurance for the Central States Health and Welfare Fund and Pension Fund, and as of the date of his recent conviction for taking a kickback from a Pension Fund loan, was still serving as a consultant to the fund. Dorfman businesses have received millions of dollars in loans from the Pension Fund and both he and his attorney Harvey Silets have received substantial fees in connection with Pension Fund loans. In 1970 alone the Silets law firm received $95,000 in fees. Dorfman has continued to expand his business empire. One of his recent ventures was Aetna Resources, Inc., a high-risk loan company in New York City. Two of his business associates in the company were Nick Tweel of Huntington, West Virginia, and James Hoffa, Jr.

At Local 710 in Chicago the late John T. "Sandy" O'Brien has been replaced as head by William Joyce, who draws a salary of over $100,000 a year. A member of the local, Robert Barnhisel, has led a five-year rebellion of dissident members against what he claims is gross mismanagement, denial of union democracy and pension fund inadequacies. Meetings of the dissident group are often disrupted by strong-arm men from Local 710 and the dissidents themselves have been subjected to continuous harassment and layoffs from their employment.

In St. Louis Morris Shenker, although no longer head of the Crime Commission, has made millions of dollars in fees in connection with the placement of loans from the Teamsters Pension Fund.

The loan activities of the Pension Fund have been even worse since Hoffa's conviction for defrauding it. The fund continued to pour millions of dollars into Las Vegas hotels and mob-controlled gambling casinos. When Morris "Moe" Dalitz and other racketeers who controlled the Desert Inn in Las Vegas decided to sell out because of increasing federal surveillance of their activities, they moved to La Costa, near San Clemente, California, and built Rancho La Costa Country Club with $27,000,000 in loans from the Pension Fund. The club has become a mecca for racketeers from all over the country. Allen Dorfman has a home on the property.

There has been no meaningful monitoring of the Pension Fund by the federal government since Hoffa's conviction in Chicago. No remedial changes were instituted internally and neither the Department of Justice nor the Labor Department followed up in an effective way to determine whether the plundering of the fund continued. The fund continued to pump over 70 percent of its assets into speculative real estate loans; many of the loans continued to go bad; and the conniving and kickbacks went on as if nothing had happened, as evidenced by the conviction of Allen Dorfman and what follows below.

The only exception to the lack of attention by the federal government was in the Southern District of New York, where Robert Morgenthau stayed on as the United States Attorney until late 1969 and continued to probe into the fund's operations. The results of his efforts give some indication of how the fund really works as a slush fund for the mob, and what might be found elsewhere in the country if anyone bothered to look.

It is a familiar pattern. In a series of loans from the fund, kickbacks of roughly 10 percent were made in cash. The kickbacks were split among a group that in every instance included underworld figures. The middleman for these loans was David Wenger, the accountant for the fund, who received half of the kickbacks. During the period 1968 to 1970 convictions were obtained in six separate trials in connection with these loans. There was a $90,000 kickback on an $875,000 loan for the construction of the Fairlawn Memorial Hospital in Fairlawn, New Jersey. The recipients were Johnny Dio's uncle, James Plumeri, accountant Leonard Russo, labor relations man Jack McCarthy and Wenger. The same group received cash kickbacks in the same amount for another $875,000 loan to a bowling alley in Queens, New York. They were convicted in the first case and pleaded guilty in the second.

Wenger, Russo and Plumeri were among a group that split up another $42,000 kickback on a $700,000 loan for a shopping center in Florida. Another member of the group was Salvadore Granello, a hoodlum who was murdered before he could go to trial. The others pleaded guilty.

A $1,800,000 loan to the Cashmere Corporation in Cleveland netted $180,000 in cash to a group that included Sam Berger, who had been involved in the original paper local operation, Jimmy Plumeri and Floyd Webb, a Teamsters official, since deceased, who was a trustee on the Pension Fund when the loan was granted.

Mobsters Salvadore Granello and Jimmy Plumeri, along with Johnny Dio's brother Frank Dioguardi and David Wenger, pleaded guilty to dividing up a $60,000 kickback on a $900,000 loan for the Midland General Hospital in Dallas. Finally, Wenger and one other person were convicted in another trial in connection with a $1,500,000 loan to Mid City Properties, Inc., in Detroit. Eleven other co-defendants, including some of the major underworld figures in Pittsburgh and Detroit, were acquitted.

The chief government witness in all of these trials was Herbert Itkin, a New York attorney who worked for a number of years as an undercover agent for both the CIA and the FBI. David Wenger told Itkin that he split his half of the kickbacks with Hoffa. It was Itkin who had been the FBI's source concerning the payments being made to Labor Department official Morris Emanuel in return for information about government investigations of Hoffa and other Teamsters officials in 1963 and 1964. At that time the FBI did not want to surface Itkin, who had been present when the payments were made to Emanuel, because he was furnishing valuable information to both that organization and the CIA. In 1965

Emanuel was confronted with the information by Department of Labor officials and given the choice of resigning or facing prosecution. He resigned.

Itkin finally abandoned his undercover status when he testified in the New York trial of Tony "Ducks" Corallo and political leader Carmine DeSapio on charges of shaking down the Con Edison Company. James Marcus, an aide to Mayor John Lindsay, was also indicted but pleaded guilty and cooperated with the government. Both Corallo and DeSapio were convicted and are serving their terms in the federal penitentiary at Danbury, Connecticut. Marcus was sentenced to a term at the Lewisburg Prison. One day as he was sitting in the cafeteria talking to another prisoner, Jimmy Hoffa walked up and shouted at the man talking to Marcus, "What are you doing talking to that fink?" Marcus was transferred shortly after to another prison for his own safety.

Herbert Itkin still lives on a military base and is accompanied by protecting United States deputy marshals wherever he goes. He hopes someday soon to move away and change his identity. Robert Morgenthau, who was probably the most effective United States Attorney in the country in the prosecution of organized crime and white-collar crime cases, is now practicing law in New York City.

The present federal laws governing the activities of pension funds are woefully inadequate. This has been recognized by Congress for some time. Each year new legislation is introduced to tighten the controls over operations of these funds, to give the workers a vested interest in the funds and to make the reporting requirements more meaningful. But each year the proposed legislation languishes in congressional committees and dies. There are currently pending some thirty variations of such bills sponsored by the Administration, Senator Jacob Javits of New York and Representative John Dent of Pennsylvania but there is little hope of early enactment.

As the law now stands, a pension fund is not required to report to whom loans are made or the amount of individual loans. The borrower is not required to report what he does with the money. The workers, for whom the funds are supposed to exist, have no vested interest in them. There is often no reciprocity between funds. A man can work for forty years driving a truck as a Teamsters member and end up with little or no pension because he happened to have been transferred, often without choice, from one local to another.

This last problem was documented in a series in the *Chicago Tribune* in March, 1971, by reporters Ronald Kozial and James Strong. Sixty-three-year-old Derman Vestal, a member of the Teamsters Union for thirty-two years, was found working as a dishwasher against the advice of his doctor to supplement his Social Security payments because he was ineligible for a pension. He had begun working as a truck driver in Des Moines in 1937, had transferred to Local 705 in Chicago in 1954 and then to Local 710 in 1962. Because there was no reciprocity between the pension funds of the locals, Vestal was declared ineligible for a pension. The reporters found another Teamster, Clarence Spellman, age sixty, selling newspapers to survive. Spellman had suddenly gone blind one day while driving his truck. He applied for his pension but was told that he was ineligible because he had transferred to a different local three months earlier.

Locals 710 and 705 have their own pension funds and are not a part of the Central States Pension Fund. Although locals covered by the Central States Fund do have reciprocity and some locals outside the fund have reciprocity with the fund, they often do not have such with each other. The result is a situation of total confusion wherein the Teamsters member suffers, sometimes tragically.

On the other hand, officials of most Teamsters locals, and of the International, are neither confused nor suffering. There are pension plans on top of pension plans for many of these Teamsters officials. Often, the more different union offices one holds, the more pension plans by which he is covered. Jimmy Hoffa did not have to worry about reciprocity or anything else when he cashed in his lump-sum pension for $1,700,000.

Although the information required by law to be filed annually by pension funds is inadequate, it is also revealing. In forms filed with the Department of Labor for the year ending January 31, 1971, the Central States Southeast-Southwest Areas Pension Fund showed assets of $800,000,000. Of that amount $586,000,000—over 70 percent—was invested in real estate loans and mortgages. Although contributions to the fund for that year totaled $153,000,000 and total receipts were a staggering $314,000,000, the assets increased by only $90,000,000. The simple conclusion is that although the rate of contributions and the number of members covered has increased steadily, the fund has consistently lost money. For some reason, perhaps because the fund is so big and has grown steadily, the fact that it is losing money each year does not seem to bother anyone. Administrative expenses for 1971 were over $2,000,000, of which $800,000 was for salaries, $600,000 for fees and commissions and $700,000 for "other administrative expenses." Another $210,000,000 was for "purchase of assets and real estate," but there was no explanation as to what that means.

It is what the filed forms do not reveal, because it is not required, that is more pertinent. The form filed for the year 1964 did not indicate that a $500,000 loan had been made to the Home Juice Company in Detroit which had been taken over by racketeers when the owner could not pay a gambling debt. Nor did it show the first loan for $9,000,000 to Moe Dalitz and his friends for the La Costa Country Club, or that Allen Dorfman was one of the agents for the loan.

The report for the year 1965 did not show a $15,000,000 loan to Caesar's Palace in Las Vegas, or that the applicant was Jay Sarno, the owner of the Atlanta Cabana Motor Hotel, or that one of the agents was, again, Allen Dorfman. Nor did it show a $10,500 loan to Hoffa's pal Paul Allen, the head of the Riggers Union in Detroit, for "purchase of the Hazel Park Cab Company." It also omitted the fact that a person known as Martha *Lewis* received a share of a $30,000 fee for the placement of a $2,000,000 loan for the Kirwood General Hospital in Detroit.

The 1966 report did not mention two loans totaling almost $5,-000,000 to Allen Dorfman's Reliable Insurance Company; $6,000,-000 in loans to the Lodestar and United Holding Company of Las Vegas; and $18,000,000 in loans to corporations controlled by Morris Shenker's friend and business associate, Irving Kahn of San Diego. The $1,800,000 loan to the Cashmere Company which netted $180,000 in cash kickbacks to Sam Berger, James Plumeri and Teamsters official and Pension Fund trustee Floyd Webb was not in the report.

Unreported loans in 1967 included $200,000 to the Villa National Bank in Denver, of which Allen Dorfman was an official, and a $440,000 loan to Villa Investments, also in Denver. The agent on the former loan was Jacques Schiffer. Also, that year, there was an additional $3,750,000 loan to the Lodestar and United Holding Company of Las Vegas and a $1,470,333 loan to the Sierra Memorial Hospital in Los Angeles. Two of the applicants on the latter loan were Cal Kovens and Martha Louis. On February 14 a loan in the amount of $62,500 was approved for Chattanooga attorney Harold Brown and Sam Pettijohn. The latter had been one of the persons who assisted in obtaining the affidavits from bellhops and prostitutes alleging that the jurors in Hoffa's Chattanooga trial had been drunk and promiscuous. The agent for this loan was the law firm of Harvey Silets, Allen Dorfman's attorney.

In 1968 Irving Kahn's corporation in San Diego received another $9,500,000, Lodestar and United Holding in Las Vegas another $1,138,500 and La Costa Country Club another $18,200,000 in loans.

These are just a sampling of loans over the five-year period following the conviction of Jimmy Hoffa and his associates for their manipulation of the fund. It is not my intention to imply that the existence of these or other loans was wrongfully withheld from the reports. There is no requirement, as the law now stands, that they be included. It is quite clear, however, that the law should be changed to require that such loans be reported individually and in detail. The new legislation proposed by Senator Javits contains such a provision. In spite of the convictions in Chicago eight years ago, the fund continues to operate in a manner that violates established sound investing standards, enriches a small group of cronies, and permits substantial cash kickbacks to racketeers, and an accountant, a consultant and a trustee of the fund. How many other kickbacks have there been that have not been detected? By what stretch of whose imagination can a fund of this size—now reaching $1,000,000,000—be allowed to continue in this fashion? The trustees of the fund, both union and management representatives, should have to account to the 400,000 Teamsters members whose pensions depend on a sound exercise of fiduciary responsibility.

There is nothing in the President's commutation order to prevent Jimmy Hoffa from becoming, like Allen Dorfman, a consultant to the fund, nor for that matter, from resuming his position as a trustee. He is precluded only from "the direct or indirect management of a labor union." The Pension Fund is not a labor union. Likewise, under the Landrum-Griffin Act, there is nothing to prevent Hoffa from holding union office, since the crimes for which he was convicted are not included among those that prohibit a person from holding such office. As in the case of pension funds, there have been yearly attempts to amend the Landrum-Griffin Act to improve some of its deficiencies, such as broadening the list of crimes the conviction for which is a bar to holding union office. But this effort likewise never gets out of committee.

So long as both the legislative and executive branches of our government, which have jurisdiction over these matters, continue to allow political considerations to take priority over remedial action there can be no real change in the status quo. It is an accepted fact on Capitol Hill that legislation that might be offensive to organized labor rarely gets out of the labor committees. It is also unreasonable to assume that an Administration that has entered into an obvious political alliance with the Teamsters Union will be very concerned that its infiltration by racketeers and the abuse by some of its officials of their trust and their members make it little different from what it was fifteen years ago. When officials of the Department of Labor and the Department of Justice are asked why there has been no major investigation of the Teamsters Pension Fund in the past eight years, they say, "I guess it's just too big."

Meanwhile, Jimmy Hoffa waits impatiently. Officials of the Department of Justice acknowledge that there may be no way of enforcing the prohibition against union activity that was a condition of Hoffa's commutation, once he is free of parole supervision in March, 1973. The grand strategy at the present time is to move the timetable up even earlier. It calls for first overturning the Chattanooga conviction by the appeal from Judge Wilson's denial of the latest motion for a new trial or by an affidavit from Ed Partin. The claim would then be made that the five-year sentence for the Chicago conviction has already been served. The hope would then be for a Presidential pardon, leaving Hoffa eligible to reclaim the presidency of the union.

A short while ago Hoffa made a suprise appearance at a meeting of 1000 stewards of Local 710 in Chicago. He told the cheering audience that "the year 1972 will be an eventful year" and that "I hope soon I will be successful in securing a release from the controls I have and I will be able to speak out." He said that he hoped to return to the Teamsters Union, since it was the only occupation he had known. It was not an idle boast.

Recent events tend to indicate that Hoffa has reason to hope that he will soon receive a pardon from President Nixon and will then be in a position to reassume control of the Teamsters Union. There has been a series of moves which appears to be designed to pave the way for such action by the President and to make it more palatable. The new arrogance in those moves, on the part of both the Administration and Hoffa and his associates, leaves little question any longer of their conspiracy.

First, a small group of attorneys in the Department of Justice was secretly designated to start laying the ground work for a Presidential pardon. Their mission is to attempt to portray the Test Fleet case in Nashville as so unjust a prosecution that Hoffa could be said to have been justified in tampering with the jury. Similarly, they are seeking to show that the Sun Valley case was defective, thus clouding the Pension Fund case that evolved from it.

Next, the carrot and stick approach is again in operation in connection with Ed Partin. Partin was scheduled to go to trial in Houston on October 10, 1972, on the charge that he threatened Wade McClanahan. United States Attorney Gerald Gallinghouse has indicated that he would personally try the case for the government. Partin also faces a subsequent retrial of the one remaining count in the antitrust case. Judge Batton recently recused himself from this case and was replaced by Judge Manuel Real of Los Angeles. Again, as in the original replacement of Judge West by Judge Murray, the usual channels were bypassed, and now instead of a judge from Montana, there is a judge from California to hear a case which originated in Louisiana. One week after Judge Real took the case, D'Alton Smith called Partin and suggested he come to Los Angeles. Smith said that he thought he knew how to handle the situation. Partin was keenly aware that Smith had correctly predicted his own lenient treatment by Judge Real.

Then, Nick Morrissey, the persistent Boston Teamsters official, offered Partin a simple solution to his problems. If Partin would sign an affidavit—this time merely stating that he did not give the FBI permission to bug his car when he met with Ewing King prior to the jury-tampering indictment of Hoffa in 1964—a federal grand jury would be quietly empaneled and Partin would be given immunity from all the charges pending against him. The bugging of Partin's car is the focal point of Hoffa's latest pending appeal, scheduled for a hearing on October 18. Partin would be expected, of course, in addition, to tell the grand jury the "truth" about Nashville and Chattanooga.

This rather unorthodox panacea was to be arranged by Presidential assistant Murray Chotiner and Department of Labor official Donald Nagle, acting on Chotiner's instructions, with behind the scenes assistance from President Nixon's attorney friend Charles Rhyne and former President Eisenhower's Chief of Protocol Wiley Buchanan. The cast continues to change but never ceases to be fascinating.

Finally, Jimmy Hoffa was to earn the gratitude of the American people and the President by obtaining the release of American prisoners of war in North Vietnam. Hoffa's newfound agent, William Taub, representing himself as Hoffa's attorney, not only obtained audiences with Presidential advisor Henry Kissinger and the Deputy Attorney General of the United States, but actually succeeded in obtaining permission from the United States Parole Board for Hoffa to visit Hanoi and a validated passport from the Department of State. Hoffa and Taub would have been quietly on their way, had the story not leaked to the press, at which point Secretary of State William Rogers intervened. The embarrassment to both Hoffa and the Administration was heightened when it was discovered that William Taub was not an attorney and had a long record as an expert con man. It was a temporary setback.

Meanwhile, Frank Fitzsimmons is still the general president of the International Brotherhood of Teamsters. Fortified by his close relationship with the White House, the formerly docile Hoffa ally has shed some of his subservient ways. He has decided he likes his new power and respectability and intends to keep them. He has reminded Hoffa loyalists and potential dissidents that he signs their paychecks and that he, not Hoffa, is running the union.

President Nixon appears to have the best of both worlds. In his first and only nationally televised appearance since being released from prison, Hoffa spoke in favor of the President's reelection and he continues to hope for a pardon. Fitzsimmons continues to bask in the warmth of the President's friendship. He has been appointed by the President to the Board of Directors of the Communications Satellite Corporation and his wife has been named to serve on the Arts Committee of the Kennedy Center for the Performing Arts. On July 17 Fitzsimmons gathered the International Executive Board together at the La Costa Country Club and they formally endorsed the candidacy of Richard Nixon for reelection to the Presidency. They thus complied with a commitment made when the President agreed to commute Hoffa's sentence and release him from prison. Then they drove from the mecca for the mob that the Pension Fund built thirty-five miles north to the San Clemente White House for poolside photographs with the President of the United States.

President Nixon obviously hoped that the 2,000,000 Teamsters members and their families would follow their leaders into the

Nixon camp, Jimmy Hoffa hopes he will soon have his pardon, and Frank Fitzsimmons keeps looking over his shoulder.

Meanwhile the coffers of the corrupters continue to grow and the victims increase in numbers and in their feelings of hopelessness.

Index